Making Sense of Media:
A Cultural-Historical Approach

Making Sense of Media

A Cultural-Historical Approach

Robert Henry Stanley

Table of Contents

Preface 1
1. Copying Concerns 7
2. News Media 43
3. Shifting Standards 80
4. Media Law 112
5. Movie Matters 156
6. Sound Visions 194
7. Television Culture 225
8. Ethnicity 263
9. Gender 285
10. Web Culture 321
Endnotes 349

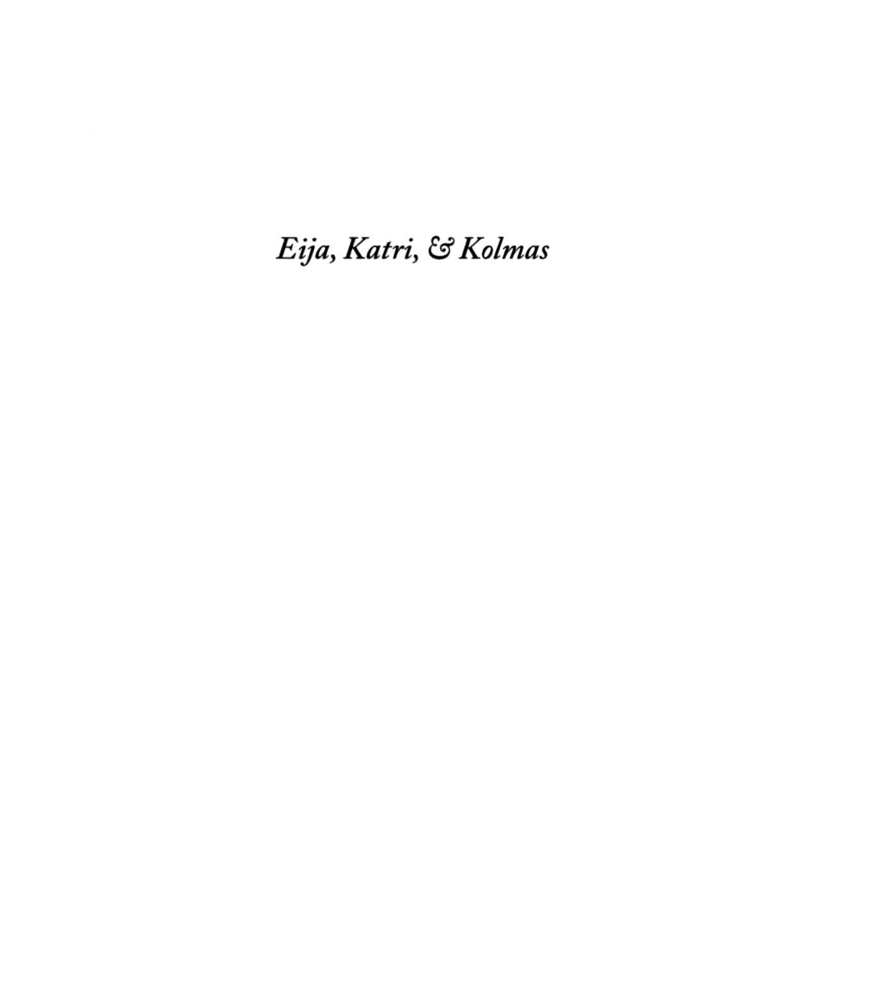

Eija, Katri, & Kolmas

Preface

Taking a stab at writing an introductory media studies textbook is ambitious, some might say, foolhardy, given the broad range of issues and subject matter this field encompasses. Such a foundation text has to be accessible, well organized, clearly written, and, most of all, engaging, thought-provoking, and conducive to class debate and discussion. This task is all the more daunting since the primary target readership is already absorbed and distracted by the very media under consideration.

This very absorption and fascination open up opportunities for harnessing attention and directing it toward a greater understanding of how the communications media and the forces that shape their content affect people's lives. What the media cover, how they cover it, and what they ignore may undercut the achievement of crucial matters such as climate control, universal healthcare, affordable housing, income opportunities, equitable taxation, and global conflict.

At perhaps no time in our history has the systematic study of the content and contours of media messages within the context of the legal, political, economic, and cultural factors been more urgent and necessary. In unprecedented ways, politicians, propagandists, and peddlers of goods and services are all trying to affect the three-pound organ in our skulls. Comprised of cells called neurons, hundreds of billions of them, linked to one another in a vast network of brain tissue with more synapses or connections in a cubic centimeter than stars in the Milky Way. Our brain's circuitry determines our hopes, fears, great ideas, stereotypes, prejudices, senses of humor, and desires, our very understanding that we even exist at all. When its synapses or neural connections change, so do we.

Cultural/Historical Lens

This foundation text focuses on the various forms of "communications media"—the objects, devices, and mechanisms for preserving, copying, and moving ideas, images, and information through space—within legal, political, economic, and cultural factors. All approaches to the study of media, or any other academic inquiry area, are necessarily guided by some implicit or explicit assumptions. They shape the types of questions asked and the kinds of evidence used in answering them and structure and organize all research and analysis.

A guiding premise of our analysis is that a cultural-historical lens provides the best perspective for understanding the contours and content of the various media forms and the range of forces that shape them. The term culture, rooted in agriculture, has multiple interpretations resulting from its usage within a range of discourses. In an aesthetic sense, it refers to the most significant artistic achievements of humankind. Typically, such great works are decidedly European in origin. For our purposes, as an analytical concept, the term culture is most usefully defined as a process by which we produce "meaning"—the rational and irrational responses someone or something evokes, including images, interpretations, and feelings.

Culture, distilled to its essence, is how we make the world meaningful. The various meanings generated from media practices, conventions, and forms reside in specific historical contexts. They determine the significance of everything from images of dogs and cows to movie scenes to statues honoring explorers and military leaders. The aim is to unveil the social divisions and cultural conflicts that often gave rise to the diverse meanings of such familiar forms of media artifacts and practices.

The underlying assumption of this text is that meaning, culture, and stereotyping interact through practices, conventions, rituals, and artifacts in a historical context. Through a cultural-historical lens, scrutinizing such matters as media portrayals, stereotypes, and legal, economic, and social constraints generate insights into the meanings, values, and often-contradictory social and political effects of public discourse. This framework also facilitates consideration of a wide range of theories, analyses, and research, and opens up many avenues of inquiry for further investigation.

The kinds of meanings any act or element may evoke are learned and perpetuated in culture through such institutions as family, religion, media, law, and government. Different cultural groups think, feel, and act differently. A dog in one culture may be a pet, but in another something to have for dinner. A cow may be sacred or the source of hamburgers depending on cultural values and traditions. There are no scientific standards for considering one cultural group's perceptions and interpretations as intrinsically superior or inferior to another's.

 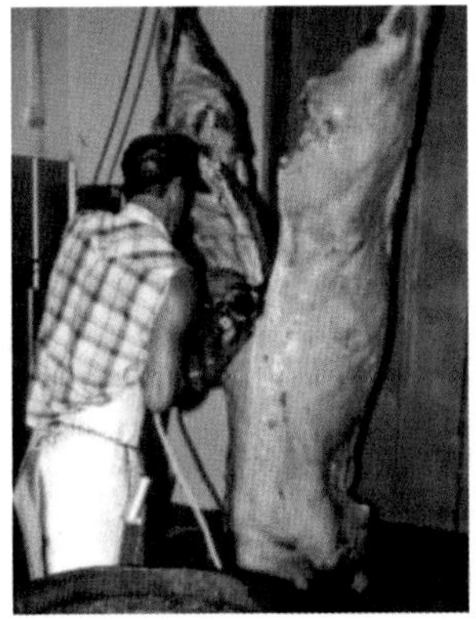 

Social-Scientific Approaches

Media researchers often conduct surveys and experiments on single works turning the results into percentages and making predictions. The basic approach begins with identifying a problem. Second, reviewing related research and theories and developing a working hypothesis. Third, determining appropriate methods or research design, collecting information, or relevant data. Fourth, analyzing results to see if the theory is verified. And, finally, interpreting them to determine if they explain or predict the problem. The touchstones for this kind of research are objectivity (no researcher bias), reliability (through replication), and validity (whether the study measures what it claims to measure).

Turning phenomena into numbers, academicians under pressure to publish have done much of this "quantitative" research. And only definitive results are likely to get scholarly journal acceptance. As a consequence, such studies limit the kinds of problems considered. The wording of a hypothesis must make it testable. Terms must be precisely defined, such as "the term attitude in this study refers to a predisposition to behave in a particular way." The subjects, usually undergraduates, are typically given paper-and-pencil tests before and after watching or observing some media event to see whether attitudes or whatever changed. Scores of studies employing social scientific methods concluded the effect of a single media event on the individual was minimal – the mismatch between the subject and approach skews such findings.

Survey research has similar shortcomings. While useful in specific areas like determining the program, product, or political preferences, surveys are limited in the kinds of knowledge they provide. This method can only assess phenomena that respondents are conscious of and willing or able to disclose. Such individual responses often obscure more than they reveal. They lack consideration of how these responses might reflect broader cultural patterns or how the structure of society may condition them. Common concerns in media studies such as the impact of movie and television depictions of women and minorities are not amenable to even the most refined and sophisticated survey techniques.

Categories and Stereotypes

The form and content of media doubtlessly affect individuals but do so among and through a nexus of mediating factors and influences. News, advertising, entertainment, public relations, propaganda, and other forms of social and public expression circulating through a wide range of media outlets play a large part in shaping and reinforcing stereotypical classifications through which we navigate everyday experience.

Coming from constant cultural exposure, stereotypes, as applied to people, refer to fixed ideas about how a particular group thinks or behaves and focuses on factors such as age, race, ethnicity, gender, religion, and nationality. We sort out and lump together people in many other ways, such as their vocation, attire, facial features, and general appearance. They are a pervasive form of everyday experience.

When we categorize, we also polarize or divide into sharply contrasting classifications. Things identified as belonging to the same category seem more similar to each other than they are, while those in different types seem more diverse than they are. The unconscious mind, recent neuroscientific studies suggest, transforms subtle nuances and fuzzy differences into clear-cut distinctions. We generate meaning through such oppositions, interpreting someone or something in terms of what it is not.

Underlying mechanisms of mind, stereotypes are the natural outcome of human perception, the mental activity of organizing the input of the senses (sight, hearing, touch, taste, and smell) into categories and interpretations. Categorization is a strategy we use to process our environment more efficiently. It is one of our most critical mental activities, and we do it all the time. Our tendency to categorize, while simplifying our environment and making it easier to maneuver, may also cause us to react to a social group or category rather than the actual person. The challenge is not how to stop categorizing. Instead, it is to become aware of when we do it in ways that inhibit the recognition of individual uniqueness and determine what factors are causing us to do so.

Provisional Knowledge

In this complex media environment, categorization is far too complex to discern any single chain of causes and effects. Causal connections are more like a woven fabric than a chain. In the interaction of the primary means of communication, interpretation, culture, history threads cross and re-cross to form an intricate weave not readily unraveled. This text focuses on those central threads that seem to reveal patterns recognizing the possible distortions implicit in those choices.

The primary concern is with the generation and circulation of meanings, not on any effect of a single media message. The conclusions drawn tend to be tentative and provisional, part of a continual process of discovery, opening up areas for substantive critical discussion and consideration. Such analysis proves nothing. Instead, it heightens awareness of how we might interpret media messages that work to our detriment and others. The approach is nonpartisan, but the intent is to provoke social and political discussion—precisely what an introductory text in media studies should do.

The general writing style is informal and narrative. Although not geared to a specific academic level, the general concepts should be readily accessible to those taking basic and advanced courses in media studies. Looking up the meanings and pronunciation of unfamiliar words is an excellent way to expand and sharpen language skills. Every chapter incorporates aspects of law, history, economics, culture, advertising, public relations, and propaganda essential to a foundation text and directly relevant to assessing the interactions of media and meaning. The book gives particular attention is matters concerning gender, ethnicity, social class, and war propaganda. Thumbnail images sprinkled throughout at strategic points highlight material and aid retention.

About the Author

Dr. Robert Henry Stanley is Professor of Film and Media Studies at Hunter College of the City University of New York. In a similar vein, *Making Sense of Movies* is among his previous five published books. His professional activities have included coordinating faculty/industry seminars for the International Radio and Television Society, moderating panel discussions for media professionals, and serving on the board of directors of the New York World Television Festival. He also served for many years as a judge for the International Emmy Awards of the National Academy of Television Arts and Sciences, and a judge and moderator for the Edward R. Murrow Brotherhood Awards.

Acknowledgements

This section of a book sometimes resembles the longwinded acceptance speeches at the old Academy Awards shows. With that caution in mind, I shall keep the expression of appreciation short. First off, I want to thank my dear wife, our daughter, and grandson, whose enduring love and support make it all worthwhile. John Hartley Whalen lent his eagle eye for spotting typos and the like to every chapter. Never without his book of sonnets, he inspired me to work more Shakespeare into the text. Cherouk Akik and Melissa Lent did a close reading of several chapters and offered astute comments and criticisms.

A heartfelt thank you is also due to the many excellent students in my primary and advanced media studies courses. Their pertinent questions, insightful comments, and cultural concerns helped immensely in sharpening my approach to the sometimes complex and unsettling subject matter.

Book designer Avery Mathews did a splendid job with the cover jacket and the integration of thumbnail images into the textual material. Sensing the Grim Reaper lurking nearby, I had neither the time nor inclination to pursue a publisher. While getting critiques from scholars around the country is worthwhile, the process invariably involves publisher pressure to put the material into a worn-out mold resulting in a media text bearing little difference from what's already abundantly available. Writing with no one looking over my shoulder with the bottom line in mind proved liberating.

Chapter 1

Copying Concerns

The shifts in human perception and understanding wrought by advances in copying technology are invariably subtler and less discernible than a cultural change resulting from a political revolution. The full impact of new ways of storing, replicating, and spreading ideas, images, and information is only apparent in retrospect, after reverberating across the culture.

Of course, to be sure, potentially disruptive new copy-making media will not—in themselves—uproot long-held cultural beliefs and practices. Who uses the tools and techniques, their specific uses, and the constraints placed on them will be decisive factors. All the same, while new media of expression initially function to fulfill current needs, they invariably have unintended and unanticipated cultural consequences that transport people into a future of unknowns.

Before the invention and widespread use of printing from movable metal type facilitated making multiple copies, people's ways of categorizing, creating a sense of themselves and others, came primarily through direct experience or anecdotes, verbal stories, and recollections of those in the same orbit with equally limited knowledge or perspectives. This situation began to change with books and other printed materials, making literacy and education possible, gradually fracturing the foundation of the religiously-inspired worldviews of the Middle Ages and ultimately opening the way to the often-perplexing, contradictory categorizing in the current media-saturated environment.

Prelude to Printing

Writings, artifacts, and rituals are the keys to unlocking the cultural chambers within which those in the distant past resided. Recreating any aspect of history from such limited indicators is fraught with problems, sparking endless arguments and disagreements. Events, characters, and settings are recreated based on available historical data. New evidence may undermine existing explanations, requiring reinterpretations of a historical account in an ongoing process of assessment and reevaluation.

The retrieved records to construct a historical narrative, like fictional fare, are ordered and linked by cause and effect. As social, political, and cultural influences change, the old consensus, based upon limited evidence, might no longer be considered historically valid in explaining such particulars as cause and effect, motivation, and self-interest, challenging the established, accepted, or traditional.

Another hazard of constructing a narrative history from inevitably highly limited building blocks is an overload of the negative. Historical records are much like the contents of a daily newspaper, filled with affliction, misfortune, corruption, assault, murder, mischief, and misadventure. The normal does not make the news or become part of the historical record, notes Barbara Tuchman in *A Distant Mirror*.[1] Mindful of this bias toward the negative, she stresses that the hundred years preceding the invention of printing from movable metal type marked an unusually calamitous time in Europe.

The medieval bubonic plague, known as the Black Death, began in 1331 in China, as did by most accounts the current viral pandemic. A strain of bacteria residing on fleas carried by black rats killed half of China's population. From there, it swept along trade routes to Europe, North Africa, and the Middle East. In the years between 1347 and 1351, the disease wiped out at least a third to half of all Europeans passing from infected person to infected person through respiratory droplets much as Covid19 does these days. In England alone, it killed so many people that the population didn't climb back to its pre-plague level for almost 400 years.

Adding to the death toll and disruption, England and France waged a war that, with many truces and renewals, lasted over a hundred years. Papal schism and simony were marks of the growing corruption and secularity of the Roman Catholic Church. Increased poverty and misery fanned peasant and proletarian insurrection. Freebooting companies of brigands plundered and pillaged the countryside with impunity. Authority was at a low ebb as the exercise of political power shifted uneasily among the religious leaders, wealthy landowners, and embedded royal dynasties.

By the middle of the fifteenth century, feudalism was in sharp decline, papal authority was on the wane, and the dictates of commerce increasingly shaped the course of human lives and relationships. In various countries, aristocrats were joining forces with an emergent capitalist class to accelerate secular trends and to centralize the functions of government. Innovations in print technology can be seen as both the outcome and the agent of these developments.

Meaning in the Middle Ages

In medieval times, baptism, marriage, and burial ceremonies enveloped each stage of the life cycle couching in comforting spiritual symbolism the harsh reality that we are all born, lust, and must die. Splendid religious pageants rivaled the spectacle of circuses. Sculpture, music, painting, and stained-glass windows reminded the faithful of the joys of eternal salvation. The steeples of the Roman Catholic Church, the largest international institution at the time, towered above the pastoral flock, like secular skyscrapers today, imposing symbols of power and influence.

A testimony to the enduring power of such religious symbolism, in September 2018, when flames shot through the roof of Notre Dame Cathedral, nearly all the French media outlets expressed sorrow over the loss. A jewel of medieval Gothic architecture, the mystical light filtering through its stain-glass windows might turn even an ardent atheist into a true believer. Although few attend Mass regularly in this mainly Roman Catholic country, clarion calls for the cathedral's rebuilding echoed across the landscape from Paris to coastal Saint Nazaire.

Throughout medieval Europe most communication took place primarily in a communal context. The consensus in the community and intense pressures for conformity acted upon the individual, from birth on, to narrow still further the range of acceptable beliefs and behavior. There was also likely to be a high degree of social visibility and scrutiny, which insured compliance. The vast majority of people were illiterate, and manuscript production had been conducted almost exclusively in monasteries.

As a result, even if more people were able to read, texts tended to be both religious and orthodox. Novelty, change, and independent thought were not sought or encouraged. The scarcity and expense of parchment, which was the principal material used for writing, tended to minimize secular challenges to a religious view of the universe. The spread of Islam around the eighth century had cut off supplies of papyrus, the tall aquatic plant in the Nile region of Egypt used as a writing surface.

Commerce and its corresponding need for increased communications began to undermine the old order of things as early as the eleventh century. At that time, there was increased commercial activity accompanied by a revitalization of city life. The towns and cities that had survived the Germanic invasions at the beginning of the medieval period had become sparsely populated and economically dependent on agriculture. With the expansion of commerce, ancient urban centers grew dramatically in population and area, and new towns appeared in many places.

Literacy rates increased as commercial transactions necessitated the growing use of contracts, bills of exchange, and business correspondence. There was also an upsurge in lay education, due partly to the increased demand for more literate men capable of handling the growing complexities of commerce. But other factors were also at work.

By the middle of the twelfth century, Western Europe had found itself awash in new knowledge, recovered from the ancient Greek world by way of the Muslims. In addition to these strong classical influences, fresh and innovative aspects of Islamic and Byzantine culture also had their impact. In response to these developments, great universities emerged in Paris, specializing in theology; in Palermo, Salerno, and Montpellier in medicine; and in Bologna in law. Then others followed, among them Oxford and Cambridge in England. The growth of commerce and education increased the need for more efficient production of writing materials.

Writing Surfaces

Invented by the Chinese in the second century C.E., papermaking techniques moved slowly along the Silk Road, a network of lucrative silk trade routes connecting the East and West. An indication of where regions thrived and prospered, its journey across Asia, and northern Africa into Europe took over a thousand years. Once arriving in medieval Europe, a backwater of cultural progress, it served to accelerate the expansion of commerce and education and played a crucial role in advancing the development of the printing press.

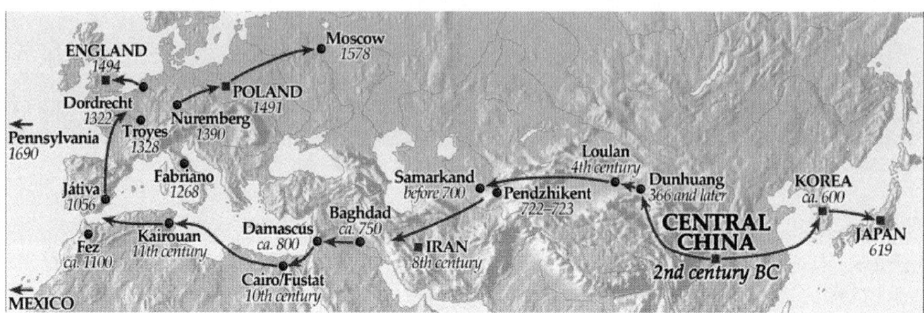

Mostly Arab Muslims turned papermaking into a significant industry. Paper mills flourished across the Islamic regions of the world. Unlocking the mysteries of paper, industrious Arabs employed linen rags saturating and fermenting them in water, as a substitute for the bark of the mulberry the Chinese used. By manufacturing paper on a large scale, devising new methods for its production, they accomplished a feat of essential significance in copying.

The *Koran*'s first paper manuscript to survive dates from 972, but by this date, the use of paper had become standard for most books and documents. Medieval Islamic libraries had hundreds of thousands of volumes far outstripping the relatively small monastic and university libraries in the West. Islamic Amazigh residing in Spain probably introduced techniques for paper manufacture into Europe in the twelfth century. Papermaking centers appeared in Italy after 1275, and France and Germany in the 14th century. By the fifteenth century, papermaking techniques had reached England.

Most writings about the paper trail refer to the Berbers' role, but, as a colleague from the region explained, this designation carries negative connotations. The Romans applied it to all peoples, not them, and therefore uncivilized. Arab colonizers struck another blow to the dignity of the people in the region. They used the epithet Berber as a reference to the sound of sheep and other farm animals. This digression is all by way of saying the Amazigh, ethnic groups mostly indigenous to North Africa, transported papermaking techniques into Europe, paving the way for the printing press.

Although the use of paper was neither as attractive nor as durable as parchment, it was more practical and less expensive. A typical 150-page manuscript on parchment required preparation of the skins of about a dozen sheep.[2] Writing on paper surfaces had the added advantage of being difficult to erase, an important consideration when records and documents had to be secure from forgery. Ample supplies of paper accommodated the new social needs, making possible the rise in commercial and university manuscript production and the growth of the international book trade. In Paris alone, some 10,000 lay scribes were practicing their craft by the middle of the fifteenth century.[3]

Social, political, economic, religious, and technical developments made Europe ready by the 1450s for the invention of the printing press. During the eleventh century C.E., the Chinese also invented a movable-type technique using carved clay baked into hard blocks that were then arranged onto an iron frame and pressed against an iron plate. While allowing for rearranging for each new page, this method and subsequent Korean movable type proved impracticable. The costly process was labor-intensive, given that the ancient Chinese alphabet of ideograms has thousands of characters, as opposed to the more concise, alphabetical script used in Western languages.

Movable Metal Type

Steeped in debt from a previous financial mishap, the German goldsmith Johannes Gutenberg recognized an economic opportunity in the growing demand for books, contracts, calendars, pamphlets, and the like. Working in the city of Mainz on the Rhine River, the industrious Gutenberg developed printing from movable metal type to make money from mass-producing relatively inexpensive products. Born with the surname Gensfleisch, the inventor of printing, like Donald Trump's father, sought a more forceful and marketable moniker. Herr Drumpf and Gutenberg both understood the power of naming and sound symbolism.

Mechanical Duplication

Drawing on his knowledge of metallurgy, and Europe's longstanding phonetic alphabet of twenty-six letters, based purely on phonemes or vocal sounds pronounced in a particular order to generate meaning, he created type mold of just the right width and uniform height. Reconfiguring the durable reusable letters allowed him to make many different pages at a relatively low cost. The other vital elements were paper, modified oil-based ink, and a winepress, traditionally used to crush grapes for wine and olives for oil, retrofitted into his printing press design.

His shop turned out calendars, pamphlets and other ephemera. Roman Catholic clergy became his most profitable patrons when he printed thousands of "indulgences" for the purchase of salvation, not only to the living but also to the dead. Granted increasingly for money with little regard for actual repentance, indulgences became a conspicuously crass means of ecclesiastical fundraising. The hallmark of his printing press, in the early 1450s, working with a staff of about twenty, Gutenberg turned out some 180 or so copies of the two-volume Vulgate—the fourth-century Latin translation of the Bible. To print these many copies took about three years.

What has come to be called the "Gutenberg Bible" was huge and mimicked the design of the scribal bibles in much the way e-books imitate printed works in the modern era. Each of the 1,300 pages contained forty-two lines of text in Gothic type, with double columns, some having letters in color. Like manuscripts of the time, it had no punctuation or indentation of paragraphs. Arranging the letters in a type tray took a full day for a single page of text, but the durability of the letters and the tray itself

provided for a more cost-saving approach, producing books and other printed materials at a much cheaper cost than contemporary methods. Metallic compounds may be responsible for the intensity and sheen. Gutenberg printed as many as sixty of them on costly vellum. The first book produced with movable metal type was the Kindle of its age in that it marked the early stage of a new medium.

Few records exist from this time about Gutenberg, but details of his invention are in the lawsuit testimony of a former financial backer suing for repayment. This testimony describes his type, inventory of metals, and kinds of molds. The movable-metal-type inventor ultimately lost the case with his backer seizing his equipment as collateral. Records of his later years are as sketchy as his early life. Remaining in Mainz, he ceased any efforts at printing after 1460, possibly due to impaired vision dying at age seventy about eight years later. His recognition as the inventor of one of the most significant copying machines in human history only came at the start of the sixteenth century, over three decades after his death.

Book Distribution

Gutenberg's invention didn't realize its profit potential until a distribution network for books emerged. Many enterprising German printers looked for more promising markets, eventually arriving in the great trade center of Venice, the central shipping hub of the Mediterranean in the fifteenth century. They produced books, including editions of the works from classical antiquity, with a brilliant type design that went far beyond earlier techniques, blending ancient and modern influences to achieve more profound originality of form and content and created the first large-distribution mechanism for printed books.

By the 1490s, Venice, a city in northeastern Italy, on a lagoon of the Adriatic Sea, was the book-printing capital of Europe. Along with religious texts and literature, the ships brought breaking news from across the known world. The Venetian printers sold four-page news pamphlets to sailors, and when their ships arrived in distant ports, local printers would copy and hand them off to carriers who would rapidly transport them off to dozens of towns. With literacy rates still very low, locals would gather at the pub to hear a paid reader recite the latest reports, typically ranging from bawdy scandals to war reports, demonstrating a growing market for news of all sorts.

The printers of Venice, uniquely situated on a group of 118 small islands separated by canals and now linked by over 400 bridges, in 1482 also hit upon a "killer app" for the platform of metal type—the "pocketbook" for individual reading. The accessibility and portability of the pocketbooks helped the spread of literacy and brought in a great profit, especially through the sale of secular books.

As the cost of books dropped, less wealthy members of society could gain access to this once exclusive and rare luxury item. Soon not only wealthy merchant families but also many medium-sized towns could boast of having a library. Yearly book fairs became a common occurrence in some of the major cities in Europe. The development of such printing protocols as standardized spelling, grammar, and syntax facilitated communication. Trade among European capitals and Asia introduced print practitioners in Europe to the new method of paper manufacturing using discarded rags, a much cheaper process than the vellum formerly used in the West.

Although scribal culture persisted for hundreds of years afterward, the personal printed book would over time fundamentally change the mindset of medieval readers. "All thought draws life from contacts and exchanges," writes French scholar Fernand Braudel. "Printed books accelerated and swelled the currents which the old manuscript books had kept within narrow channels."[4]

Reading became a private activity, the antithesis of communal thought and behavior contributing to a new sense of individuality with liberating intellectual effects. Alarming Church leadership, scientific findings became "printed and replicable" on a large scale, threatening religious orthodoxy. Those so inclined could now carefully read the words of great thinkers for themselves--pondering, questioning, considering, and perhaps doubting.

The availably of the printed word and the corresponding growth of literacy fostered social separation and fragmentation—much the way smartphones and internet connections do these days. The old medieval worldview shaped by tribal, mystical, and sacramental experiences like baptism and communion slowly began to fade into the background. Whereas the acquisition of insights and information in an oral culture required repetition, printing freed the mind for original and creative thought. No longer being bound by the pragmatic concern of retention resulted in a shift in perception and understanding accelerated by religious reforms.

PRINTING & PROTEST

In the context of this emerging print culture, a young Wittenberg professor named Martin Luther drew up his set of ninety-five theses attacking the sale of indulgences and various practices of the Roman Catholic Church and posted them on the door of the Castle church on the eve of All Saints Day late in October 1517. By most accounts, his only intent was to start a productive debate with his academic colleagues. Most significantly, he later had them printed and sent to his friends in several cities, translating from Latin into local languages. He used broadsheets to spread his protestations, the same large format that developed into the newspaper.

English cleric and scholar John Wyclif (1320-84) had condemned ecclesiastical wealth, avarice, and hypocrisy, anticipating much of the thunder of Luther's reform ideas. And influenced by Wyclif's protests, the Czech John Hus (1369-1415) had denounced the deceptive use of indulgences and founded a reformed church in Bohemia. But it was the printing press in Luther's arsenal that gave his words such explosive proportions.

The shifting power structure in sixteenth-century Germany allowed his protestations to be printed and spread with few impediments. The central authority, the Holy

Roman Emperor, lacked the supremacy to control all the regional authorities within his territories. One of those officials, Saxon Prince Frederick III, used his political influence to protect Luther against both the Catholic emperor and the pope. For German princes, moreover, backing the reformer often coincided with a compelling financial temptation—the seizure of Catholic wealth.

Much of Luther's prodigious production of polemic writings and sermons appeared in print. In effect, he became the first European intellectual to "go viral," creating the momentum for an unprecedented wave of changes in religion, thought, society, and politics throughout the world. The religious upheaval ignited by printing presses of Wittenberg did not subside until nearly half of Western Christendom had broken away from the Roman Catholic Church becoming "Protestant," as the supporters of Luther's protestations came to be called. The most stable authority known to Europeans in the Middle Ages was challenged, shaken, and eventually splintered. With area after area becoming Protestant, those in the upper reaches of the Catholic hierarchy launched a major counteroffensive to stem the corrosive effects of printer's ink.

A Papal Council convoked at Trent, an imperial city in northern Italy, met on and off for eighteen years between 1545 and 1563 to reaffirm and redefine traditional doctrines. Among the council's more significant actions were the inauguration of the Index of Prohibited Books designed to prevent the reading of heretical literature by unauthorized persons. This period also saw an even more significant role for ritual and iconography in Roman Catholic communications. Churches were all the more elaborately adorned with paintings, stained glass, and sculpture.

In contrast, Protestant reformers in northeastern Europe sought to establish a literate, visually iconoclastic culture. They whitewashed church murals and replaced them with the Ten Commandments; removed church statues; and smashed stained-glass windows substituting clear panes instead. Paintings and sculptures venerating the Virgin Mary were destroyed as well, with some Protestant sects eventually rejecting the whole notion of the virgin birth entirely.

The image was grappling with the printed word, without realizing the strength of the latter. The old heresy of individualism was becoming the new orthodoxy. The introduction and widespread use of the printing press eventually disrupted the whole cultural underpinning of the medieval power structure seemingly snapping the synapses that sustained it.

Latin Loses Ground

The potent mix of printing and Protestantism played a significant part in the linguistic development of modern Europe. Latin, the lingua franca of ecclesiastical authority, had dominated the written word throughout most of the medieval period. As the laity sank into illiteracy following the fall of the Roman Empire, this created a situation of enormous cultural significance. It meant that the language of formal learning, literature, and religion was different from the vernacular—the words that were spoken by most people. An increasingly literate middle-class public, unfamiliar with Latin, sought out books and other printed materials in their own vernaculars, contributing to the rise of new national identities.

In the first fifty years or so of printing, the age of the so-called "incunabula," Latin still dominated the publishing field. But as the market for published materials spread, articles and books began to be printed in the vernacular of the various regions of Europe. The prodigious output of the printing presses in the new Protestant countries was in the vernacular, greatly facilitating literacy among the laity. Different Protestant denominations were eager to propagate their doctrines. To this end, they established schools for the general population, where even the son of a cobbler or a peasant might learn to read the Bible and other books in the vernacular.

Thoughts that had remained dormant for centuries flowered once again in this soil made fertile by printers' ink. For millennia, science was a largely solitary pursuit. Great mathematicians and natural philosophers were separated by geography, language and the sloth-like pace of hand-written publishing. Not only were handwritten copies of scientific data expensive and hard to come by, they were also prone to human error.

Science took significant leaps forward in the sixteenth and seventeenth centuries. When developing his revolutionary sun-centric model of the universe in the early 1500s, the Polish astronomer Copernicus relied not only on his heavenly observations but also on printed astronomical tables of planetary movements. The Italian astronomer, physicist, and engineer Galileo's discoveries with the telescope revolutionized astronomy and paved the way for the acceptance of the Copernican heliocentric system.

Still, his advocacy of that system explicitly contradicted Holy Scripture. For his heresy in claiming that earth orbits the sun, the Roman Catholic Church sentenced him to life imprisonment. He served his sentence under house arrest and died at home after an illness. Despite such scientific setbacks, the next several centuries witnessed the emergence of a culture increasingly shaped by print technology and its progeny.

As the age of scribes gave way to that of printers, the pride of authorship took on a new significance. Many medieval churchmen regarded hubris as the guiltiest of sins. The religious authorities sought to suppress the individual ego entirely seeing medieval art and literature for the greater glory of the Almighty. In compliance, writers and artists of the age usually did not affix signatures to their works.

The move toward secularization served to alter that situation. It is indeed hard to imagine such Renaissance figures as Boccaccio or Machiavelli submerging their identities in the collectivity of the group. But the conditions of scribal culture had helped to keep the ego in check. Printing, suggests Marshall McLuhan in *The Gutenberg Galaxy*, helped to release the ego by providing "the physical means of extending the dimensions of the private author in space and time."[5]

The spread of multiple copies of printed material enabled academics, wealthy merchants, and intellectuals of comfortable means to collect personal libraries. Scholars sifted, clarified, and developed this written heritage. "Once old texts came together within the same study, diverse systems of ideas and special disciplines could be combined," explains Elizabeth Eisenstein. "Increased output directed at relatively stable markets, in short, created conditions that favored, first, new combinations of old ideas, and then the creation of entirely new systems of thought."[6]

Aristotle & Shakespeare

A copying machine match between Aristotle and Shakespeare, along with other wordsmiths, saw the birth of speech and drama programs during the last century. Several of these popular departments, especially prominent in the midwest, metamorphosed into media studies. Some rhetorical types fell in with a fast crowd of number crunchers to create the field of mass communication, an increasingly distant cousin ever since media mated with film studies, whisked away from art, theatre, and literature. The availability of printed materials made these matches eventually possible by providing an easy and relatively less expensive access to a broader range of ideas and information.

"Typographical fixity," to use historian Elizabeth Eisenstein's term, had finally broken down the cycle of unearthing, losing, and finding classical texts.[7] The retrieval and duplication of the ancient Greek philosopher Aristotle's writings in ethics, poetics, rhetoric, political theory, metaphysics, and the philosophy of science, had a profound effect on a nascent media studies and overall intellectual development.

Roots of Media Studies

Aristotle's highly influential treatise, *Rhetoric*, the faculty of finding in every given case all the available means of persuasion, provided the framework for public speaking instruction, one of the "seven liberal arts" of the Middle Ages.[8] Aimed at imparting general knowledge and developing broad intellectual capacities, the areas of study in the medieval European university curriculum included grammar, rhetoric, and logic (the trivium) and geometry, arithmetic, music, and astronomy (the quadrivium). The three tenets underpinning of rhetorical analysis, ethos, logos, and pathos, provide a framework for dissecting and validating or debunking ethical, pathetic, and logical appeals of arguments. Ethics or ethos entails calls to intelligence, virtue, morals, and the perception of trustworthiness. Pathos or pathetic appeals play to the emotions and deeply held beliefs drawing audiences into the subject matter. They give a sense of personal stake and are often the catalyst that drives readers and listeners into action. Logos or logical appeals focus on reasoning, evidence, and facts to support an argument. They involve more rational strategies and often strengthen the impact of pathos.

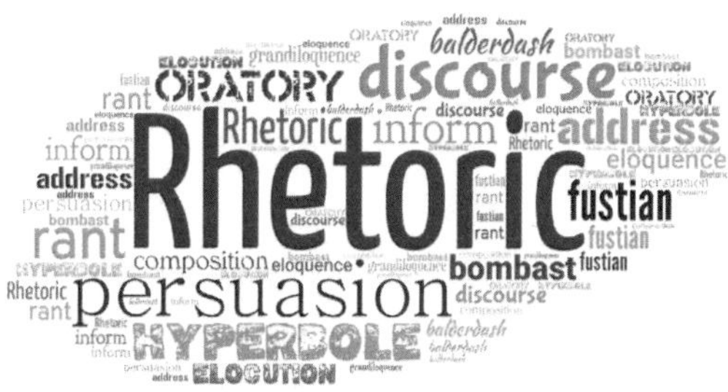

Through the late 19th century, the art of rhetorical persuasion played a central role in Western education in training orators, lawyers, counselors, historians, and politicians. While classical techniques provided the tools for trained speakers to be effective persuaders in public forums and institutions, contemporary rhetoricians investigate human discourse writ large, including journalism, digital media, fiction, history, and the more traditional domains of politics and the law. The ways people influence and persuade one another are cornerstones of the developing discipline of media studies.

Mastery of the analytical skills gained from a liberal arts curriculum arguably provides the best critical and creative mindset for maneuvering in the ever-evolving job market and economy of today's digital universe. A classroom culture rooted in liberal arts focuses on full personal development rather than specialized knowledge in a career pursuit. In the process, life becomes more meaningful, filled with meaning, fostering an ecumenical worldview.

Most of Aristotle's writings continue to be studied, and his work remains a powerful current in contemporary philosophical discourse. Whether the esteemed philosopher's strong defense of slavery, belief in women's inferiority, and opposition to the concept of intrinsic human dignity deserves classroom consideration is a source of contemporary debate and dispute not only in the hallowed halls of academia but also on the pages of popular publications.[9]

Reproducing Shakespeare

A significant media studies contributor, long-dead William Shakespeare remains a crucial component of college curricula. Although none of his manuscripts survive, high school and university students have been able to study his plays and sonnets across the decades and centuries due to the printing press. His works—both poetic and dramatic—often appeared in print before the 1623 publication of the First Folio, the most reliable text for about twenty plays, and a valuable source for many of those previously published. He used more than 20,000 words in his plays and poems, and by combining words, changing nouns into verbs, adding prefixes or suffixes, and so forth likely invented or introduced at least 1,700 words into the English language.

Shakespeare's literary longevity is testimony to the contemporary cultural importance of his works. Studying his judicious use of metaphor, and other rhetorical tools, along with his rhythmical blank verse, greatly enhances verbal facility and stylistic flare. His methods of dramatic irony, language signifying the opposite of what's said, often serve as sarcasm, as in the opening scene of *Richard III*, or as tools of humor to convey an incongruity ridiculing or deprecating an idea or course of action.

The more extensive works of the "Bard of Avon," a title in recognition of his stature, invite reinventions and new interpretations. As a fifteen-year-old schoolboy, Orson Welles put on an ambitious adaptation of *Richard III*.[10] A book of the bard's complete works a constant companion, his creative project evolved into an original but unwieldy mix of Shakespeare's plays.[11] This teenage undertaking foreshadowed his legendary Mercury Theatre productions of the 1930s.

In 1936, at age twenty, Welles adapted and directed Shakespeare's *Macbeth*, about the downfall of a usurper in medieval Scotland, encouraged in his actions by three witches. He moved the play's setting from Scotland to a fictional nineteenth-century Caribbean island, recruited an entirely black cast, and substituted Haitian voodoo rituals for Scottish witchcraft. The "Voodoo Macbeth," as the press dubbed the production, created a sensation when it opened Harlem, launching Welles's meteoric directing career. After astonishing New York theatergoers with several bolder stage productions, he departed for Hollywood in 1939, where he made *Citizen Kane* (1941), a shining example of the American cinema at its best.

The "pure cinema" movement aside, a bard-like love of words, and images attract many to enacted screen drama, a collaborative endeavor.[12] The director and his crew magically bring the world of Elizabethan theatre to full-bodied life in the critically acclaimed *Shakespeare in Love* (1998). The essence of this paean to the power and appeal of stage drama (and by extension the cinema) resides in the strikingly inventive screenplay of Marc Norman and Tom Stoppard.

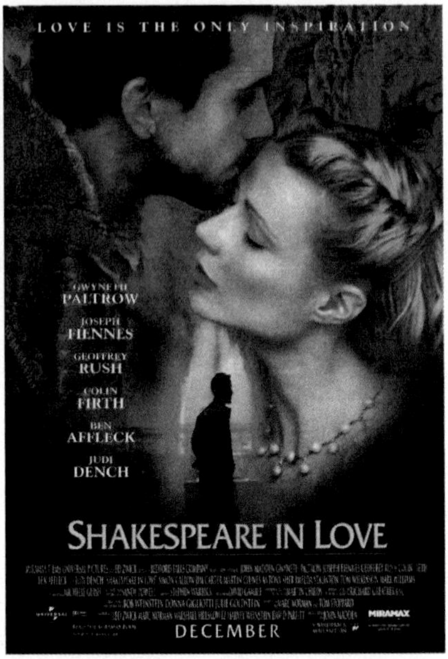

The writing team steadfastly adhered to the scant facts known about Shakespeare and his early life and times. But they constructed their romp of sex, sacrifice, and sonnets around a fanciful premise. We are aware young Will is destined to become perhaps the greatest dramatist the world has ever known. In 1593, London theatre aficionados saw him only as a struggling hack, playing second fiddle to the more esteemed Christopher Marlowe.

As house writer for the Rose Theater, Will Shakespeare (Joseph Fiennes) is struggling with his new play, a comedy with the working title "Romeo and Ethel, the Pirate's Daughter." He has difficulty dashing off a single page of blank verse. His writer's block worsens when he catches his promiscuous paramour Rosaline (Sandra Renton), engaging in "country matters" with another man. She is hardly the inspiration he needs to turn out the "greatest love story" of all time.

Cleverly crafted bits abound throughout the screenplay. As did the Bard of Avon, the scriptwriters use the double entendre—words and phrases with a double meaning or interpretation—to avoid saying anything overly sexualized. When Will consults a shrink (Antony Sher) to overcome his waning prowess with words, the "indelicate" meaning of the figure of speech is barely cloaked. While the hourglass is running, for the fifty-minute session, the woeful Will laments with lyrical flourishes that it is as though he has a broken quill. As if the organ of his imagination is dried up. As if the proud tower of his genius collapsed. After he likens his writing attempts to trying to pick a lock with a wet herring, his doctor gingerly inquires: "Tell me, are you lately humbled in the act of love?"

When again taking quill to parchment, having resolved his impotence, Will, after a false start, is gloomily auditioning actors when a passionate young thespian catches his fancy but flees to her tony residence. The pursuit is on, with the youth turning out to be Viola De Lesseps (Gwyneth Paltrow), an heiress with an adventurous soul on the verge of an unwanted arranged marriage. She loves poetry and theater and longs for a wild, uninhibited romance. Disguised as a young lad, she wins Romeo's role (women were not permitted to act on stage). Will later spots his muse at a dance, is smitten, and eventually figures out that she's the "male" actor with the wispy mustache he cast as Romeo (he's attracted to "him" as well).

Once the passionate affair, and satiric playfulness, are underway, Will's production begins to evolve and grow, deepening into the romantic tragedy that will become *Romeo and Juliet*. During the play rehearsal sequence, the language flows seamlessly back and forth between scenes of their erotic embraces and the next scene on stage. While "necking and petting," quaint euphemisms for a wide range of sexual behavior, they utter sweet nothings that sound almost Shakespearean. Faithful to the bard's formula, the path of true love, alas, is strewn with pitfalls and unassailable obstacles. His affair of the heart ultimately doomed, a despondent Will decides to darken the play's ending.

Printing as Mass Production

Printing from movable type became the archetype of mass production—the first mechanization of an elaborate handicraft, casting replicas of metal type in vast quantity. It established the main principle of letterpress printing, notes S. H. Steinberg in *Five Hundred Years of Printing*. And it introduced to Europe, "more than three centuries ahead of its general adoption by industry, the theory of 'interchangeable parts' which is the basis of the modern mass-manufacturing technique."[13]

Copying Errors

Scribes copied manuscripts by candlelight in dark dank monasteries. Errors were likely common but only on a single text at a time. The ability to record, retrieve, and transmit information on a huge scale created new concerns for accuracy. In a 1631 reproduction of the beautifully written *King James Bible*, often called the "Wicked Bible," one simple typographical error in the Book of Exodus cost its printers a month's salary and their printing licenses.

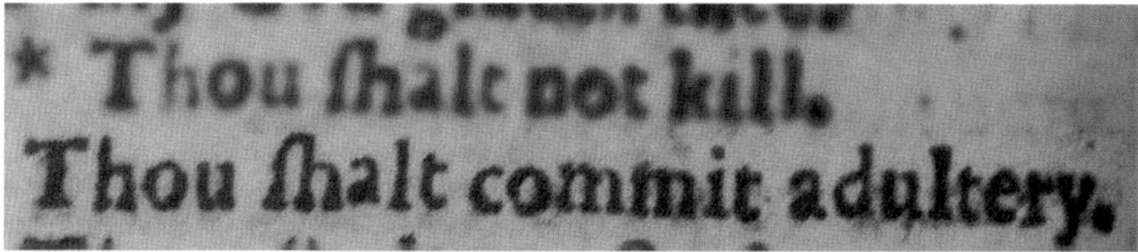

The passage the publishers misquoted was the Seventh Commandment, which should have read, "Thou shalt not commit adultery," but the word "not" was omitted, thus changing the sentence into "Thou shalt commit adultery." This error appeared in multiple copies. Authorities destroyed most of them, and the number still in existence, considered highly valuable by collectors, is thought to be relatively low. One copy containing the misprinted commandment is in the collection of rare books in the New York Public Library.

The dictate not to commit "adultery" would seem among the most obvious, easiest of the commandments to comprehend. In contemporary society, the word means any act of sexual intercourse outside of marriage or, perhaps a bit more narrowly, any act of sexual intercourse between a married person and someone who is not a spouse. A look at the original meaning reveals a lot about attitudes toward women that manifests itself in modern times in a range of ways.

The ancient Hebrews had a very restricted understanding of the concept of adultery, limiting the definition to just sexual intercourse between a man and a woman who was either already married or at least betrothed. The marital status of the man was irrelevant. Thus, a married man was not guilty of adultery for having sex with an unmarried or unengaged woman. At the time women were often treated as little more than property—a slightly higher status than the slaves. Because women were like property, having sex with a married or betrothed woman was regarded as misuse of someone else's possession.

Halting Heresy

The first measures to control printing were introduced just a few decades after the emergence of printing technology. In early sixteenth-century England, Protestant publications from abroad contributed to a growing disaffection with papal power. But it was Henry VIII's desire for a legitimate male heir, more than any other factor, that led to the establishment of the Anglican Church. Catherine of Aragon, his wife of eighteen years, had borne only a daughter, Mary.

When it became apparent that she would bear no more children, Henry sought papal approval to have his marriage annulled so that he could remarry. (He was to marry six times, in all.) When the pope refused his request, the irate king persuaded a subservient Parliament to make him, not the pope, head of the Church of England. However, Henry VIII was no Protestant. He continued to support the Catholic position on all doctrinal points except that of papal supremacy. He persecuted with equal severity Protestants and Roman Catholics alike who refused to acknowledge his spiritual leadership.

During Henry VIII's reign, he constructed an elaborate framework of official state control to stem the flow of heretical literature. In 1529, a list of prohibited books was instituted under secular authority. On Christmas Day in 1534, Henry VIII issued a proclamation requiring printers to have a royal permit before setting up shop. In 1538, he extended licensing to all books printed in the English language and prohibited the importation of printed books.

Despite such measures, the Henrician Reformation ultimately resulted in the establishment of an Anglican Church that was more Protestant than Catholic in orientation. The reign of Henry's young son Edward VI, saw publication of a Book of Common Prayer and forty-two articles of faith; they were clearly Calvinist in flavor. But Catholicism briefly reemerged to a position of preeminence when Mary Tudor, Catherine of Aragon's daughter, succeeded to the throne. "Bloody Mary," as she was called, had some 300 Protestants burned at the stake.

In her effort to restore Catholicism, Queen Mary chartered the Stationers' Company and limited printing rights to the members of that guild. Comprised of printers, publishers, and dealers in books, it became the cornerstone of the English licensing system. Founded in 1403 and incorporated in 1557, this guild, empowered with search, seizure, and even limited judicial functions, dominated London's trade in printed books during the sixteenth and seventeenth centuries. In effect, controlling the right to copy became a method of censorship.

Censorship Under Pressure

After civil war broke out in England in the 1640s, many in the upper reaches of that society came to see social literacy as a contributing factor in the social disruption. There was a growing realization that literate people, as Stone points out, "are far harder to govern and exploit than illiterate, for the simple reason that it is extremely difficult to make sure that they never develop a taste for subversive literature."[14]

The conflict between royalists and parliamentarians, and among competing factions on the parliamentary side, had been augmented by an enormous outpouring of printed materials. The system of state censorship virtually collapsed under the onslaught. The arbitrary and tyrannical Court of the Star Chamber, so named because its meetings were held in a room at the Palace of Westminster that had gilt stars on its ceiling, was abolished in 1641. The effectiveness of the Stationers' Company as the controlling authority in the printing industry was also destroyed.

Among the more eloquent proponents of unlicensed printing in the civil war period was the poet John Milton. His 1644 prose polemic *Areopagitica* asserts: "And though all winds of doctrine were let loose to play upon the earth, so Truth be in the field, we do injuriously by licensing and prohibiting to misdoubt her strength," he boldly asserted. "Let her and Falsehood grapple; who ever knew Truth put to the worse in a free and open encounter?" But Milton's concept of free expression was quite limited.

A few pages after this often-quoted passage, he expressed little toleration for, "Popery and open superstition which as it extirpates all religions and civil supremacies, so itself should be extirpated." (However, he would try "to win and regain the weak and misled.") Nor could he conceive of condoning that which was impious or evil, or against faith or manners. And blasphemy, atheism, and libel were not among "the winds of doctrine" that he would "let loose." Later, Milton himself became an official censor.

Milton was an adherent of the Independents, a radical minority of Puritans—a Calvinist sect that sought to "purify" the Anglican Church of all remaining traces of Roman Catholicism. After the Puritans under Oliver Cromwell came to power, the Anglican Church, the House of Lords, and the monarchy were all legislated out of existence. Cromwell eventually wielded a sovereignty that was far more despotic than any of his royal predecessors. By the time of his death in 1658, many in the country had grown weary of Puritan austerities.

The next two years saw most of the old institutions restored, but many bitterly fought issues remained unresolved. Neither king nor Parliament had clear supremacy; sharp economic and religious differences still prevailed. The traditional censorship system based on state licensing that the government reinstituted in 1662 remained intact for thirty-one years. Moreover, Parliament still maintained restrictions against reporting its proceedings and kept controls against treason and "seditious libel" intact.

Seditious libel was a particularly damaging way of controlling expression, broadly defined to allow the suppression of all criticism of those in power. Any publication intended to bring the king into disrepute, incite disaffection against him or the government, raise discontent among the people, or promote feelings of ill will between different classes was categorized as seditious libel.

The truth of what was said made little difference. Indeed, the higher the truth, the more serious the libel, since such a charge could cause more considerable discontent among the people than a false one. Such restrictions aside, the abandonment of licensing in 1694 was a significant step forward. While still subject to charges of seditious libel, the government did not control books and journals before publication.

Colonial Press

Early colonial administrators in America were well aware of print technology's disruptive potential. In 1671, Sir William Berkeley, who governed Virginia for thirty-eight years, succinctly stated his views, doubtlessly held by many of the Crown's officials: "But I thank God we have not free schools nor printing, and I hope we shall not have [them] these hundred years," he said. "For learning has brought disobedience and heresy and sects into the world, and printing has divulged them and libels against the government."[15]

Characterizing the early development of a free press as a heroic struggle against such tyrannical views is standard; there is much evidence to support this perspective. In the eighteenth century, demands for freedom of the press in America were directed primarily against British colonial rule. Many American rebels indeed found inspiration in the enlightenment ideas of Voltaire, Rousseau, and English philosopher John Locke, commonly known as the "father of liberalism." John Milton's Areopagitica also enjoyed wide circulation in this period.

Provocative pieces in the *New York Weekly Journal* under the pseudonym "Cato," the pen name of two antimonarchists, were especially critical of New York's corrupt, inept governor, Sir William Cosby. In 1734, under Cosby's order, the sheriff arrested the *Journal*'s publisher, John Peter Zenger, and the attorney general accused him of "raising sedition."[16] When a grand jury refused to indict the publisher, he charged him with libel in August 1735.

After the chief justice found his first counselor in contempt, he removed him from the case, leaving the defendant in prison for more than eight months. His wealthy backers secretly arranged for famed Philadelphia lawyer Andrew Hamilton to defend him. One of the most astute and able advocates in the colonies, he turned the case into a cause célèbre with the public's interest growing to a fever pitch.

Well into the winter of life, his white wig falling to his shoulders, the histrionically inclined Hamilton argued eloquently for the cause of liberty. The defendant, asserted Hamilton, could not be found guilty unless what he printed was indeed libelous. To be libelous, said Hamilton, the words themselves must include seditious and malicious falsehoods. He told the jury in ringing tones: "It is not the cause of the poor printer, nor of New York alone, which you are now trying. No. It may, in its consequences, affect every freeman that lives under the British government on the main of America." In his concluding remarks, Hamilton directed the jury to do its duty by striking a blow for the cause of liberty—the liberty "both of exposing and opposing arbitrary power ... by speaking and writing-

truth." Palpably exhausted, Hamilton limped to his chair.

The chief justice charged the jury with a few awkwardly phrased remarks about their obligation not to go beyond the fact of publication, leaving the issue of seditious libel to the justices. The jury retired, only to return ten minutes later with a unanimous verdict of not guilty.

The judge did not set the decision aside, although it was certainly within his power to do so. The jury had gone beyond its mandate in direct contradiction of the law. Less a clarion call for freedom of expression, the outcome probably reflected the disdain many colonists felt for governor's corrupt practices. Whatever the reasons, at the time, no distinct separation of powers existed. Printers and editors were hauled before hostile legislatures and assemblies—held in contempt and jailed and fined.

The eighteenth-century crusade for freedom, viewed through a less rose-colored prism, can be seen as an effort to legitimize a new capitalist class challenging the royal authorities to advance its economic interests. A group of wealthy merchants and landowners backed the "cause of the poor printer," seeking a more significant share of control in the colony's affairs. They had initially set up Zenger's newspaper as a vehicle for expressing their interests and views.

From this vantage point, unclouded by patriotic rhetoric, the fight for a free press appears more like the calculated product of expediency than the enlightened result of principle. The passage of the Stamp Act of 1765 evoked the wrath of newspaper publishers. Many considered this legislation, which placed a hefty tax on the paper used in publishing, to be highly inimical to the functioning of a profitable press.

Typical of the militant newspapers was the *Boston Gazelle and Country Journal*, to which Samuel Adams was a frequent contributor. As a polemicist, Adams had few peers. He instilled in his readers with a fierce hatred of England. Not averse to dipping his quill in the venom of vituperation, he gave lurid descriptions of British soldiers beating small boys, violating matrons, and raping young girls. English officials denied these charges, in vain. Bostonians quickly came to resent the presence of soldiers bitterly.

John Dickinson, a colonial journalist, argued outright for the sanctity of property rights and free enterprise. His capitalist viewpoint was expressed in a series of articles entitled "Letters from a Farmer in Pennsylvania," printed in the *Pennsylvania Chronicle* and reprinted in other newspapers throughout the colonies. Although Dickinson was opposed to revolution, he strongly favored home rule for the provinces and resented English control over foreign trade. Dickinson had nothing but contempt for radicals fomenting revolution; nevertheless, he did more than any other writer, except Samuel Adams, to bring on the War for Independence.

The war had united large property owners, merchants, bankers, and manufacturers long with small farmers and wage earners in a common cause. Not all elements of American society, however, were encompassed in the stirring words of the Declaration of Independence: "We hold these Truths to be self-evident, that all Men are created equal, that their creator endows them with certain unalienable rights, that among these are Life, Liberty and the Pursuit of Happiness."

Penned by Thomas Jefferson, one of eight American presidents who owned slaves while in office, the phrase "all men are created equal" meant men and not women. Nor were equality and unalienable rights intended for all men—for living in the rebellious colonies were slaves, indentured servants, and Native Americans. The Declaration's claims for freedom and equality didn't include any of these men, let alone women. During his lifetime, Jefferson owned several hundred slaves. Some forty-one of the fifty-six of those who signed the historical document were slaveholders. In 1776, slavery was legal in all thirteen of the new states.

Highlighting the hypocrisy of the revolutionaries, former slave Frederick Douglass in a July 5th, 1852 speech in Rochester, New York called the celebration of independence a sham; the boasted liberty, an unholy license; the claim of national greatness, a swelling vanity; the sounds of rejoicing empty and heartless. No recording exists of how he delivered such stirring sentiments as "above your national, tumultuous joy, I hear the mournful wail of millions."[17] Mincing no words, Douglas, a key leader of the abolitionist movement, noted no nation on the earth is guilty of practices more shocking and bloodier than those of the people of these United States. He recognized that the American Revolution espoused high principles and made significant progress in realizing them, but condemned the hypocrisy of tolerating the massive injustice of slavery, which so blatantly contradicted those principles. His rebuke is not a matter of judging historical figures by modern standards but of holding them up to the professed principles at the time.

Commercial and Partisan Press

During the late 1700s and early 1800s, newspaper publishing bore little likeness to the institution it is today. Typically, papers had a small circulation, with scant staff to reproduce them on clunky hand-cranked presses. Even in the larger urban areas, the owner of a newspaper usually served as the reporter and editor with apprentices helping with printing and delivery. There was no job description of "journalist" or any of the prevailing standards of verification, independence, or accountability.

For the most part, a political and commercial press intended for well off and politically engaged readers dominated journalism. Bankrolled by political parties or affluent subscribers, newspapers provided political commentary and information about domestic and world markets. In the nineteenth century, as the United States gained higher industrial output, the rapidly expanding economy created an enormous demand for information. Entrepreneurs wanted to know about market conditions and those political vicissitudes affecting the flow of raw materials and manufactured goods. By 1830, there were some 700 or so newspapers in the country, sixty-five of them dailies.

The competition in New York City was particularly keen. Of the eight morning papers competing for advertising and circulation by 1828, five of these were devoted exclusively to commercial affairs. In just the previous year, two new morning newspapers appeared, the *Journal of Commerce* and the *Morning Courier*. The latter soon merged with the *Enquirer* to become the formidable *Courier and Enquirer.* In its earliest years, the flamboyant James Watson Webb, who engaged continuously in journalistic jousts with his newspaper rivals, edited this combined newspaper.

The *Journal of Commerce* became the *Courier*'s single most active competitor. Both newspapers maintained their schooners to meet incoming ships, which brought foreign newspapers. The other morning papers in New York belonged to an association organized for the express purpose of sharing such expenses. An intense rivalry emerged. By 1831, maintenance of news boats reached a combined cost of $25,000.

Advertising revenue helped to defray this expense. Ads in the *Courier and Enquirer*, for instance, were often so numerous that it had to print additional pages. The primary profit came from subscription sales. Since the average subscription cost about $8 to $10 a year, large circulations were out of the question. Individual copies could be purchased at the printer's office for 6¢ an issue. But even this price precluded a general readership since the average worker only earned about 85¢ a day.

Hamilton-Jefferson Press Battles

As the nineteenth century dawned, with the constitutional system now in place, what has come to be called the "partisan press" reflected a sharp schism between the two distinctive political parties that had emerged after the revolution, the Federalists and Republicans (later Democratic-Republicans). A significant division between the nascent parties concerned how broadly or narrowly the new constitution should be interpreted.

Led by such pen warriors as Alexander Hamilton, ill-born, well-married, and decidedly ambitious, the Federalists favored a broad, expansive reading with a strong centralized government empowered to check the imprudence of democracy. The Republican position, expressed by to-the-manor-born Thomas Jefferson, among others, preferred a narrower constitutional scope that allowed for a league of more or less independent states. Hamilton and Jefferson fought for their positions on the battlefield of the nation's newspapers. The Federalist press attacked Jefferson and his allies mercilessly, while the Republican newspapers did likewise to Hamilton and his cadre.

The journalism of this era was not only partisan but, in what may have a familiar ring, also often fabricated, overheated, and sometimes scandalous. Jefferson and Hamilton were remarkably erudite, cultured men. In addition to reading and writing learned tomes, they enjoyed playing such instruments as the violin, harp, and pianoforte. At the same time, they supported a press that libeled, vilified, and berated with abandon. It is no small irony, notes media historian Eric Burns in *Infamous Scribblers*, "that the golden age of America's founding was also the gutter age of American reporting, that the most notorious presses in our nation's history churned out its copies on the foothills of Olympus."[18]

An editorial in a Hamilton-backed Federalist newspaper, the *Gazette of the United States*, exemplifies the nasty, personal nature of partisan attacks in late 18th-century America. Written under the pen name "Phocion," an ancient Greek statesman, it attacked the pretensions and demagogic tendencies of 1796 presidential candidate Thomas Jefferson. The campaign between him and the presidential incumbent John Adams became highly acrimonious.[19]

In an October editorial in the *Gazette*, the unidentified author, who turned out to be Hamilton himself, went so far as to accuse Jefferson of carrying on an affair with one of his slaves. Such personal attacks continued unabated. Some six years later, Republican journalist James Callendar (with secret funding from Jefferson) claimed Hamilton had repeated sexual encounters with another man's twenty-three-year-old wife (she and her husband had conspired to blackmail the middle-aged Hamilton).[20]

During the presidential election of 1800, Callendar, perhaps the most poisonous of the print warriors, assailed then-President John Adams with such colorful epithets as "repulsive pedant" and "a hideous hermaphroditical character." In a nasty game of tit for tat, supporters of Adams returned fire, spreading rumors that Jefferson was an atheist from whom the God-fearing would have to hide their bibles.

The vitriolic Callendar was charged, tried and convicted under the 1798 Sedition Act, which made it a crime to utter "any false, scandalous and malicious" statements against the Government of the United States, the President, or members of the Congress or "to incite against them the hatred of the good people of the United States." In a pamphlet advocating the election of Jefferson over Adams, Callendar had accused Adams of contriving "a French war, an American navy, a large standing army, an additional load of taxes, and all the other symptoms and consequences of debt and despotism." "Take your choice," he concluded, "between Adams, war and beggary, and Jefferson, peace and competency."[21]

Under tenants of this act, which flies in the face of current-day interpretations of the First Amendment, the government did not have to prove that the alleged seditious writings were false. Instead, the accused had to disprove the charges. His attorneys argued to no avail that this legislation should be construed to apply only to false statements of facts and not to reports of political opinion.

At the time the sedition law was enacted, war with France seemed imminent, and rumors of French espionage and seditious activities were rampant. The legislation was used, however, in an attempt to suppress all criticism. The Federalists prosecuted twenty-five persons and convicted ten, all in patently unfair trials. When Thomas Jefferson ascended to the presidency in 1801, they were all pardoned, including Callendar.

In 1802, when then-President Jefferson snubbed his request for a political appointment, the spurned Callendar turned on his onetime benefactor. Writing in a Richmond newspaper, he claimed the president had kept one of his slaves as his concubine, and that her adolescent son bore a striking resemblance to the president himself.

Such rumors had long been circulating, but the onetime Republican's article put them squarely in the public arena. The story continued to dog the president for the remainder of his term in office, although few historians credited the charges. Recent DNA testing revealed that the widowed master of Monticello, built with slave labor, had almost certainly fathered six children with Sally Hemings, a slave on his sprawling estate. Hemings herself was likely the half-sister of Jefferson's deceased wife, Martha. Upon his death, the flawed founder did not free the people he enslaved, other than those in the Heming's family, including several of his offspring. He sold everyone else to pay off his considerable debts.

For the most part, the tone of the partisan press softened as the century progressed. Many journalists among the founders moved on to other endeavors. Well into middle age, Alexander Hamilton was a notable exception. Soon after Jefferson ascended to the presidency in 1801, a vexed Hamilton, now out of power, lost little time before assailing his archenemy.

Writing under the pseudonym Lucius Crassus, an ancient Roman orator, Hamilton, in response to Jefferson's First Annual Message to Congress, found foolishness or betrayal or worse in just about every topic the president covered. On the hot-button issue of immigration, for instance, he vehemently opposed the president's call for an easy path toward naturalization. After Hamilton died in a duel with Vice President Aaron Burr in Weehawken, New Jersey on July 11, 1804, newspapers became less partisan. His death marked the passing of an era.

Right to Make Copies

The mass production of printed materials transformed the whole notion of authorship, making writing a potentially profitable enterprise. A right to copy or copyright is a form of "intellectual property"—any work of authorship, invention, and discovery, or other original creation that may be protected by law. The United States Constitution, Article I, Section 8, Clause 8, is the basis for a proprietary right of control over literary or other artistic creations as well as inventions granted by the federal government for a limited time. The applicable section reads, [The Congress shall have power] "To promote the progress of science and useful arts, by securing for limited times to authors and inventors the exclusive right to their respective writings and discoveries." The primary purpose is to encourage creative production for the ultimate benefit of society at large.

Copyright law protects an "intangible" creation, one that can't be touched or held or locked away for safekeeping. To be protected, the creator must "fix" the work in a tangible medium of expression for a more than transitory period. A draft of a novel on paper, the "rushes" from a movie before editing, a snapshot on film or a digital camera's flash memory, all are "fixed" works within the meaning of copyright law.

The law protects the form of expression, its presentation. A reporter's style, the manner of presenting the facts, can be copyrighted, for example, but not the events in the story. Other journalists may use the same information to write their news stories. Once the copyright expires, the work falls into the public domain, meaning it is essentially public property and can be used freely by anyone without permission or royalty payments.

As one might expect of a former colony in the British Empire, a great deal of the

American legal system is grounded in English law. The 1710 Statute of Queen Anne, the first legislative copyright act in Anglo-American history, triggered decades of debate over the meaning of its various provisions. Functioning as a supreme court of sorts, the British House of Lords ruled in 1774 that copyright is no longer a publisher's right but rather an author's right, albeit a right of limited duration.

As interpreted, the law granted the creator of a work fourteen years of exclusive rights and legal protections preventing others from copying, distributing, or selling it without permission. These rights could be renewed for another fourteen years if the creator was still alive to do so. The Copyright Act of 1814 extended more rights for authors but did not protect them from reprinting outside the country.

The Berne International Copyright Convention of 1886 finally protected authors among the nations who signed the agreement. This legally binding arrangement automatically protects copyrights for creative works when written or recorded on some physical medium. Although the United Kingdom signed in 1887, it did not implement large parts until 100 years later. The United States did not become a signatory until 1989.

Duration of Protection

American copyright law traces its lineage back to the Queen Anne statue, a major influence on the first federal law protecting creative works, the Copyright Act of 1790. It required registration of a work to receive copyright protection. Providing the author with the sole right and liberty of printing, reprinting, publishing and vending, the length of copyright protection was likewise short, fourteen years, plus the ability to renew one time for fourteen more, only available if author was alive. Congress extended renewal for a second term to include an author's heirs some twelve years later. And, in 1831, it extended the first term to twenty-eight years but renewal period stayed the same.

By the dawn of the twentieth century, whole new vistas lay open for the rapid world-wide circulation of ideas, intelligence and, with new means of public transportation, even the movement of people themselves. Many members of Congress were aware of the necessity of encouraging authorship as a profession, a way of earning a livelihood from writings. Under the 1909 Act, copyright had a 28-year term, followed by a possible renewal and extension of the copyright for another 28 years.

Abandoning the two-term scheme and renewal system in the Copyright Act of 1976, Congress extended all existing copyrights by nineteen years. The new act protected works created after 1978 for the life of the author or creator plus fifty years. After this period, work falls into the public domain and may be copied by any person for any reason without payment of royalty to the original owner. It protects "works for hire," those done as an employee or under contract, for seventy-five years after publication. Further expanding protection, in 1992, Congress dropped the renewal requirement for all works created before 1978.

Until 1989, when the United States joined the Berne Convention, still the world's primary international copyright agreement, the failure to affix a copyright notice (Copyright © 2020 by Robert Henry Stanley), meant the automatic loss of most copyright protection. Today, a copyright notice is not required to protect a work; once a work is created it is protected. To sue for infringement requires registration, however. To register a copyrighted work with the federal government, the owner must fill out the proper registration form, pay a small fee, and deposit two complete copies of the work with the Copyright Office.

Copyright & the Courts

To promote innovation and ensure consistency across states, the framers decided that copyright infringement would be adjudicated at the federal level. Knowledge of the federal court system is essential for an understanding of decisions in copyright infringement cases. Congress created all federal courts save for the United States Supreme Court, which is the only court specifically established by the Constitution.

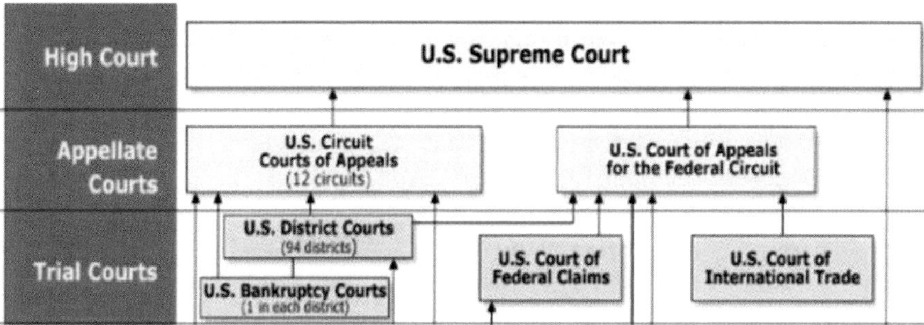

The national court system has three tiers or levels. The point of entry is usually one of the ninety-four U.S. District Courts. These trial courts are the "workhorses" of the federal system. For a court to consider a case, three conditions must apply: a legitimate controversy ripe for adjudication, parties in the case have "standing"—a direct interest in the outcome, and the claim must fall within the court's jurisdiction or sphere of influence.

At the next level are the thirteen U.S. Courts of Appeals: the eleven numbered courts correspond to regions of the country. The two unnumbered courts, both located in the nation's capital, are the District of Columbia court, for such matters as appeals of rulings by administrative agencies, and the Federal Circuit court, responsible for patents, trademark, and copyright appeals, among several other things of significance to media practitioners.

These "appellate" courts can affirm or negate lower court decisions, dismiss appeals, remand them to trial courts, and reverse with an order to lower courts to dismiss. At the summit of the system is the Supreme Court of the United States. Presidents nominate, and a majority of the Senate confirms judges in the federal system. At all three levels, these are lifetime appointments. While trial courts deal with questions of fact and law, appellate courts generally focus exclusively on matters of law.

Since the losing parties are entitled to at least one appeal consideration, the intermediate appellate courts have little discretion over whether to accept cases from the trial level. In criminal cases, the prosecution can't appeal or retry an accused person on the same (or similar) charges following a valid acquittal of those found guilty. Legitimate reasons might include the allowance of inadmissible evidence, flawed jury selection, or incorrect instructions. A successful outcome generally results in a new trial.

As many as 10,000 cases may be appealed to the U.S. Supreme Court yearly, although it generally hears only 75 to 100 of these. Most cases come to the Supreme Court by appeal when one party submits a petition requesting the review of a lower court's decision. When deciding to hear such a request, the court grants a "writ of certiorari," roughly meaning, "to be more fully informed." In granting such a writ, four of the nine justices must believe that errors in the procedure have happened in the lower court—called "the rule of four."

Once the Supreme Court accepts an appellate case, all nine justices sit together to consider the arguments of the contending parties. Each side presents its evidence in the form of a brief, which is a document that gives the facts of a situation, summarizes the lower court's decision, and argues the party's opinion. The court can also grant oral arguments, during which both parties have thirty minutes to present their cases in person before the court. The justices then convene to discuss the matter before handing down their holding.

There are several types of opinions that the court can hand down. The most common is the majority opinion, which states the decision of the majority of the court, usually at least five of the justices with one serving as the author. A plurality decision is when fewer than five support the ruling but not the rationale. A decision sometimes comes in a brief, unsigned statement, called a per curium decision, Latin for "by the court," in which five or more members of the court issue a ruling collectively. The two types of individual opinions are concurring, one or more members who voted with the majority, but for differing legal reasons, and dissenting, the opposing arguments of one or more justices who voted against the majority.

Retroactive Copyright Protection

Under American law, the copyright owner (who is often not the creator of the work) has the absolute right to change a work without the consent of the creator. The 1992 Auto-Renewal Act made renewal automatic for works first published between 1964 and 1977. All works under copyright would be accorded the maximum term then available. In 1994, in Section 104A, Congress restored copyright in foreign works that were still protected in their origin countries but not in the United States.

The Sonny Bono Copyright Term Extension Act added twenty-years to the first fifty years. Named after the former entertainer turned congressman, the extension applied retroactively. As amended, the 1976 law extended the two terms of twenty-eight years of 1909 legislation, increasing the second term of twenty-eight years to sixty-seven years for a total of ninety-five years. The earliest works to benefit from the extension were those published in 1923. Congress passed this extension mainly to get in line with European Union standards so as not to lose this significant export market.

Internet publisher Eric Eldred wanted to post Robert Frost's poems on his website, which contains public domain literature. Joined by a group of commercial and non-commercial interests who relied on the public domain for their work, he challenged the retrospective extension claiming Congress had violated the "limited times" provision of the constitution. After losing at the district and appellate court levels, Eldred appealed to the U.S. Supreme Court, which granted certiorari, agreeing to hear the case.

In her 6-3 majority opinion, Justice Ruth Bader Ginsberg rejected Eldred's "for limited times" argument rationale, stating the amendment reflects the reality that Americans are living longer. Refusing to apply constitutional free-speech standards to limit Congress's ability to confer copyrights for limited terms, she noted the court shouldn't second-guess the legislative branch. She also stated the extension is in harmony with a 1993 European Union directive instructing its members to establish a baseline copyright term of life plus seventy years. And to deny this longer term to the works of any non-EU country whose laws did not secure the same extended time.

Protections Provided

Under the "first sale" doctrine, when copyright owners sell lawfully made copies of works, purchasers can put them in the trash or sell them for profit because these acts don't involve making copies. Throwing a copyrighted work in the trash or selling it even for a profit is perfectly legal because these acts don't involve making copies. Although to be protected a work must be fixed in a physical medium, owning a "copy" of a work is not the same thing as owning the copyrights in the work.

Copyright does not protect titles, slogans, names, or short phrases. Nor are ideas or facts protected, only the expression of them. The telling of news stories, their style, and manner of presentation, is protected but not the facts themselves; other journalists may use them with impunity. If there are only one or very few ways to express an idea, courts deem the expression "merged" with the concept and grant no protection against copying. This doctrine prevents copyright from being used to monopolize ideas.

The selection and arrangement of facts (e.g., in databases) can be protected as a "compilation." In that event, copying the underlying facts is not an infringement, so long as the copier does not appropriate the creativity residing in selecting or arranging the facts. It follows that extracting facts or data from a web site (so-called "screen scraping") is usually not a copyright violation, although it may violate the site's terms of use (which may or may not be enforceable under contract law). And if automated software "robots" or "spiders" collect masses of data from a website, its owner might also assert a state law claim for "trespass to chattel" or movable personal property.

The individual who wrote or created the work initially owns the copyrights in a work with a notable exception. Under the "work made for hire" doctrine, employers own the rights to works created by employees within the scope of their employment. Depending on contractual specifics, nonemployees commissioned to create work may own the copyrights even though someone else paid for it.

A homeless charity, the Community for Creative Non-Violence, commissioned James Earl Reid to do a sculpture for display at a Christmas Pageant in Washington. D.C. Called "Third World America," it depicted a homeless family sleeping on a grate in the street. Reid contented he owned the copyright and therefore had the right to profit from reproductions of the stunning sculpture.

Reid had used his own tools, worked in his own studio, received no regular salary or benefits, and had only a short-term relationship with the homeless charity that commissioned the sculpture. Justice Thurgood Marshall giving the court's opinion held he was an independent contractor, not an employee, so the "work made for hire" provision

did not apply.[22] These kinds of cases often turn on the wording of the contract.

Over the decades, Congress expanded the subject matter of copyright law to embrace a wide range of works, whether published or unpublished. These include literary or textual works of all kinds (including novels, short stories, biographies, articles, news stories, poems, outlines, letters, email messages, etc.), pictorial, graphic and sculptural works (including sketches, paintings, photographs, drawings, designs, etc.), musical, dramatic and choreographed works (songs, telephone ring tones, plays, TV shows), sound recordings (performances of songs, public speeches, books on tape), computer programs, most websites, and various other digitized works.

Elements for Proving Liability

Copyright holders who choose to bring a suit must prove three elements, originality, access and substantial similarity. Released in November 1970, "My Sweet Lord" made George Harrison the first of the Beatles to have a solo No. 1 on the Billboard Hot 100. A few months after its release, Bright Tunes Music, the publisher of Ronnie Mack's "He's So Fine," a 1963 hit for the New York "girl group" the Chiffons, sued the former Beatle for copyright infringement.

In September 1976, a United States District Court heard testimony by Harrison and expert witnesses. Analyzing both songs' music, the presiding judge concluded in somewhat of an overstatement, "it is perfectly obvious to the listener that in musical terms, the two songs are virtually identical."[23] He found Harrison "subconsciously" plagiarized the Mack song. After saying he believed he did not do so deliberately," the judge noted that "My Sweet Lord" is the same song as "He's So Fine" with different words, a bit of an overstatement. Since Harrison had access to "He's So Fine," this is, under the law, he concluded "infringement of copyright, and is no less so even though subconsciously accomplished."

Tricky transactions affected the outcome of the case. In 1978, before the court decided on damages in the case, Harrison's former manager Allen Klein, who had represented him earlier in the proceedings, purchased the copyright to "He's So Fine" from Bright Tunes. In 1981, the court decided the damages amounted to $1,599,987, but that due to Klein's duplicity, Harrison would only have to pay him $587,000 for the rights to "He's So Fine"—the amount his crafty former manager had paid Bright

Tunes for the song.

Copyrights can be transferred only by an express assignment in writing. This requirement governs exclusive licenses as well as assignments of the entirety of a copyright. The copyright holder owns a "bundle of rights"—to reproduce the work in copies; prepare derivative works based on the original; distribute copies to the public; or display and perform it publicly. A violation of any of these rights involves the payment of "damages" or financial compensation.

The plaintiffs, those bringing the suit, may ask the defendants, or alleged violators, to pay for damage suffered, as well as for the reimbursement of profits made by "infringers" from pirating the protected work. When plaintiffs experience no actual loss, they may seek statutory damages—those prescribed by the copyright statute range from $750 to $150,000 per infringement depending on the infringer's culpability.

Fair Use Doctrine

The 1976 statute in seeking to balance guarantees of free speech and press with the copyright protection includes a "fair use" provision. The concept of fair use enables copyright law to coexist with freedom of speech protections and looks to prevent copyright from being used as a weapon rather than its stated purpose: to incentivize creativity. Section 107 of the 1976 act outlines four factors for courts to consider when determining fair use: (1) The purpose and character of the application, including whether such use is for commercial or nonprofit educational purposes. (2) The nature of the copyrighted work. (3) The amount and substantiality of the portion used concerning the copyrighted work as a whole. (4) The effect of the use upon the potential market for, or value of, the copyrighted work.

In assessing fair use under the statute, the courts explore all four factors and weigh the results together in light of copyright purposes. While seemingly straightforward, these factors don't provide very much in the way of guidance. No bright line exists that separates the protectable expression from the non-protectable material in a work of fiction. What precisely is a judge supposed to consider regarding the purpose and character of the work? What about the nature of the copyrighted work makes a use fair or not? Congress didn't create the fair use section to define new legal concepts, but rather codified 150 years of judicial practice, with all its uncertainty intact, into a few sentences.

A landmark case, illustrating the application of these factors concerns the memoir of Gerald Ford, who became president after Richard Nixon resigned in the face of likely impeachment charges. His first significant act upon taking office was to grant a full pardon to Nixon for his role in the Watergate scandal. In 1977, after losing a close election to Democrat Jimmy Carter, Ford contracted with Harper & Row, to publish his memoirs. As they were nearing completion, the publisher negotiated a prepublication agreement with *Time* magazine to excerpt 7,500 words from Ford's account of his pardon. Before Time released its article, the *Nation*, using approximately 300 words from the manuscript, scooped the story.

As a result, *Time* reneged its agreement, and the publisher sued the *Nation* for copyright infringement. The case eventually made its way up to the U.S. Supreme Court, the highest tribunal in the land. In a 6-3 opinion, Justice Sandra Day O'Con-

nor, writing for the majority, the court held that the *Nation*'s use of verbatim excerpts from the unpublished manuscript was not "fair use."[24] The majority opinion held that the unpublished nature of work is a key, though not necessarily determinative, factor tending to negate a fair-use defense.

The high court said the 1976 Copyright Act clearly recognizes the right of first publication for an author. It also declined to expand fair use to create "what amounts to a public figure exception to copyright" in response to the defendant's First Amendment argument. In a 1992 amendment, Congress allowed that unpublished works might fall under "fair use," making right of first publication less significant.

Additionally, Justice O'Connor ruled that although the excerpts constituted a quantitatively insubstantial portion of the memoirs, they represented "the heart of the book." Finally, noting that the effect of the use upon the potential market for the copyrighted work was the "single most important element of fair use," she found that the defendant's use "directly competed for a share of the market" and presented "clear-cut evidence of actual damage." The "crux of the profit/nonprofit distinction is not whether the sole motive of the use is monetary gain," she noted, "but whether the user stands to profit from exploitation of the copyrighted material without paying the customary price."

A critical fair use distinction involved using technology to record programs off the air for personal purposes but not for resale. In the 1970s, Sony developed the Betamax videotape-recording format. Fearing this new technology would lead to widespread copying, Universal Studios and the Walt Disney Company sued Sony and its distributors in a California district court in 1976. They alleged that because the device has copyright infringement potential, they were liable for any violation committed by its purchasers. The district court ruled for Sony, on the basis that noncommercial home recording was fair use, but, on appeal, the ninth circuit court reversed.

In 1984, the U.S. Supreme Court Justice John Paul Stevens, writing the five-member majority opinion, held that such use as recording a show for viewing at a more convenient time, so-called "time-shifting," did not violate copyright law.[25] Even though users of the equipment could contravene copyright, substantial non-infringing uses of the technology can protect its creators from being liable for copyright infringement. The ruling proved a boon to the home-video market, as it created a legal haven for the recording technology, permitting viewers to select their show date and curtain time.

Transformative Use

Like many before him, Pierre N. Leval, then-District Court Judge for the federal district court for the Southern District of New York was frustrated by the unpredictable outcome of fair use cases on appeal. After the Second Circuit overturned two of his decisions, the frustrated judge wrote what would become a highly influential 1990 *Harvard Law Review* article calling for replacing the ad hoc and arbitrary with a new standard providing greater consistency.

When the district court judge wrote the law journal piece, he likely didn't imagine that, just four years later, it would contribute to what would become one of the most important fair use decisions in American copyright history. In *Campbell v. Acuff-Rose Music*, the high court seemed to heed his call, focusing not only on the small quantity taken from the copyrighted work but also on the commercial and transformative nature of the defendant's use.[26] The case dealt with the hip-hop band 2 Live Crew, which, in January 1989, had released the song "Pretty Woman," a raunchy parody of the 1964 Roy Orbison and William Dees song "Oh, Pretty Woman."

The copyright holder of the Dees-Orbison composition, Acuff-Rose Music, a firm formed by a Grand Ole Opry star, Roy Acuff and Fred Rose, a singer, pianist, and songwriter, filed a lawsuit claiming that 2 Live Crew's parodic version was an infringement. Though the district court initially ruled in favor of 2 Live Crew, a central fixture in the Miami hip-hop scene, the appeals court overturned that decision holding the commercial nature of the parody gave it a presumption of unfairness.

In a unanimous decision, the high court held that no infringement occurred because the defendant added new meaning and message rather than merely superseding the original work. In turning the pretty woman into a "bald-headed," "hairy," and "two-timing" creature, the hip-hop band imitated the musical style of the original with deliberate distortion or exaggeration for comic effect.

While we might not assign a high rank to the parodic element, Justice David Souter stated, delivering the opinion of the court, the song reasonably could be perceived as commenting on the original or criticizing it, to some degree. It "juxtaposes the romantic musings of a man whose fantasy comes true, with degrading taunts, a bawdy demand for sex," commenting on "the naiveté of the original of an earlier day, the rejection of a sentiment ignoring the ugliness of street life and the debasement that it signifies."

Emphasizing an aggregate weighing of all four fair use factors, this decision represented a modification of the high court's earlier view in *Harper & Row* that the fourth factor was "the single most important element of fair use." The new creation would likely not affect the original work, Souter stated, so the copyright owner would not suffer financial harm. Still, commercial concerns will weigh heavily in favor of the defendant in an infringement lawsuit. The more the parody transforms the work it mimics,

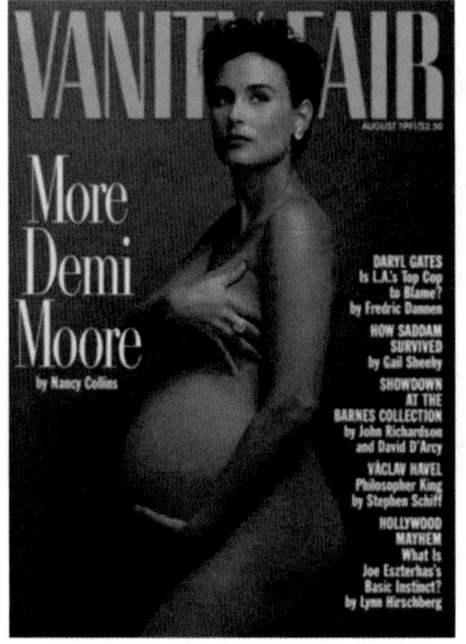

the more likely it is fair use. A tribute to Judge Pierre N. Leval's influence on the outcome, the high court's decision cited his article repeatedly.

The standard for determining whether a kind of use is transformative remains a bit blurry. Still, courts have provided some examples of works that meet or fail this test, sometimes involving seemingly trivial matters. One such case concerned the August 1991 issue of *Vanity Fair* magazine. It featured famed photographer Annie Leibovitz's cover image of a naked very pregnant Demi Moore in profile brimming with the beauty of nascent life. Her right hand and arm cover her breasts, and her left hand supports her baby bump—a pose evocative of Sandro Botticelli's "The Birth of Venus."

Two years later, as part of its promotional campaign for *Naked Gun 33 1/3: The Final Insult*, the third in a series of slapstick comedies starring Leslie Nielsen as an inept detective, Paramount commissioned an ad agency to create a photograph of its star's face superimposed over the body of a pregnant woman. The agency's creative team digitally altered the photo to make the skin tone and shape of the body more closely match those of Demi Moore on the Vanity Fair cover. The movie studio used the digitized image with the "DUE THIS MARCH" teaser in a magazine ad campaign launched in early 1994.

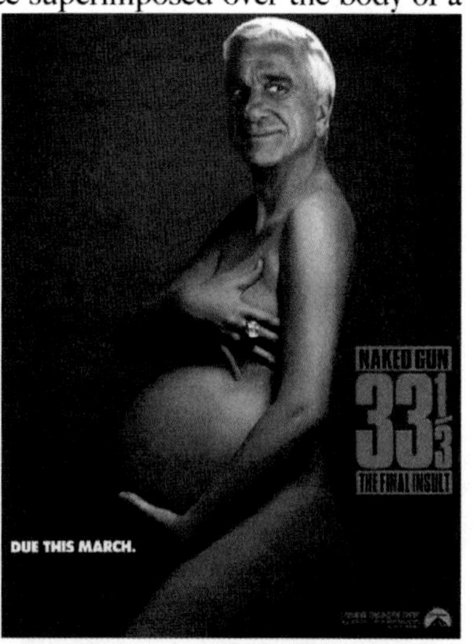

Leibovitz sued for copyright infringement, arguing that she was entitled to licensing revenue from the photograph. At the southern district court of New York trial, the presiding judge found the use to be fair, and granted summary judgment, a ruling without a jury, in favor of Paramount. On appeal, the United States Court of Appeals for the Second Circuit affirmed.[27] While conceding that the commercial purpose of the movie ad weighs against it, the appeals court nonetheless concluded it qualifies as a fair-use parody under the *Campbell v. Acuff-Rose Music* "transformative" precedent. Finally, the court found that the photographic parody did not serve as a market substitute, especially since the plaintiff conceded that the use did not interfere with any potential market for the original or derivative works.

The appellate court took particular note that, while the composition and posing of the models are the same, other elements are different. In the movie publicity photo, the light is more garish, including sharper contrasts and brighter colors while in the *Vanity Fair* cover photo, the lighting is warmer and more subdued. It also highlighted such differences, as the picture of the ring on the publicity model's right-hand is flashy and much larger than the ring Moore is wearing on her right hand. The expressions on the faces are also dissimilar: Moore's face has no trace of a smile, while Nielsen's bears a mischievous smirk.

A case involving Patrick Cariou's book of his photographs of the Rastafarian community in Jamaica further expanded the concept of transformative use. When Richard Prince incorporated some of these photos into his paintings, Cariou sued him in the southern district court of New York, which held that Prince's works were infringing. In April 2013, the Second Circuit reversed the district court decision, finding that most of Prince's appropriation art was "transformative" to a "reasonable observer" and, therefore, fair use. In particular, the appeals court found that the lower court erred in requiring that the appropriating artist claim to be commenting on the original work, and found the creations to be transformative if they presented a new aesthetic.[28]

Copyright & Censorship

The Suntrust Bank, owner of Margaret Mitchell's 1936 Civil War novel *Gone with the Wind* sought a restraining order in federal district court to stop Houghton Mifflin from publishing and distributing Alice Randall's 2001 parody, *The Wind Done Gone*. To debunk the romanticized, whitewashed mythology perpetrated by the author, she appropriated the characters, plot and major scenes from the original. Her book celebrates emancipation not only from bondage but also from myths, customs and stereotypes. After a hearing, the district court granted the motion, preliminarily enjoining Houghton Mifflin from further production, display, distribution, advertising, or sale of Randall's book.[29]

Citing the Leval law journal article, the Eleventh Circuit appellate court focused on the extent to which a critic may use the protected elements of an original work of authorship to communicate her criticism without infringing the copyright in that work.[30] While noting appropriation of numerous characters, settings, and plot twists, the appeals court found that the newer book was a parody, specific criticism of and reply to the Mitchell bestseller.

Cutting to the crux of the matter, it held that the story is "transformed," providing a social benefit by shedding light on the earlier work and posing little risk of market substitution. The more transformative the new creation, it noted, the less the significance of other factors. After the appeals court vacated an injunction against publishing the book, the parties settled the case in 2002. Mitchell's estate dropped the litigation against the publisher in an exchange of an unspecified donation to Morehouse College, a private historically black men's college in Atlanta, Georgia. The book's cover bears a seal stating, "The Unauthorized Parody."

Digital Millennium Copyright Act

Although computers and a rudimentary internet existed when Congress passed the current copyright law, its members did not take these media into consideration.

As a result, courts have struggled to apply statutes and copyright concepts to these newer technologies. Digital media especially pose a significant challenge. Digitized material can be copied quickly, easily, and cheaply via the internet with each copy being every bit as good as the original. Once reproduced and shared, others can make their copies and further distribute them in an almost endless chain

Lawmakers have responded by passing a series of measures to tighten protection, the most significant being the 1998 Digital Millennium Copyright Act. This legislation implemented World Intellectual Property Organization treaties, and insulates internet service providers and other intermediaries from copyright infringement liability for material posted by others. It also outlaws the manufacture, importation or sale of devices used to circumvent encryption codes. The law carries criminal penalties of a $500,00 fine and a five-year jail term.

Among other measures, the law authorizes the Librarian of Congress to create limited exemptions to the anti-circumvention provisions every three years to spare those whose fair use of some copyrighted materials otherwise would have been affected. These include circumventing "digital rights software" to incorporate short excerpts from movies into new works for criticism and comment in documentary filmmaking and educational purposes and other noncommercial uses.

The act's "safe harbor" provision requires internet service providers to implement a notice and takedown procedure. The process entails the copyright owner (or the owner's agent) sending a takedown notice to a service provider requesting that the provider remove material that is infringing their copyright(s). A service provider can be an internet service provider (e.g., Comcast), website operator (e.g., eBay), search engine (e.g., Google), a web host (e.g., GoDaddy) or other types of online site-operator.

The procedure can get complicated. If the providers fail to respond promptly, they may forfeit protection making them vulnerable to potential secondary liability for assisting with copyright infringement. When removing content, they must notify the party who put up the post. A poster objecting to the takedown can file a counter-notice with the service provider, and inform the copyright holder. If the parties can't agree, the matter may go to court for determination.

An illustrative example of the notice-and-takedown process concerning fair use involved a twenty-nine second video a mother uploaded to YouTube in 2007 of her thirteen-month-old son dancing to Prince's "Let's Go Crazy." The song's copyright holder, Universal Music Video, filed a takedown notice with the online video-sharing platform prompting it to remove the video. When Lenz challenged the takedown, YouTube restored it.

Later that year, the mother, with the help of the Electronic Frontier Foundation, an international non-profit digital rights group, successfully sued Universal Music. Before claiming copyright infringement, the United States Court of Appeals for the Ninth Circuit, affirming a district court ruling, held that copyright holders must consider fair use in good faith before issuing a takedown notice for content posted on the internet.[31]

While still complicated and challenging, the notice and take down process got greater clarification in a case initiated in March of 2007. The media conglomerate Viacom sued YouTube and its corporate parent Google in the U.S. District Court for the Southern District of New York seeking more than $1 billion in damages. It claimed the popular video-sharing site was engaging in "brazen" and "massive" direct and secondary copyright infringement by allowing users to upload and view thousands of unauthorized clips of entertainment programming.

Some two years later, the district court judge granted summary judgment in favor of YouTube, holding that the safe harbor provision protects the video-sharing site, requiring it to remove infringing material once aware of it but not to seek out infringements. Viacom appealed to the U.S. Court of Appeals for the Second Circuit, which vacated the lower court ruling.[32] Instead, it ruled that Viacom had presented enough evidence against YouTube to warrant a trial but did uphold the decision it was not required to look for materials that might infringe copyright. It sent the case back to the lower court, which again granted summary judgment in favor of YouTube. Viacom appealed once more, but before the second circuit could hear the case, the parties settled without any money changing hands.

Digital Avatars

Any creative illustration fixed in a tangible medium is eligible for copyright, including the ink designs displayed on human flesh. Whether copying or reproducing a tattoo qualifies as fair use is still unsettled law. A recent case sheds some light on the matter. Take-Two, a primary developer, publisher, and marketer of interactive entertainment and video games, develops and publishes products through its wholly-owned subsidiaries, 2K and Rockstar Games. They annually release an updated simulation video game that depicts basketball with realistic renderings of different National Basketball Association teams that include the players' tattoos.

What constitutes the "fair use" of these indelible skin decorations became a legal matter when Solid Oak Sketches acquired the licensing rights to LeBron James, Kobe Bryant, Kenyon Martin, DeAndre Jordan, and others from multiple tattoo artists. In 2016, the company filed suit in the District Court for Southern of New York against the game developer. The lawsuit alleged the illegal, unauthorized use of its tattoos as they appear on the digital avatars of the famous players in the basketball simulation video game.

In a March 2020 decision, the district court granted the video game developer's motion for summary judgment. It found the digital replication of basketball players' tattoos in a game does not constitute copyright infringement.[33] Courts make such a ruling when the undisputed facts and the law clarify the impossibility for one party to prevail if the matter were to proceed to trial. The court considers all designated evidence in the light most favorable to the party opposing the motion.

In this case, the district court judge found that at no point during the video clips provided by Take Two were the tattoos discernable to the viewer. They were either out of focus, blocked by another player, or obscured by player movement. As a result, no reasonable trier of fact, i.e., a jury, could find the tattoos as they appear in NBA 2K to be "substantially similar" to the tattoo designs licensed to Solid Oak. On all four factors of fair use, the court found in favor of the defendants.

On the first factor, the character and purpose of the use, the court ruled that the defendant's application was "transformative," an increasingly crucial consideration because of the tattoos' reduced size they were not recognizable. The court separately found that the defendants used the skin images to accurately depict the players—a very different purpose from the original intent of the inked sketches as expression through body art.

On the nature of the copyrighted work, the second factor considered, the court found that the tattoos were more factual than expressive because they reflected common representations. Concerning the third factor, the amount and substantiality of the use, the court found that copying the entirety of the tattoos was justified by the "transformative" purpose of "creating a realistic gaming experience."

Finally, on the highly significant fourth factor, the effect of the use on the potential market for or value of the copyrighted work, the court found that the video games' application did not substitute for the original. The use was transformative from the original purpose. Still, the plaintiff had failed to show "that a market for licensing tattoos for use in video games or other media is likely to develop." With a great deal of money at stake, this ruling is likely to be challenged in the federal appeals court, although given the robust and conclusive district judge's opinion, a reversal is far from a slam dunk.

Peer-to-Peer File-Sharing

Any unauthorized use of copyrighted works by a "third party" can constitute a "secondary" infringement liability if there's knowledge of the infringing acts and facilitation of the infraction. Liability for contributory infringement attaches if someone aids the violation with knowledge of the infringing laws. Vicarious infringement occurs if the defendant had the right and power to control the infringing activity and received a direct financial benefit. Finally, one is liable for inducement of copyright infringement if evidence shows that one distributed a device or technology to promote its use to infringe copyright by clear expression or other affirmative steps taken to foster infringement defenses to copyright infringement.

In a 2005 case, the high court unanimously ruled that peer-to-peer file-sharing networks such as Grokster and Steamcast are potentially liable for copyright infringement if they intend for their customers to use software primarily to swap songs and movies illegally.[34] In his majority opinion, Justice David Souter held that producers of technology who promote the ease of infringing on copyrights could be sued for "inducing" copyright infringement committed by their users.

In so ruling, Souter sought to leave in place the principles of the 1984 Sony Betamax case, protecting VCR manufacturers from liability for contributory infringement, noting that this case was "significantly different" because of evidence that file-sharing sites were trying "to cause and profit from" copyright by "inducing" infringement. The considerable disagreement among the justices in concurring opinions over whether the case is substantially different from the Sony case, and whether the precedent established by Sony should be modified leaves a broad grey area, with the lower courts left to work out what constitutes encouraging copyright infringement.

Google's Book Project

Google scanned millions of books, indexed the contents, and provided both library users and the public with the ability to search through them.

Though many of the books were under copyright protection, it did not obtain permission from the copyright owners to scan them. An epic legal battle between authors and publishers and the internet giant over alleged copyright violations dragged on for years. A federal judge for the southern district of New York, in 2011, rejected the settlement over concern it would "release Google (and others) from liability for certain future acts.

Meanwhile, the parties focused on whether Google was protected by the fair use doctrine. As part of that briefing, in August 2012 the Electronic Frontier Foundation filed a brief supporting Google's fair use defense. Three associations representing over 100,000 libraries joined it. The statement pointed out several factors favoring fair use including that Google Book Search is a reference tool that helps people find books, and serves the public benefit.

In late 2013, the same district court granted summary judgment in favor of Google, dismissing the lawsuit and affirming the Google Books project met all legal requirements for fair use. The authors appealed to the Second Circuit Court of Appeals. Writing for a unanimous three-judge panel, Pierre N. Leval upheld the judgment, ruling that "the purpose of the copying is highly transformative, the public display of text is limited, and the revelations do not provide a significant market substitute for the protected aspects of the originals."[35] The U.S. Supreme Court subsequently refused to revive a challenge to Google's digital library of millions of books, turning down an appeal from authors who said the project amounted to copyright infringement on a mass scale.

Despite the project's inability to achieve full potential, Google's scanning created some important junctions in an ever-expanding web of networked research. The Google Books corpus provides a cornucopia of resources. Scholars can tap into it using computational analysis to look for patterns in large amounts of textual material, for instance—without breaching copyright. And with initiatives like Project Gutenberg, the oldest digital library of out-of-copyright books, an avid reader can download books ranging from *Fanny Hill* to *Finnegan's Wake* for free to ponder on a digital tablet or mobile phone.

Future Directions

Without a doubt, the capacity to digitize, making an infinite number of copies, each identical, will continue to erode copyright protection. The trade-off is that fair use and safe harbor protections have allowed internet companies like Wikipedia, the free online encyclopedia created, edited, and verified by volunteers worldwide, to grow and prosper, providing invaluable access to a broad range of knowledge. While not without serious problems, profit-oriented social media platforms like Facebook, Instagram, and Twitter have connected millions of people across the planet. In addition to its powerhouse search engine, the multinational tech giant Google offers dozens of services designed for work and productivity.

The direction of the future is digital, as one-click "reproducibility" transforms how we see and understand our environment and ourselves. The quickly done duplication and transmission of words and images to a vast number of destinations will increasingly influence cultural change in unexpected and unanticipated ways.

The numerous advances in copying and sharing make a potentially empowering path to a politics of collective action. In Minneapolis, in spring 2020, a police officer pressed his knee on the neck of a handcuffed man lying prone on the street, while his fellow officers did nothing to stop him. The moment would only have existed for those present if an onlooker hadn't captured it on a smartphone. Those digital images percolating across social media platforms iconized the victim into a symbol of slavery, segregation, and oppression across the decades and centuries dating back to 1620 when the first boatload of slaves arrived on the Virginia colony's shores.

In a matter of weeks, long taken-for-granted statues, monuments, and other expressive media forms celebrating enablers of enslavement moved to the forefront of news coverage and consciousness. In response to the lethal choking, the "Black Lives Matter" chant echoed through power and privilege corridors. A coalition of progressives pushed the country into uncharted territory, calling not only for racial justice but also for affordable housing, expansion of public transit, universal health care, free public colleges, and clean, renewable energy sources. How pervasive or profound the changes demanded by this fervent chorus will be, or how the protestations will influence the culture in general, is impossible to predict.

Chapter 2
News Media

Modern newspapers are one of the most significant dividends of the invention and widespread use of the printing press. They satisfy our need to know things we cannot experience personally. And bear witness to extraordinary events, disseminate specialized knowledge, shape cultural trends, expose corruption, and often trigger public debate. They spread information on a broad scale and cover a range of events that affect people's lives locally, regionally, nationally, and across the world.

Selling Attention

These functions of the newspaper evolved in the nineteenth century. Beginning with the publication of the *New York Sun* in 1833 by a twenty-three-year-old job printer, Benjamin H. Day's four-page half-tabloid-sized paper was unlike any publication that had gone before, emphasizing local occurrences, particularly those of a sensational nature. For the purchase price of one penny, every day people could read stories of murder, mishap, and mayhem.

By appealing to the city's rapidly expanding working-class, including many newly arrived immigrants, the enterprising publisher began to capture a broad and ever-widening readership. In the process, he not only created a whole new definition of newsworthiness but an entirely new business model as well. As the readership grew, he sold their attention to advertisers. In other words, his readers were his product. This way of making money has been a guiding principal in the development of not just newspapers but of most communications media.

The sale of attention Day set in motion applies with equal force not just to sensational sheets but also to glossy magazines, electronic media news divisions, social media sites, and such august institutions as the *Wall Street Journal*, the *New York Times* and the *Washington Post*.

When using Google, we become its product, what the search giant sells to advertisers. The more we click, the more it knows, making our attention all the more saleable to select sellers of goods and services. The harvesting of human attention and reselling it to advertisers has become an essential component of our economy. "Existing industries have long depended on it to drive sales," notes law professor Tim Wu. "And new industries of the twentieth century have turned it into a form of currency they can mint."[36]

A vital ingredient in the *Sun*'s success was marketing. In essence, to be sold, attention must first be harvested, a useful crop metaphor for something that has become a "commodity" like wheat or crude oil, a product to be bought and sold in the marketplace—the arena of competitive or commercial dealings.[37] The data-selling business would make former New York City mayor and failed presidential candidate Michael Bloomberg a billionaire eighty times over.

The *Sun* was the first newspaper in the United States to be hawked on the streets by newsboys, known as "newsies," who bought papers in bulk from the publisher, initially for 67¢ a hundred. Mostly from poor immigrant families, these ragged lads and occasional lassies were not allowed to return unsold newspapers, so frequently worked until very late at night. From the mid-nineteenth to the early twentieth century in the United States newsies were the leading distributors of papers to the general public. While morning editions of newspapers were often delivered directly to subscribers, newsboys on the streets sold most of the afternoon editions.

To stay competitive, Day hired a full-time reporter, an unemployed printer, George W. Wisner, who ferreted out what he thought would be newsworthy local happenings and wrote engaging articles about them. Covering the police court in the early morning hours each weekday, Wisner had a novelist's eye for telling detail.

In a few lines, Wisner was able to capture the parade of drunks, wife-beaters, confidence men, shoplifters, and streetwalkers who appeared before the magistrate. Day became so reliant on him that he agreed within weeks of hiring the reporter to split the paper's profits applying his share toward partial ownership. While retaining the title of senior editor, Day increasingly devoted his attention to the business side.

In addition to crimes and minor wrongdoings committed by ordinary people, the newspaper also reported on such personal events as suicides, deaths, and divorces. It gave the first account of an average person taking his own life. Such reporting made it an integral part of the community and the lives of its mostly lower-income readers, whose attention sellers of goods and services increasingly wanted to attract. The popularity of this coverage left little doubt advertisements rather than subscription fees could support a newspaper.

Slippery Satire

As a craft, satire runs the risk of being taken seriously rather than ironically, seen as confirming and supporting the target of its ridicule. In 1835, *New York Sun* journalist Richard Adams Locke set out to satirize the conventional wisdom among astronomers of the time who not only believed that the moon was populated but also the planets, all the stars, and even the elliptical orbiting comets shooting across the sky.

They assumed this because God would not have created these celestial bodies without also creating intelligent beings there to appreciate them.

To send up what seemed to him a silly assumption, Locke wrote a seven-article series that, through a skillful blend of fact and fiction, presented a tale of life on the moon a contemporary reader would likely find farfetched. The series started with a detailed account of the telescope used for the lunar explorations and purported to tell of the "Great Astronomical Discoveries, lately made by Sir John Herschel at the Cape of Good Hope." Subsequent articles explained the moon's geology, geography, and natural history.

The carefully paced narrative culminated with the revelation that bat-like men and women inhabited the lunar surface. They spent their happy hours in collecting various fruits in the woods, in eating, flying, bathing, talking, and fornicating in public. The paper also published the series as a pamphlet that included a lithograph of the supposed landscape of the moon, with the man-bats eating, flying, bathing, and loitering about upon the summits of cliffs.

As Locke later explained in a letter critical of religious astronomy, "he was continuously astonished, and horrified, at the credence given to this fairy-tale version of astronomy, this '*pseudo* philosophy' that dressed itself so extravagantly in the robes of piety and faith." Furthermore, "he was convinced that if its power remained unchecked, it would continue to erect its baneful influence on future generations of young minds."[38]

Instead of laughing over the concocted tale, or picking up on its pointed critique of the religion-science linkage, other newspapers reprinted the articles, often with favorable comments on the magnitude of the discovery. The series managed to fool not only the average reader but some members of the scientific community as well. The prestigious higher-education institution Yale, named after a slave owner and trader, even sent a delegation to New York to investigate the report.

Why was the story so convincing? Why did readers so willingly suspend disbelief? There are some plausible explanations. Such a revelation seemed to confirm there was a benevolent God and that they were not alone in the universe. And Locke's use of scientific terminology, along with his continual references to various forms of authority, certainly added an essential element of authenticity to the tale.

Perhaps most significant of all, current research confirms that people want and seek out corroboration, not contradictions of deeply held beliefs. When provided with something new, we tend to accept what reconfirms our preconceived notions, and assess contradictory evidence with a jaundiced eye, notes a neuroscientist. Based on carefully conducted studies, she explains that "presenting people with information that contradicts their opinion can cause them to come up with altogether new counterarguments that further strengthens their original view."[39] The life-on-the-moon series is often labeled hoax, not satire. But Locke intended ridicule, not deliberate deception.

Stance on Slavery

The city in which the Day built his news business was a rich mosaic of colors, cultures, and communities. Since slave labor was not a crucial element of the northern economy, most states in that region passed legislation to abolish slavery. New York State slew this monster slowly to ease the hardship on owners. They had ample time to sell their human chattel in slave states if they wished. In 1799, it passed legislation that freed slave children born after July 4th of that year but indentured them until they were young adults. Some eighteen years later, it enacted a new law that would free slaves born before 1799 but not until 1827. Under the Fugitive Slave Act of 1793, New York was still required to honor the property rights of slave-state residents. In this way, in effect, slavery continued to exist in a state even after it had been abolished.

Officials in Manhattan returned runaway slaves to their owners and continued to tolerate or ignore racism, discrimination, and rigid segregation in churches, courtrooms, public schools and facilities as well as on city buses and ferries. Such practices must have made visitors from below the Mason-Dixon Line feel right at home in the big city. In the summer months especially, wealthy Southern families headed north to Manhattan with slaves in toe. With the sight of enslaved blacks a common occurrence on the city's streets, strangers might easily assume they were in a slave state.

While otherwise apolitical and nonpartisan, the *New York Sun* took a strong stance against slavery, providing detailed coverage of the city's slave trade. It published compelling stories of captured runaways and the misery of slave marriages severed on the auction block. After recounting the story of a sundered couple, quoting the slave's bewailing of the injustice of his lot, George Wisner went on to challenge his readers directly. What would be your feeling, he queried, if a white woman was forcibly separated from her husband to live as the chattel and perhaps paramour of a black man?

The suggested miscegenation aside, it was a bold scenario to pose in a city dependent on slave-produced cotton. In southern states like Virginia, advocacy of abolition was punishable by fines and imprisonment.[40] And mob violence against opponents of slavery was not uncommon in both the North and South. In St. Louis, Missouri, in the mid-1930s, threats forced the publisher of a religious newspaper to shut down after he condemned a racist mob for burning a black man alive. After moving to Alton, Illinois, a "free" state rife with racism, he was shot and killed while fighting a warehouse fire. An angry mob had set it ablaze trying to destroy his newly purchased printing press.[41]

Wisner's scenario could have had severe economic repercussions as well since many of the newspaper's Irish immigrant readers were engaged in a bitter competition with blacks for jobs. This ongoing tension erupted in violence in July 1863, with the passage of federal law to draft white men to fight in the Civil War. The protests against the conscription law turned into a race riot on the lower eastside, with white rioters, mostly Irish immigrants, attacking and killing black people. The military did not reach downtown until the second day of rioting. By the time they arrived, mobs had lynched, tortured and mutilated eleven black men, murdered many more, destroyed over 100 buildings and homes, and burned an orphanage for black children to the ground.

Now the *Sun*'s de facto editor, Wisner did not let these growing tensions deter him from pursuing his brand of radical politics. He printed several articles, editorials, and even gloomy poems on the horrors of slavery and provided sympathetic coverage to the city's small but passionate abolition movement. Despite such a stance, week after week, the *Sun*'s readership grew.

Violent-Death Enticements

In May 1835, an experienced journalist, Scottish-born James Gordon Bennett, with a university education in economics, launched the *Morning Herald*. He lamented the upscale journalism of the day with its seriousness of tone, party affiliations, and stolidly serene solemnity. When he had worked as Washington correspondent for the *New York Enquirer*, he recognized the public at large would not buy a severe paper at any price.

Almost from the outset, to draw reader attention, the *Herald* put a premium on coverage of violent death—suicides, murders, deadly fires, riots, executions, and the like. In April 1836, Bennett ran a front-page story of the grisly murder in an elegant brothel of prostitute Helen Jewett. She was struck on the head three times with a sharp object, most likely a hatchet. After inflicting the lethal blows, the murderer then set fire to her bed. The *Herald* drew groundbreaking attention with lurid descriptions of the murder along with its coverage of the alleged killer's apprehension, his subsequent trial, and the not guilty verdict after less than an hour of jury deliberation.

Move Toward Modern Journalism

For all his brutal crime stories, Bennett recognized the value of reporters and news reports for the society at large, as well as a way to increase readership seeking to be informed as well as shocked, titillated, and generally distracted from the daily grind. Setting a template for modern journalism, he wrote the first daily column on the stock market, and conducted interviews with newsmakers.

Among Bennett's other journalistic innovations were the use of maps to illustrate war reports and putting the news on the front page rather than the second. To expand coverage, he hired a phalanx of correspondents to gather and report noteworthy events, a category constantly expanding. He even established bureaus outside the country and brought new emphasis to the arts and cultural events. By 1845, the *Herald* was the most popular and profitable daily newspaper in the United States.[42]

At the height of the American Civil War, Bennett was employing more than sixty reporters. And he pushed his staff to make sure the *Herald* published "dispatches" or reports from the battlefield before any of its competitors.[43] The irascible Bennett ceded control of the newspaper in 1867 to his eccentric son James Gordon Bennett, Jr., prone to naked carriage rides, public urination, and having a lifelong obsession with owls. Under his stewardship, the Herald continued to be very successful. Regular contributors to the newspaper included Mark Twain, who wrote over 200 articles during his long tenure.

Three years after assuming command, the younger Bennett, to expand reader attention even more, hired the renowned journalist/explorer Henry Morton Stanley to find Dr. David Livingstone. The Scottish missionary and explorer had gone to Africa,

intent on finding the source of the Nile, Africa's longest river. But for several years no one had heard from him. Stanley eventually arrived on the east coast of Africa in early 1871 and organized an expedition to head inland.

In November 1871, the unflagging Stanley finally encountered Livingstone. The report of his cleverly casual greeting, "Dr. Livingstone, I presume?" may have been apocryphal, but it became part of the lexicon for many decades afterward. The paper's financing of Stanley's successful quest to find Livingstone in Africa's interior won it international acclaim. Illustrators around the world imagined the encounter. In the 1870s, the New York Herald was one of the most widely read and influential papers in the world.

Wild-Animals-Run-Amok Hoax

To draw attention to a potential danger, the *Herald* purposely deceived its growing readership—"fake news"—with a "positive purpose." In November 1874, it ran a front-page article with the screaming headline AWFUL CALAMITY.[44] Running over 10,000 words and occupying six full columns, it told of wild animals escaping from the Central Park Zoo (called the "menagerie" at the time), at the center of the densely populated island of Manhattan. Pumas, panthers, lions, tigers, and even a rhinoceros, it claimed, were running amok around the city, wreaking havoc wherever they went.

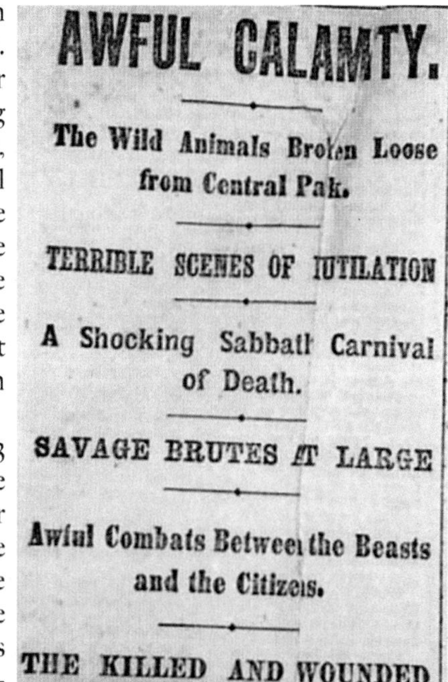

AWFUL CALAMTY.

The Wild Animals Broken Loose from Central Pak.

TERRIBLE SCENES OF IUTILATION

A Shocking Sabbatl Carnival of Death.

SAVAGE BRUTES AT LARGE

Awful Combats Betwee the Beasts and the Citizens.

THE KILLED AND WOUNDED

One "eyewitness" reported he had seen a lion ripping apart four small children. Another told of several animals fighting over the lifeless body of the zookeeper tossing him around like a rag doll. At press time, according to the account, the death toll stood at forty-nine with another 200 or more injured. Only if readers read carefully to the end would they have learned that the entire report was a hoax intended to jolt people out of their apathy to do something about the poor state of the zoo's security before an actual calamity occurred.

The paper's managing editor in an 1893 *Harper's Weekly* article acknowledged he was responsible for the hoax.[45] The editor claimed that the idea came to him after he witnessed a leopard almost escape while being transferred from an animal carriage into its cage in the menagerie. He saw it as "a harmless little hoax, with just enough semblance of reality to give a salutary warning."

By all accounts, the hoax caused widespread panic throughout the city. The police mobilized. The National Guard was called in to control the chaos. Reporters were dispatched to cover the shocking incident. For its part, the *Herald* feigned surprise when the article provoked such an enormous reaction, but it was wholly unrepentant. By way of apology, it simply inserted a short article into the next issue, titled "Wild Beasts," urging that safety precautions at the menagerie be improved.[46] After all, the article contained a disclaimer at the bottom saying it is pure fabrication.

The "wild beasts wreaking havoc in the streets" concoction ranks as one of the most notorious media deceptions of the nineteenth century. In the immediate aftermath, evidence of the new journalistic standards emerging, newspapers across the country roundly rejected the *Herald's* defense of concocting the fictional story to spotlight a public danger. While admitting that the animals confined in the Central Park Zoo were clearly in flimsy cages, the *New York Times* characterized the article as an intensely stupid and unfeeling hoax and printed letters from readers claiming to have been terrified by the story.[47] In the long term, it is not difficult to see how such fabrications by mainstream publications do damage to the credibility of all news media.

Dailies Spread

The low-priced dailies quickly spread to other urban areas. The *Boston Daily Times* appeared in 1836, and within several weeks of publication could claim a circulation of 8,000. That same year saw the launching of the *Philadelphia Public Ledger*, whose sale of papers soon climbed to 20,000, some ten times that of its nearest competition. The *Baltimore Sun*, founded in 1837, witnessed its circulation jump to over 10,000 within nine months. These penny papers gave new meaning to Marshall McLuhan's notion of the vernacular as a PA system par excellence.

Better printing techniques and faster productive capacity kept pace with rising circulation figures. The web press, invented in 1871, printed on both sides of the paper fed into it from large rolls. The Linotype machine, first available in 1886, cast rows of the type directly from molten metal, allowing for much higher speed and convenience in the production of newspapers.

The resounding success of the penny press model for making money was a clear sign of the big business and advertiser-supported enterprise that journalism was to become. The production of large daily newspapers increasingly occurred in substantial industrial plants requiring significant capital investment to build and operate. The faster and faster print technology necessary to turn out many thousands of papers every day, combined with the costs of gigantic rolls of paper, and employing a large staff of reporters and managerial personnel, precluded establishment of a newspaper in an urban center without considerable finance. Newspapers had become an institution, an organized body playing a vital role in the life of the nation.

Magazine Exposés

First adopted in 1731 by a publisher aiming at "gentlemen," the term "magazine" derives from the Arabic for "storehouse"—on the analogy of a military storehouse of varied material. Colonial magazines documented early aspects of American life, concerns over taxation, state vs. federal power, and similar such matters. Over time, such publications appeared on a regular schedule, contained a variety of articles, financed by advertising, a purchase price, prepaid subscriptions, or sometimes all three of these means. Passage of the Postal Act of 1879 lowered postage rates putting magazines on equal footing with newspapers delivered by mail. By the end of the century, magazine circulation flourished, advertising revenues soared, capturing reader attention, and building a national marketplace.

Discouraged with newspaper superficiality, journalists sought out magazines where they could write in-depth about broader issues. By the dawn of the 1900s, reformed-minded publications such as *Collier's Weekly*, *Munsey's Magazine*, and *McClure's Magazine* were already in wide circulation and read avidly by the growing middle class. Among the most steadfast reporters of this era, former schoolteacher Ida Tarbell set a new standard for investigative journalism.

McClure's Magazine

VOL. XX *NOVEMBER, 1902* NO. 1

THE HISTORY OF THE STANDARD OIL COMPANY

BY IDA M. TARBELL

Author of "The Life of Lincoln"

CHAPTER I—THE BIRTH OF AN INDUSTRY

ONE of the busiest corners of the globe at the opening of the year 1872 was a strip of Northwestern Pennsylvania, not over fifty miles long, known the world over as the Oil Regions. Twelve years before, this strip of land had been but little better than a wilderness its only inhabitants the lumbermen, who every season cut great swaths of primeval pine and hemlock from its hills, and in the spring floated them down the Allegheny River to Pittsburg. The great tides of Western emigration had shunned the spot for years as too rugged and unfriendly for settlement, and yet in twelve years this region avoided by men had been transformed into a bustling trade center, where towns elbowed each other for place, into which the three great trunk railroads had built branches, and every foot of whose soil was fought for by capitalists. It was the discovery and development of a new raw product, petroleum, which had made this change from wilderness to market-place. This product in twelve years had not only peopled a waste place of the earth, it had revolutionized the world's methods of illumination and added millions upon millions of dollars to the wealth of the United States.

Petroleum as a curiosity was no new thing. For more than two hundred years it had been described in the journals of Western explorers. For decades it had been dipped up from the surface of springs, soaked up by blankets from running streams, found in quantities when salt wells were bored, bottled and sold as a cure-all—"Seneca Oil" or "Rock Oil," it was called. One man had even distilled it in a crude way, and sold it as an illuminant. Scientists had described it, and travelers from the West often carried bottles to their scientific friends in the East. It was such a bottleful, brought as a gift

GEORGE H. BISSELL

The man to whom more than any other is due the credit of what is called the "discovery" of oil; for it was he who first took steps to find its value and to organize a company to produce it. It was he, too, who suggested the means of getting oil which proved practical. After the oil company which he organized obtained oil in the Drake well, he aided in establishing the needed industries and institutions in the new country.

3

Tarbell wrote a series of articles for *McClure's* about the behemoth Standard Oil Company and the rapacious practices its patriarch, John D. Rockefeller, who controlled ninety percent of the nation's oil industry by the 1880s. He held this monopoly for nearly twenty-five years, making him one the wealthiest Americans in history with an accumulated capital between $300 and $400 billion in today's current dollars. Like the high-tech firms today, his company became an integral part of people's lives. Nearly every household in the nation used oil as a light source.

Carefully researched and written in a fair-minded fashion, Tarbell's essays detailed the oil company's rise to power and its quashing of threats to its domination through bribery, deception, intimidation, and outright thuggery. The nineteen-part series was published in book form in 1904 as The History of the Standard Oil Company. Five years later, the U.S. Supreme Court found the company had violated the Sherman Antitrust Act, causing its breakup into

some thirty-four constituent entities (some of which still have among the highest levels of revenue in the world). In the aftermath of Tarbell's scathing indictment, Rockefeller became one of the most detested people in the nation, a symbol of everything that had gone wrong with industrial capitalism. In a crucial role, still played today, several imaginative cartoonists regularly ridiculed him and his control over government agencies in what became a forceful rhetorical tool for progressive causes.

Public Relations

The modern "spin" machine, better known as public relations, churning out propaganda emerged early in the twentieth century to counter negative publicity resulting from investigations into predatory practices and corporate corruption. Promoting products, persons, and political positions, as well as corporate and individual image polishing, is divided into distinct but intertwined fields, advertising, and public relations. Advertising entails identifiable and controllable paid media access. In contrast, public relations ploys appear without cost as news or information, but media outlets decide the kind of coverage if any.

To polish the family's badly tarnished image, the Rockefellers turned to public relations pioneer Princeton-educated Ivy Ledbetter Lee, master of such now standard persuasive techniques as the news conference, the press release, and the staged event to attract media coverage. Sole son and scion of the family fortune, John D. Rockefeller Jr., father of the five famous Rockefeller brothers, owned a controlling interest, forty percent of the stock, and sat on the board as an absentee director of the Colorado Fuel and Iron Company in Ludlow, Colorado. The oppressed miners worked under appalling conditions and lived in company-owned towns. Their employers controlled the stores where they bought their groceries and supplies, the churches, the schools, even the courts.

Long indifferent to worker welfare, Rockefeller sought Lee's expertise in April 1914 to burnish the family reputation, when tactics to stop strikes and union organizing erupted in a tragedy at the mining company. In the summer of the previous year, United Mine Workers began to organize the eleven thousand coal miners. Most were first-generation immigrants from Italy, Greece, and Serbia; many hired a decade prior, to replace workers who had gone on strike. In August, the union extended invitations to mining company representatives to meet about their grievances—including low pay, long and unregulated hours, and corrupt practices, but management rebuffed the overtures. Colorado law required many of the rights they sought but remained unenforced. A month later, eight thousand Colorado mineworkers went on strike.

The strike stretched on for months culminating in a violent confrontation between the miners and the Colorado state militia, summoned by Rockefeller surrogates to end the work stoppage. Four militiamen brandished a machine gun at some of the striking miners. At some point, shots were fired—accounts as to who initiated the first salvo are inconsistent—and a daylong gunfight resulted. The state's militiamen raked the colony with machine guns and then set fire to the tents housing the families of the miners killing thirteen residents attempting to flee.

Discovered among the ruins the following morning was the makeshift infirmary where four women and eleven children had sought to escape the fighting by hiding in a cellar-like pit. All the children and two of the women died. The incident sparked ten days of violence in the surrounding coalfields, resulting in at least fifty-three deaths. While accounts vary, a cruel and inhuman action had occurred. Picked up by the national press, and striking many as a consequence of unchecked corporate might, the coverage further inflamed hatred against the Rockefeller name.

In a full-scale publicity campaign, Lee took several measures to spin the story. He prepared press releases to discredit the United Mine Workers, claimed the infirmary deaths stemmed from inadequate ventilation, described the militiamen as defenders of law and property, organized a much-publicized visit by Rockefeller Jr. to Ludlow, and promoted a new labor agreement that improved conditions at the Colorado mine. His maneuvers opened the way to wallpaper over the brutal conflict. In the aftermath of the tragic events, company towns waned, and stricter labor laws, actually enforced, appeared on the books. An antidote to corporate greed, support for unions nationwide reached an all-time high in the 1930s.

In the years ahead, Lee presented a more humanized version of the wealthy family doing a complete makeover of John D. Rockefeller Sr., who had a well-deserved reputation as a ruthless, profit-driven tyrant who would crush anyone in his way. Bodyguards had to surround him when he went to church. Even some charitable organizations returned his money as tainted.

By the 1930s, Lee had gradually transformed the Rockefellers into widely regarded and revered humanitarians and philanthropists. The elderly Rockefeller's predatory practices faded from public memory as he became beloved for handing out shiny dimes to children (in the pre-arranged presence of the press). He lived to a ripe old age, and with the passing years, came honors and respect from the United States and around the world. The family name became synonymous with philanthropic giving, and several of Rockefeller Junior's sons ran successfully for high government positions.

The repackaging of the ruthless Rockefeller through a host of tax-exempt charitable foundations, aside from being a clever bit of public relations, provided a way of multiplying the family fortune and influence. The vast amounts of cash generated, at the taxpayers' expense, enabled the Rockefellers to control to a large extent the direction and focus of science, education, politics, medicine, economics, law, media outlets, and a thousand other things in the United States and abroad. Philanthropists use the similar ploys to reduce taxes and exercise influence to the present day.

Dubbed by author and muckraker Upton Sinclair as "Poison Ivy," Lee courted further controversy representing the Soviet Union and German chemical giant IG Farben trust closely tied to Adolph Hitler and the Nazi regime, which ultimately put his reputation into a tailspin. Among other measures, he launched a publicity campaign that urged diplomatic recognition of the Soviet Union by the United States and other nations in the 1920s. And early in the following decade, he did public relations work for IG Farben in the United States and promoted the international sales of its chemical products.

Of course, Lee couldn't know at the time that the Soviet Union and Nazi Germany would become tyrannical, war-driven dictatorships or that the chemical trust would play a prominent part in the Nazi extermination of Europe's Jewish population. Prompted by his unsavory overseas clientele, Congress passed the Foreign Agents Registration Act in 1938. Anyone representing a foreign power is now required to register with the Justice Department.

Rise of Press Associations

The older papers seeing news and the newspaper as a source of essential information and forum for debate on substantial issues were incensed by the penny papers aggressive newsgathering, sensational stories, and blatant methods of promotion. All the same, the competition they created could not be ignored. By 1848, the mounting expense of carrier pigeons, pony express, railroads, and harbor boats to meet incoming ships, along with telegraph tolls made cooperation among newspapers an economic necessity.

Associated Press

In that year, several influential newspapers in New York, among them the *Sun*, *Herald*, and *Courier and Enquirer*, joined forces to share the costs of procuring national and international news. Each newspaper remained independent but was served by a jointly formed organization that came to be called the Associated Press (AP). This new association soon achieved a commanding position in the newspaper industry. It employed reporters in all the principal cities in the United States and Canada.

Having priority arrangements with the owners of the telegraph wires, a technical advance having a significant impact on the news business, allowed the organization to sell its dispatches to newspapers outside New York. The inland newspapers, in such cities as Chicago, Louisville, Cincinnati, St. Louis, and New Orleans joined the service. Subscribers were compelled to foreswear the use of rival agencies. Out of this arrangement national associations eventually developed.

In the late 1860s, the emergence of the Western Associated Press, made up of midwestern dailies, challenged the New York group's autocratic control and emphasis on news of interest mainly to the seven charter members. As a result of court pressure, the two associations reorganized in 1900 as a nonprofit cooperative. Members shared the cost of exchanging news and paid the association's news staff, which collated regional coverage and augmented it with additional information. These days the nonprofit Associated Press operates over 260 news bureaus in more than 100 countries around the globe.

United Press International

In 1907, the Scripps newspaper chain's creation of the United Press Association (UP) as a privately owned enterprise for the gathering and dissemination of news broke the monopoly hold of the Associated Press. In addition to supplying its own newspapers, Scripps made the service available to those papers not admitted to the rival press association. Two years later, the Hearst organization developed a third major news service, the International News Service (INS). United Press and the International News Service merged in 1958, forming United Press International-UPI.

For much of the second half of the twentieth century, UPI's newswires, photo, news film, and audio services provided material to thousands of newspapers, magazines, and radio and television stations. At its peak, UPI had more than 2,000 full-time employees, 200 news bureaus in 92 countries, and some 6,000 media subscribers. When afternoon newspapers, its principal client category, diminished in number the wire service went into decline. With a change in ownership in 1982 came sharp staff cutbacks. Near the turn of the century, UPI sold it broadcast client list to its rival, the Associated Press. Operating on a much smaller scale, it now concentrates mostly on smaller market niches.

Overseas News Agencies

For news from abroad, many of the larger publications during the nineteenth century relied on overseas newsgathering agencies to service the rapidly growing information needs of government and business. Three news agencies—Reuters of England, Wolff of Germany, and Havas of France (later to become Agence France-Presse)—divided up the world of news among themselves.

The foreign correspondent became a familiar figure on the colonial landscape. Like explorers of an earlier epoch, these overseas reporters in many respects were de facto agents in the expansion of empire. "A generation of explorer-adventurer-reporters grew up, 'gentlemen followers' of colonial wars, half-spies for London and Paris, half-entertainers for the news-reading public whose imagination was fired by accounts of their exploits," writes Anthony Smith.[48] Foreign reporting reflected a Western orientation that was often insensitive to the indigenous culture of overseas territories before their domination by the colonial powers.

Foreign correspondents fed the business community's need for commercial and political information and supplied general readers with dramatic stories and romantic adventure. By definition, news was seen to arise from the exceptional, not the commonplace. There was a growing emphasis on discreet, isolated events. This practice of abstracting only bits and pieces of information about the environment served to obscure the legacy of colonialism and the historical circumstances of industrial development. Emphasis on conflict and civil strife further helped to strengthen the imperial bent of Western journalism.

Such practices prevail to the present day. Contemporary Western journalists still tend to think of news in terms of an aberration rather than normality. The concentration on the exceptional over the commonplace invariably results in a stereotypical view of the world at large. In less developed countries, in particular, disasters, famines, wars, military coups, and political corruption tend to be the only aspects of life likely to make their way to Western news media.[49]

Victorian Era Internet

During the ninetieth century, the massive increase in industrial production and world trade created a pressing need for a new type of information, prices of raw material, lending rates, stock market quotations and the like. The advent of the electric telegraph greatly facilitated gathering and circulating such data and statistics. In the 1830s, drawing on the work of others, painter-turned-scientist Samuel Morse perfected the process.

Morse adopted a simple key to make and break an electrical circuit, which produced a clicking sound of long or short duration depending on the operator's timing. A pen or stylus marked a motor-driven tape in accordance with the pulse of current in the circuit. He developed a code of combinations of "dots and dashes" corresponding to the letters of the alphabet. A frequently used letter such as "e" is represented by a simple dot. The combination for the less frequently occurring "q" is dash-dash-dot-dash. A skilled operator was soon able to send or receive thirty-five or more words a minute utilizing the code.

After a series of public demonstrations of his electrical marvel in 1838, Morse petitioned Congress for an appropriation to build an experimental line. In 1844, with a government subsidy of $30,000, he installed the first operational copper-wire telegraph line between Baltimore and Washington, D.C. that broke the bond between communications and transportation. Sitting at a table in the old Supreme Court chamber in Washington, he tapped out to his assistant in Baltimore the dramatic query "What hath God wrought?"—a prescient Bible verse from the Book of Numbers signaling the influence of electronic media on people's lives for centuries to come.

Just inside the 72nd Street and Fifth Avenue entrance to Central Park on the left is the imposing Samuel F.B. Morse statue that depicts the American inventor and painter standing on a large pedestal. His one hand rests on a single-wire telegraph, and the other clasps a strip of Morse code. The unveiling of the bronze statue on June 10, 1871, initially located in the Mall area, drew some 10,000 people, including a large contingent of telegraphers from across the country who identified themselves by wearing badges made of white ribbon.

The tribute proved timely. Morse died ten months later at his winter home in New York City. Like so many celebrated in publicly displayed sculptures, he had some less-than-admirable attributes. A leader in the anti-Catholic and anti-Irish movement, in 1836, he ran unsuccessfully for mayor of New York City under the anti-immigrant Nativist Party's banner. By the 1850s, Morse had become a well-known defender of slavery, considering it to be divinely sanctioned.

Whatever his faults or moral failures, Morse's invention of sending messages by electrical energy became an increasingly important part of the nation's social and economic development, and the rest of the world's as well. The growth of this electronic marvel was explosive, as Morse's licensees or competitors using other patents rapidly strung wire. The Baltimore-Washington line soon connected to New York and Philadelphia. Separate telegraph trunk lines followed: New York to Boston, Buffalo, the Great Lakes, down to New Orleans and all points west. The island of Manhattan became the communications nexus for most of the country.

An intricate interlacing of terrestrial and submarine telegraph cables followed already established transportation routes around the world. In 1851, underwater cable connected England with the European continent. Some fifteen years later, a transatlantic cable joined England and North America. By the 1870s, a global telegraphic network was in place providing electrical links to newspapers, stock exchanges, and commodity markets so that the news of price changes affected the whole market system at once. With most of the major industrial centers connected, the world of business and commence shrunk faster and further than ever before as time annihilated space.

The cables that spanned the oceans and continents affected a wide range of practices. Everything from diplomacy to commerce to newsgathering required rethinking. Businesses extended operations abroad. New forms of crime emerged. Codes created were soon cracked. A deluge of data inundated users of this expanding web of wires. The exchange of electrical impulses even sparked romances.

Western Union

From the outset, telegraphy was a capitalist enterprise in the United States. Morse had offered to sell his invention to the American government, but, when Congress demurred, he and his associates sought private funds. There followed a period of intense rivalry; some fifty or so telegraph companies sprung up, a few for no other reason than to sell stocks. Cutthroat competition became the order of the day. Through an aggressive policy of acquisitions, Western Union eventually emerged out of the confusion in a position of supremacy. By 1866, this company had acquired 50,000 miles of line and was well on its way to becoming a monopoly in the telegraph industry.

Western Union's board members included such tycoons as John Jacob Astor and William H. Vanderbilt. Control of the nation's web of wires was a key to wealth and power. For instance, in 1875, Representative Charles A. Sumner of California charged that information regarding sudden changes in market prices was often withheld from San Francisco until insiders could make a profit. In 1881, Jay Gould—that most rapacious of robber barons—took control of the giant telegraph company. Gould, who at the time also owned the *New York World*, used his privileged access to commercial intelligence ruthlessly. "He scanned the telegraph, or manipulated it, as an open book to the secrets of all the marts," writes Matthew Josephson.

On several occasions, Congress tried to break Western Union's monopoly hold over the flow of information to little avail. It considered more than 70 bills designed to reform the telegraph system in the decades following the Civil War, but Western Union was able to muster strong opposition. Congressmen in both major political parties who were friendly to Western Union's interests received unlimited supplies of "franks"—forms providing free telegraph service. The franking privilege was a strong inducement for government officials to favor the telegraph company, because it allowed them to keep in touch with constituents, particularly during campaigns.

Wireless Telegraphy

Italian-born Guglielmo Marconi expanded the turn-of-the-century internet with his remarkable invention of wireless point-to-point telegraphic communication. In 1895, he demonstrated through the use of a Morse key, the transmission of dots and dashes (long and short electrical impulses) via radio waves. Combining technical genesis with business acumen, Marconi, with wealthy backers, set up companies first in England and then the United States. This company soon dominated American point-to-point, ship-to shore communications.

Unknown at the time, the distance radio waves travel increases at night when the ionosphere, the layer above the earth, contracts. The waves bounce back and forth between the ionosphere and the earth's surface greatly increasing the range of a signal. Canadian-born inventor Reginald Fessenden made major advances in radio communication, especially in receiver design, as he worked to develop audio reception of signals.

Using a General Electric generator in Newfoundland, Canada, Fessenden broadcast human voice and music to ships at sea on radio waves on Christmas Eve 1906, astonishing wireless operators over a wide area and a range of hundreds of miles. The following year, American Lee De Forest invented and patented the three-element "Audion" vacuum tube, which could both receive and amplify electrical signals. It significantly improved the reception and transmission of radio waves.

Telephony

Within a few years of telegraphy's consolidation, another electric marvel appears—the telephone. The first words inventor Alexander Graham Bell sent in 1875: "Mr. Watson, please come here I want you" signaled the start of another communications revolution. Bell rushed to the U.S. Patents Office, beating another inventor, Elisha Gray, by two hours. In 1877, the triumphant inventor and his associates founded the Bell Telephone Company, eventually rebranded as the AT&T Corporation.

AT&T's far-sighted Theodore Vail, who became president in 1885, helped set up the Western Electric subsidiary to build telephone equipment and oversaw the first long-distance system from Boston, Massachusetts, to Providence, Rhode Island. Seeking other opportunities, Vail left in 1889 five years before Bell's telephone patent expired, which sparked the sprouting of small telephone companies across the country. In 1907, banker J.P. Morgan, through a series of rapid maneuvers, acquired control of AT&T, now the holding company for the entire Bell system, and enticed Vail, off making money in Argentina, back into the telephone fray with his old title of chief executive.

An advocate of "enlightened" monopoly, Vail dealt with the problem of competition in several ways. He committed the company to build a long-distance system that would cross the entire United States — doing this required in scientific research, which led to the development of AT&T's own laboratory, Bell Labs. He also cooperated with competitors, leasing them the use of AT&T's phone lines.

In 1913, Vail's settlement of a federal lawsuit sounded the death knell for openness and competition. That same year, after Lee de Forest began to suffer financial setbacks, Vail bought his vacuum-tube patents, including the Audion, which significantly amplified telephone signals. These patents allowed the company to build the first coast-to-coast telephone line. In the 1920s, this web of wires would make AT&T a significant player in the emerging broadcast system.

Changing Urban News Environment

Expanding Readers

Some three decades into the nineteenth century, what constituted news and newsworthiness began to undergo another dramatic transformation as newspapers sought to grab the attention of the rapidly expanding immigrant population. Steel plants, oil refineries, railroad links, expanding factories, and a growing labor force all emerged during late nineteenth century industrial expansion.

Factories needed workers and people were immigrating to the United States by the millions. Between 1870 and 1900, the population almost doubled. The move from farm to factory helped swell the growth in emerging urban centers. The influx of people tended to concentrate in the industrial Northeastern states. There were some fifty-eight cities with a population of more than half a million by the 1890s.

Transport Nexus

The whole New York area was fast becoming the gateway to a complex nexus of trade routes. The shipyards on both sides of the East River estuary tidal water, with dozens of piers along each, turned out vessels running the range from clippers to sloops, and schooners to tugboats. The prodigious output of wooden boats of all kinds provided jobs for thousands of skilled artisans. More than fifty piers jutted as well into the Hudson River, which flows into New York Bay and past the west side of Manhattan. Opened in 1825, the 363-mile Erie Canal linked the Hudson River in Albany to Lake Erie in Buffalo. This engineering marvel created the first transportation system between the Eastern Seaboard and the western interior of the United States that didn't require portage. The construction of additional canals linked the Erie Canal to Lake Champlain, Lake Ontario, and the Finger Lakes.

As the city became the fulcrum of the cotton trade, it drew merchants, shippers, auctioneers, bankers, brokers, insurers, and countless others to the burgeoning urban center. As a corollary to becoming dominant in shipping and commerce, it became the banking and stock market capital of the nation. The economy of New York was almost as dependent on slavery as that of the plantation owners. The cotton trade helped it develop into the most important port in the hemisphere by the 1830s. As the cotton kingdom flourished, so did its economic connections with New York City whose merchants dominated the transatlantic trade of this "white gold." Cotton comprised some forty percent of all the goods shipped out of its port.

The invention of the cotton gin in 1793 not only made cotton a significant industry but also sharply increased the need for slave labor. Some significant small plantations spread across the south from Florida to central Texas. An act of Congress that outlawed the importation of African slaves passed in 1807 and President Thomas Jefferson signed into law.[50] But the prohibition against importing African slaves did nothing to quell the domestic traffic in slaves and the interstate slave trade.

Planters purchased pickers at premium prices from slaveholders in states outside the area conducive to cotton growing like Virginia, Tennessee, and Kentucky. The huge debt incurred tightened the link between the city and the plantation owners. At the center of finance, New York banks mostly provided loans to buy more land and slaves. Some of Manhattan's most prominent families making at least part of their fortunes from slave-produced cotton had surnames like Morgan and Vanderbilt. Archibald Gracie used cotton profits to build Gracie Mansion, now the residence of the city's mayors.

The economy of Brooklyn, which by mid-century had grown to become the nation's third-largest city, was also closely tied to slavery. The products of slave labor filled warehouses along the East River estuary. In the 1850s, sugar refining was Brooklyn's largest industry. The massive factory building of the Domino Sugar Refinery, located on the Williamsburg waterfront, once produced more sugar than any other place on the planet.

In what newspapers reported as progress, after years of haphazard planning and a series of deadly cholera outbreaks, beginning in 1849, municipal officials invested in a complex sewage system piping human waste into the brackish East and Hudson rivers, turning them into cesspools instead of letting horse manure and feces float in pool on the streets. The excrement in the streets from humans and horses polluted all the wells. A massive engineering project to divert water from sources upstate, construction of the Croton Aqueduct between 1837 and 1842 brought a dependable supply of pure water propelled by gravity into New York City.

The population in the city was fast approaching four million by the beginning of the new century. The pace of life quickened, technical advances stepped up, and mobility, both social and geographic, gained momentum. The municipal transportation technology of the day was elevated trains. They were pulled by large, dirty, and heavy steam-powered locomotives, which sparked and screeched their way up and down the aboveground tracks. Located along Second, Third, Sixth, and Ninth Avenues, these elevated trains allowed people to live, work, shop, and play in different neighborhoods. Most Manhattan residents soon lived within a ten-minute walk to an elevated train. A small army of "news butchers," a colloquialism of uncertain coinage, walked through the train cars selling newspapers, snacks, fruit, cigars, and other products to the passengers. Toward the end of 1938, the city shut down the Sixth Avenue El, which ran past Radio City Music Hall, replacing it with a subway line still in operation.

Pulitzer's New York World

Along with the expansion of canals and railroads, and the urban transport nexus, progress in papermaking and the invention of the rotary printing press allowed for enormous growth in newspaper circulation. By the 1880s, newspaper publisher Joseph Pulitzer reached an enormous readership.[51] A Hungarian-born immigrant who had learned the newspaper business in Saint Louis, Missouri, the industrious Pulitzer established a reputation for combining sensationalism with crusading journalism. In 1883, he bought the *New York World*, a newspaper whose influence had declined. At the time of the Pulitzer purchase, the *World* had a circulation of perhaps 15,000. Within two years circulation had soared to 100,000, and by 1887, it passed the quarter-million figure.

Several factors contributed to the *World*'s remarkable success. Beyond sensational stories, it met a need at a time when New York's expanding population was moving from the crowded tenement houses below fourteenth street toward the north of the island. Its use of bold headlines and bright illustrations, together with its emphasis on relatively simple words and sentence structure helped to attract a broad general readership. Another magnet for readers was its diverse coverage: stories of sex, scandal, crime, and disaster; extensive political and financial reports; special features for women; a whole department for sports; crusading editorials.

A comic strip called "Hogan's Alley" proved to be enormously popular. Its motley cast of characters included a baldheaded, jug-eared, buck-toothed street urchin called the "Yellow Kid." He wore an over-sized yellow nightshirt that bore quippy observations in a broad stereotypical New York dialect. His popularity not only boosted circulation but also ignited a sales boom. The newspaper made vast amounts of money from selling Yellow Kid playing cards, dolls, broaches, ice cream, bottle openers, sheet

LI HUNG CHANG VISITS HOGAN'S ALLEY.

music, and even cigarettes. One of the first examples of sales linked to a character, it would hardly be the last. (The movie companies that feature Marvel comic-book heroes, for instance, rake in far more money from merchandising than they do from box- office ticket sales.)

The newspaper launched several spectacular publicity stunts. In 1885, for instance, the *World* itself made news when it raised $100,000 mostly from the nickel-and-dime contributions of its working-class readers, many of them immigrants, to build a pedestal for the Statue of Liberty. A year later, testimony to the power of the press, the neoclassical copper sculpture (now green from oxidation) with torch-bearing arm aloft, a broken shackle and chain at its feet, stood high at the entrance to New York Harbor. A plaque inside the pedestal's base, added in 1903, contains Emma Lazarus' sonnet, "New Colossus," with its now-famous lines, "Give me your tired, your poor, your huddled masses yearning to breathe free." She wrote the poem to help raise money for the pedestal. (The plaque has resided in the island museum since 1986.)

These stirring words came to symbolize for many a message of hope and freedom for immigrants coming to America. At the time the statue was unveiled, however, the 1882 Chinese Exclusion Act barred the Chinese for ten years from entering the United States. Extended until 1943, it was the first federal law ever to ban immigrants based on race or nationality but not the last. In the years ahead, Korean, Japanese, and Eastern and Southern Europeans "yearning to breathe free" would be subject to strict quotas or outright bans.

Earlier in the century, states like Indiana and Illinois passed laws barring the immigration of free blacks. Other states carved out of the Northwest Territory from Ohio to Michigan passed laws as well making blacks unwelcome. Free blacks crossing borders into these states ran the risk of being sold as slaves. Most of these anti-immigration laws were not reversed until well after the end of the American Civil War.[52]

NELLY BLY

A reporter for the *New York World*, Elizabeth Cochrane writing under the pseudonym Nellie Bly, would go to incredible lengths to expose wrongdoing and malfeasance. Accompanying the population growth in Manhattan was a burgeoning underclass of convicts, the poor, the sick, and the mentally ill. In 1828, the city purchased an island in the East River from the Blackwell family to build a jail and an asylum.[53] The mental hospital consisted of two wings meeting at a right angle, joined in the center by an octagonal tower. One side was for men and the other for women. The central octagon housed staff apartments, offices, and parlors. (The structure still stands, converted into condominiums.)

Bly feigned insanity so she could get committed to the Women's Lunatic Asylum to investigate reports of neglect and brutality, foul food and unjust confinement. With the exception of torture, the enterprising reporter later wrote after experiencing such deplorable conditions firsthand, nothing would produce insanity quicker than "to take a perfectly sane and healthy woman, shut her up and make her sit from 6 A.M. to 8 P.M. on straight-back benches, do not allow her to talk or move during these hours, give her no reading and let her know nothing of the world or its doing, give her bad food and harsh treatment, and see how long it will take to make her insane."[54]

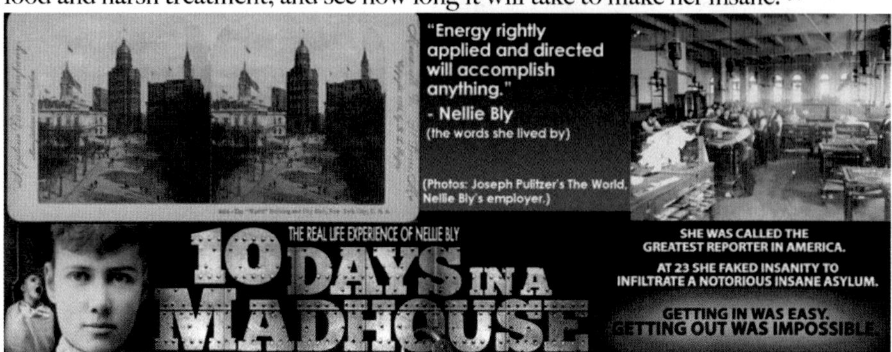

After ten days, the asylum released Bly at the *World*'s behest. Within a week of her release, the newspaper ran the first part of her exposé, entitled "Behind Asylum Bars," followed the next Sunday by "Inside a Madhouse." Newspapers throughout the country reprinted the articles. Shortly after, the paper published the two-part story in book form as *Ten Days in a Mad-House*. The exposé caused a sensation, resulting in a grand jury investigation and an $850,000 budget increase for the mental institution to implement reforms. The asylum staff transferred or discharged several of the wrongly committed women.

In 1889, Pulitzer sent Bly around the world to see if she could beat the travel time of Jules Verne's fictional character Phineas Fogg in *Around the World in Eighty Days*. The newspaper offered a free trip to Europe to the person whose guess came closest to the actual time it took Bly to circle the globe. The contest drew nearly a million estimates. Traveling by ship, train, rickshaw, sampan, horse, camel, and burro, Bly returned to a cheering crowd in under seventy-three days. Her stories about the people and lands she encountered en route made her one the most famous females on the planet, an inspiration to women during an era when marriage or a menial job was considered their only appropriate option.

Historian Daniel Boorstin would later call these kind occurrences "pseudo-events," by which he meant events arranged or brought about for the sake of the publicity they generate. Such staged events take the form of press conferences, trial balloons, background briefings, organized protests, public spectacles, and the like. Since the early twentieth century, noted Boorstin, "a larger and larger proportion of our experience, of what we read and see and hear, has come to consist of pseudo-events."[55] Those in a position to create such events tend to set the agenda for local, regional, and national matters of discussion, as the enormous nationwide racial-justice marches in mid-2020 demonstrated.

Hearst's News Empire

Pulitzer's principal competitor, William Randolph Hearst, entered the news business in 1887. His father, George Hearst, a mining millionaire and U.S. senator from California, gave his only son the *San Francisco Examiner*.[56] Some eight years later, after turning the *Examiner* into a moneymaker, Hearst purchased another newspaper, the *New York Journal*. It would become the second in a long list of media holdings that he acquired in the next decade of his life.

Using his wealth and privilege, Hearst built a massive communications empire. Eventually, he owned over two-dozen newspapers nationwide with nearly one in four Americans getting their news from one of his publications. Under his control, the *Journa*l soon outdid the *World* in sensationalism, selling newspapers by printing giant headlines over lurid stories featuring crime, corruption, sex, and innuendo.

To gain a competitive edge, Hearst lured away R.F. Outcault, creator of the famous *New York World* comic strip featuring the Yellow Kid. The move fueled the already heated rivalry between the two press magnates. In response, Pulitzer hired another artist to create a second Yellow Kid. To many critics, the so-called "Battle of the Yellow Kids" signaled an even deeper decline of journalistic integrity. A more staid newspaper editor dubbed the false, ill-researched, and frequently distorted reporting among sensationalist newspapers of the 1890s "yellow journalism."

Scion of a vast fortune, Hearst was determined to build circulation by catering to urban working people, many of whom were recent immigrants. His newspapers favored labor unions, progressive taxation, and municipal ownership of utilities. They featured abundant drawings, advice to the lovelorn columns, and sentimental stories.

Supporting Irish and German readers in particular, long marginalized in Protestant America, the paper condemned British influence and spread fears about the "yellow peril" of Asian immigration.[57] Some of his detractors have even accused Hearst of instigating the Spanish-American War merely so he could report it. Although such a charge simplifies complex causal components, it is not without some degree of truth.

Fermenting War

Historians have long debated the causes of this war. To quell an armed uprising in its Cuban colony, Spain had sent some 200,000 troops to the island. Economic devastation, notably the destruction of sugar cane production, was widespread. The Cuban uprising aggravated economic conditions in the United States, which in 1893 had entered a severe recession that would last nearly five years. Toward the end of the century, advances in technology and expanding economic globalization were making an urbanizing public with the time and education to read newspapers anxious about how long the United States could remain isolated and unarmed.

Hearst's jingoistic coverage of a Cuban insurgency did much to provoke pro-war sentiment. Late in 1896, for instance, he sent celebrated journalist Richard Harding Davis and noted painter-sculptor Frederic Remington to Havana to cover the conflict between Cuban insurgents and Spanish authorities. Under Madrid's control for nearly 400 years, tensions on the island colony were coming to a boil.

After a short time, the rotund Remington, perhaps reluctant to pass through

Spanish lines to reach the Cuban insurgents, requested to be relieved of the assignment. The intrepid Davis stayed on traveling across the island colony. His reports told of a landscape blighted by blazing fields of sugar cane and of civilian casualties resulting from neglect and starvation in Spanish detention camps.

In February 1897, Davis filed a story about Spanish police boarding a U.S. vessel bound for New York in order to search three young Cuban women who were suspected of carrying insurgent dispatches. The journal featured his report on page one under the five-column headline: "DOES OUR FLAG PROTECT WOMEN?" The second page of the report featured a half-page Remington drawing.

Imagined from New York, it showed one of the women naked and surrounded by policemen searching her clothing. It was the kind of stuff that built circulation—nearly a million copies of the newspaper were sold. But it was not an accurate depiction of what had taken place. Davis, who had reported that female officers had searched, was outraged when Hearst printed that it had been male officers of the law. After this episode, he resigned and refused to work for Hearst again.

Pulitzer sent reporters to interview the Cuban women when they arrived in the United States. The women made it clear that matrons, not police officers, had searched them. Seizing on the opportunity to embarrass its competitor, the *World*, under the headline: "THE UNCLOTHED WOMEN SEARCH BY MEN WAS AN INVENTION OF A NEW YORK NEWSPAPER," exposed the *Journal*'s distortion of the facts.

Undeterred, Hearst continued to foment war. In January 1898, when the American battleship Maine exploded in the harbor of Havana, taking the lives of 256 American sailors, the *Journal* offered a $50,000 reward for information leading to the arrest and conviction of the perpetrators. It presented a seven-column drawing of the ship anchored over mines, and a diagram showing wires leading from the mines to a Spanish fortress on shore under the screaming headline: "THE WARSHIP MAINE WAS SPLIT BY AN ENEMY'S SECRET INFERNAL MACHINE."

Such flights of fancy shot the circulation of the *Journal* well past the one million mark. Three days after the sinking, the Journal proclaimed in bold type: "THE WHOLE COUNTRY THRILLS WITH WAR FEVER." The actual cause of the explosion would later be revealed to have been an accident. Despite uncertainty about the cause, both Hearst and Pulitzer published what turned out to be a bogus cable from the captain of the ship to the assistant secretary of the navy informing him that the disaster was no accident. Newspaper circulation soared, and readers increasingly clamored for war.

Getting little newspaper attention, segments of the business community, with some $450 million in agricultural investments at stake, had long been interested in wresting Cuba from the declining Spanish Empire. Spurred on by bankers and arms merchants eager to protect assets and reap a windfall, in April 1898, President William McKinley declared war on Spain even though the government had most of the minuscule American Army spread around the country.

As a short-term measure, McKinley authorized three volunteer cavalry regiments each comprised of 800 to 1,000 soldiers. They were to be drawn from the ranks of men whose skills and life experiences made them predisposed to martial pursuits. The most famous of the three, the First United States Volunteer Cavalry, was the only one sent to Cuba. Reporters soon dubbed it the Rough Riders. It was a unique group of volunteers ranging from Ivy League athletes to Arizona cowboys led by no less a figure than future president Theodore Roosevelt. Under his leadership, they helped secure victory in Cuba in a series of gripping, bloody fights across the island that made front-page news across the country. Their charge in the Battle of San Juan marked a turning point in Roosevelt's life, one that led directly to the White House.[58]

Reporting now for the *New York World*, among other publications, Richard Harding Davis contributed considerably to the legend surrounding Roosevelt and the Rough Riders. More than 16,000 men fought in the Cuban campaign, but there was only one regiment that mattered for much of the American public. A trustbuster, pioneer conservationist, and staunch suffrage supporter, the much-admired Roosevelt has fallen out of favor in recent years. Critics have pointed to his opinions about racial gradation, his support of eugenics, and his imperialist inclinations.

The short, decidedly lopsided war effectively ended with the surrender of Spanish forces at the port city of Santiago de Cuba, where American warships had blocked the harbor. The two nations agreed to a cease-fire the following month and formally signed the Treaty of Paris in December. Whatever motives may have led to the war, the United States acquired Puerto Rico, Guam and the Philippines. It paid Spain $20 million to cover its ownership of the Philippine infrastructure. During this time, the United States annexed several island possessions spanning the globe, including Hawaii and American Samoa.

With cable tolls, salaries, and dispatch boats to transport reporters, covering the 113-day war proved to be extremely expensive. The *World* employed three vessels; the *Herald* had five; and *Journal* at various times used ten steamers, yachts, and tugboats as dispatch vessels; the *Evening Journal*, the ill-bred sister publication of the *Morning Journal*, issued as many as forty extra editions a day. The deployment of newsboys was indispensable. Without their swift distributing power, all the effort and expense in reporting the war would have been for naught. Pulitzer came to regret his role in the rush to war, but Hearst expressed no qualms at all about his sensationalist coverage.

American troops next fought a counterinsurgency in the Philippines using many of the same brutal tactics the Spanish had employed in Cuba, racking up more bodies than the American Civil War. The Asian archipelago didn't get civilian rule until 1913. Sounding like the imperialistic British, American leaders justified this fight as a noble effort to civilize and uplift Filipinos. The United States had heeded British novelist and poet Rudyard Kipling's appeal in the infamous poem, "White Man's Burden," for Americans to take on the obligation of an empire, as had Britain and other European nations. The Filipino fight set the pattern for future American forays into foreign lands.

Newspaper Diversity

A financial news service for private clients, founded in 1882 by Charles H. Dow and Edward T. Jones, evolved later in the decade into the *Wall Street Journal*. Circulation remained small until the 1940s, when the paper broadened its coverage of business and finance to include all events of international and national importance affecting the business community. Eventually, multiple printing plants and domestic satellite relays gave to the newspaper a national readership of well over a million people. It is now part of Rupert Murdoch's News Corporation. The *Christian Science Monitor*, founded by the Christian Science Church of Boston in 1908, also emerged as a nationally read newspaper of distinction. This daily pioneered an interpretative approach to problems and trends in regional, national, and international affairs. These days, it is an online newspaper.

The leading daily in the Midwest was the *Chicago Tribune*, which first appeared in 1847. Under the control of Joseph Medill, who with his partners purchased the paper in 1855, it challenged the *New York Herald* in flamboyant personal journalism. It was a vitriolic publication; despite its overt emphasis on moral values, it did not hesitate to use the power of mass circulation to pour invective on those with whom it disagreed. But its circulation soared; then as now, the *Chicago Tribune* was considered a newspaper with a strong conservative, its critics call it reactionary, point of view. It was anti-labor and defended the status quo with vigor. Robert McCormick and Joseph Patterson assumed control of the newspaper in 1914. Under McCormick's direction (until his death in 1955), it became one of the best-written, most forceful dailies in the country.

Other areas outside New York and the Eastern seaboard also had newspapers of distinction. William Rockhill Nelson and Samuel E. Morss established the *Kansas City Star* in 1880. (Ill health soon caused the latter to leave the newspaper business.) This superb publication shunned sensational coverage. It showed what a news outlet could accomplish when it determines to drive corruption out of a city by exposing its perpetrators to public view through the instrumentality of the press.

Nelson battled politicians and gamblers and campaigned vigorously for improving the quality of life in the rough-and-tumble town of Kansas City, Missouri. By the time of his death in 1915, the *Star*'s circulation had climbed to 170,000. After Nelson's heirs died, the employees purchased the *Star* and a companion paper. They remained under employee ownership for over fifty years. The newspapers came under corporate control in 1977. Now part of the Knight-Ridder/McClatchy publishing empire, recently fallen into bankruptcy, the *Star* remains one of the great newspapers in the United States.

In general, by most accounts, the newspapers that sprang up in the West and the South were not paragons of journalistic excellence. The *Denver Post*, a sober publication these days, was launched on sensationalism and a series of stunts and crusades. In San Francisco, the *Chronicle* was an enterprising and exemplary endeavor until challenged by the emergence of William Randolph Hearst and the *San Francisco Examiner*, a newspaper that typified the overwrought, shocking, and frequently lurid journalism of the period.

CRIMINAL COMPLICITY

A downside of selling attention can be complicity in bigotry and blind hatred to meet reader expectation. In the South, many newspapers played a significant role in the racial terrorism of the late nineteenth and early twentieth centuries, which saw thousands of blacks hanged, burned, drowned, or beaten to death by white mobs. The organizers of a lynch mob that burned a black tenant farmer at stake in 1921 observed standard protocol when they notified newspapers early in the day that they planned to kill him as painfully as possible. This practice gave editors time to produce special editions that provided the time and place so would-be spectators could attend such horrific events. A reporter in attendance for the *Memphis Press* described the victim's suffering in lurid detail.[59]

This unsavory role of newspapers in the South surfaced dramatically in spring 2018 when the nearly two-centuries-old *Montgomery Advertiser* printed a front-page mea culpa for its lynching coverage. The apology coincided with the opening in Montgomery, Alabama, of a museum dedicated to the legacy of slavery and a memorial honoring the thousands of lynching victims. The first capital of the Confederate States of America, the city had been notably slow to atone for its sordid racial history. In October 2019, the city elected its first black mayor. On the cusp of celebrating its 200 years as an incorporated city, some sixty-percent of its 200,000 residents are black.

The decades following the end of the Civil War saw a few black-owned newspapers emerge below of the Mason-Dixon line, the informal name of the antebellum boundary between the free (Northern) states and the slave (Southern) states. With his brother, Frank, as co-owner, Alexander Manly published the *Daily Record* in Wilmington, North Carolina. By the late 1890s, this bustling port city had 20,000 residents; its population was majority black, with a rising middle class. A progressive enclave surrounded by reactionary forces, its multi-racial government included black council members, police officers, and magistrates.

An interracial coalition of white populists and black Republicans had prevailed in the 1896 state elections. The disenfranchised Democrats were determined to regain power in the upcoming November 1898 gubernatorial elections. The *Daily Record* publisher gave them a rallying cry to stave off another political defeat. In response to a speech supporting lynching black men who slept with white women, Alexander Manly wrote an editorial stating that many white women, rather than being raped by black men, willingly had consensual sex. It ignited outrage across the South with calls to lynch the light-skinned Manly, partially descended from a slave owner, his pale complexion testimony to the hypocrisy and sexual exploitation of female chattel on antebellum plantations.

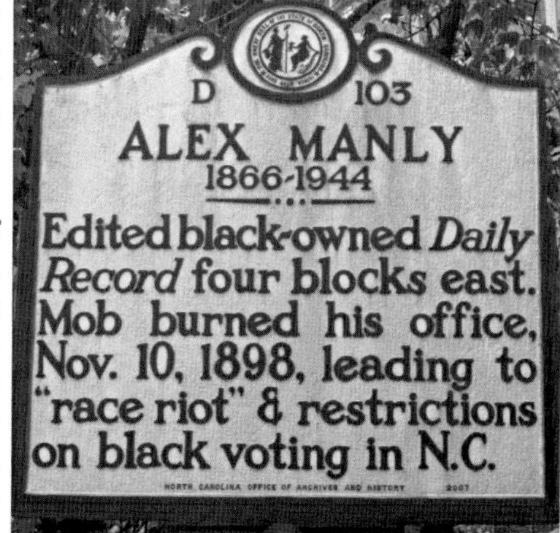

In Raleigh, North Carolina, Josephus Daniels, publisher of *News & Observer*, the state's largest newspaper, conspired with like-minded Wilmington Democratic political leaders and plantation aristocracy to use the editorial to provoke a violent coup d'état. Newspaper editorials, raucous rallies, cartoons, fabricated news stories, and widely distributed pamphlets accused black men of exhibiting ill-will and disrespect for whites in public, labeled them as corrupt and unjust and often referred to their assumed lust for white women.

Focusing their rage on Manly's editorial, and hell-bent on lynching him, more than 2,000 heavily armed white supremacists swarmed through Wilmington's streets. They torched the *Record* office, destroyed homes and businesses, terrorized women and children, and killed at least sixty black men, throwing the bodies in the Cape Fear River, which ran red with blood for days. The attackers forced city officials to resign at gunpoint and replaced them with Democratic leaders, who banished prominent blacks and sympathetic whites. Hundreds of terrified black families fled to surrounding swamps and forests. Fortunately for Manly, a white friend warned him about the plot to lynch him. Because of his European heritage, he was able to pass for white, which helped him escape from the encircled city.

This brutal insurrection, notes the author of *Wilmington Lie*, halted gains made by blacks and restored racial discrimination as official government policy, cementing an apartheid agenda in the region for another half-century.[60] Two years after the death and destruction, and the overthrow of a duly elected city government slated to be in power for another year, Daniels backed a new constitutional amendment that barred most of the state's black residents from voting. An unrepentant white supremacist, the influential newspaper publisher served as U.S. Secretary of the Navy during World War I and was U.S. Ambassador to Mexico under President Franklin Delano Roosevelt.

Anxieties about white women coupling with black men touched as nothing else the raw nerve of racism. Fear of miscegenation reared its ugly head in Tulsa, situated on the Arkansas River between the Osage Hills and the foothills of the Ozark Mountains in northeast Oklahoma. Newspapers like the *Tulsa World* and *Tulsa Tribune*, along with other publications, stoked long-simmering racial tensions, portraying the predominantly black Greenwood district of the city as rife with sleazy jazz joints, speakeasies, and a hotbed of racial mixing.[61] An inflammatory front-page story entitled "Nab Negro for Attacking Girl in Elevator," appeared in the May 31, 1921 edition of the *Tulsa Tribune*. The unsubstantiated accusation of attempted rape provided the pretext for one of the worst incidents of racial violence in American history, rivaled only by the wholesale slaughter of indigenous peoples.

After the arrest of the black man, spoiling for an evening's lynching, a crowd convened at the courthouse, where officials barricaded him on the top floor for protection. Denied weapons at the National Guard armory, whites-- including some police--broke into a sporting goods store across the street from the courthouse, grabbing guns, ammunition and just about everything else in sight. Three carloads of armed black men appeared on the scene to prevent the illegal hanging. After an exchange of gunfire with the mob, outgunned and outmanned, they retreated to Greenwood to defend against the coming onslaught.

Called the nation's "Black Wall Street" by Booker T. Washington, its economy fueled by an oil boom, Greenwood in northwest Tulsa was one of the most prosperous black communities in the United States. The black-owned *Tulsa Daily Star*, small but spirited and bold, promoted equal rights and opportunities. Challenging racism and fighting against injustice, the newspaper urged the area's black residents, including those living in shacks and shanties without indoor plumbing, to fight for their rights and leverage their political clout. Providing leadership and influence in shaping Tulsa's black community, the law-trained editor and publisher, A.J. Smitherman, didn't hesitate to criticize the perceived wrongdoings of the bustling city's white officials and administrators.

This distrust between city officials and the leading black voice in the community lay bare the volatile racial climate in Tulsa. Acting out long-smoldering antipathies, a horde of white residents, many deputized by city authorities, descended on the district attacking black residents at will and looting and torching businesses. By the time the bloody conflagration ended, the rampaging ragtag mob on the ground and in the air pilots of crop duster planes dropping incendiary devices destroyed over thirty square blocks.

Homes, churches, hotels, restaurants, drugstores, schools, medical offices, public libraries, hospitals, and the *Tulsa Daily Star*'s offices and printing plant lay in rubble, its publisher forced to flee, relocating in the northeast. Over 800 sustained injuries, and an estimated 10,000 blacks were left homeless, with many moved to temporary detainment camps subject to harassment and humiliation. Although challenging to pinpoint precisely, the death toll may have been as high as 300. The all-white grand juries in the 1920s-era court system and a complicit press precluded any possibility of justice for the victims of this murder and mayhem.

The post-Civil War South could boast of a few outstanding, white-owned high-minded newspapers. When Henry W. Grady became part owner and managing editor of the *Atlanta Constitution* in 1880, for example, he helped to develop that publication into one of the best-written, best-edited newspapers in the country. The University of Georgia's School of Journalism, which offers the annual George Foster Peabody Broadcasting Awards, is named after Grady. Another excellent newspaper in this generally lackluster area was Henry Patterson's *Louisville Courier-Journal*, which—like the *Atlanta Constitution*—championed the rehabilitation and development of a vigorous South.

Selling Sober Attention

Newspapers in several American cities—including Boston, Chicago, Denver, St. Louis, and San Francisco—adopted many of the features and content characteristics of yellow journalism. Penny papers of a soberer sort also made their mark. Horace Greeley's serious and high-minded *New York Tribune* first appeared in 1841. He would continue as its editor for the next thirty years. During Greeley's tenure, perhaps reflecting his puritanical upbringing, the paper had a strong moralistic tone. Among the many causes he promoted was the abolition of slavery.[62]

A mix of partisan and penny press in outlook and orientation, the *Tribune* was the dominant Whig Party and then Republican newspaper in the United States. In addition to editorials promoting multiple reforms, the paper provided political news, special articles, lectures, book reviews, book excerpts and poetry. Greeley hired an impressive roster of editors and feature writers, including women's rights advocate Margaret Fuller, who later became famous in their own right. For some eleven years, starting in the early 1850s, the *Communist Manifesto* author Karl Marx served as the *New York Tribune*'s London correspondent tackling a range of issues from social inequality and starvation to the slave and opium trades.[63]

In many ways Greeley was an idealist envisioning a virtuous citizenry who would eradicate corruption. Such high ideals notwithstanding, as with most of the penny papers, the *Tribune* was hardly averse to building circulation and advertising revenue by carrying accounts of crimes, petty offenses, and moral transgressions. But it was careful to present this material under the guise of cautionary tales. While the daily's circulation early on trailed its rivals the *Sun* and the *Herald*, neither could match the huge success of its weekly edition. First published in September of 1841, the weekly enjoyed a wide popularity in small cities and towns, and by 1860 could boast of a circulation of some 200,000.

Stalwart Times

Two *Tribune* alumnae, George Jones and Henry Jarvis Raymond, launched the *New York Times* in the fall of 1851. Under Raymond's editorship, the *Times* avoided the extremist viewpoints and sensationalist stories that were common in the press the 1850s, a period rife with factional and sectional hatreds. A politician as well as a journalist, he was elected lieutenant governor of New York.

After contributing to the demise of the Whig Party, active in the period from 1834 to 1854, Raymond played a significant role on the formation of the Republication Party (then the more progressive party opposing the spread of slavery). A strong Lincoln supporter, he prepared the incumbent president's 1864 platform, and also served one term in the House of Representatives. After being denied a second term, he returned to active newspaper work. During his tenure, the *Times* gained a reputation for sobriety, moderation, and balance.

With Jones at the helm, following Raymond's death at age forty-nine, the newspaper's influence grew in 1870 and 1871, when it published a series of exposés on William "Boss" Tweed, leader of the city's Democratic Party—popularly known as "Tammany Hall" (from its early 19th-century meeting headquarters). Those revelations led to the end of the corrupt Tweed Ring's domination of New York's City Hall.

In the 1880s, the paper gradually transitioned from supporting Republican Party candidates in its editorials to becoming more politically independent and analytical. This shift caused it to lose a portion of its more progressive readership. It regained ground within a few years, but a severe economic depression that lasted almost four years brought it to the brink of bankruptcy.

PROMOTING WORLD WAR

The efficacy of engaging in attention-grabbing promotional campaigns was not lost on supporters of global conflict. When England went to war with Germany in August 1914, the British government engaged in systematic propaganda on a global scale, drawing the United States among others into war with an avalanche of pamphlets, books, speakers, movies, and the like, all presenting one-sided versions of the complicated origins of the conflict and the righteousness of its actions. In what came to be called "atrocity propaganda," tales of the spike-helmeted Germans cutting off the hands of children, boiling corpses to make soap, and crucifying prisoners of war enjoyed broad circulation in the news media.

At the height of the First World War, a German official sent a secret Western Union telegram sent to the government of Mexico. It promised the Mexicans a military alliance if the United States entered the war against Germany and helped it recover the territories of Texas, Arizona, and New Mexico lost in the Mexican-American War. If it had reached the Mexican government, the course of the war could have changed forever. But the British intercepted the telegram and passed it along to the American government. The intercepted telegram, its contents depicted by cartoonists, justified President Woodrow Wilson's entry into the war, a boon for American business interests.

When the United States entered the fray in April 1917, declaring war on Germany, the *New York Times* and the *New York Herald*, were both staunchly anti-German. While the *Herald*'s editorials were practically a mouthpiece for the Wilson administration, the *Times* took a more reasoned approach. "The chief public service of the *Times* in the war," writes the author of a behind-the-scenes history of the newspaper, "was that from the very beginning it understood where the rights and wrongs of the conflict lay, it was able to justify its position by sound argument. It never ceased to maintain that position with all the vigor which its editors were able to command."[64]

The pro-war stance of these papers was evident not only on editorial pages but also in the selection and placement of stories, sizes of headlines, and the use of illustrations. Other leading papers in the city like the *Tribune* were also strongly pro-Ally. The *Sun* and the *Evening Post* maintained a more impartial position on their editorial pages. By sharp contrast, the Hearst-owned newspapers across the country, along with his influential International News Service, were stridently anti-British.

In response to negative coverage, the British government cut off the wire service's use of cables or the mails to transmit dispatches from London and expelled its correspondents. Other nations aligned with the British took similar restrictive measures. With a firm attachment to the British Empire and Commonwealth, the Canadian government barred all Hearst newspapers from the country.

Soon after American entry into the war, President Woodrow Wilson launched a systematic campaign to promote support for the wartime effort, which required at least a million men in uniform ready to fight. When only 73,000 volunteered, a large majority in Congress voted for compulsory conscription. By executive order, Wilson established the Committee on Public Information (CPI), the nation's first federal propaganda agency, to muster support for the war. From within the government, its membership included the secretaries of war, state, and navy.

To oversee the new propaganda apparatus, Wilson appointed journalist George Creel, a well-connected critic of corporate excess and government corruption. Under his leadership, the CPI organized a public relations and advertising program of considerable proportions to sound the constant drumbeat for defeating the enemy. Among other measures, the agency created colorful posters that appeared in store windows around the nation, catching the attention of the passersby for a few seconds.

Depictions designed to demonize the German, inciting anger and fostering feelings of hatred, appeared not only on posters, but also in pamphlets, sketches, films, and cartoons. In many instances, they employed the word "Hun," a slang term for Germans to suggest they are beasts or subhuman intent on raping and pillaging. Common slogans included "Down with the Hun!" or "No Mercy for the Hun!"

After prodding from the CPI, the Hollywood studios produced jingoistic movies like *The Claws of the Hun* (1918), *The Hun Within* (1918), *The Prussian Cur* (1918), *Outwitting the Hun* (1918), and *The Kaiser Beast of Berlin* (1918) that depicted the Germans as evil incarnate. In *Till I Come Back to You* (1918), Belgian children are shipped to Germany to work in munitions factories, where they are whipped and starved into submission. A purported "inside look" at the atrocities of Prussian prison camps is provided by *My Four Years in Germany* (1918). In *Hearts of the World* (1918), a once-idyllic French village is occupied by depraved Prussians who plunder and rape at will. Perhaps the most virulent example of this hate-the-Hun propaganda, *The Heart of Humanity* (1918), featured Eric von Stroheim as a German military officer who, in the process of trying to rape a young nurse, tosses the baby in her care out of an upstairs window.

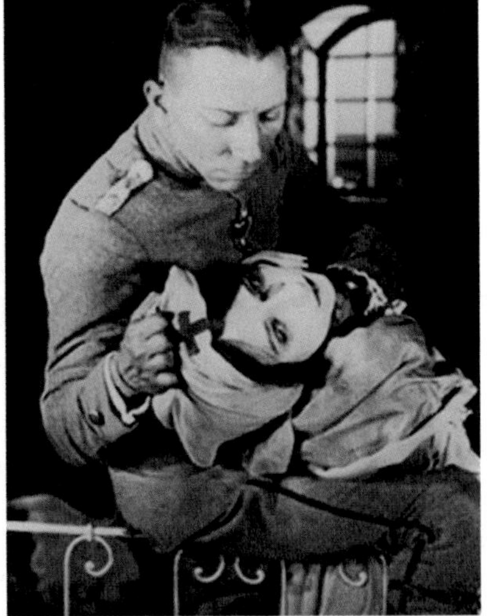

Such movies and sensational news coverage contributed to a climate of hysteria and blind hate in which everything German came under assault. Sauerkraut became "liberty cabbage." German musicians, actors, and writers couldn't find work. The music of Bach and Beethoven disappeared from the programming of civic orchestras. And Americans of German descent who didn't change their names were subject to persecution. Although the vast majority of Germans living in the United States had no responsibility whatsoever for the war, all the vials of wrath produced against their country of origin poured upon them. (Even King George, to rid the royal family of its German taint, changed his surname from Saxe-Coburg-Gotha to Windsor in 1917 and Anglicized the names of his relatives in the royal court.)

CORPORATE IMAGE POLISHING

During the First World War, chemical companies were among the principal pecuniary beneficiaries. The American chemical conglomerate, DuPont de Nemours, Inc., commonly known as DuPont, early in the last century, had a monopoly on the manufacture of gunpowder for the military. Presented with substantial evidence from a disgruntled former employee of collusion and conspiracy, in summer 1907, the U.S. Department of Justice charged DuPont and the other powder companies with "maintaining an unlawful combination in restraint of interstate commerce" in violation of the Sherman Anti-Trust Act.

The outcome was hardly disruptive of its profit stream. The chemical giant ended up keeping its monopoly over gunpowder manufacture, the target of the anti-trust action in the first place. It went on to make a fortune during the First World War by supplying the European Allies and later the U.S. Army with millions of rounds of small arms and high-powered explosives for artillery shells.

After the war ended, the petrochemical industry turned to the consumer market to maintain profits. The ironic "better living through chemistry" became the Dupont's motto for the 1940s and 1950s as pesticides, plastics, chemical beauty products, and miracle cleaning products became all the rage. These chemicals entered the consumer market without any tests to determine how all these new chemicals would impact humans, animals, and our environment. The screen drama *Dark Waters* (2019) affectingly shows the devastating effect DuPont's toxic chemical waste had on a West Virginia town.

From 1935 to 1953, DuPont sponsored the bland but popular anthology historical series *Cavalcade of America*, which later moved to television, playing from 1952 to 1957. The series helped polish DuPont's corporate image, tarnished after a 1930s Senate investigation into munitions profits during "the Great War," or perhaps more accurately "the Chemist's War." It revealed that the company, promoting "better living through chemistry" had derived more than a billion dollars from war contracts between 1914 and 1918 for a profit of close to $240 million. As a result, its stock value soared.

The German company Bayer has long run warm, soft-focused ads and comfort-inducing commercials highlighting the social benefits of its aspirin and other products. In fall 2019, under the slogan "Why We Science," it launched a series of TV commercials along with digital and social media to show the value of its products, from healthcare to agriculture, in consumer's lives. Few people would ever suspect from these uplifting ads that the company has a dark, sinister past.

Bayer and other chemical manufacturers (both Allied and German), manufactured chemical weapons in the First World War, including chlorine gas, which had horrific effects in trench warfare. The global pharmaceutical company's image-polishing campaigns have obscured a host of sins, among them using Jewish slave laborers during the Second World War. As part of the IG Farben chemical trust, it invested in Zyklon B; the gas used to kill 100,000s of Jewish men, women, and children at Auschwitz, the largest mass extermination factory in human history—its building bankrolled by Deutsche Bank. One of its scientists assisted the infamous "angel of death" Josef Mengele with genetic experiments on children.

A marriage made in hell, in May 2018, the Trump Administration Justice Department approved Bayer's $63 billion merger with agriculture giant Monsanto, inventor of the controversial herbicide Roundup, and a significant producer of genetically engineered crops. Along with Dow Chemical and several other chemical companies, it made Agent Orange for use by the U.S. military as part of its deadly defoliation warfare program in Vietnam, causing terrible human suffering and enormous environmental damage. Testifying to the success of the aspirin seller's image polishing campaign, they called the combined companies simply Bayer, avoiding negative associations with the Monsanto name.

Devastating Death Toll

In the global storm of the First World War, some 10 million expired on the battlefield, among them 50,000 American soldiers. The two sides fought bloody, horrific battles for months, sometimes conquering only a few meters of mud. The terrifying new tactics and technologies, including poison gas attacks, minefields, airstrikes, and the unspeakable misery of trench warfare, marked a turning point of modern military conflict. Perhaps as many as another twenty million people died of hunger and disease related to the war. Cities all across Europe lay in ashes with their economies in ruin. Such devastating death and destruction, far from making the world safe for democracy, created a cultural breeding ground for war, terror, and dictatorship.

Clouding the cause of the death count, at the height of the war in early 1918, one of history's most lethal influenza viruses erupted in an overcrowded army camp in Haskell, Kansas and moved east with American troops as they headed to Europe.[65] Unseen since the dark days of the bubonic plague, the contagion raged across the globe, emptying city streets and filling gravesites on six continents. The Allies dubbed the pandemic the Spanish flu, primarily because it received more considerable press attention in Spain. Neutral in the war, it didn't impose the wartime censorship and repressive measures of the American government and other combatant nations to maintain morale and stifle dissident voices.

Priming for War

By the war's end, propaganda was a fact of modern society, an almost spiritual force that could manipulate the thoughts and behavior of those most susceptible to its influences. The wartime campaign to win hearts and minds seemed to validate the prevailing belief that propaganda works best when it confirms and reinforces the already accepted, explaining the efficacy of patriotic appeals. The same education system teaching literacy also imbues in students a blind patriotism, the seedbed of international disputes. Every morning they pledge allegiance to the flag, the foremost symbol of American nationalism. They sing the national anthem at assemblies and are assigned textbooks that as a rhetorical article of faith depict American achievements as the noblest among nations.

Most history textbooks, notes a well-documented critique, shaded by politics, provide irrelevant and even erroneous details while omitting crucial facts and questions antithetical to a particular point of view. Such an approach to teaching is likely to make students more not less vulnerable to distortions and fabrications, turning off those regions in the brain that regulate critical thinking, self-awareness, and rational behavior. The study of history, the author concludes, will become useful, relevant, and intellectually stimulating to students "when their teachers and textbooks stop lying to them."[66]

The indictment implicates grade, middle, and high school teachers, but also publishing companies, school boards, and influential interest groups with an agenda served by withholding disagreeable truth from developing minds. Many elementary and high schoolteachers are not only underpaid and overworked but must also contend with poorly prepared students and overcrowded classrooms. And teacher-training programs often fall short in preparing future educators to identify the insidious ways propaganda is spread through textual materials as well as news coverage across the country.

Modern Times

When Adolph Ochs, the son of German-Jewish immigrants, purchased the *New York Times* in 1896, its circulation had dropped to 9,000. Under his stewardship, it expanded coverage of financial news, market reports, real estate transactions, and other activities of interest to men of commerce and industry. Ochs unabashedly supported such conservative measures as the lowest tax-rate consistent with good government and no more government than was essential to protect society. He saw little role for government in local affairs in a city plagued by fifth, poverty, and dehumanizing want and misery.

This pro-business orientation soon found a large readership. Within a year, circulation had reached 25,000, and advertising kept pace. In 1898, Ochs dropped the purchase price of the *Times* from three cents to a penny—thereby making it accessible to a broader readership. Within three years, circulation had jumped to more than 100,000, securing the newspaper a solid place in American journalism.

Under the guidance of Ochs, the *Times* achieved international scope, circulation, and reputation but its coverage of dictators sometimes fell far short of journalistic excellence. Reporting from Moscow from 1922 to 1941, British-born Walter Duranty overlooked or rationalized some of Josef Stalin's worst atrocities. His denial of the widespread famine most notably in Soviet Ukraine was especially egregious.

Duranty not only denounced reports of starvation as an exaggeration or malignant propaganda but also attacked the credibility of a British journalist who had witnessed the starving firsthand. Many years later, there were calls to posthumously and symbolically strip him of the Pulitzer Prize he received in 1932 for a series of reports about the Soviet Union. In response to *Stalin's Apologist* (1990), a highly critical biography of Duranty, the *Times* acknowledged in a signed editorial that his articles denying the famine constituted "some of the worst reporting to appear in this newspaper."[67]

After Ochs died in 1935, his son-in-law, Arthur Hays Sulzberger succeeded him as the publisher. He shared his father-in-law's imperative that the newspaper be impartial to all social and ethnic groups, especially the Jews. The publishers reportedly worried that extensive coverage of issues facing Jewish communities in the United States and abroad would negatively affect the paper's reception, as the tide of American anti-Semitism rose dramatically during the Depression.

In this climate, the newspaper gave scant attention to the Nazi persecution of Jews, a charge to which it later conceded. The fear of having the Times branded a "Jewish newspaper" conveniently coincided with U.S. government policy during the height of the Third Reich that downplayed the plight of Jewish victims and refugees. Such matters seemly didn't fall under its "all the news that's fit to print" slogan, adopted by family patriarch Adolph Ochs soon after taking over the paper. If the *Times,* along with other influential news outlets had spotlighted Nazi atrocities against Jews, perhaps the nation might have awakened to the barbarity far sooner than it did.

Anonymous Sources

The lifeblood of journalism, sound information, often comes from sources who won't talk unless promised confidentiality—something journalists are ordinarily reluctant to do. Typically, at mainline news media outlets, a single unnamed source is rarely enough to go ahead with a story, there must be two sources with the same firsthand knowledge. And one of a handful of top editors must sign off on its use before publication.

The granting of source anonymity usually takes place under tightly controlled circumstances, with checking and corroboration, and most journalists work hard to get stories right. Reporters and editorial staff do make mistakes, of course, with the breakdown of the vetting process sometimes having dire consequences. The *New York Times* coverage leading up to the 2003 Iraq War highlights the risk of loosening the checks and balances. Seemingly hoodwinked, the ordinarily conscientious Pulitzer-prize winning veteran reporter Judith Miller wrote many front-page accounts of the existence of "weapons of mass destruction" in Iraq, all based on anonymous sources.

Miller's story about Iraq's possession of aluminum tubes designed for the manufacture of nuclear weapons offered as its sole attribution "unnamed administration sources." On the same morning the piece appeared, Vice-President Dick Cheney, on "Meet the Press," cited it to support his assertion Iraq was building weapons of mass destruction. Not only did the story turn out to be patently false but turned out to be planted by the vice-president's chief of staff, one of the journalist's principal unidentified sources.

Allowing an anonymous high-placed source to run amok, Miller woefully failed in the pursuit of truth. She did again with another of her unidentified primary sources, Ahmad Chalabi, a convicted embezzler on the payroll of the State Department and the Department of Defense. An outspoken lobbyist for the war with Iraq over ten years before the invasion, the American government eventually accused him of being an agent of the Iranians.

Such flawed journalism continued in the weeks after the war began in earnest. Such incautious reporting and editing were hardly a trivial matter. The death and destruction and overall human cost of this war were devastating. Putting the brakes on journalistic leaps of faith, the *Times* minimized the use of unidentified sources, and justified within stories its decisions to do so.

Overlooked

The newspaper of record fell short in other ways as well. Since the inception of the *New York Times* in 1851, white men have dominated the obituaries. The women "overlooked" included such acclaimed figures as the poet Sylvia Plath, the writer Charlotte Brontë, and the photographer Diane Arbus. It also ignored the deaths of accomplished women of color.

Among those whose passing went unnoticed was former slave Ida B. Wells, whose investigative reports focused on lynching and structural racism. And the Harlem Renaissance literary star Nella Larsen didn't get recognition on the paper's obituary

page either. Her novels concern black middle-class families and the debilitating pressures of race.

Whether neglectful or purposeful, a judgment call of an editor who didn't deem such deaths newsworthy is impossible to say with any certainty. Beginning in late 2017, the *Times* obituary staff sought to rectify this situation.[68] Diverging from the traditional obituary style, writers have become creative in their accounts, generally not even mentioning the deaths until toward the end of the belated obituaries.

As part of a month-long tribute to "important L.G.B.T.Q. figures," at the end of May 2019, the *Times* ran a belated obituary of the sculptor Emma Stebbins.[69] She designed the bronze eight-foot-tall Angel of the Waters statue atop the Bethesda Fountain surrounded by four cherubs representing "health," "purity," "peace," and "temperance," Unveiled in Central Park in 1873, it celebrated the flow of fresh water into the city. Recipient of the first public art commission ever awarded to a woman in Manhattan, Stebbins drew her inspiration from the story in the Gospel of John about an angel giving curative powers to the waters of Bethesda in Jerusalem.

When she got the commission, the belated obituary notes, Stebbins resided in Rome with her lover Charlotte Cushman, a leading performer of Shakespeare's play on the British and American stages known for playing both male and female roles. The group of artists and writers forming a circle around Cushman was among the first generation of women to forge careers in the arts and develop same-sex relationships. Stebbins and Cushman eventually exchanged private marriage vows. After dying in 1876, the grand star did merit a *Times* obituary, without any mention of her partner. Describing Cushman as "the virgin queen of the dramatic stage," it noted, "She was ugly beyond average ugliness."[70]

Changing Times

Under Sulzberger's leadership, and that of his son-in-law (and successor), Orvil Dryfoos, the newspaper extended its breadth and reach with crossword puzzles, a fashion section, and an international edition. Ochs's grandson, Arthur Ochs "Punch" Sulzberger, took command after Dryfoos died in 1963, leading the *Times* for almost thirty years. In the mid-1970s, he introduced sweeping changes in the organization of the newspaper and its staff and brought out a national edition transmitted by satellite to regional printing plants. He also added individual weekly sections on various topics supplementing the regular news, editorials, sports, and features.

Still with a Sulzberger at the helm, owing mainly to its well-respected journalists, columnists, and editorial personnel, the reliable news reports continue to be supplemented by informed and insightful opinion pieces. The paper has not flinched from coverage of the administration of President Donald Trump, despite his Twitter taunts and threats. And its columnists and commentators have hardly been timid about documenting the occupant of the Oval Office's moral laxity, ineptitude, narcissism, deception, lack of empathy, obstruction of justice, the ongoing embrace of dictators, and inflammatory rhetoric.

The separation of news from opinion has long been an ingrained part of the *Times* culture. Yet, some see the paper's preoccupation with the president and his Republican enablers as causing it to lose all pretense of impartiality. Conservative columnist Michal Goodwin, an early advocate of a Trump presidency, contends that a succession of managing editors relaxed the rules resulting in coverage reflecting the leftist bias of reporters.[71] He singles out Dean Baquet, the *Times*' executive editor since 2014, as the principal culprit in undercutting the paper's credibility.

The defining moment of decline, Goodwin contends, came in August of 2016. At that time, its media correspondent implied that Donald J. Trump is a demagogue playing to the nation's worst racist and nationalistic tendencies. That he cozies up to anti-American dictators and that he would be dangerous with control of the United States nuclear codes. As a working journalist, if you believe these things, he asserts, "you have to throw out the textbook American journalism has been using for the better part of the past half-century, if not longer."[72]

Instead of restricting the correspondent to writing about sports or food or fashion, anything but politics, Goodwin notes, Baquet's reaction was precisely the opposite. That column, the current managing editor said, "nailed" his thinking, that Trump had "challenged our language," declaring the quest for fairness over, saying: "I think that Trump has ended that struggle," adding: "We now say stuff. We fact-check him. We write it more powerfully that it's false."

All of a sudden, claims Goodwin, himself a former *Times* reporter, the newspaper abandoned "standards of fairness and impartiality that Adolph Ochs established and that every publisher and editor since had tried to uphold." Ironically, now a *New York Post* columnist and Fox News commentator, two of the most biased news outlets in the nation, Goodwin is seemingly advocating that the *Times* report the president's lies, distortions, and fabrications without correction or qualification. Nothing in the "canons of journalism" requires reporters to serve as stenographers and treat deceptions as straight news. The blatant disregard his current employer demonstrates for the norms of truth and civility are hardly a model for journalism worthy of emulation.

Still Standing

The *New York Post*, founded by Alexander Hamilton in 1801, as the *Evening Post*, exemplifies some of American journalism's best moments and, more recently, its worst. William Cullen Bryant joined the newspaper as a reporter in 1826. In addition to his growing distinction as a poet, Bryant was also by then an experienced writer of prose, having published more than fifty critical essays.

The poet, lawyer, and journalist became the chief editor and principal owner two years later. In his editorials, he not only supported the right of workers to strike but also defended religious minorities and immigrants and promoted the abolition of slavery.[73] With his ironic wit and clear-headed arguments, he cut to the heart of the issue at hand. Over the next half-century, under his direction, the *New York Post* would become one of the most respected newspapers in the city.

After changing hands several times, the paper became part of Rupert Murdoch's media empire, which includes Fox News. He imported the sensationalist journalism style of many Australian and British newspapers typified by such *Post* headlines as "Headless Body in Topless Bar." More recent covers include the salaciously suggestive "Bezos Exposes Pecker." This headline story refers to Amazon's Jeff Bezos's allegations that *National Enquirer* boss David Pecker tried to blackmail him with nude photos of his married lover. A gossip-hungry tabloid, the *Post* these days stands as substantial testimony that the history of journalism is hardly a straight line drawn inexorably toward progress.

Chapter 3

Shifting Standards

Journalists have to navigate a force field of pressures from a range of political and economic interests: government, business, politicians, corporate owners, advertisers, public relations practitioners, and protest organizers. And they must do so in a way that makes the news appear to be credibly providing a public service. On any given day, around the globe, all sorts of things occur—armed conflicts, riots, frauds, deceptions, murders, romances, weddings, domestic violence, political speeches, protests, suffering, hardship, and so on.

In many respects, these matters don't exist beyond those experiencing them directly unless they get reported. Few of us would know about such things as starvation, bombing raids, defense spending, deception, or skullduggery if the news media ignore or are unaware of them. The role, power, and importance of the news media in a democracy are generally not in dispute. An underlying premise is that reliable information is the vital axis linking the government and governed.

In trying to maintain trustworthiness, the mainstream news media espoused the standard of impartial reporting, often labeled objectivity, soon after the turn of the twentieth century. This standard called for the news media to develop a consistent method of evaluating information—a transparent approach to evidence—so that outside pressures as well as personal and cultural biases would not undermine the accuracy of their work.

This norm served not only as a guide for gathering, editing, and reporting news but also as a marketing device to deflect criticism, and appeal to a wider audience as a way to increase revenue. The standard criteria for impartial or objective reporting include separating fact from opinion and maintaining an emotionally detached neutral vantage point with fairness and balance. In other words, the method, not the journalist, is objective.

The stylistic standards of impartiality include maintaining a third-person point of view (No use of "I"), sparse use of adjectives (so as not to convey one's feelings about a subject), and an inverted-pyramid story structure—a way of front-loading answers to what-who-where-when-how elements of an event. Its tenets are starting with a conclusion and then building on how it came about—the details, arguments, and opinions—throughout the rest of the story. But the what, where, when, who and how story structure hides a whole constraining framework of choices and interpretations. Only a tiny fraction of events each day gets reported. Who counts as newsworthy? "What" occurrences and "where" merit attention? Whose responses and reactions to what happened to deserve inclusion? Such decisions are subjective.

The facts of any event are elusive. As media analyst Michael Schudson explains what gets reported, "are not aspects of the world, but consensually validated statements about it."[74] Reporters rarely witness something deemed newsworthy directly. Even when they do, editors typically require they turn to reliable witnesses or authoritative sources rather than their observations for verification.

These are fundamental principles of journalism, an often-helpful approach news organizations use to highlight that they are trying to produce something obtained by objective methods. This kind of reporting makes the presentation, not the coverage itself, ostensibly impartial. But reporters and editors invariably must select what events to cover, how to cover them, the kinds of questions asked, the slant of the sources consulted, and the words and terminology employed. All of which are shaped by often-unexamined values, beliefs, and assumptions.[75]

The recognition of such predispositions prompted many in the news media to develop a consistent method of testing information—a discipline of verification. The admonition to verify and validate factual statements about events in line with professional benchmarks before publishing hardly approaches the standard rules of evidence, as in the law, or an agreed-upon method of observation, as in the conduct of scientific experiments. Among other things, the ability of journalists to confirm "the facts" or verify the evidence in any situation has notable limits because they can't subpoena sources and put them in jail if they lie or possibly check the validity of every assertion.

What's in a Letter?

The stylebook of the Associated Press, which gathers news reports and sells them to subscribing news firms, has long been the standard bearer of journalistic writing style. One of the primary factors propelling changes in this catechism is cultural pressure. By mid-2020, across the country, a chorus of voices rising to a crescendo has proclaimed that Black (not black) lives matter to them. Heeding the call to capitalize Black as recognition of respect and justice, this press association, and other major media outlets, have stopped using the lowercase letter in referring to those of sub-Saharan African ancestry. To many, the capitalization signifies the difference between a color and a shared culture.

Despite its imprecision in referring to an entire continent, the African-American classification remains an acceptable usage. At this point, the stylebooks of the major news media outlets don't call for capitalizing "white" or "brown" as cultural designations. The adjective brown describes a wide range of cultures, and hate groups have appropriated the word white in uppercase to signify supremacy. Anointing one category of people with an uppercase creates a potentially prejudicial

imbalance. An incident involving a woman facing a charge of filing a false police report after she claimed a birdwatcher threatened her in Central Park during a dispute over her dog provides a case in point. In an update, the *New York Times* reported that the Manhattan district attorney's decision "to charge a white woman with filing a false police report against a Black man in Central Park..." does not have his support.[76] Imagine the reverse situation of a Black man who filed a false report against a white woman. The uppercase use appears to be emphasizing his racial category to his detriment.

BALANCED NEWS

By most accounts, such letter lopsidedness aside, the overwhelming majority of journalists at significant mainstream outlets—national magazines, newspapers, public radio programs—do their best to provide coverage that is fair, accurate, and balanced. But too often in the attempt to be impartial, at least within the sphere of legitimate controversy, reporters and editors, wading in the mainstream, give equal weight to all views on controversial issues of public importance even when one side of an argument is mostly accurate. In trying to distinguish between balance, impartiality, neutrality, and, crucially, the best attainable version of the truth, many media outlets tie themselves into knots resulting in often misleading coverage.

In the 2016 presidential race, for example, the major media news outlets gave extensive coverage to the improprieties of sexual misconduct and unethical behavior pervading Republican Donald Trump's campaign. Many "balanced" their adverse reports on him by providing comprehensive coverage of his Democrat opponent Hillary Clinton's use of a private email account while serving as Secretary of State (something her predecessor Colin Powell admitted to doing as well).

Reports on President Trump's alleged impeachable offenses appeared in the news daily. The Murdock-owned business-oriented *Wall Street Journal* broke the story of a government whistleblower's allegations. The intelligence official alleged the president pressured the head of Ukraine to investigate Joe Biden falsely claiming that as vice president, he stopped Ukrainian prosecutors from pursuing a case involving his son.

To deflect attention, President Trump spun a fake scenario about House Intelligence Committee Chair Rep. Adam Schiff, who spearheaded the investigation, plotting "a scam" with the whistleblower to bring down his presidency. The actual events debunk Trump's claims. Neither Schiff nor the whistleblower did anything wrong. Nonetheless, the president's skewed spin got broad coverage. His tagging the Democratic representative with the sobriquet "Shifty Schiff" also captured a lot of media attention. (After House Democrats impeached the president, a Republican majority in the Senate, calling no witnesses, acquitted him.)

The environmental debate provides a case for why the practice of giving balanced coverage to demonstrably invalid positions for the sake of supposed balance fails both journalism and the general public. The overwhelming empirical scientific evidence that humans are causing global warming is often given equal play with the tiny minority of skeptics or deniers. Merely presenting polling data or the dubious claims of pundits for the sake of balance can skew the debate in ways that work against understanding this complex issue. Juxtaposing skeptic and scientist on the same television screen gives them equal weight as well

The seemingly greater emphasis in news coverage on "climate change" rather than "global warming" further clouds comprehension. The two terms describe different aspects of the environmental problem. As focus-group research suggests, the more abstract "climate change" doesn't sound as dire or scary as global warming, although hard evidence about how often, by whom, and in what context these terms appear in the news is in scant supply. Whatever label is applied, giving credence to profit-driven denials and equivocations, if the vast majority of scientists are right in their dire predictions, contributes to an existential threat to civilization.

When used, the term global warming is often misinterpreted to mean no more cold weather and no more snow. To the contrary, global warming can increase snowfall, because warmer air can hold more moisture. Although the average temperatures are rising, it still gets cold in winter, so we always get snow. Whatever the weather of the moment, the threats from heat waves, floods, and extreme storms resulting in the loss of human life are mounting as attempts to curb carbon omissions face fierce opposition.

It is little wonder confusion reigns supreme, especially given that the world's five largest publicly-owned oil and gas companies spend an estimated $200 million a year on lobbying to control, delay or block binding climate legislation. They standardly use spin to cloud the near-total scientific consensus that the climate crisis is critical and that without drastically curtailing carbon emissions, it will trigger repercussions across the planet for thousands of years.

Format Imbalances

The format itself of primary presidential debates fosters false equivalencies by putting the ill-informed on the same platform as the learned in ways that may favor the emotional assertions of the former. At the September 2015 CNN-sponsored debate among Republican presidential primary candidates, the exchange between medical doctor Ben Carson and real estate mogul and reality TV star Donald Trump highlights how emotion can eclipse reason even when involving a logically lopsided matter in ways that have troubling implications for impartial journalism.

"Dr. Carson, Donald Trump has publicly and repeatedly linked vaccines, childhood vaccines, to autism, which, as you know, the medical community adamantly disputes," the moderator said, pitching him a slow ball down the middle. "You're a pediatric neurosurgeon," highlighting his credentials. "Should Mr. Trump stop saying this?" Bunting rather than hitting a homerun, Carson began hesitantly. "Well, let me put it this way," he replied. "There have been numerous studies, and they have not demonstrated that there is any correlation between vaccinations and autism."

After Carson further fudged his response, the equivocations sowing seeds of doubt, Trump responded. "Autism has become an epidemic.... It's gotten totally out of control," he claimed. A "beautiful child, went to have the vaccine... a week later got a tremendous fever, got very, very sick, now is autistic." He also maintained that the

vaccinations babies and children get were similar to those "pumped" into "a horse." Although Trump's anecdotal argument boiled down to a single instance and intuition, even a prominent neuroscientist, Tali Sharot, watching the exchange reacted viscerally and illogically to the businessman's baseless assertions. Images of a nurse inserting a horse-size syringe into her tiny baby would not fade from her mind. "Trump tapped into my very human need for control and my fear of losing it," Sharot explains, having written extensively about emotion, influence, and decision-making. "He gave me an example of someone else's mistake and induced emotion, which helped align the pattern of activity in my brain with his, making it more likely to take his point of view." Additionally, amplifying her irrational reaction, "he warned of the dire consequences of not following his advice."

The neuroscientist's instinctive reaction highlights the perils of providing significant media platforms that pit the unsound and ill-informed against unadorned reasoned discourse. Citing several studies, she notes that unvarnished facts, hard data, statistics, and the like, won't prevail if the news media don't also address people's needs, desires, emotions, and motivations. Every instant of every day, all kinds of images and symbols assault our senses, transmitting 11 million bits of information to our brains.

This three-pound organ in our skulls has a remarkable capacity to ignore, but we are always paying attention to something.

As did Aristotle in his ancient treatise *Rhetoric*, Sharot cautioned that combining solid logical reasoning with proper emotional appeals is essential to getting and holding attention. The "tsunami of information" inundating us "can make us even less sensitive to data because we've become accustomed to finding support for absolutely anything we want to believe."[77] As the long-ago philosopher stressed, pathos is as essential as logos and ethos in the rhetorical toolbox.

Unanchored Images

With inventions of the camera and celluloid roll film in the nineteenth century, nascent news photographers developed an affecting pictorial means of documenting events. But while the photographic image offers a visual awareness of the world outside direct experience, it is abstracted and unanchored. Unlike words and sentences, camera images don't provide us with an idea or concept like "the ocean," only a particular fragment of the here-and-now, a wave at a specific moment.

A photograph presents the world as an object, while in a language, it is presented as an idea, explains media critic Neil Postman. "There is no such thing in nature as 'man' or 'tree.' The universe offers no such categories or simplifications; only flux and infinite variety."[78] The photograph's distance from everyday reality can be seen from its distortions of time and space; its two-dimensionality; its selection and omission of objects through the framing of the camera's lens. Photos only get meaning with context; it is through language that they become understandable.

The importance of context for making sense of events has clear implications for the practice of photojournalism, which entails collecting, editing, and presenting visual news material for publication or broadcast to augment a news story. What to shoot, how to frame it, how to edit it, and how to present it are constant considerations.

War photography has always been a genre that relies on staged events. It was rare when a photograph could capture something spontaneous. Subjects were carefully composed and staged to capture better images in a complicated creative process involving lighting, lenses, film stock, camera placement, and other such factors.

Mathew Brady was one of the most celebrated nineteenth-century American photographers. He was best known for his portraiture and documentation of the American Civil War. In deciding what to shoot, he and his talented team of wartime photographers rearranged bodies of dead soldiers to create a clearer picture of the atrocities associated with battle. For example, on the battlefield at Gettysburg, Pennsylvania, his team shifted around the bodies of dead Union soldiers for dramatic effect. Shot by Timothy H. O'Sullivan in July 1863, the stage-crafted photo won wide acclaim for its authenticity under the title "Harvest of Death." By 1864, *Harper's Weekly* reproduced his team's photos promoting the notion photographs could serve as published documents preserving history.

The *New York Daily News* was one of the first newspapers in the United States to regularly feature photos. The tabloid-sized paper had a cover rather than a front page and contained condensed news in a simplified, easily absorbed format with big images, huge headlines, and sensationalistic stories. The cover photo was selected to arrest the attention of potential readers. For much of its history, the newspaper spoke to and for the city's working class. It offered a titillating mix of crime stories and hard-hitting coverage of public issues. The eye-catching covers attracted commuters, and the tabloid format made the paper more comfortable to handle while standing or sitting in a crowded bus or train car.

DAILY NEWS EXTRA EDITION

NEW YORK'S PICTURE NEWSPAPER

DEAD!

One of its most startling cover photos appeared in the January 13, 1928 issue. It featured convicted murderer Ruth Snyder strapped in the electric chair at Sing Sing Correctional Facility in Ossining, New York. The Queens New York City housewife's path to electric current surging through her body began when she took up with a married corset salesman. After persuading her husband to get life insurance, forged, so it paid extra for death caused by an unexpected act of violence, she enlisted the hapless salesman to murder him. A reporter for a related newspaper with a hidden ankle camera snapped the picture at the moment of execution. It ran the next day under the headline "Dead!" For decades after, those attending this fatal method of punishment had to lift their pant legs for camera checks. The case was the inspiration for the novella *Double Indemnity*, adapted for the screen in 1944 as a stylish film noir starring Barbara Stanwyck.

The heyday of photographic storytelling was roughly from the 1930s to the 1950s. During that period, *Life* was the leading photo-essay magazine in the United States. At the time of the magazine's launch in 1936, the United States was in the Great Depression. Adolf Hitler was firmly in power in Germany. In Spain, General Francisco Franco's rebel army was at the gates of Madrid. The German Luftwaffe pilots and bomber crews gave Franco air support. And Italy's Benito Mussolini annexed Ethiopia in the quest to become a global power.

Taken in late 1943, but not published until some ten months later, the disquieting image of three dead Americans partially-buried in the sand at Buna Beach in New Guinea, with military censor approval, for the first time appeared in *Life* during World War II without the bodies draped, in coffins, or otherwise covered up. The government permitted the magazine cover photo fearing American public complacency about the war in which an Allied victory was far from certain.

For the most part, the weekly magazine ignored ominous events. It filled its oversize 11 × 14-inch pages with frivolous but attractively reproduced images, using beautiful engraving screens, high-quality inks, and glossy paper. Most likely its best-known photograph is that of a nurse in a sailor's arms, taken on August 14, 1945, as they celebrated "Victory over Japan Day" in New York City. In the post-war years, it published some memorable images of events in the United States and the world. But, as the 1950s drew to a close, the magazine's halcyon days were over as television drew away viewers and advertising dollars.

Photojournalism continues to shape perceptions of reported events. A range of dramatic images emerged from the Vietnam War, many of which still resonate in the culture. Photojournalist Eddie Adams captured one of the most famous images of the war—a South Vietnamese general summarily executing a young man on a Saigon street. His snub-nosed pistol is already recoiling as the lad's face contorts from the force of a bullet entering his skull, the camera capturing the precise moment of death. The image was reprinted around the world and came to symbolize for many the brutality and anarchy of the war.

The unanchored photograph did not—nor could it—explain the circumstances on the streets of Saigon on the first of February 1968, two days after the forces of the People's Army of Vietnam and the Viet Cong launched the "Tet Offensive," a significant escalation and one of the most extensive military campaigns of the war. Heavy street fighting had pitched the capital of South Vietnam (Republic of Vietnam) into chaos when its military caught a suspected Viet Cong squad leader at the site of a mass grave of more than thirty civilians. Believing he murdered the wife and six children of one of his colleagues, the war-hardened general executed the benign-looking captive on the spot without hesitation.

Among the most horrific images emerging from the war in Vietnam, or any armed conflict, for that matter, is Associated Press photographer Nick Ut's 1972 shot of terrified children, including a screaming naked girl, fleeing their napalmed village. This captured fleeting moment in time becomes all the more heart wrenching with the added context that the American-backed South Vietnamese air force had mistakenly dropped the incendiary chemical mixture. It has become an icon of conflict photography. The news media rarely show the twisted faces and scorched bodies of warfare's victims. The military's tragic mistakes are typically described with such deodorizing euphemisms as "friendly fire" and "collateral damage."

New Journalism

The "new journalism" of the 1960s and 1970s surely affected impartial reporting. But how it did so beyond stylistic changes is difficult to discern. What this phrase, whose use has a long history, meant apart from the use of literary techniques depended on who employed it. The primary ingredients included a subjective perspective, a writing style reminiscent of long-form nonfiction, and intensive reportage in which journalists immersed themselves in the stories they wrote about.

This literary style of journalism first appeared in such magazines as *Esquire*, *New York*, and *Rolling Stone* in nonfiction pieces by such acclaimed writers as Tom Wolfe, Hunter S. Thompson, Joan Didion, and Norman Mailer. These writers believed alternative forms of journalism were required to deal with the deep fissures rending the social fabric. They more-or-less rejected standard rules of reporting and injected something to give it life. This injection entailed various ways of combining the vividness of fiction with straight news reporting.

Such news writing generated a great stir at the time. With the benefit of hindsight, several of these often-lengthy pieces appear more than a tad pretentious and self-aggrandizing. In the coverage of the 1960s "protest movement," several seemed incapable of distinguishing between police doing their jobs and behaving as "merciless oppressors." This general ideological fault line marked a sharp divide among those lumped together as "new journalism" practitioners.

The irrepressible Tom Wolfe was perhaps the first to comment critically on this cleavage. In a *New York* essay titled "Radical Chic: Dinner at Lenny's," he lambasted a

benefit for the Black Panthers, a revolutionary political organization, hosted by Leonard Bernstein and his wife, Felica, already known as prominent anti-war and civil rights activists.[79] The piece makes their fashionable leftism seem silly if not downright dangerous. Among the "cocktail-party revolutionaries" who gathered at the famed New York Philharmonic conductor's posh Park Avenue triplex were some of the wealthiest movers and shakers of the New York creative community along with several members of the Black Panther Party.

The soiree was intended to raise money for twenty-one Black Panther members charged with conspiring to kill police and concocting various bomb plots around New York. They had been held without trial for nine months, with bail set so high it was effectively impossible for them to pay, and without resources to prepare for their defense. After listening to the party's manifesto and solicitations for the prisoners, the well-heeled guests dug deep into their pockets to pay for legal fees and to support the families of the imprisoned.

By the mid-1970s, the writing was on the wall. Among the various factors contributing to the new journalism's impending demise were well- below-par imitation and unbridled self-indulgence. While good storytellers are in demand at any time, perhaps only the cultural upheaval of the late 1960s could have produced the poetic prose dazzle of the white-suited Tom Wolfe or the drug-addled Hunter S. Thompson. The legacy of new journalism, whatever its essence, is most evident these days in the slightly ironic, first person features that are a staple of many general-interest magazines.

Concentric Spheres

A useful analytical framework for assessing reportorial norms and practices is to divide the journalist's world into three concentric spheres—consensus, legitimate controversy, and deviance.[80] The area of consensus contains viewpoints on which there are widespread agreement and taken-for-granted shared values and assumptions. In the legitimate controversy sphere, journalists recognize that rational and informed people hold differing views. These matters are the most significant to cover, and also ones upon which journalists feel obliged to remain neutral and impartial, as much as possible, eschewing support for or against a particular position.

For much of the 1960s, coverage of the war in Vietnam fell within the consensus sphere. The three television networks were hardly critical of the war and gave minimal coverage to the nascent antiwar movement. In addition to deriding its dissenters, comedian Bob Hope served as a cheerleader for the war in his annual Vietnam Christmas specials aired on NBC every January. An hour-long 1967 CBS documentary on the American air war in Vietnam was rhapsodic about the aerial bombing with the narrator cavalierly commenting, "Civilians are always killed in war." In his critical review of the program, *New Yorker* TV critic Michael Arlen, regarded it as mostly propaganda followed by brief interviews with critics of the bombardment. One might conclude, he noted, that the network "is another branch of government, or of the military, or of both."[81]

While serving three tours as head of the CBS Saigon bureau between 1964 and 1966, Morley Safer gave revealing reports from the thick of the combat. In 1965, one incident captured on camera showed U.S. Marines setting fire to village huts in dirt-poor Cam Ne while the villagers, mostly women and children, scurried away. One striking sequence showed a Marine flicking a Zippo cigarette lighter to burn down the huts. After a heated debate among CBS officials, "The CBS Evening News" with Walter Cronkite aired two-minutes of the footage complete with crackling huts and terrified villagers. Few primetime viewers had ever seen U.S. troops act with such blatant indifference to human suffering.

By many accounts, President Lyndon B. Johnson was obsessed with how television covered the war. He monitored the newscasts on banks of three televisions in the Oval Office—one tuned to each major network. Upset by the short Safer segment, the next morning, he called CBS president Frank Stanton to berate the network complaining it had "shat on the American flag." The president demanded to know why CBS would use a story by Safer, a Canadian with "a suspicious background."

Realizing that effective policy abroad requiring significant sacrifices had to rest on a solid political consensus at home, the Defense Department made it clear to CBS that Safer was subsequently persona non grata. Such crises encouraged news outlets to censor themselves, withholding images and information that might deviate from consensus viewpoints and reflect badly on the war effort.

By the summer of 1965, CBS news president Fred Friendly had reached the conclusion shared by his network colleagues and others in the profession "that journalism was failing to explain the complexities of the Vietnam War."[82] Still, Safer's narrated footage of chilling indifference would echo across the media landscape. Torching a village or field came to be called a "Zippo mission," while scenes of setting villages on fire appeared in many Vietnam War movies.

The *New York Times* reporter David Halberstam, one of a group of journalists (including Neil Sheehan and Peter Arnett, among others) who earned the ire of the Kennedy and Johnson administrations for his reporting of what he viewed as the truth about Vietnam—that the United States was slowly and steadily getting entangled in a conflagration it couldn't win. The tone more about winning than withdrawing, his hawkish articles on the weakening military situation and the problems facing the

South Vietnamese government so rankled official Washington that, in October 1963, President John F. Kennedy asked the paper's publisher to transfer Halberstam out of Saigon, the capital of South Vietnam.

After leaving the *Times* in 1967, Halberstam wrote for *Harper's* magazine. He later authored several highly praised books, including the ironically titled *The Best and the Brightest*, an extensively researched indictment of American policy in Vietnam and American policymakers. The stewards of the Vietnam fiasco Halberstam profiles had impressive pedigrees. McGeorge Bundy, the national security adviser, was a legend in his time at Groton, the sharpest lad at Yale, and dean of Harvard College.[83]

Bundy's deputy, Walt Rostow, was a child prodigy, always the youngest to do something, whether at Yale, M.I.T., or as a Rhodes scholar. Robert McNamara, the defense secretary, was the youngest and highest paid Harvard Business School assistant professor of his era. He later made a mark as a World War II Army analyst, and, at age 44, became the first non-Ford to lead the Ford Motor Company. Their senseless, foolhardy exercise of power gone awry resulted in the needless loss of 58,220 Americans and countless Vietnamese.

Legitimate Controversy

American military involvement in Southeast Asia gradually moved from the consensus to the legitimate controversy sphere. The shift stemmed from the growing dissonance between official assurances and news stories about American military failures as reporters moved, unescorted, from unit to unit as the action dictated. The content of the reportage turned mainstream opinion against the war, not some news media epiphany or awakening to the immorality of the conflict. A consistent, single-minded, morally based editorial stance about the cruel and brutal behavior wrought by the conflagration appeared mainly in fringe publications.

With American casualties steadily mounting, and seemingly no end in sight, by 1968, the establishment itself—and the nation as a whole—was sharply divided over the war. Newspapers like the *New York Times* and the *Washington Post* along with the then three major broadcast television networks, took an increasingly skeptical if not critical stance toward the failure of President Lyndon Johnson's war policies in Vietnam. When CBS News avuncular anchor Walter Cronkite, an on-the-air war booster, declared the United States might have to accept a stalemate, coverage had undoubtedly shifted firmly into the sphere of legitimate controversy with a focus more on military mastery than human misery.

After Richard Nixon ascended to the presidency in 1968, the criticism that the news media had a distinctly liberal slant in the tone and selection of news coverage intensified. In a November 1969 speech in Des Moines, his vice president Spiro Agnew, in no uncertain words, strongly denounced the three major broadcast television networks as a tiny, hostile, "enclosed fraternity of privileged men elected by no one." Some two-thirds of the more than 150,000 letters, phone calls and telegrams received at the three television networks in response to the speech were pro-Agnew. While executives fretted about the public hostility, someone at NBC put the matter in perspective. All the adverse reactions, he noted, amounted to less than one-fourth of the outraged public responses to the network's cancellation of Star Trek.[84]

A week later, the vice president went to Montgomery, Alabama for his second condemnation of the news media, this time singling out the *New York Times* and the *Washington Post* for being biased in the selection and presentation of the news, and warning that there was "a trend toward monopolization of the great public information vehicles and the concentration of more and more power over public opinion in fewer and fewer hands" as newspapers began buying up radio and television stations, magazines and other publications (a cause of concern for many liberal journalists and scholars as well).

Adding to the cultural divisiveness, in early spring 1970, a massive nationwide student strike permeated the media landscape with walkouts from college classrooms in response to the United States expansion of the Vietnam War into Cambodia. The protests would climax with national guardsmen killing four students at Kent State University in Ohio. Photojournalist John Filo's image of an agonized looking young woman with one arm raised kneeling over the dead body of an unarmed student reverberated around the globe. The fatal shootings triggered immediate and massive outrage on campuses across the country. More than four million students participated in organized walkouts at hundreds of universities, colleges and high schools, the largest such strike in the history of the United States. The student strike further galvanized public opinion over the war raging in Vietnam.

Judging from the violent confrontations, widely covered by network news, a significant swath of the American public opposed the anti-war movement. In early May 1970, a few days after the Kent State killings, when college students and other peace protesters gathered on Wall Street and Broad Street to hold a vigil, some 200 angry construction workers flanked them. With the police doing little to interfere, they singled out longhaired "hippie" types, beating them with their "hard-hat" helmets and other equipment. This harrowing event signaled the changing class base of both the Republican and Democratic parties, notes a recent book on the incident.[85] The resulting polarizing of politics into hardened left and right, prevailing to the present day, helps explain the improbable presidency of Donald J. Trump—a scion with a stereotypical stevedore's speech patterns.

With its emphasis on the dramatic, the television news media implicitly took sides, mainly ignoring working-class grievances. Nothing excuses the brutal beatings and vicious attacks. Still, the blue-collar worker bore the brunt of such well-intended but ill-considered liberal efforts as preferential affirmative action and forced school busing outside designated districts, and were much more likely to be drafted than those in the privileged classes.

Middle and upper-class youth often got deferments or skipped service altogether with notes from doctors of phony "foot spurs" and the like. And most screen depictions were hardly ego-boosting for the working-class crowd. In movies like *Joe* (1970), the title character, a blue-collar bigot, seemed barely a step above a Neanderthal. During a hippie-commune confrontation, he unwittingly kills his daughter. On its heels appeared the satirical family sitcom *All in the Family*, with that television avatar of ethnic bigotry, foul-mouthed working-class Archie Bunker.

Garnering a great deal of attention on the evening television news, pro-war construction workers disrupted the Wall Street area every day for two weeks, often to cheers from sympathizers in the financial industry. The demonstrations culminated in a massive march through lower Manhattan backing the war and the Nixon administration's policies. An estimated 100,000 or more steamfitters, plumbers, ironworkers, and other laborers from nearby construction sites like the nascent twin towers waved American flags, engaged in fervent oratory, sang patriotic tunes, and displayed "anti-peacenik" placards. Many had served in past wars and military conflicts and viscerally despised what they perceived as a bunch of pampered, longhaired, flag desecrating, draft dodging malcontents.

Seizing the moment, among other measures, the Nixon Administration and its well-heeled cadre of corporate backers organized an "Honor America Day" on July 4, 1970, in the nation's capital. Organizers deliberately avoided any mention of the country's major issues, like Vietnam, racism, and drugs. A crowd-pleasing roster of A-list names and public figures, such as Red Skelton, Jack Benny, and Kate Smith attended the event. In service of diversity, the event included musical performances from young country star Glenn Campbell and singer Teresa Graves, a black performer who appeared on *Laugh-In*. The sight of staunch right-wingers like the Reverend Billy Graham, comedian Bob Hope, and saccharine bandleader Lawrence Welk on the platform signaled the event's partisan, pro-Nixon, pro-war slant.

As the crowd gathered near the Lincoln Memorial for the event's morning religious service, presided over by the forceful Graham, an evangelical with an immense following of the faithful, protesters behind them started a "smoke-in," lighting up joints that were red, white and blue and waving Viet Cong flags. "Before this is over," Bob Hope quipped, "I may need some of that stuff myself." Using a woven flag as a metaphor, Graham urged listeners to "check the stitches of poverty that bind some of our countrymen," while stressing a robust commitment to God and warning against drug use, decadence, and permissiveness. A few hundred dissidents, intent on disruption, some completely nude, waded waist-deep into the reflecting pool and launched into antiwar

chants during the service. Angry members of the National Socialist White Peoples Party, all looking very white, taunted and threatened them.

An estimated 350,000 attendees, mostly white and middle-aged, gathered near the Washington Monument for entertainment. Court jester Hope hosted the staged event. Real estate magnate, golf companion to presidents, the ultra-rich comedian was a cheerleader for the troops from World War II, through Vietnam, to the Gulf War. His humor helped conservative Americans process changing mores, from new roles for women in the workplace to the counterculture revolution of the 1960s.

A paid oil company promoter, opposing industry divestiture, among other such dubious activities, Hope was hopelessly out of touch not only with the concerns of the protesters but with the troops as well. During his 1969 Christmas tour in Vietnam, soldiers booed when he relayed Nixon's promise of a solid plan for ending the war. The stand-up comic became increasingly less relevant, although still headlined prime-time television specials into his dotage. By the time the once-beloved star died in 2003, two months after he had turned 100, his reputation had suffered severe damage from revelations of his sexism, philandering, and homophobia.[86]

Stage-managed political theater became a hallmark of Richard Nixon's successful presidential campaigns. The now-disgraced former Fox News head, the late Roger Ailes, who subsequently worked on the successful campaigns of Ronald Reagan, George H. W. Bush, and Donald J. Trump, orchestrated the president's 1968 victory, stressing style over substance. The wily media consultant targeted disgruntled blue-collar workers and southern white Democrats opposed to civil rights legislation and went to work through television, making the stiff Nixon more likable and accessible to voters.

Among the image-making techniques he employed were farcical Q&A forums, prearranged telecasts in various cities during which Nixon responded to carefully chosen questioners selected from supportive audiences who cheered the candidate's answers.[87] Journalists were not allowed to attend, but could only watch in a separate room, although the format mimicked a press conference. The shows were also usually broadcast on local stations only so Nixon could repeat his answers across states.

During the Washington demonstrations, news cameras captured rampaging youths smashing windows, slashing tires, dragging parked cars into intersections, even throwing bedsprings off overpasses into the traffic below. The ferocity of the outbursts, which got extensive media coverage, convinced many middle-class Americans that the nation was on the verge of revolution. As a result, due in part to the televised chaos, an odd coalition of angry blue-collar workers, disillusioned southern Democrats, ambitious evangelicals, captains of industry, and other self-styled paragons of law-and-order saw Nixon defeat progressive George McGovern in forty-nine of the fifty states.

A great deal of the suffering, death and destruction in Southeast Asia occurred during the Nixon Administration, which had secretly expanded its bombing campaign into Cambodia, causing devastating and long-lasting effects. Making this all the more tragic, as widely reported early in 2017, documents from an aide seemed to confirm long-time speculation that Richard Nixon had tried to dismantle a Vietnam peace initiative to help his 1968 presidential campaign.

Deviance Sphere

Within the outer sphere of deviance, the news media tend to reject topics and claims. They see them as unworthy of fair consideration either because they're unfounded, taboo, or of such minor consequence that they don't merit coverage. As a result, those who make such claims are typically treated as marginal, laughable, or dangerous individuals and groups whose positions on issues fall far outside a range of variation deemed to be legitimate.

Labeling the Al Qaeda agents who, on September 11, 2001, crashed jetliners into the twin towers of the World Trade Center and the Pentagon as cowards and terrorists falls clearly into the consensus sphere. Comedian and commentator Bill Maher, late-night ABC-TV host of the show *Politically Incorrect* at the time, deviated from the norm treating the 9/11 attacks as legitimate controversy.

A panelist said that he didn't think the terrorists were "cowards," as President George Bush had described them. Maher replied: "We have been the cowards – lobbing cruise missiles from two thousand miles away. That's cowardly. Staying in the airplane when it hits the building. Say what you want about it. Not cowardly. You're right." The comment sparked a huge controversy, and soon, advertisers began to pull out. ABC eventually canceled the popular show. (Within a year, *Real Time with Bill Maher* debuted on subscriber-supported Home Box Office where his sharp satire attracts several million viewers weekly.)

Coming into Sharper Relief

The recent media coverage of the Confederate statuary controversy highlights how the designation of concentric spheres can shift over time. During the past several years, rallies and protests over statues, murals, and monuments, many now see symbolizing a painful legacy of colonial expansion and racial discrimination, have thrust these enduring tributes into the national spotlight. Long ignored by news outlets, and textbook authors, these once taken-for-granted media of expression raise perplexing questions of meaning and interpretation.

General Lee/Jim Crow Conflict

The biggest brouhaha concerned a bronze statue in the once-sleepy college town of Charlottesville, Virginia. The Confederacy's top general, General Robert E. Lee, is astride a horse, both green from oxidation, a memorial to the glorious past for some, a standard-bearer for a white supremacist future for others. Advertised as "free speech" rally, hundreds of white nationalists, joined by figures like former Ku Klux Klan leader David Duke, demonstrated in support of the statue, slated for removal. Media outlets put most of the protesters further into the sphere of deviance when counter-demonstrators ignited a clash that culminated with several injuries and the death of a young woman. The statue had been erected in 1924, almost sixty years after the Civil War ended. Some residents and city officials, along with civil rights groups, saw it as a symbol of the "Jim Crow era" designed to intimidate blacks.

The name Jim Crow, from an antebellum minstrel routine, came to be a derogatory epithet for blacks. In the late 19th and early 20th centuries, white Democratic-dominated state legislatures enacted Jim Crow laws that enforced racial segregation in the Southern United States in public schools, public pools, phone booths, public transportation, restrooms, restaurants, drinking fountains, hospitals, asylums, jails, and even residential homes for the elderly and handicapped. Erecting statues of confederate leaders, along with naming streets, hospitals, and military bases after them struck many as part and parcel of an intimidation campaign to keep black people living in fear.

The contemporary news media treated those who ignored or were ignorant of this history with scorn and derision. President Trump, for instance, at an impromptu August 2017 news conference, attributed the violence in Charlottesville over the removal of the Lee statue to protesters and counter-protesters alike asking: "What about the 'alt-left' that came charging at, as you say, the 'alt-right,' do they have any semblance of guilt? What about the fact they came charging with clubs in hands, swinging clubs, do they have any problem? I think they do." He added: "You had a group on one side that was bad and you had a group on the other side that was also very violent. Nobody wants to say it, but I will say it right now."

The former vice president, Joe Biden, then a leading 2020 Democratic presidential candidate, slammed Trump over his remarks. His response contradicted his vote in 1975 to restore citizenship to Lee. Voting along with him were a who's who of staunch segregationists. For the most part, reporters working in the traditional news media dismissed Trump's off-the-cuff equation out of hand as uninformed at best and undeserving of follow-up or full investigation. This dismissal gained credence when not only Democrats but also several Republicans were quick to pan his remarks. Reports of Biden's hypocrisy or changed viewpoint got lost in the rapidly changing news cycle's swirling mists.

The majority of the 700 or so Confederate statues sprinkled around the country appeared decades after the Civil War ended. The most significant spike occurred between 1900 and 1920 and another peak in the 1960s as the civil rights movement gained steam. A carving on Stone Mountain in Georgia, the birthplace of the modern KKK, is the largest Confederate memorial in the United States, with officials at the 1972 unveiling calling it the eighth wonder of the world. The 158-foot-tall monument depicts General Robert E Lee, Lt. General Thomas "Stonewall" Jackson, and Confederate President Jefferson Davis astride their horses Blackjack, Traveler, and Little Sorrel.

The dedication ceremony featured then vice-president of the United States, Spiro T. Agnew. His purpose in appearing, he told the assembled group, was to recall those principals of loyalty, dignity, and honor that shine through the men commemorated in the bas-relief sculpture. Most media coverage of the unveiling ceremony neglected to mention the property's owner and the original sculptor were Klansmen. A popular tourist attraction, the stone carving can be viewed from the observation deck, on the memorial grounds, at the reflecting pool, or while ascending the mountain in a cable car. The imposing sculpture has long been a lightning rod for controversy. In mid-2020, a local NAACP branch organized a widely reported protest at the site to demand its removal.

Altogether the United States has over 1500 Confederate memorials, mostly in the South, but some are also in the North. Some ten military bases contain the names of Confederate officers as well. Like any form of expression, statues generate multiple meanings, depending on the beliefs and backgrounds of observers. Many people want these Confederacy tributes to remain in place—embracing a "lost cause" credo that the war was a struggle to defend a state's right to secede from the union and save the gentile Southern way of life. Its proponents give short shrift to such facts as the states seceding from the union included some four million enslaved people.

Although the Confederate constitution enshrines the right to own slaves, organizations like Sons of Confederate Veterans, headquartered in Columbia, Tennessee, see its mission to celebrate and preserve southern heritage. Among other things, they maintain gravestones, erect monuments, and promote the study of Civil War history. Notable members of the nonprofit endeavor have included Pat Buchanan, politician and commentator, Clint Eastwood, actor and movie director, and Harry S. Truman, thirty-third President of the United States.

At various times during the year, such as Robert E. Lee's birthday and Confederate History Month, the Sons of Confederate Veterans gather along Monument Avenue in Richmond, Virginia, the capital of the old Confederacy, donning period military regalia and uniforms. The statues along this posh avenue include the usual suspects, Jefferson Davis and Virginian Confederate veterans of the Civil War like Robert E.

Lee, J.E.B. Stuart, Thomas "Stonewall" Jackson, and Matthew Fontaine Maury.

Reflecting a growing awareness that protecting slavery was central to the war, early in 2017, a city commission voted to remove Davis's towering statue, toppled later by protesters, and put signage around the other figures. The purpose of the signage is to explain the biographies of the men and their changing meaning more fully. Some three years later, amid renewed protests, state and city officials decided to remove them altogether.

Amid the outcry for racial justice across the country, in late June 2020, Mississippi's governor signed a bill into law to stop flying the state's flag. First adopted in 1894, it incorporates a Confederate battle emblem—a red background, with a blue X lined with thirteen white stars. Many of the state's residents, especially its sizeable black population, see it as a symbol of white supremacy, much like Confederate monuments that have come down elsewhere around the South.

Perhaps as many as 700,000 lives were lost in the Civil War, and countless numbers maimed. The rest of the Western world somehow managed to end slavery without the brutality and bloodshed by both northern and southern combatants. For the most part, the shifting currents from consensus to controversy to deviance in mainstream news coverage of the supporters of Civil War memorials set in motion by the white supremacist rally in Charlottesville has not morphed into a debate or discussion about tributes to Union generals.

Widening Arc

The initial focus on Confederate symbols has now moved on to a wider arc of figures, with public displays celebrating everyone from Christopher Columbus to George Washington to Theodore Roosevelt under critical scrutiny and physical attack. Presiding over the entrance to the American Museum of Natural History in New York since 1940, the composition of the bronze equestrian statue of Roosevelt flanked by African and Native American figures signifies for many a painful legacy of colonial expansion and subjugation. In the fall of 2017, a collective called Monument Removal Brigade spattered red paint on the huge base of ten-foot-high sculpture. Amid widely reported growing public controversy, in June 2020, the museum's administration announced that it requested city officials remove the statue.

Some historical tributes have been damaged or destroyed; others forklifted into storage; still others left in place to await an uncertain fate. In June 2019, after half a century of sporadic debate and protest, the San Francisco Board of Education voted unanimously to whitewash the thirteen murals depicting the life of George Washington that line the halls of a high school named for the first president because they include scenes of slaves at work in the fields and barns of his estate, and a dead Native American that appears in three of the murals.[88] Some minority students at the high school along with their parents complained that the images are degrading. The work of a radical Russian émigré, the stunning murals imply that Washington not only owned slaves but also supported western expansion into lands occupied by Native Americans. The artist painted them in the mid-1930s under the Works Progress Administration's auspices, which created jobs for the unemployed suffering through the Great Depression.

Like any work of art, these murals hardly tell the whole story. The enormous wealth and privilege of George and Martha Washington come from over 500 slaves, but the country's first president did change his views on slavery. Despite having been an active slaveholder for fifty-six years, becoming one at age eleven, he struggled with slavery. He frequently spoke of his desire to end the practice. When he and wife would no longer benefit, near the end of his life he decided to free his slaves, the only "founding father" to do so. In his 1799 will, drawn up three months before his death, he left directions for the eventual emancipation of his slaves after the passing of his wife.

Columbus Controversy

The assault on statues as powerful and hurtful symbols of systemic racism challenged what the mainstream news media long regarded as taken-for-granted shared values and assumptions. Among a number of racially charged tributes, one of the most contested is Christopher Columbus. The federal holiday honoring this intrepid explorer and navigator came about because President Benjamin Harrison proclaimed it as a one-time national celebration in 1892 in the wake of a bloody New Orleans lynching that took the lives of eleven Italian immigrants.[89]

Darker-skinned southern Italians, particularly Sicilians, suffered much of the same egregious discrimination as former slaves. They were, at times, shut out of schools, movie houses, and labor unions, consigned to church pews set aside for black people, and derided in the streets with nasty ethnic epithets. In 1937, at the behest of the Knights of Columbus, a Roman Catholic fraternal service organization, President Franklin D. Roosevelt proclaimed Columbus Day an official U.S. holiday.

Rallying around their ethnic ancestor's holiday and celebratory statuary in places like Columbus Circle in Manhattan, presumably allowed Italian-Americans to paint a flattering portrait of themselves into the public record. As virtually every schoolchild learns, Columbus and his courageous crew sailed the ocean blue in 1492 on the Nina, Pinta, and Santa Maria, a benign image the news media consistently reinforced over the decades. But in recent years, in light of scholarly revelations about the Genoa-born voyager, the coverage of him has shifted from consensus sphere into that of legitimate controversy.

This pivotal, influential explorer, who historians use to divide the past into epochs, classifying the Americas before he arrived as "pre-Columbian," turns out to have been a nasty piece of work. Much of the teaching and reporting about Columbus is the stuff of myth and legend. Invariably left out of the coverage is his initiation of the trans-Atlantic slave trade, sending several dozen Taíno people as slaves from the Caribbean to Spain and later many hundreds more, including children.

The historical details of Columbus's voyages to the Americas near the turn of the fifteenth and sixteenth centuries churn the stomach. He and his crew plundered the island of Hispaniola (now the site of Haiti and the Dominican Republic.). They demanded food, gold, spun cotton, as well as sex from the native women. In addition to putting the indigenous population to work as slaves in his gold mines, Columbus also seized and sold women and girls, some as young as nine, as sex slaves.

To ensure the cooperation of the natives, he and his crew meted out severe punishment for even minor infractions. Leaving no doubt of their capacity for cruelty, the occupiers cut off the ears or nose of natives, sending them back to their villages for all to see the disfigurement. When the natives finally rebelled, they were mowed down, set upon by dogs, and skewered on pike and sword.[90] In recent years, several states and municipalities have scrapped the Columbus Day holiday. Instead, they celebrate "Indigenous People's Day" or "Native American Day."

Getting scant coverage in schoolbooks let alone by news media outlets until the last few decades, ripping off the blinders hiding the explorer's unsavory history of oppressing and enslaving indigenous people prompted assaults on monuments to him in various parts of the country. Early in June 2020, for example, protesters using ropes toppled a statue of him in Richmond, Virginia's Byrd Park, setting it ablaze and then throwing it into a nearby lake.

A Columbus statue in Boston's North End, erected in 1979, is a frequent vandalism target. In 2006, persons unknown beheaded it, and in 2015 doused it in fake blood and spray-painted the words "Black Lives Matter" on the back of its pedestal. Someone knocked the head off again in June 2020 amid nationwide demonstrations for racial justice. In August 2017, unidentified persons adorned the bronze sculpture of Christopher Columbus in New York's Central Park with red paint and added graffiti about not tolerating hate. Since the advent of nationwide protests in mid-2020, patrol cars have been keeping vigil around the clock.

PROFESSIONAL JOURNALISTS

The emergence of impartiality, at least in the legitimate debate sphere, as a widely adopted standard occurred in tandem with recognition of journalism as a profession. The National Press Club, formed in 1908, fosters ethical standards for the gathering and reporting news. The following year witnessed the appearance of the first chapter of what became the Society of Professional Journalists. And in 1922, newspaper editors started the American Society of Editors, the first nationwide professional journalism association.

Throughout the nineteenth century, journalists entered the field as apprentices, starting most often as copy boys and cub reporters. The first time that journalism got recognition as an area of academic study was in 1908 when the University of Missouri initiated a four-year course of study. New York's Columbia University followed suit four years later, offering the study of journalism as a graduate program, endowed by newspaper publisher Joseph Pulitzer. Its awards bearing his name are among the most prestigious in the country.

Journalism is now a standard course of study in colleges and universities across the United States with the aim of fostering news media to function as the "fourth estate," a sobriquet suggesting the press's supposed watchdog role over the legislative, executive, and judicial branches of government. To keep up with the demand of aspiring reporters and their professors, textbooks and other materials on the subject of journalism increased. Soon the stacks were filled with anecdotal, biographical, and historical studies specifically on the subject of journalism and its practitioners.

In the fall of 2006, the City University of New York's graduate school of journalism admitted its first class. Housed in the former headquarters of the *New York Herald Tribune* on West 40th Street, it boasts a newsroom with seats for 130, a broadcast studio, several multimedia editing suites, a library, and a research center 1,500 books on journalism, as well as numerous classrooms. In June 2018, Craig Newmark, founder of Craigslist, donated $20 million to the school's foundation to enhance its mission of training skilled, ethically-minded, and diverse journalists. The journalism school now carries his name, a bit ironic. His free online classified-ad service virtually wiped out this revenue source for newspapers, already struggling to survive.

Most journalism programs have upped their game. Typical of nationwide trends, Northwestern University's Medill School of Journalism's curriculum integrates multimedia storytelling into all reporting classes. Students must also master law cases and quantitative skills. Once only offering a nuts-and-bolts curriculum, Columbia School of Journalism students now must take legal, historical, and ethical courses. With journalism moving mainly online, legal discussions surrounding copyright get more considerable attention. Students often take classes at the university's prestigious law school. At one of copyright professor Jane Ginsberg's pizza-fueled luncheon seminars in spring 2019, a panel of experts talked about Pierre N. Leval's 1990 *Harvard Law Review* article and the impact of the high court's interpretation of "transformative use" in the *2 Live Crew* case, significant for storytellers in the newsroom and courthouse.

Exposing Wrongs

In a democracy like the United States, the newspaper and its broadcasting, cable TV, and online offspring play a crucial part in monitoring and reporting on corporate, government, institutional, and individual abuse and overreach, and are critical to ensuring fair and just laws and legal procedures. To fulfill this role, reporters and editors turn to the time-tested touchstones of relying on persistent digging, careful interviewing, searching for corroborating documents, and especially verification from several reliable sources.

With these professional yardsticks, investigative reporters can identify and assess wrongdoing without sacrificing impartiality and fair-mindedness. These investigative projects may require months or even years researching and preparing a report, which will then go through a rigorous editorial review, at least in the mainstream media. In-depth investigations are not only time-consuming but also expensive and may not yield anything publishable.

To ferret out evidence of suspected misdeeds, and expose incompetence, corruption, and outright lies, reporters spend countless hours analyzing lawsuits and other legal documents: tax records, government reports, regulatory reports, corporate financial filings, and databases of public records. They also conduct numerous interviews with on-the-record sources as well as, in some instances, with sources wishing to remain anonymous (for example, whistleblowers). At its best, investigative reporting can provide valuable revelations, connecting the dots that people in power generally do not want to be connected. And, in the process, holding those engaging in unethical or fraudulent behavior to account.

Clearly taking a point of view, in 1971, CBS ran *The Selling of the Pentagon*, an expose of pro-Vietnam War government propaganda and on the relationship between the defense department and its corporate contractors. Controversy over the show—especially accusations that interviews had been edited in a way that distorted the meaning of what had actually been said—brought about a congressional investigation of the production processes for documentaries. Ultimately, Congress failed to obtain, as they had requested, CBS's production materials beyond the finished program that aired, but the investigation did result in the network tending to tread more carefully in the future.

Woodward/Bernstein

President Richard Nixon's skullduggery would get its comeuppance with the arrest of five men for breaking into the Democratic National Committee offices at the Watergate Complex in Washington, DC. That one of the burglars was on the payroll of the president's reelection committee intrigued two young reporters at the *Washington Post*, Bob Woodward and Carl Bernstein.[91] They did old-fashioned legwork to unravel who was behind the break-in. Aided by an unidentified source, dubbed Deep Throat, they uncovered a series of political crimes and "dirty tricks" that connected the burglary back to the White House. Able editors, exacting managing editor Ben Bradlee, and the paper's owner Katharine Graham gave them crucial support.

The talented news team's articles ultimately led to indictments of forty administration officials. Eventually, before their bestselling book's publication, fallout resulting from the *Post* revelations forced the president to resign, highlighting why in-depth, watchdog reporting is so critical to social accountability and an effectively functioning democracy. The president and his unethical acolytes engaged in theft, illegal wiretapping, slush funds, and obstruction of justice, along with campaign espionage and sabotage.

60 Minutes

Debuting in 1968 on the CBS television network, the initially bi-weekly series *60 Minutes* pioneered such engaging albeit at times ethically questionable investigative journalism procedures and techniques as re-edited interviews, hidden cameras, and "gotcha" visits to the home or office of an investigative subject.

In addition to presenting personality profiles, the seasoned reporter hosts do "hard news" investigative reports on a wide range of topics but the focus on individual malefactors tends to preclude any serious consideration of broader blue-collar and middle-class concerns such as rising income inequality, globalization and outsourcing, robotics replacing workers, the decline of coal mining, and low-wage chain stores and online retailers driving out small business. Reports have ranged from the potential psychological damage of playing video games to the possible benefits from the resveratrol in red wine to Congressional insider trading that led to reform legislation.

Despite irregular scheduling, due to the network's National League Football contractual obligations, the program's hard-hitting reports divided into two or three long-form pieces attracted a steadily growing audience, particularly during the waning days of the Vietnam War and the gripping unfolding events of the Watergate scandal.

With changes in the Federal Communications Commission's prime-time rules then in effect, the newsmagazine secured an early slot in the network's Sunday evening program lineup and with the addition of more youthful and conventionally attractive correspondents to the reporting team, it became a strong rating hit and, eventually, a general cultural phenomenon. From 1978 to 2011, the program usually ended with a (usually light-hearted and humorous) commentary by Andy Rooney expounding on topics of wildly varying import, ranging from international politics, to economics, and to personal philosophy on everyday life.

Pedophile Priests

Through meticulous research, including extensive door-to-door interviews, the *Boston Globe*'s "Spotlight" team gradually unearthed a story of widespread sexual abuse of children by pedophile priests. Initially, investigating allegations against a unfrocked priest accused of molesting more than eighty boys, who was moved around several times, the Spotlight team begin to uncover a pattern of widespread sexual abuse of children involving dozens of Catholic priests in Massachusetts, and an ongoing cover-up by the city's archdiocese.

The dogged team eventually uncovered a conspiracy to hide the facts that went all the way to the Vatican itself. Those in the upper reaches of the Roman Catholic Church knew that the abuse of children was taking place and moved the predatory

priests to other parishes to continue their molestations. Seemingly more concerned about its reputation and influence than the well-being of young parishioners, the Boston archdiocese gave hush money to families of the victims.

In early January 2002, *Boston Globe* readers picked up their local paper and saw the front-page headline: "Church Allowed Abuse by Priest for Years." The story, written by a reporter on the investigative "Spotlight" team, was massive in word-count and impact, but it was just the beginning. Two more Spotlight stories on the same topic ran that day, with more to follow. The sustained uproar from the stories led to archbishop stepping down in disgrace. (Pope John Paul II gave him a position in Rome). A year later, the Spotlight team's shocking exposé became the basis for a compelling, insightful movie on investigative journalism stressing the sometimes crushingly tedious gumshoe part of a reporter's job.

By shining a light into the very darkest places of human depravity, these revelations may prove to be one of the most important pieces of factual storytelling of our time. In the years since the Spotlight team began its investigation in 2001, the Vatican received reports of several thousand credible cases of child abuse by priests around the globe. In 2014, for example, the bodies of 800 babies and children were uncovered in a septic tank "grave" at a former home for unmarried mothers run by the Roman Catholic Church in Ireland. In recent years, numerous dioceses around the country have become embroiled in scandal over the handling of clergy sexual abuse.

Bogus Remedies

Among the advertisers of the nineteenth and early twentieth centuries in the United States were promoters of "patent medicines," over-the-counter remedies or "nostrums" to cure or prevent everything from venereal diseases, tuberculosis, and cancer to cholera, scarlet fever, chronic abscesses, and ill-defined gynecological ailments. They marketed their products, an elixir, tonic or liniment, as medicine. Such nostrums were typically of unproven effectiveness and questionable safety. Sellers of liniments claimed the snake oil they contained cured or alleviated all kinds of pain, making the snake oil salesman a lasting sobriquet for a charlatan.

DEATH'S LABORATORY

The bogus and exaggerated claims of the patent medicine pioneers eventually generated profound distrust along with alarming press coverage. The early June 1905 issue of *Collier*'s, a widely read national weekly, contains a major exposé of the patent medicine fraud. Its cover features a striking illustration a skull, bookended by cash bags, filled with patent medicine bottles above the heading "Death's Laboratory." Among other unsettling matters, the text below the heading tells of colicky babies fed laudanum, an alcohol-based pain remedy containing morphine sulfate prepared from opium. A precursor to "targeted advertising," the pushers of this potion scoured newspapers for birth announcements and then sent free samples to new mothers. Those who received these freebies had no idea the ingredients could be poisonous, and dozens of infants got severely ill and died.

The Progressive Era, a period of widespread social activism and political reform across the United States spanning the 1890s to the 1920s, saw an increase in federal regulations. In 1906, President Theodore Roosevelt signed into law the act that created the Food and Drug Administration (FDA) to oversee product safety but legal challenges thwarted the agency's actions almost from the outset.

Some five years after the FDA's creation, the U.S. Supreme Court ruled that the 1906 act did not apply to false statements of drug efficacy.[92] In response, a year later, Congress passed an amendment adding "false and fraudulent" claims of "curative or therapeutic effect" to the federal agency's mandate. It also required labeling of the quantity or proportion of such specified narcotic substances as alcohol, morphine, opium, cocaine, and heroin. But the courts continued to narrowly define these powers and requirements, among other things, setting high standards for proof of fraudulent intent.

Heightening the importance of the news media's watchdog and investigative functions, many newspapers and magazines published exposés of the useless and potentially dangerous concoctions promoted as medicine. In addition to the creation of state agencies, such exposure led to the formation in 1914 of the Federal Trade Commission "to challenge any unfair methods of competition... and unfair or deceptive acts or practices in commerce."

In a 1975 amendment, Congress increased the agency's authorization allowing it to seek redress for consumers and civil penalties for repeat offenders. It also increased the agency's authorization to pursue violations "affecting commerce" rather than just those "in commerce." Under the 1914 Clayton Act, the FTC also enforces federal antitrust laws that prohibit anticompetitive mergers and other business practices that restrict competition and harm consumers.

As a law enforcement agency, like other such agencies, the FTC lacks punitive authority. Although not permitted to punish violators—that is the responsibility of the judicial system—it can issue cease and desist orders and argue cases in federal and administrative courts. Its authority now extends to internet swindles, deception, and unfair business practices, such as telemarketing fraud or price-fixing schemes. Like the FDA, the President appoints the five commissioners with the approval of the Senate to serve for seven-year terms.

As might be expected, depending on the political climate, legal challenges and congressional revisions weakened the agency's mandate. Although its basic authority to police false and deceptive advertising remains intact, the regulatory agency's limitations are illustrated by the 1960s Geritol marketing campaign claiming the product would cure "tired blood" resulting from iron deficiency. After a lengthy investigation, in 1965, the FTC ordered its makers, the J.B. Williams Company, to stop running the ads, stating that tiredness is not a reliable indicator of iron deficiency, and the product would do little to remedy run-down feelings. When the company, a Nabisco subsidiary, started making the claims again, the agency brought a suit settled with a payment of a $125,000 fine.

By the time of the settlement, the promotion of Geritol had moved to suggestiveness rather outright verifiable claims. Its ads featured a radiantly healthy young woman saying such words as, "I'm in love, and I take Geritol." She explained that looking after one's self is essential, so she got plenty of rest, enough sleep, and took Geritol every day. Some of these ads presented clinging young couples giving, as media critic Eric Barnouw put it, "the impression that their love life was ecstatic, and interrupted only momentarily to film a commercial."[93] The resounding success of the seeming FTC-proof campaign, he notes, points to the increasing irrelevance of regulatory reviews that tend to be word-oriented.

The patent medicine promoters pioneered advertising appeals that were later used for other products. Almost from the outset, Listerine's owners also marketed it as a preventive and remedy for colds and sore throats. In 1976, in a rare period of zeal, the Federal Trade Commission ruled that these claims were misleading, and that the product had "no efficacy" at either preventing or alleviating the symptoms of sore throats and colds. The FTC ordered its owner, now Warner-Lambert, not only to stop making the claims, but also to include in the next $10.2 million worth of Listerine ads specific mention that "Listerine will not help prevent colds or sore throats or lessen their severity." The regulatory agency seldom imposes such "corrective advertising" these days.

Explosive Revelation

The 2008 race for the White House unfolded like something from the realm of fiction. Despite blanket news coverage, a discredited scandal sheet, the *National Enquirer* broke a significant story the mainstream media missed entirely. In October 2007, it reported that former North Carolina Senator John Edwards was having an affair with a video maker, a woman he picked up in a hotel bar and hired to cover his campaign. His only defense was to call the paper "tabloid trash," the accusation enough so the exposé got no traction in traditional news outlets and almost none in the blogosphere.

The explosive revelations could hardly have surprised his campaign workers. He and his cancer-stricken wife fought, in front of staffers, about the affair numerous times. At one point, in such a state of fury, she deliberately tore her blouse in the parking lot of a Raleigh airport terminal, exposing herself. "'Look at me,' she wailed at him then staggered, nearly falling to the ground."[94] This occurred well before the major news outlets took the reports of the affair seriously.

Dogging the presidential hopeful every move, in July of the following year, the tabloid ran a photo-documented article claiming to have caught Edwards visiting his mistress, and their alleged illegitimate child at a hotel in Los Angeles. National news outlets finally picked up on the allegations reporting on how they might affect his chances of being selected as a running mate in Barack Obama's 2008 presidential bid. His political career in shambles, Edwards eventually admitted to the extended affair and the paternity of his paramour's baby girl.

Less soap-opera like but far more worrisome, in February 2014, print journalist Glenn Greenwald and documentary filmmaker Laura Poitras, among others, launched *The Intercept*. It is the online news publication that initially served as a platform to report on the documents released by National Security Agency (NSA) whistleblower, Edward Snowden. Based on his revelations, it exposed the NSA's involvement in targeted killings. Among other things, it detailed the flawed methods that are used to locate targets for lethal drone strikes, resulting in the deaths of innocent people.

Global Investigations

A significant development in investigative journalism in the twenty-first century has been the global investigations carried out by cooperating news organizations and freelancers. They revealed the deep and pervasive corruption of the global financial system. An anonymous source released 11.5 million documents in 2015 detailing financial and attorney-client information for over 214,000 offshore entities. These documents, some dating back to the 1970s, were from the Panamanian law firm and corporate service provider Mossack Fonseca, which specializes in all kinds of legal, semi-legal and not-really-legal subterfuge designed to horde, hide and launder the fortunes of the very rich.

Journalists from 107 media organizations in eighty countries analyzed the personal financial information of the law firm's wealthy clients, including public officials and celebrities. They found clear evidence of fraud, tax evasion, and avoidance of international sanctions. After more than a year of analysis, the first news stories were published in early April 2016 along with 150 of the documents themselves—dubbed the "Panama Papers" because of the country from which they originated. The project marked an important milestone in the use of numerical data software tools and wireless, cellular, and broadband technologies. These enable people or organizations working together to complete a task or achieve a goal independent of location.

A year later, this global consortium's "Paradise Papers" investigation revealed how wealthy individuals and major corporations hide assets outside their countries to save on taxes. The list of hundreds of people whose confidential transactions have been disclosed by the Paradise Papers includes politicians, business tycoons, entertainment and sports stars, and some of the largest companies on the planet, among them Facebook, Twitter, Apple Inc., The Walt Disney Company, Uber, Nike, Walmart, Siemens, McDonald's, and Yahoo!. The torrent of unreported cash that washes through tax havens and secret bank accounts around the globe directly affects the well-being of society by robbing governments of funds to pay for education, health care and infrastructure.

Downsizing and Concentration

The essential role of quality journalism and the retraction of traditional ways of supporting it is exacerbated by shifting ownership patterns. The handful of large firms that oversee the vast majority of organizations dedicated to the publication of news and related information has dramatically downsized. A staving bottom line caused the closing of hundreds of papers and cutting tens of thousands of reporting jobs. And surviving newspapers are increasingly laying off or reducing reporters' salaries they can no longer afford to pay.

In 2018, the Tribune Company (briefly rebranded Tronc), a Chicago-based publishing firm that owns the *Los Angeles Times* and the *Chicago Tribune*, acquired all of the outstanding interests of the *New York Daily News*. It fired the newspaper's top editor and cut the newsroom staff by half. In recent years, the giant GateHouse Media, owner of 154 daily newspapers in thirty-nine states, has shrunk newsrooms as well. It's done this while pursuing shareholder value, in part by consolidating operations in regional hubs and merging newspapers.

A growing number of news firms have slashed pay, laid off or furloughed staff, cut production of print editions, or shut down altogether. The watchdog of local reporting is slowly dying as the cuts at the local level go on unabated. In March 2020, Poynter's *Tampa Bay Times*, acknowledging severe financial stress, announced it was suspending print editions except on Sundays and Wednesdays while furloughing at least fifty employees. Those at the helm seemed to be prodding loyal print readers, many of them older, to consider the website or an e-replica edition as an alternative.

When local papers are fatally wounded, corrupt local politicians and municipalities will likely feel free to steal or pollute the air, water sources, and other aspects of the already fragile environment. Sharp personnel cuts and dwindling resources translate into fewer reporters monitoring the city council, checking court dockets, scrutinizing school board meetings, and the like. When the presses stop rolling, even everyday matters such as touchdowns scored, local heroes honored, and townsfolk dying, will likely go unnoticed.

In the news business for nearly a century, Gannett's formidable chain of newspapers includes the nationally distributed *USA Today*, along with more than 100 other publications in small, midsize, and large cities nationwide. Early in 2019, the firm slashed journalism jobs all across the country. The cuts were not insubstantial. The *Indianapolis Star*, for instance, let go of three seasoned journalists, including well-known columnist Tim Swarens. Six journalists at the *Bergan Record* in North Jersey faced the ax after nine others took an early retirement buyout. On and on, the cuts continued. News of the axing leaked out on Twitter and across newsrooms, but just how many felt the steel blade is uncertain.

To many observers, the old news firm seemed to be trimming down for a possible purchase, which occurred later that summer. The New Media Investment Group, a holding company that controls GateHouse Media, bought Gannett in a transaction valued at roughly $1.4 billion. The combined company, under the Gannett name, publishes more than 260 daily newspapers in the United States, along with over 300 weekly publications in forty-seven states. An affiliate of the New York investment management firm Fortress Investment Group owned by SoftBank, a Japanese conglomerate, oversees the news media operations. The emerging global information empire seems ever-more far removed from the fourth estate aspirations of the journalism profession.

Early in February 2020, the publisher of the *Miami Herald, Kansas City Star*, and dozens of other regional dailies, McClatchy, whose origins date to 1857, filed for bankruptcy protection. The move foreshadows further cost-cutting and staff reduction for one of the most prominent players in local journalism. The 163-year-old family publisher controlled by Chatham Asset Management sold some newspapers to another chain, Digital First Media, now known as MediaNews Group owned by Alden Global Capital.

In practice, buying a newspaper company in semi-distress to cut costs can mean large-scale firings, weakening or destroying unions, and seizing pension funds. Among the most predatory purchasers is Alden Global, a Manhattan-based hedge fund with investment earnings domiciled in the tax-lenient Cayman Islands. With a mostly foreign clientele, Alden has been investing in American newspapers since 2009. Through its majority control of the MediaNews Group, a management company, the hedge fund owns 200 or so daily and weekly papers, including the *Denver Post, St. Paul Pioneer Press, San Jose Mercury News, Los Angeles Daily News*, the *Boston Herald*, and New Jersey's *Trentonian*.

A rising crescendo of critics accuses Alden of slashing jobs and sucking profits from the newspapers while starving them of the resources without any regard for their long-term future. The largest newspaper in Colorado, the Pulitzer-prize winning *Denver Post*, as a case in point, has become a shadow of its once-robust self. Its eviscerated newsroom went from more than 200 journalists to two-dozen or so, with squeezing out as much profit as possible the principal aim. In March 2018, Margaret Sullivan, the media columnist for the *Washington Post*, called the profit-driven hedge fund "one of the most ruthless of the corporate strip-miners seemingly intent on destroying local journalism."[95]

Voracious hedge funds like Alden/MediaNews manage to curtail independent journalism without telling editors and reporters what to write or not write. Deprivation, it turns out, is at least as effective as outright censorship to silence alternative voices. The hedge-fund playbook strategy entails taking over an existing company for a short time, cutting costs by firing employees, running up the substantial debt, extracting the wealth, and then moving on to the next target, sometimes leaving retirees in a lurch without earned pensions. Meanwhile, a remarkable number of news operations are now bankrupt or extinct.

Of those print editions of newspapers and magazines still standing, virtually all have suffered dwindling readership and the loss of advertising revenue. The venerable *Boston Globe* and its sister paper, the *Worcester Telegram & Gazette*, dropped ninety-six percent from $1.8 billion when the *New York Times* bought the papers in 1993 to $71 million at the time it sold them in 2013.

PAY WALLS PAY OFF

To stay afloat, the *New York Times* cast off every nonessential entity, trimming the size of the newsroom, reducing a dividend paid to members of the Sulzberger family, and borrowing $250 million from the Mexican billionaire Carlos Slim. Amid the deepening crisis in journalism, the enfeebled "old grey lady," refusing to abandon the unsteady vessel, put up a metered pay wall in 2011, initially providing twenty articles a month for free, now reduced to fourteen; beyond that, requiring readers to purchase a subscription plan. The pay wall paid off, with five million subscribers and stock rebounding by 2020 to nearly triple what it was six years earlier.

The company's expanding online readership more than compensated for the sharp drop in printed newspaper sales. Its podcast, called *The Daily*, now attracts over one million or so listeners a day. In June 2019, the company debuted *The Weekly*, a television show on the FX network in which a half-hour episode each week features one of the paper's reporters focusing on a pressing issue of the day. It draws on investigative reports, political scoops, and cultural dispatches of the paper's 1,700 journalists scattered across 160 countries—an impressive number in an industry where total employment nationally has been steadily dropping.

To shed more light on the inner workings of the paper, the *Times* is running a series of posts explaining some of its journalistic practices. A summer 2019 piece in the newspaper focused on how reporters and editors wade through the thick stream of distortions, exaggerations, prevarications, and outright lies that prevail in presidential politics these days.[96] The company, according to the most recent data, has more digital subscribers than the *Wall Street Journal*, the *Washington Post*, and the 250 local Gannett newspapers combined.[97]

Paywalls seem to have become a significant trend among big publishers. In addition to the *New York Times*, the *Wall Street Journal*, *Washington Post*, and the *New Yorker*, among other publications, have erected them as well. Typically, readers have free access to a limited number of articles each month as a lure; beyond that, they must purchase a subscription plan. These metered paywalls have been a godsend for quality reporting, with highly reliable and reputable national newspapers and magazines, attracting substantial revenue influxes, after limited unpaid monthly access. Among other matters, steady subscription revenue permits investments in exposing wrongs of all kinds.

With print readership and advertising collapsing, old media valuations are not what they used to be. In 2013, Amazon's Jeff Bezos purchased the Washington Post, the leading newspaper in the nation's capital, for $250 million, a fraction of what the esteemed but floundering publication was worth a decade earlier. Undeterred by low expectations, the hugely wealthy internet entrepreneur hired as executive editor Martin Baron, who oversaw the *Boston Globe*'s Spotlight investigative team. Under Baron's leadership, readership has exploded, the newsroom has grown significantly, and content has become more suitable for the digital world.

One of the *Post*'s skilled team of investigative reporters, Craig Whitlock broke the "Afghanistan Papers" story.[98] He based his reporting on a trove of notes and transcripts generated by a federal project examining the root failures of the most protracted armed conflict in American history. In addition to hundreds of candid quite volatile interviews, the documents included a new cache of memos written by former Secretary of Defense Donald Rumsfeld. They revealed the extent to which American leaders misled the public on their efforts to hunt down Osama Bin Laden, rout the Taliban, expel Al Qaeda, install democracy, and undo corruption.

After a three-year legal battle, in the face of frequent stonewalling, Whitlock got the unclassified documents under the Freedom of Information Act. This law, enacted in 1966, requires the full or partial disclosure of previously unreleased information and materials controlled by executive branch government agencies upon request. The raw material and his accompanying analysis paint an unflattering picture of a nearly two-decade-long military intervention that has failed to achieve many, if not most, of its goals, and of government officials who deceived the American people about that failure.

The story lay bare that winning was never clearly defined and that senior officials failed to tell the truth about the war in Afghanistan throughout the protracted, trillion-dollar military campaign that saw the loss and suffering of countless lives. As a three-star general who served as the White House's Afghan war czar conceded, they did not understand Afghanistan and didn't have "the foggiest notion" of what they were doing. Military leaders struggled to articulate who they were fighting, let alone why, while offering assurances that the mission was on track.

Never settled were such crucial matters as whether al-Qaeda or the Taliban was the enemy and if Pakistan functioned as friend or foe creating confusion for American troops in the field. Perhaps most damning, the report states, the United States under three administrations turned a blind eye as the Afghan power brokers—government leadership, warlords, drug traffickers, and defense contractors—wallowed in fraud and mass corruption plundering with impunity.

While the *Washington Post* and the *New York Times* have had success with digital subscribers, local newsrooms continue reporting declining profits, leading to layoffs as readers abandon ink and paper in favor of news apps and websites. Print advertising revenue has plummeted, and the money most publishers have made from digital advertising has fallen short of what newspapers used to bring in from print ads.

Robust Reporting Capsizing

News websites hosted by the mainline media companies have been competing with reputable alternative news sources. Many of them, like BuzzFeed, Vice, *HuffPost*, Mashable, and the titles under Vox Media, became quite formidable in size and scope. The online news outlet BuzzFeed, for instance, developed an impressive reportorial team and body of work worthy of attention.

After a period of significant growth, attracting hundreds of millions of dollars in venture funding, and building sizable newsrooms staffed with highly skilled reporters and editors, they've had a bumpy ride traversing the rapidly shifting media landscape. Long darlings of the digital-media revolution, these once-thriving firms now face the harsh realities of figuring out a viable business model.

With Google and Facebook dominating the penny-press method of making money from selling attention to advertisers—absorbing much of the revenue derived from digital advertising—some of these one-time successful sites have had little choice but to shutter their virtual doors. Others like BuzzFeed slashed staffs, including dozens of journalists at its money-losing but prestigious news division. Although severely banged up, it is still afloat amid the rubble of bold upstarts now gone, even though its founding editor-in-chief Ben Smith jumped ship to become the *New York Times* media columnist in 2020.

At the core of this digital disruption are the failures of the attention-selling model at the local level for financing news, information, and investigative journalism. To satisfy a starving bottom line, numerous local newspapers around the nation, grappling with the loss of classified advertising, declining print circulation, and diminishing ad revenue, switched to metered paywalls, but with much less success. The coronavirus is likely to accelerate the demise of many local news outlets, with shuttered local businesses like retail stores and movie theatres depriving them of advertising revenue infusions.

The current crisis is an auspicious time to make a painful but necessary shift, asserts the *Times*'s new media columnist, Ben Smith, a proponent of non-profit, local news publications. "Abandon most for-profit local newspapers, whose business model no longer works, and move as fast as possible to a national network of nimble new online newsrooms. That way, we can rescue the only thing worth saving about America's gutted, largely mismanaged local newspaper companies — the journalists."[99] Certainly, letting newspaper chains fade away to pave a path for a future that is all digital and mostly nonprofit is an issue that merits a lot more study and debate before jumping on this bandwagon.

The role, power, and importance of the news media in a democracy are generally not in dispute. An underlying premise is that reliable information is the vital axis linking the government and governed. Many people rely on honest, authoritative, fact-based reporting that can help them understand challenges of these turbulent times as advertising revenue is plummeting, and news organizations are facing an existential threat.

Such touchstones of solid journalism as checking factual statements, attributing accurately, minimizing the use of anonymous sources, uncovering new information, and exposing falsehoods remain essential hallmarks guiding gathering, editing, and reporting in reliable print, broadcast, and online news outlets. In this new digital era, the need has never been higher for skilled journalists with no particular bent beyond basic decency to distill complex events, filter through factual statements to pull out the essential aspects, and to condense lengthy arguments into understandable stories.

Chapter 4
Media Law

Although widely touted as a bulwark of democracy, in many ways, the fourteen of the forty-five words of the First Amendment to the Constitution: "Congress shall make no law... abridging the freedom of speech or of the press" are a somewhat limited mandate. The generation who adopted the Constitution, the Bill of Rights, and the early state constitutions did not believe in a broad scope for freedom of expression.[100] For much of its history, this amendment played a bit part, confined to a small and often irrelevant role.

During the nineteenth century and well into the twentieth, as the barons of big business got more prosperous, nearly half the working population of the U.S. labored long hours in appalling conditions, going home to filthy slums at night. In the face of strikes and the demands for the overthrow of capitalism, state authorities used sedition, criminal anarchy, and criminal conspiracy laws repeatedly to suppress expression by labor organizers and left-wing political radicals along with pacifists, slavery abolitionists, religious minorities, early feminists.

Repressive Measures

After American entry into the First World War, Congress passed and President

Woodrow Wilson signed into law the Espionage Act of 1917 prohibiting spying, interfering with the military draft and making false statements that might impede military success. Violation is punishable by a maximum fine of $10,000 or by imprisonment for not more than twenty years or both. It gives the Postmaster General authority to impound or to refuse to mail publications that he determined to be in violation of its prohibitions.

In what resulted in a landmark case, socialist Charles Schenck mailed over 15,000 leaflets to men listed in newspapers as having passed their draft board examinations. The leaflets declared the draft violated the Thirteenth Amendment prohibition against involuntary servitude calling a conscript little better than a convict—deprived of his liberty and his right to think like a free man.

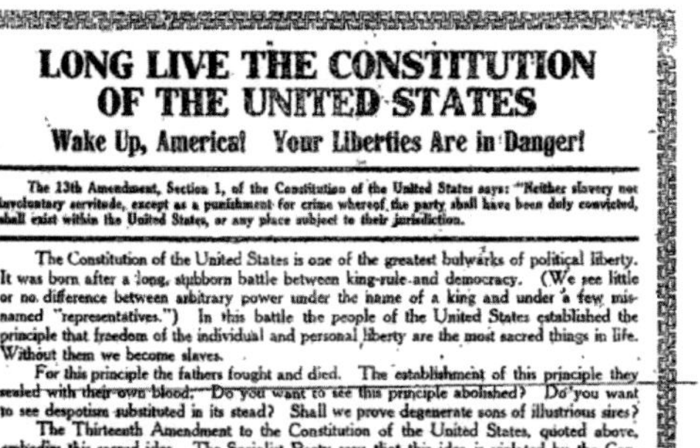

LONG LIVE THE CONSTITUTION OF THE UNITED STATES

Wake Up, America! Your Liberties Are in Danger!

The 13th Amendment, Section 1, of the Constitution of the United States says: "Neither slavery nor involuntary servitude, except as a punishment for crime whereof the party shall have been duly convicted, shall exist within the United States, or any place subject to their jurisdiction.

The Constitution of the United States is one of the greatest bulwarks of political liberty. It was born after a long, stubborn battle between king-rule and democracy. (We see little or no difference between arbitrary power under the name of a king and under a few misnamed "representatives.") In this battle the people of the United States established the principle that freedom of the individual and personal liberty are the most sacred things in life. Without them we become slaves.

For this principle the fathers fought and died. The establishment of this principle they sealed with their own blood. Do you want to see this principle abolished? Do you want to see despotism substituted in its stead? Shall we prove degenerate sons of illustrious sires?

The Thirteenth Amendment to the Constitution of the United States, quoted above, embodies this sacred idea. The Socialist Party says that this idea is violated by the Conscription Act. When you conscript a man and compel him to go abroad to fight against his will, you violate the most sacred right of personal liberty, and substitute for it what Daniel Webster called "despotism in its worst form."

The war effort, they maintained, was a cunning conspiracy, and citizens should not be sent to foreign shores to shoot the people of other lands. While urging the public to disobey conscription in strong but reasoned arguments, they advised only peaceful action. The government charged him with conspiracy to violate the Espionage Act of 1917 by attempting to cause insubordination in the military and obstruct recruitment. Convicted of violating this law, he appealed because the statute violated the First Amendment.

Writing for a unanimous court, Justice Oliver Wendell Holmes, sporting a luxuriant white handlebar mustache, concluded that courts owed greater deference to the government during wartime, even when constitutional rights were at stake.[101] He concluded that the First Amendment does not protect speech that approaches creating a "clear and present danger" of a significant evil that Congress has power to prevent, even though the alleged danger hardly seemed clear or present.

Without any evidence of an adverse effect, the seventy-seven-year-old Holmes, regarded by many as having the best legal mind on the high court, reasoned that the widespread dissemination of the leaflets was sufficiently likely to disrupt the conscription process. Perhaps most remembered, he compared the leaflets to falsely shouting "fire!" in a crowded theatre, not permitted under the First Amendment. This shaky analogy doesn't hold up to scrutiny. Shouting fire is the same as pulling an alarm, an action not speech at all. It is hardly logically analogous to a reasoned pamphlet expressing opinions regarding the military draft. A pamphlet is an invitation to think; the theater shout is a directive to run.

The same unanimous high court upheld the twenty-year sentence of prominent socialist the towering six-and-a-half-feet Eugene Victor Debs, by most accounts a great orator, for giving a blistering albeit abstract anti-war speech before a packed crowd at a park in Canton, Ohio.[102] While providing a typical speech that criticized capitalists and blamed big business for pushing the country into war and profiting

from it, he carefully avoided saying anything construed as an effort to disrupt the draft. Making a sweeping indictment, with shades of Senator Bernie Sanders, he castigated the "master class" for always declaring wars. In contrast, the "subject class" has had "nothing to gain and all to lose—especially their lives." "You need to know," he assured his listeners, "that you are good for something more than slavery and cannon fodder." Running for president from prison in 1920, he received almost a million votes. After the whirlwind of war hysteria subsided, on Christmas day 1921, President Warren G. Harding freed Debs along with twenty-three other dissidents.

The conflict raging in Europe seemed to demand a single-minded devotion on the American home front to the immense task of converting the peacetime economy and consciousness to the stringent requirements of war. Protestations against the conflagration could result in harsh punishment. A 1918 amendment to the act, the Sedition Act, adding nine new offenses, made it a crime to "utter, print, or publish any disloyal, profane, scurrilous or abusive language about the form of government, the Constitution, the armed forces, military uniforms or the flag."

With this far more extensive range of disloyal expression to draw upon, overzealous federal authorities wielded censorship powers capaciously and ruthlessly. Calling the military draft unconstitutional, criticizing the war bond drive, the president, war profiteering, anti-German violence, or even stating that the war was in opposition to the teachings of Christ—all became a crime. The government prosecuted close to 2,000 people, and nearly 900 of them went to jail.[103] One of the more severe sentences, considering the infraction, U.S. filmmaker Robert Goldstein got a ten-year prison term in a federal penitentiary for depicting an ally, Great Britain, in a highly unfavorable light in his Revolutionary War epic, *The Spirit of '76*. The story concerns George III's mistress and her efforts to become "Queen of America." His conviction, and confiscation of the movie turned on single scene showing Redcoats bayoneting a baby and carrying an unwilling maiden into a bedchamber. (A presidential pardon set Goldstein free after eighteen months). In mid-December 1920, the government repealed the Sedition Act, actually a set of amendments, but the espionage act itself is still on the books.

Amendment Incorporation

Not until 1925, did the U.S. Supreme Court "incorporate" parts of the First into the Fourteenth Amendment.[104] Adopted after the Civil War to protect the rights of freed slaves, this 1868 amendment makes every person born in the United States a citizen. It guarantees everyone equal protection under the law. On top of that, it prohibits the states from denying a "person" life, liberty, or property without due process of law. The courts defined the fundamental principle of procedural "due process" as ensuring that all levels of government operate within the law and provide fair procedures for everyone.

By making the First Amendment's provisions protecting freedom of speech and press binding on the states as well as the federal government, the high court opened the way to later advances in civil-rights and censorship struggles. Most of the provisions in the Bill of Rights are now applicable to all branches of government at all levels, but with few exceptions they do not restrain the private sector. Companies like CBS, Comcast, or Facebook are not legally bound to eschew censoring media content.

The words in these two amendments provide an essential lesson in the generation of legal meanings. Every judge or justice begins with the text when interpreting the law. In the 1925 case, a five-four decision, the majority held the word "liberty" in the Fourteenth encompasses "speech" and "press" in the First Amendment. In other words, two open-ended concepts are subsumed under an equally ill-defined abstract notion, the constitution itself providing no basis for making sense of either of them. Such unanchored judicial interpretations determine the meaning of the text rather than the other way around, with far-reaching and unforeseen consequences serving very different social and political agendas.

Corporate Persons

The Fourteenth Amendment's provisions, as interpreted by the 1925 court majority, have not only exponentially expanded the protection of civil rights for all Americans but corporations as well. In an 1886 railroad case, the U.S. Supreme Court recognized corporations as "persons" enjoying many of the same prerogatives as individuals.[105] During oral arguments, the chief justice commented that the provision forbidding a state to deny to any person within its jurisdiction the equal protection of the laws applies to corporations. Although not part of the holding, a clerk added it to the official opinion. In later cases, this off-the-cuff comment would stand as a precedent. In 1886 alone, the high court invalidated 230 state laws designed to regulate corporations.

The suppression of anyone thwarting wealth and privilege was justified by such abstract ideals like patriotism, personal liberty, freedom, and independence. With the benediction of the courts, corporations used the "due process" clause as a reactionary economic tool to prevent state legislatures from meddling in such matters as trade, contracts, and employment reforms like setting of minimum wages or maximum work hours. This interpretation prohibiting government prosecution that affects certain fundamental rights, subverted the amendment's original intent to accommodate corporate profit margins. The liberty granted corporations as persons, in effect, gave them a license to exploit. Sanctifying this interpretation of due process, the U.S. Supreme Court overturned many state reform laws, resulting in the spread of sweatshops and child labor abuse.

The much-vaulted concept of liberty came to mean release from any restraints or responsibility, free from civic duty, from taxation, from the mutual obligation to the public welfare in general. Such a conception, wrapped in the robes of legal sanction, protects and perpetuates wealth and privilege for the relatively few, bearing little resemblance to a belief that the state should work to provide all Americans with the freedom that comes from a stable and prosperous life. Of course, advocates of minimal government involvement in the affairs of business and commerce, even when they promote poverty and inequality, claim they too are defenders of liberty—the vagueness of the term allowing multiple interpretations.

Challenges to the due process dogmas began in the 1930s when the Great Depression put millions out of work and on the breadlines. Following the sudden deaths Chief Justice William Howard Taft and Associate Justice Edward T. Sanford, the United States Supreme Court adopted a more moderate view with the appointments of Owen T. Roberts and, as the new chief justice, Charles Evans Hughes.

This change in composition moved a majority of the high court away from the reactionary judicial activism that had undermined the working class, the civil rights of minorities, and free speech, and toward a more progressive era of judicial restraint. Signaling this shift, in *West Coast Hotel v. Parrish* (1937), in a 5-4 decision, the high court upheld a state minimum wage law for the first time.[106]

Citizens United

Whatever the high court's composition, it has reaffirmed the legal fiction of corporate personhood many times over the decades. In the 2010 *Citizens United* case, the most sweeping expansion of corporate rights yet, the U.S. Supreme Court in a five-four ruling held that political speech by corporations is a form of free speech covered under the First Amendment.[107] The case arose after Citizens United, a conservative non-profit organization, sought to air and advertise a film critical of Democratic presidential candidate Hillary Clinton shortly before the 2008 Democratic primary elections.

The five-four-majority opinion, penned by Justice William Kennedy, held that the "speech clause" bestowed no special protection on the news media as an industry. (The court passed on clarifying the "press clause.") The matter at hand was the 2002 Bipartisan Campaign Reform Act (better known as the McCain-Feingold Act). Separating corporations into media and non-media categories, this act prohibited any non-media corporation or labor union from making an "electioneering communication" within thirty days of a primary or sixty days of an election, or making any expenditure advocating the election or defeat of a candidate at any time.

In striking this provision, the high court's decision prohibits the government from restricting independent expenditures for political expression by corporations, including nonprofit entities, labor unions, and other associations. The majority opinion was joined in full by Chief Justice John G. Roberts, Jr., and Justices Antonin Scalia and Samuel A. Alito and in part by Justice Clarence Thomas. Roberts and Scalia also filed separate concurring opinions, while Thomas concurred in part and dissented in part.

In a lengthy and impassioned dissenting opinion, Justice John Paul Stevens argued that the framers of the Constitution had sought to guarantee the right of free speech to "individual Americans, not corporations," and expressed the fear that the ruling would "undermine the integrity of elected institutions across the Nation." The high court's "blinkered and aphoristic approach to the First Amendment," he warned, "will undoubtedly cripple the ability of ordinary citizens, Congress, and the States to adopt even limited measures to protect against corporate domination of the electoral process." Justices Stephen Breyer, Ruth Bader Ginsburg, and Sonia Sotomayor joined his forceful dissent.

Later rulings would trash other campaign finance restrictions equating them to prior restraint. The striking down limits on the amount of money that individuals could give to organizations that expressly supported political candidates spurred the rise of "super PACs," exerting a growing influence on local, state, and federal elections. Like stage magicians engaging in the sleight of hand, to avoid disclosing donors' identities, some super PACS re-registered themselves with the Internal Revenue Service (IRS) as tax-exempt "social welfare" organizations. In another common strategy, such entities retain their status under the tax code but accept large donations from essentially sham social welfare institutions created to collect and distribute anonymously donated money.

As a result of *Citizens United* and its progeny, writes Jane Mayer in *Dark Money*, "the American political system became awash in unlimited, untraceable cash."[108] In her well-documented account, the investigative journalist illuminates how, perhaps as never before, big corporations, the wealthy, and the powerful use their money, technical expertise, along with skilled lobbyists and lawyers, not only to influence elections but also to help write the laws and regulations, and affect the selection of the judges and justices interpreting them. Most states elect some judges, although each of these sovereign entities has a different set of guidelines governing how they fill local and state-level judiciaries.

High Court Jurisprudence

The supreme law of the land, the U.S. Constitution says little about the composition, qualifications, or even the number of justices comprising this august body. Congress decides such matters, initially setting the number at six but eventually raising it to ten. In 1869, it dropped the number to nine, eight associate justices and chief justice, constant to the present day.

In order of seniority, Clarence Thomas, Ruth Bader Ginsburg, Stephen Breyer, John Roberts, Samuel Alito, Sonia Sotomayor, Elena Kagan, Neal Gorsuch, and Bret Kavanagh comprise the current court. John Roberts is Chief Justice of the United States (his official title). These nine are among the most influential people on the planet, yet many among us can more easily identify the members of a rock band than the composition of the nation's highest tribunal.

In interpreting the constitution, the current justices more-or-less fall into two broad camps with a lot of wiggle room. In one camp, a faction embraces the doctrine of "original intent," holding justices should conform to the meaning the Congress intended. Another faction believes in "textualism," considering only the words of a statute, not the intent of the lawmakers who wrote them. Those taking either or some mix of these two approaches are generally labeled "conservative." Those in the other camp, usually identified as "liberal," build from the language of the framers but take an "expansive view," arguing that the constitution is a living document whose vague and ambiguous eighteenth-century language allows for changes in interpretation, as time and circumstance require.

These divisions are fluid depending on the matter at hand. In the 1970s, for example, conservative justices left behind the text and the framers. They began to rule that the First Amendment protected commercial speech, like advertisements, even though such expression had never enjoyed such constitutional protection before. The "commercial-speech doctrine," still a tenet of the right, does not extend to untruthful and misleading advertising or ads promoting illegal products or services.

The justices agree far more often than they disagree. All the same, differences in judicial philosophy and approach have the members of the nation's highest tribunal at times seeming to jump around every which way. Consider the case of a thirty-two-foot tall Latin cross on public land in Bladensburg, Maryland, bearing a bronze plaque with the names of forty-nine soldiers from the area killed during the First World War. Tax dollars fund the maintenance, repair, and other care the cross requires. The matter before the high court concerned whether this statue on public property at the center of a busy intersection violated the First Amendment's "establishment clause." This clause, together with the "free exercise clause," forms the constitutional right of freedom of religion. The relevant legal text is: "Congress shall make no law respecting an establishment of religion, or prohibiting the free exercise thereof...".

The meaning of these vague clauses caused legal concern since first being applied to the states in 1947. The high court initially articulated the three-pronged "lemon-test" in 1971, which holds that government action violates the establishment clause if it lacks a secular purpose, has its primary effect as promoting or inhibiting religion, or fosters an excessive entanglement of government with religion.[109] While criticized and modified through the years, its three prongs remain the primary criteria lower courts apply in establishment clause cases, such as those involving government aid to parochial schools or the introduction of religious observances into the public sector.

By a vote of 7-2, not settling on a single test, the high court held that longstanding monuments with religious symbols, no matter how imposing, do not violate the establishment clause and can remain in place because they acquire additional layers of secular meaning in subsequent years.[110] Alito wrote the "plurality opinion"—a majority agree with the ruling but not the reasons. Joining him were Roberts, Breyer, and Kavanaugh. Kagan joined Breyer in a concurring opinion. Thomas and Gorsuch concurred in the judgment, each writing separately.

Ginsburg wrote a dissenting opinion, joined by Sotomayor, saying in essence that a Christian cross is not suitable to honor those of other faiths who died defending their nation regardless of how long ago it had been put up. The fractious decision in this Latin cross case, highlighting hardly neutral agendas, provides little guidance for lower courts or for such contentious "establishment" matters as tax dollars funding religious schools.

The religion clauses have been honored in the breach ever since the election to the presidency of Republican Dwight D. Eisenhower in 1952. The new president made religion in American central to American culture inaugurating new traditions like the National Prayer Breakfast and other trappings of Christianity associated with the White House. And a compliant Congress, neutering the First Amendment, added the phrase "under God" to the Pledge of Allegiance and made "In God We Trust" the country's first official motto.

Throughout much of high court's history, men alone made the often-crucial decisions affecting every major area of American life. The first woman to serve, Sandra Day O'Connor, didn't penetrate this male bastion until President Ronald Reagan appointed her in 1981. After graduating in 1952 from Stanford Law School, one of the top law schools in the country, she had difficulty finding a paying job as an attorney because of her gender. At that time, most law firms would hire only men.

Ruth Bader Ginsberg joined O'Connor on the court some twelve years later. She was one of just nine women to attend Harvard Law School in 1956, and one of her professors made her painfully aware that she wasn't welcome. Although she was a top-notch student at Harvard and Columbia Law, which she later attended, upon graduating leading law firms turned her down, and she received worse pay and worse treatment than her male colleagues in the workforce.

A forerunner in the fight for gender equality, Ginsberg gradually emerged as the court's foremost advocate for women's rights. She rocketed to pop culture prominence in 2013 after a series of fiery dissents in gender-related cases inspired an NYU law student to link Ginsberg with rapper Biggie Smalls by bestowing on her the sobriquet "The Notorious R.G.B."[111]

Limited Mandate

At first glance, the free speech-press mandate seems clear. After a closer reading and upon further reflection, the underlying complexities rise to the surface, raising ongoing questions that have nagged the legal system over the last two centuries. Does the right to speak one's mind include the right to use offensive language to start a fight or incite a riot? Does it extend to aggressive symbolic actions involving no written or spoken words, like burning the nation's flag? Is the right to publish sexually graphic, hateful, or libelous material protected? How about the right to condemn the American government? In deciding such matters, the majority of the high court has never interpreted the First Amendment in absolute terms. Among the limitations on speech and press are such categories as incitement to violence, actual or "true" threats, obscenity/child pornography, false commercial claims, slander and libel, privacy rights, and copyright law. These exceptions all affect how "the news" is gathered, edited, and reported.

Struggles for freedom of expression can be better understood when viewed in the cultural-historical context of competing classes, alliances, and factions than abstract-universal objectives. The inherent vagueness of freedom of expression guarantees allow for multiple meanings depending on political perch.

Prior Restraint

Sir William Blackstone's treatise on English law was highly influential on the framers of the United States Constitution and its first ten amendments. In his four-volume *Commentaries on the Laws of England* (1765–1769), he elucidated the rights of individuals against government, including a necessary restriction on government from suppressing the press to inform the public. Although Blackstone recognized the right of the government to punish immoral, blasphemous, treasonable, seditious or scandalous libels, he also stood firmly in favor of an extensive freedom of the press and an absolute prohibition on prior restraint of publication.

Minnesota Morality

Blackstone's presumption continues to serve as one of the foundational principles of First Amendment jurisprudence. The matter of prior restraint first came before the high court in a case involving Minneapolis of the 1920s, rife with gambling, bootlegging, prostitution, racketeering, and gangland murders. The city's "respectable" newspapers, with many reporters on the take, turned a blind eye on the widespread corruption. The co-publishers of the *Saturday Press*, Howard A. Guilford, and Jay M. Near, had no such qualms about exposing wrongdoing. They claimed Jewish gangsters were "practically ruling" the city, the chief of police was taking bribes, and the governor was incompetent.

With a penchant to provoke people in power, they practiced a brand of journalism that, as Fred Friendly in *Minnesota Rag* puts it, "tattered on the edge of legality and often toppled over the limits of propriety."[112] The weekly's scurrilous accounts of wide-spread city corruption teemed with anti-Catholic, anti-Semitic, anti-black, and anti-labor prejudices. Despite such bigotry, a great deal of what the two men published was accurate or, at least, more so than not.

The Saturday Press

A Direct Challenge to Police Chief Brunskill

The Chief, in Banning This Paper from News Stands, Definitely Aligns Himself With Gangland, Violates the Law He Is Sworn to Uphold, When He Tries to Suppress This Publication. The Only Paper in the City That Dares Expose the Gang's Deadly Grip on Minneapolis. A Plain Statement of Facts and a Warning of Legal Action.

Respectfully Submitted

Future three-term Minnesota governor Floyd B. Olson, attorney at the time for Hennepin County, in which the twin cities of Minneapolis and St. Paul are located, secured an injunction under a 1925 Public Nuisance Law to prohibit the publishers from printing and distributing future issues. Guilford and Near appealed their case up through the Minnesota appeals court system—losing each round, and then to the U.S. Supreme Court, which agreed to grant certiorari.

The newly appointed chief justice, Charles Evans Hughes, wrote the five-four-majority opinion in Near's favor.[113] After reviewing the facts, he concluded state's statute imposes an unconstitutional restraint upon publication, citing four main reasons. First, it "is not aimed at the redress of individual or private wrongs. Remedies for libel remain available and unaffected." Second, it "is directed not simply at the circulation of scandalous and defamatory statements with regard to private citizens, but at the continued publication by newspapers and periodicals of charges against public officers of corruption, malfeasance in office, or serious neglect of duty." Third, its "aim is not punishment, in the ordinary sense, but suppression of the offending newspaper or periodical." Finally, it not only operates to suppress the offending newspaper or periodical but to put the publisher under an effective censorship.

Like Blackstone centuries earlier, Hughes made a distinction between prior restraint and subsequent punishment. In dealing with abuses of the media in criticizing official misconduct, the latter is an appropriate remedy if consistent with constitutional safeguards. Prior restraint is unconstitutional except in extreme situations (ex: obscenity or protecting national security), and the government carries the burden to prove the validity of exceptions. He concluded that although miscreant purveyors of scandal may abuse liberty, "does not make any the less necessary the immunity of the press from previous restraint in dealing with official misconduct." The issue of prior restraint is central to a series of landmark cases involving motion pictures.

Censoring Cinema

The intensity of the movie experience prompted agents of social control (politicians, police, religious leaders and the like) since the early nineteenth century to contain its potential meanings and influence, particularly with regard to sexual matters. At the very time the cinema was becoming an agent of ideas and a source of social controversy, government officials were subjecting it to increasingly intense scrutiny.

Movie censorship boards in the United States had begun to spring up soon after the turn of the century. The first municipal ordinance, passed in Chicago in 1907, empowered the chief of police to issue permits for the exhibition of movies. He was invested with the right to withhold permission for those movies deemed immoral or obscene. State censorship boards began to appear beginning in 1911. The first state to pass a censorship law was Pennsylvania; Ohio and Kansas followed suit in 1913, and Maryland did so in 1916. In March 1921, New York State passed a bill permitting prior restraint of movies. The personal predilections of state and local authorities frequently provided standards for judgment. A confrontation with a censor could be costly, resulting in mutilated prints, adverse publicity, and lost revenue.

Early in 1915, the Detroit-based Mutual Film Corporation challenged the constitutionality of the state censorship commissions of Ohio and Kansas in a trio of cases that went all the way to the U.S. Supreme Court.[114] Among other matters, Mutual claimed that the statutes under which these commissions operated infringed on the liberties of speech, opinion, and press guaranteed by both the state constitutions and the First Amendment to the U.S. Constitution.

In the lead case, from Ohio, the high court ignored Mutual Film's reliance on the First Amendment's speech and press provisions, which did not apply to the states until 1925, and concentrated instead on the pertinent provision of the Ohio constitution guaranteeing freedom of speech and press. Although acknowledging the importance of freedom of expression, the justices found little that linked movies to the traditions of the print media. Movies, they noted, "may be used for evil," that "a prurient interest may be excited and appealed to," and that some things "should not have pictorial representation in public places to all audiences." They conceded that movies were "mediums of thought," but then so were many other things, such as "the theater, the circus and all other shows and spectacles."

After explaining that a long history of precedent permitted extending police power over such forms of entertainment, the nine justices unanimously concluded: "It cannot be put out of view that the exhibition of moving pictures is a business pure and simple, originated and conducted for profit, like other spectacles, not to be regarded, nor intended to be regarded by the Ohio constitution, we think, as part of the press of the country or as organs of public opinion."

In the Kansas case, the outcome was the same. To the argument that the statute "violates the Bill of Rights of the United States and the State of Kansas," the high court responded that censorship of movies did not "abridge the liberty of opinion." Movies were mere entertainment, and therefore not entitled to legal protection. If censors didn't like what they saw, they could cut a movie to death. These decisions served as the rule of law for the next thirty-seven years.

These cases were heard in the federal courts because they involved disputes between parties from different states. Under its power in article III, paragraph two, of the U.S. Constitution Congress authorized federal district courts to hear civil cases exceeding $75,000 (amount set by congressional legislation) in which the parties are "diverse" in citizenship, which generally indicates they are from different states. In deciding diversity cases, federal trial judges must apply the statutory and case law of the state in which they sit, as if they were a court of that state. For federal jurisdiction to apply, complete diversity is required. None of the plaintiffs can be from the same state as any of the defendants.

Movies didn't begin to enjoy greater First Amendment freedom until 1952, following New York's attempt to ban the Italian-made film *The Miracle* because state officials considered it sacrilegious. Written and directed by Roberto Rossellini, it dramatizes the story of a simple-minded peasant woman (Anna Magnani) who is impregnated by a bearded stranger she believes to be Saint Joseph. She considers her pregnancy a miraculous gift from God. However, after apprising her fellow villagers of this "miracle," she is subject to derision and ridicule. To escape this treatment, she hides out in a nearby cave until she is about to give birth. She then goes to the town church, where her baby boy is born. The forty-minute movie ends with the new mother reaching for her child while murmuring, "My son! My love! My flesh!"

The motion picture division of the New York State Education Department that since 1927 had been vested with full authority to preview all movies shown in the state licensed *The Miracle* first without English subtitles and then with them, in 1949 and 1950, respectively. The movie opened at the Paris Theatre in New York City late in 1950 with two French films, as part of a trilogy called *The Ways of Love*. Within two weeks, the city's Catholic commissioner of licensing declared *The Miracle* "officially and personally blasphemous" and ordered it removed from the screen.

In the meantime, the Roman Catholic Church's Legion of Decency, formed in

1934 to make Hollywood repent, had condemned the movie as a "sacrilegious and blasphemous mockery of Christian and religious truth." New York's archbishop also denounced the film and urged Catholics not to patronize the theatres showing it. Following this indictment, members of the Catholic War Veterans picketed the Paris Theatre. The manager of this little art house even received bomb threats.

Claiming to have been deluged with hundreds of letters, postcards, and telegrams protesting the showing of *The Miracle*, the New York Board of Regents ordered a special three-member subcommittee to review the movie. When this group found it to be sacrilegious, and therefore in violation of state law, its American distributor, Joseph Burstyn, was ordered to appear before the board to show cause why his license should not be rescinded.

Burstyn refused to appear on the grounds that the board lacked the authority to revoke a license once it had been granted. After reviewing the movie, the full board unanimously agreed that it was sacrilegious and revoked his license. After the New York courts upheld the board's decision, he turned to the highest tribunal in the land for redress.

Late in May 1952, a unanimous U.S. Supreme Court ruled that the New York law prohibiting sacrilegious expression was an unconstitutional abridgment of free speech and free press.[115] The high court stated that the standard of sacrilegious was "far from the kind of narrow exception to freedom of expression which a state may carve out to satisfy the adverse demands of other interests in society."

The broad, all-inclusive definition of sacrilegious given by the New York courts, said the high court, sets the censor "adrift upon a boundless sea amid a myriad of conflicting currents of religious views, with no charts but those provided by the most vocal and powerful orthodoxies." The court further held that the state had no legitimate interest in protecting the various religions from distasteful views sufficient to justify prior restraint.

Although the Supreme Court put the moving picture within the pale of constitutional protection, explicitly reversing the 1915 *Mutual* decision, those working with this powerful medium of expression were not afforded the same safeguards as print practitioners. Noting that each method of expression tends to present its own peculiar problems, the justices permitted a variable standard. Moreover, the issue of whether all prior licensing of movies is in itself unconstitutional was left unresolved.

All the same, throughout the decade, the high court, in a series of cases, continued to erode the powers of licensing boards. One of the major foreign films to run afoul of the censors was a British-French coproduction of *Lady Chatterley's Lover*, imported to the United States in 1959 by Kingsley International Pictures. Although this movie version of D. H. Lawrence's controversial novel contained no explicit sex scenes, it was clear in revealing that Constance Chatterley, in despair over the emptiness of her life, had an adulterous relationship with her paralyzed and impotent husband's gamekeeper. The licensing board of the state of New York refused to grant a permit for the movie. In support of its position, it cited a state law that made it illegal to show a movie "which portrays acts of sexual immorality, perversion, or lewdness, or which expressly or impliedly presents such acts as desirable, acceptable or proper patterns of behavior." Rather than make any cuts, Kingsley appealed to the New York Board of Regents. Its

decision to support the censors was later annulled by an appellate court, upheld by the Court of Appeals of New York, its highest tribunal, and eventually considered by the nation's court of last resort.

The U.S. Supreme Court was unanimous in ruling against the New York censors, though the justices were not in agreement on the reasons for doing so.[116] A five-member majority focused on the position of the state's highest court of appeals that the law under which the licensing board acted requires "denial of a license to any motion picture which approvingly portrays an adulterous relationship, quite without reference to the manner of the portrayal."

What New York had done, in effect, was to prevent the exhibition of a movie because it advocated the idea that adultery under certain circumstances may be appropriate. For the majority of the court, this construction could not be allowed to stand because the Constitution "protects advocacy of the opinion that adultery may sometimes be proper, no less than advocacy of socialism or the single tax." Subsequent rulings by the nation's highest tribunal sounded the death knell for municipal and state censorship boards.

By the end of the 1950s, the constitutionality of prior restraint of movies was in doubt. The highest courts in Ohio and Massachusetts had invalidated the licensing laws in their respective states. Only four states continued to maintain censorship boards, Kansas, Maryland, New York, and Virginia. Finally, in 1961 the U.S. Supreme Court ruled on the constitutional status of licensing per se in a case involving *Don Juan*, a movie version of Mozart's opera Don Giovanni. Its distributor, Times Film Corporation, had decided to challenge Chicago's censorship ordinance.

After paying the licensing fee, the distributor refused to submit the movie to Chicago's superintendent of police for previewing. When the city, in turn, refused to grant a license for exhibition, Times Film appealed the decision in the federal courts, charging that Chicago's licensing system and prior restraint of movies in general were unconstitutional. Both the federal district court and court of appeals dismissed the complaint.

In a five-to-four decision, the U.S. Supreme Court upheld Chicago's power to license movies, ruling that such prior restraint was not in itself necessarily unconstitutional.[117] The majority stressed that neither the specific standards nor the stipulations of the Chicago ordinance was at issue in this case. The high court also took care to limit the scope of its ruling, stating that no "unreasonable strictures on individual liberty" should result from licensing movies before they are exhibited.

After citing historical examples of abuses of prior restraint, the dissenting minority concluded that the majority's decision "officially unleashes the censor and permits him to roam at will, limited only by an ordinance which contains some standards that, although concededly not before us in this case, are patently imprecise."

The *Times* ruling left open the question of what standards may be employed by censorship boards in judging the acceptability of movies. The high court moved toward clarifying this matter four years later, when it unanimously reversed the conviction of a Baltimore theatre owner for showing the movie *Revenge at Daybreak* (1952) without a license.[118] It threw out the Maryland censorship statute, stating that it did not provide adequate procedural safeguards "against undue inhibition of expression." Henceforth, said the Court, censors must make licensing decisions expeditiously, provide proof that a movie is illegal before rejecting it, and allow for prompt judicial review.

With these stipulations spelled out, movie censorship boards around the nation began to collapse. Maryland was the one state that persisted in licensing movies. It rewrote its censorship statute to comply with the high court's new requirements. Among other provisions, the revised law required licensing decisions to be made in fifteen days.

At all three levels, the federal courts found this narrowly drawn statute to be constitutional.[119] But the legal climate for movies had clearly changed. In 1981 even Maryland decided to get out of the censorship business. For all practical purposes, this marked the end of governmental attempts at prior restraint of movies in the United States.

Pentagon Papers

The issue of prior restraint of the press came to the fore again in 1971 when the *New York Times* began to publish excerpts from top-secret documents revealing deliberate deceptions about United States involvement in Southeast Asia over four decades. The official title of the study was the "Report of the Office of the Secretary of Defense Vietnam Task Force," later dubbed the Pentagon Papers. A repentant hawk, Daniel Ellsberg, former Marine Corps officer, Harvard Ph.D. in economics, and strategic analyst at the military-funded RAND Corporation think tank, and the Department of Defense, had been an early supporter of U.S. involvement in Indochina and had worked on the preparation of the 1967 study. As the Vietnam War dragged on, with more than 500,000 U.S. troops in Vietnam by 1968, and further buildups planned, he became disillusioned with American involvement in Southeast Asia. After secretly photocopying large sections of the report, Ellsberg approached several members of Congress, none of whom acted. In March 1971, while working as a senior research associate at the Massachusetts Institute of Technology's Center for International Studies, Ellsberg gave portions of the report to Neil Sheehan, a reporter at the *New York Times*, which after reviewing the report, published a series of scathing articles based on its most damning secrets.

ew York Times

NEW YORK, SUNDAY, JUNE 13, 1971

Vietnam Archive: Pentagon Study Traces 3 Decades of Growing U. S. Involvement

Among other matters, these documents revealed that four

administrations were deliberately deceptive about American involvement in Southeast Asia. The Truman administration gave military aid to France in its colonial war, thus directly involving the United States in Vietnam. In 1954, President Eisenhower decided to prevent a communist takeover of South Vietnam and to undermine the new communist regime of North Vietnam. John F. Kennedy broadened American commitment, actively helping to overthrow and assassinate South Vietnamese president in 1963. For his part, Lyndon B. Johnson intensified covert warfare against North Vietnam and began planning to wage overt war in 1964, a full year before the depth of U.S. involvement was publicly revealed.

In the 1964 presidential campaign against Republican Barry Goldwater, Johnson promised, "American boys will never fight a war Asian boys should be fighting themselves," while secretly conducting airstrikes over Laos, raids along the coast of North Vietnam, offensive marine actions, and building military bases for 500,000 troops. The study concluded before Richard Nixon ascended to the presidency, but he feared making it public would hurt efforts to fight the ongoing conflict and broker a peace agreement.

The first of Sheehan's articles based on the study appeared in the newspaper in the summer of 1971. When attempts failed to get the paper to stop publishing, after the third daily installment appeared, the Nixon Justice Department obtained in U.S. District Court a temporary restraining order against further publication of the classified material, contending that further public dissemination of the material would cause "immediate and irreparable harm" to U.S. national defense interests.

The newspaper appealed, and the case began working through the court system. In the meantime, the *Washington Post* began publishing its series based on the top-secret study. The government's attempt to obtain a restraining order against the newspaper in the D.C. federal court failed. The appeals on both sides went to the highest tribunal in the land.

The U. S. Supreme Court, two weeks later on expedited appeal, ruled 6-3 against the Nixon administration because it failed to meet the "heavy burden of proof" necessary for prior restraint.[120] The high court did not say the *Times* and *Post* had a right to print this story under the First Amendment's mandate that "Congress shall make no law... abridging the freedom of speech or of the press...." Its unsigned or "per curium" opinion pointed to sharp disputes among the court's members. All nine justices wrote individual opinions, disagreeing on significant substantive issues. Hardly a ringing declaration against even temporary press restraint, such a fractured decision provided little guidance for the future.

The war-weapon figures are staggering. In Laos alone, between 1964 and 1973, in 580,000 bombing missions, some 260 million cluster bombs rained down, about 2.5 million tons of munitions—equivalent to a planeload of bombs dropped every eight minutes, twenty-four hours a day, for nine years, nearly seven explosives for every man, woman, and child in the country. By the end of the war in Southeast Asia, the American military had dropped seven million tons of bombs on Vietnam, Laos, and Cambodia, more than twice the number of explosives dropped on Europe and Asia during the Second World War.

After the high court ruled against it, the Nixon Administration had Daniel Ellsberg

"All the News That's Fit to Print"

The New York Times

LATE CITY EDITION

VOL. CXX ... No. 41,431 — NEW YORK, THURSDAY, JULY 1, 1971 — 15 CENTS

SUPREME COURT, 6-3, UPHOLDS NEWSPAPERS ON PUBLICATION OF THE PENTAGON REPORT; TIMES RESUMES ITS SERIES, HALTED 15 DAYS

and an alleged accomplice indicted on criminal charges, including conspiracy, espionage, and stealing government property. The trial began in 1973 but ended in a dismissal of the charges after prosecutors discovered that a secret White House team (dubbed "the plumbers") had burglarized Ellsberg's psychiatrist's office in September 1971 to find damaging information that would discredit him.

The whole affair gave rise to two opposing narratives reflecting the deep polarization of American society since Vietnam. To one side, Ellsberg is a traitor who betrayed his country and escaped punishment thanks only to skullduggery. To the other, he is a heroic figure risking his freedom to halt needless bloodshed. Much the same division applies to the *Times* for publishing the top-secret document.

Judge-Made & Statutory Laws

In broad terms, the concept of "the law" refers to a system of rules and regulations to guide human behavior and sanctions to enforce them. The edifice of our legal system includes constitutions, statutes, executive orders, administrative agencies, federal departments, and the common law and law of equity (injunctions and restraining orders) developed by the judiciary.

At the state and federal level, constitutions reign supreme over statutory law because they are the foundation for the government itself. They typically accomplish three things: a plan for establishment and organization of the governing body of an individual state or the nation as a whole; outline responsibilities, duties, and powers of its various components; and guarantee certain rights to the people.

In most of the fifty states, constitutions specify a tripartite structure similar to the federal government—congressional, executive, and judicial. The individual states are sovereign entities with the ability to make their laws except when they conflict with the United States Constitution. The text of this document includes a "supremacy clause" that requires state courts to follow federal law when conflicts arise between it and state constitutions or other state law.

Among the variety of laws affecting the work of media practitioners are the common law developed in England during the twelfth century, and those derived from legislative bodies—municipal councils, county commissions, state legislatures, and the U.S. Congress. The purpose of statutory law is to anticipate problems that may affect large numbers of people. Called ordinances at the city level and statutes at the state and federal level, they are meant to serve as guidance to people before they act. Criminal law, in particular, must give people fair warning that specific behavior is illegal before punishing them for engaging in it, so it is always statutory. Some 95 percent of all cases occur at the state level.

The common law—also known as case law—has widely impacted the process of gathering, editing, and reporting events deemed newsworthy. The defining characteristic of this oldest source of American jurisprudence is a reliance on precedent, what Latin-prone lawyers refer to as *stare decisis.* Meaning "to stand by matters decided," this mandate serves to maintain the law's stability. The part of the case that establishes the precedent is called the holding. This is the court's decision regarding the legal question presented. Sometimes courts say outright, "We hold that...." More often, one must sift through a lot of text to find the "golden nugget." The rest of the stuff can be informative but is not legally binding.

Whether a precedent is binding depends on the court's hierarchy and jurisdiction. The two types of authority are "personal"—the court's right to exercise its control over the parties involved in a case, based on residences in or contacts with a particular area, and "subject matter"— the specific issues that a court is empowered to decide.

Judges in the same jurisdiction are obliged to make their rulings as consistent as reasonably possible with previous judicial decisions having similar issues or facts. A Wisconsin state court ruling is not binding on a California judge. For a court to consider a case, three conditions must apply: there must be a legitimate controversy that is ripe for review; the parties in the case must have standing, which is a direct interest in the case; and the issue at hand must fall within the court's jurisdiction or sphere of influence.

The writers of the constitution accepted most of the English common law as the starting point for American law. Situations still arise that involve rules laid down in cases decided more than 200 years ago. Each case decided by a common law court becomes a precedent, or guideline, for subsequent decisions involving similar disputes. These decisions are not binding on the legislature, which can pass laws to overrule unpopular court decisions. Unless these laws are determined to be unconstitutional by the Supreme Court, they preempt the common law precedent cases.

Much of the common law, which varies from state to state, became incorporated into statutes. These days judges create and establish precedents under the common law prerogative mostly in the areas of contracts (agreements between two or more parties that are enforceable by law) and torts (civil wrongs that result in legally actionable harm or injury). The aspects of tort law relevant to the media include libel, invasion of privacy, and right of publicity.

When seeking deeper pockets, plaintiffs can sue not only those directly responsible for a tort but also their employers, meaning not only reporters but also news organizations may be liable. This liability stems from the old idea that the master is responsible for the servant. Cases involving torts and contracts typically occur at the state level.

LIBEL LAW

One of the exceptions to the First Amendment mandate that "Congress shall make no law... abridging the freedom of speech, or of the press...." concerns libel, a tort regulated through state law that involves harm to reputation, causing someone to be shunned, or exposing that person to hatred, contempt, or ridicule.

All fifty states have libel laws, which include statuary and common or judge-made law. While the basics of libel law are similar in every state, the details, like how much time you have to file a libel lawsuit, or what plaintiffs have to do to prove their reputation has been damaged, can vary. Typically, media outlets lose libel cases at trial level but often prevail on appeal—a very expensive process.

Most states recognize two types of libel. With *libel per se*, a statement is obviously damaging, libelous on its face. Stating someone is a criminal, disreputable in business, sexually promiscuous (especially a female), or suffers from a communicable disease constitutes libel per se. The negative implications are only evident in *libel per quod* when the plaintiff introduces additional facts to show damage to reputation. The words or phrases involved maybe harmless in themselves, but become libelous because of connected circumstances.

A person who initiates a libel case, the plaintiff, must prove (1) *publication* or republication, (2) *identification*, the words were of and concerning the plaintiff, (3) *defamation*, the material is damaging to reputation, (4) *falsity*, the content is untrue, (5) *fault*, some level of negligence, error, or defect of judgment, and (6) *damage*, harm that goes beyond mere embarrassment, such as loss of income, denial of employment, documented depression, or social opprobrium.

Publication occurs when one person, in addition to the writer and the person defamed, sees or hears the material. A republication of defamatory remarks constitutes a new libel. The defamatory statements may appear in local, regional, or national outlets, as well as on a personal website, a blog, a social networking platform, or even through an email. News vendors, bookstores, libraries, and the like are generally exempt from such lawsuits, regarded as vendors or distributors, not publishers.

So are internet service providers for the material originated by others. And most social media platforms, such as Twitter and Facebook, are protected from libel lawsuits by a provision of the Telecommunications Act of 1996, which means that they are not considered to be publishers of the content of their users. As sites and services increasingly exercise more editorial control just as a publisher would do, this immunity might be forfeited.

With regard to *identification*, the plaintiff can be recognized by name, nickname, photograph, or references that would identify only one person. The falsity and fault requirements depend on whether the plaintiff is a private or public figure. A private person plaintiff must prove *falsity* only if the statement is a "matter of public concern." As for *fault*, a private person must prove that the publisher of false statements acted negligently. In contrast, a public figure plaintiff has a higher hurdle to prove fault. The yardstick for a libel being committed is how the alleged false statements at issue would affect a "reasonable person" viewing the plaintiff.

Under the concept of "absolute privilege," government officials enjoy immunity from libel suits based on remarks uttered or written as part of their official duties. Journalists, among others, are protected by a "qualified privilege" if the material comes directly from the report of a privileged proceeding or document that is published or broadcast accurately. Naturally, a dead person can't sue, nor can the deceased's relatives unless the departed initiated the suit before dying at least in those states with "survival statutes." Something to keep in mind when reading tell-all biographies with explicit and salacious details.

The issue of damaging reputations of the dead come to the fore with the theatrical release of *Richard Jewell* late in 2019, a movie about the planting of a bomb packed with nails at the 1996 Summer Olympic Games in Atlanta, Georgia. Numerous news reports had hailed the title character as a hero for his discovery of the bomb, leading to the clearing of people around the bomb, significantly limiting casualties. Jewell went from hero to villain when, according to the movie, a crude and coarse *Atlanta Journal-Constitution* reporter offered sex to an F.B.I. Agent in exchange for information about the investigation. She sidles up to him at a bar, but he abruptly rejects her request. When she moves her hand along his inner thigh, he soon relents, revealing that Jewell is under suspicion. Grateful for this scoop, she brazenly asks, "want to get a room, or just go to my car?"

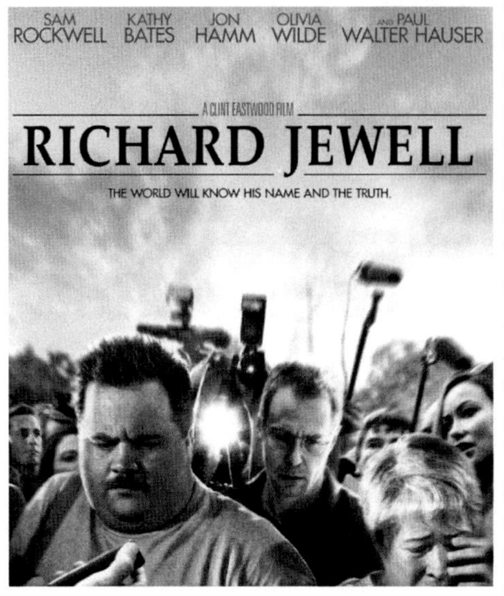

Nothing in the source material for the movie suggests this scene ever happened. What is telling, the movie's makers use her real name, she died in 2001, while giving a fictitious one to the F.B.I. Agent. In the light of libel law, they were able to use the old sex-for-a-story trope with impunity from liability, damaging the dead reporter's reputation for some cinematic titillation.

Weaponizing Libel Law

To thwart criticism, government officials sometimes weaponize libel law as well. In perhaps its most significant decision on freedom of the press, the U.S. Supreme Court declared in *New York Times v. Sullivan* that "debate on public issues should be uninhibited, robust, and wide-open," noting that it may well include "vehement, caustic, and sometimes unpleasantly sharp attacks on government and public officials."[121] The high court added that because "erroneous statement is inevitable in free debate," even false statements of fact must sometimes be protected.

The case originated in early 1960 when the *New York Times* published a full-page advertisement by supporters of Martin Luther King Jr., entitled "Heed Their Rising Voices," that criticized the police in Montgomery, Alabama, for their mistreatment of civil rights protesters. The advertisement had several factual inaccuracies, such as the number of times King had been arrested during the protests, what song the protesters had sung, and whether or not students had been expelled for participating. In paragraph six, the ad states: "Again and again the Southern violators have answered Dr.

The New York Times.

Heed Their Rising Voices

Your Help Is Urgently Needed . . . NOW !!

COMMITTEE TO DEFEND MARTIN LUTHER KING AND THE STRUGGLE FOR FREEDOM IN THE SOUTH

King's protests with intimidation and violence. They have bombed his home, almost killing his wife and child. They have assaulted his person. They have arrested him seven times." This paragraph contains ambiguous antecedents opening it up to different interpretations. "They bombed...." "They arrested...." implies both pronouns have the same precursor, and only the police make arrests. The police were not implicated in bombings and made efforts to apprehend those who were.

L.B. Sullivan, Commissioner of Public Affairs for the City of Montgomery, Alabama, who had oversight responsibility for the police, claimed the false accusations made in the ad against the police had harmed his reputation. In response, he sued the *Times* for libel in the local county court for defamation. The courtroom was thick with racial prejudice. It had segregated seating, lawyers used racial epithets, and the trial judge spoke openly of "white man's justice."

The trial lasted only three days. As might be expected, the jury returned a verdict in favor of Sullivan with $500,000 in damages. The *Times* appealed the judgment to the Supreme Court of Alabama, which stated the newspaper acted "irresponsibly." It then turned to the U.S. Supreme Court, which agreed to hear the case.

The stakes were exceedingly high. The *Sullivan* case, notes Anthony Lewis, legal correspondent for the *Times* during this period, was merely the first salvo in a concerted campaign to stifle media criticism.[122] Two stories by *New York Times* reporter Harrison Salisbury prompted another round of libel action, asking for total damages of $3,150,000 against the *Times* and $1,500,000 against Salisbury. Nor was the *Times* the only target; by the time the high court decided the *Sullivan* case, southern officials had brought nearly $300 million in libel actions against the press.

The U.S. Supreme Court's ruling removed the threat of all these cases. In March 1964, in a unanimous 9–0 decision, it held that the verdict violated the First Amendment. Explicitly, it adopted the "actual malice" test. Public-official plaintiffs had to prove that a false statement was made "with the knowledge that it was false or with reckless disregard of whether it was false or not." It made clear that the public official suing for damages had to prove the existence of actual malice "by convincing clarity." In the light of this ruling, Sullivan decided not to seek a new trial and the other libel actions brought by southern officials soon dissipated.

Since the decision's issuance in 1964, the U.S. Supreme Court has extended its higher legal standard for defamation to all "public figures." Celebrities or people with ready access to the mass media as well as those who have thrust themselves into a significant public controversy must also prove actual malice.[123] The high burden of proof public-figure plaintiffs face makes it hard for them to win a libel lawsuit in the United States.

The different standards exist because public figures are often at the center of matters of public concern that the news media should report on as part of their "watchdog" role on the government. If journalists, however defined, could be punished for every error published about a public figure, they might avoid reporting on controversial subjects that concern the public. The public would lose access to crucial information. Also, public figures generally have greater access to the media in order to counter defamatory statements.

The more significant freedom journalists enjoyed after *Sullivan* and similar cases may have prompted the news industry to modify its impartiality standards. The fair coverage of rivals or disputants, the cornerstone of journalistic principle, has not been rejected by the mainstream media but rather reimagined, permitting reporters and editors to make judgments about the news but requiring that they do so dispassionately and based on careful verification.

Privacy Rights

While every culture has norms guiding what is acceptable, the private lives of individuals are often at odds with such normative behavior, so they select what they reveal about themselves to avoid any possible humiliation or mistreatment. For example, a gay man working in a highly conservative company might choose not to disclose his sexual orientation. If someone were to reveal this personal aspect of his life, he might seek legal recourse in the courts.

Unlike libel law, dating back to antiquity, a right to maintain privacy, as a legal concept, is a fairly recent invention. An 1890 *Harvard Law Review* essay, authored by Samuel Warren and future high court justice Louis Brandeis, sparked the legal community's interest in media prying into private lives.[124] They were chagrined by such recent inventions as "instantaneous photography" as well as the emergence and widespread circulation of newspapers leading to invasion of the "sacred precincts of private and domestic life."

The two Boston lawyers proclaimed "the press is overstepping in every direction the obvious bounds of propriety and of decency. Gossip is no longer the resource of the idle and of the vicious, but has become a trade... which can only be procured by intrusion upon the domestic circle." They called for nothing less than the creation of a new legal course of action aimed at protecting the right of privacy, primarily a "right to be let alone"—as part of the full protection in person and in property.

From these high-level origins emerged the tort of public disclosure of private fact. To establish such a claim, a plaintiff, the person bringing the suit, must establish that the fact was indeed private, that it was widely publicized, that a reasonable person would find the revelation offensive, and that the material was not of legitimate public concern or interest. In some states, like New York, for instance, there is no actionable legal claim for public disclosure of private facts, and no remedy is available.

In most states, however, a legal claim for public disclosure of private facts is actionable, although several significant differences between jurisdictions will affect the strength and scope of the claim. In California, for example, the plaintiff must also

prove the defendant disclosed private facts with reckless disregard for the reasonable offensiveness of the disclosure. In other states, the "legitimate public concern" element is not one for the plaintiff to prove, but is a defense available to the defendant.

Consider the case of Oliver Sipple, who, in the autumn of 1975, deflected a gun held by Sara Jane Moore, a forty-five-year-old bookkeeper and five-times-divorced mother of four, who was trying to assassinate President Gerald Ford. The *San Francisco Chronicle* speculated that Sipple's homosexuality, no secret in the city's predominantly gay section where he resided, might explain why the president never publicly thanked him for his heroic act, and many other news outlets across the nation picked up the speculative story. A distraught Sipple took offense since this was the first time most of his family and old Marine buddies learned of his sexual orientation. After publication of the article his family rejected him. He filed a disclosure of private fact suit against the *Chronicle* in a California court. His claims failed in part because the revelations were not sufficiently private, and his sexual orientation was newsworthy.[125]

SLAPP Suits

Simply filing a lawsuit can, in and of itself, have a chilling effect on the freedom of speech and press. News media frequently defending themselves against frivolous lawsuits aren't focusing entirely on reporting controversial stories. In what has come to be labeled SLAPP suits, an acronym for strategic lawsuits against public participation, companies use the threat of a prolonged legal battle to censor, intimidate, and silence critics.

SLAPP suits aim to burden defendants with costly judicial procedures until they abandon their criticism or opposition. Only a few of the cases go to trial, and the defendants win ninety percent of the time. Still, deep-pocketed plaintiffs can extend the intimidation through extensive discovery requests, affidavits, and appeals that require a great deal of time and resources.

In recent years, some thirty states passed anti-SLAPP statutes, many empowering courts to dismiss lawsuits intended to chill protected expression and award attorney fees to the target. Of course, this means twenty states don't, and with the absence of federal anti-SLAPP legislation, in many instances, the plaintiffs can file a suit in one of those jurisdictions to bully critics into silence. In libel, the traditional standard is that any court in any locale where the statement at issue could be seen or heard may have jurisdiction—the authority to decide on a legal matter.

A privacy SLAPP suit knocked out Nick Denton's Gawker Media, a fleet of sites covering the romps of the rich and famous valued at as much as $300 million to $400 million.[126] Setting the lawsuit in motion, the firm's often tasteless, insensitive tech blog in 2007 put up a post that exposed then little-known technology investor Peter Thiel as gay. Although an open secret in the close-knit community of the Silicon Valley elite, the billionaire, a founder of PayPal and the first backer of Facebook, believed his sexuality to be private, not for public exposure.

Seeking revenge, Thiel bankrolled wrestler Hulk Hogan's $100 million invasion of privacy suit against the celebrity gossip site over an online article containing a thirty-second video. It shows Hogan (né Terry Gene Bollea) having consensual sex with the wife of his best friend, radio shock jock Bubba the Love Sponge Clem (his legal name). Lawyers for Gawker argued that the professional wrestler had long been a flashy celebrity who, in radio appearances and other venues, frequently discussed details of his sex life, including the pornographic video, stoking public fascination that made the topic newsworthy.

A Florida jury awarded Hogan $140 million in his lawsuit in March 2015, sending Gawker Media and Denton into bankruptcy and then killing off gawker.com altogether. The most massive invasion of privacy payday ever against a major media company, and perhaps the first-ever to bankrupt one, it led in August of that year to the fire sale of Gawker Media to Univision for $135 million. The endgame may well have been a verdict that was either slashed or overturned on appeal, but instead, Denton settled the Thiel-funded case for $31 million shutting the legal process down.

Erotically-Oriented Expression

In the United States, at the time of the First Amendment's adoption, laws against sexually explicit material did not exist. An abundance of risqué material of was widely available. Long before Carrie Bradshaw's erotic musings in *Sex and the City*, there was Benjamin Franklin, creator of the first gossip column in what would become America. His juicy tidbits ranged from a cuckold husband seeking revenge to a Casanova constable climbing in the wrong bedroom window. In a column from 1745 titled "Advice on the Choice of a Mistress," Franklin advised bachelors to seek out corporal pleasure with older women. They "hazard no children," he wrote, and "are so grateful" for a young man's attention. Referring to what is below the "girdle," he added, "it is impossible...to know an old from a young one."

Naughtiness in Early America

Such sexism and ageism notwithstanding, the libidinous Franklin showed the way to attracting attention with salacious stories. Naughty tittle-tattle of all sorts enjoyed wide currency. Rumors swirled around Dolley Madison, the wife of the dour, diminutive fourth president. Some seventeen years his junior, the flamboyant Dolley called attention to herself donning feathered turbans, rouged cheeks, and décolletage gowns without the traditional tucked handkerchief to shield her cleavage.

The First Lady's flouting of convention struck many in the partisan press as an insult to proper women, held as symbols at the time of a nation in its purest form. Several Federalist newspapers accused her of adultery and promiscuity, some even claiming her allegedly impotent husband made her and her equally vivacious sisters sexually available, as it were, to foreign dignitaries and members of Congress.[127] The rumors only subsided after she became the heroine of the War of 1812, saving George Washington's portrait, a narrative that she carefully crafted herself.

In this spicy media environment, authorities made no serious effort to interfere with salacious expression, no matter how lewd, erotic, or pornographic. The widely-read John Cleland novel, *Memoirs of a Woman of Pleasure* (aka *Fanny Hill*), initially published in London in 1748, for example, sees sexual deviance as an act of pleasure, rather than something that was merely shameful. Having a loving husband and children, a middle-aged Frances "Fanny" Hill, now a rich Englishwoman recounts the "scandalous stages" of her earlier life as a prostitute starting at age fifteen. This epistolary novel—first published in two parts—features just about every sex act imaginable, (the fantasies of regular readers of *Cosmo* excluded.) An illustrated edition of Fanny Hill led to one of the nation's first obscenity trials when, in 1821, the Massachusetts Supreme Court ruled against two men who had been printing copies of the book. Most legal cases at the state level revolved around images.

Cleansing American Culture

As the nineteenth century progressed, "obscenity laws" became more common. Prosecutions rose and ebbed with the major religious reform movements during the century. Congress passed the first federal obscenity statue in 1842, a customs law regulating the importation of obscene materials. The adoption of comprehensive federal obscenity legislation to supplement earlier efforts owes much to religious moralist Anthony Comstock, head of what came to be called the New York Society for the Suppression of Vice.

The crusading Comstock's campaign against sexually explicit material won backing from some of the nation's wealthiest men, including banker J. P. Morgan and soap-and-toothpaste magnate Samuel Colgate. In 1873, Comstock almost single-handedly lobbied through Congress a statute that prohibited mailing or importing from abroad of any "obscene, lewd, lascivious, or filthy book, pamphlet, picture, paper, letter, writing, print, or other publications of an indecent character."

The federal legislative body provided no definition of obscenity. The new law also prohibited the mailing of any material concerning birth control or abortion. Officially called the "Act of the Suppression of Trade in, and Circulation of, Obscene Literature and Articles of Immoral Use," those convicted of violating this postal statute could receive up to five years of imprisonment with hard labor and a fine of up to $2,000. Federal agencies such as the Bureau of Customs and the Post Office Department were the most vigilant and vigorous in executing this legislation.

From the year of the of the law's enactment in 1873, known as the Comstock Act, he served without pay (until his death 1906) as a special agent of the U.S. Post Office Department. As an unpaid postal inspector, Comstock worked with zeal to enforce the new law under which many were prosecuted. In his efforts to purify and morally uplift society, that same year, he also founded the New York Society for the Suppression of Vice to monitor compliance with state laws and work with the courts and district attorneys in bringing offenders to justice. He had thousands arrested for circulating obscene materials and even claimed credit for causing suicides.

Hicklin Standard

By the turn of the century, twenty-four states passed similar statues, many more stringent than the federal law. In an 1896 decision, the U.S. Supreme Court seemed to conflate indecency and obscenity.[128] Lew Rosen had been convicted under the Comstock Act for mailing "indecent" pictures of females. In upholding his conviction, the high court accepted a trial judge's use of the British "Hicklin rule" for determining whether a work is obscene. In the 1868 case from which this rule emerged, the British court defined obscenity as that which has the tendency "to deprave and corrupt those whose minds are open to such immoral influences, and into whose hands a publication of this sort may fall."

Under this standard, an entire work could be suppressed even if only a few of its passages were found to be obscene. The high court's recognition of the Hicklin rule made the "most susceptible person" criterion for determining obscenity the accepted one in both federal and state courts in the early twentieth century. The high court didn't officially abandon this broad benchmark until 1957, when it declared in *Butler v. Michigan* that it unconstitutionally restricted adults to only those materials suitable for children.[129]

Attempts at Redefining Obscenity

Beginning in 1957, in *Roth v. United States*, along with its companion case *Alberts v. California*, the U.S. Supreme Court attempted to redefine obscenity and set standards for applying its definition.[130] The operator of an erotic material business in New

York City, Samuel Roth was convicted under the Comstock Act for sending "obscene, lewd, lascivious or filthy" materials through the mail, advertising and selling a publication called American Aphrodite ("A Quarterly for the Fancy-Free") containing literary erotica and nude photography. David Alberts, who ran a mail-order business from Los Angeles, was convicted under a California statute for publishing pictures of "nude and scantily-clad women." The U.S. Supreme Court granted certiorari.

In a 5-4 decision, the high court rejected the Hicklin test and defined obscenity rather vaguely and abstractly as the material, applying contemporary community standards, that must, taken as a whole, appeal to a prurient interest in sex. Although conceding the federal law was far from clear or straightforward, Justice William Brennan, Jr., writing for the majority, upheld the convictions, concluding that when applied according to the "proper standard for judging obscenity," the words obscene, lewd, lascivious or filthy "give adequate warning of the conduct proscribed."

While reaffirming that obscenity fell outside First Amendment protection, Brennan remarked "sex, a great and mysterious motive force in human life, has indisputably been a subject of absorbing interest to mankind through the ages." As a vital aspect of human interest and public concern, he noted that "sex is not synonymous with obscenity, and the mere portrayal of sexual matters in art, literature, and scientific works does not automatically remove such expression from the protection of the First Amendment." He included within the sphere of constitutional safekeeping "all ideas having even the slightest redeeming social importance." Although eventually refined, this qualification paved the way for broader protection of free expression.

In his concurring opinion, Chief Justice Earl Warren expressed concern that "broad language used here may eventually be applied to the arts and sciences and freedom of communication generally." Still, he agreed that obscenity is not constitutionally protected. Justice John Marshall Harlan II dissented in *Roth* but concurred in *Alberts* because while states had broad power to prosecute obscenity, the federal government did not.

Justice Hugo Black, joined by William Douglas, wrote a dissenting opinion, stating he could "understand (and at times even sympathize) with programs of civic groups and church groups to protect and defend the existing moral standards of the community." He could even "understand the motives of the Anthony Comstocks who would impose Victorian standards on the community." Still, he nonetheless concluded that "when speech alone is involved," the government cannot, consistent with the First Amendment, "become the sponsor of any of these movements."

A footnote in the majority opinion explains that material of a prurient (from a Latin word meaning "to itch") nature has "a tendency to excite lustful thoughts" and create "lascivious longings." What do such thoughts and longings entail? Most dictionaries define lust in terms of intense or unrestrained sexual craving. What specific depictions of sex, which the court itself noted, is "a great and mysterious motive force in human life," is likely to evoke such unrestrained cravings? How is that judgment to be made? By what standard? And whatever criteria are applied, why should the government have the right to exercise any control over the moral content of a person's thoughts?

Slippery Guidelines

Following the high court's 1957 decision, the issues of what kinds of materials were actually obscene and how they could be controlled soon became one of the most recurrent matters taken to the courts for resolution. The elderly, erudite members of the country 's highest tribunal found themselves devoting an inordinate amount of time to sexually explicit movies, books, and magazines.

When movies were among the exhibits in obscenity cases, several of the justices and most of the clerks went either to a basement storeroom or to one of the larger conference rooms to see firsthand the source of the alleged prurience. One aged justice, whose eyesight was failing, watched from the front row, able to make out only the general outlines. His clerk or another justice would describe the action on the screen. "By Jove," he would exclaim. "Extraordinary."[131]

The justices tried on a number of occasions to clarify and refine the concept of obscenity but found themselves sharply divided over its meaning, engaging in dissenting and concurring opinions that would muddy the already confusing issue. In slightest redeeming social importance, the high court struck down the conviction of Nico Jacobellis who managed a movie theater in Cleveland Heights, Ohio, that had shown a French film called *Les Amants* (*The Lovers*) containing one explicit three-minute sex scene.[132] While ruling that the movie was constitutionally protected they could not agree as to a rationale, yielding four different opinions from the fractured majority. In his now famous concurring opinion, Justice Potter Stewart stated, referring to hard core pornography, that: "I know it when I see it, and the motion picture involved in this case is not that."

Trilogy of Cases

In a sweeping effort to establish clarification, in 1966, the high court decided a trio of cases on the same day: *Memoirs v. Massachusetts*, *Mishkin v. New York*, and *Ginzburg v. United States*. The first case in this trio involved John Cleland's infamous novel *Memoirs of a Woman of Pleasure* (aka *Fanny Hill*), controversial since it was published in London in 1748.

The Attorney General of Massachusetts successfully sought an equity suit against the book only, not the publisher, to limit its availability. In a stunning six-to-three decision, reflecting the changing moral tenor of the time, the U.S. Supreme Court held that *Memoirs of Woman of Pleasure* was not obscene and put forth a revised three-part definition of obscenity: (1) prurient interest in sex; (2) patent offensiveness; and (3) utterly without redeeming social value.[133] A word change in the latter component significantly expanded constitutional protection. The work at issue no longer needed to have "importance" but a mere modicum of social value. Only a "plurality" of the high court agreed on this definition so it wasn't binding on the lower courts.

In *Mishkin v. New York*, Edward Mishkin had been convicted of violating New York's obscenity statute for his dominant role in several enterprises engaged in producing and selling allegedly obscene books—some fifty them. Depicting such deviations as fetishism and sadomasochism, they had such catchy titles as *Mistress of Leather*, *Cult of the Spankers*, *Screaming Flesh*, and *Dance of the Dominant Whip*. He contended that books depicting such "deviant" sexual practices could not be obscene because they did not appeal to the prurient interest of the "average person." Faced with this rather ingenious claim, the high court upheld his conviction changing "average person" to "intended and probable recipient group."[134]

In *Ginzburg v. United States*, the third case in the trilogy, the defendant, Ralph Ginzburg, had been fined $28,000 and sentenced to five years in prison for mailing modestly erotic works: *EROS* (classy hardcover magazine), *Liaison* (bi-weekly newsletter) and a short book, *The Housewife's Handbook on Selective Promiscuity*. Even though the publications per se were not obscene, the high court upheld his conviction claiming he had engaged in the sordid business of "pandering," that is, "the business of purveying textual or graphic matter openly advertised to appeal to the erotic interest of customers."[135]

As an example, Ginzburg had sought mailing privileges from the postmasters of Blue Ball and Intercourse Pennsylvania, and Middlesex, New Jersey, for the obvious purpose of promoting his materials "on the basis of salacious appeal." The analysis of the publications focused almost entirely on Ginzburg's marketing. Among other points, the decision noted, "the commercial exploitation of the sexual nature of the materials was relevant in determining the "ultimate question of obscenity," because it suggested that he was exploiting their prurient appeal.

In his dissenting opinion, Justice John Marshall Harlan II, named for his grandfather who also served on the high court, criticized this expansion, as the materials would not be obscene without these external factors. The majority opinion, he contended, sustains Ginzburg's conviction on "the express assumption that the items held to be obscene are not, viewing them strictly, obscene at all." During his sixteen-year tenure, Harlan's unwavering belief in judicial restraint, federalism, and the separation of powers had a powerful effect on his opinions, especially his First Amendment jurisprudence.

Loosening Standards

A year or so later, the high court's holding in *Redrup v. New York* added to the confusion, overturning obscenity convictions in three cases arising out of the sale of sexually-explicit paperback books and magazines carrying such names as *Lust Pool*, *Shame Agent*, and *High Heels*.[136] In a brief per curium, or unsigned opinion, it announced that with each justice applying his own definition of obscenity, a majority of the justices had concluded, after toting up the votes, that the materials were not obscene. Its inability to articulate a definition of obscenity that could command a majority of the justices led to an era of disarray among the lower courts. Over the course of six years, it disposed of some thirty-one cases with per curium opinions.

A case involving suspected bookmaker Robert Eli Stanley clouded the matter of obscenity even more. The police searched his home in Atlanta, Georgia, in an effort to seize betting paraphernalia. They found none, but instead discovered three reels of eight-millimeter film containing pornography in a desk drawer in an upstairs bedroom. Stanley was arrested, charged, and convicted for violating a Georgia law prohibiting the knowing possession of obscene material.

In its unanimous 1969 decision *Stanley v. Georgia*, the U.S. Supreme Court overturned Stanley's conviction ruling that based on the First and Fourteenth amendments, the private possession of obscene material could not be held as a crime.[137] The decision stated unequivocally that government "has no business telling a man, sitting alone in his own house, what books he may read or what films he may watch."

The high court considered the matter of profanity in public in its 1971 decision in *Cohen v. California*.[138] At the height of protests against the war raging in Vietnam, Paul Robert Cohen was arrested in 1968 for wearing a jacket bearing the words "Fuck the Draft" in a corridor of the Los Angeles county courthouse. Arguing that his message was protected by the First Amendment, he was convicted under the state's penal code of maliciously and willfully disturbing the peace and sentenced to thirty days in jail. The California Court of Appeal upheld the conviction.

After the state's highest court denied review, the U.S. Supreme Court granted a writ of certiorari. Writing for the majority, in a 5–4 decision, Justice Harlan reversed the appellate court's ruling, explaining that this was not an obscenity case, because for the states to "prohibit obscene expression, such expression must be, in some significant way, erotic." He acknowledged that some observers would surely be offended by Cohen's expression and that some parents might be upset. But "outside the sanctuary of the home," he noted, we are often subject to "objectionable speech."

Pornography Moves Mainstream

With an agreed-upon meaning of obscenity increasingly elusive, by the dawn of the 1970s, even hardcore sex films were receiving nationwide exposure. One of the most successful releases of this sort was the sexual smorgasbord *Deep Throat* (1972). Featuring close-ups of actual copulation, fellatio, and cunnilingus, its satirical storyline revolves around a woman (Linda Lovelace) who's unable to achieve sexual satisfaction until her deranged doctor (Harry Reams) discovers that her clitoris is not in the usual place. The film's popularity helped launch a brief period of celebrity interest in explicit pornography, referred to as "porno chic." Even the fashion and cultural icon Jackie Kennedy Onassis was reportedly spotted leaving the World theatre after a showing of the box-office bonanza.

A New York judge with a flair for rhetorical flourish ruled this highly explicit exploration of clitoral arousal to be obscene, issuing his opinion on the film as "this feast of carrion and squalor," "a nadir of decadence" and "a Sodom and Gomorrah gone wild before the fire."[139] But prosecutors around the nation found it extremely difficult to persuade juries to ban the exhibition of any hardcore pornographic film fare. Such diverse communities as Binghamton (New York), Cincinnati (Ohio), Houston (Texas), and Sioux Falls (South Dakota) decided *Deep Throat* had redeeming social value.

Reworked Obscenity Definition

Those advocating legal restrictions on the rights of adults to read or see sexually explicit material gained support for their cause in June 1973 when a five-member majority of the U.S. Supreme Court, which by then included four of president Richard Nixon's appointees, rendered five major decisions concerning obscenity legislation and control. The lead case, *Miller v. California*, is the most significant.[140]

The majority opinion set forth revised guidelines for determining obscene material: "(1) whether the average person, applying contemporary community standards, would find that the work taken as a whole appeals to the prurient interest; (2) whether the work depicts or describes in a patently offensive way, sexual conduct specifically defined by the applicable state law; (3) whether the work taken as a whole lacks serious literary, artistic, political or scientific value." (A 1987 ruling placed the ultimate assessment of "serious value" in the hands of judges rather than juries.[141])

Of particular significance, the high court clarified that states are not required to adopt these guidelines and that they are free to establish other standards so long as they are no more restrictive than those outlined in this decision. Further, although legislatures could seek to suppress obscenity, the same majority noted that nothing in the U.S. Constitution required them to do so. In the case *State v. Henry* (Oregon, 1987), for instance, the Oregon Supreme Court ruled obscenity is a protected form of expression under the "free expression" provision of the state's constitution.

For all the efforts at greater specificity, the high court was still resorting to such indefinite and ill-defined concepts as prurient interest, patent offensiveness, and serious literary value—the meanings of which will necessarily vary depending on the experiences, outlooks, and predilections of the persons defining them. In fact, the newly refined guidelines proved to be no more definitive in practical terms than those they replaced.

Only eleven days after the *Miller* decision, the Georgia Supreme Court upheld the conviction of an Albany, Georgia, theatre manager for exhibiting *Carnal Knowledge* (1971), an R-rated movie about the sexual attitudes and obsessions of two male friends from college through middle age that a jury had found to be in violation of the state's anti-obscenity laws. The Georgia court's decision was appealed by the Motion Picture Association of America to the U.S. Supreme Court in the hope that the justices would reconsider their position allowing varying community standards of judgment.

In June 1974 the high court unanimously ruled that the movie did not meet the *Miller* standard for obscenity.[142] At the same time, the majority opinion confirmed that, although the various states may establish the whole state as the relevant community, they are not required to do so. In the absence of statewide standards, it allowed jurors to determine prurient appeal by drawing on their own knowledge of the views of the average person prevailing in the community from which they were selected.

The high court did stress that local juries do not have "unbridled discretion in determining what is 'patently offensive'" and noted that the Georgia courts in this case misunderstood the second part of the *Miller* test. The kind of material that is patently offensive, it explained, includes representations or descriptions of such things as "ultimate sex acts, normal or perverted, actual or simulated" and "masturbation, excretory functions, and lewd exhibition of genitals." With regard to *Carnal Knowledge*, the Court noted that, although "ultimate sexual acts" are understood to be taking place, there is "no exhibition whatsoever of the actors' genitals, lewd or otherwise, during these scenes," and "nudity alone is not enough to make material legally obscene under the Miller standards."

Despite various attempts at clarification and refinement, the high court's current guidelines have caused the same confusion and uncertainty, and led to the same waste of law enforcement and judicial resources that were experienced under the previous standards. It would seem a concept as elusive as obscenity—especially when it is considered in the context of artistic or social worth—defies legal definition or meaningful enforcement.

The task of devising legal mechanisms that suit the demands of one segment of society without limiting the freedom of other sectors remains as intractable as ever. Some law enforcement agencies continue to pursue purveyors of sexually explicit material. But a great many more have decided that, when weighed against such pressing problems as murder, rape, and robbery, along with the difficulty of getting a conviction, the prosecution of obscenity cases involving forewarned, consenting adults is not a high priority.

The changing tenor of the time is evident in the special counsel's 1998 report on the forty-nine-year-old President Bill Clinton's Oval Office escapades with a twenty-four-year-old White House intern, Monica Lewinsky. The Starr Report, with an advisory warning of sexual explicitness, went far beyond establishing that the president lied when he denied having sexual relations with "that woman." It included salacious specifics of various sexual encounters suggest its author, Kenneth Starr, also had as his purpose to humiliate and embarrass the president, and in the process, do the same to the intern.

Perhaps no details better illustrate the stress of salaciousness than the description of Clinton's use of a cigar as a sex toy and how he took calls from congressional members while receiving oral sex. The details of the racy report got extensive news coverage and provided late-night comedy show fodder. The entire country seemed to be talking about sex. Debates broke out about whether fellatio constituted sex. Citing the Bible, Clinton claimed it didn't, likely evoking cheers from teenage boys. Issued some two decades before the #MeToo rendering, the report's broad media coverage, no doubt painful for his wife and daughter, only seemed to enhance the promiscuous president's popularity.

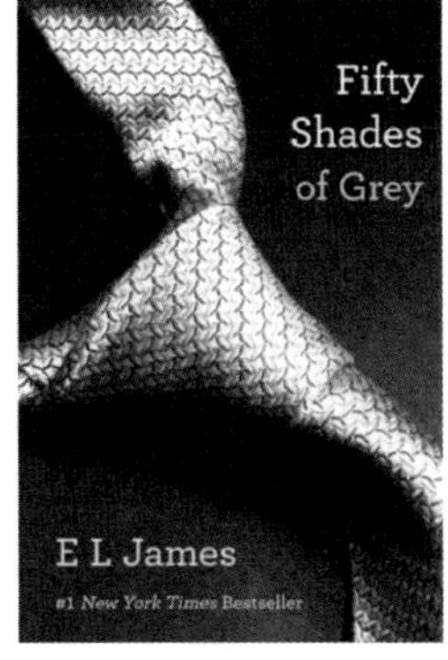

Deviance Takes Center Stage

In this new legal and cultural climate, the kinds of sexual deviance that got Edward Mishkin prison time have moved from the wings to the center stage and are evident across a wide range of media outlets. The explicitly sexual scenes involving the principal characters in E.L. James's 2011 salacious novel *Fifty Shades of Grey* feature bondage/discipline, dominance/submission, and sadism/masochism that leave little to the imagination. Morphed from web-published fan fiction into a blockbuster book and movie franchise, it is the number one bestselling book in the American book market over the past decade, according to NPD BookScan. Its progeny *Fifty Shades Darker* (2011), and *Fifty Shades Freed* (2012), occupy the second and third spots on the top-ten list of the decade's bestselling books.

The opening scene of the first episode of Showtime's *Billions* series, about the cat-and-mouse game of an ambitious federal attorney and a wealthy hedge-fund hustler, has no nudity but does demonstrate an innovative (and not-as-yet-proven-effective) treatment for minor burns. One of the male leads is on the floor securely tied while an unidentified woman straddles him to administer a golden shower on his bare chest, which she has just used as an ashtray to extinguish a burning cigarette slowly. As another case in point, episodes of HBO's hugely popular *Game of Thrones*, a medieval fantasy epic, featured rape, infanticide, cannibalism, beheading, crucifixion, castration, incest, murder, and dismemberment.

Such graphically sexual and violent series as *Billions* and *Game of Thrones* appeared on premium cable channels. Because the installation of cable involves disruption of city streets and the stringing of lines on utility poles, municipalities grant licenses known as franchises. Under the 1984 Cable Communications Policy Act, such franchisers had the authority to ban obscene or indecent cable-originated programming.

A cable subscriber challenged the constitutionality of a Miami ordinance regulating the distribution of indecent (but not obscene) material through cable television. The federal district court found the provisions of the law pertaining to "indecent material" constitutionally overbroad. On appeal, the eleventh circuit federal court of appeals held that the indecency prohibition that applies to broadcasting does not pertain to cable systems.[143] It characterized cable as a less-invasive medium without the same compelling justifications for content controls as broadcast media. The high court affirmed broadcast-cable distinction without opinion.

Regulation of Radio

The rise of national networks and the growing commercialism of broadcasting coincided with the development of radio regulation. The necessity to regulate radio signals stems from the fact that only one transmitter (which generates and sends the signals) can operate at the same time in the same place without interference. For intelligible communication to occur, just a small fraction of those wanting to broadcast can do so. Some form of selective licensing is required, given that the radio spectrum isn't wide enough to accommodate everyone who wishes to use it. With the advent of broadcasting in 1920, regulation of radio signals fell under the Radio Act of 1912, intended for point-to-point, ship-to-ship, ship-to-shore communication.

This legislation, enacted after the sinking of the luxury liner Titanic, forbade the operation of radio apparatus without a license from the Secretary of Commerce. After assuming this post in 1920, Herbert Hoover issued some 500 broadcast licenses over the next two years as the mania mounted, stimulating a demand for spectrum space, which the writers of the 1912 act had not anticipated. In response to the broadcasting boom, Hoover convened four annual radio conferences that included representatives from the giant electronic companies, various government agencies, along with smaller firms, a few inventors and engineers, and amateur radio operators. With each conference, Hoover expanded his regulatory powers.

Decisive legal developments in 1926 deprived the commerce secretary of any effective authority to regulate the radio spectrum. Without authorization, the Zenith Radio Corporation changed its hours of operation and jumped to a channel that had been ceded to the Canadian government. Commander Eugene McDonald, Zenith's president, took this action in order to force judicial clarification of the commerce secretary's authority. (McDonald's Chicago station had been allotted only two hours a week on a channel that General Electric's station in Denver could preempt at will.)

The Department of Commerce charged Zenith with criminal violation of the Radio Act of 1912. In April 1926, the U.S. District Court of Northern Illinois ruled that the provisions of this law were too vague and ambiguous to justify prosecution. Additionally, this federal court held that the commerce secretary's measures to restrict radio channels and hours of operation might be unconstitutional, since it had no basis in law.[144]

New Radio Act

When Congress assembled in December 1926, broadcasting was high on the legislative agenda. Senate and House conferees soon hammered out a compromise measure. In February of the following year, President Calvin Coolidge signed into law the resultant Radio Act of 1927. The new legislation reflected a number of Congressional concerns. Among the more significant were ownership of the airwaves, monopolistic practices, and censorship.

The new law stated in unequivocal terms the federal government's jurisdiction over the channels of interstate and foreign radio transmission. The use of such channels was to be granted to licensees for only limited periods of time. It was further provided that a license did not, in any way, confer ownership. In granting a new license or permitting the transfer of an existing one, the guiding standard was to be the "public interest, convenience or necessity"—a phrase borrowed from state public-utility laws of the late nineteenth century and from the Transportation Act of 1920.

Congress placed strict limits on the federal government's control over the content of radio transmissions. It prohibited the licensing authority from interfering with the right of free speech by means of radio communications. However, this prohibition did not extend to "obscene, indecent or profane language." Licensees were required to treat rival candidates equally, and not exercise any power of censorship over the material they broadcast.

Ringing declarations aside, these provisions would mean little unless they were enforced. The 1927 act, reflecting an accommodation of interests between the House and Senate, established a curious division of responsibilities between the commerce secretary and a newly created Federal Radio Commission (FRC). The commerce secretary retained such powers as fixing the qualifications of operators, inspecting station equipment, and assigning call letters.

In the assignment of call letters, radio stations to the east of the Mississippi River started with "W," as in WNBC, WOR, etc., and stations west of the Mississippi begin with the letter "K." Since a few stations were licensed before this plan took effect, there are a few exceptions to the "W" and "K" rule. The new five-member commission had broad administrative and quasi-judicial authority over applications for station licensees, renewals, and changes in facilities, for one year. At the end of that time, such power would revert to the commerce secretary. The commission was to continue merely as an advisory and appellate body.

The new commission got off to a shaky start. The act called for the appointment of the five commissioners by the president with the advice and consent of the Senate. Each commissioner was to represent one of five designated geographic districts within the United States. But the Senate confirmed only three of the president's appointees before adjournment. Moreover, the House failed to appropriate funds for salaries or supplies. Only through an emergency allocation of funds from the Department of Commerce was the new commission able to begin its herculean task of bringing order to the airwaves.

Congress eventually confirmed a full complement of salaried members to the commission. It also extended the FRC's authority for two successive years, thereafter making it a permanent regulatory agency. But the initial temporary status of the FRC made it susceptible to all sorts of pressures. As in other areas, the interests of the already powerful prevailed. The new law resulted in very few structural changes.

The giant electronic firms lobbied the new regulatory agency from the outset to keep out new disruptive entrants posing a threat to the existing power structure. For the most part, the FRC preserved the policies and practices of the commerce secretary. The division of the broadcasting band into low-power, local, middle-power, regional, and high-power, national, clear channels (a channel on which only one transmitter operates) continued.

Once again, the favored channels went to those firms with ample financial resources, superior technical equipment, highly skilled personnel, and first-rate legal representation. In practical terms, this meant that commercially sponsored stations were assigned most of the regional and clear channels. Stations operated by religious, educational, municipal, and other non-profit concerns remained relegated to daytime hours on low-power local channels.

Public Interest Criterion

The 1927 act provided very few specific guidelines for utilization of the broadcasting band. Congress said curiously little about commercial sponsorship. A single reference was included in the 7,000-word document, requiring the airing of an announcement as to the person, firm, or company paying for or furnishing certain broadcast material. The FRC was authorized to make special regulations applicable to radio stations engaged in "chain" or network broadcasting; however, the rationale for such regulations was not specified.

No attempt was made anywhere in the act to explain the rather amorphous concept of the public interest, convenience, or necessity. A standard of this type can be more readily applied to a public utility where the kind of service is specific—for example, gas, water, or electricity. The application of such a standard to broadcasting makes the problem considerably less tractable. Is the standard applicable to programming? If so, which "public" is to be considered? In a variegated and pluralistic society like the United States, there are likely to be many different publics when it comes to programming preferences.

The FRC grappled with these issues on a case-by-case basis. In its 1928 *Great Lakes* decision, the commission made it clear that the program service rendered by broadcasters would be considered when granting or withholding licenses.[145] The FRC denied the application of the Great Lakes Broadcasting Company for a license for a new station, on the grounds that the proposed program service would be of value interest to only a small proportion of the listeners living in the area. The commission stated that there was not sufficient room in the radio spectrum for every school of religious, political, social, and economic thought to have its separate broadcasting station.

Advertising, however, was excluded from the sanctions against special interest groups because its revenues furnished the economic support for broadcasting. Moreover, the FRC seemed to imply that programs appealing to a large segment of the listening audience were, by definition, in the public interest, convenience, and necessity. Those not served by such programming had the option of turning the dial. Of course, whether or not people listened to a profit-oriented station, its commercial imperatives in one way or another affected them. Those imperatives frequently worked to the detriment of minority interests.

Airwave Charlatan

The FRC did attempt to deal with manifestly flagrant commercial abuses. Not unlike cyberspace these days, broadcasting had attracted an assortment of fakers, quacks, and charlatans. Among the more striking to come before the microphones, and a significant figure in the development of radio regulation was John Romulus Brinkley—the infamous "goat gland" surgeon.[146]

Brinkley, who had obtained a medical degree from a diploma mill in Kansas

City for $100, used his broadcasting station—KFKB in the small farm community of Milford, in central Kansas to advertise an operation involving an implant of the gonads of a young goat inside the scrotum of human patients. The procedure was supposed to restore sexual vigor. Since sexual impotence, or "erectile dysfunction," is at times psychological, Brinkley was able to offer his listeners testimonials of positive results. The operation became so popular that he had to arrange for a shipment of goats from Arkansas.

Short on logic and reason and long on falsehoods and emotional appeals, Brinkley was on the air each day for several hours, primarily promoting his goat-gland surgery and treatment for diseased prostate glands. His station featured a broad range of entertainment fare as well. He also broadcast a program called the Medical Question Box, during which he diagnosed and prescribed medicines for his listeners solely based on letters he received from them. "Here's one from Tillie," said the diploma-mill doctor in a typical response. "She says she had an operation, had some trouble 10 years ago. I think the operation was unnecessary, and it isn't very good sense to have an ovary removed with the expectation of motherhood resulting therefrom. My advice to you is to use Women's Tonic No. 50, 67, and 61. This combination will do for you what you desire if any combination will, after three months' persistent use."[147]

To meet the growing demand for his medicines, Brinkley organized the Brinkley Pharmaceutical Association. Soon his number-coded concoctions—which contained little more than castor oil and aspirin—could be obtained from some 1500 druggists. He also developed a thriving mail-order business. From his drug operation alone, Brinkley is estimated to have grossed in excess of $700,000 a year.

Assigned a clear channel, Brinkley's station had fared well in the FRC 's allocations. But by 1930, powerful forces were arrayed against him. The *Kansas City Star* ran a series exposing his predatory practices, and medical authorities mounted a campaign to put him out of business. Later that year, on the basis of complaints filed by the American Medical Association, the FRC held a hearing on the renewal of the broadcasting license of KFKB.

As a result of this hearing, the FRC decided not to renew the station's license. Brinkley appealed the decision in federal court, claiming that the FRC action constituted censorship. In 1931, the U. S. Court of Appeals for the District of Columbia ruled that the FRC had acted within its powers. The commission had held that Brinkley's medical programs were inimical to public health and safety and therefore were not in the public interest.[148]

In its argument to the appeals court, the commission made clear that there had been no attempt on its part to scrutinize broadcast matter prior to its release and that review of past conduct did not constitute censorship. The court supported this position, holding that the commission was necessarily called upon to consider the character and quality of the service to be rendered and that in considering an application for renewal of license an important consideration is the past conduct of the applicant. Invoking the Biblical injunction "by their fruits ye shall know them," the appeals court left little doubt of the licensing authority's right to consider a station's past programming when a license renewal is sought.[149] It's a precedent for the broadcast media that prevails to this day.

Judicial affirmation of the FRC's right to review past programming practices had little immediate impact on the operations of the big commercial stations. The regulatory agency rarely refused to renew a license for anything other than the most flagrant violations. What's more, most commissioners were not unmindful of the job opportunities open to them if they cultivated the right connections. In fact, two of their number soon moved to profitable vice-presidential perches at CBS. In the years ahead, tenure with one of the regulatory agencies would often translate into a high-level position in private industry.

Communications Act of 1934

Prior to 1934, no single agency was charged with broad authority over communications. Several agencies—chiefly the Interstate Commerce Commission, the Postmaster General, and the Federal Radio Commission—partially regulated wired and radio transmissions. Congress put all interstate wired and wireless communication under the control of a single agency, the Federal Communications Commission.

The new legislation retained most of the provisions of the 1927 Act. As overseer of broadcasting, the new seven-member commission tended to follow the policies and practices of its predecessor agency. Many commissioners, well before their tenures expire, look to high paying positions at media outlets for future employment. Of course, how many have consciously used their appointments as stepping-stones to more lucrative private sector jobs cannot be confirmed with any certainty. In any event, relatively few commissioners serve full seven-year terms.

A 1952 amendment to the Communications Act prohibits commissioners who resign early from practicing before the agency for a year. But, by many accounts, this restriction is not strong enough to insulate commissioners from career considerations when they are promulgating rules or making decisions. And no such restriction is placed on FCC staff members, who—more often than not—actually make decisions that the commissioners later approve. As might be expected, large staff turnover is a common occurrence at the agency.

Whether those making decisions sometimes involving many millions of dollars always do so impartially remains a concern. In May 2011, for example, FCC Commissioner Meredith Baker, a well-respected experienced government official, accepted a job as senior vice president of governmental affairs for NBC Universal just four months after the commission approved its merger with telecommunications behemoth Comcast. Her switch in positions renewed ongoing concerns about the revolving door between regulatory agencies and private sector companies. Whatever her motives, the abrupt change from the regulator to the voice of the regulated has the appearance of impropriety.

The domain of administrative law encompasses technical orders and rules created by governmental agencies to deal with complex problems requiring specialized knowledge. Among the 100s of federal and state agencies now in existence, of particular importance to media outlets besides the Federal Communications Commission are the Federal Trade Commission, and the Food and Drug Administration. These are "independent" administrative agencies, so named because although they are part of the executive branch of government, they carry out the mandates of the legislative branch in specific government-regulated industries, such as over-the-air radio and television broadcasting. Adhering to a 1984 U.S. Supreme Court precedent, courts typically defer to reasonable agency interpretations when Congress has been silent or ambiguous on a topic.[150] Such deference generally results in upholding agency regulations.

Not only do administrative agencies have the power to make rules and enforce them with fines and other punitive measures, but they also serve a quasi-judicial function. Their administrative courts are usually the first to hear cases related to violations of agency rules. Congress provided the protocol for agency rulemaking and enforcement in the 1946 Administrative Procedure Act, which requires reasoned decision-making with explanations that are plausible and consistent. Several current justices on the high court have expressed concern about giving deference to the quasi-executive, quasi-legislative, and quasi-judicial powers exercised by these agencies.

Fairness Doctrine

Acting under the public interest standard, in a 1940 decision, the Federal Communications Commission prohibited editorializing by all commercial broadcasters.[151] Reversing itself nine years later, it articulated the "fairness doctrine," requiring broadcasters who editorialize and otherwise treat controversial issues of public importance, to do so fairly and sensibly by affording reasonable opportunities for contrasting points of view and allow the airing of opposing views on those issues.[152] In practical terms, this meant that programs on politics were required to include opposing opinions on the topic under discussion. In most circumstances, the licensee had considerable discretion to the format used in presenting an issue, the different shades of view offered, and the amount of time afforded.

In the latter half of the 1960s, the FCC developed and codified personal attack and political editorial rules to help ensure licensee fairness to issues, listeners, and candidates. These corollary rules mandated that broadcasters alert anyone subject to a personal attack in their programming and give them a chance to respond. Stations had to notify such persons (or groups) within a week of the attack. And they must send them tapes or transcripts of what was said and offer the opportunity to respond. The other rule required any broadcasters who endorsed or opposed candidates to allow other candidates for the same office reasonable chance for a response.

The doctrine sustained several challenges over the years. A lawsuit challenging it on First Amendment grounds reached the Supreme Court in 1969. The issue was whether the FCC's fairness doctrine regulations, concerning personal attacks made in the context of public issue debates and political editorializing, violate the First Amendment's freedom of speech guarantees. In a unanimous decision, although similar laws are unconstitutional when applied to the print media, the high court held that the doctrine and its correlatives were consistent with the First Amendment.

Writing for the majority, Justice Byron White stated that it is the rights of the viewers and listeners that is the most important, not the rights of the broadcasters. Referring to the scarcity of radio frequencies, he said they should be used to educate the public about controversial issues in a way that is fair and without bias so they can create their own opinions.

Although providing resounding support for broadcast regulation, the decision did note that if the doctrine's net effect reduces rather than enhances speech, the constitutional basis of it would require reconsideration. The FCC eventually decided that the fairness doctrine hurt the public interest and violated free speech rights guaranteed by the First Amendment, ceasing to enforce it in August 1987, but not scrapping the two corollary rules until the end of the century.

Regulating Broadcast Indecency

Because of its regulatory status, over-the-air radio and television has not felt the full impact of the changing moral climate of sexual expression. Regulating in the public interest, the Federal Communications Commission has particular latitude in controlling programming that threatens to undermine cultural morality. Specifically, it may enforce Section 1464 of the criminal code, which prohibits the broadcasting of "any obscene, indecent, or profane language."

The commission's enforcement powers include issuing a warning notice or letter of reprimand, imposing a monetary fine, placing conditions on renewal of a license, or revoking a license entirely (very rarely used). In exercising its authority to impose sanctions under law, it has consistently contended that broadcasting is subject to tighter strictures than other media, since it is available at the flick of a switch to young and old alike.

In the early 1970s, complaints poured into the commission concerning obscenity, indecency, and profanity resulting from a new format that had hit the airwaves dubbed "topless" radio—live telephone conversations entailing explicit sexual matters. The FCC ordered its staff to monitor such programs. In 1973, it imposed a $2,000 fine on the Sanderling Broadcasting Corporation, licensee of WGLD-FM in Oak Park, Illinois.

The station featured a midday talk show with a male moderator who invited women to call in and discuss the intimate details of their sex lives on the air. The commission concluded that a broadcast in which a female caller talked about the fun of performing oral sex on the driver of a moving car to break the monotony met the prevailing definition of obscenity in that it appealed to a prurient interest in sex and was patently offensive to the contemporary community standards of the broadcast media.

The regulatory agency stressed that this definition was being applied to the special case of radio broadcasting: "This is peculiarly a medium designed to be received and sampled by millions in their homes, cars, on outings, or even as they walk the streets with transistor radio to the ear, without regard to age, background or degree of sophistication."[153]

The licensee elected to pay the forfeiture, and did not appeal. But the Illinois Citizens Committee and the Illinois Division of the American Civil Liberties Union petitioned the Federal Court of Appeals in Washington, D. C., for review. This court found in favor of the FCC, noting that the probable presence of children in the audience is relevant to a determination of obscenity.

Seven Dirty Words

Does the pervasive presence of radio and television justify a more limited First Amendment protection for broadcasters than for print practitioners? The first full U. S. Supreme Court review of the issue came in 1978. The case on which the high court ruled involved a broadcast by WBAI-FM, a listener-supported station in New York City owned by the Pacifica Foundation. Early one afternoon in 1973, the station, in a program about language, featured a twelve-minute selection from a comedy album by George Carlin, in which the comedian discussed the "seven dirty words" that could not be said on radio or television.

The words describe female organs, excrement, sexual intercourse, sodomy, and incest, which Carlin described as the "ones that will curve your spine [and] grow hair on your hands." He gave examples of their current usage and varying meanings, and provided a bit of etymological background on some of them. For instance, in commenting on the ancient Anglo-Saxonism for the sex act, Carlin noted: "It's a great word, fuck, nice word, easy word, cute word, kind of. Easy to say. One syllable, short u, fuh ends with a kuh. Right? A little something for everyone. Fuck. Good word. Kind of a proud word, too. Who are you? I am FUCK. FUCK OF THE MOUNTAIN. Tune in again next week to FUCK OF THE MOUNTAIN."

The comedy monologue, preceded by a warning about the potentially offensive words, had been played during a program about contemporary society's attitudes toward language. The FCC received a complaint from a man who happened to hear the broadcast on his car radio. He noted that his young son was with him when he listened to the show and that "any child could have been turning the dial and tuned in that garbage." (It later turned out that the man was a member of the media watchdog group Morality in Media and that the "young son" whom he said was with him in his car when they heard the monologue was fifteen years old at the time.)

Acting on that single complaint, the FCC ruled that the language used in the Carlin monologue was "indecent," because it depicted sexual and excretory activities and organs in a manner patently offensive by contemporary community standards for the broadcast media at a time of day when children were likely to be in the audience. The commission reprimanded the station and issued a "declaratory order" forbidding the broadcast of indecent language. The Pacifica Foundation, licensee of WBAI-FM, appealed the FCC order and, in March 1977, the Court of Appeals for the District of Columbia ruled that the agency's ban was an unconstitutionally vague and overbroad exercise in censorship. The FCC then appealed the decision to the U.S. Supreme Court.

In July 1978, in a decision that aroused considerable controversy, a five-member majority of the high court held that the FCC may regulate the broadcasting of words that are patently offensive, even though they are not obscene.[154] Associate Justice John Paul Stevens, writing for the narrow majority, cited the broadcast media's "uniquely pervasive presence in the lives of all Americans." And stated that the fact that broadcasting is "uniquely accessible to children, even those too young to read" as the reasons for restricting the First Amendment rights of broadcasters.

In so supporting the FCC action, the majority seemed to affirm a more restrictive rationale for broadcast regulation, based on the intrusiveness of radio and television rather than on the scarcity of spectrum space. "Patently offensive, indecent material presented over the airwaves confronts the citizen, not only in public," wrote Justice Stevens, "but also in the privacy of the home, where the individual's right to be let alone plainly outweighs the First Amendment rights of an intruder."

Civil libertarians could find some consolation in the court's emphasis on context, as well as content. Justice Stevens suggested, for instance, that an occasional expletive in the telecast of an Elizabethan comedy would not justify the imposition of sanctions. Time of day was also an important consideration. The court implied that the case for regulation would be far weaker if allegedly patently offensive material was broadcast late at night. Recalling an earlier case in which it was noted that a "nuisance" may be the right thing in the wrong place—like a pig in the parlor instead of the barnyard," Justice Stevens stated: "We simply hold that when the Commission finds that a pig has entered the parlor, the exercise of its regulatory power does not depend on proof that the pig is obscene."

In a sharply worded dissent, Associate Justice William J. Brennan pinpointed the cultural conflicts inherent in any FCC foray into the regulation of program content. "As surprising as it may be to individual Members of this Court," he asserted, "some parents may actually find Mr. Carlin's unabashed attitude towards the seven 'dirty words' healthy, and deem it desirable to expose their children to the manner in which Mr. Carlin defuses the taboo surrounding the words." He accused the majority of "a depressing inability to appreciate that in our land of cultural pluralism, there are many who think, act and talk differently from the Members of this Court, and who do not share their fragile sensibilities."

Despite its victory in the *Pacifica* case, the FCC exercised considerable restraint over the next decade. It held that prohibitable "indecent" language consisted only of the repeated use of Carlin's "seven dirty words" between the hours of 6:00 a.m. and 10:00 p.m., when children are most likely to be in the audience. Applying this time-of-day standard, the regulatory agency brought no indecency enforcement actions over the next decade or so.

Exposed Flesh & Fleeting Expletives

In what might be called "the bare breast brouhaha," every corner of the broadcasting world felt the vibrations from the split-second exposure of Janet Jackson's right breast at the 2004 Super Bowl halftime show. Performing "Rock Your Body" alongside "surprise" guest Justin Timberlake with him pursuing her around the stage, she'd pause periodically, bending forward, pushing her rear end into his crouch. As they began the final lines of the song, the provocative duo climbed the stairs to the center part of the stage. While singing the lyric, "I'm gonna have you naked by the end of this song," Timberlake pulled off her black leather breastplate. An estimated ninety-million viewers, at least those who hadn't blinked at the precise moment of the exposure, got a fleeting glimpse of Jackson's areola and sun-shaped nipple shield.

By many accounts, the CBS switchboard nearly exploded from the call volume. Could civilization itself survive such a sight? The FCC reportedly received 120,000 complaints, prompting it to investigate and eventually fine the network $550,000 for violating indecency rules. Most protests turned out to originate from the Parents Television Council. Its organized campaign made the regulatory commission increasingly vigilant for instances of indecency.

Following the costliest 9/19th of a second in broadcast history, and the resultant FCC crackdown, heavily-fined vulgar shock-jock Howard Stern, decided to vacate his nationally syndicated sex-charged one-hour terrestrial radio show. He signed a five-year deal worth $500 million with Sirius Satellite Radio, a subscription-based satellite radio service exempt from the FCC's broadcast regulations. At a time of increased FCC concern about airwave pollution, a frequent Stern guest, future president Donald Trump, when conversing with him often made crude and demeaning comments about women. Even his daughter Ivanka wasn't out of bounds in the twosome's salacious exchanges.

In 2006, the year Stern started his lucrative new job, Congress increased fines for indecent expression ten-fold from $32,500 to $325,000 for each incident or violation. The FCC had become more hands-on in dealing with indecency during the administration of George W. Bush, seeking to punish broadcasters in several highly publicized events. These included U2 lead singer Bono's exclamation, in accepting a Golden Globe Award, that "this is really, really fucking brilliant." Another occurred when singer-and-actress Cher, after receiving her "life achievement" trophy at 2002 Billboard Music Awards, gushed "people have been telling me I'm on the way out every year, right? So fuck 'em."

Well known for being well-known, presenters Paris Hilton and Nicole Richie, who had burst onto the entertainment scene with their 2003 mega-hit reality show *The Simple Life*, referred to a sex act and a body function during the Billboard Music Awards that same year. Other cases involved fleeting nudity. In an episode of ABC's hit television show *NYPD Blue*, for example, the nude buttocks of an adult female character were visible for some seven seconds and the side of her breast for an instant.

In its initial consideration, the FCC had reasoned that there was no violation because Bono was swearing in a non-sexual way. In 2004, however, it declared for the first time that it would treat the airing of inappropriate words and images as "indecent" even if they appeared only briefly and in passing. Applying this new rule, it held that the exclamations of the presenters and award recipients, as well as the broadcasting of fleeting nudity, violated the prohibition on indecency. In these zealous pursuits, the regulatory agency chased nudity and profanity off the airwaves.

The broadcast networks challenged the FCC's new formulation of the ban on indecent expression on two distinct grounds: that the commission adopted it improperly, and that it violated the First Amendment. The appeals court for the Second Circuit agreed, striking it down. But in *FCC v. Fox Television Stations*, decided in 2009, the U.S. Supreme Court, in a five-to-four decision, held that the new rule had correctly been enacted but did not address the constitutional issue.[155]

Three years later, after the Second Circuit again struck down the rule, in July 2010, on First Amendment grounds, the case came back to the high court for consideration of the constitutional question. In a unanimous decision, it vacated the FCC's rules on "fleeting expletives" and brief nudity saying it had not given networks adequate notice of its policies and that they were overly vague, thereby denying those fined due process of law.[156] The high court added that it saw no necessity for overruling the 1978 *Pacifica* decision because technological change overtook its reasoning.

Cyber Porn Prevails

While adults have ready access to all sorts of sexually explicit material, the question remained whether government can constitutionally shield minors from exposure to such gratification of the senses in cyberspace. The crucial consideration in *Reno v. ACLU* (1997) concerned whether government's approach to protecting minors from indecency on radio and television had applicability to the internet. The U.S. Supreme Court voted 7-2 to strike down the Communications Decency Act (CDA), a provision of the 1996 Telecommunications Act that outlawed transmissions of sexually explicit and indecent materials on computer networks to anyone under age eighteen.[157]

The Justice Department argued that the *Pacifica* ruling should control the case, but the high court, in an opinion by Justice John Paul Stevens, distinguished that decision on three primary grounds. First, unlike the airwaves, the government doesn't have the authority to restrict sexual content on the internet, which doesn't "belong" to the public and has no long-standing tradition of regulation. Second, unlike the situation in *Pacifica*, where the FCC allowed indecent programming during hours when children were unlikely to be in the audience, no similar "safe haven" was possible on the internet. Third, spectrum scarcity does not apply to the internet.

To deny minors access to potentially harmful speech, with echoes of the high court's earlier rejection of the Hicklin rule, Stevens explained, the legislation restricts "a large amount of speech that adults have a constitutional right to receive and to send to one another." Most significantly, he stated that the internet, highly pervasive and accessible, is a "unique" medium deserving full constitutional protection. This decision didn't affect Section 230 of the decency act protecting internet service providers from being liable for the words of others, and it remains the law.

As a result of a string of court rulings on the broad categories of sexually-oriented material, such as pornography (sexually explicit), indecency (patently offensive), profanity (vulgar, coarse, or sacrilege), and hard-core pornography (obscenity), the governments ban only the latter altogether. Three sections of federal law make it a felony to produce obscene material through interstate and foreign commerce knowingly or to knowingly transport obscene materials (including via a computer service) for sale or distribution purposes.[158] After over a century of censorship, the slippery legal concept of "obscenity" has mostly evaporated with prosecutions for the sale, distribution, or exhibition of even hard-core pornography a rare occurrence.

Any agreed-upon legal definition has proved elusive and perhaps irrelevant in the age of the internet. The practical reality is that advances in technology and changing social mores have overwhelmed the execution of obscenity law. Search engines will instantly find seemingly limitless websites that often offer free access to graphically explicit videos with the mere click of a mouse. These included anal sex, lesbian sex, oral sex, bondage, masturbation, sadomasochism, and just about anything else lurking in the mind's dark recesses.

Chapter 5

Movie Matters

Movies allow us to indulge our deepest wishes and hidden desires. They offer excitement without physical risk. They furnish answers to questions about how we should behave that, in an earlier era, would have been provided exclusively by the examples of people we knew. We put ourselves in the shoes of the actors, empathizing with the characters they portray and experiencing the whole range of their emotions. Our minds get caught up in the compelling images and sounds, and travel mentally, as it were, through the proscenium arch into the dramatic events played out on the screen.

A movie constitutes a separate reality of sorts, one full of seemingly living images. Those who reside in these "alternate realities" can command a great deal of our psychic energy and attention, affecting our thoughts and feelings about everything from fashion to fascism. Few forces in the world have been more influential in shaping the way we see ourselves and our social environment, and who controls this cultural machinery is no small matter of concern. These days making movies for theatrical release is a small outpost in a vast media universe run by agents, lawyers, and financiers, approving or rejecting one project of another, with little or no involvement in actual production. But from the late 1920s to the early 1950s, the legendary "movie moguls" held sway over every aspect of filmmaking from script to screen. And millions went to "the movies" at least twice a week regardless of what appeared on the screen.

The movie mogul epithet came into use about 1915 to describe the public image of these enterprising immigrants—part grand potentate, part barbarian invader.[159] Born in small towns in Germany, Hungary, Poland and Russia, they rose from such modest occupations as a furrier, haberdasher, trolley bus driver, and junk dealer to reign over celluloid empires, setting standards for shooting and editing that prevail to the present. By the dawn of 1940s, they were among the highest paid executives in the world. The rags-to-riches largely Jewish immigrants from central and eastern Europe built huge industrial complexes employing an elaborate division of labor and churned out hundreds of movies every year.

In addition to production facilities, they owned distribution networks and cinemas, hired stars, and delivered such enticements as sound and color. In the process, aided and abetted by Wall Street banking firms, this cartel of vertically and horizontally integrated corporations channeled all cinematic creativity through a set of narrow apertures. Although these companies centered production facilities in or near the once sleepy town of Hollywood, the name coming to symbolize the whole industry, they located their administrative offices in New York City, close to the center of finance. The amount of capital necessary for the conversion to sound in the late 1920s, and the economic crisis gripping the nation, led to corporate upheaval in many movie companies and a reordering of the entire industry.

Command of the Illusion Factory

When the dust had settled, eight companies dominated the industry. The Big Five—those involved in all three phases of the movie industry, production, distribution, exhibition, were Loew's-M-G-M, Warner Bros. Pictures, Paramount, Fox Film (20th Century-Fox in 1935), and RKO. Among the Little Three were Universal, Columbia, and United Artists. Of these, Universal and Columbia were producers-distributors, and United Artists was solely a distributor. These companies controlled most of the first-run theatres in major American cities where movies premiered. Through iron-clad contracts, they indirectly controlled almost all neighborhood and second-run movies houses as well.

The movie industry had become highly centralized and concentrated at the expense of smaller, less well-financed enterprises. The adoption of sound technology in the late 1920s and the expansion of distribution networks and theatre chains had made these companies much more dependent on their principal sources of financing, particularly the Morgan and Rockefeller banking interests. As the economic crisis in the nation worsened, movie firms slipped out of the hands of the founders and into those of the backers.

Some foes of high finance's dealings in the movie industry turned to the works of the at-once revered and reviled German political philosopher Karl Marx to understand the implications of this involvement. One of the revolutionary nineteenth-century thinker's most significant passages for media analysis appears in *The German Ideology* of 1845, an early work written jointly with his lifelong friend and collaborator Friedrich Engels when Marx was in his late twenties. "The class which has the means of material production at its disposal," they argued, "has control at the same time over the means of mental production, so that thereby, generally speaking, the ideas of those who lack the means of mental production are subject to it."[160]

This notion of owning the means of "mental production" opens up several possible avenues for empirical investigation. These include the connection between ownership and control, the relations between producers and owners, the process through which ideas favorable to the already powerful make their way into movies, news shows, and other entertainment fare, as well as the dynamics of reception involved as audience members adopt these ideas as their own.

Marxist-inspired studies of the movie industry in the 1930s tended to take such passages as accepted doctrine rather than as guidelines, and they focused only on the issue of ownership of the means of production. Using elaborate charts and detailed financial data, two British analysts showed how, through control of sound recording systems and ownership of the major companies, the most powerful financial groups in the United States, if not the capitalist world had gained nearly complete control over the movie industry. "Whether the movies will regain their former financial success," they ominously concluded, "ultimately depends on whether the Morgans and the Rockefellers will find it in their interest in the increasing change in American life to provide the masses with the type of pictures that alone will induce them to flock to their cinemas."[161]

Although these analysts provided useful insights into potential sources of control over the process of moviemaking, they said nothing about how such control might actually work. Nor did they give any indication of why financiers would want to make movies that "the masses" find unappealing. There is little reason to doubt that for banker and studio executive alike the ability to make money was the principal yardstick of success—as much money as possible. The path to profit was in the production of movies with broad audience appeal eschewing anything provocative or disruptive that might diminish box-office revenues.

When the movie industry became another bastion of big business, the men of Wall Street did attempt to play a direct role in running some of the studios. The result of such meddling hurt profits, as financial wizard Joseph P. Kennedy (presidential father to be), himself a wheeler-dealer in moviemaking, pointed out in a 1936 study of Paramount. Given carte blanche, he interviewed virtually everyone with a significant role in turning out movies. In the process, Kennedy found gross mismanagement and inefficiency at all levels. Although he likely wanted the Paramount presidency himself, the bankers and creditors controlling the company's board of directors, which he had advised shaking up, passed on him taking over but did put other seasoned movie men into positions of power.[162]

By the end of the 1930s, men experienced in the entertainment business ran all the major movie companies. Each studio functioned like a small fiefdom ruled by a feudal lord whose power over his charges was absolute. His ultimate weapon was to banish one of his minions from the manor. Rigid organization and tight production schedules allowed most studios to operate smoothly and efficiently. Virtually every aspect of production functioned effectively in an interlocking structure. Since production was "institutionalized"–built into the rules and routines of the moviemaking process, hardly any opportunity existed for challenging the inequities of the capitalist system even though many with radical inclinations were on the studio payrolls.

Each major studio made between forty and fifty feature films a year. To turn out that many movies required immense staff. Most production personnel were under long-term contracts, the connective tissue of the studio system, including producers, directors, screenwriters, cinematographers, art directors, costume designers, sound recording experts, and other technical staff. While under contract, an employee could not quit joining another studio, refuse to work on an assigned project or renegotiate for increased compensation.

Beneath the glittering cloak of glamor and fame's dazzling allure, a star's lot gradually took on the reality, if not the appearance, of serfdom with all the gradations of servitude. Ruling the studio lots like satraps, the movie moguls or their underlings could order leading players to alter facial appearances, change hairstyles, body weight,

and clothing choices, modify biographical details, and assume new names often anglicizing them. Kirk Douglas started life Issur Danielovitch, Edward Robinson as Emanuel Goldenberg, Doris Day as Doris Kapplehoff, and Margarita Carman Cansino metamorphosed into the alluring Rita Hayworth.

If stars refused to play a role, the studio would suspend without pay, and when they returned to work, the time away was added to their contracts. In addition to holding them to heavy work schedules, the studio required them to attend publicity functions and promote their pictures. Contracts usually allowed for stars to be loaned out or rented to other studios. The lending studio generally received about 75 percent more than the star's actual salary to compensate for its temporary loss. The borrowing studio benefited from the star's services without incurring the cost of a long-term contract.

The conditions of moviemaking were more exacting at some studios than at others. At Warner Bros. Pictures, the emphasis was on fast and efficient production. Unit supervisors tightly managed the whole production process in what amounted to a factory-like, assembly-line approach to moviemaking. Producers, directors, writers, actors, cinematographers, editors, and technical staff were shuffled relentlessly from project to project. Studio supervisors strictly limited vacations and canceled them at a moment's notice. Although individual directors could exercise some discretion, supervisors ordinarily kept them on a taut leash.

Curtailing Content

In the 1920s, an impatient and indecorous spirit seemed to possess the population—especially the young. F. Scott Fitzgerald, oracle of what came to be called the Jazz Age, saw the whole of society going hedonistic. The "flapper" with her short skirt and hair and her painted face competed with the virginal girl next door as the feminine ideal. Although Prohibition was the law of the land, bathtub gin flowed freely, and speakeasies sprang up everywhere. The saxophone replaced the violin as the dominant instrument at dances. Young and old alike intimately embraced as they moved in syncopation to the sensual sounds. The roar of automobile engines sounded a clarion call to the libido as well. Many affluent young people apparently thought nothing of jumping into the car and driving off-away from the prying eyes of parents, chaperons, and neighbors.

The movie industry and the mishaps and malfeasances of its derelict denizens became a focal point for the fury of those who felt the nation was sinking into a moral abyss. Frightened industry leaders hired the politically well-connected Will H.

Hays, elder in the Presbyterian Church, former chairman of the Republican National Committee, and current postmaster general, to head the Motion Picture Producers and Distributors of America (MPPDA)—a new trade association created to supersede previous, less effective attempts to counteract the threat of government censorship of movies and to create favorable publicity for the industry.

Under his leadership, this mouthful of an organization quickly launched a successful public relations campaign to defeat a Massachusetts censorship bill subject to a referendum. Publicized by press agents as "movie czar," Hays was, in fact, no more than an employee of the studio heads whose job was to promote integrity and generate profits in the movie industry. As part of its public relations campaign, the Hays Office—the MPPDA's moniker —initiated several measures. A "morals clause" in all contracts permitted studios to discharge an employee at the first warning of "moral turpitude." In addition to establishing Central Casting to regulate extras' employment, the industry purged its rolls of prostitutes, people with criminal records, and those who pursued their calling on the casting couch.

Other measures included the production of publicity shorts showing stars as regular folks whose lives were not terribly different from those of their fans. Industry insiders knew better. One short looked in on gamin-like Marion Davies as she cleaned her modest apartment. There was no hint that she was press magnate William Randolph Hearst's mistress and lived with him in medieval splendor at Hearst Castle in San Simeon, California. Another presented leading lady Alma Rubens at home with her mother. She was, in fact, a heroin addict and in a few years would be dead. The industry also launched a publicity campaign to discourage young women from migrating to the movie capital, and it sponsored a Studio Club to house female aspirants already in Hollywood.

As the industry's mail-order Moses, Hays sought to halt Hollywood's worship of false gods. He took several measures to dissuade producers from making movies that might provoke censure. He got them to submit synopses of all plays, novels, and stories for scrutiny before filming, and he set up a Studio Relations Committee to keep them informed about the kinds of material various states considered censorable.

This agency codified a list of "Don'ts and Be Carefuls" in 1927 based on a study of the specific rejections and deletions made by municipal and state censorship boards. The list of "Don'ts" contained eleven items that could not be depicted on the screen: profanity (either by title or lip); licentious or suggestive nudity; illegal drug trafficking; any inference of sexual perversion; "white slavery" (the interstate transportation of women for immoral purposes); sex hygiene and venereal diseases; childbirth; children's sexual organs; ridicule of the clergy; willful offense to any nation, race, or creed; and "miscegenation" or interracial coupling.

The list of "Be Carefuls" comprised twenty-five subjects. Areas in which special care needed to be exercised included such things as the use of the flag, international relations, arson, firearms, theft, robbery, brutality, murder techniques, methods of smuggling, hangings or executions, sympathy for criminals, sedition, cruelty to children or animals, the sale of women, rape or attempted rape, "first-night" or honeymoon scenes, a man and woman in bed together, deliberate seduction of girls, the institution of marriage, surgical operations, the use of drugs, and excessive or lustful kissing. These two lists of admonitions were based on precedent, not principle, and provided little immunity from what promised to be enduring and worsening censorship problems for the movie industry.

With the general introduction of sound in 1929, criticism of movie content magnified. Some of the loudest complaints about immorality in talkies came from Catholics, who were twenty million strong by the late 1920s, roughly seventeen percent of the population. Because the Catholic Church wasn't divided into diverse denominations, it was far more capable of unified action than were Protestant groups. When movie dialogue began to offend this ecclesiastical giant, the Hays Office swiftly acted to placate it. Early in 1930, industry leaders adopted a revamped and expanded version of the "Don'ts and Be Carefuls" by a Jesuit priest and a lay Catholic publisher of a trade journal for movie exhibitors.

Production Code

Officially called the Motion Picture Production Code, this new set of guidelines detailed various offenses that could not be committed against middle class morality. For example, the audience was never to be enticed into sympathizing with crime, wrongdoing, evil, or sin. No aspect of the law-divine, natural, or human-was ever to be ridiculed. Vulgarity, obscenity, and profanity were to be avoided. The sanctity of marriage and the home was to be upheld. Although adultery and illicit sex were recognized as occasionally necessary plot devices, they were not to be explicitly treated or justified, or attractively presented. Sexual relationships, even within marriage, were to be downplayed. Any display of excessive or lustful kissing and embracing was prohibited.

Hays hailed the new self-regulatory rules for moviemaking as a clear indication of the industry's ability to police itself responsibly in the era of talking pictures. But enforcement mechanisms once again proved to be weak. The major companies agreed to submit each movie they produced to the Studio Relations Committee before sending it to the laboratory for printing. If a movie was found to violate any provision, it could not be released until necessary changes were made. A panel of three members, selected on a rotation basis from the principal producers, served as an appeals board with the power to overrule the decisions of the committee. Because they knew that their own movies might come under scrutiny, the members of the rotating panel were often reluctant to support deletions in rival productions.

Frisky "Fallen" Women

Cinematic depictions of illicit love affairs, risqué situations, off-color conversations, and frisky "fallen" women caused great consternation. Few movies at the time dealt

with sexual matters more blatantly than *Baby Face* (1933). A sultry Barbara Stanwyck plays a working-class predator who uses her body to bargain for career favors moving up floor-by-floor, sexual conquest by sexual conquest, into the upper reaches of a banking firm. Like other "fallen-women" features, it shows no actual sex. Camera work and the musical score suggest what was happening. After each of the title character's assumed sexual conquests, the camera tilts a few floors farther up the side of the bank building, usually accompanied by a honky-tonk rendition of "St. Louis Woman."[163]

The Roman Catholic Church, apparently disillusioned with the Hays Office's failure to enforce the new code, conducted a vigorous campaign to reform screen conduct. At their annual convention in 1933, Catholic bishops decided to organize a national Legion of Decency. Catholics in the 104 dioceses nationwide were entreated to repeat or sign a pledge condemning the corrupting effect of salacious movies on public morals. A Catholic boycott of movie theatres in Philadelphia brought national attention to the ecclesiastical crusade. Theatre boycotts were threatened in other locales as well. Box office receipts tumbled in heavily Catholic neighborhoods, especially in the big cities, and the message went out to the movie industry that it was time to seek salvation.

Production Code Administration

With remarkable alacrity, the Catholic Church obtained the power to exert a strong moral influence over movies. In this regard, it has often been criticized for imposing sectarian principles on a pluralistic society. But the Catholic moral posture wasn't very different from that of other major religious, civic, and educational groups at the time. The Legion of Decency campaign to reform the movie industry quickly garnered support from major Protestant and Jewish groups. It also received ringing editorial endorsements from newspapers across the country.

The marshaling of such a large and solid body of highly influential groups and institutions strongly and actively opposed to prevailing production practices could not be ignored by the movie industry without dire economic consequences. The big studios, already caught in the throes of the deepening depression, heeded the call to repent. In the summer of 1934, the Hays Office disbanded the Studio Relations Committee and replaced it with the more formidable Production Code Administration (PCA). The members of MPPDA agreed not to release or distribute any movie unless it received a certificate of approval signed by the director of the PCA. To keep this new enforcement machinery well oiled, producers were charged a fee based on the total production cost of each picture submitted for approval.

The PCA was empowered to impose a $25,000-per-day fine against any defiant MPPDA member who sold, distributed, or exhibited a movie not bearing the seal of approval. An advertising code became binding the following year, with a fine ranging from $1000 to $5000 for failure to honor its dictates. In addition, the MPPDAs' Title Registration Bureau, which had been established in 1925 to eliminate duplication of movie titles, had the authority to prohibit the use of salacious, indecent, or obscene titles.

Will Hays placed Joseph Ignatius Breen, a devout Catholic and father of six, in charge of the new self-regulatory apparatus. The rotund Breen's hail-fellow manner hid a deep-seated obsession with Jewish influence in the movie industry. By the 1930s, Jews occupied positions in the upper reaches of Hollywood far out of proportion to their numbers in the general population. Of the eight leading companies, men of orthodox Jewish parentage ran six, and Jews played important roles at most stages in the development of the other two. The operators of the major theatre chains and most powerful talent agencies were Jewish, as well. So were the lawyers who transacted most of the movie industry's business.

Aside from basic bigotry, the reasons for Breen's preoccupation with this strong Jewish presence in the movie colony are far from clear. A recent study suggests that Jews had a conservative and even anti-Semitic influence on the making of movies.[164] The studio heads hesitated to hire Jewish actors and made them change their names when they did employ them. They also discouraged the use of Jewish themes and characters. Their ethnicity supposedly made them so insecure that they hungered for esteem, respectability, and, most of all, assimilation. The principal way to achieve this, they believed, was to have their movies reflect an understanding and acceptance of broadly shared American values.

The new director of the PCA didn't see it this way at all. Breen attributed almost everything he didn't like about the movie industry to the Jewishness of its leaders, whom he referred to at various times as "dirty lice" "the scum of the earth," a "foul bunch, crazed with sex...and ignorant in all matters having to do with sound morals."[165] His correspondence is replete with such remarks and reveals a great deal about his attitudes toward the studio heads during his long tenure as industry watchdog. He seemingly saw himself as the one man who could curb the sinful ways of the Jewish movie moguls, and he was quick to notify them if he felt they were circumventing the code's moral mandates.

For all his bigotry, Breen was not indifferent to the box office. Producers could-and often did-finagle and maneuver. Moreover, despite what he said behind their backs, Breen was polite if not deferential in his dealings with industry leaders. Men whose benediction could bestow fame and fortune, and whose disfavor could bring banishment, were not about to tolerate ethnic epithets from an employee—even if an entire legion of irate Catholics came to his support. To a considerable extent, Breen was successful in alleviating licensing tensions. In the process, however, the PCA became more restrictive than many of the state and municipal censorship boards. Loose morals, exposed flesh, and bedroom antics were soon in scant supply on screens across the country.

Newsreels

Moviegoers got a cinematic glimpse of world events through newsreels that provided a source of current affairs, information, and entertainment. A form of the short documentary film, they were typically part of a movie theatre's bill of fare from the 1910s into the 1960s, with a running time of about ten to fourteen minutes.[166]

Most movie studios had a newsreel division. Although they were more a product of show business than journalism, newsreels occasionally presented events of great magnitude. They covered such events as the burning of the Hindenburg, the assassination of Alexander I of Yugoslavia, the Lindbergh kidnapping and subsequent trial of Bruno Hauptmann, and the Japanese bombing late in 1937 of the American flat-bottomed gunboat USS Panay while it was anchored in the Yangtze River. The incident occurred after its military forces had invaded China, where they later massacred some 300,000 civilians and prisoners of war in the city of Nanking (now known as Nanjing).

In the spring of 1935, a new hybrid appeared on movie screens across the country called *The March of Time*, based on the thirty-minute weekly radio news series broadcast from 1931 to 1945.[167] Combining documentary footage and dramatic recreations, it appeared in movie theatres from 1935 to 1951, produced once a month by Time Inc. at the cost of $50,000 to $75,000 per issue. Running about twenty minutes, it had well-constructed scripts and used the full panoply of feature-film techniques and technology. Music was carefully arranged and, at times, composed.

In 1938, it began to focus on a single theme within each production. It presented issues with open partisanship, not attempting even pseudo-objectivity. The intent was to maintain a controversial and stimulating cinematic vehicle to arouse an audience that had come to regard news in the movies as soporific. Segments dealt with breadlines and poverty, with demagogic politicians and bureaucrats, with unemployment, and with the shadows of war, among other pressures of the day.

In January 1938, *The March of Time* released its first single-topic issue. It was probably the most controversial release this organization ever put out, not because of the single-topic format but because the subject was "Inside Nazi Germany, 1938." Footage from Nazi Germany included shots of Jews sitting on isolated yellow benches set aside for them, and of anti-Jewish graffiti painted onto shop windows around the city. The producers supplemented these shots with reenactments. They included propaganda activities, military men pursuing training, an elderly German couple listening with trepidation to a Hitler radio address, political prisoners, concentration camps, German censors examining mail, and a storm trooper collecting funds from a homemaker.

The isolationist outcry that arose over this depiction of Nazi Germany echoed even in the halls of Congress. Movie exhibitors were reluctant to show pictures that touched on European or Asian politics. Many regarded the exhibition of such a film as giving Hitler a forum for addressing the U.S. public. But the film was a strong indictment of the Nazi leader and his brutal anti-Semitic policies, and the newsreel was, by now,

firmly ensconced in the programs of thousands of movie houses. For the next three years, many of the *March of Time* releases, unabashedly anti-Fascist, championed greater American involvement in the European crisis. At its peak, an estimated twenty-five million U.S. moviegoers a month saw the provocative newsreels.

Such revelations about the persecution of Jews in Nazi Germany were unusual in the media environment of the 1930s. Deep-seated anti-Jewish sentiment had long been rife in American society. Jews suffered discrimination in employment, at social clubs and resort areas, with quotas on enrollment at colleges, and in the purchase of specific properties. Such prominent figures as Henry Ford, whose mass production techniques transformed the auto industry, relentlessly scapegoated Jewish Americans for many of the nation's ills.

According to a poll in the late 1930s, some sixty-percent of Americans agreed with statements describing Jews as scheming, dishonest, and avaricious. In a fairly typical expression of the common view, novelist Raymond Chandler, a Los Angeles resident who knew Hollywood well, wrote to his English publisher, "I've lived in a Jewish neighborhood, and I've watched one become Jewish, and it was pretty awful.[168]

Anti-Nazi Features

The diversionary feature-film fare of the major studios had helped to mitigate the harsh realities of the 1930s. Moviemakers generally avoided any topics touching on war-related matters or international politics for fear of losing foreign markets. For most studio heads, exhibiting few business few scruples, the bottom line took priority over the barbarity of Nazism, continuing to do business with the Nazi regime long after they were aware of its agenda.[169] All the same, as the threat of Nazism mounted, some studio executives undertook projects that were decidedly political in orientation.

An innovator of sound movies, the Warner brothers, apparently hating Nazis more than they cared about German grosses, led the way with *Confessions of a Nazi Spy* (1939), an espionage thriller based on actual trial evidence about officials in the Third Reich and their American operatives waging secret warfare against the United States. The movie gained an added aura of authenticity through ominous narration and other documentary devices such as the judicious use of actual newsreel footage of the 1939 German-American Bund rally in Madison Square Garden to increase the effectiveness of the message. Perhaps most controversial at the time, this cinematic salvo suggested that German consulates were fronts for waging secret warfare against the country.

In retrospect the spy melodrama may appear to be rather tame, but it stirred up a storm of protest at the time of its release. The German consulate filed an official complaint, charging that it was part of a broad U.S. conspiracy. Bund leader Fritz Kuhn threatened the Warner studio with a $5-million lawsuit, and German diplomatic forces openly worked to suppress the movie in the United States and abroad. When shown in a predominantly German-American section of Milwaukee, an angry band of pro-Nazi sympathizers burned the theatre to the ground. Eighteen Latin American and European nations banned the movie outright. However, within the countries comprising British Empire it was shown without a single cut.

After war erupted in Europe in 1939, closing the continental market, the movie industry released a flock of anti-Nazi features. *The Mortal Storm* (1940) chronicles the difficulties of a German middle-class family divided in its loyalties when the Nazi regime comes to power. In *The Man I Married* (1940), an American woman who visits Germany in 1938 with her German-American husband and their small son, experiences the fanaticism of the Nazis. A British big-game hunter in *Man Hunt* (1941) stalks Adolf Hitler to his Berchtesgaden retreat just for sport. He aligns the Nazi fuehrer in his telescopic sight but fails to shoot since he had deliberately neglected to load his rifle.

One of the most provocative anti-Nazi pictures of the period was *The Great Dictator* (1940), a seriocomic representation of the Hitler mythology in which Charlie Chaplin played a dual role, appearing both as a humble Jewish barber and as Adenoid Hynkel, the ranting, posturing dictator of Tomania. Their paths cross toward the end of the movie. The barber, mistaken for the dictator, takes his place before the microphones. During the six-minute oration, packed with political innuendo and thinly veiled contemporary implications, he urges, "Soldiers! Don't give yourselves to these brutes who drill you...treat you like cattle, and use you for cannon fodder."

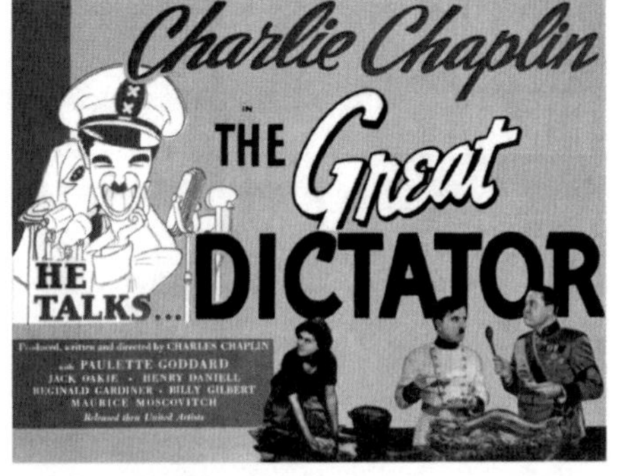

Within the dramatic fiction, of course, Chaplin's Jewish barber is addressing the citizens of Tomania, but his words are aimed directly at the movie audience. To those attuned to the comic actor's antiwar political affinities, phrases like "cannon fodder" must have carried clear echoes of the isolationist allegations that President Franklin D. Roosevelt was planning to sacrifice American lives to defend British imperialism. This opposition to military action must have escaped those accusing Chaplin of warmongering.

Joining the growing antiwar chorus was Roosevelt-appointed U.S. ambassador to Great Britain, Joseph P. Kennedy. The longtime wheeler-dealer in the movie industry told studio executives to stop demonizing the Germans. Because if the country entered into the war, he cautioned, the blame would fall on Hollywood Jews for hoodwinking the nation. His attack on Jewish movie producers, notes his biographer, was so "intemperate," so "provocative," so "uncalled for" that those present suspected some ulterior motive was in play—perhaps a ploy to scare them out of the business so he could get back in again.[170]

Some of the congressional anti-Hollywood sentiment had shades of anti-Semitism as well. In a national radio speech broadcast from St. Louis, Missouri, Republican Gerald Nye of North Dakota warned that the movies had become gigantic engines of propaganda to rouse war fever in America and plunge the nation to its destruction. The intemperate Nye went on to list the heads of the major movie companies, stressing their Jewish surnames, and noting, "in each of these companies there are several production directors, many of whom come from Russia, Hungary, Germany, and the Balkan countries." Are you ready, he demanded, "to send your boys to bleed and die in Europe to make the world safe for this industry and its financial backers?"[171]

The isolationist outcry culminated in hearings before a Senate subcommittee investigating war propaganda in movies.[172] The fiery senator from North Dakota led the offensive, referring to the film fare he considered interventionist in orientation as vicious propaganda. But when pressed, Nye was unable to recall even the names, let alone the plots, of the movies he wanted the committee to condemn. It turned out that he hadn't seen most of those he excoriated. Other isolationist opponents of Hollywood proved equally ill informed.

The most telling testimony came from Fox studio head Darryl F. Zanuck, who began by pointedly mentioning his deep Methodist roots in Wahoo, Nebraska. He argued forcefully that Hollywood pictures were powerful sales vehicles for the American way of life, not only to America but also to the entire world. They sold this way of life so effectively, he asserted, that the first thing the dictators who took over Italy and Germany did was to ban them. When he finished speaking, the Senate gallery erupted in applause. Everything that followed was anticlimactic. The subcommittee did not meet again after the United States went to war, rendering the entire matter moot.

Government Propaganda

After the American government started drafting men, it commissioned a series of seven documentary films designed to persuade inductees of the necessity for combating the "Axis Powers"—Japan, Germany, and Italy. They consisted mostly of existing footage, including newsreels, captured enemy records of the battle, clips from Hollywood features, and footage from Nazi propaganda films like *Triumph of the Will* along with bits of staged action.

An anonymous army of artists and artisans worked as writers, editors, narrators, composers, and conductors. Famed moviemaker Frank Capra, the only screen credit, produced and directed most of them under the umbrella title "Why We Fight." The War Department supervised the re-enacted parts for which no relevant footage was available. And the Disney studio did the animated maps and diagrams that give scope to the live-action sequences and clarify and relate otherwise random material. Blackness seeped menacingly across the map to illustrate the spread of aggression. Such standard narrative techniques as exposition, mounting action, climax, and denouement provided the dramatic form.

PRELUDE TO WAR

The first installment, *Prelude to War*, shown in movie theaters throughout the country served to persuade the public of the need to become involved in the war and ally with the Soviet Union. Rife with stereotypical images, it compares the "free" and "slave" worlds: The free world of the Allied nations honors life, liberty, and the pursuit of happiness. The slave world of the Axis nations respects only tyranny, brutality, and strict obedience to the leader and threatens to envelop the entire planet. According to the narration, righteousness and Christian commitment to protect countries unable to defend themselves compelled Americans to preserve freedom by fighting the Axis nations.

While the screen showed images of Axis leaders Hitler, Mussolini, and Hirohito, the narrator intoned: "Take a good look at this trio. Remember their faces. If you ever meet them, don't hesitate." Like most wartime propaganda, the films were simplistic and emotional hiding as much as they revealed. "In depicting all allies in 'free world' terms," notes Eric Barnouw, "many unpleasant problems were simply ignored."[173] The shortcomings of American idealism, such as a segregated army, were likewise concealed or disregarded.

The War Department's Information and Education Division conducted a series of experiments on the effectiveness of some of the seven indoctrination films.[174] A research team of social scientists gave subjects a questionnaire to measure factual knowledge, opinions, and overall attitudes. They then divided them into experimental groups and a control group, all but the control group saw a film in the "Why We Fight" series, and all subjects were then measured again.

The effects were, for the most part, minimal. The films were moderately successful in teaching smarter soldiers about events leading up to the war but, according to the pencil-and-paper test administered after viewing, had no power to fire up soldiers with enthusiasm for the war or to create lasting hatred for the enemy or establish confidence in the Allies. The findings indicated modest amounts of opinion change on certain specific points. But more general attitudes toward the war, its aims, and why the United States was involved in the conflict remained largely unaffected.[175]

Decades of research have since confirmed that significant changes occur when a range of media repeatedly focus on a particular matter and are relatively consistent in presenting a uniform interpretation. The minimal effect of single propaganda pieces seemed to "add up" during the Second World War to a significant impact. Some 16,000 movie houses around the country committed to the exhibition of U.S. government propaganda shorts on a wide range of subjects. Various federal agencies produced short films designed to sell war bonds by instilling feelings of fear and loathing toward the Japanese.

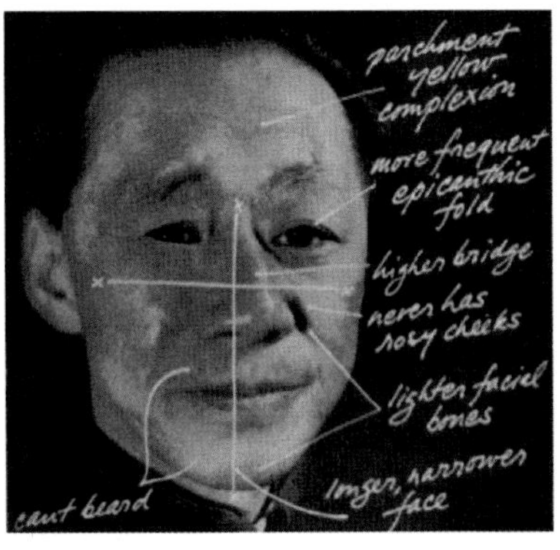

JUSTICE *DENIED*

A particularly nasty example of this type of propaganda is called *Justice* (1943), in which Japanese soldiers are shown tossing babies with their bayonets. (The shooting of this scene took place in the old Paramount studios in Astoria, New York, which had been taken over by the military during the war.) Such staged scenes combined with actual footage of the aftermath of the Japanese attack on China. In the closing segment, a narrator intones: "Every tank kills a Jap. How about it, folks, have you killed a Jap soldier today?" (The actual brutality of Japanese soldiers in China may have far exceeded the depictions in American propaganda films.[176])

Propaganda films like *Justice* along with posters, feature films, radio shows, and other media fare appear to have released a kind of contagion of irrationality. It spread to the Japanese people in general (justifying saturation bombing of cities like Tokyo), as well as to Japanese Americans (many who had never been in Japan) and, finally, failing to discriminate between the varieties of Asian cultures, to all Asian Americans. Indiscriminate acts of violence against South East Asians, in general, became commonplace. Chinese people, in particular, were singled out for abuse.

To "dispel some of the confusion," shortly after Pearl Harbor, *Life* magazine ran a photo essay on "How to Tell the Japs from the Chinese."[177] Mug shots of a representative of each group, accompanied by arrows and asides, served to highlight the distinctions. The comparisons entailed such features as the Japanese model's massively boned head and face, and flat, pug nose (which betray his "aboriginal antecedents") and the Chinese representative's longer, more delicately boned visage and finely bridged nose.

INSTRUCTIONS TO ALL PERSONS OF JAPANESE ANCESTRY

Living in the Following Area:

All that portion of the City and County of San Francisco, State of California, lying generally west of the north-south line established by Junipero Serra Boulevard, Worchester Avenue, and Nineteenth Avenue, and lying generally north of the east-west line established by California Street, to the intersection of Market Street, and thence on Market Street to San Francisco Bay.

All Japanese persons, both alien and non-alien, will be evacuated from the above designated area by 12:00 o'clock noon Tuesday, April 7, 1942.

No Japanese person will be permitted to enter or leave the above described area after 8:00 a. m., Thursday, April 2, 1942, without obtaining special permission from the Provost Marshal at the Civil Control Station located at:

1701 Van Ness Avenue
San Francisco, California

The Civil Control Station is equipped to assist the Japanese population affected by this evacuation in the following ways:

1. Give advice and instructions on the evacuation.

One wonders for whom this lesson in physiognomy was intended. Certainly, bomber pilots and soldiers in the field had no need for such instruction. Perhaps it was for the hooligans who were harassing and attacking people of both Japanese and Chinese ancestry.

The irrationality pathogen infected liberal politicians as well. The Roosevelt Administration sent 120,000 Japanese Americans—two-thirds of them U.S.

citizens—to internment camps in such desolate places as Heart Mountain, Wyoming, Minidoka, Idaho, and Topaz, Utah. For legal grounds, the government turned to the antiquated Alien Enemy Act of 1798, which permits a president to apprehend, intern, and otherwise restrict the freedom of "alien enemies" upon declaration of war or actual, attempted, or threatened invasion by a foreign nation. The federal government attempted to justify these internment camps in a propaganda piece titled *Japanese Relocation* (1942). Images of huddled families with belongings in tow belie the narrator's assurances that this forced relocation was being done "with real consideration for the people involved." "All of this was done," notes Geoffrey Stone in *Perilous Times*, "even though there was not a single documented act of espionage, sabotage, or treasonable activity committed by an American citizen of Japanese descent or by a Japanese national residing on the West Coast."[178]

Although the precise number is in dispute, thousands of German and hundreds of Italian ancestries also suffered confinement, deportation, repatriation, registration, travel restrictions, familial disruption, and property confiscation. Pressured by the United States, Latin American governments collectively arrested many German and Italian as well as Japanese ancestries, shipping many of them back to this country for internment.

In a now widely repudiated ruling, the United States Supreme Court upheld the exclusion of Japanese Americans from the west coast military area during the war.[179] Some two and a half years after signing the executive order mandating Japanese internment, in 1944, President Franklin D. Roosevelt rescinded it. The government closed the last of the internment camps by the end of 1945. The former internees faced a hostile racial environment.

Image Arsenal

As the ominous shadow of war enveloped all of Asia and Europe in its darkness, the movie industry marshaled it talents and production resources to combat the enemy on the propaganda front. The power of the motion picture to persuade and propagandize came front and center during the Second World War, which the United States entered in December 1941 following the Japanese attack on Pearl Harbor in Hawaii, then an American-controlled archipelago in the North Pacific Ocean.

Whatever the patriotic purposes, the primary aim of movie production continued to be profit. Burdened by union organizers and weak box-office returns for some big-budgeted movies, Walt Disney entered into a contract with the American government to develop thirty-two animated shorts. Its animation apparatus operated in high gear, turning out film fare of incalculable value to the American government's propaganda effort.

Disney may have built his business around a rodent named Mickey, but it was Donald Duck who proved to be the most popular during the war years. In *Der Fuehrer's Face* (1942), Disney employed familiar images and symbols to ridicule the regimentation of German life under the Nazis. The irascible Donald Duck dreams that he is in Nutzi Land. He lives in a house that bears a striking resemblance to Adolf Hitler. Everywhere in sight are swastikas: on the dial of the alarm clock, on the walls of his humble dwelling, and even in the shape of the shrubbery around it. He is abruptly awakened by a bayonet-toting martinet. "Up dumkopf!" he roars, "you will have the privilege of working twenty-eight hours a day for the Fuehrer."

After a hurried breakfast of ersatz food (the bread loaf is made of wood), Donald marches to his job at a munition factory weighted down by a big bass drum marked with the Nazi insignia. Along the way, he passes a fire hydrant shaped liked a swastika. In the course of the day spent screwing down bomb casings, the distraught duck goes berserk, and a close-up of his face rotates and explodes into a surreal nightmare world in which images of him are pounded as they move down the conveyor belt. Following another explosion, dozens of his images fall, settling finally into his sleeping form. When he awakens with a start, still half asleep, Donald sees the shadow of an outstretched arm and starts to respond with a "Heil" but then realizes it is the arm of a miniature Statue of Liberty. The film seemingly concludes with his heartfelt expression of appreciation that he is a citizen of the United States. But the closing iris opens again just long enough to show a close-up of Hitler getting hit in the face with an overripe tomato.

Before the animated anti-Nazi propaganda short film's release, Spike Jones and His City Slickers recorded a highly successful version of its theme song, "Der Fuehrer's Face," parodying the Nazi anthem, the "Horst Wessel Song." Unlike the cartoon, noted for parodies of popular songs of the time, some Spike Jones versions contain the sound effect of flatulence (often called the Bronx Cheer) with each "Heil!" to show contempt for the Nazi leader.

The sheet music cover bears the image of little Donald Duck throwing a tomato in a caricature of Adolph Hitler's face. In the Spike Jones recording, the chorus line, "Ja, ve is the Supermen" is answered by a soloist's "Super-duper super men!" effeminately delivered suggesting the prevalence of epicenes among the self-proclaimed Nazi master race. In the animated short, these lines are flatly delivered but with effeminate gestures by Hermann Göring.

Among other government agencies, the Treasury Department enlisted Donald Duck's help to remind people to pay their taxes. The Tax Revenue Act of 1942 put many people on the tax rolls for the first time. There were no mechanisms early in the war for withholding income tax from people's salaries before they were paid. Workers had to be encouraged to put some money aside for the quarterly payment of taxes.

In *The New Spirit* (1942), an eight-minute short, Donald is shown listening to the radio, with the American flag waving in the pupils of his eyes. In a patriotic fervor, he implores the radio to tell him how to aid the war effort. At first, the answer ("By paying your taxes") enrages the web-footed patriot; but, when he is informed of the power of his taxes to purchase armaments ("taxes to beat the Axis"), he gladly sets about calculating his income tax. Working as an actor, Donald has earned $2501. He finds that he owes $13 in taxes (he has three dependents—his adopted nephews) and immediately rushes to the nation's capital with his contribution in hand.

The short was so successful in getting people to pay their taxes that the treasury department commissioned Disney to make a sequel. An estimated twenty-six million people saw *The New Spirit*, and thirty-seven percent of them reported, in a Gallup poll, that it affected their willingness to pay taxes.[180] Called *The Spirit of 1943*, it presents Donald Duck as the typical worker on payday. His mind divides into two personalities: the gentle, thrifty Scotsman, and the irresponsible "zoot-suited" spendthrift. The zoot-suit look featured a wide-brimmed hat, baggy but tight-cuffed trousers, and an oversized jacket with heavily padded shoulders. Popular with poor black and white youths in the large cities, most associated the dress style with Mexican teenagers—or pachucos, as they were called in Los Angeles.[181]

During World War II, long-standing prejudice against Mexicans coalesced into hatred of the zoot-suiters. Around the time the Disney studio was producing this short, the press reported clashes between sailors stationed in southern California and the Mexican teenagers. When a zoot-suiter knifed a sailor, naval personnel went on a rampage, beating up anyone who was wearing the hated outfit. The Los Angeles City Council responded by passing an ordinance forbidding the wearing of zoot suits within city limits.

Playing on this kind of adverse publicity, the zoot-suited spendthrift in *The Spirit of 1943* is associated with the Nazi cause. He and the Scotsman engage in a tug-of-war over the mind of Donald, one urging him to spend his money frivolously and the other imploring him to save it so he can pay his taxes ("thanks to Hitler and Hirohito taxes are higher than ever before"). Both lose their grip and fly in the opposite direction. The Scotsman smashes into a wall whose plaster falls away to reveal lines of red bricks and white mortar and a window of stars on a blue field in a composition that suggests an American flag. In sharp contrast, the zoot-suited spend-

thrift hurtles into the Idle Hour Club, whose swinging doors are in the shape of a swastika. When he emerges, his bow tie is shaped like the Nazi symbol as well, and he blows swastika-shaped smoke rings. He also sports a Hitler-like brush mustache and forelock.

Rather than succumbing to his pleas, Donald smacks him back into the nightclub, its door shattering into a giant V for victory. After the enlightened duck pays his taxes, a narrator explains over-animated visuals of American guns, airplanes, and ships destroying the enemy how the money will serve to bury the Axis powers and preserve democracy.

Despite humorous elements, the overall tone of many Disney shorts is decidedly somber and grim. In *Education for Death* (1943), adapted from a 1941 book of the same title by Gregor Ziemer, the focus is on the indoctrination of a German lad named Hans as he grows from a young schoolboy into an adult soldier. At elementary school, his teacher tells the class a Nazi version of the Sleeping Beauty story. It depicts Adolph Hitler as the knightly prince rescuing an obese, overly amorous Brunhilde (the goddess of composer Richard Wagner's Ring cycle operas). "The moral of this story," a narrator notes, "seems to be that Hitler got Germany on her feet, climbed onto the saddle, and took her for a ride."

In another classroom sequence, a Nazi instructor uses the parable of the wolf and the rabbit to illustrate the world belongs to the strong. When Hans shows sympathy for the rabbit, he is swiftly punished and subjected to reeducation. After a montage of book burnings, smashed church windows, and Bibles, they all dissolve into *Mein Kampf* (My Struggle), Adolph Hitler's autobiographical account of his philosophy and plans for conquest. The film concludes with a chilling sequence in which marching children transform into goose-stepping Nazis. Wearing blinders and manacles, they finally dissolve into rows and rows of gravesites.

Cartoonish Combatants

For the most part, wartime movies depicted the Japanese as inhumanly, cruel, and sadistic. In *Behind the Rising Sun* (1943), whose setting is the Sino Japanese War of the 1930s, Japanese soldiers toss babies into the air and bayonet them, molest women and insert needles under their fingernails, and string men up by the wrists until the blood vessels in their arms burst. In several wartime movies, there were calls for the total annihilation of Japan.

In depicting Germans, Hollywood's emphasis tended to be on Nazi characteristics rather than on those of the population as a whole. Screen Nazis typically spoke with thick guttural accents, shouted "*schweinhund*" at the slightest provocation, and religiously said "heil Hitler" when greeting one another with kicking boot heels and outstretched right arms.

They seemed to derive particular pleasure from tormenting older people and brutalizing attractive young women. In *Hitler's Children* (1943), a lurid exposé of the Hitler Youth, young girls willingly submit to Aryan men (with or without the benefit of clergy) impregnating them to sustain the "master race." Those who refuse are ticketed for sterilization, or worse. One of the holdouts is a German girl (Bonita Granville) raised and educated in America whose taste of democracy has made her utterly resistant to Nazism. In the movie's pivotal scene, her defiance results in a public flogging, her hands tied to the base of a flagpole, and the back of her blouse ripped open. After the first few lashes, the man she loves (Tim Holt) interrupts the flagellation, bringing death to them both.

Watchful Bureaucrats

Throughout the war years, movies were made under the watchful eye of government bureaucrats. Having a domestic and an overseas branch, the Office of War Information (OWI) promoted public understanding of the war, coordinated government information activities, and acted as liaison with the various media outlets. Its Bureau of Motion Pictures oversaw government filmmaking and dealt with the movie industry. Among other services, it supplied moviemakers with the special information needed for the production of war-related film fare.

The motion picture bureau tried to influence movie content as well by analyzing and evaluating projects, suggesting story subjects and plot lines, and exerting pressure on the industry to secure cooperation. But its requests to see scripts prior to production initially met with strong opposition from the major studios. The bureau also raised the wrath of a conservative coalition of Republicans and southern Democrats that regarded the OWI and its subsidiaries as imprudently pro-Roosevelt and perilously liberal if not leftist. Thus, in 1943, an increasingly hostile Congress cut off almost all funding for the OWI's domestic operations.

All the same, the motion picture bureau still enjoyed considerable economic leverage to shape the output of the movie industry. Its advisory authority was augmented by another wartime agency, the Office of Censorship, which was empowered to bar the export of movies deemed detrimental to the war effort. In an effort to fortify foreign distribution dividends, most of the major studios eventually acceded to the bureau's request to see scripts prior to production. From mid-1943 until the end of the war, according to one scholarly account, "OWI exerted an influence over an American mass medium never equaled before or since by a government agency."[182]

Self-Censorship in Decline

During the Second World War, while the federal government attended to politics on the screen, the Production Code Administration continued to focus on flesh, not fascism. The entire social fabric of American society seemed to unravel during the war years. Millions of young people, cut loose from community ties, experienced much greater sexual freedom. Marriage, birth, and divorce rates soared. Many women working in factories and war plants enjoyed unprecedented social mobility and personal and economic freedom.

In the face of this wartime upheaval in gender relations, the PCA remained steadfast in its efforts to maintain cinematic morality. When reviewing a feature film for code approval, Joseph Breen did not simply demand deletions; he also worked to effect changes in the entire moral outlook of the screen drama. But as the war years took their toll on the moral fabric of America, Breen occasionally deviated from his earlier standards. Prior to the war, for instance, he had warned studios away from James M. Cain's sharp, brooding novella of adultery and murder, *Double Indemnity*. In the fall of 1943, however, he approved a somewhat sanitized screenplay of the story with hardly a murmur. Such concessions inspired other moviemakers to push the moral parameters.

Having an aversion to showing bodily functions, Breen remained steadfast on prohibiting the depiction of toilets or any hint of urination. He ordered a scene cut from the courtroom drama *The Paradine Case* (1947) because it showed a commode in a jail cell. He also denied a seal of approval to the Italian-made *The Bicycle Thief* (1948) in part because of a scene showing a boy (his back to the camera) trying to urinate against a wall. Even canines couldn't relieve themselves. In *The Best Years of Our Lives* (1946), he demanded the excising of a scene in which a dog wet the floor. The industry watchdog, notes a social history of the movies, seemed bent on curing the cinema of incontinence.[183]

The postwar period witnessed the gradual abandonment of the production code, precipitated by adverse antitrust rulings, the rise of independent production, the importation of foreign films, and the dramatic decline in box-office receipts as people moved to the new suburbs and turned to television and other divertissements. Joseph Breen remained in charge of the PCA, but he was clearly out of touch with the changing social reality. By the time he retired in 1954, the entire self-regulatory structure was on the verge of collapse. Highlighting Hollywood hypocrisy, that year, the cinema's moral custodian received a special Oscar for "his conscientious, open-minded and dignified management of the Motion Picture Production Code."[184]

In the 1950s, when any depiction of sex in books, movies, or magazines was tightly constrained, the general assumption seemed to be that the government could legitimately forbid materials that the majority deemed indecent or obscene. This assumption came into question as social attitudes about human sexuality began to change with the popularity of publications like *Playboy*, whose first issue had a nude centerfold of Marilyn Monroe. It was only one of the waves of racy new magazines, books, and movies. Cheap and often quite erotic paperbacks were readily available for purchase at newsstands, dime stores, and local drugstores. Grace Metalious's 1956 novel *Peyton Place*, an exploration of such previously suppressed topics as lust, incest, adultery, and abortion, became a runaway bestseller.

Restraining the Red Menace

Once the "hot war" ended, the "cold war" with the Soviet Union resumed in earnest. At the height of tensions in the 1950s and 1960s, all the major media outlets promoted the dangers of communism. The now infamous *My Son John* (1952) is perhaps most crazed and excessive of the batch of the virulent anti-Communist propaganda movies made during this period. The unfolding story revolves around the parents (Helen Hayes and Dean Jagger) of a young man, John (Robert Walker), who appears to have

succumbed to the temptations of communism.

Most of the action takes place in the home of the Jefferson family, a dark breeding ground of oedipal conflict, motherly love, and fatherly anguish. The mismatched couple have three sons. Two are masculine ex-football heroes who heroically march off to war. Their arrogant, somewhat effeminate intellectual brother misses church and family dinners to spend time hanging around with his former professor. He ridicules his father's patriotism and his mother's religious devotion. While on a trip home from his job in the nation's capital, his parents begin to suspect he's become a subversive, a spy for the Communists, or perhaps something even more heinous, a homosexual.

Lumping together spies, subversives and homosexuals was a common practice at the time. While John doesn't come right out and acknowledge his sexual orientation, he expresses disdain for heterosexuality when his overly attentive mother asks him if he has a girlfriend. Following him back to D. C. to do some detective work, she discovers to her horror that he is a Communist agent. In the meantime, John has promised to give the commencement speech at his alma mater.

Just as the FBI is about to arrest him, he realizes the error of his ways. Remorseful, he decides to tape-record his final confession about how he has been duped by the Communists singling out higher education as the "poison" that led him to subversive activities. In the climactic final scene, the graduating college students intently listen to his cautionary tale played from the tape recorder after his death at an empty podium illuminated by a shaft of light that seems to emanate from the heavens.

Many movies displayed and embraced an atmosphere of perhaps unparalleled fear of the red menace. The titles leave little doubt about the anti-communist thrust of such features as *The Red Menace* (1949), and *I Was a Communist for the FBI* (1951). In the bulk of the anti-communist movies, virtually every character is a stereotype, and seemingly every other line of dialogue is a patriotic speech. In the juvenile political thriller, *Big Jim McLain* (1952), John Wayne and James Arness star as stick-figure HUAC investigators hunting down communists in post-war Hawaii organized labor scene.

Duck and Cover

The cultural climate of irrational anxiety in the late 1940s and 1950s as the East-West arms race intensified was conducive to duck-and-cover drills, dog tags for school kids, and backyard bomb shelters. Perhaps subconsciously, entertainment fare reinforced at an early age the hatred and fear of communism or socialism of any kind. Augmenting such fearfulness, in 1951, the newly formed Federal Civil Defense Administration (FCDA) commissioned a nine-minute film designed to prepare schoolchildren to take protective action in the event of a nuclear strike.

The short begins with an animated sequence featuring a pith-helmet-wearing cartoon turtle named Bert ("who was very alert"), then switches to live footage as a narrator explains what to do immediately after seeing a bright flash of light. To protect them from a nuclear blast, youngsters dive under desks, seek cover while walking to school, riding a bicycle, on a school bus, and picnicking. In the age of nuclear warfare, although only the United States had dropped atom bombs, the horrifyingly absurd caution conveyed that children might be annihilated anytime, anyplace, without warning save a flashing light unless they rapidly ducked and covered themselves.

The FCDA distributed this terrifying film to schools as well as a shortened version to local television stations nationwide, which aired it as public service announcements. Adding to the terror, by 1952, New York City's school board spent $159,000 on equipment and materials to produce 2.5 million metal identification tags for all public and private school students to wear at all times. By April of that year, Army-style metal dog tags were distributed to every child from kindergarten to fourth grade. Many other city school boards across the country soon followed suit. The unspoken purpose being that they would help distinguish children who were lost or killed in a nuclear explosion. The federal government later sent many of these frightened youngsters to Vietnam, under the bogus banner of making the world safe for democracy by eradicating communism in southeast Asia.

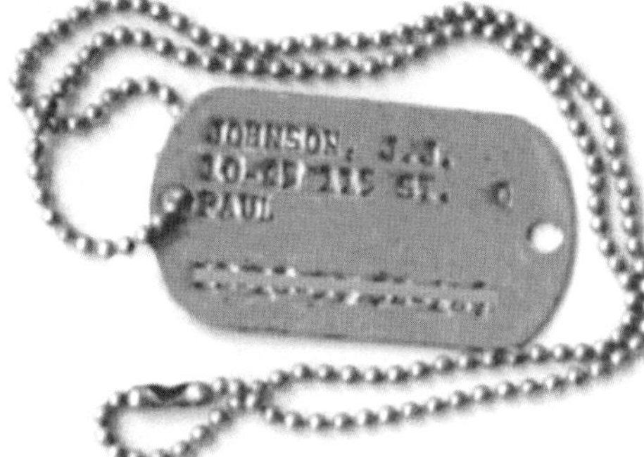

Codes to Ratings

The higher legal freedom accorded to movies in the postwar period eventually led to a significant overhaul of the movie industry's self-regulatory mechanisms. The Motion Picture Association of America (MPAA), the trade organization's name simplified in 1945, changed the code for screen conduct in 1956 and again a decade later to allow moviemakers more considerable latitude in the representation of all aspects human experience.

The groundbreaking 1966 screen adaption of Edward Albee's award-winning play *Who's Afraid of Virginia Woolf?* had a level of profanity and sexual implication unheard of in movie theatres at that time. Replete with dialogue that violated the standard moral guidelines, the movie, featuring superstars Elizabeth Taylor and Richard Burton, contained such expressions as "hump the hostess" that the faithful framers of the old production code never imagined would be at issue. Released with the cautionary "Suggested for Mature Audiences," it foreshadowed the movie industry's general acceptance of the need for a classification system.

A strong impetus for such an industrywide system came in April 1968 when the U.S. Supreme Court, in two cases handed down the same day, ruled that state and local authorities have the right to protect minors from exposure to subject matter permissible for adults. In *Ginsberg v. New York*, the high court, Justice William Brennan writing for the 6-3 majority, held that the government could constitutionally protect children from exposure to material that is "obscene for minors."[185] The matter concerned magazines that depicted female nudity not considered obscene for adults.

In the other decision, the U. S. Supreme Court rejected a film classification ordinance in Dallas, Texas, because it failed to provide sufficient guidance to those in the motion picture industry and to members of the city board who had to decide whether the movies were suitable for minors.[186] The committee classified films as "suitable" or "not suitable" for young persons, defined as anyone under sixteen. A large theatre chain in the southwest, Interstate circuit, challenged the ordinance as being unconstitutionally vague.

Ignoring the board's ruling that *Viva Maria*, a 1965 comedic adventure starring Brigitte Bardot and Jeanne Moreau, was "not suitable for young persons," Interstate deliberately exhibited the movie without imposing age restrictions on the audience. Set in the early 1900's Central America, more slapstick than salacious, the characters the two famous French stars play lead a revolution, blow things up, and invent the striptease mid-chanson. A county court upheld the board's designation, and the Texas Court of Appeals affirmed the lower court decision.

The high court, reversing the ruling, held that the vagueness of the ordinance violated the First and Fourteenth Amendments but did not preclude acceptance of a more carefully crafted age classification scheme. Writing for an 8-1 majority, Justice Thurgood Marshall, echoing the *Ginsberg* ruling, held that a state "may regulate the dissemination to juveniles of, and their access to, material objectionable as to them, but which a state clearly could not regulate as to adults."

Seeing the writing on the wall, as it were, in the fall of 1968, the MPAA—in conjunction with the International Film Importers and Distributors of America (IFIDA) and the National Association of Theatre Owners (NATO)—scrapped the rickety production code. They adopted in its place a national system of voluntary classification, the Code and Rating Administration (CARA)—now referred to only as "the rating board." Most mainstream producers and distributors agreed to submit their pictures for the rating before commercial release.

Located in Los Angeles, the board's members serve for a two-or three-year term. The MPAA's president, who selects the board's chair, does not participate in, nor may he or she overrule, its decisions. (In March 2011, former Connecticut Senator Christopher Dodd became the latest MPAA chief.) The appointed chair, in turn, selects the other members of the panel, based on such vague criteria as a shared parenthood experience, intellectual maturity, and the capacity to put themselves in the role of most parents when they make their decisions. Having specialized knowledge of movies is not a criterion. The composition of this panel at any given time is a closely guarded secret, lest moviemakers try to influence the outcome of the classification process.

Initially, the four designations were: G, suggested for general audiences; M, indicated for adults and mature young people; R, restricted-persons under sixteen not admitted unless accompanied by a parent or adult guardian; and X, persons under sixteen not admitted. Early in 1970, the MPAA changed the M rating (thought to be confusing) to GP, all ages admitted-parental guidance suggested.

At the same time, it increased the R and X age limits to seventeen. Two years later, the MPAA changed GP to the current designation: PG, parental guidance suggested, some material may not be suitable for pre-teenagers. It withheld its seal—which validates the rating—from any movie that received an X designation. In the summer of 1984, it added the PG-13 rating—cautioning parents to give careful consideration for attendance of children under thirteen.

Among the factors considered are thematic content, visual treatment, and the use of such elements as language, violence, sex, and nudity. With the new rating system and more permissive legal climate, nude scenes, simulated sex, and explicit language eventually became commonplace in American cinema. And the makers of mainstream movies now had the latitude in dealing with a wide range of adult matters, sometimes able to negotiate a less restrictive rating with only one or two minor cuts.

The rating board has been able to exert influence over producers through its power to impose restrictive designations. The major movie companies were particularly sensitive to the stigma of an X rating, denied mall showing and newspaper advertising. In their contracts with independent producers, they usually stipulated that all movies must receive either an R or a less restrictive rating. As a consequence, the X rating eventually fell into disrepute, becoming identified in the public mind with pornographic films. The nicer-sounding NC-17—no one under seventeen admitted—replaced it in 1990. In the delicate process of protecting children without limiting what adults may watch, only the MPAA's rating board remains as a regulator of mainstream theatrical releases.

Hollywood Reimagined

The growth of independent production accelerated when the industry's system of vertical integration (the capacity to produce, distribute, and exhibit movies under a single corporate umbrella) began to break apart, and the big studios underwent retrenchment and reorganization. In 1944 the Justice Department reactivated its antitrust suit. The case eventually made its way to the U.S. Supreme Court, which ruled in 1948 that the vertical structure of the major companies violated federal antitrust laws.[187] The high court remanded the question of theatre ownership to the federal district court in New York City where the case had originated. In 1949 this court decided that separation of production and distribution from exhibition was the appropriate remedy.

The five vertically integrated companies—beginning with RKO and continuing with Paramount, Warner Bros., Twentieth Century-Fox, and Loew'sM-G-M—signed consent decrees that broke the corporate chains linking production and distribution to exhibition. Although trumpeted as a major triumph for government trustbusters, this court-imposed dismantling did little to prevent the development of new concentrations of control. The theatre chains maintained their dominance in exhibition even though they were required to divest some of their holdings. But the distribution of movies, the key to controlling production, continued to be dominated by the established studios.

Foreshadowing the commercial practices prevalent today, many of the big Hollywood studios embarked on a policy of financing, marketing, and distributing movies made by independent producing units. The move to independent production gained impetus from United Artists, which by the 1950s had evolved into a company run by lawyers. The studios provide some financing, assist in such particulars as renting studio space and preparing contracts, guaranteeing promotion and distribution, and to do so with a minimum of front office interference. As actors, writers, directors, and producers increasingly turned to this form of production, the studio head was relegated to determining which of these people to sign to short-term contracts for picture deals.

The 1960s witnessed a fundamental change in the control structure of the movie industry. The erratic earnings of the big studios, dating from the advent of television, made them highly susceptible to mergers and corporate takeovers. Those seeking to gain a hold in the movie industry were attracted by the potential profits from television production, large movie libraries, real estate assets, and musical and literary copyrights. Because voting stock had become widely dispersed, executive cadres at the studios had only a tenuous hold on the corporate reins. This resulted in a constant ebb and flow of managerial personnel.

Disruptions at the once-mighty M-G-M, with its trademark lion roaring at the start of every movie, were especially severe. Its production chief, Louis B. Mayer, had been forced to abdicate his throne in 1952 and had failed in a later bid to regain power. The production policies of his successors did little to boost revenues. During the next decade, the studio underwent several stressful managerial changes, causing the ailing lion to become increasingly arthritic and enfeebled.

After being pursued by various corporate suitors, M-G-M was acquired in 1969 by Las Vegas-based financier and casino owner Kirk Kerkorian. The new management he put in place virtually liquidated the studio, selling thirty-eight acres of its Culver City backlot, as well as theatres in Australia, South Africa, and the United Kingdom. They abruptly canceled movie projects, slashed personnel, leveled historical sets, and turned the company's collection of props, costumes, and other musty memorabilia over to an auction house. A pair of the iconic ruby-red slippers Judy Garland wore in the 1939 movie *The Wizard of Oz* when she clicks her heels together three times to return home to Kansas fetched a reported $15,000. The four known existing pairs are now worth millions.

Much of the money drained from the studio went into the construction of the M-G-M Grand Hotel in Las Vegas. The once-proud lion, although prosperous in his old age, now presided over roulette wheels, craps tables, and slot machines. Resuscitated several times over the years, the studio never again regained its position in the top ranks of the Hollywood hierarchy. Most of the major companies, weakened by internal strife and disorder, were assimilated into complex corporate enterprises beginning in the 1960s.

Film School Directors

A new generation of talented moviemakers—among them Francis Ford Coppola, Brian de Palma, George Lucas, Martin Scorcese, and Steven Spielberg—gave Hollywood a fresh creative energy in the 1970s. Most of them had studied film history, aesthetics, and production as formal academic subjects in graduate programs in Los Angeles and New York. And all of them shared an abiding love of both old Hollywood movies and innovative European and Japanese cinema.

As might be expected, their directorial styles tended to mix the conventional with the experimental. While periodically pursuing personal projects with limited appeal, they derived strength and creative influence not by subverting the established mode of visual storytelling but by expanding its stylistic parameters. Their movies often surged with ingenuity and creative vitality. By the same token, most of these movies manifested strong narrative structure, clear characterizations, careful camera work, tight editing techniques, and a superb command of dramatic action.

These young moviemakers initially enjoyed a high degree of autonomy and creative freedom. Many movie pundits began to proclaim the advent of a "new Hollywood" dominated by directors rather than studio bosses. Although the idea of a director-dominated movie industry was seductive and gained lots of media attention, the shifts in creative control proved to be short-lived and superficial. Those pushing the parameters of moviemaking conventions too hard soon found themselves marginalized.

The big studios might have given directors with a proven track record some measure of creative freedom, but they relinquished little of their ultimate power over the production process. By allowing a director to assume greater responsibility for a movie, executives could shift the blame for financial failure away from themselves. As a result, at the start of the 1980s, when big-budget projects made with a minimum of front office interference began to bomb at the box office, studio management quickly chided director indulgence and assumed closer control over the making of movies.[188]

During the past several decades, the movie industry gradually became more open to diverse directorial talent. Unlike in the old studio era, many minority group members have secured directing jobs. After several years of mind-numbing television roles, black actor Carl Franklin, at age 37, returned to school, obtaining his MFA degree in directing in 1986 from the AFI Conservatory in Los Angeles. He first made his mark at the helm of the low-budget *One False Move* (1992), a crime thriller about three misfits who commit six brutal murders throughout one night in Los Angeles as they seek a cache of money and cocaine. Excelling in crime thrillers, Franklin directed the highly atmospheric *Devil in a Blue Dress* (1995), starring Denzel Washington as a novice private eye in post-World War II Los Angeles. He adapted the screenplay himself from the Walter Mosley novel of the same title. Some eight years later, he directed *Out of Time* (2003), with Washington playing a Florida police chief investigating a vicious double homicide before he falls under suspicion. Like so many directors, much of Franklin's work has been on television shows over the last decade.

Asian American directors like Ang Lee, who first achieved acclaim with such understated movies as *Sense and Sensibility* (1995) and *The Ice Storm.* (1997) have also flourished in the American cinema. To direct *Crouching Tiger, Hidden Dragon* (2000), the Taiwan-born Lee returned to his roots in China. Filmed in the Mandarin Chinese language and released in the West with subtitles, this highly choreographed martial arts movie earned both plaudits and substantial profits. Some of his most acclaimed work explores repressed hidden passions. In *Brokeback Mountain* (2005), Lee won accolades for his cinematic depiction of two modern-day cowboys (Heath Ledger and Jake Gyllenhaal) who fall into a forbidden and secretive sexual relationship.

Women moviemakers, in general, have made significant inroads in Hollywood in recent years. An alumna of both New York University and the American Film Institute, Amy Heckerling's first directorial effort, the coming-of-age comedy *Fast Times at Ridgemont High* (1982), about teenagers indulging in sex, drugs, and rock n' roll, scored big at the box office. Her next movie, *Johnny Dangerously* (1984), a gangster spoof, flopped financially, but later garnered a substantial cult audience. After a few silly but sometimes solid hits, in 1995, she wrote and directed the career-defining *Clueless*, reworking and updating Jane Austen's *Emma* as a 1990s comedy of wealthy teenagers living in Beverly Hills. It won the National Society of Film Critics Best Screenplay award. In recent years, the Bronx-born writer-director has likewise done many television shows. Hollywood is the dream factory, Heckerling once resignedly remarked, and no one dreams about older women.[189]

Some female directors have displayed sensibilities that are difficult to categorize. Writer-director Kathryn Bigelow covers a wide range of genres. Her movie *Strange Days* (1995) is a dazzling but uneasy mix of socially relevant issues and futuristic action. For her work on *The Hurt Locker* (2009), an intense drama about a bomb-disposal unit in Baghdad facing increasingly dangerous situations, Bigelow became the first woman to take home the prized Oscar for Best Director. She received numerous accolades for her direction of such movies as *Zero Dark Thirty* (2012), about the decade-long hunt for and capture of al-Qaeda terrorist leader Osama bin Laden, and *Detroit* (2017), dramatizing the brutal and bloody 1967 riot in the motor city.

Canadian filmmaker and screenwriter Mary Harron's movies include *American Psycho* (2000), a perversely amusing look at the mind of a serial killer (Christian Bale) who seems to have stepped off the pages of GQ. It contains moments of lacerating violence that could repulse even the most ardent horror film fan. Harron co-wrote the movie with Guinevere Turner. They also co-wrote her film *The Notorious Bettie Page* (2005) based on a 1950s pin-up model and sex icon, a target of a Senate investigation because of her risqué bondage photos. Her direction of such movies as *The Moth Diaries* (2011), a teenage Gothic horror tale with a lesbian storyline, gained her recognition as a feminist filmmaker, a label she doesn't embrace.

Despite the window of opportunity opening wider for women, directing mainstream big-budget movies is still dominated by white males. Although female membership in the Directors Guild of America has shot up, of the 113 directors attached to the 100 top movies of 2019, a full 89.4 percent were male, and 10.6 percent had a woman occupying the director's chair. While up from the previous year, this situation persists even though several studios have women in key production positions. For the first time, in the 2018-19 season, women or directors of color helmed half of all television episodes.

Analyzing Movies

The big studio production units refined character types, dramatic designs, shooting strategies, and editing techniques to facilitate emotional involvement of audiences around the globe. Most artists and artisans in Hollywood's ateliers increasingly saw themselves as "bound by rules that set stringent limits on individual innovations." They generally agreed that "telling a story is the basic formal concern," with the aim toward "realism" and "artifice" concealed through unobtrusive filmmaking techniques and stress on the continuity of action. And the stories themselves should be "comprehensible and unambiguous," possessing "a fundamental appeal that transcends class and nation."[190]

Story Structure

The cinematic mode of visual storytelling honed in the heyday of Hollywood prevails to the present, as a leading film scholar documented, exploring a range of movies from the 1960s through the turn of the century. "All art forms have certain structural templates," he notes. While movie conventions "aren't as stringent as the rules governing the Petrarchan sonnet," they adhere to "fairly firm standards of plot construction and characterization."[191] The typical movie, even in the current era of bloated blockbusters, follows specific paths of action designed to facilitate clarity of expression and heighten emotional involvement.

At the most basic level, a causal chain of events is set in motion by the motives and conflicts of characters with whom we are encouraged to identify or empathize. The unfolding action raises questions about these characters that require answers. With few exceptions, at least two specific courses of action ordinarily emerge, one of which almost invariably involves heterosexual romance. The central characters' primary goal is to win or keep the love of a member of the opposite sex.

Other lines of action are usually related to this romantic aspect so that a small number of characters become involved in several interdependent developments. The subsequent conflicts and complications build to a climax and resolution. Although events may appear out of chronological sequence, the enacted story has a clear beginning, middle, and end. Any remaining loose ends are likely to be tied up in a brief denouement or concluding scene. Such recurring patterns provide the promise of something new based on something familiar. Having an underlying sense of what is likely to happen, we can direct our attention at how, when, and with what new twist it will happen.

A central character's motives provide the principal focus of interest. As in all dramatic forms, conflict is the driving force of movies. Dissension near the beginning arising from obstacles preventing a character from achieving desires or fulfilling needs undergoes increasingly intense and suspenseful development before reaching a climactic conclusion. Such conflict can develop between characters with conflicting motives, between characters and their surrounding conditions, or through a single character's contradictory impulses.

Three-Act Template

For analysis purposes, a useful assumption is that most movies separate into three distinct acts or divisions.[192] Although not identified by name or marked by clear breaks in the action, these divisions nonetheless seem to occur in a remarkable number of movies. In general, the first act or major division introduces the principal characters, suggests something about their personalities, and sets up a significant problem or conflict that requires resolution. Suspenseful moments, such as questions that need answers, generally serve to stimulate interest. Toward the end of this act, perhaps twenty to thirty minutes into a two-hour movie, there commonly occurs a significant turning or plot point-an event or incident that spins the action in a new direction.

In *Thelma and Louise* (1991), when the two title characters (Geena Davis and Susan Sarandon) spend a weekend together, they unwittingly enter a lustful wolves world. Once on the interstate, bullied, and submissive housewife Thelma is determined to let her hair down and have some fun. She pleads with her pal to stop at a honky-tonk bar for a drink. Before long, Thelma, drunk and giggly, is dancing with a local lothario (Timothy Carhart). In the parking lot, despite her tearful pleas, he begins to assault her sexually. Her pal Louise comes out toting the gun Thelma packed for protection, and thwarts the rape attempt. The would-be rapist's misogynous slurs provoke her to fire a bullet directly at his chest. Her extreme response to the insults marks the first significant turning point and brings down the curtain on the first act.

The second act, roughly half of the typical movie, basically develops the conflict or struggle established by the end of the first act. Several minor plot points may occur as protagonists strive to achieve goals and encounter various obstacles. About eighty-to-ninety minutes or so into the movie, another major turning point brings matters to a head and initiates the resolution in the third act. Whether a quiet moment or an action-filled event, this turning point drives the story to its climax or highest point of dramatic tension.

In *Thelma and Louise*, the second major turning point occurs as the outlaw pair is driving on a moonlit highway through the imposing mesas of Monument Valley, Marianne

Faithfull's affecting "The Ballad of Lucy Jordan" playing on the soundtrack. In the silence of the desert, looking at each other, they realize for the first time that there is no going back. The final act brings the action to its peak emotional pitch and caps off the process begun in the first act with remaining questions answered.

The last division of *Thelma and Louise* provides the answer to the compelling question of what will happen to the two fugitives from justice. They come to the end of the road. Behind them is a small army of law enforcement agents, and the imposing Grand Canyon looms ahead. Rather than surrender, they decide to drive off the cliff. When Louise puts the car in gear and floors it, they sail over the edge. The image freezes. Suspended in space, the two seem to defy gravity. They have become free spirits.

Not carved in stone, the three-act scheme separated by turning or plot points roughly one quarter and three-quarters of the way through the unfolding action serves as a set of flexible guidelines for analytical purposes. As an enacted screen drama unfolds, pressing questions invariably arise about the characters and situations through what happens or is posed explicitly in the dialogue. Such internal queries serve to generate suspense and structure anticipation about possible outcomes. While answers to some implicit questions come fairly quickly, others sustain interest until the closing scenes.

Shooting & Editing Schemes

Over the decades, moviemaking entailed greater use of moving cameras, wide-angle and telephotos lenses, shorter scenes, and more close-ups and concise, quicker edits, but the basic production techniques still hold sway. Skillful camera work and editing generally afford the optimum vantage point on the unfolding action. The range of perspectives can move back-and-forth across a continuum from the objective to the subjective. With the objective point of view, individuals, events, and locations are shown neutrally, and not from any character's vantage point. They may be presented in a distant wide-angle view, approximating how we might see them on a stage, or in varying degrees of closeness.

With the subjective point of view, the camera position suggests something shown from the angle of vision of a character in the previous shot. Such shots can also indicate the physical or psychological state of someone. Blurred images, for example, might signal the point of view of someone hit over the head. A subjective point-of-view shot is typically joined together with two objective shots to suggest the vantage point of a specific character.

The perspective changes every time the composition of the frame changes, whether by moving the camera, adjusting the lens, or altering the angle or position of the camera relative to the subject. Camera angles can range from a bird's-eye view (directly above) to a worm's-eye view (directly below). Such camera angles can be employed to enhance a range of feelings. They often convey attitude, giving us a sense of what the subject feels about the surrounding people or objects. The higher the angle, the more a feeling is intensified.

In general, low-angle shots generate in us a sense of weakness, impotence, and diminution. The angle imbues the subject with an air of dominance, power, or authority. Perhaps this reaction is related to childhood memories of looking up at parents and other authority figures. Conversely, when aimed downward, the camera simulates the point of view of a tall person, and the subject is diminished in stature and put in a subordinate position. Again, the resonance of past experiences and responses creates this effect. Of course, appropriate responses always depend on context.

The moviemaker can single out faces to bring emotional weight to the unfolding story. Close-ups are especially useful for conveying emotion, allowing the smallest reaction of a player, the slightest quirk of the lips, the tiniest lift of the eyebrow, or droop of the shoulders and almost invisible tensing of the muscles. Shifting patterns of light and shadow carry strong emotional and symbolic overtones. They can be exploited within a single shot or from scene to scene. Contrasts between light and dark can set a mood even before any action has occurred. Within a single shot, one character may appear in bright tones and another in shadows or dark tones to suggest something about their traits or their emotional or dramatic situations.

Movies are less removed from reality in superficial ways these days. When the industry turned to talkies, the studios fostered among its players a not-quite-British, not-quite-American style of speaking. As Swedish-born Ingrid Bergmann urges, "Play it, Sam. Play 'As Time Goes By,'" in *Casablanca* (1942), her staccato "t's" and stretched out "a's" lending a musical flavor to rising and falling of the voice as she speaks. The glamor and grandeur in her lilting vocal pattern and pronunciation is not a real accent but an affectation, a hybrid of aristocratic British speech and standard American English. Taught in upscale New England prep schools or mastered for theater productions, it suggested a certain out-of-the-ordinary above-the-rabble quality.

The appearance of star players also had aspects of discernible artifice, lighting them in ways that made their faces appear to emanate rather than reflect light. That such facial lighting usually had no identifiable source in a scene served to enhance this impression. To stay with the same example, the veteran cinematographer for *Casablanca* used such "star lighting" techniques to enhance Ingrid Bergmann's screen allure considerably. Soft lighting accentuates her cheekbones, and delicate shading of her high forehead directs attention to her expressive eyes. Whenever the camera closes tightly on her face, filters, makeup, and subtle illumination effects combine to make her appear to be as submissive as she is seductive.

Perhaps more than any other single factor, it is the visual style of the lighting that provides the thread uniting the untidy taxonomy of film noir, or "dark cinema." The action typically occurs in the dark, shadowy worlds of shabby train stations, dimly lit cocktail lounges, remote hilltop mansions, and rundown hotel rooms lit with flashing neon signs. Interior sets are usually dark, with foreboding shadow patterns from Venetian blinds often lacing the walls. The ambiance of *Out of the Past* (1947) serves as a veritable textbook of noirish lighting techniques. The elaborate tonal qualities of the

black-and-white imagery serve to accentuate shifting moods, emotions, and subtle air of menace. The world-weary private eye (Robert Mitchum) works his way through a twisted plot involving brutal killings and unscrupulous females. The stress is on tone and mood, the murky moral milieu he inhabits and how it affects him. The sensual play of light and shadow on the principal female character's face (Jane Greer) suggests unfathomable depths.

The evocative power of darkness can contribute to mood and meaning in myriad ways. There are many instances in movies where the lights not turned on are as significant as those that are. Reducing or eliminating fill lights to soften the shadows can produce ominously stark patterns of light and dark. Spotlight positioning can generate scary or menacing shadows on an actor's face. Under lighting comes up from below a subject, casting shadows upward and creating a ghoulish look. In photographing *The Godfather* (1972), cinematographer Gordon Willis used top lighting shining down directly above the title character (played by Marlon Brando) to give his eyes the look of dark sockets—mysterious, unnatural, incomprehensible, and a little frightening.

Color photography also can affect the emotional tone or atmosphere of a movie in subtle ways. Moviemakers can draw upon a rich palette of colors to set the overall mood of a scene, convey psychological states, or evoke a sense of nostalgia or a period feel. Light sources and images are warm or warmer as they move toward red (the reddish glow of candlelight) and colder as they move toward blue (the bluish cast of fluorescent lamps).

Director Spike Lee employed changing patterns of color and light intensity in *Malcolm X* (1992) to convey the different moods of the title character's life. Working with cinematographer Ernest Dickerson, he bathes the early Boston street scenes of the movie in a mellow, sepia-toned sunlit glow and then shifted to a colder, more bluish hue for the views in prison. When Malcolm (Denzel Washington) becomes a Muslim, the images are very stark. The talented cinematic team considerably soften the clarity during his journeys to Mecca and the Sahara. In many critical moments of his life as a public figure, they intersperse color photography with black-and-white, quasi-documentary footage.

Moviemakers usually employ many camera setups for the separate shots comprised in most scenes. Each new set up of the camera may involve changes in the lighting scheme, the deployment and movement of actors, the angle and position of the camera (and possibly lenses and filters), and the placement of microphones. Because of the amount of time and organization entailed in these activities, moviemakers typically film together shots requiring the same basic setup, even though they may appear in different parts of the scene. The simplest of scenes can involve intricate camera setups that are quite time consuming to execute.

The components of continuity editing include "matching" successive shots with ongoing action, graphic similarities, connecting glances, or familiar sounds. In a visual match, actors, objects, and other compositional factors retain their approximate positions from shot to shot. Eyeline matches, connecting the separate glances of the speakers, let the audience know what each speaker is looking at or talking to even when they are not shown together on the screen. A match-on-action continues a physical action from one shot to the next without any disorienting jumps. (Common sounds from shot to shot further help to conceal cuts.) The effectiveness of matching depends on its smoothness. Directors must employ specific shooting strategies to ensure that editors have the necessary footage to create a smooth, logical flow from shot to shot within a scene.

As the French-Greek rooted term "melodrama" suggests, music has been an essential element of movies almost from the outset, even the earliest silent films accompanied by a piano or small ensemble. The judicious use of musical accompaniment helps set the pace of the action, communicates mood, serves as a substitute for dialogue, sustains tension, and gives a sense of dramatic continuity. The infinite flexibility and variability of music allow for the evocation of a wide range of moods and feelings. Veteran composer Nino Rota used original material and excerpts from a score he wrote for an Italian production to create *The Godfather*'s hauntingly evocative musical score. From the movie's opening "Godfather Waltz," performed on a single trumpet, to the richly orchestrated arrangement accompanying the closing credits, the score interlaces with intricate melodies and passages associated with different moods and characters.

To a large degree, music helps determine the extent of our involvement in any movie and can often evoke strong emotional responses. The spirited music of the wedding sequence and the nostalgic waltz to which Don Corleone and his wife dance (both composed by Carmine Coppola, the director's father) stand in sharp contrast to the edgy piano chords that heighten tension in several scenes. A short eleven-note piece for flute, piano, and clarinet serve as the musical motif for Michael's rise to power in the Corleone family.

Early in the baptism sequence, a solo organ modulates through a series of major chords. As scenes showing preparations for the killings intermingle with ones showing the sacred service, the tone becomes slightly more ominous through the modulation to a minor chord. The organ sounds gradually change into the passacaglia from Johann Sebastian Bach's Passacaglia and Fugue in G Minor. This rather sad work sets the mood for the multiple murders that follow.

Genres

Most movies fall into some genre, or recognizable category, such as westerns, crime sagas, horror films, romantic comedies, musicals, and science fiction thrillers. Although the concept of genre enjoys wide currency, the actual basis for distinguishing between various kinds of movies is hardly clear or consistent. Film analysts have categorized genres in multiple ways, but a dominant factor has been the subject matter. Gangster films chronicle the rise and fall of criminal figures as they struggle against police and rival gangs, and war movies are concerned with battles, bloodshed, and behind-the-lines maneuvers.

Other genres get defined in terms of rhetorical intentions. For example, spy thrillers offer suspense; comedies aim to amuse, and horror films seek shock and disgust. Another method of categorization focuses on formal elements. Musicals employ songs and dances. Domestic melodramas involve strong expressions of emotion. The critical factors in film noir include dim, low-key lighting, disorienting visual schemes, and unbalanced compositions; epics utilize wide-screen formats, vivid color, sweeping movement, elaborate costumes, and a "cast of thousands."

From a critical standpoint, classifying movies into specific generic categories can best be viewed less in terms of particular and exclusive elements and more in terms of analytical usefulness. Many films, in fact, don't fit comfortably into self-contained, consistent generic frameworks. The romantic crime thriller *Out of the Past* (1947) and the moody western *Pursued* (1947) both contain film noir elements. Putting these two movies in the same analytical category, regardless of how it is labeled, focuses on the stylistic, narrative, and thematic affinities they possess.

Thematic Template

A scholarly analysis of mainstream movies suggests thematic developments often turn on the incompatible values and beliefs of the settled and the unsettled existence—the individual versus community, movement versus stability, and competition versus cooperation.[193] The intense psychological pull of these opposites suggests the irreconcilability of involvement with others, maintaining a high degree of autonomy and independence, having an adventurous life and enjoying domestic tranquility, and ambitious careerism and a stable family situation. Despite the comforting denouements of many movies, part of the appeal of watching them is that there are no easy choices. A lifestyle that promises adventure and freedom also opens up the possibility of loneliness and anonymity. In devotion to family and community lingers the potential for predictability, boredom, and frustrated desire.

Of all the generic categories, the western is most indicative of these narrative undercurrents in many ways. In the typical western, these dichotomies are transformed into wilderness and civilization, with the "frontier" as the dividing line, and structurally associated with such opposing values as freedom versus restriction, pragmatism versus idealism, tradition versus change, and self-interest versus social responsibility.[194] These elements take concrete form in such characters as the gunfighter, the marshal, the farmer, the Indian, the housewife, and the barmaid. They're also evident in such items as shoes and boots, tea and whiskey, trains and buckboards, aprons and gun belts, and hats and headdresses.

Any technique, image, gesture, or event may have thematic implications. The values associated with the unsettled life are typically manifested in a male protagonist who is self-reliant—a social outsider generally free of entangling relationships. Women usually mean trouble for this type. Even loving and loyal women are likely to challenge his way of life by posing the threat of marriage and the settled life. This man seems most comfortable with other males who share his disdain for domesticity.

The standard-bearer of the settled life, in contrast, is most often a male protagonist who is comfortable in society and enjoys being with women. He is likely to be married, to feel responsible for the welfare of the community at large, and to pursue collective action. The conflict of values inherent in frontier claims of both unlimited freedom and social conformity generally achieve dramatic resolution in ways that are emotionally satisfying.

Rugged Individualism

The quintessential western hero actor John Wayne stomped the sagebrush in Saturday-morning serials and cheap action pictures, gradually honing his natural attributes into a distinctive screen persona. His role as the Ringo Kid in the classic western *Stagecoach* (1939) propelled him into the top ranks of box office stars—a position he maintained for the next several decades. During the 1940s and 1950s, as a study of the star suggests, Wayne's screen persona came to symbolize the popular conception of American manhood and individualism as it had evolved in the first half of the century.[195] In such roles as a ruthless empire builder in *Red River* (1948) and a relentless ex-Confederate soldier in *The Searchers* (1956), his rough features and granite-like demeanor conveyed a sense of inner strength, the quality that arguably comes closest to the secret of his enduring screen success. In combination with other attributes, such as sensitivity and amiability beneath a hard exterior, this proved to be magic for many moviegoers and television viewers.

The mantle of rugged old west individualism passed to Clint Eastwood, who started his screen career as a bit player in such sci-fi/horror films as *Tarantula* (1955) and *Revenge of the Creature* (1955). He first garnered national attention four years later costarring on the TV series *Rawhide* as a young hunk cattle driver trying to get his herds to market in the face of rustlers, nasty weather, and all manner of other difficulties.

The lean, laconic Eastwood catapulted to international fame in 1964 by starring in an Italian-made western made in Spain. Two more such big box-office draws quickly followed. The kind of isolated figure he cut in role after role seemed to tap into some deep strain in American culture and history. For several decades, he infused a sense of solitariness into even stock and two-dimensional characters. From the squinty-eyed gunslinger in *A Fistful of Dollars* (1964), *For a Few Dollars More* (1965) and *The Good, the Bad and the Ugly* (1966) to the craggy-faced former killer of terrifying reputation in the revisionist western *Unforgiven* (1992), Eastwood resonated with audiences across generations and national boundaries.

The classic plot formula of the loner who rides in from the wilderness, enters a troubled frontier community, and leads a group of homesteaders in its struggle to prevail over the covetous cattlemen or hostile Indians who are holding back the advance of civilization reoccurred in a variety of theatrical releases in the fifteen or so years following the Second World War. By removing the impediments to civilization, this imposing symbol of frontier freedom and autonomy becomes anachronistic. So he drifts off to some unspecified land further into the wilderness, his life of solitude and self-determination only temporarily disrupted.

In *Gunfighter Nation*, cultural historian Richard Slotkin argues that the western genre offers the most precise articulation of America's myths—those symbolic narratives that express the culture's central beliefs, political struggles, and social uncertainties.[196] They contain the conceptual categories that inform words and practices and provide a means of explaining problems that arise in the course of historical experience. He sees the frontier myth as amplified and refracted through post-World War II western novels, movies, and television series as the foundation of American thought and history affecting notions of democracy, heroic action, destiny, gender, and race and helping to forge American political conceptions about the world in general.

Although vague about matters of cause and effect, Slotkin not only links the frontier myth to America's attempts to expand into the Caribbean, thwart the forces of Communism in Europe, and project its power into Southeast Asia but also to specific metaphorical thought and language. He notes, for example, that not long after President John F. Kennedy proclaimed the "New Frontier," government officials sent CIA agents they called "cowboys" to infiltrate Cuba. American troops fighting a "frontier" war in Vietnam were encouraged to think of South Vietnamese peasants as "settlers" requiring rescue from the "savagery" of communist "Indians."

Such verbal displays of the frontier myth are not just a matter of language, but also a process of internally organizing or understanding an aspect of the external world in ways that make it familiar. Casting Vietnam in terms of the western frontier, a part of mythical history dear to many Americans, conjures up a place free from the stifling conventions and untethered by the legal and social constraints associated with civilization and may give free rein to the worst human instincts.

Urban Frontier

Although the western genre virtually disappeared from the large screen in the late 1970s and 1980s, even a cursory glance at movies of this period suggests that the appeal of ad hoc individualism remained strong. Its enduring allure can be seen in the cinematic exploits of such "disguised" western antiheroes as Clint Eastwood's Dirty Harry and Charles Bronson's lone vigilante in *Death Wish* (and its sequels).

The characters in these urban crime dramas share a spiritual bond of sadness and solitude with the classical western hero, but they are far more resigned to the conditions imposed by contemporary circumstances. Whereas the gunfighter of the classic western strives to establish a pristine rule of order, these embittered loners simply seek to carve out a small space for themselves in which something like traditional justice

can prevail. They have no expectation of ever quelling the forces of evil. In the harsh world they inhabit, the very social institutions the western heroes fought to establish have been suborned by greed and cupidity. A malefactor may be subdued, but society remains as sour as ever.

In *Death Wish* (1974), a mild-mannered New York City architect (Charles Bronson) turns wild-west-like vigilante after three thugs invade the apartment by posing as deliverymen, kill his wife and rape and sodomize his grown daughter. After returning from a business trip, he learns from his son-in-law that his daughter is severely depressed from the trauma of the assault and has become catatonic. When he discovers that a client has given him a handgun as a gift, he loads it and takes a late-night walk during which an armed mugger accosts him. He shoots him, and in a state of shock, runs home and vomits.

The next night, recovered and revengeful, he stalks the mean streets of the urban frontier on the prowl for muggers, hoodlums, and other predators lurking in parks and subways. In the course of the next few weeks, he shoots several miscreants, some who provoked him, and others when he sees them attacking innocent people. As street crime in New York City declines, the media trumpet him as a hero, prompting law enforcement authorities not to apprehend him when they learn he is the serial killer. They offer only one option: get out of town for good. He heads west to Chicago. His gun-like finger pointing gesture at the airport suggests he will resume his vigilante crusade, moving on as it were to the next "frontier town" where his services are needed.

The police in a crime-ridden precinct featured in *Fort Apache, The Bronx* (1981), feel like troops at a frontier outpost surrounded by hostiles. Highlighting the inhospitable conditions, a drug addict shoots two rookie cops at the movie's beginning. At the center of the story is a hard-drinking veteran officer (Paul Newman) who, with his novice partner, attempts to maintain law and order in the mostly Puerto Rican community to no avail. Alleged police brutality sparks rioting. During the mayhem, he and his partner witness a fellow cop tossing a teenager off a roof to his death.

Breaking the "blue code," the police veteran is shunned when he reports the roof killing. His new nurse girlfriend dies from a heroin overdose. He has a battle of will with his commanding officer who sees blind brutality as the answer to urban blight. The killer of the two cops is never found, despite mass arrests and interrogations. On the verge of quitting the force, he spots a purse-snatcher fleeing from a house he burglarized. He and his partner give chase, and the image freezes as he leaps to tackle him.

The basic structure and character types of the classic western reappear in various guises across many different genres and periods. In generically dissimilar movies, a self-reliant loner reluctant to become involved with others eventually joins forces with someone who has a strong sense of mutual commitment and social responsibility. Paralleling the trajectory of the classical western, all of these movies tend to favor ad hoc individualism over the civilizing values of family and community. Most of what happens is pinned to the self-reliant loner's emotional point of view and take its logic from his perspective.

Current Cinema

The advent of glittering technologies altered the entire movie industry as digitizing moved from the wings to center stage. The typical director these days uses high-definition digital cameras to capture images with fidelity akin to that of the 35-millimeter film without the degradation of visual quality that is inevitable when films are transferred from negatives to master prints and then to third-generation copies shown in theatres. Whether on a large screen or a small one, every run of a digital movie will provide pristinely, flicker-free images devoid of lint, scratches, and torn sprockets.

In addition to enhancing viewing experiences, and allowing for more credible computer-generated imagery, industry-wide adoption of digital cinema significantly reduced the amount of time and money it takes to distribute movies to exhibitors. Sending copies of videos to theatre operators on disk or digital tape, or beaming them via satellite saves a big chunk of the estimated billion dollars the big studios used to spend each year making, insuring, and shipping large film prints. These new distribution methods and exhibitions create more excellent cinematic choice by opening more avenues for smaller, independent works.

The viewing of movies at home is now the norm; the pandemic accelerated the transition from multiplex to the living room. The internet, a vast network of tens of thousands of interconnected sub-networks with no single owner or controlling authority, links millions of computers worldwide. The World Wide Web organizes and standardizes the data flowing through these electronic pathways and lets individual computers tap into one another. Accessing the internet has become so simple and straightforward that most Americans and millions worldwide now make their way around the many movie websites. The growth of streaming services has earned the home the preferred place for watching movies and other forms of enacted storytelling.

Chapter 6

Sound Visions

In what's often called radio's "golden age," the 1930s and 1940s, producers and performers, with the intimacy of the home as their stage, created a "movie projector of the mind," turning the use of sound into a distinctive communications medium of broad reach and appeal. Almost from the outset, profit-driven corporate interests concerned with the bottom-line carefully orchestrated the gratifying and intoxicating activity of radio listening, of creating mental images of how persons, places, and things look.

Not unlike the penny press of an earlier era, radio's underlying business model was grabbing and holding audience attention and selling it to advertisers. As the voice of corporate America, broadcasting's adoption of the market and commercial values spawned a culture that cemented its power, in the words of antitrust law professor Tim Wu, defining "the basic tenor of the times, the ambiance in which things happen, and ultimately the character of a society."[197]

The "public airwaves" is a catchy phrase, implying the ether's intended for the welfare or well-being of all segments of the society. Such commonweal language aside private corporations—stations, networks, ad agencies, and advertisers—emerged as the real rulers of this first of the electronic media to divert minds from the root causes of the harsh conditions and gross inequalities of everyday life.

These profit-oriented custodians of radio (and later television) waves developed program formulas, business practices, ratings, and demographic surveys designed to deliver audience attention to advertisers while provoking as few people as possible. To a former advertising copywriter turned scathing critic commercial broadcasting, the whole system seemed "a conspiracy of silence" on any aspect of social life that did not contribute to the objectives of the advertiser.[198]

Early Broadcast Advertising

In August 1922, AT&T launched WEAF in New York City and filled its airwaves with the first radio commercial. A spokesperson for the Queensboro Corporation extolled tenant-owned apartment houses in a ten-minute presentation (some sources say fifteen minutes). He rhapsodized about "the green fields and the neighborly atmosphere, right on the subway without the expense and trouble of a commuter, where

health and community happiness beckon," and enjoined listeners to hurry to the Hawthorne Court apartment complex in Jackson Heights in Queens, New York.[199] Comprised of seven buildings along 76th street and another seven along 77th street, between 35th Avenue and 37th Avenue, it was the first planned garden and cooperative apartment community in the United States and still stands out in the neighborhood of mostly multi-unit buildings with cramped quarters not uncommon. Recent decades saw the area became a microcosm of cultures worldwide, with street vendors and food courts offering highly diverse ethnic fare.

As a result of this ten-minute sales pitch, Queensboro sold many apartments, proving direct advertising could be successful. By the end of 1922, WEAF could claim thirteen advertisers, including department stores R.H. Macy and Gimbal Brothers. Tangible evidence of an extensive listenership came in January 1923 when, following a talk by movie star Marion Davies on "How I make up for the movies," sponsored by the beauty product Mineralava, which offered a free autographed picture of the cinema star. Hundreds of requests poured into the station.

Moving cautiously into the new medium, most sponsors merely linked their names to particular programs. Every effort was made not to offend. The management at WEAF prohibited a vacuum cleaner manufacturer from using the line "Sweep no more, my lady," for fear that lovers of the song "My Old Kentucky Home" might get upset.[200] It also held up a toothpaste-sponsored program while it considered the propriety of mentioning on the air so intimate a matter as the care of teeth. Such sensibilities seem a world away from the feminine hygiene and erectile dysfunction commercials that routinely air on the broadcast media these days. As the time-for-sale system spread rapidly, sponsored concerts competed with catchy jingles for audience attention.

Dissident voices largely disappeared from the airwaves as profit-driven corporations assumed control of broadcasting. Critiques of banks and businesses, subjects such as socialism, and virtually any ideas likely to provoke social unrest got short shrift. *Brooklyn Eagle* associate editor H. V. Kaltenborn who had a weekly current events series on WEAF, later wrote based on his experiences that radio's chief purpose had become "to make money for those for those who control and use its mechanical devices."[201]

Broadcast Networks

The basic pattern for radio broadcasting—one that would later be followed by television—was firmly set during the mid-1920s when AT&T sold its broadcast assets, including WEAF, to the Radio Corporation of America. This sale was the first indication that private corporations could sell the public resource through which stations transmitted for private gain. The telephone company would continue to profit indirectly from broadcasting by leasing its high-efficiency cable lines for the interconnection of broadcast outlets.

In the same year that AT&T consummated the sale of its stations, RCA organized a central broadcasting subsidiary—the National Broadcasting Company. With the acquisition of WEAF and AT&T's other broadcast assets, NBC owned two outlets in New York City and other locations. Rather than duplicate programming on two stations in the same broadcast area, NBC set up two semi-independent network operations—the "Red" network and the "Blue" network to control and centralize the radio medium by connecting stations nationwide networks.

A radio network exploits the economy of scale by interconnecting stations to carry the same programming through an organization that also produces and provides the shows. The interconnection of stations and the centralized programming coincided with the general consolidation and standardization of goods and services nationwide.

National advertisers, who found the newly established NBC networks a most efficient sales vehicle for standardized products, soon set the scale for air time costs. Their ability to pay hefty amounts for access to the airwaves ensured them a privileged position in the nation's broadcast system. As one might expect, given its corporate parents, NBC's programming practices did nothing to hinder the established order. Other firms own most of the station "affiliates" in a network. By law, no organization could hold more than seven stations; regulators considerably liberalized such ownership rules in recent decades. Those stations without a network affiliation are called "independents." By the mid-1930s, some one-third of network programming was advertiser supported, with about half of all revenue coming from ten advertising agencies.

Within a year or so of NBC formation, an operating company called Columbia Phonograph Broadcasting System emerged, a merger of the fledging United Independent Broadcasters and the Columbia Phonograph Company. One of the first major clients of the new network was the Congress Cigar Company, makers of La Palina cigars headed by Samuel Paley. When the year-old system ran out of money, William Paley, the advertising manager of his father's cigar company, secured controlling interest becoming at age 27, its president.[202] Proving to be an astute businessman, by the early 1930s, he turned the operation into a success through various maneuvers.

CBS paid each affiliated station on an attractive sliding-scale basis for access to its airwaves. In effect, stations licensed to serve local communities had turned over their facilities to the national network. NBC was quick to follow CBS's lead when it started to lose affiliates to the rival organization. The local station had but to flick a switch, permitting programs and revenues to flow into its facilities. It could also sell time to local advertisers. Affiliation with one of the national networks turned local broadcasting into a bonanza.

The business success of NBC and CBS encouraged unaffiliated stations and regional networks to unite. In 1934, several advertisers urged WOR (New York City) and WGN (Chicago) to link up for simultaneous broadcasts. This arrangement allowed advertisers to reach large population centers without having to pay for coast-to-coast hookups.

Soon WXYZ (Detroit) and WLW (Cincinnati) decided to join the other two metropolitan stations. That same year, all four stations officially united as the Mutual Broadcasting System. It was incorporated to carry on the business of selling advertiser time and coordinating the exchange of programs—including that enduring icon of American culture *The Lone Ranger*, a masked man who, with "an Indian rode the plains, searching for truth and justice."

Broadcasting's Diversions

The program fare of radio increasingly defined the reality of people's lives, as the auditory sense moved to center stage. Media historian Susan J. Douglas notes that the absence of imagery is the most significant strength of radio, allowing "people to bind themselves so powerfully to this device." The medium's extension and magnification of our auditory sense have discernible effects on the way we see the world at large and ourselves. "When information comes solely through our auditory system," she explains, "our mental imaging systems have freewheeling authority to generate whatever visuals they want"[203]

By the 1930s, the radio set had become the country's most important piece of household furniture, and a new cultural phenomenon as millions tuned in the vacuum-tube-filled box to hear the same network shows, in large part produced by ad agencies on behalf of their corporate clients. Everyone involved in this profit-making endeavor to attract and hold the attention of millions was not likely to undercut stockholder dividends or load still higher costs on the consumer by observing standards of ethics, morals, and taste. Challenges to this system invariably failed because the electronic instruments essential for shaping and organizing public opinion nationwide were in the hands of its corporate custodians.

Ad Agencies

Ad Agencies took form in the 1830s as brokers for the sale of space in the print media. By the 1920s, they had become institutions of considerable resources and importance. With growing importance came a new sense of self-importance. Bruce Barton, a partner in Batten, Barton, Durstine & Osborne, was even so bold as to suggest in his best-selling book of the mid-1920s, *The Man Nobody Knows*, that if Jesus Christ were around in modern times he would be an account executive in an ad agency. The book offered an image of Jesus as a go-getter, the first modern salesman, who "picked up twelve men from the bottom ranks of business and forged them into an organization that conquered the world."[204] Radio broadcasting provided an extremely effective means of promoting standardized products of all sorts. The makers of canned soups, packaged desserts, cigarettes, brand-name coffee, and other mass-produced items were soon lining up to sponsor shows. The vast revenues this generated enabled producers to offer

programs and performers that kept listeners riveted to their radio sets residing in a realm of make-believe unconducive to reasoned discourse.

The advertising agencies producing radio fare tended toward traditional values and attitudes, especially in relation to politics and cultural change. As emissaries of some of the most powerful corporations in the United States, the ad industry's political and cultural stance could scarcely have been otherwise. Albert Lasker of the Lord & Thomas agency, for instance, counted among his clients such firms as General Electric, RCA, Cities Service, Commonwealth Edison, and Goodyear. Lord & Thomas was one of the first of the big agencies to set up a radio department. J. Walter Thompson, McCann-Erickson, Young and Rubicam, Benton and Bowles, BBD&O, and scores of other agencies soon followed suit.

For their regular services, agencies received fifteen percent of the broadcast time, matching the fee paid by newspapers and magazines for space sales. For putting together programs, agencies added a second fee of fifteen percent of production costs to a client's bill. (Sponsors, in turn, passed these costs hidden in the retail price of the products on to consumers.) This practice gave agencies the incentive to escalate the costs of broadcasting time and move into the programming area. While the networks could decide when and what kinds of programs they would transmit, the agencies and their clients held the purse strings and generally called the shots.

In 1933, when NBC, one of the first and largest tenants, moved into the sixty-six-story RCA Building, all thirty-five of its studios had a special soundproof booth from which sponsors or agency representatives might supervise the production of programs. Built at the cost of $250 million, in many ways, this imposing Art Deco-styled skyscraper that forms the centerpiece of Rockefeller Center in Midtown Manhattan symbolized the new mega business era of broadcasting. (In 2015, new corporate owner, Comcast, renamed it the Comcast Building—often shortened to 30 Rock.)

Adverting Guru

Like the impressionist painter Picasso, advertising pioneer Claude C. Hopkins turned some of his most famous works in minutes or days. Starting his career as a patent-medicine promoter, he pushed such products as Dr. Shoop's Restorative promising a cure for such ailments as dystopia and constipation. He also promoted Liquozone, a germicide costing nearly nothing to make, that he claimed could relieve or cure everything of dandruff and diphtheria to malaria and malignancy. The enormous success of this bogus nostrum made Hopkins not only wealthy but in significant demand. Hired by ad agency powerhouse, Lord & Thomas, he insisted copywriters research a client's merchandise to create "branding," singling out a product from the rest of those on the market as unique and "demand engineering," fostering a desire for something that might not otherwise exist. Full of himself and his calling, Hopkins boasted in a speech that promoters like himself sway millions changing the currents of trade, building up new industries, and creating customs and fashions. Our names are unknown, he asserted. But there isn't a home, in a city or hamlet, where some human being is not doing what we demand.[205]

While with Lord & Thomas, old huckster Hopkins conceived of the idea of popularizing orange juice as a drink filled with the magic ingredient Vitamin C. His advertising campaign for the Southern California Fruit Exchange (later the brand Sunkist) headlined, "Drink an Orange," explained that orange juice was "a delicious beverage—healthfulness itself." Splashed with warm light, a typical ad promoting the beverage as an elixir for infants depicts a doting mother seated with a rosy-cheeked newborn in a posture for nursing. Instead, she is feeding the baby spoons of orange juice. The ad copy states: "Orange juice is regularly prescribed for the diet of tiny babies because physicians know its purity and food value." Largely as a result of such advertising and promotion, millions of Americans became convinced that their health depended on drinking a glass of orange juice at breakfast every day. Hardly having infant curative effects, orange juice is a harmful substitute for breast milk. And unlike a fiber-filled orange, the juice quickly turns to glucose in the blood stream increasing of a range of maladies when drunk in large amounts. After retirement from Lord & Thomas, capping off his career as president and chairman, in 1923, Hopkins published his manifesto *Scientific Advertising*, gaining the former patent-medicine promoter prestige and emulation, regarded among peers as one of the foremost figures in the history of marketing.

Promoting Products

Product promotion took many forms. Dramatic situations were commonly used to support the sale of soap. The American Tobacco Company, the maker of Lucky Strike cigarettes, tried a variety of sales pitches on the programs it sponsored. Women were encouraged to "reach for a Lucky instead of a sweet" as an aid to weight reduction. This firm became one of the first to buy testimonials (including one from a famous opera singer who didn't even smoke). A cigarette brand reminded listeners of its name and merit with a tobacco auctioneer's chant and the oft-repeated slogan: "L.S./M.F.T., L.S./M.F.T. Lucky Strike means fine tobacco. Yes. Lucky Strike means fine tobacco."

Augmenting its "Reach for a Lucky instead of a sweet" advertising slogan, the Company hired public relations practitioner Edward Bernays. He enlisted photographers, artists, newspapers, and magazines to promote the slim female as the ideal of femininity, no doubt to the chagrin of confectioners. When surveys showed that women objected to Lucky Strikes because the green package with its red bull's-eye clashed with the colors of their clothes, he swung into action to make green fashionable. There followed a green fashion luncheon, a green-themed charity ball attended by upper-crust women donning green gowns, and innumerable window displays of green suits and dresses.

Products were glorified in jingles, as well. Pepsi-Cola stressed economy in its singing commercial: "Pepsi-Cola hits the spot! Twelve full ounces, that's a lot. Twice as much for a nickel, too." Premium offers, usually redeemed by sending in the box top from the sponsor's product, became a prevalent sales gimmick on shows aimed at women and children. General Mills, the sponsor of Jack Armstrong, the All-American

Boy, offered young listeners such things as whistle rings and secret decoders in return for box tops from Wheaties breakfast cereal.

Vaudeville Comedy Shows

Makers of canned soups, packaged desserts, cigarettes, brand-name coffee and other such mass-produced items sought to reach the largest possible audiences. To meet advertiser demand, programmers turned to the production values of vaudeville. The repertory of this theatrical entertainment format, which was especially popular in the early twentieth century, included song-and-dance routines, acrobatics, animal acts, mimed and slapstick comedy, juggling, blackface skits, parodies, impersonations, and monologues. A large part of the aesthetics, and a lot of the talent for commercial broadcasting (and motion pictures) came from vaudeville.

Variety shows, relying heavily on the vaudeville format, became a network staple during the 1930s. A comedian or a singer who could be readily identified with the sponsor's product usually hosted these shows. Jack Benny, Eddie Cantor, Ed Wynn, Burns and Allen, and Jimmy Durante were among the veterans of vaudeville to gain enormous popularity on the airwaves. A juggler by the name of John F. Sullivan left vaudeville for broadcasting and, calling himself "Fred Allen," achieved lasting fame with his one-liners and clever repartee.

Advertisers strove for a close association between product and performer. Comedian Ed Wynn was the Texaco Fire Chief. The comedy team of George Burns and Gracie Allen meant Maxwell House coffee; ventriloquist Edgar Bergen and his wooden dummy Charlie McCarthy, Chase and Sanborn, another coffee company. The "personality" announcer, who could push a product and play a role in the script, became a prominent feature of many programs. Announcers like Don Wilson (Jack Benny) and Bill Goodwin (Burns and Allen) became celebrities in their own right.

Budgets for popular variety and comedy shows often ran to a quarter-million or more a year. General Foods, the maker of Jell-o, paid Jack Benny $10,000 a week, thirty-nine weeks a year, for his "proven ability to sell an ungodly amount of his sponsor's merchandise."[206] Benny created the appealing on-the-air character of the self-confident skinflint who constantly makes a fool of himself. Much of his humor derived from placing this character in well-contrived situations so that laughter could be evoked not so much from what he said, but because of the circumstances in which he said it.

Benny's radio show for General Foods debuted in 1934. Three years later, vaudevillian Eddie "Rochester" Anderson signed on as his brash valet, chauffeur, and frequent comic foil.[207] The white master and black servant comedy routines they did carry traces of blackface minstrelsy. Lest these roots get obscured, in a fall 1936 broadcast, called "Doc Benny's Minstrel Show," the entire cast spoke in a "black" dialect. As Benny's valet, Anderson was subservient to all the characters in the show, addressing them in his uniquely identifiable gravelly voice with the honorific "Mr." or "Miss" before their surnames. Anderson's role retained many of the minstrel stereotypes (lazy, gambler, drinker), and the humor often had racial tinge, but the writers usually had the references come from his character. In one episode, for instance, Rochester complains that Benny wants him to compensate for the lack of a radio in his rattletrap by singing. And at 8:00, he retorts, he wants me to do "Amos and Andy." Even though he often got laughs at Benny's expense, his subordinate manservant status was always evident. Such seemingly harmless humor sponsors could comfortably support.

Quantifying Listeners

Profit-oriented networks, and ad agencies producing the programs required data that could be quantified and generalized: Who listened to what; when; and with what economic effect? Unlike newspapers and magazines, radio reached unseen multitudes not measurable in terms of circulation sales figures. At first, fan mail was used to determine program listenership. But by the 1930s, audience surveys based on telephone samples increasingly determined not only advertising rates but program content as well.

One of the earliest attempts at estimating audience size was made in 1929 by Archibald Crossley, a market research specialist. It used a simple recall method in which he asked respondents what programs they listened to the previous day. He called people in the early evening, finding their names in public telephone books. The sample excluded those with unlisted numbers or without phones. Despite the limitations of this technique, the Association of National Advertisers and the American Association of Advertising Agencies met it with favor. As a result, in 1930 they established a program rating service called the Cooperative Analysis of Broadcasting (CAB), under the direction of Crossley.

Clark-Hooper, Inc., a market researcher in the newspaper and magazine field, introduced second rating service in 1934. (In 1938, Clark-Hooper split into two companies, and C. E. Hooper continued the radio rating service.) Hooperatings employed the telephone "coincidental" method (coinciding with the call). The contacted individuals would be asked to supply information only about what station they were tuned at the time of the call and to what program they were hearing. They also provided the name of the program's sponsor, and the number of men, women, and children listening to the radio at the time the telephone rang.

Every day of the week, operators in thirty-two cities conducted coincidental interviews continuously from 8:00 a.m. to 10:30 p.m. A statistical analysis of the telephone sample established national ratings. Hooper also provided ratings for programs in individual cities. The company provided regularly published reports to both the buyer and the seller of radio time.

Hooperatings soon superseded CAB as the dominant rating system. (The CAB abandoned its recall method for concurrent telephone calls after 1941, but was unable to compete against Hooper and discontinued its service within five years.). Since telephone ownership in the 1930s tended to be related to economic status, poorer households were grossly underrepresented in the Hooperatings. Nor did the sampling include rural residences. Nevertheless, advertiser-supported programs that did not do well in the Hooperatings went off the air. Not all listeners in radioland were created equal. The consequences for programming content it can safely be said were more conservative than revolutionary.

Crime and Detective Shows

The entertainment fare on advertiser-supported broadcasting also mimicked the emotionalism and sentimentality of melodramatic theatre and the plot contrivances of formulaic dime novels and magazine stories, popular art forms that had taken shape with the advent of industrialization and urbanization. Crime series, especially those featuring well-known fictional detectives, became an important staple of the networks' schedules. With rare exceptions, these series had formula plots, stereotyped characters, surface conflicts, and predictable denouements. In each episode, a noble protagonist sought to catch and/or kill some evil and villainous person or persons. The credibility of both the characters and the actions was usually sacrificed for suspenseful effect. Sophisticated use of sound served to heighten the appeal.

The 1930s saw an eruption of detective series, with nearly every fictional sleuth being presented in a radio version. There were Sherlock Holmes and Dr. Watson, Ellery Queen, Nick and Nora Charles, Philo Vance, Bulldog Drummond, Martin Kane, and even Mr. Moto. Each advertiser adapted these fictional characters to fit its own needs. In *The Adventures of Sherlock Holmes*, which early in the decade was sponsored by a coffee manufacturer, Dr. Watson would sip some of the sponsor's product before beginning his tale of adventure and intrigue.

Broadcasting bolstered the image of law enforcement agencies as well. In 1935 Philips H. Lord, a radio actor and producer, launched the short-lived *G-Men* series with scripts based on the files of the Federal Bureau of Investigation. J. Edgar Hoover was one of the first public officials to recognize the potential of entertainment programming to promote law-and-order politics. Over the years, he came to cooperate with many producers in order to promulgate an image of the FBI as a champion of justice. But he was displeased with Lord's emphasis on gunplay at the expense of patient investigative work; so, after twenty-six weeks, he ended the bureau's association with the show.

Philips H. Lord lent an air of authenticity to his shows by employing actual police officials to serve as commentators. The *Gangbusters* series, which premiered in 1936, was hosted by the former superintendent of a state police force. Much of the raw material for the show's half-hour scripts came from the police reporters who covered crime cases in various parts of the country. Any of a score of free-lance writers worked on each episode, blending fact and fiction to promote "America's crusade against crime." Sirens screeching in the night, the clattering of submachine guns, and other such sound effects helped to ensure emotional participation.

Another Lord series, *Mr. District Attorney*, was loosely based on the career of Thomas Dewey in New York City. It went on the air in 1939 featuring nameless prosecutor who served as "champion of the people, defender of truth, guardian of our fundamental rights to life, liberty, and the pursuit of happiness." At the opening of each episode, listeners were assured in ringing tones of the crusading crimefighter's unflinching dedication to law and order within a framework of justice and fair play: "And it shall be my duty as District Attorney not only to prosecute to the limit of the law all persons accused of crimes perpetrated within this county but to defend with equal vigor the rights and privileges of all its citizens." A comic-book spinoff hit home the message as well.

None of these shows referred to the ruinous financial crisis that prevailed throughout the nation. Sponsors shunned any suggestion that the causes of crime might have some economic roots. The good/bad guy formula itself served as a mechanism for such content control. The same cut-to-pattern characters and conflicts could be found in adventure series and western shows as well. The "crime doesn't pay" dictum—may have reinforced the prevailing power suggests a media historian, by blending this serious lesson within a diverting context, and repeatedly illustrating that anti-social villains must reform, go to prison, or face execution to make "the society of the propertied" secure and enduring.[208]

Youngsters were also enlisted in the radio war against crime. In the hours after school, on Saturday mornings, and in the early evenings, the airwaves were filled with adventure programs aimed specifically at children. Comic strip characters like Terry and the Pirates, Don Winslow of the Navy, Superman, and ace detective Dick Tracy were given fuller realization on radio with the voices of actors, music, and sensational sound effects.

Out of the dark recesses of some radio writer's imagination came such urban vigilantes as the Green Hornet, Captain Midnight, and that "mysterious aide to the forces of law and order," the Shadow, who was, "in reality, Lamont Cranston, wealthy young man about town who, years ago in the Orient, learned the hypnotic power to cloud men's minds so that they could not see him."

For millions of young people, the stirring sounds of the "William Tell Overture" meant another episode of the Lone Ranger who, with his faithful Indian companion, Tonto, led the fight for law and order in the early West. This show provided the incentive for organizing the Mutual Broadcasting System (MBS), which carried it on stations not affiliated with the three major radio networks—NBC Red, NBC Blue and CBS.

Daytime Serial Dramas

Daytime serial dramas, more popularly known as "soap operas" because of their sponsorship by soap manufacturers, also enjoyed enormous popularity during the 1930s. Such serials constituted nearly 60 percent of all network daytime programming, by the end of the decade. Some serials had a remarkably long radio run. *The Romance of Helen Trent* was on the air from 1933 to 1960. This serial told the story of a thirty-

five-year-old star-crossed Hollywood dress designer who "when life mocks her, breaks her hopes, dashes her head against the rocks of despair, fights back bravely, successfully, to prove what so many women long to prove in their own lives, that because a woman is thirty-five—or more, romance in life need not be over, that the romance of life can extend into middle age, and beyond."

The promise of fulfilling romantic fantasy filled the daytime airwaves like some heady perfume. The ultimate achievement for the soap-opera heroine the serials hit home daily lies in finding Prince Charming and wedded bliss, despite the harsh truth that this blueprint left many real-life women stranded if their husbands died or divorced them. Over the years, Helen shared her innermost secrets with devoted listeners in heartbreaking fifteen-minute slices. Movie moguls, directors, attorneys, oilmen, millionaire ranchers, and even a mad hypnotist pursued her as she tried to find love in a world full of calamity, danger, and wickedness. The series ended after over 7200 episodes, Helen's demise in a balcony collapse just before returning her most beloved suitor.

Appeal of Serials

The popularity of radio serials aroused interest among social researchers. One study found that the average listener tuned in regularly to 6.6 different serials. What did listeners find appealing about these serial dramas? A survey conducted mainly among homemakers by a social psychologist led her to conclude that the stories had become an integral part of many women's lives. They provide temporary emotional release, escape from the dull routines of everyday life, and "a model of reality by which one is taught how to think and how to act."[209] One woman indicated that she used a face cream advertised on Helen Trent "because she is using it, and she is over thirty-five herself and has all these romances." Some 61 percent of those interviewed said they used merchandise advertised on the serials they followed.

This kind of research was useful to the custodians of commercial broadcasting, but it necessarily ignored questions of more considerable cultural significance. For instance, what historical circumstances led women to turn to radio serials for emotional release, escape, or social guidance? Could there possibly be a functional link between soap operas and the romantic songs of misty-voiced minstrels that titillated the sexual fantasies of bored aristocratic ladies in the twelfth century?

Such broad cultural concerns are not amenable to even the most refined and sophisticated survey techniques. While useful in specific areas like determining program or product preferences, surveys are limited in the kinds of knowledge they provide. This method can only assess phenomena that respondents are conscious of and willing or able to disclose. Individual responses often obscure more than they reveal. They lack consideration of how these responses might reflect broader cultural patterns or how the structure of society may condition them.

Martian Invasion

Creativity enjoyed freer rein in unsold periods especially at CBS under William Paley who, along with other innovative offerings, put young New York actor and director named Orson Wells and his Mercury Theatre group on the radio network in 1938. The group's new takes on classic plays like Shakespeare's *Julius Caesar* reimagined as a commentary on the rise of fascism gained critical acclaim if not large audiences. In most *Mercury* productions, it was Welles himself who narrated. His sonorous baritone voice could produce narrative passages of amazing rhythmic dexterity.

On the cover of *Time* magazine only months earlier, the 23-year-old Welles, along with writer Howard Koch reworked the plodding Victorian narrative about a Martian invasion of earth, H.G. Wells's *War of the Worlds*, into a gripping faux newscast with real moments of shock and excitement. The program, aired on Halloween night in 1938, made headlines with its news-bulletin format to interrupt dance music and inform listeners of the destruction being wrought in New Jersey by invading Martians.

Based on little more than anecdotal evidence, newspapers were replete with stories of "widespread" panic, of police being "swamped" by fearful callers, of parish priests "inundated" with requests from parishioners seeking confession, and of people digging old gas masks out of the closet for protection. Few, if any, of these anecdotal reports were ever investigated and confirmed.[210] A small percentage of listeners may have been frightened, and some perhaps even panicked. Many of those who did had tuned in late and missed apparent clues that it was fiction, and a large percentage assumed the U.S. was under attack by Germany, not Mars. But the evidence hardly shows that panic overtook tens of thousands of people throughout the country.

Bill Dock, a New Jersey Farmer, preparing to fight off the invading Martians. Image from Life Magazine, November 1938

A *Life* magazine photograph of a New Jersey farmer, shotgun at the ready, prepared to fight off the invading Martians, went the 1930's equivalent of viral even though the photo looks posed. Newspapers and magazines may well have exaggerated the panic to control better the upstart medium of radio that was becoming the dominant source of breaking news by the late 1930s. By some estimates, newspapers around the country ran over 12,500 stories about its impact. Such attention hardly seemed warranted since such data as exist, mainly C. E. Hooper's shaky telephone coincidental reports, indicates that only two percent of national respondents tuned into the broadcast. The rest were most likely listening to ventriloquist Edgar Bergen's *Chase and Sanborn Hour*, one of the most popular programs on radio, or not tuned into anything at all.

DAILY NEWS FINAL

FAKE RADIO 'WAR' STIRS TERROR THROUGH U.S.

"War" Victim

"I Didn't Know".

Assuming widespread panic, a Princeton University social psychologist and his research team set out to answer why so many people acted so irrationally when the circumstances reported were so improbable.[211] They concluded that, among other elements, critical ability and education level determined how listeners responded to the broadcast. Still, they interviewed only 135 people in depth. Most had been frightened by the show. And all came from New Jersey, which precludes generalization to the public at large because this was hardly a "random sample" in which every member of the population studied has an equal chance of being selected. The conclusions are even more suspect since beyond not studying a diverse group of listeners, the team relied heavily on mail and clippings from sensational newspaper reports related to broadcast. Further tainting the results, they conflated being "frightened," "disturbed," or "excited" by the program with being "panicked."

Airwave Orators

The four major radio networks, NBC Red, NBC Blue, CBS and MBS along with a variety of local stations provided a plethora of quiz shows, comedies, musical variety fare, live sporting events, mysteries, westerns, dramas, thrillers, and adventure series to stimulate the imagination. These networks also brought the disembodied voices of politicians, preachers, celebrities, educators, and product promoters into people's homes for the first time.

Fireside Chats

Few politicians used the medium to more significant advantage than Franklin D. Roosevelt, faced with the problem of how to heal the ailing nation without undermining the existing economic system or the personal freedoms essential to democratic rule. Soon after his election to the presidency in 1932, a banking crisis confronted the country as frightened depositors threatened to withdraw their savings. He closed the banks and then asked for radio time to address the American public. Taking to the airwaves, Roosevelt explained warmly and intimately how he and the American people together would meet the crisis, telling listeners that it was safer to keep money in a reopened bank than under the mattress. "I want to talk for a few minutes with the people of the United States about banking," he began. "I want to tell you what has been done in the last few days, why... and what the next steps are going to be." He ended

his gentle explanation by assuring the listening audience, "It is your problem no less than it is mine. Together we can't fail." It was a touching and perhaps surprising innovation of collective destiny endowing him with the wisdom and concern of a savior.

The wealthy Roosevelt had a cultivated "mid-Atlantic accent," blending aristocratic American and British inflection and pronunciation. The elocution teachers at the kind of posh upper-class prep school he attended embraced this accent as the "proper way" of speaking. His patrician-sounding voice probably struck some as haughty and supercilious. But, by most accounts, the reassuring radio addresses, dubbed "fireside chats," did much to help propel New Deal legislation through Congress and avert a collapse of the capitalist system. During his first year in office, he gave four radio talks altogether.

Intimate Propaganda

The personal intimacy of radio broadcasting reaching listeners at home made it a potent force for social and political movements. During the depths of the Depression, silver-tongued agitators took to the airwaves. With his folksy southern accent, Huey Long, an early Roosevelt supporter who eventually turned against the president, built a national following through the effective use of radio. First as governor of Louisiana and then as U.S. senator, Long often used radio to promote his controversial positions. "Hello friends, this is Huey Long speaking," he typically began. "And I have some important things to tell you. Before I begin I want you to do me a favor. I am going to talk along for four or five minutes, just to keep things going. While I'm doing it I want you to go to the telephone and call up five of your friends, and tell them Huey is on the air."

Setting in motion a massive social movement, Long was a corrupt politician who ran his state like a personal fiefdom, even after he went to Washington. With a political machine that controlled every government job in the state, from the highest to lowest positions, he made ample use of this power to pack the state government with allies who would do his bidding.

His palliative "Share Our Wealth" program promised to provide every family with an income of $2,500 per year and a homestead worth $5,000, through confiscatory taxes on great fortunes. Share-Our-Wealth clubs soon spread into 8,000 cities, towns, and villages, providing a strong foundation for his presidential ambitions. Democrats feared that he could poll three or four million votes on a third-party ticket, and possibly even throw the 1936 election to the Republicans. All such fears abated in September 1935, when Long was killed by an assassin's bullet. Roosevelt won reelection by a landslide.

Like the German Führer, Adolph Hitler, who became chancellor of Germany in

1933, many radio orators placed the blame for the nation's woes on Jews and communists, often conflated into one group. Among the most persuasive and provocative was ebullient Father Charles E. Coughlin.[212] His parish, the Shrine of the Little Flower in Royal Oak, an industrial suburb near the northern edge of Detroit, served only twenty-eight families when he began broadcasting over WJR in Detroit in 1926. His magnetic voice, with its Irish brogue, and the rousing sermons he delivered, attracted a considerable following. As the Depression deepened, Coughlin increasingly turned his attention to political themes accusing the citizenry of scorning the essential family and national doctrine of Jesus Christ. His assertions, with the ring of future popularizers, didn't spare the corporations either, blasting them for mistreating working families and warning of the dangers of the "concentration of wealth in the hands of the few." Foreshadowing the later McCarthyism script, he claimed that American communists infiltrated many levels of government and corporate leadership, and lashed out at the "Bolshevism of America."

For a time, CBS became the inflammatory priest's pulpit—at regular commercial rates. His bold attacks on international banking and his overtones of anti-Semitism prompted network officials to request advance scripts. He responded with a broadcast accusing CBS of censorship. His suggestion that listeners write to the network in protest resulted in a deluge of mail. The network brass soon worked out a plan to dispose of the increasingly demagogic priest, while at the same time seeming to open the airwaves to even greater religious freedom. It scheduled a regular CBS Church of the Air and invited all denominations to share the radio pulpit free of charge, on a rotating basis. Henceforth, no time was to be sold by the network for religious purposes. CBS did not renew Father Coughlin's contract.

When NBC likewise refused to sell him time, the rabble-rousing "radio priest," as he came to be called, organized his own hookup of stations. By the mid-1930s, his anti-government, anti-Wall Street, anti-Semitic diatribes could be heard weekly by upward of forty million listeners around the nation. At the peak of his power, his income from contributions amounted to some $500,000 a year. He had an uncanny knack to connect emotionally with sympathetic audiences, and seize upon vague anxieties percolating in American culture for many decades.

With a steady stream of donations, he expanded his radio network into a virtual empire. Disillusioned with Roosevelt's failure to take over the nation's banking system or implement other of his proposed reforms, he formed a hardline anti-Communist, isolationist organization called the "Christian Front." When the United States began publicly opposing the German Nazi regime of Adolf Hitler, Coughlin turned on Roosevelt entirely, accusing him of advocating "international socialism," and praising Hitler and Italy's Benito Mussolini as "anti-Communist fighters." Echoing Nazi minister of propaganda Joseph Goebbels, he claimed that Marxist atheism in Europe was a Jewish plot.

In 1936, Coughlin formed the National Union for Social Justice and its attendant political branch, the Union Party—his aim to unseat the president. During the next two years, he moved increasingly over the edge in blatantly anti-Semitic rhetoric and his attacks on international bankers. His weekly magazine, *Social Justice*, read by millions, even reprinted the *Protocols of the Elders of Zion*, a hoax document at the heart of a long-debunked, anti-Semitic conspiracy theory.

During the 1940 presidential election, the "radio priest" viciously attacked Roosevelt, calling him "the world's chief warmonger," and speaking approvingly of Adolph Hitler, praising Nazi persecution of the Jews. "When we get through with the Jews in America," he chillingly crowed, "they'll think the treatment they received in Germany was nothing."[213]

When the United States entered the war at the end of 1941, the National Association of Broadcasters, the industry's powerful trade association, arranged for Coughlin's broadcasts to be terminated. And, at Roosevelt Administration's behest, the U.S. Post Office refused to deliver his weekly newspapers. Perhaps fearing his pro-Nazi sympathies would lead to formal charges of treason, in May 1942, Coughlin quietly announced that he was severing all political ties "on orders from Church superiors." Although he continued to write pamphlets about the dangers of communism until his death in 1979, his impact on American political thought ended in the first months of the war.

Influential propagandists, Huey Long and Father Coughlin, had instinctual abilities to communicate their ideas to susceptible audiences. They seized upon vague anxieties, notes historian Alan Brinkley that had afflicted American society for many decades, among them, the fear of concentrated corporate and government power, the concern about the erosion of community and personal autonomy, and the threat to traditional American values.[214] Having faded so quickly from the public ear, how powerful and ominous they once had seemed is easy in the ensuing years to forget as is how the radio medium's inherent capacity for intimacy makes it potent force for propagandizing in modern society.

Wartime News

During the latter half of the 1930s, as broadcasting gradually replaced newsreels and newspapers as the principal sources of information about current events, what people heard increasingly defined the reality of their lives. The fleeting sounds of radio transmission are very different from the permanence of information on the printed page, which can be carefully read and assessed.

News "bulletins" and news broadcasts became more commonplace, bringing the latest information about national and world affairs directly and immediately into American homes and earlobes. In 1933, for example, stations broadcast on-the-scene interviews following an assassination attempt against president-elect Franklin D. Roosevelt to a widening American audience. Radio reporters covered critical political events like presidential conventions and election night returns, the results sent out over the airwaves to listeners.

Early in the decade, the national networks paid scant attention to providing daily news coverage. But CBS's coverage of such events as the 1932 presidential election alarmed newspaper publishers. In April of the following year, the Associated Press withdrew all service to the networks, under pressure from the publishers. The United Press and the International Press Service quickly followed suit compelling radio networks to set up their news operations.

At NBC, A.A. Schecter became a one-person news department. His newsgathering for Lowell Thomas's evening newscast consisted primarily of making telephone calls. At the time, its parent company, Radio Corporation of America (RCA), had two semi-independent network operations, NBC-red and NBC-blue. With advertisers preferring the red, the blue became a dumping ground for talk shows and similar fare that might win favor with the FCC, the agency regulating broadcasting.

CBS set up a more extensive news organization, the Columbia News Service, under the direction of former United Press editor Paul White. White established news bureaus in major American cities and had the managers of these bureaus line up stringers (part-time reporters). CBS also subscribed to the services of the British Exchange Telegraph and the Chinese Central News Agency for coverage of Europe, Asia, and parts of South America. General Mills agreed to pay for half the cost of the CBS-operated news service if weekly expenses didn't exceed $3,000. The food company sponsored daily newscasts on the network.

Newspaper publishers, concerned about the success of the Columbia News Service, retaliated by dropping the program listings of local CBS affiliates. They also put pressure on the sponsors of CBS shows. These tactics got results. CBS decided to seek peace with the publishers. NBC, with its makeshift news operation, was even more amenable to negotiation. In December 1933, representatives of the broadcast and newspaper industries met at the Hotel Biltmore in New York City and arrived at a compromise. CBS agreed to disband its burgeoning news operation, and both networks promised to refrain from newsgathering in the future.

At network expense, a special Press-Radio Bureau would be set up to cull material from the three wire services for broadcast use. The actual broadcasting of news was to be confined to two five-minute periods daily, one in the morning after 9:30 a.m. and the other at night after 9:00 p.m. These newscasts could not be sponsored. Radio commentators were to be restricted to generalizations and news more than twelve hours old.

The agreement seemed to signal a total victory for the publishers. But they had overlooked a simple maxim: When there is sufficient demand for something in a competitive economy that demand will be met. Non-network stations were able to attract listeners to longer newscasts; this, in turn, led to the formation of new and independent newsgathering agencies, such as the Transradio Press Service.

In 1935, the UP and INS joined the competition to sell news to radio stations. The AP didn't follow suit until the end of the decade. But for all intents and purposes, the compromise agreement had come apart. Soon, even the stations that subscribed to the Press-Radio Bureau were permitted to present news summaries as early as 8 a.m. and as late as 6 p.m. After a few years, the much-maligned bureau quietly expired.

By the late 1930s, radio broadcasting was becoming the dominant source of breaking news. Owned by William S. Paley, wealthy son of a cigar magnate, CBS was struggling to keep up with NBC. Paley came to see news programming as an area where his growing network might be able to gain an advantage. He hired two print journalists, Ed Klauber, and Paul White, to run CBS's news unit. Under their watch, the network increased the frequency of its news reports and launched news-and-commentary programs hosted by Lowell Thomas, H. V. Kaltenborn, and Robert Trout.

In March 1938, as German armies marched into Vienna, CBS responded with a landmark broadcast, the first World News Roundup. Live reports from correspondents stationed in London, Paris, Berlin, and other European capitals were its signature feature. Edward R. Murrow and William L. Shirer managed the complex operation for the network. Radio correspondents often scooped the newspapers with reports of significant events. William L. Shirer of CBS and William Kierker of NBC witnessed the French surrender at Compiegne Forest in the same wagon-lit in which the German capitulation of 1918 had taken place. Later, in a joint half-hour broadcast, the two reporters provided American listeners with a vivid description of the extraordinary scene.

As the United States entered the war in late 1941, the earnest and personal recounting of experiences by the radiomen, many of whom were later to develop into deans of the news analysis business, made the war a very real and affecting experience for listeners on the home front. Intensified public interest in news, particularly news about the war, proved especially beneficial to CBS, where Klauber and White had built a talented stable of reporters. Led by Edward R. Murrow, they specialized in vivid on-the-spot reporting and developed an appealing style of broadcast journalism, affirming CBS's leadership in the news.

By the beginning of the Battle of Britain, large-scale attacks on civilian populations by Nazi Germany's air force, CBS assigned Murrow to provide full-time radio coverage of air assaults and coordinate the company's European reporting network. He created a network of Europe-based radio correspondents, known as the "Murrow Boys," many of whom would become household names in their own rights.[215]

When correspondents returned home for a brief rest, the network publicity machinery moved into high gear, making sure their derring-do polished the image of the company picking up the tab. The CBS cadre feted William Shirer, for instance, when he returned from Germany in 1940, with parties, receptions lecture tours. All the attention won him a lucrative book contract. His account of his broadcasts from Germany, *Berlin Diary*, became an immediate bestseller. He later wrote the hugely successful *The Rise and Fall of the Third Reich*. Millions have read this comprehensive history of Nazi Germany and scholarly works have been citing it for over five decades.

Radio correspondents became charismatic figures. During the London blitz, when the Nazis sent as many as a thousand planes a day to bomb the beleaguered city, Murrow, a speech major in college, broadcast on-the-spot descriptions of the devastation, revolutionizing the very style of radio news into "factual storytelling." He became the first bona fide star of broadcast news, cutting a dapper figure as he walked London streets. His deep, resonant voice seemed to match his accounts' gravity as he reported from a rooftop on the overhead bombing. Without any plan or preparation, Murrow's

"This is London" broadcasts during the Nazi aerial bombardments gave listeners a visceral, emotional sense of being there. "The lights are swinging over in this general direction now," he began reciting into a microphone. "You'll hear two explosions. There they are. That was the explosion overhead, not the guns themselves," he observed in easy to grasp short sentences. "I should think in a few minutes there may be a bit of shrapnel around here." Countering the tide of U.S. isolationism, his riveting rooftop reporting did much to win popular support for America's entry into the war.[216]

Before American entry into the war, such tunes as "The Last Time I Saw Paris," evoking nostalgia for a peaceful pre-war Paris, and "Boogie Woogie Bugle Boy," charting a young soldier's military experiences, became popular on radio and enjoyed large record sales. As the nation became immersed in the war, patriotic or war-related music such as "Praise the Lord and Pass the Ammunition," "Comin' In on a Wing and a Prayer" and "You're a Sap, Mr. Jap," filled the airwaves. Big bands, most famously the orchestra headed by Glenn Miller, and entertainers such as Bob Hope performed before thousands at military bases. These shows aired on the radio to listeners from Maine to California.

Wartime Censorship

In times of war, controlling public discourse that an enemy might exploit to undermine the conduct of military operations, strategic policy, or homeland defense, becomes as important as managing official secrets. Congress passed legislation in 1938 that gave the president the authority to define which types of military information needed security protection. Citing this law, President Roosevelt issued an executive order, in May 1940, to establish the Office of Censorship. Its purpose was to supervise information published or broadcast that had any relation to wartime conditions.

For the most part, newspapers and broadcast stations censored themselves, withholding any information that might be of value to the enemy. Early in 1942, the censorship office issued a Code of Wartime Practices that listed the type of materials not permissible for presentation. For example, it prohibited information concerning weather conditions. German submarines were known to be operating off the East Coast of the United States, raising fears that boat commanders could use weather news to determine whether there would be any sailings from seaports.

The government banned as well information about troop, ship, or plane movements, the location of military bases or fortifications, and all but the most comprehensive reports concerning damage from enemy attacks or about casualties incurred by the U.S. or Allied forces in combat with the enemy. It asked broadcasters additionally to eliminate any "man-on-the-street" or other interview-type programs in which people other than station employees or well-known local citizens could have access to a microphone. The purpose of this was to prevent the use of such programs for the transmission of coded messages. Quiz shows, telephone request programs, notices of club meetings, and amateur hours virtually disappeared from the air. The networks were especially zealous in adhering to the code restrictions.

During the war years, there was a high degree of cooperation among broadcasters and government officials. The National Association of Broadcasters, the industry trade association, promulgated a code in December 1941, forbidding the use of "frenzied news flashes," vivid dramatizations of the news, and "hysterical mannerisms" that might unduly affect the listener's peace of mind. In February 1942, at the suggestion of the White House, radio programmers launched a thirteen-week series called This Is War. Norman Corwin, a veteran writer-director at CBS, supervised each of the half-hour programs in the series. These were carried simultaneously on 700 of the nation's 924 radio stations through the facilities of all four networks.

The first program, "How It Was with Us," extolled the peace-loving, pure nature of the American people. Movie actor Robert Montgomery, as narrator, proclaimed America's essential goodness—even though "we happen to be pretty good with a gun." To audiences familiar with western movies, this philosophy and attitude were easy to understand and put the war into terms that clarified the desirable behavior and reactions. Subsequent programs saluted the armed forces and evoked the nature of the enemy. Maxwell Anderson, Stephen Vincent Benet, and Philip Wylie were among the literary luminaries who contributed scripts.

Radio was ready-made for propaganda purposes. Some ninety-percent of the American people could be directly reached by radio at home. The Office of War Information, established by President Roosevelt in 1942, incorporated the information activities of several pre-war agencies and included radio and motion picture bureaus.[217] Among the most pressing problems facing the federal government on the domestic front was the shortage of workforce. After years of grappling with high unemployment, the United States found itself without sufficient workers for its round-the-clock war plant production.

The OWI's radio bureau, seeking to rectify this situation, suggested that serial characters appear in war-related jobs.[218] Several producers and writers complied. Peggy Farrell of Front-Page Farrell was one of the first soap opera heroines to work in a war plant. Several serials soon followed suit. Stella Dallas's war plant job led to involvement with secret formulas and enemy agents. Researchers did not attempt to determine just how many women were persuaded by these serials to enter the workforce. But given the strong identificatory appeal of radio heroines, the number was probably considerable.

In 1942 the popular daytime serial Our Gal Sunday added the character of a black soldier. Returning intermittently during furloughs, he functioned primarily to provoke conversations between Sunday and her husband about the loyalty of black service members to the United States. That same year, another daytime serial, The Romance of Helen Trent, contained an extended episode involving the heroine of the title. She was gravely injured while attempting to save a truck loaded with war goods. She was rescued and treated by "a Negro doctor." In gratitude, she later found the doctor a job as a physician in a war plant. This plot development opened the way for several more discussions among the characters about the competency, loyalty, and patience of black Americans.

The war provided subject matter for several evening adventure shows. The Whistler, David Harding-Counterspy, The Man Called X, and The FBI in Peace and War, among others, did weekly battle with enemy agents and black-marketeers. In 1942, the title character in Mr. District Attorney began battling Nazis. As in the movies, stereotyped forces fought for the United States. The enemy seldom seemed like a threat to primary institutions. Sophisticated sound effects subsumed ideological conflicts.

Many popular children's shows shifted to war-related themes. Robust and intelligent comic-book police detective Dick Tracy, on network radio from 1934, became involved with the French underground. Captain Midnight fought the foes of freedom in Japanese-occupied China. Jack Armstrong, "the all-American boy," became all-American in Pan-America; the Nazis captured little Orphan Annie. She subsequently outwitted them; Superman did battle against the nefarious activities of domestic traitors. The shows urged youngsters likewise to save fuel, collect scrap, and otherwise aid the war effort.

Broadcasting and advertising emerged from the war more tightly intertwined than ever before. In terms of profit, the war was for radio good business: Total advertising revenues jumped 85 percent from 1941 to 1945, resulting in before-tax profits topped 1940, earnings by 120 percent. The president of the National Association of Broadcasters asserted in 1945 that radio belongs along with "the local dairies, laundries, banks, restaurants and filling stations as a member of the town's business family."[219]

Industry Disruption

During the Second World War, radio and other media outlets were cooperative with the government. Still, wartime relations between the broadcasting industry and federal agencies were, at times, less than harmonious. Behind the façade of unity, a bitter battle ensued between the FCC and the networks. With no direct control over these national operations, the commission, concerned about concentration, aimed its reform measures at affiliated stations. Among other means, the federal agency limited affiliation to two years and prohibited stations from affiliating with any organization operating two networks.

In practical terms, RCA would have to spin off either its red or blue network into an independent company. CBS and NBC challenged the commission's authority in the courts, and in 1943, the U.S. Supreme Court ruled in favor of the regulatory agency.[220] RCA sold the NBC blue network to Edward Noble, the Lifesaver candy tycoon, who changed its name to the American Broadcasting Company. As part of the deal, he got all the programs and personalities contractually bound to the network. The genesis of ABC created another competitor in radio, where several shows on the blue network had a steadfast audience and the burgeoning television industry.

In the postwar period, television stations and household sets multiplied across the country, giving rise to substantial structural and operational changes in the radio industry. Another factor affecting broadcasting was the rise of FM radio, which could transmit music on the stereo and allowed for much better fidelity on high and low notes. The result is the emergence of an all-about-the-music ethos as musical programs of all kinds moved away from the more inferior quality AM band.

Radio Music

Long a staple of radio, popular music came to dominate scheduling as other forms of entertainment fare shifted to television. The nostalgic, sentimental, and romantically idealized popular radio and recorded music from the 1930s to the mid-1950s by many accounts served as a soothing antidote. One of the first performers to exploit the intimacy of the microphone early in the broadcast era, Bing Crosby, "collaborated with the electric current as though he were romancing a woman," notes longtime jazz critic. He played "the mike with a virtuosity that influenced every singer to follow, grounding it as a vehicle of modernism."[221] His mellifluous, resonant baritone, a direct extension of conversation, came just as naturally to him as talking, or even breathing, or so it seemed.

The prominent purveyors of American popular love songs Bing Crosby affected include many Perry Como, Frank Sinatra, and even Elvis Presley, who recorded more than a dozen of Crosby's signature hits. A former barber, Perry Como's warm baritone singing sentimental songs in a soft, low voice, came to characterize popular music in the 1940s.

The skinny young crooner Frank Sinatra's mournful wartime love songs, such as "I'll Walk Alone," evoked swoons from "bobbysoxers"—teenage girls wearing rolled anklet socks. His soft, throbbing voice, tapping a strong undercurrent of post-pubescent sexual desire, threw young girls into a frenzy, weeping, screaming, and shrieking rapture. Protecting him from his fervid female fans, a squad car full of police officers accompanied him everywhere. After a career decline and a shift to movies, Sinatra enjoyed a resurgence of popularity in the late 1950s, setting mature female hearts aflutter, releasing a string of successful albums under his record label, Reprise Records

The Ink Spots achieved global fame in 1939 with such sentimentality as "If I Didn't Care," featuring Bill Kenny's sweet, high tenor voice with Orville "Hoppy" Jones's basso talking and Charlie Fuqua, and Deek Watson providing harmony. Accompanying themselves on three tenor guitars

and a cello, picked and slapped by Jones like a double bass, they created romantic magic with the simple, saccharine lyrics: *If I didn't care more than words can say/If I didn't care, would I feel this way?/If this isn't love, then why do I thrill? And what makes my head go 'round and 'round/While my heart stands still?* The unique musical style of The Ink Spots presaged several new genres, especially doo-wop—a form of a cappella vocal group harmony with an engaging melodic line to a simple beat using nonsense phrases. The singing group's other tender love ballads from 1939 include "My Prayer," "Memories of You," and "I'm Gettin' Sentimental Over You." During the 1940s, they had over thirty hits at or near the top of the charts.

Most romantic songs of the period contained little hit of sexual desire, let alone lust. A notable exception is Peggy Lee's sultry purr and intimate and insinuating phrasing in such songs as "Fever" captures both the heated ecstasy and the heartache of romantic relationships. *When you put your arms around me/I get a fever that's so hard to bear/You give me fever/you give me fever/when you kiss me/fever when you hold me tight (you give me fever)/Fever in the mornin' fever all through the night.* The 1940s were the singer, songwriter, composer's heyday in a career spanned six decades.

The chemistry that ignites lustful desire also evokes pangs of jealousy, erratic behavior, and irrationality, along with a host of other less-than-positive moods and emotions. Clarion-voiced song stylist Frankie Laine, who hardly needed a microphone, captures this torment in his 1951 hit "Jezebel." *If ever a pair of eyes promised paradise/Deceiving me, grieving me, leaving me blue/Jezebel, it was you/ Could be better had I never known a lover such as you/Forsaking dreams and all for the siren call of your arms.*

Laine's raw, emotionally charged delivery and an intense vocal style owed nothing to the soft, sentimental crooning of a Crosby, Como, or Sinatra. Unlike such smooth balladeers, he would bend notes and stress each rhythmic downbeat. The brash vibrancy and coarse accent of his songs heralded the rock "n" roll music that was to come.

Scandal-Ridden Rock

The sound of the drum aroused the hidden primitive as sentimental love songs receded before the insistent rhythmic, sensuous beat of what evolved into music labeled rock 'n' roll. In the 1950s, the depiction of gender relations in music started to shift toward lyrics and sounds less romantically adorned as radio disc jockeys, or DJs exerted considerable influence over the airwaves.

By far, Alan Freed, the strongest record spinner, first gained local celebrity status in 1951, hosting a show on a Cleveland radio station devoted to "rhythm & blues." Record producers coined this term to replace the designation "race music," the standard catchall phrase to describe most music made by blacks at the time. Unlike most of his competitors, Freed played the recordings of black artists rather than the cover versions of white performers.

Many of the songs Freed promoted pushed the limits of what was deemed acceptable on the radio medium, among them the Dominoes recording of "Sixty Minute Man." Featuring Bill Brown's bass voice, the singer boasts of his fantastic sexual prowess: *Well, listen here, girls,/I'm telling you now/They call me loving Dan/I'll rock 'em, roll 'em all night long/I'm a sixty-minute man.* The verb phrase rock and roll, a common euphemism among blacks since the mid-1910s, meant, "to have sexual intercourse." By the 1920s, "rocking and rolling" became a popular double entendre referring to either dancing or having sex. Freed appropriated the phrase to describe the amalgamation of rhythm and blues and country music he played during his show.

A former truck driver born in Tupelo, Mississippi, Elvis Presley moved rock 'n' roll from the backwaters to the mainstream. His music career began in Memphis in 1954, recording at the Sun Records studio of Sam Phillips, who wanted to bring the sound of black music to a broader audience. With Presley singing and playing rhythm acoustic guitar, accompanied by lead guitarist Scotty Moore and bassist Bill Black, they created an up-tempo, backbeat-driven fusion of traditional country music and rhythm and blues in "That's All Right." It became highly successful, first in Memphis, then throughout the southern United States. The music giant RCA Victor acquired Presley's contract and released his recording of "Heartbreak Hotel" in January 1956. It became a number-one hit in the United States. His seductive looking low-riding eyelids, soft-edged facial features, front-heavy blondish pompadour (later dyed jet black accompanied by facial cosmetic refinements), and energized rendering of songs, and sexually provocative body movements during stage performances made him enormously popular—and highly controversial.

Presley's success provided a pathway for black rock 'n' roll performers like Chuck Berry. A significant influence on evolving rock music, Berry refined and developed rhythm and blues with such 1950s hits as "Maybelline," "Roll Over Beethoven," "Rock and Roll Music," and "Johnny B. Goode." By the end of the decade, with his dazzling guitar solos and showmanship, Berry had become a high-profile established star with several hit records, movie appearances, and lucrative touring venues. But a propensity for females barely beyond pubescence soon brought his career crashing down. In December 1959, in St. Louis, Missouri, police arrested him under the 1912 federal Mann Act for allegedly having sexual intercourse with a 14-year-old Apache waitress. A jury founded him guilty, and, after several failed appeals, he served the better part of two years in prison.

Like Berry, piano-playing rocker Jerry Lee Lewis also had a fatal sexual attraction to young girls, and by several accounts, an insatiable appetite for female flesh. Lewis made his first recordings in 1956 at Sun Records in Memphis, another of rock and roll's pioneers. His version of the honky-tonk ballad "Crazy Arms" sold well in the South, but his piano-pounding rollicking 1957 hit "Whole Lotta Shakin' Goin' On" that shot him to fame worldwide. He followed this with "Great Balls of Fire," "Breathless," and "High School Confidential."

Signaling today's rockers, his live performances were increasingly wild and energetic—brutalizing the piano, playing with his feet, standing on, crawling under, and even setting it on fire, working teenage audiences into a heated frenzy. Nicknamed "the Killer" for his stormy personal life, a highly publicized marriage to his thirteen-year-old first cousin threw his career in a tailspin from which it never fully recovered.

Such scandals contributed to early rock 'n' roll's notoriety. Another factor traces to a long history in the United States of fearing race mixing and lynching black men because of their perceived desire for white women. To have young, teenage white girls screaming to someone like brash "Little Richard" Penniman with a sax-packed black band as he's singing "Tutti Frutti" was surely disconcerting for many white middle-class parents. His appearance alone must have caused consternation, with his heavy makeup, colorful costumes, and processed hair that stood anywhere from six inches to a full foot above his forehead,

A song the flamboyant rocker had polished in black clubs across the South, the original version leaves no doubt about its erotic aspects: *Tutti Frutti, good booty / If it's tight, it's all right/And if it's greasy, it makes it easy*. With its opening cry of *A-wop-bop-a-loo-bop-a-wop-bam-boom*, Little Richard's recording, even with sanitized lyrics, is a potent mix of gospel, blues, and boogie-woogie with a distinctive rock beat and rhythm, topped off with a loud-volume vocal style suggesting sexual power. His recordings and concert tours cracked the color line, drawing black and white teenagers together despite attempts to sustain segregation. His effeminate mannerisms notwithstanding, he attracted large female audiences, many tossing panties toward the stage during his performances. With his record sales waning in the United States, he went on tour in Europe in 1962. The opening act for him at some venues featured an English rock band formed in Liverpool in 1960. Sporting odd upside-down bowl-like haircuts, they called themselves the Beatles.

The bowdlerizing of songs like "Tutti Frutti" and other popular entertainment forms was nothing new. The verb "to bowdlerize" traces back to early nineteenth-century physician Thomas Bowdler. Upset by passages in Shakespeare's works, he turned out an expurgated edition removing or modifying passages that struck him as risqué, vulgar, or otherwise objectionable. Much to the chagrin of literary critics of the day, he applied his literary eraser broadly. Within eleven years of his death in 1825, the verb bowdlerizes referred to as expurgating books or other texts.

Many radio stations around the country bowdlerized the primal sound of rock music as well. They refused to play or promote black performers singing anything other than saccharine hymns to hormonal upheaval. Such prejudice provided opportunities for white singers like wholesome, clean-cut appearing Pat Boone with his signature white bucks and argyle socks. The catalyst for his career was a string of cover songs originated by black artists, including "Tutti Frutti," the legacy of segregation never affording them the same amount of success or remuneration. In the early years of rock 'n roll, Boone's covers were usually commercially more successful than the originals, even though his smooth vocal delivery was more reminiscent of crooners than the raspy, full-throated yowl of Little Richard. Never one to miss an opportunity to bowdlerize a music genre, Boone's 1997 album, *In a Metal Mood: No More Mr. Nice Guy*, covers hard rock and heavy metal songs in a jazz/big band style. It became his first hit album in thirty-five years, although displeasing some of his older, longtime fans favoring his religious songs.

The rock 'n' roll musical genre underwent notable changes with the advent of the Beatles. The combined talents of John Lennon, Paul McCartney, George Harrison, and Ringo Starr made them one of the most influential bands of all time. With roots in 1950s rock and roll, the guitar virtuosity of Chuck Berry, along with other pioneer rockers like Elvis Presley and Buddy Holly, as well with the steel-string acoustic guitar playing and close harmony singing of the Everly Brothers, significant influences, the group incorporated elements of classical music and traditional romantic ballads in innovative ways. They expanded domestic success with their hit, "Love Me Do," recorded in 1962.

Within a few years, the Beatles were international stars, leading the "British Invasion" of the United States. In the fall of 1965, they released McCartney's poignant composition "Yesterday" from the album *Help!*, as a single in the United States. Featuring his vocal and acoustic guitar, together with a string quartet, it became one of the most covered songs in popular music history. From 1965 onwards, as McCartney began to supplant Lennon as the dominant musical force in the band, they produced

increasingly innovative recordings. Along with *Rubber Soul*, a significant advance in the band's music and lyrics' refinement and profundity, they released the *Revolver* and *Sgt. Pepper's Lonely Hearts Club Band* albums. They enjoyed further artistic acclaim and commercial success with the White Album and Abbey Road.

After the group's break-up in 1970, all four members enjoyed success as solo artists. Lennon was shot and killed in December 1980, and Harrison died of lung cancer in November 2001. McCartney and Starr remain musically active. Even the most ardent fans must find it a bit disconcerting to hear these two septuagenarians singing lyrics from "I Saw Her Standing There," such as *Well, she was just seventeen/you know what I mean.* A self-taught musician with a versatile broad tenor vocal range, McCartney composed the catchy song in 1962 when barely out of his teens.

The age of classic rock 'n' roll is long over, integrating into pop music, and gradually receding before edgier forms like heavy metal and rap that burst onto the music scene in the 1980s, brash, misogynistic, and drenched in debauchery. The artists themselves maintained strict "gangster" personas, and most of the genre's biggest names were known drug dealers, many of them convicted criminals. In recent years rap music evolved into a uniquely genuine voice in the culture that speaks out against police brutality and social injustice.

Talk Radio

By the early years of this century, a plethora of chatty radio personas of different political stripes filled the airwaves with partisan perspectives. With regularly scheduled syndicated programming from March 2004 to January 2010, the progressive Air America network, under various names, featured news reports, guest interviews, and monologues by on-air personalities, among them Al Franken and Rachel Maddow.

From the outset, the network faced fierce headwinds, plagued by a raft of problems, a charity-loan scandal, contract disputes with affiliates and employees, continual changes in ownership and management, and smaller, less powerful, under-performing broadcast signals. The only all-progressive talk radio network in the nation never got an even keel. With liabilities far outweighing assets, it filed for bankruptcy in fall 2006. During the insolvency, pivotal on-air personality Al Franken gave up his show of three years to run for the U.S. Senate. Meanwhile, longtime host Rachel Maddow started moving toward television, appearing as a guest host and panelist on MSNBC, and eventually anchoring a week-night prime-time program on the cable news channel. Unable to stay afloat, the left-tilting Air America network went under at the beginning of 2010.

Air America's ratings never came anywhere near those of right-wing talk titans like Rush Limbaugh. His nationally syndicated show became the model for scores of imitators. A daily call-in program that blends news, talk, and partisan analysis, it goes far beyond left-right political discourse. The charismatic Limbaugh, sharp, fluent and authoritative, is often characterized as conservative, but this is a misnomer since his frequent radical and reactionary rants hardly reflect any commitment to the traditional values and ideas of conservatism or to the truth for that matter.

The revenues for right-wing radio have taken a hit in recent years. Several significant advertisers fled the programs whose hosts routinely use coarse, inciteful, or inflammatory language. A polarizing figure, Limbaugh, has insisted it's unfair to hold white Americans accountable for slavery, blamed gay marriage for the decline of Christianity, and frequently applies the epithet "feminazi" to describe supporters of women's rights. He lost all propriety early in 2012 when he called Georgetown law student Sandra Fluke a "slut" and "prostitute." She had testified before the House Democratic Steering and Policy Committee in support of mandating insurance coverage for contraceptives. He made numerous similar statements over the next two days, leading to the loss of many local and national advertisers.

Chiming in on the coronavirus pandemic, without any evidence, Limbaugh suggested it was a plot hatched by the Chinese to destroy the entire American economy. The audience for Limbaugh and other right-wing hosts is in no small degree older, and the factional over-the-air format is having difficulty attracting younger listeners. The demographic categories advertisers eagerly want to reach are Gen X'ers and Millennials. Most in this age range are doubtlessly only vaguely if at all aware of the aging Limbaugh (suffering from stage-four long cancer) or phalanx of other fact-light but spin-heavy radio and television talk-show pundits and pontificators.

At the behest of her husband, First Lady Melania Trump awarded Limbaugh the Presidential Medal of Freedom during the State of the Union address in early February 2020, an honor he now shares with Mother Teresa, Joseph Lowery, and the crew of Apollo 13. President Trump lavishly praised the recipient of the nation's highest civilian honor but neglected to mention how he's used his radio platform for over twenty years, fifteen hours a week, to fuel the vicious toxicity that characterizes our moment.

Public Radio

The leading public television and radio broadcasters, the Public Broadcasting Service (PBS) and National Public Radio (NPR), operate as technically separate entities. The system currently receives some funding from both federal and state sources. But generally, most financial support comes from underwriting by foundations and businesses ranging from small shops to large corporations, along with audience contributions via pledge drive—derisively called an "electronic tip cup." Neither government nor corporate funding has ever been sufficient to encourage much risk-taking, and the safeguards against a business or political static have proved uncertain.

Given the shaky state of affairs in public radio and television, it is little short of remarkable that the system can claim some absolute triumphs. Among the many worthwhile shows on public radio is *Morning Edition*. Some regional public radio networks and local stations also produce locally focused content under their Morning Edition banner. For a quarter-century or so, genial Bob Edwards hosted the morning show.

Produced and distributed by National Public Radio in Washington, D.C., it offers intelligent, non-partisan reporting and analysis. Steve Inskeep, David Greene, and Rachel Martin are the hosts. They take listeners around the country and the world with multi-faceted stories, up-to-the-minute news, background analysis, interviews, and commentary every weekday morning.

The show draws on reporting from correspondents based around the globe, and producers and reporters in various locations in the United States NPR member-station reporters across the country. Independent producers and journalists throughout the public radio system supplement this reporting. Inskeep and Martin host from NPR headquarters in Washington, D.C., and Green from its studios in Culver City, California. Owing to effective coordination, on a typical morning, listeners hardly suspect they are not all in the same studio together. It airs weekday mornings and runs for two hours, and many stations repeat one or both hours. The show feeds live from 05:00 to 09:00 ET, with feeds and updates as required until noon.

The entire news team is exemplary, accentuating the enduring value of news outlets that are forceful and investigative while remaining politically independent and fair-minded, whatever the focus of attention. Veteran journalist Steve Inskeep is an exceptionally astute and skilled interviewer who asks well-informed, probing questions and responds with on-target follow-ups. The interviewees cover a reasonably broad range of political and ideological points of view.

In one controversial segment during the 2016 presidential campaign, he interviewed white supremacist and former Ku Klux Klan leader David Duke. He is someone in the sphere of deviance rejected by most mainstream journalists as being unworthy of impartial consideration. The interview's primary intent was to explore why Duke and his supporters were attracted to Republican presidential nominee Donald Trump. As might be expected, Inskeep and NPR came under sharp attack for giving prime airtime and legitimacy to someone like David Duke.

Some listeners accused NPR of attempting to "smear" Donald Trump. To provide insight into a marginalized group of Trump supporters, Inskeep relied on recognized expertise, moral authority, and simple common decency. At the same time, he was also quite precise in presenting candidate Trump's statements disavowing this support. Ignoring repugnant ideas doesn't make them disappear. Isolation causes them to become worse or more intense as they get reinforced and magnified in the cocoons of cyberspace. The open forum for diverse and even extreme points of view appears to be working. The highest-rated news program on radio, *Morning Edition*, is holding onto its audience when declines are the norm across the fractionalized media landscape.

Probing Podcasts

The podcast is proving to be a promising media outlet for a range of topics. For the uninitiated, podcasting is a free service permitting internet users to pull audio files from a dedicated website to listen to on their computers or smartphones. Just as blogging has enabled almost anyone with a computer to play reporter or provocateur, podcasting allows virtually anyone to become a radio disc jockey, talk show host, recording artist, or an investigative journalist.

The *Serial* podcast's first-season dove deep into the murder of Hae Min Lee, a Korean-American high school senior who disappeared on January 13, 1999. When her body was found four weeks later, authorities determined she'd been killed by manual strangulation. Within a year, her ex-boyfriend, Adnan Syed, was convicted of the crime and sentenced to life plus thirty years.

Although long proclaiming his innocence, not uncommon for convicted killers to do, his case generated only local interest until it became the subject of the *Serial* podcast in 2014, which brought international attention to the murder and to Syed's subsequent trial. In July 2016, a Maryland judge vacated his conviction and ordered a new trial. A special appeals court upheld this ruling but the Maryland Court of Appeals overturned it, and Syed remains behind bars serving his original sentence.

The popularity of *Serial*'s first season sparked a boom of cold-case imitators. This serialized long-form format proved to be especially conducive for investigative reporting. Pushing the perimeters of the cold-case mold, the seasoned five-person investigative reporting team of the podcast "In the Dark," produced by American Public Media, creates sound-rich, immersive audios, studded with literary details.

The ten-episode first season, exploring a kidnapping/murder, was released in September and October of 2016, with updates offered in December 2016 and September 2018. The second season, whose episodes spanned from May 2018 through June 2019, explored the murderer conviction of Curtis Flowers, who had been tried repeatedly for the killing of four people in a furniture store in Winona, Mississippi—and sentenced to death after the sixth trial.

As the saga unfolded, the focus sharpened on the inequities of the criminal justice system. Running around an hour, released once a week, the episodes poked holes in the forensic evidence and raised questions about an informant who said Flowers had confessed to him. In the latest episode, the show also shredded the alibi of a second suspect. Looking at 6,700 jurors over 25 years of district attorney's tenure, the reporters found that prosecutors in the district, which is 40 percent black, were four times as likely to strike black jurors as white ones. In the six trials Flowers endured, some sixty-one of the seventy-two jurors were white.

This kind of painstaking research contributed to the U.S. Supreme Court's decision in June 2019 that the district attorney in the case had violated the U.S. Constitution. Episodes of the podcast's two seasons have been downloaded over fifty million times. Along the way, it received a Peabody Award and became the first podcast to win a George Polk Award, one of investigative journalism's most prestigious prizes.

Chapter 7

Television Culture

Time and again, we turn to television's panoply of digital dazzle for comfort, diversion, and even enlightenment. Viewers can choose from an unprecedented range of programming. An occasional trip to a movie theatre provides interruption from the daily routine. But television in all its forms, including a broad range of movies, has become the daily routine, a pervasive presence in people's lives. Wielding our remote controls, we select the show date and curtain time for an extensive choice of entertainment fare of every type.

Over-the-Air Television

Such a variety of programming from many places around the globe would have been unimaginable to the viewer of conventional broadcast television in an earlier era when three profit-driven corporate-owned networks, CBS, NBC, and ABC, enjoyed a seemingly impregnable monopoly over daytime and primetime. With their roots in radio, these organizations connected stations nationwide and relied on advertisers to support mostly paint-by-number variety shows and formulaic series and serials.

The programs carried by airwaves into homes across the country had unprecedented reach and influence. From the mid-1950s through the 1970s, over-the-air television was a historic anomaly with routinely huge audiences mostly watching the same "common dominator" programming at the same time more than ever before or ever since. The advertiser-supported structure assured that no unorthodox and heretical ideas would interfere with profits or political objectives. Many of the advertisers, global conglomerates engaged in bribes, subsidies to foreign political parties, and negotiating for CIA interventions, were dedicated to supporting diversionary fare that distracted from world affairs, lulled critical faculties, and contributed to a climate of political complacency.

Most of the program formats and major stars made a smooth transition to network television. The vast majority of shows bore little resemblance to the social and economic realities of the everyday world or explored perspectives in different interest groups, geographic areas, or cultural communities. The very success of mass entertainment lies in large part in the collapse of cultural contradictions and divergent political positions into the prevailing consensus. The programming process itself creates and fosters narrow and restrictive perimeters, reducing nearly all the offerings to shallow, albeit at times attention-riveting appeals.

The inanely amusing reached new heights with the *I Love Lucy* series, starring Lucille Ball and Desi Arnaz. His engaging screen personality along with her madcap antics and canny comic timing did much to overcome the rather low order formula writing. Many of the plots revolved around Ball's hairbrained housewife character's desperate desire for a career in show business and her willingness to do anything, no matter how absurd, to get her foot in the door.

Predictably, for one reason or another, all of her silly schemes failed—such empty-headedness hardly a role model for female viewers. Attracting an estimated ninety-million viewers weekly, this funny, albeit regressive depiction of gender relations propped up a patriarchal cultural perspective. Skillfully filmed with three cameras, like a stage play, the 179 half-hour episodes produced during its original network run still play on stations across the country and in television markets around the world.

The trove of politically bland but sometimes socially astute comedy fare included *Your Show of Shows* featuring seasoned performers Sid Caesar and Imogene Coca, who offered subtle pantomimes and often hilarious character sketches. The inventive comic genius behind the show, the rubber-faced Caesar, was responsible for coming up with many of the verbal exchanges during which he and his costar lampooned pretenses, clichés, and platitudes. Carl Reiner and Howard Morris appear in many of the sketches. The multi-talented Reiner wrote for the show as well as being part of a raucous stable of scribes that at one time or another included such future luminaries as Mel Brooks, Woody Allen, Neil Simon, and Larry Gelbart. The skits skewered everything from opera to health-food fads. Talented guest stars like Art Carney and Ray Bolger added to the antics. Caesar usually got the best lines with Coca playing second fiddle like a virtuoso. They both could bend their flexible faces into wide range of recognizable character-types. He had an uncanny ability to imitate sounds—a slot machine, an elevator, a dial phone, a slamming door, even an elephant with hay fever.

Among the most successful primetime shows was *Toast of the Town* (later called *The Ed Sullivan Show*), an amalgam of variety features supplemented with classical music and dance, hosted by a wooden, stone-faced newspaper gossip columnist named Ed Sullivan. As though speaking to a crowd at a football stadium, he would introduce each act in a voice pitched to the highest register. His was one of the few variety programs not predictable from week to week. One week viewers might see Hungarian ballet dancers on another movie clips of M-G-M stars singing and dancing. While having little talent himself, he was an astute judge of entertainers but kept their performances

with prevailing moral parameters of family fare.

When Elvis Presley first appeared on the show in the fall of 1956, the cameramen shot him only from the waist up because his pelvic gyrations were considered too sexually suggestive for television. The host had previously turned down an opportunity to hire the provocative performer for $5,000 but realized his mistake when the show's ratings tumbled on the evening Presley appeared on a rival variety program. For three appearances on the *Sullivan Show*, he got the unheard-of sum of $50,000.

The rock singer had already appeared six times on the Dorsey brothers' *Stage Show* between January and March 1956 on the short-lived DuMont Television Network. Despite popular offerings such as the *Arthur Murray Party*, *Cavalcade of Stars*, *Life Is Worth Living*, and *The Ernie Kovacs Show*, the network never found itself on solid financial ground. Unlike its competitors, it had no stable of radio stars to draw on and suffered perennial cash shortages.

DuMont's biggest hurdle may have been an insufficient number of VHF stations up and running to support a fourth network. The technical limitations of the coaxial cable and microwave links lines maintained by AT&T weakened its competitive position as well. The service provider didn't have enough circuits for signal relays to the affiliates of four networks at the same time. The company fought an uphill battle for program clearances outside its three owned-and-operated stations in New York City, Washington, D.C., and Pittsburgh.

Competition for affiliate stations had heightened in 1953 when the FCC approved the merger of the shaky ABC network with deep-pocketed United Paramount Theaters. When deciding which system to join, station owners were more likely to choose CBS, NBC or ABC as their primary affiliate. Even with a gyrating Elvis generating a sizable teenage viewership, DuMont's executives had already decided by the summer of 1955 that the network was no longer viable. It went dark a year later. Its old Manhattan production facility is now the Fox Television flagship station.

The young Presley's raw power in his *Stage Show* appearances was rarely evident in the many movies he made over the years. A notable exception is the tough New Orleans-set crime drama *King Creole* (1958). Although plot-heavy, Presley gets to sing thirteen songs. They're all knockouts, especially the sultry *Trouble* that his character sings while working as a busby in a sleazy Bourbon Street nightclub. The number is completely integrated into the moment through the scene's visual composition.

Standing before an all-black Dixie band, Presley begins to sing staring in the direction of the club's odious owner who pressured him to perform: *If you're looking for trouble/You came to the right place/If you're looking for trouble/Just look right in my face/I was born standing up/And talking back/My daddy was a green-eyed mountain jack/Because I'm evil, my middle name is misery/Well I'm evil, so don't you mess around with me.* At first, he's restrained, but as the taunting lyrics intensify, his hips and legs begin to revolve to the music, and the look on his face shifts from disdain to delight in his performance. A series of recurrent camera angles show him in medium closeup in visual interaction with the club owner and the audience as a whole.[222]

Crime shows became a television staple as well. Jack Webb, creator and star of *Dragnet* (which had premiered on radio in 1949), successfully transferred the low-keyed documentary style of this show to television. Loosely based on actual cases taken from the files of the Los Angeles Police Department, the series stressed the mundane nature of most police work. Its understated, matter-of-fact approach and its use of world-weary, flat-sounding voices were much imitated-and later parodied. With each episode shot on film, the *Dragnet* series ran on NBC-TV from 1952 to 1959.

Most early network television shows were live, causing problems in gauging time. To present a television show "live," that is, at the instant of its occurrence, generally involves the use of multiple television cameras to capture the continuous action. The director, watching a bank of monitors, showing the image on the air at any given moment, tells the camera operators to different positions or adjust a turret of several lenses, editing by switching camera images at any given time.

This procedure is quite different from traditional feature filmmaking where fifty or so master scenes are broken down into six or seven smaller ones, making more than 300 scenes in all. The director sets up each scene fragment and, after rehearsal, shot them separately using a single camera. A completed feature film might consist of 700 or 800 separate shots. Cost efficiency compels a director to shoot scenes out of sequence. The action must follow the expensively constructed sets, for example, instead of the reverse as occurs in the final editing. To avoid having high-priced stars idle, directors shoot the scenes in which they appear in close sequence.

Anthology Drama

The big hit TV shows were aired mostly live from New York because the biggest audience was on the East Coast. With on coaxial cable available for transmission, the rest of the country saw a "kinescope," a film recording of a television broadcast with very poor resolution. The smaller audiences of the early 1950s permitted some experimentation, and so the variety shows, westerns, crime melodramas, and situation comedies coexisted with other formats, such as the anthology series. This format has its roots in the legitimate theatre, with each program presented as a complete drama.

Most of the anthology series were produced live, with all editing (camera switching, in this case) being done while the program was in progress. Several cameras would cover the production, from different angles and distances. Each was equipped with a turret of several lenses so that the camera operator could switch from a long view to a close-up. Operators wore earphones through which they received instructions from the studio control room, where a bank of screens provided the director with the images being picked up by the cameras. A separate monitor showed the camera image on the air at any given moment. Surveying the various monitors, the director issued supplementary instructions to the camera operators, who were already working from notes prepared in advance of the performance. Split-second decisions determined what went out over the air. Unlike moviemaking, a second or third take wasn't possible if somebody flubbed a line or a microphone came into view. Many colleges have similar but more state-of-the-art setups to teach television news reporting and the like.

Tiny studio facilities placed a premium on close-ups and intimate situations. With a cable-filled floor to maneuver, psychological rather than physical confrontations became a necessity. Usually, scripts were selected only if they required a small cast, a minimum of set constructions, few variations in lighting, and the most elementary variety of camera shots to generate an appropriate emotional response. While there were landmark offerings among these programs, many affecting audiences with impressions that endure to this day, such as *Marty*, *A Man Is Ten Feet Tall*, and *Twelve Angry Men*, anthology programs were not uniformly excellent or, for that matter, regularly entertaining. They did though more than any other television form, draw upon issues of universal concern, offering glimpses of what television might aspire to give viewers insight into the tensions, fears, and anxieties of ordinary people.

Paddy Chayevsky's May 1954 Goodyear Television Playhouse teleplay *Marty* concerns the mundane and ordinary life of a lonely butcher from the Bronx (Rod Steiger) still living with his mother, eager for him to marry and have a son. He's long-desired female affection but despairs ever having a romantic relationship as he heads toward middle age. "I'm a fat little ugly guy and girls don't go for me, that's all," he poignantly tells his mother. After despairing about how to spend the weekend, and then suffering another humiliating rejection when he calls a young woman to ask her out, he finally decides to attend a social at the Waverly Ballroom. At a dance, he connects with Clara (Nancy Marchand, later of *The Sopranos*), a dowdy-looking school teacher, just ditched by her blind date—who offered Marty "five bucks if you take this dog home for me." And in their mutual misery, after some awkwardness, they form a romantic bond, laying bare the shallow but widely-held illusion that passionate love and affection stem solely from surface attractions.

These glimpses of everyday reality, so rare in television's make-believe world, may well have contributed to the demise of this type of programming. Advertisers have always been in the business of selling magic. Commercials invariably provide "a solution as clear-cut as the snap of a finger: "a new pill could solve the problem, deodorant, toothpaste, shampoo, shaving lotion, hair tonic, car, girdle," notes a broadcast analyst.[223] The sharp contrasts between the visions shown in the commercials and the harsher realities in the anthology drama content may have caused advertisers to abandon this type of program as a sales vehicle—the contrast made the commercials seem fraudulent.

Although clear causal connections are elusive, the shift toward more standard program fare suggests that network executives and advertisers alike became increasingly contemptuous of nuance and ambiguity. Another factor was expansion into foreign markets requiring programs that were quickly transplantable to other cultures as scores of countries launched commercial systems. The most successful authors of anthology dramas and adaptations caught the shadings and subtleties of everyday American speech, but these nuances were often incomprehensible to an overseas audience.

In contrast, "episodic series" de-emphasizing dialogue in favor of action could be dubbed with little difficulty. Such series, with each episode a variation of a specific formula, have one or more reoccurring characters but not the continuing story of a serial. Once the creators established character types and dramatic thrust, any number of writers can contribute to each episode. With content more manageable, the episode series come to dominate the primetime schedules of the three networks. Such series could later be "syndicated"—licensed on a station-by-station basis. Successful series in syndication can cover production costs and profit, even if the "first-run" on network primetime is not profitable. An even more compelling reason for jettisoning the anthology format is that the percentage of the viewers dropped precipitously as the sale of television sets skyrocketed. With huge audiences, programmers ran the risk of losing viewership or offending with a slow-moving dramatic offering. The safer bet to grab and hold audience attention was to go with a suspenseful quiz show or an action or adventure series.

Quiz Scandals

Long a staple of radio broadcasting, the quiz format made a smooth transition to television with a considerable boost in the ante. The prizes of these new shows were unprecedented. On *The $64,000 Question*, the first of the big-money quiz shows, a losing contestant would get a Cadillac as a consolation prize. The resounding success of this show, debuting on CBS in summer 1955, spawned over a dozen imitators.

With a little luck, and a trove of esoteric trivia at the quick, overnight riches and acclaim seemed easily achievable. One of the new game shows, *Twenty-One*, that pitted contestants against each another, began to climb in the ratings when Charles Van Doren, a sincere, appealing-looking Columbia English instructor, showed up to compete. A seemingly shy but well-informed challenger, with a patrician manner, he eventually defeated the reigning champion Herb Stempel, whose abrasiveness and flawed facial features had made him unpopular with audiences. A disgruntled Stempel later complained that he and his bogus victor had been given answers in advance and coached to heighten the suspense.

His unsupported claims didn't ignite enough sparks to draw media attention until match-fixing in another game, *Dotto* (connect the dots to identify an image) gained publicity in August 1958. FCC probes, grand jury proceedings, Congressional hearings, and lawsuits led to networks taking the reins canceling big-prize quizzes and replacing them with episodic film series and "public interest" documentaries. A formal congressional subcommittee investigation convened in the summer of 1959 revealed the rigging of *Twenty-One*, along with several other such shows. After initially denying he had taken part in any deceptions, a chastened Van Doren, his reputation badly tarnished, later conceded that he would give almost anything to reverse the course of his life. He admitted he had agonized in a moral and mental struggle to come to terms with his betrayals. Such chagrin over cheating seems quaint and old-fashioned in an age when duplicity and deception are the coins of the realm.

Mythical Old West

Westerns became a major staple in network primetime programming soon after television burst onto the scene in the postwar years. The archetypal social outsider is at the center of *Cheyenne*, a western that debuted in 1955 on the ABC network along with *Casablanca* and *King's Row* playing on alternate weeks under the umbrella title Warner Brothers Presents. The Warner production unit, to keep its costs low, shot most of the episodes in five or so days and supplementing studio sets with old film footage. After an unknown actor named Clint Walker clicked as Cheyenne Bodie, the archetypal laconic drifter softened with a gentle disposition, the network dropped the other two shows. The series became simply *Cheyenne* and enjoyed a seven-year run on ABC. Other than the title character, it had no continuing characters, although several actors frequently appeared in guest or bit roles. The theme song contains the melancholy lyrics: *Cheyenne, Cheyenne, where will you be campin' tonight? Lonely man, Cheyenne, will your heart stay free and light? Dream Cheyenne of a girl you may never love. Move along, Cheyenne, like the restless clouds up above....* In each episode, he wanders westward, trying to avoid trouble but to no avail. The success of the series set off a stampede of imitators.

During the 1950s, western series like *Gunsmoke, Wagon Train, Big Valley, The Virginian, Have Gun Will Travel, Yancey Derringer,* and *Bonanza* dominated network television prime-time schedules. In *Wanted: Dead or Alive*, broadcast from 1958 to 1961, soon-to-be-superstar Steve McQueen played a Civil War veteran with a sawed-off rifle as a holstered weapon making his living as a bounty hunter in the frontier of the 1870s. By the close of the decade, some thirty westerns aired weekly in prime-time slots.

Some had remarkably long runs. Featuring James Arness as Marshal Matt Dillion, a plain-spoken lawman in everyday work clothes, *Gunsmoke* was a central part of the CBS-TV prime-time schedule for twenty years (1955-1975). The tall stoic town marshal likes saloonkeeper Kitty (Amanda Blake), and she obviously would want to marry him, but their romance is short-lived, only one episode in the long-lived series. Like many in its aging audience, the western series suffered from hardening of the arteries in its later years.

Advertisers increasingly pursued a younger demographic, the eighteen-to-forty-niners raising families, buying houses, moving up the corporate latter, and paying for all kinds of products and services. CBS network brass decided to axe the western series in 1967, but William Paley, the company's founder, and a big fan, got wind of it while on a Caribbean vacation.[224] Even though it had denture-wearer demographics, the series went back into the evening schedule, where it stayed for another eight years.

Cowboys for Kids

Saturday afternoon movies and primetime programs set in the historical west aimed at youngsters appeared on television from the outset. When silver-haired actor William Boyd's career fell on hard times, he donned a black hat, black shirt, black boots, and two big revolvers, and galloped onto the screen as Clarence E. Mulford's pulp-western hero Hopalong Cassidy of the Bar 20 Ranch.

Starting in 1935, Boyd appeared in dozens of these inexpensively produced westerns that became staples of the Saturday matinee theatrical circuit. Unlike the novels, in the screen version the cowboy Galahad in black attire was clean-living and wholesome, using neither tobacco nor alcohol, and always playing fair on the side of law and justice. His drink of choice was sarsaparilla, a once-popular soft drink made from smilax plants. Western movie mainstay George "Gabby" Hayes originally played his grizzled sidekick.

When the franchise's producing company decided to cease making Hoppy movies, the prescient Boyd, with only a six-grade education, had the acumen to bank his future on television. He mortgaged everything he owned in 1944 to buy character rights from Mulford and the backlog of the movies in which he had starred. When the movies appeared on NBC-TV beginning in 1949, Hopalong Cassidy became a small screen sensation and a hero to hordes of youngsters across the country.

By the 1950s, William Boyd Enterprises developed extensive international distribution deals, resulting in the dubbed or subtitled western hero atop his majestic white horse Topper riding across big and little screens throughout Europe and Latin America. His screen success made Boyd a star, lucrative licensing and endorsement deals and made him wealthy. The Hopalong phenomenon included comic strips in hundreds of newspapers worldwide, highly profitable comic books, and thousands of licensing tie-ins that left little doubt about the merchandising potential of the television medium. The

enterprising Boyd made millions from royalties on the sale of toy six-shooters, holsters, hats, kerchiefs, roller skates, candy bars, and even soap products.

Coonskin Caps

Original television westerns aimed at juveniles ignited a merchandising mania as well. In mid-December 1954, ABC premiered the first installment of three separate one-hour westerns on the *Disneyland* program called "Davy Crockett: Indian Fighter." The title character (played by Fess Parker) of this Disney-produced telecast was a Tennessee backwoods gun-for-hire. His cinematic exploits championed the westward move that led to the death and disruption of Mexican and indigenous peoples. The stunning loss of life and level of violence depicted was unprecedented in a genre primarily intended for youngsters. Shootings, knife fights, and brutal hand-to-hand combat abounded. The nation was in the grip of a Davy Crockett craze by the time the third episode in the initial trilogy aired. Disney's theatrical release, an edited compilation of the first three episodes, *Davy Crockett, King of the Wild Frontier*, reaped a box-office bonanza as well. Three versions of the show's theme song, "The Ballad of Davy Crockett," were in the top ten selling recordings of the *Billboard* magazine weekly charts in 1955. Since Disney couldn't trademark the historical name or likeness of the real-life frontiersman, several companies jumped on the big-bucks bandwagon, turning out Crockett-related products en masse.

Over a thousand different products flooded the market everything, from bath towels and ukuleles to underwear and wristwatches, the most iconic and biggest-selling item being the imitation coonskin cap. By the time two additional episodes appeared in the *Disneyland* anthology series, the colossal commercial boom had already dissipated. Seemingly every youngster across the United States had donned an artificial fur cap, carried a rifle and powder horn, and sung such stirring albeit racist lyrics as *Them redskin varmints us volunteers'll tame/'Cause we got the guns with the surefire aim.*

Cowboy Branding

Advertising campaigns strive to create a unique name and image for products in the mind of consumers. Initially promoting Marlboros as an accessory to female fashion and sophistication, in 1954 its maker Philip Morris went all-out for the male market to compete with the three other top cigarette brands. It wanted to reposition the brand with a new "crush proof" box and new stronger filter so that it would appeal to the much larger men's market. To accomplish this task, the company enlisted Leo

Burnett, a Chicago advertising executive with an impressive track record of promoting products. He designed a campaign that associated Marlboros with a variety of "men's men," rugged men doing manly work, sea captains, cowboys, and athletes all sporting wrist tattoos—accountant and professor types need not apply. Burnett ultimately decided the way to expand the market was to associate Marlboros with the folklore of the Old West. Cowboys took the reins in 1962. The advertising campaign's aim was to make the cigarette part of cowboy regalia symbolizing freedom and autonomy. His creative division dressed the models dragging on a cigarette in a Stetson hat, button-up shirt, jeans, boots, spurs and maybe a vest, poncho or chaps for good measure in picturesque untamed terrain.

Beginning in late 1963, the campaign featured real working cowboys as well as models. In the same year, it started using the majestic theme music from *The Magnificent Seven* (1960). In one television commercial a wild stallion is portrayed as stealing a rancher's best mares. A cowhand is in hot pursuit. The rancher is shown lighting up a Marlboro and thinking about what is happening. Suddenly he whistles for the cowhand to stop the chase and he comments, seemingly to himself, "You don't see many wild stallions anymore . . . they're the last of a rare and singular breed." Then over a crescendo of music the announcer's voice says, "Come to where the flavor is. Come to Marlboro Country." The slogan promised the ordinary man the prospect of transforming himself into, or at least associating himself with, a rugged and macho cowboy merely by lighting up this Philip Morris product. Associating the cigarette with the vast mythology about the American west proved an immediate success. The Marlboro Man's image of masculinity, autonomy, and freedom, with its implicit but not blatant sexiness, indirectly countered the increasing health concerns about smoking.

Mad Men *Cautionary*

Recapturing the 1960s ad agency atmosphere, cigarettes were an enticing feature of *Mad Men* (2007-2015). The acclaimed basic cable period piece featured an abundance of sex, drinking, and chain-smoking in the office and at home. After sex with his latest conquest, philandering Don Draper (Jon Hamm) invariably enjoys a cigarette. Most of the main male characters have cheated on their spouses and can be seen smoking several times over the course of an episode.

In some ways a cautionary tale, the link between smoking and cancer lurks in the smoke-filled atmosphere from the start to the finish of the popular small-screen drama. In the pilot episode, Draper, in charge of the Lucky Strike account, has to come up with a clever way to push this perilous product after the 1960 *Reader's Digest* report linking cigarettes and cancer along with other maladies. Saving the day, he pitches the misleading slogan "Lucky Strikes are toasted," used in actual ads dating back to the late 1920s. Never mind that all brands are exposed to radiant heat, "Advertising," he assures the client, "is based on one thing: happiness."

Some four seasons into the series, timed with the release of the first Surgeon General's report in 1964 warning that "Cigarette smoke is causally related to lung cancer," Draper attempts to save the ad agency from bankruptcy by writing a screed about severing its relationship with Lucky Strike, no longer wanting to push a deadly product. The manifesto runs as a full-page announcement in the *New York Times*. Despite the report's dire warning, most of the principal characters continue to light up, but by the penultimate episode, Draper's ill-fated ex-wife Betty (January Jones), long depicted as a heavy smoker, is diagnosed with terminal lung cancer, an X-ray of her disease-clogged organs appearing on the screen.

Cigarette Challenge

By the early 1960s, the issue of tobacco smoking and its adverse effects on the public health began to generate a great deal of public discussion. Cigarette commercials associated smoking with vigor, success, and romance but said nothing about the lingering illness and death it causes. In late 1966, attorney John Banzhaf III asked the CBS-owned flagship in New York City to provide airtime for announcements against smoking. When the station refused, he filed a "fairness complaint" with the FCC arguing that the station ran great quantities of pro-smoking messages and that, as a public service, it should be required to show an equal number of anti-smoking messages free of charge.

The FCC found validity in this argument. In early June 1967, it stated that the public should hear an anti-smoking viewpoint. However, it required only the ratio of one anti-smoking message for each of the four cigarette advertisements. The tobacco industry appealed against this decision, but the United States Court of Appeals upheld it and the United States Supreme Court declined to hear the case. Various governmental and voluntary health organizations made extremely creative spots and provided them to stations.

They proved so effective, Congress decided to ban tobacco ads on television after 1970. The ban took effect at midnight on Jan. 2, 1971 to give the cigarette companies a final chance to advertise on TV during the New Year's Day college bowl games. When cigarette advertising shifted primarily to print media anti-smoking announcements all but vanished from the airwaves.

Following the cigarette decision, environmentalists and others challenged product advertisements for cars, snowmobiles, public utilities and gasoline engines saying they raised controversial issues. In 1974, deluged with complaints, the FCC declared its decision on cigarette advertising was unique and not applicable to the promotion of other products.

As early as the 1950s, tobacco companies were aware—thanks to their research—that their products were hazardous and addictive. Still, they waged a prolonged and frequently successful campaign to suppress and blur the facts consciously, and knowingly deceiving the public for decades to keep making money. The same methods and very often the very same individuals did the same thing for acid rain, DDT/chemical manufacturers, and now global warming. Such tactics included sending dubiously credentialed experts out into the world to disguise dishonesty as reasonable doubt.

"We just don't know." "The science is complicated." "We need more research."[225]

Between 1950 and 1994, those harmed by cigarettes filed over 800 lawsuits against the various tobacco companies. Had they been successful, these suits, setting a precedent for others to follow, would have effectively crippled the tobacco industry, and may have even bankrupted them as well. Many states began to follow suit and filed their own documents against tobacco, claiming a loss of Medicare funds due to the care of patients with smoking related diseases.

In November 1998, the four largest American tobacco companies and the attorneys general of forty-six states, five territories and the District of Columbia signed the tobacco "master settlement" agreement. The states settled their Medicaid lawsuits against the tobacco industry for the recovery of their tobacco-related health-care costs. They also exempted the companies from private tort liability regarding harm caused by tobacco use.

In exchange, the companies agreed to curtail or cease certain tobacco marketing practices, as well as to pay, in perpetuity, various annual payments to the states to compensate them for some of the medical costs of caring for persons with smoking-related illnesses. The money also funds a new anti-smoking advocacy group, called the American Legacy Foundation (AFL) that is responsible for such campaigns as "truth in advertising."

The creative team from the two firms awarded the ALF's "truth movement" contract to develop the television advertising campaign have turned out wrenching ads designed to deconstruct the images long associated with cigarette ads. A TV ad aimed at Virginia Slims, a Philip Morris product, is set outside a major tobacco company. Protesters run around setting up two podiums and microphones. Bystanders watch, unsure of what is happening. On one podium is posted a placard with the letter "Q". On the other is the letter "A". A large advertising poster is unraveled, featuring Virginia Slims, with the line, "Find Your Voice."

At the Q platform a woman addresses the street. "Tobacco companies have been targeting women for the past seventy years, asking us to find our own voice. Today my friend Grace has a question for you guys." Grace comes to the microphone and speaks through her artificial larynx, "Is this the voice you expected me to find?" The camera moves to the A platform where no one is there to answer the protesters. Silence. The text comes up, "Ask Questions. Seek Truth."

Show Biz Investigations

Labor strife, rebellious exhibitors, restricted foreign markets, and anticommunist purges plagued the movie industry and spilled into small screen shows as well. Toward the close of the Second World War, a jurisdictional dispute involving the union affiliation of set decorators escalated into an industrywide strike. It dragged on for eight months, and strikers and studios alike acted brutally at times. A principal target of the strike action, the Warner studio used tear gas and water hoses to disrupt the picket lines. Many in the movie colony attributed the disruptions to communist agitation within the unions.

The Motion Picture Alliance for the Preservation of American Ideals, formed in

1944 to exorcise the communist demon from Hollywood, called for a government investigation of subversive activity in the movie industry. Along with producers, directors, writers, and set designers, its membership included such stars as Gary Cooper, Clark Gable, Robert Taylor, Barbara Stanwyck, and John Wayne. Principal funding for the group came from the heads of the major studios and press baron William Randolph Hearst. When postwar Soviet-American relations soured, it gained many new converts to its cause.

In the ensuing Cold War, the House Un-American Activities Committee (HUAC), created in 1938 to investigate alleged disloyalty and disruption, launched an all-out, no-holds-barred assault against supposed subversive activities in the movie industry. In May 1947, a subcommittee of HUAC, which had half-heartedly investigated Hollywood twice before, held closed hearings at the Biltmore Hotel in Los Angeles to examine the extent of the American Communist Party's influence in the movie industry. Most of the witnesses who testified were members of the Motion Picture Alliance for the Preservation of American Ideals.

The following October saw the beginning of public hearings in the Caucus Room of the old House of Representatives office building in the nation's capital. Scores of reporters, many equipped with movie cameras, were on hand to cover the spectacle. Klieg lights hung in clusters from two massive chandeliers, providing illumination worthy of a studio soundstage. Uniformed police were on guard outside the hearing room to control the crowd that congregated in the corridors to catch a glimpse of the movie stars in attendance.

During the first week of the hearings, twenty-four "friendly" witnesses testified before the subcommittee. Among them were top studio heads, who tried to justify wartime movies, released mostly in 1943 when the Soviet-American alliance stood at its height, that depicted the former superpower in a favorable light while airbrushing out the insidious aspects of its repressive regime.

An evasive Jack L. Warner contended he knew of nothing in *Mission to Moscow* (1943) that was in any way deceptive or subversive. Based on the memoirs of Joseph E. Davies, once the American ambassador to the Soviet Union, this misguided movie glosses over Josef Stalin's bloody political purges and treats his 1939 alliance with Hitler as a purely tactical maneuver to buy time. It even justifies Russia's invasion of Finland as part of some vague master strategy. As a result of this assault, in the three-and-a-half-month "Winter War" of 1939-1940, the small Nordic country had to cede among other areas control of Karelia, on freshwater Lake Lagoda, displacing some 400,000 Finns—something the movie neglects to mention.

In support of M-G-M's much criticized *Song of Russia* (1943), in which Robert Taylor stars as a concert conductor on tour in the Soviet Union, Louis B. Mayer argued that it was merely a romance featuring a Russian setting and the music of Tchaikovsky. All the same, the movie did tend to idealize everyday life in the Soviet Union. Sightseeing in Moscow, for example,

Taylor's character enthuses, "I can't get over it. Everyone seems to be having such a good time." While revealing very little in the way of subversive screen content, the proceedings did provide some amusement. Staunchly anti-unionist Walt Disney, who had battled the Cartoonists Guild to the brink of bankruptcy, described attempts to subvert his studio and have Mickey Mouse follow the party line. Screen Actors Guild president Ronald Reagan, future leader of the free world, declared that Red threats had led him to pack a gun.

The following week, the "unfriendly" witnesses had their turn. Nineteen had been subpoenaed, but only eleven were called to testify. After denying Communist Party affiliation, playwright Bertolt Brecht made a precipitous retreat to what was then the German Democratic Republic. The remaining ten included producer Adrian Scott, director Edward Dmytryk, and screenwriters Alva Bessie, Herbert Biberman, Lester Cole, Ring Lardner Jr., John Howard Lawson, Albert Maltz, Samuel Ornitz, and Dalton Trumbo. They all based their refusal to cooperate on the First Amendment, which states that Congress has no right to make any law restricting free speech or peaceful assembly, and therefore presumably no right to investigate anything involving these matters.

Each went to the stand, gave his name, address and occupation, attempted to read a prepared statement denouncing the subcommittee investigation, and then, after that had been ruled inadmissible, declined to answer the question as to whether he was, or ever had been, a member of the Communist Party. Only screenwriter Albert Maltz was permitted to read his entire statement. His credits included *Pride of the Marines* (1945), which criticized wartime profiteering, discrimination against Jews, and the harsh treatment of returning soldiers in the workplace.

Some of the so-called unfriendly witnesses were quite hostile when they appeared before the subcommittee. John Howard Lawson, founder and first president of the Screen Writers Guild, was especially unruly and arrogant. He was dragged shouting from the witness stand. After each witness left the stand, a subcommittee investigator read a lengthy dossier into the record detailing his alleged Communist Party affiliations. In November 1947, each was cited for contempt of Congress. Despite the First Amendment defense, they were indicted, arraigned, tried, and found guilty. In the spring of 1950, the U.S. Supreme Court refused to review their convictions. All went to federal prison to serve sentences of up to a year, thereby gaining a prominent place in the folklore of the left as the "Hollywood Ten."

Red Channels

The fledgling medium of television was easily traumatized. Three ex-FBI agents, sensing an opportunity, were quick to capitalize on the trepidations rife in this developing branch of the popular arts.[226] They published a widely circulated newsletter called *Counterattack*, which listed the alleged communist activities and sympathies of those prominent in commerce and industry. Executives in the advertising and television industries responded with particular alacrity to the accusations being made, prompting the *Counterattack* forces to focus most of their energies on the entertainment field. The ex-government agents issued a special edition of *Counterattack*, a paperback book called *Red Channels*, which read like a virtual Who's Who of show business. It listed

151 performers, with "citations" of their alleged communist activities and sympathies. Fear permeated the television industry. Performers were dropped from shows without explanation. Actors, writers, directors, and producers found themselves unemployable, as media organizations began to compile blacklists. Industry personnel were made accountable for their actions and affiliations.

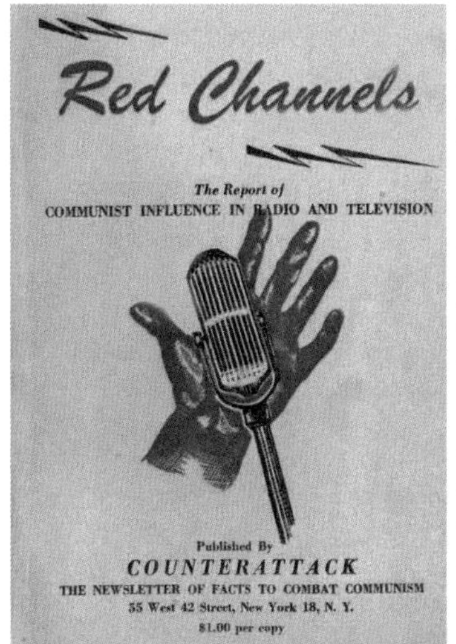

Those called upon to explain their citations were only employable if their responses to the inquisitors proved acceptable. Many were given neither the opportunity to contest the charges nor the opportunity to gain further employment. Writers could and did find work under pseudonyms; the plight of actors both male and female was particularly onerous, since the only salable thing they had was their identity. Many turned to alcohol. Some, in total desperation, committed suicide.

Executives at the television networks summarily dismissed anyone who might generate controversy or jeopardize advertising revenues. Once blacklisting was institutionalized, it expanded and soon went far beyond the names published in *Red Channels*. The practice was complicated by the unique structure of broadcasting. In the movie industry, most hiring was still concentrated in the major studios; in television, in contrast, networks, program packagers, advertising agencies, and sponsors all had a voice in deciding who was to be employed. The fear of reducing audience numbers or associating advertised products with causes or individuals that might be deemed offensive crippled creativity and impelled a retreat into formulaic programming.

STRUCTURAL CONSTRAINTS

In most instances, the affiliate was more than happy to accept network programming, because the slick, professionally produced offerings attract the large audiences that enable each affiliate to demand high rates from its local advertisers. The network makes time available in each program for the affiliates to sell to advertisers. For carrying (the industry term is "clearing") its programs and commercials, the network generally gives the affiliated stations approximately thirty percent of the rate that they would receive by selling to advertisers directly.

An affiliated station does not make most of its profits from this network compensation. The bulk of a station's revenue derives from two sources: the sale of local time in and around the network programs, and the sale of local time on its own presentations in those hours when the network programs are not carried. Although the affiliate is dependent on the network for program material, the arrangement is symbiotic: Without the audiences provided by the local stations, the networks could not reach the mass audiences that validate the high advertising rates that constitute the profit income .

As a whole, the affiliates wield power over the networks. By law, they can reject any network offering. If a substantial number of affiliated stations reject a network program, it can mean a drastic reduction in advertising revenue. Network expenses are fixed, regardless of the size of the audience. It costs no more to reach forty million people than it does to reach ten million people. Affiliate clearance, then, means bigger and bigger profits. Full program approval means maximum benefits.

To ensure affiliate acceptance, the networks, for the most part, excluded ethnic minorities from the primetime schedule in anything other than subservient roles. Little was said about sexual activity in the public arena of network broadcasting, either. For example, in the mid-1960s, Dick Van Dyke Show, although married, the principal characters Rob and Laura Petrie slept in twin beds to diffuse any explicit connotation that they had physical intimacy. Direct references to non-normative heterosexuality were excluded from network programming altogether. Kept out as well were coarse language about bodily functions, sexual activity, or profaned sacred words.

Playing by the Numbers

Once a program whether news or entertainment is on the air, the two sets of numbers that provide the quantitative yardstick of success or failure are known in the industry as the "rating" and the "share." The rating represents the percentage of households tuned to a particular program in a given time period, from the universe of households equipped to receive television signals. For a national or network program, the universe is the total number of television-equipped households; for local ratings, it is the number of TV households in the station's coverage area. If *NBC Sunday Night Football* has a national average audience rating of 13.7, for example, this figure means that an estimated 13.7 percent of the nation's 119.6 million or so television households were tuned to that program during an average minute of its telecast or watched a DVR playback on the same day.

The share (short for "share of the audience") is a comparative and, hence, a competitive figure representing how programs performed relative to the other programs in the same period. Whereas the rating is a percentage of all TV households, the share is based only on those households using television at a specific time. Let's say, for purposes of illustration, that there are 100 television households in the United States. If thirty of them tuned to NCIS, it would have a 30.0 rating. But of those 100 TV-equipped households, only sixty are using television during NCIS's time slot, which means that NCIS has thirty out of the sixty homes with sets in use or a fifty-percent share of the audience.

A. C. Nielsen Company, a retail surveyor for food and drug firms, entered the audience measurement field in the 1940s. It had a method for determining listenership through the use of a mechanical instrument called the "Audimeter," which attached to radio sets. Designed by several MIT professors, the device made a record on tape whenever the set was turned on. The position and length of the lines drawn on the tape indicated time of day the set was turned on, the time it was in operation, and the stations to which it was tuned. Nielsen's sample eventually included 1,100 households across the country. Initially, the company's field representatives collected the paper tapes on a biweekly basis.

Unlike telephone interviewing, the Audimeter did not depend on viewer recall or honesty. This device also permitted audience measurement of a much higher cross-section of the population. However, the Nielsen system had several shortcomings. The Audimeter recorded when the set was on, but not the actual audience or even if anyone was listening. If someone forgot and left the house without turning off the radio, the tape would continue to register the station as having an audience. There were other, more disturbing factors concerning the composition of the sample population.

From the outset, the sample did not adequately represent blacks and other minorities, because the company didn't place Audimeters in racially and ethnically segregated, low-income households. This omission did not upset the sales strategies of the major ad agencies or their clients. The impoverished slum dweller was not part of the buying public that they were trying to reach. This Nielsen practice prevailed well into the television period. Even if a program of particular interest appealed to those living in the nation's poor households, the rating system would not have given any indication of that interest.

Nielsen adapted the Audimeter to television and undertook several refinements. All the same, it registered even if only the family dog watched, or someone put the sound turned down to make the glow from the set a romantic nightlight. To get demographic data, Nielsen had more-or-less randomly selected viewers to keep a diary physically recording the shows they watched. Lower-rated stations and shows claimed the memory-dependent diary method was biased and inaccurate. The growing variety of channels exacerbated the problems of poor program recall and flawed meter measurement.

As complaints about its system of measurement mounted, in 1986, Nielsen introduced what it called a People Meter, an electronic device that recorded real-time viewing to solve the problem. The way it works is that a meter is attached to each set. Each family member in a sample household is assigned a personal "viewing button" on a remote-control unit that identifies age and sex. If the TV is turned on and viewers don't identify themselves, the meter flashes to remind them. Additional buttons on the meter enable guests to participate in the sample by recording their age, sex, and viewing status into the system.

Nielsen also started refining and tweaking its random sampling methods to compensate for the dramatic changes in demographic diversity across the country over the past several decades. In reaction to census shifts and requests from some industry sectors, Nielsen along with other similar firms additionally adjusted to the new reality of many watching and listening while on the move by employing such devices as a "portable people meter." People clip the unit to clothing. It detects hidden audio tones within a station or network's sound stream, logging each time it finds such a signal.

Provocative Entertainment Fare

The year 1968 saw the killing of civil rights leader Martin Luther King, Jr. and patrician presidential candidate Robert F. Kennedy, riots and protests on campuses across the country, the outbreak of violence among police and protesters during the Democratic convention in Chicago, and the launch of the Tet Offensive in Vietnam.

Tellingly, that same year, the second-highest-rated television show in the United States was *Gomer Pyle, USMC*, a series following the activities of a Marine Corps private that never mentioned the Vietnam War. And the fourth highest-rated *Mayberry R.F.D.*, set in a small North Carolina town, made no reference to racial segregation or discrimination. But commercial imperatives sometimes conspire with, as well as against, expanding the range of expression.

By the late 1960s, demographic data had become more important to network advertisers than gross headcounts. Ratings researchers began to break down the viewing audience for individual programs according to specific demographic characteristics, including age, ethnicity, education and economic background. As a result, the networks started to stress prime-time shows aimed at urban and suburban residents in the 18-to-49-year-old range, because they—presumably—spend the most money.

In the pursuit of this younger demographic, after the 1970–71 season, the networks canceled longtime staples on the television landscape favored by older working-class viewers, among them *The Ed Sullivan Show*, *The Lawrence Welk* Show, *The Red Skelton Show*, *The Andy Williams Show*, and even everybody's favorite cinematic canine *Lassie*. Such traditional sitcoms as *That Girl* and *Hogan's Heroes* also left the air at the end of that season, as did several lingering variety programs. Many such nostalgia-tinged primetime programs had been on the air since the 1950s or earlier, harking back to an imagined simpler time when everyone "knew their place" in the social hierarchy.

All in the Family

The baby boomer generation—younger, better educated, with more disposable income—became the desired target audience of advertisers and program producers. Even though the boomers grew up watching television shows of the 1950s and 1960s, their tastes and values were often in marked contrast to that of their middle-class parents. Subjects previously excluded from television entertainment fare began to appear with regularity.

The CBS network, seeking programming with the potential to tap the young adult and urban market aired *All in the Family*, modeled after a hit BBC-TV series, *Till Death Do Us Part*, in which the central character is a cockney hatemonger. Bud Yorkin and Norman Lear, a producing-writing-directing team with a long list of credits, bought the adaptation rights and took the concept to ABC. Carroll O'Connor played Archie Bunker exceptionally well. Camera close-ups captured every nuance of emotion in his expressive face—incredulity, exasperation, astonishment, and even vulnerability. It was the latter trait that seemed to belie the character's blunt language and blasphemies. For all his surface simplicity, the bigoted Bunker was a complex comic creation.

The subject matter dealt with many topics that were taboo on television. In the opening scene, for instance, son-in-law Mike Stivic (Rob Reiner) tries to persuade his wife Gloria (Sally Struthers) to have Sunday morning sex while her parents Archie and Edith Bunker (Jean Stapleton) are in church. When the Bunkers come home early—Archie didn't like the sermon— Mike greets them zipping up his trousers as he descends the stairs from the second-floor bedrooms. Interspersed throughout the episode were Archie's attacks on welfare chiselers, Jews, blacks, and atheists, among others.

Unlike the idealized sitcom families of the 1950s and 1960s like *Leave It to Beaver*, *The Donna Reed Show*, and *Father Knows Best*, the Bunkers fought the cultural and generational battles typical of the era in the living room of their Queens, New York low-rent bungalow. Although the show featured a typical sitcom living-room setting everything looked and sounded different. Shot on videotape, it had a visual immediacy unprecedented in television sitcoms. Its characters were loud and sometimes brash, and the language used was often profane, racist, or otherwise offensive.

The network received relatively few complaints and even some compliments. The initial reviews were mixed. Critic Cleveland Amory writing in the big-selling program schedule *TV Guide* waxed enthusiastic: "Not just the best-written, best-directed and best-acted show on television, it is the best show on television." The strongest condemnation came from John Leonard, writing under the byline "Cyclops" in *Life* magazine. He called it "a wretched program" in which "bigotry becomes a form of dirty joke."[227]

Network brass had little vested interest in such reviews. Commercial television is in the business not of creating critically acclaimed programs, but of supplying audience attention to advertisers. "To the critic," as industry analyst Les Brown noted, "television is about programs. To the broadcast practitioner, it is mainly about sales. This explains why most critics have nothing important to say to the industry and why, among all the critics in show business and the arts, the television reviewer is probably the least effective."[228]

All in the Family was a slow starter; but, by summer reruns, it took the lead in the ratings race. In its first full season, it was the most watched series in the nation, a position it held for five years. While maintaining its situation comedy format, the show tackled such serious topics as bigotry, molestation, impotence, menopause, draft evasion, cancer, and death. The predominant battering ram, *All in the Family* broke down the restrictions placed on television content during the preceding twenty years.

While widely hailed as enlightened program fare, as incarnated by Carroll O'Connor, Archie's bigotry becomes little more than the misguided mutterings of an ignorant, almost lovable lout. At the same time, the series repeatedly pokes fun at his potbellied, beer-guzzling, workingman ways. When he mispronounces a word, as Michael Parenti points out in *Make-Believe Media*, "generous offerings of prerecorded audience laughter accompany this." The implication is that a malapropism uttered by a working-class person "deprived of a decent education—is a cause for great merriment."[229]

Breaking More Ground

Weekly series such as *The Mary Tyler Moore Show* (the trials and tribulations of a thirtyish career woman working in a midwestern television station newsroom), *M*A*S*H* (the hijinks of some cynical civilian surgeons who have been drafted for service in the Korean War), and *Hill Street Blues* (the grim reality of police work in an urban ghetto) also broke new ground. The latter show, in particular, deftly handled disturbing issues while maintaining a sense of humor. Its emphasis on characters rather than cases, and its convincingly realistic dialogue and insightful but restrained pathos, served to underscore the stubborn sameness of a large part of the television schedule.

While the redefinition of the desirable audience in the early 1970s did expand the perimeters of appropriate content for television programming, the new candor prompted reactions from several fronts, and demonstrated larger divisions within social and cultural communities. In part as a result of these divisions, however, special interest or advocacy groups began to confront the networks about representations and content that had not been present before 1971.

Candid discussions of sexuality, even outside of traditional heterosexual monogamy, became the focal point of many shows. For some social groups which had had very little, if any, visibility during the first twenty years of American broadcast television, the broadening of program boundaries were a mixed blessing. The inclusion of gay, black, and Latino people in programming was preferable to their near invisibility during the previous two decades, but advocacy groups often took issue with the framing and stereotyping of the new images.

In contrast, conservative groups opposed the incorporation of topics within content that did not align easily with traditional American values or beliefs. In particular, the American Family Association decried the increasing presentation of non-traditional sexual behavior as acceptable in broadcast programming. Other groups rallied against the increased use of violence in broadcast content. As a result, attempts to define the limits of appropriate content became an ongoing struggle as the networks attempted to balance the often-conflicting values of marginal social groups.

The critical and commercial success of "relevance programming" had paved the way to entirely new areas of content. Although such programs thrived, yet another scheduling trend became evident during the mid-1970s. A changing cultural climate, brought on in part by the American defeat in the Vietnam War, the Watergate scandal, and rising conservative influence, led some network executives and television producers to conclude that a large segment of the viewing audience might be ready to return to escapism.

Time-Warped Nostalgia

In the 1976–1977 season, *All in the Family* lost its five-year perch at the top of the ratings. A bland but amusing high school comedy, *Happy Days* (1974–1984), set in the 1950s, before the Watergate scandal and the Vietnam War, moved to the top of the ratings. Other nostalgic fare such as *Laverne & Shirley* (1976–83), set in the early 1960s, *The Waltons* (1972–1981), a Depression-era saga of a mountain family, and *Little House on the Prairie* (1974–1983), rural life in the late 19th century, also reached large audiences during this period. As its title suggests, *Happy Days* reverted to the old television tendency of providing amusing make-believe divorced from reality.

The faithful viewer of such nostalgic fare resided in a time warp of sorts redolent of when American women were encouraged to stay in the kitchen wearing gingham and awaiting the breadwinner's return. Many women, in fact, supported conservative American family and religious values, among the most influential, Phyllis Schlafly. A

major force in American politics and culture, opposing women's liberation and abortion, she stalled passage of the Equal Rights Amendment by linking it with the Right to Life movement.[230] The chief scourge of feminism, her anti-ERA crusade attracted tens of thousands of women into the conservative fold. A prolific writer, her bestselling books included polemics against liberal Republicans. Staying active in conservative causes, at age ninety-two, she coauthored an influential 2016 book making a case for the candidacy of Donald Trump.

Reflecting a trend across media, the latter half of the 1970s saw what pundits dubbed "jiggle TV," featuring young, attractive, often scantily clad women (and later men as well). Among the series in this category was *Love Boat* (1977–86), a romantic comedy set on a Caribbean cruise ship and *Charlie's Angels* (1977–1981), three undercover female detectives donning beachwear and various kinds of revealing attire. Other similar titillating trifles included *Three's Company* (1977–1984), with the then-tantalizing premise of two young women and a man sharing an apartment, and *Fantasy Island* (1978–1984) for fulfilling romantic dreams and desires.

With the nationwide spread of cable systems, which amplify broadcast signals, UHF was no longer an obstacle to establishing a viable fourth television network. In 1986, media mogul Rupert Murdoch's News Corporation bought 20th Century Fox and six major market UHF stations television stations in six of the top ten markets to launch the Fox Broadcast Network. Its edgy, youth-oriented program fare and sports offerings included the crude humor of *Married with Children*, the excitement of NFL games, the witty social commentary of *The Simpsons*, and sexy youth programming like *Beverly Hills 90210*. From 2004 to 2012, it could boast of being the highest-rated broadcast network in the highly coveted 18–49 demographic.

Television News

Like the creators of theatrical newsreels, television news producers construct real-life stuff with the tools and techniques of moviemaking. Cinematic considerations mold both local and national news programs. As in movies, the emphasis is on personality, action, drama, and conflict. The producers of television news deliberately design scene fragments to evoke emotional responses. Videotaped events are shaped into narrative-dramatic structures and edited in ways that heighten their emotional appeal.

Issues are defined and presented in terms of personalities. As in westerns and crime thrillers, the focus tends to be on individual malefactors. Conflicts are a struggle between good and evil or right and wrong, not between competing ideas and worldviews. Lighting, camera placement, editing, and other cinematic techniques serve to intensify the spectacle and dramatic effect.

Local TV News Shows

At the local level, broadcast television stations gear their news coverage towards viewers residing in areas in which the stations operate. The stories have a strong regional focus and, like the old penny papers, stress crime, and aberrant social behavior in general. National or international stories may also make the top stories, but the local significance is typically featured. The multiplicity of possible news items accumulating throughout a day is whittled down and winnowed out by selection, editing, and inference designed to entertain rather than enlighten.

Weather reports also play a very important role in local news as they are found in every local newscast. Compared to national news, local news provides more in-depth, regular and frequent coverage of weather reports relevant to a station's viewing area. Traffic reports are featured especially during weekday morning newscasts. Sports news is also a major regular feature during evening newscasts, especially for local sports teams. A station typically produces around five to seven hours of local news on weekdays and airs fewer hours on weekends. Some stations focus more on hard news than others.

Despite superficial coverage, local news shows can be quite engaging. In 1968, WABC-TV's "Eyewitness News" debuted, turning staid news broadcasting on its head. Before this broadcast viewers got their news from one anchor, invariably a man, sitting behind a desk. At the local WABC station on-air reporters, including women and members of marginalized groups chatted with one another in what became known as "happy talk." Within a year and a half, the local news program catapulted from dismally low ratings into the market's top spot, a position it has yet to relinquish.

Over the years, its reporters have shown a singular flair for comfortably interacting in front of a camera while reading from a teleprompter (an ability few can master). Longtime co-anchors Bill Ritter and Liz Cho, along with meteorologist Lee Goldberg constitute the current three-member news team, with various sportscasters completing the four-member panel. The three have charming chemistry as they interact during the news and weather reports. Such chemical connection is no small matter with conventional over-the-air television viewership on a downward spiral and the scramble for dwindling local news audiences fiercely competitive.

Exposing McCarthyism

In 1952, newscaster Edward R, Murrow and producer Fred Friendly made the transition to the fledgling medium of television with their *See It Now* broadcasts. This news documentary, which featured Murrow on camera, made its debut over the CBS television network on November 1951. In the first show, Murrow noted in his introductory remarks that he and co-producer Friendly were "an old team trying to learn a new trade." Over time the program series, which moved to an early evening time slot during the 1952-53 season, tackled more sensitive topics eventually casting a critical light on the outrages of that whole political phenomenon called "McCarthyism."

The term is the catchall for the cold-war paranoia that prevailed in the United States during the 1950s. The junior senator from Wisconsin, Joseph R. McCarthy, whose name came to symbolize the era, was particularly zealous in his pursuit of alleged communists and subversives in U.S. public and private life. The practices that McCarthy's name came to stand for arguably had more to do with postwar expansionism than with the abusive activities of any one individual.

Buttressed by the wartime boom, U.S. businesses began to move aggressively into new markets around the globe. The concept of a "free world" became the corporate creed. Freedom of the seas, markets, trade, and the media was the pennon of the postwar period. Through such measures as the Truman Doctrine, U.S. foreign policy aimed to curtail and contain the spread of communism, while simultaneously expanding U.S. business interests abroad. All too often this necessitated such unpopular measures as shoring up the regimes of odious dictators. This policy of expansionism abroad required justification at home so a war-ravaged Soviet Union was presented to Americans as posing a direct threat to their national security. The military was especially active in whipping up a tempest of fear.

Murrow and Friendly were never so bold as to expose the roots of postwar paranoia. But they did take on Senator Joseph R. McCarthy, who had a knack for dominating the news cycle with sensational, typically groundless accusations. Reporters turned into stenographers, helping to fuel his rise to prominence with extensive, often-respectful coverage without context or analysis.

Longtime media critic James Aronson noted that although many reporters came to loath McCarthy as a cynical liar and power manipulator, they nevertheless accepted, and editors published, the information he waved at them. "Such reports," he chides, "if their content proved to be false, might have been excused once or twice on the grounds of deadline or overzealous reporting." Conscientious reporting went out the window "when this happened day in and day out for four years, when every reputable Washington correspondent knew the disseminator was a proved liar, there was no shred of an excuse."[231]

Despite such uncritical coverage, by the time *See It Now* presented a special report on the junior senator from Wisconsin in March 1954 his power was already in decline as opinion pieces in the news media increasingly labeled him a dangerous demagogue. The program consisted primarily of juxtaposed McCarthy film footage that highlighted his inconsistencies and his often wild, unsubstantiated attacks. McCarthy was shown browbeating witnesses at Congressional committee hearings, contradicting himself, and resorting to innuendo and malicious remarks.

A key sequence involved the testimony of Reed Harris, an employee of the U.S. Information Agency, who appeared before McCarthy's Senate Permanent Subcommittee on Investigations to answer questions. Among other things, it wanted to know about a book he had written in 1932 while an undergraduate at Columbia University. The footage from this hearing, referred to as "a sample investigation,' showed the junior senator at his browbeating worst. McCarthy singled out a passage from the book, which referred to the institution of marriage as an antiquated and stupid religious phenomenon.

Columbia suspended Harris from his classes as a result of the book, and McCarthy established that the American Civil Liberties Union had supplied him with an attorney. He asked if Harris was aware that the ACLU listed him as a subversive front. Murrow pointed out that neither the attorney general, the FBI, nor any other federal government agency had ever listed the ACLU as subversive. Throughout the telecast, Murrow did not pay even lip service to journalistic objectivity. At the close, he said: "This is not the time for men who oppose Senator McCarthy's methods to keep silent. We can deny our heritage and our history, but we cannot escape responsibility for the result."

The following week the show featured a second McCarthy expose, in which viewers saw the senator and his minion Roy Cohn (later a mentor to Donald Trump) badgering and bullying a seemingly bewildered witness named Annie Lee Moss, who was suspected of being a communist. When Mrs. Moss was asked if she had ever heard of Karl Marx, she responded: "Who's that?" The Senate hearing room shook with laughter-not at her but, as Fred Friendly explained it, "at the ludicrous situation of this pathetic, frightened woman, suspended from her job, being interrogated as though she were Mata Hari."[232] The program clearly reinforced McCarthy's image as a dangerous demagogue. However, it should be noted that, four years later, the Subversive Activities Control Board reported that Annie Lee Moss had indeed been a member of the Communist Party.[233]

Early in April, McCarthy, accepting an offer of free time, presented a filmed half-hour rebuttal that strongly attacked Murrow. He characterized the journalist as "the cleverest of the jackal pack which is always found at the throat of anyone who dares to expose individual communists and traitors." There's a certain irony in this attack, because Murrow clearly had cold-warrior credentials. He was an ardent supporter of the Truman Doctrine, favored more spending on armaments, argued for a stronger military presence in Europe, and even advocated the right of a president to send military forces abroad without congressional approval.[234] It's testimony to the tenor of the times that a man like Edward R. Murrow would be labeled a communist sympathizer.

Viewer response to the McCarthy programs was immediate and polarized. CBS was deluged with thousands of telegrams and telephone calls. The general reaction was one of praise for the position taken against McCarthy, but there were also bitter denunciations of Murrow and the network. Threats were even made against Murrow's eight-year-old son Casey; and, for years afterward, the boy always had to be met at school and escorted home.The McCarthy-Murrow encounter became a national spectacle. Murrow was regarded in some circles as "that traitor." Some months after the McCarthy telecasts, Murrow was the principal speaker at the annual Junior Chamber of Commerce ceremony to honor the year's "ten outstanding young men." As he rose to speak, one of the young men walked out in protest. He was Robert F. Kennedy who, for several months, had served as counsel to the senatorial committee of Joseph McCarthy.[235]

Throughout the continuing controversy, Alcoa remained steadfast in its sponsorship of

See It Now. It even held firm when the tobacco industry, a major purchaser of aluminum foil, objected to a two-part report on cigarettes and lung cancer. But the company's priorities were changing. Competition in the aluminum industry was increasing, and the company had decided to enter the consumer market. Since it would no longer be just a wholesaler, public controversy assumed much greater importance. At the end of the 1954-55 season, Alcoa bowed out and *See It Now* was dropped from the weekly network schedule.

Network Television News

Network television news began modestly in the late 1940s. In spring 1948, CBS launched the fifteen-minute *Douglas Edwards With the News*. Over some fourteen years, he covered such events as the Miss America Pageant (five times), the attempted assassination of Harry S. Truman in November 1950, and the coronation of Elizabeth II in June 1953. He also received wide praise for his coverage, on both camera and radio, of the sinking of the SS Andrea Doria in July 1956. But by the end of the decade, viewership levels for the Edwards broadcast weakened severely as his anchor rivals began to attract a broader audience.

One of the "Murrow Boys" team of war correspondents, Walter Cronkite, replaced the respected Douglas in 1963. His seemingly intuitive sense of the proper balance between gravitas and show business made him a valuable asset in commercial television, a voice of certainty in an uncertain world. Anointed in a 1972 poll as "the most trusted man in America," he set a standard for accuracy, fairness, and dependability.

During one of the most volatile periods of American history, Cronkite dominated the television news industry. His avuncular and authoritative baritone guided viewers through such traumatic and enthralling news events as the assassinations of John F. Kennedy, the Rev. Dr. Martin Luther King Jr., and Robert F. Kennedy; the civil rights struggle in the South; the turbulent 1968 Democratic National Convention in Chicago; the first walk by a man on the moon in 1969; the Vietnam War; and the Watergate scandal.

On NBC's fifteen-minute *Camel News Caravan*, launched in the summer of 1949, anchor John Cameron Swayze, boutonnière intact, presented verbal reports supplanted with film clips. The set featured an ashtray on the desk in front of the newscaster and the Camel logo behind him. Near the end of each telecast, he went "hopscotching the world for headlines," dispatching a grab bag of items in a sentence or two. Then the suave Swayze would conclude with "That's the story, folks. Glad we could get together." It was the first newscast to use in-house produced film footage rather than movie newsreels. The show also drew upon government-supplied films for coverage of world events.

In the fall of 1956, seasoned journalists Chet Huntley and David Brinkley replaced Swayze; witty and well matched, they become the first TV news stars. Located in New York City, Huntley handled the bulk of the general news most nights. Brinkley co-anchoring from the nation's capital specialized in Washington-area topics such as the White House, U.S. Congress, and the Pentagon. Critics considered the sharp but somewhat solemn Huntley to possess one of the best-broadcast voices in the business. And Brinkley's dry, often witty, news writing provided viewers a contrast to the

often-sober output from rival evening newscasts. The anchors gained great celebrity with surveys showing them better known than many movie stars or even the Beatles.

Until the 1970s, the ABC television network had fewer affiliate stations, as well as a weaker prime-time programming slate, to be able to support its news operations.[236] Its first evening news program *News and Views*, launched in 1948, had a shaky existence. In fall 1952, ABC began experimenting with a more extended evening newscast, *All-Star News*. As a result of low ratings, the network returned to the traditional evening news format and premiered *John Daly and the News* a year later.

Before anchoring this news show, Daly had a long and successful radio news career at CBS. He reported on the Franklin Roosevelt administration as a White House correspondent in the late 1930s. During the Second World War, he was the CBS network's chief correspondent in Italy.[237] After he left the anchor's desk in 1960, ABC struggled to find someone to compete against Huntley-Brinkley and Walter Cronkite.

During the middle of the decade, ABC put youthful Peter Jennings in the network anchor's chair. With this Canadian-born journalist at the helm, the show continued to rank third in viewership behind news programs on CBS and NBC, so his tenure didn't last long. A well-polished cosmopolitan, Jennings returned to anchor the ABC newscast in early fall 1983, a position he held for over twenty-one years.

Early in September 1963, the CBS Evening News expanded its newscast from fifteen to thirty minutes; Huntley-Brinkley followed suit a week later. Lacking resources, ABC didn't stretch its news program until January 1967. While this expansion meant the networks could sell more advertising slots, it resulted in further shrinkage of time available for local news scheduling.

All three of the television networks wanted to expand to forty-five minutes or even a full hour to justify the enormous expense of gathering the news. Even a quarter-hour would have brought in many millions in advertising fees. But local station managers served notice that they would not tolerate further encroachment of their financial territory. "If CBS announced it was going to 45 minutes, and wouldn't make the minutes optional," a station executive exclaimed in 1976, "I'd cut my wrists and jump out the window."[238] Most network-affiliated stations continue to oppose any expansion of national newscasts.

These days many prefer to wade in the roiling waters of social media for news and opinion. But seasoned journalists like NBC's Lester Holt still give largely older, albeit fewer viewers, dramatic slices of life, distilled through television's national news outlets, some semblance of continuity, cohesion, and congruence. Their mellifluous tones and pontifical manner create an aura of reasoned intellect.

Whatever journalistic skills these performers may possess, their primary asset is the ability to remain composed in front of a camera under all circumstances. They remain show business assets even though no longer enjoying the same celebrity status as rock or movie stars. We assess their thespian skills, comment on their appearance, and evaluate their phrasing and intonation. The events they present may disappear from memory, but the characters they create—their screen personae—remain in our mind.

Gulf War Coverage

Serving tidbits of news on a small platter of time invariably contributes to stereotyping and reductionism. Such malnourishment of the mind is a recipe for shallow thinking, especially dangerous when propaganda is the main item on the media menu. In August 1990, Iraq invaded and occupied Kuwait over oil pricing and border incursion that the hugely wealthy emirate refused to negotiate. Soon after the invasion, the Kuwaiti royal family in exile launched a massive propaganda campaign denouncing the occupation and mobilizing public opinion in the western hemisphere in favor of war to free its black-gold rich country.

Among other measures, the royal family retained the services of the large, politically savvy Hill & Knowlton PR firm, which crafted a campaign that purposely misleads Congress to help justify the bombing of Iraq. As past propaganda campaigns confirmed, a dramatic theme repeatedly reinforced across media outlets proved how to sway hearts and minds. Like the British in "the Great War," the campaign's underlying thrust became the time-tested atrocities canard, the crueler, the better, and especially easy to fake and fabricate.

Toward this end, the public relations practitioners arranged for hearings by a "congressional human rights caucus," unencumbered by legal sanctions that would make witnesses hesitant to fabricate. A key witness, a fifteen-year-old girl identified as simply Nayirah, sobbingly testified that while volunteering in a Kuwait City hospital, she saw Iraqi soldiers stealing incubator cribs callously leaving the premature babies on the cold floor to die. The blockbuster testimony got extensive media coverage throughout the world, on television and radio talk shows, and at the UN Security Council. Tear-filled Nayirah turned out to be the daughter of the Kuwaiti ambassador to the United States. She had left Kuwait long before the Iraqi soldiers arrived. "Lying under oath in front of a congressional committee is a crime," acidly notes John MacArthur, who first exposed her identity, "lying from under the cover of anonymity to a caucus in merely public relations."[239]

The waging of war to push Iraq's invading army from Kuwait cost billions of dollars and required an unprecedented, massive military mobilization. With prodding from Pentagon public relations personnel, network television news producers, always mindful of selling attention, gave this brutal assault the dramatic shape and heady rush of a *Star Wars* movie. Each of the over-the-air three networks in operation at the time introduced its war coverage with music, a logo, and a title-"War in the Gulf" on CBS, "America at War" on NBC, and "Crisis in the Gulf" on ABC and CNN. Impeccable casting contributed to the skein of cinematic melodrama.

Allied commander General Norman Schwarzkopf seemed like a hero right out of an oversized Han Solo mold—manly, smart, sensitive, and resourceful. Even seasoned reporters jockeyed for proximity to him, despite his utter disdain for members of the press, treating them with a contempt reserved for enemy forces. The evil villain of the small-screen drama, the Iraqi leader Saddam Hussein, appeared to have about as much warmth and charm as Darth Vader. The network coverage of the devastating assault on Baghdad consisted mostly of antiseptic images. Bombs and missiles appeared to strike their designated targets with the precision of laser swords.

The Bush administration had succeeded in relegating most of the news media to almost complete compliance with its propaganda aims. Veteran war correspondent, CNN's Peter Arnet, the only reporter to directly provide live coverage from the ground in Baghdad, especially during the first sixteen hours of the bombing, captured the blitzkrieg's horrors with air-raid sirens blaring and bombs exploding in the background during his dramatic reports. Although forty foreign journalists were present at the Al-Rashid Hotel in Baghdad at the time, only the around the clock cable news channel CNN possessed the means—a single phone line connected to neighboring Amman, Jordan—to communicate the aerial assault to the outside world.

Before the assault ended, American planes flew more than 109,000 sorties, raining 88,000 tons of bombs, the equivalent of seven Hiroshima's, and killing millions randomly across the country. Hardly surgical, from Basra to Bagdad and beyond, the bombing severed every service essential to survival, water supplies, electricity, transport roads, and the gasoline reserve. Entire blocks in numerous residential areas saw the damage or destruction of hospitals, mosques, and churches. The immense toll of human suffering can't be quantified.

Metaphors & Propaganda

Understanding and experiencing one kind of thing in terms of another is the essence of metaphor, a primary means, with stereotypes, of making sense and generating meaning.[240] Unless in poetry, like Emily Dickenson's evocative, *I felt a funeral in my brain*, most metaphors are almost always unnoticeable. They're just like the air we breathe, usually invisible. We unconsciously assimilate the metaphorical connections by imitating those around us, repeating them ourselves until they seem natural.

The catchy phrase "neurons that fire together wire together" nicely captures the way repeatedly activating the same circuits makes an association permanent. In American English, a remarkable number of metaphors have war connotations: "The parties *launched* a diplomatic effort." "The neighbors agreed to a *truce*." "Every day is an uphill *battle*." "The senate became the *battleground* for stem cell lobbyists." "The press *bombarded* the president with questions." "They work at the *front lines* of the war on poverty." "He is *mobilizing* a significant campaign against child exploitation."

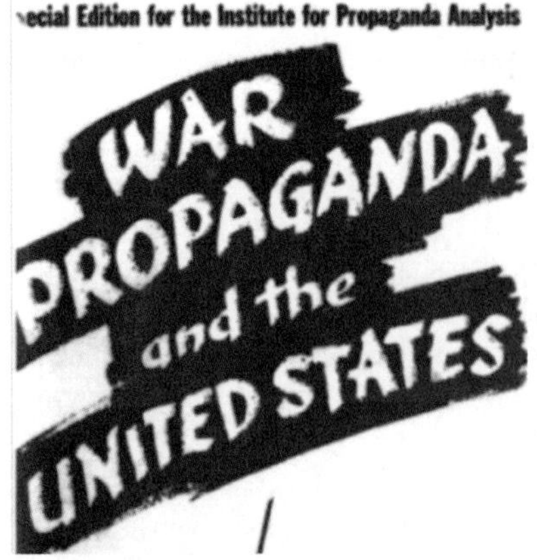

Most of the tools in the standard propaganda playbook have metaphoric elements. In the late 1930s, the short-lived Institute for Propaganda Analysis, to promote critical thinking, published seven "devices" or propaganda analysis techniques with metaphorical aspects.[241] These include: name-calling, glittering generality, transfer, testimonial, plain folks, card stacking, and bandwagon. The "bandwagon" device aims toward persuading the target audience to jump on, as it were, become a part of a popular movement, or be left behind. It capitalizes on the human need to be part of something more substantial, by creating the illusion that widespread support exists.

In "card stacking," specific facts that threaten a position are deliberately omitted or rationalized away, making an argument appear conclusive. The term originates from gambling and occurs when players try to "stack" decks in their favor. With the "plain-folks" pitch, politicians, labor leaders, businessmen, educators, and preachers seek to win support and confidence by presenting themselves as ordinary people. To establish trust and boost credibility, "testimony" draws on renowned, respected, or admired figures to endorse people or positions.

A "glittering generality" is an emotionally appealing slogan or simple catchphrase closely associated with highly valued concepts and beliefs. These generalities are invariably vague, with multiple meanings, and have positive connotations. Such words and phrases like "liberty," "democracy," "freedom," "patriotism," are so vague and abstract as to be meaningless. A form of verbal belittlement, the technique of "name-calling" entails using derogatory tags and phrases to create a negative opinion about someone or something.

The "transfer" or association technique, the most directly metaphorical ploy, refers to connecting positive or negative qualities of a person, entity, object, or cultural value to make someone or something else more acceptable or discredit them. Associations with such visual symbols as a flag, cross, Uncle Sam, or swastika serve to stir emotions, making critical thinking more difficult. A common practice transposes vivid images of comforting cultural myths far removed from reality to an unknown product despite no logical connection or association, as the Marlboro ad campaign made apparent.

Tropes to Topple Tyrants

Even in this era of social neuroscience, with appeals aimed at the unconscious, the old propaganda ploys still have traction. During the buildup to Persian Gulf War, the Bush Administration employed the well-tread technique of transfer, repeatedly connecting Saddam Hussein with Adolf Hitler. The comparison made the Iraqi dictator into the essence of evil, a threat to all humanity, but when the brief war ended, he and his regime remained in power.

To topple this "Hitler-like menace," one of the propaganda ploys of President George W. Bush, whose father led the first incursion into the Persian Gulf, was the glittering generality. Under the banner of "Operation Iraqi Freedom," Bush the younger claimed a new regime in Iraq would be a dramatic and inspiring example of freedom for other nations. Too often in wartime, abstractions like "fighting for freedom" translate into "scuffling off this mortal coil"—to borrow a euphemism for death from Shakespeare's *Hamlet*. The tried-and-true techniques of propaganda were part and parcel of the steps leading up to the 2003 war in Iraq. After the 9/11 attack on the World Trade Center and Pentagon, spins and shams linked Iraq's leader, Saddam Hussein, to the al Qaeda terrorists and the possession of weapons of mass destruction—neither claim turned out to be true.

In *The Greatest Story Ever Sold*, cultural critic Frank Rich unravels the latticework of deception and manipulation leading up to the second Iraqi war.[242] One after another, administration officials distorted, exaggerated, or fabricated evidence. Vice President Dick Cheney asserted that the Iraqi regime aids and protects terrorists, including members of al Qaeda. Bush and Cheney stressed that Iraq possesses chemical and biological weapons and seeks nuclear weapons. National security adviser Condoleezza Rice engaged in scare tactics warning, "We don't want the smoking gun to be a mushroom cloud."

Working from weak evidence, Bush's Secretary of State Colin Powell speaking at the United Nations declared that Iraq possessed biological weapons. "My colleagues, every statement I make today is backed by sources, solid sources." These are not assertions. We're giving you facts and conclusions based on reliable intelligence, he bogusly claimed. "There can be no doubt that Saddam Hussein has biological weapons and the capability to produce more, much more rapidly." For dramatic effect, he held up a vial he said could contain anthrax, a deadly bacterium.

Rich's step-by-step account shows how the Iraqi freedom public relations campaign manipulated the news media to fulfill the goal (set months before the 9/11 attacks) of toppling Saddam Hussein to achieve a regime change more to the liking of the Bush administration. The PR practitioners steadily replaced reality with a scenario of the White House's invention and intimidated the Democrats into complicity. The mainstream news media that should have exposed these fictions, he notes, were too often rendered ineffectual by the administration's relentless barrage of public relations salvos.

When the United States along with coalition forces attacked Iraq in 2003, the Pentagon had some 7,000 public relations specialists at the ready. In many ways, master of spin Victoria Clarke, an alumna of PR giant Hill and Knowlton, became the defense department's voice. She held a series of regular meetings with several of Washington's top private public relations specialists and lobbyists. The strategy group, tasked with developing a propaganda plan for the upcoming war in Iraq, proved remarkably successful in securing press cooperation to spread its message. Images and stories of troops providing food, medical aid, and other assistance to Iraqi—and even to wounded Iraqi soldiers—emerged quickly.

Embedding journalists, staging showy briefings, emphasizing visual and electronic media, and making good television out of it were essential to fighting the propaganda war. As the Assistant Secretary of Defense for Public Affairs, Clarke oversaw daily press briefings and formulated the idea of "embedded journalists" to get more sympathetic reporting. By no means a new phenomenon, Clark took embedding to new levels. The 100s of embedded media personnel had a significant impact on the subsequent coverage. Reporters remained with the same battalion throughout their assignment, getting to know the soldiers in a personal way, becoming accepted members of a "band of brothers."

Further diminishing impartiality, the embedded reporters heard about the soldiers' fears and families and were also dependent on them for protection. They offered the public a kind of credibility that government spokespeople didn't possess. With tightly controlled access to the battlefield, reporting consisted mainly of green-hued images from night scopes and the shaky footage from hand-held cameras. These jumpy videos created compelling but distracting footage rather than the visceral images of destruction. The real sacrifices, horrors, and staggering loss of human lives remained remote.

Cable Television's Expanding Options

The dominance of the three networks, when they accounted for more than ninety-five percent of prime-time viewing, is long gone. These days they garner less than forty-percent of the television audience. The fragmentation of viewers, and compartmentalized cultural orientations accelerated with the growth of cable television, which originated as Community Antenna Television (CATV). In the late 1940s, to bring television broadcast signals to remote communities, appliance store dealers and electronics firms, among others, built strategically located super-antennas and ran wires to individual homes. The advantages of making such connections included no over-the-air interference as well as increased channel capacity.

The American landscape eventually became dotted with cable systems that were not only picking up distant signals but originating program fare as well. Such developments alarmed broadcasters, concerned that competition was diluting or fractionalizing audiences resulting in a diminution of profits. At the urging of the National Association of Broadcasters (NAB), an influential Washington lobby, the Federal Communications Commission froze cable expansion in urban areas and prohibited cable systems from bringing in programs from distant independent stations and piping them into three-station markets.

A cable system in the southwest challenged these restrictions in court. The U.S. Supreme Court held that they were permissible because the cable company's retransition over-the-air TV signals fell under the commission's charge to regulate radio and television, which gives it parallel authority to supervise cable.[243] During the 1970s, FCC lifted most of its restrictions when evidence accumulated that cable systems were doing little if any damage to established broadcasters. A decade of disputes dissipated after the passage of the 1976 copyright law. Under this statue, a small portion of the cable operators' revenues is divided among those who own the copyrights on the programs picked up and piped into homes.

The proliferation of cable in the 1980s and the 1990s only exacerbated the conflicts over programming and censorship. Because of a different mode of distribution and exhibition–often referred to as "narrowcasting—cable television has been able to offer more explicitly sexual and violent programming than broadcast television. The broadcast networks, competing with cable for attention, loosened restrictions on programming content, including partial nudity, more graphic violence, and coarse language. This strategy seems to have been partially successful in attracting viewers, as evidenced by the popularity of adult dramas such as NYPD Blue. However, this programming approach has opened the networks to further attacks from conservative advocacy groups who have increased the pressure for government regulation, i.e., censorship of objectionable program content.

Cable Talk

The round-the-clock cable news services are contributing to the declining importance of the over-the-air network news shows. Founded in 1980 by media mogul Ted Turner, the CNN cable news channel's current weekday schedule consists mostly of rolling news stories during daytime hours, followed by in-depth news, interviews, and commentary during the evening and primetime hours.

Although impartiality may be in the eye of the beholder, by most accounts, CNN generally verifies and validates factual statements in its news coverage and analysis in line with professional benchmarks, and draws on a wide range of experts and political veterans with differing opinions. No longer positioning itself between MSNBC and Fox on the political spectrum, its evening talk-program lineup with Chris Cuomo and Don Lemon at its center has seen audience share grow in recent years as the news channel moved to the left, but still lags behind its more partisan cable competitors.

Started in 1996 by Microsoft and General Electric's NBC unit (now the Comcast-owned NBCUniversal), the MSNBC around-the-clock news channel offers comprehensive coverage and commentary. A series of changes in management and internal disputes over the direction of the network resulted in a bumpy first few years. Still, its ratings took off during its extensive coverage of the impeachment of President Bill Clinton.

A low point in its stab at balancing viewpoints, MSNBC featured "The Savage Nation," an erratic and abrasive right-wing conspiracy talk-show host Michael Alan Weiner, known by his professional name Michael Savage. From the outset of his stint at MSNBC, the Gay & Lesbian Alliance Against Defamation (GLAAD) urged sponsors to stop advertising on the show. The one-hour call-in program began airing in March 2003 and ended abruptly some four months later when the network canceled it after Savage told what turned out to be a prank caller, "You should only get AIDS and die, you pig...."

Over the years, the cable news outlet's talk offerings gradually moved toward a progressive or left-leaning political stance. At the heart of its evening lineup these days is cerebral Chis Hayes and the heavily credentialed Rachel Maddow, the first openly lesbian anchor to host a major prime-time news program in the United States. While titling far to the left at times and prone to long-windedness, Maddow is a decisive interviewer with an analytical mind and keen grasp of complicated matters.

The Australian-American tabloid tycoon Rupert Murdoch launched Fox News in 1996 with former Republican spinmeister Roger Ailes at the helm (forced to resign in 2016 amid multiple accusations of sexual abuse). The wily Ailes seemed to many an odd choice to head a news network since he had no background in journalism and frequently expressed his low regard for reporters.

Under his stewardship, Fox gradually became a strongly partisan national cable television news outlet, typically looking at issues and events from a right-angle primarily in its opinion, programming, and in its selection and treatment of "hard" news." And adding to the skepticism about its journalistic mission, the network brass required on-camera women, mostly blonde, to wear revealingly tight clothes and spiked heels, and sit behind transparent desks. Several former female anchors later publicly stated they saw the skimpy outfits as a degrading way to dress undercutting their credibility as journalists. With delivering attention to advertisers in mind, the news producers picked and attired these anchors more for display than reporting skills.

Tough-minded and ecumenical interviewers like Chris Wallace are exceedingly rare on television, especially in the Fox universe. In mid-July 2020, President Trump sat for an interview with Wallace, who fact-checked his falsehoods at every turn. "That's not true, sir," he politely retorted when Trump falsely asserted that the United States has the lowest coronavirus mortality rate. Given how rare it is for the president, surrounded by sycophants, to be called out so plainly during a televised interview—let alone one on Fox—this simple retort acted as a brake, forcing him to backtrack and defend himself. He fumbled Wallace's polite but firm questions and follow-ups one after another, flailing around to find a fabrication. His usual evasion, badgering, or dashing off doubtful statements all failed him.

A model for astute interviewing, the admirably well-prepared seasoned journalist had the facts down cold, and he also knew how to deploy them. In an amusing yet telling exchange, the free world leader once again boasted about his high score on a cognitive ability test. Wallace said that he, too, took this test. "It's not," he wryly remarked, "well, it's not the hardest test. They have a picture, and it says, "what's that" and it's an elephant." Once again fumbling for words, Trump responded: "No, no, no... You see, that's all misrepresentation."[244]

Fox Nighttime Lineup

By far the most-watched American news channel, most of Fox's evening lineup of moderators brings to mind the vitriolic partisan exchanges that prevailed in newspapers during the early days of the nation's founding. Among its most provocative nightly political talk show hosts is Tucker Carlson, an alumnus of CNN and MSNBC. In mid-2020, at the height of the demonstrations against police brutality, he singled out the Black Lives Matter movement for particular scorn, dismissing demonstrators as "criminal mobs."

In the same vein, the seasoned provocateur also accused a Texas police chief of "sounding more like a therapist than a cop," and ridiculed a CNN special for children about racism featuring Elmo, the popular *Sesame Str*eet puppet. Major advertisers stopped running adding on his high-rated evening show, shifting ad-buys to other programs on Fox in the face of mounting criticism of his incendiary monologues. Two years earlier, after fulfilling purchase contracts for the time slot, many advertisers had done the same when Carlson stated U.S. immigration policy makes the country "poorer, dirtier and more divided."

His hateful rhetoric during a June 2020 show is typical of the vitriol propelling his partisan commentary. Under chyrons like "WE HAVE TO FIGHT TO PRESERVE OUR NATION & HERITAGE," he shouted at images of Senator Tammy Duckworth and Representative Ilhan Omar calling them "vandals" set on plundering American culture. In attacking Omar, "recused from a squalid Kenyan refugee camp," he leaned into the nativist trope of the ungrateful immigrant: "But Ilhan Omar is not grateful. She hates us for it." His broadsides against the Muslim congresswomen that began soon after her election endanger not only her and but also other immigrants like her. She requires extra security when she travels because of sustained threats to her life.

His adjectives aimed at Duckworth included "coward," "moron," "callous hack," "fraud," and "unimpressive." Such demeaning comments sparked a storm of protest and bolstered ratings. As she pointed out in a *Times* op-ed piece, she's a combat veteran who earned a Purple Heart after her Black Hawk helicopter was hit with a rocket-propelled grenade causing her to lose both legs. Mincing no words, she wrote, "attacks from self-serving, insecure men who can't tell the difference between true patriotism and hateful nationalism will never diminish my love for this country — or my willingness to sacrifice for it, so they don't have to. These titanium legs don't buckle."[245]

With roughly four million viewers, among the biggest audience in cable talk, Sean Hannity pounds on the fair-and-balanced scale unabashedly. An Oval Office mouthpiece, he dismisses all criticism of its current occupant as anti-Trump paranoia. The glib talk show host, prone to fact evasion and fabrication, even echoed and amplified the president's repeated wholly unfounded assertion that the coronavirus was a hoax as the number of confirmed cases steadily climbed. The smooth-talking Hannity is hardly alone on the cable news network in spreading doubt and disinformation.

In her turn in the ten o'clock slot, fact-free Laura Ingraham was quick to challenge the wisdom of those preaching social distancing, implying, more or less, that it was an overreaction. Her irresponsible statements like lest we not forget China caused this infection, echoed and magnified by the president, place people of Chinese ancestry in even greater jeopardy of attack. As might be expected, this is the channel to find ardent defenders of the Trump Administration's considerable cuts to the Center for Disease Control's budget in the two years before the coronavirus crisis. Those fed mostly on Fox News, right-wing talk radio, and organized internet rumor-mongering are bound to become misdirected and ill-informed.

What constitutes something as credible must be hard to discern. The tweeter-in-chief, displeased by some of the cable network's coverage, taunted the blunt-truth reporting of Shepard Smith. In what struck many as an unlikely coincidence, soon after his attorney general met with Rupert Murdoch in fall 2019, the longtime news anchor departed the network, further shortening the distance between the reporting produced by its newsroom and the partisanship of the primetime cheerleaders.

HBO's Axios What Matters

The leader of the free world tends to have a tough time with interviewers other than sycophantic never-ask-a probing-question Sean Hannity. Soon after the inept way he handled Wallace's pointed but polite questions, the president sat down for an HBO interview with Australian journalist Johanne Swan of Axios (from the Greek meaning worth), the news website founded in 2016 by former Politico executives.[246] Swan deferentially but repeatedly exposed his fabrications through simple follow-up questions.

During the interview, the president denounced recently deceased civil rights icon Representative John Lewis, and implied the Civil Rights Act was a mistake. He even wished deceased child predator Jeffrey Epstein's associate and alleged accomplice, Ghislaine Maxwell, well in her criminal prosecution. He seemed bewildered by Swan's point that the United States has had more people die from the pandemic per capita than many other countries. When asked about additional efforts to contain the coronavirus pandemic, he callously responded, "It is what it is. ... It's under control as much as you can control it." He also claimed "manuals" and "books" say not to test too much, but when asked what manuals, he changed the subject. Perhaps like political foe Joe Biden, he might get in less trouble by staying in hibernation.

Premium Channels

The steel-and-glass canyons of cities provided an incentive to construct cable systems as well. In 1965, cable pioneer Charles Dolan won a franchise to build a cable television system in the Lower Manhattan section of New York City. The new operation, soon to be called Sterling Manhattan Cable, was the first urban underground cable television system in the United States. Sterling eventually become Time-Life's subsidiary Time Warner Cable, spun off in 2009 and merged into Charter Communications seven years later.

In fall 1972, Dolan, and media partner Time-Life, launched Home Box Office (HBO). Early programming ranged from football games to the Pennsylvania Polka Festival. Three years later, HBO, now under Time-Life's control, began to transmit recent movie releases, uncut and without commercial interruption, via satellite to the many cable television systems springing up across the country.

Lawyer and businessman Gerald Levin, soft-spoken and seemingly unassuming, replaced Dolan as the company's president and chief executive officer. Under Levin's leadership, the premium service flourished. He eventually become CEO of the entire Time Warner corporation. In 2,000, he brokered a merger between AOL and Time Warner. At the time, AOL was *the platform*, the prime entry point into the internet. Between 1993 and 2001, its subscribers grew from 200,000 to almost thirty million. It provided direct internet via dialup service but broadband was rapidly expanding access to the World Wide Web.

The $350 billion merger turned out to be one of the biggest debacles in business history. When the share price plummeted, Levin retired from this iconic wreck with a reported $300 million in hand to become director of the Moonbeam Sanctuary, a spiritual wellness retreat in Southern California. AOL spun off from Time Warner in 2009. Verizon Communications acquired it six years later. HBO and its parent company are now a subsidiary of AT&T's WarnerMedia. In recent years, HBO has become an original-programming powerhouse with series like "Game of Thrones," "True Blood," "Boardwalk Empire," "The Newsroom," "Veep," and "Big Little Lies."

Competitors such as *Showtime* also create a wealth of original programming. Its list of entertainment fare includes *Billions*, *Shameless*, *The L Word: Generation Q*, *Penny Dreadful: City of Angels*, and the eight-season *Homeland* series set in the Middle East. Some of these shows, especially the latter, have generated considerable controversy for the way they treat sensitive political and cultural concerns.

Streaming Services

With the arrival of broadband internet, enabling transmission of high-quality images and sounds, streaming services triggered a seismic shift in the movie and television landscape. Starting as an online DVD store, Netflix introduced video-on-demand streaming of movies and television shows in 2007 and has since grown into a globe-spanning behemoth of enormous reach and appeal. It spends billions annually on new entertainment fare and has nearly 160 million subscribers worldwide. To qualify for Academy Award nominations, Netflix shows movies like *The Irishman* (2019) in theaters for a few weeks before they take up permanent residence on its streaming platform.

Other services like Hulu and Amazon Prime Video soon followed Netflix's lead into this new promised land of profits. So did streaming services such as BritBox and Acorn TV carving out narrow niches to satisfy particular passions. On a much broader scale, toward the end of 2019, Disney launched Disney Plus. The two other substantial old-line media companies—NBCUniversal and WarnerMedia—have entered the streaming fray as well. While the hunt for the next new binge-worthy hit never ends, the streaming revolution revived interest in old movies of all kinds as well as mostly forgotten over-the-air television shows.

Conglomerates in Command

These days, huge conglomerates like AT&T, Verizon, and Comcast mostly control cable systems. Their computerized nerve centers downlink program channels from satellites 22,300 miles above the earth. They are then relayed through underground coaxial or fiber-optic cables into homes through converter boxes. Municipalities and other local governments grant franchises to companies authorizing the construction and operation of cable systems.

AT&T established a network of subsidiaries in the United States and Canada that held a phone service monopoly, authorized by the government throughout most of the twentieth century. The Department of Justice filed an antitrust suit against AT&T in the fall of 1974, charging that it had used its dominant position in the telecommunications market to suppress competition and enhance its monopoly power. AT&T settled the lawsuit in 1982 through a consent decree. Without admitting wrongdoing, it agreed to divest its regionally dispersed companies offering local and regional services, called "baby bells" at the time, as well as to the divestiture and dissolution of Western Electric manufacturing subsidiary.

Several independent companies emerged, including Southwestern Bell Corporation later SBC Communications. In 2005, SBC purchased its former parent AT&T Corporation and took on the company's branding, with the merged entity naming itself AT&T Inc. and using its iconic logo. The current AT&T reconstitutes much of the former Bell System and includes ten of the original twenty-two baby bells along with the long-distance division. In early 2019, a three-judge panel of the United States Court of Appeals for the District of Columbia Circuit rejected the government's challenge to AT&T's $85.4 billion merger with Time Warner, a blockbuster deal that makes the combined company a significant player in the entertainment industry.

After the economic crisis in 2008, the federal government encouraged buyouts and mergers, by making debt cheap and keeping merger enforcement tepid. Those conditions catalyzed a significant concentration in cable systems, mobile phone carriers, and several other industries, leaving many sectors of the American economy with just a handful of behemoths. In *Captive Audience*, law professor Susan Crawford uses the 2011 merger of Comcast and NBC to show how such media powerhouses engage in anti-competitive practices, cutthroat lobbying methods, measures that stall broadband advances, and the use sports programming to dominate the internet.[247]

Among the other matters, Crawford highlights the difficulty of blocking vertical mergers, the revolving door between regulators, and the regulated, and the FCC's failure to designate internet access as a common-carrier utility. And heavily lobbied state legislatures, she notes, impedes municipal fiber network deployment—the laws in some nineteen states prevent cities from creating their broadband networks.

Like the 1930s Marxist analysts of movie company ownership by the Morgan and Rockefeller banking behemoths, Crawford says little about what such conglomerate control might mean for diverse entertainment fare. Whether for banker or studio executive, the ability to make money remains paramount. In the pursuit profit, most media companies employ a two-pronged approach to production—financing expensive movies aimed at as many people as possible and supporting less expensive, more adventurous projects.

A Comcast subsidiary, Universal Filmed Entertainment, distributes movies produced by Amblin Partners domestically and in select international territories. The Amblin partnership includes billionaire Jeff Skoll's Participant Media, behind such worthwhile climatic endeavors as *An Inconvenient Truth* (2006), climate calamity, *Food, Inc.* (2008), cruel and greedy corporate food producers, CITIZENFOUR (2014), whistleblower Edward Snowden saga, and *Spotlight* (2015), the cover-up of priest predators. Bashing billionaires has become a blood sport of sorts on the political left of late. Such blanket denunciation hardly applies to Skoll, a Canadian internet entrepreneur, and first eBay president who continues to use a big chunk of his several "1,000 million dollars" to fund movie projects that deserve kudos, not condemnation.

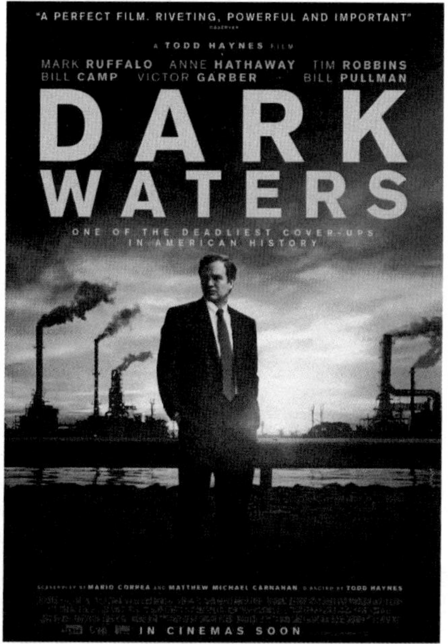

One of Participant's recent projects, *Dark Waters* (2019), is a suspenseful thriller based on actual events about the giant chemical company DuPont's dumping of the fluorocarbon PFOA, a toxic chemical used in the making of Teflon, into the water supply Parkersburg, West Virginia.[248] The focus is on the lawyer (Mark Ruffalo), who sues DuPont, the city's biggest employer in a class-action suit on behalf of the 70,000 locals adversely affected. Despite mounting evidence of the toxic fluorocarbon's dangers and calls for regulation, related "forever chemicals" are still produced in the United States. These chemicals are likely in the blood of ninety-nine percent of Americans, with firefighters and men and women in uniform at even higher risks of exposure.

The appeal of such progressive entertainment fare hardly rivals the iron-fist grip on viewership of over-the-air network television, an era of programming for huge audiences conceived as being in the cultural center. The advent of cable TV, communication satellites, smartphones, and instantaneous global communication using the internet and the World Wide Web fostered social separation and fragmentation—much the way the availability of the printed word and the corresponding growth of literacy did in medieval times. In the fragmented media environment these days, a significant segment of the nation watches or listens to anything at once only a few times at years at best.

Chapter 8

Ethnicity

We spend a large part of each day residing in an alternate reality of entertainment fare. Our synapses are replete with snatches of lyrics, tunes, themes, dialogue, and conscious and nonconscious memories of countless songs, sitcoms, crime shows, comedies, quiz programs, and movie melodramas of all sorts. Such entertainment fare affects how and what we think and feel about everything from crime to courtship to those whose skin color and facial features differ from our own.

Faraway Galaxy

The movie industry has long relied on racial and ethnic stereotypes, catering to and shaping the prevalent perceptions and prejudices, whether conscious or otherwise, amongst its target audiences, who are increasingly younger with each passing decade. These damaging depictions show up in the most unexpected places, even among digital denizens of the faraway galaxy depicted in *The Phantom Menace* (1999).

The dimwitted, computer-animated amphibian Jar Jar Binks, with his big lips, bulging eyes and a broad nose, comes right out of Hollywood's bag of black caricatures. His ineptness and cowardice in the face of danger is a running joke throughout the movie. He steps in animal dung, gets his tongue stuck in an electrical socket, lards his speech with malapropisms, and says things like "Yousa Jedi not all yousa cracked up to be" and "Why mesa always da one?" (The way he says "mesa" sounds suspiciously like "master.") His floppy ears resemble dreadlocks, and his vocal inflections suggest a West Indian patois (black stage performer Ahmed Best provided the voice of this Rastafarian amalgam of negative screen stereotypes).

Other negative stereotypes are also likely to be evident in this movie, at least to the initiated. A fat, buffoonish character named Boss Nass, seemingly a caricature of a stereotypical African chieftain, rules the Gungan tribe to which Jar Jar Binks belongs. (Commenting on his planetary neighbors, the Naboo, Nass notes: "Dey tink dey so smartee, dey tink dey brains so big.") Most Gungans wear flared trousers and share Jar Jar's bouncing lope.

Few ethnicities escape heavy-handed stereotyping. An intergalactic "yellow peril" is conjured up by the slit-eyed, faux-Asian-accented Neimoidians. These cunning and duplicitous hive-dwellers have exceptional organizing abilities and command a labyrinthine organization of bureaucrats and trade officials.

When the Jedi knights attempt to repair their broken spaceship, an insect-like junk dealer named Watto stymies them. He has a hooked nose that curves to his chin, speaks with an accent that carries distinct echoes of Yiddish, and has acquired a small fortune in currency, slaves, and other possessions through shrewd deal making and well-placed wagers. Only through the bravery of young Anakin Skywalker (Jake Lloyd) do the Jedi get the parts they need. The towheaded youngster is emancipated but separated from his mother, who still belongs to the money-grubbing junk dealer.

The resurrection of old stereotypes as fantasy figures in *The Phantom Menace* highlights the long history of denigrating minorities and marginalized groups in popular cultural forms. Such harmful stereotypical representations still enjoy wide circulation in contemporary culture. Old movies and television shows on such venues as Netflix, Amazon prime video, YouTube, and American Movie Classics abound with these negative stereotypes.

Distorting Depictions

The mental categories that simplify the complications of the real world also provide a shortcut to character development. In the early days of cinema, makers of movies used to comb the streets looking for easily identifiable social types to serve as extras. Supplying extras became formalized in 1925 with the creation of Central Casting, the principal source of stereotypical characters for decades. In common parlance, at least among older folk, someone who looks like a particular type is often characterized as being "straight out of central casting."

Actors and in varying degrees the rest of us establish personae-- assumed specific public images, or personae (an ancient Greek theatrical term referring to the masks actors wore to convey various emotions), that reinforced the roles they played. The public images of leading players especially were carefully nurtured and sustained through role assignments and coordinated publicity campaigns. The persona and the person behind the mask could be closely connected or bear few similarities beyond physical attributes.

Such recognizable stereotypes are mental images shared by those who hold a collective mindset within a particular culture, or significant sub-group within that culture, defining and labeling specific social groups or categories based on very few traits or characteristics. All who reside in the alternate reality of make-believe media have many skewed mental images of people, places, and things.

The alternate realities across media outlets tend to marginalize minorities, erasing significant differences among racial and ethnic groups traversing broad geographic areas. For the most part, they were treated as comic relief or represented as villains. And when central to plot developments, their portrayals tended toward the negative.

Once identified and dissected, stereotypes reveal expressions of otherwise hidden beliefs and values. These unconscious assumptions undoubtedly play a significant role in shaping, reinforcing, and altering perceptions of socially dispossessed ethnic groups. The offerings of the make-believe media resound with stereotypical representations. This prevalence makes examination of them an effective means of tracking how feelings and attitudes associated with some specific social category of people can change over time and the factors that foster such change.

Indigenous Populations

Native Americans typically appeared as little more than savage beasts of the wild intent on massacring peaceful white settlers. Even when nonaggressive, stoic Native Americans of few words paint them as one-dimensional, lacking the full range of emotions that other ethnicities display. While males are mostly in warrior regalia, females appear as maidens sexually available to white men. Although cause and effect are difficult to confirm, indigenous women have suffered from high rates of sexual assaults from whites. Whooping war parties attacking stagecoaches and wagon trains of dauntless pioneers have long been a staple of westerns and served to explain, sanctify, and justify a protracted bloody history of racism and deceit against this indigenous population. An underlying assumption of westward expansion in the nineteenth century is that the North American continent belonged to the United States by a combination of divine right, practical need, and the assumed superiority of the American way of life and system of rules and regulations.

The early 1970s saw a cinematic shift in the depiction of Native Americans soon after chilling reports appeared in the news media of atrocities committed by American troops in Vietnam. Movies such as *Little Big Man* (1970), *Soldier Blue* (1970), and *Ulzana's Raid* (1972) depict savage whites massacring pure and hapless Native Americans. Overtly antiwar polemics permeate *Little Big Man*. Its plot structure hinges on the reminiscences of 121-year-old Jack Crabb (Dustin Hoffman), who survived Custer's last stand at the Battle of Little Big Horn. A bracing antidote to encrusted misconceptions, the blustering, egomaniacal George Armstrong Custer depicted here is a far cry from the heroic figure played by dashing Errol Flynn in *They Died With Their Boots On* (1941).

Whether this shift carries a broader cultural resonance is difficult to discern. Why were Native Americans now being shown in a sympathetic, if not pathetic light? Were such depictions reflective of growing disillusionment and disgust with the Vietnam War and the mythology that supported it? Efforts to determine how shifts in any genre's political orientation reflect changing perceptions of social and historical events, or to assess the part such variations play in shaping those perceptions, result in tentative and speculative conclusions. Nonetheless, they are thought-provoking and may lead to new ways of making sense of others and ourselves.

Latinos

The category "Latino" encompasses all the people of Latin America, a vast area including Central and South America, that is hardly homogeneous in natural or cultural characteristics. Although Latinos constitute the largest minority group in the United States, they too have been characterized very narrowly, unlikely to be cast as lawyers, doctors, or other professionals. Mexicans were invariably depicted either as brutal bandits or endearingly lazy cowards with funny accents. Highly sexualized "Latin lovers" or exotic, sensual temptresses, framed as having fiery temperaments, are among the other common Latino stereotypes.

In such silent movies as *Blood and Sand* (1922), Italian-born Rudolph Valentino fixed the stereotype of the Latin lover as the possessor of primal sexuality, tinged with violence and danger. Mexican-born Dolores Del Rio exemplified the female counterpart in movies like *Down to Rio* (1933) and *In Caliente* (1935), playing mysterious characters whose allure arouses amorous appetites in ways that elude Anglo women. Variations on these male and female stereotypes have had many screen incarnations over the decades. When these screen portrayals lose luster, others such as eternal virgins, gang members, or drug dealers are at play. Gina Rodriguez, as the title character in the television series *Jane the Virgin*, is a recent example of a Latina as "virginal" or "passive."

To expand screen opportunities, those with Latino-sounding names sometimes not only changed appellations but also transformed themselves entirely. Margarita Carmen Cansino, for example, first made her mark in show business as a twelve-year-old dancing with her father, with whom she traveled around the world.[249] She won a sixth-month contract from Fox Films in 1935. Billed as Rita Cansino, she did a sensual dance in *Dante's Inferno* (1935), appeared as Egyptian servant in *Charlie Chan in Egypt* (1935), and as a Russian dancer in *Paddy O'Day* (1935). Sensing her screen potential, Columbia Pictures head Harry Cohn signed her to a seven-year contract but felt her image limited her to being cast in "exotic" roles. Acting on Cohn's

advice, Rita Cansino became Rita Hayworth, adopting her mother's maiden name. She changed her hair color to auburn and underwent painful electrolysis to raise her hairline and broaden her forehead. Promoted as the "Love Goddess," she became one of the most glamorous screen idols of the 1940s. Her signature role as the title character in *Gilda* (1946), stirring the lusts of strangers while singing the torch song "Put the Blame on Mame," overshadowed the rest of her screen performances and affected her personal life as well. Her lust-sparking sexual siren persona only a screen mask, she once famously lamented: "Every man I knew went to bed with Gilda... and woke up with me."

A Latino broke new ground on early network television. When CBS first approached Lucille Ball with the offer of turning her popular radio show *My Favorite Husband* into a television series, she was agreeable with the condition that her Cuban-born husband Desi Arnaz would be cast in the role of her fictional spouse (played on the radio by Richard Denning). The network's executives were eager to sign her, but having a Latino in every living room in America married to a white, homegrown gal was too much at a time.

Legal and de facto segregation was the norm throughout the country, and *Loving v. Virginia* making anti-miscegenation laws illegal was seventeen years into the future. The network brass bought the idea of putting a Latino with a white wife in primetime after seeing a "pilot" or sample episode of the proposed television program, now called *I Love Lucy* starring the couple made to test audience reaction with a view to the production of a series.

Italian Gangsters

Anti-Italian prejudice and hostility arose in the United States as a reaction to their large-scale immigration during the late-nineteenth and early-twentieth centuries, mainly from southern Italy and Sicily. Since the turn of the last century, Italian Americans have been portrayed with negative stereotypical characterizations. Scores of movies perpetuated the idea that Italian-Americans and organized crime go together like spaghetti and tomato sauce.

Hugely popular movies like *Little Caesar* (1930) and *Scarface* (1932) crystallized the stereotype of the Italian-American gangster. By all accounts, the percentage of Italians engaging in criminality is minuscule, yet the preponderance of movies featuring this ethnic group focus on gangsterism, even as those of Italian descent have made great strides in American society. The prevalence of such negative stereotyping is evident in movies like *The Godfather* (1972) and its progeny, *GoodFellas* (1990), and *Casino* (1995), and television programs such as *The Sopranos* (1999-2007). In director Spike Lee's movies, most notably *Do the Right Thing* (1989), *Jungle Fever* (1991), and *Summer of Sam* (1999), Italian-American characters are mostly menacing, racist thugs.

Nobel Extortionists

When moviemakers of Italian descent are at the helm, the depictions of criminals are sometimes oddly flattering and sympathetic. Consider the first of the *Godfather* movies, widely regarded as one of the greatest cinematic achievements of all time. Director Frances Ford Coppola co-wrote this mob melodrama with Mario Puzo

based on Puzo's novel of the same name. The focus is on the powerful Italian-American crime family of Don Vito Corleone played by non-Italian Marlon Brando.

The casting of Brando might seem an odd choice, but it's hard to imagine anyone other than the acclaimed actor in the title role. In creating the character of the mob boss, he affected a wheezing, aspirate voice seemingly cracked with age. His vocal inflections have an eccentric, slightly ethnic sound, redolent of the character's Sicilian origins. They are supplemented by subtle movements of his fingertips in front of his mouth and the way he raises his eyebrow at times instead of speaking. With his raspy voice, deliberate gestures, and penetrating stare, Brando manages to invest the aging but still powerful gangster with an air of wisdom and even nobility. By the time the old Don dies in his garden, he has become so endearing that we feel upset despite his lifetime of criminality.

Even with their brutal crimes, extortion, and trafficking in prostitution, the Corleone's are made to seem in many ways quite admirable. They give primacy to familial kinship ties, extended through the sacred practice of serving as godparents, operate with a strict code of honor, and have a strong sense of communal solidarity. Their activities are isolated in a moral vacuum.

In the absence of an efficacious law enforcement system, they appear to be forces of justice and protectors of the weak. Their victims are limited to characters embodying traits society frowns upon: an unprincipled Hollywood producer, a crooked police captain, family traitors, and other gangsters willing to deal in drugs (which Don Corleone regards as a "dirty business"). And there are no strong characters with competing values to provide a meaningful counterpoint to the Corleone family's moral outlook.

Middle Easterners

Americans of Arab and Middle Eastern heritage have long faced disparaging stereotypes in entertainment fare as well. Such depictions have roots dating back to the Crusades, a series of religious wars in the eleventh, twelfth, and thirteenth centuries between Christians and Muslims to secure control of holy sites considered sacred by both groups. Typical stereotypes include harem girls, scantily-clad belly dancers, and heavily-accented oil-rich sheiks. Movies such *Arabian Nights* (1942), and *Ali Baba and the Forty Thieves* (1944) are among a host of old Hollywood movies featuring Arab women as erotically-veiled dancers, whose primary purpose is male pleasure.

And, well before the 9/11 attacks, middle-eastern men were portrayed as anti-American villains, if not outright terrorists, and misogynistic brutes with backward and mysterious customs. In the first minute or so of the 1992 movie *Aladdin*, for instance, the theme song declares that the title character hails "from a faraway place, where the caravan camels roam, where they cut off your ear if they don't like your face. It's barbaric, but hey, it's home." The xenophobic 1996 box-office hit, *True Lies*, depicts Arabs as violent, anti-American zealots.

One of the longest-running Showtime series, *Homeland*, features CIA officer Carrie Mathison (Claire Danes), a top operative despite being bipolar. The condition, once identified as manic-depressive disorder, makes her volatile and unpredictable. With the help of her long-time mentor Saul Berenson (Mandy Patinkin), she often risks everything, including her well-being and even sanity, in carrying out a mission. On the premium channel for eight seasons, since debuting in 2011, the drama has proved to be one of the most ethnically biased shows on television. Since debuting in 2011, the series has proved to be some of the most damaging depictions on the small screen with every harmful trope in the stereotype grab-bag about Muslims, it paints them as a hidden danger to Americans. The compelling drama often drew salvos for trafficking Islamophobia. Without fail, Arabs, Muslims, and the whole Middle East appear sinister and suspicious.

Although appealing and sympathetic characters appear across the long-running series, the preponderance of those identified as Muslims are either terrorists or willing collaborators with American intelligence forces. For many Muslims, the final season was reportedly a cause for celebration. The lack of diverse depictions on television screens has left many vulnerable extremist attacks and propaganda. In recent years, as platforms proliferate, more Muslim actors, writers, and directors are finding work.

Imaginary of West Africans

Birth of a Nation

Almost from the time movies were first made, people of West African origin were represented as servile, ridiculous, or downright dangerous. Such stereotypes reached an apotheosis of sorts in D.W Griffith's *The Birth of a Nation* (1915), which idealizes the antebellum South. More than any other director of his time, Griffith clearly demonstrated the capacity of the motion picture to provide a coherent and compelling screen drama from disparate pieces of time and space. Running three hours, the dramatic power, eloquence, and vigor of this Civil War epic constitutes a significant milestone in the evolution of moviemaking, combining sweeping, epic events with intimate moments of joy and sorrow.

This cinematic dazzle is undeniably dimmed by the movie's racial depictions and assumptions of white supremacy. The focus is on two white families, the abolitionist Stonemans of Pennsylvania and the slave-owning Camerons of South Carolina whose lives are torn apart by the brutal war and its aftermath. At their modest Piedmont plantation, the genteel Cameron family is terrorized by a troop of black raiders, and the once idyllic South undergoes "ruin, devastation, rapine, and pillage" according to the narrative subtitles.

Both families lose sons on the battlefield while the daughters face the new black menace to white maidenhood. In reality white men posed a far greater threat to black maidenhood in the antebellum South. Because slaves were denied any rights, a black woman molested by a white man had no legal recourse. Virtually every plantation produced children of mixed race, most of whom were simply worked and sold like all other slaves.

Fears of miscegenation and loss of superior status permeate the section dealing with the Reconstruction period and the rise of the Ku Klux Klan. We see blacks "drunk with wine and power" and "crazy with joy" engaged in a reign of terror, shoving and taunting white people and flogging "faithful colored servants" senseless. We also see them holding placards promoting "equal marriage." The really vile characters are "mulatto" from the Spanish word for a young mule, seeming to suggest that interracial coupling invariably produces inferior progeny.

A particularly nasty scene opens with a still photograph of an empty South Carolina state legislature. This image slowly dissolves as the chamber comes to life full of raucous black lawmakers, bare feet on desks, swilling liquor and eating fried chicken. After these legislators enact a statute providing for interracial marriage, a group of blacks on the assembly floor is shown ogling something above them. The camera then cuts to reveal the object of this leering: a group of frightened-looking white women in the gallery.

KKK to the Rescue

In scenes building toward the suspense-filled climax, things look bleak until the noble knights of the Ku Klux Klan, "the organization that saved the South from the anarchy of black rule" ride to the rescue. White womanhood is saved, chastity remains in check, and renegade ex-slaves are pushed back, beaten, and killed. Northern and Southern whites are once again united "in defense of their Aryan birthright." Son of a Confederate officer, Griffith reaffirmed the prevalent stereotypes of the era propagated by politicians as well as historians. The Reverend Thomas Dixon, a college acquaintance of President Woodrow Wilson, arranged for a special screening of *Birth of a Nation* at the White House for him and his family.

After viewing the movie, the president reputedly responded: "It is like writing history with lightning. And my only regret is that it is all so terribly true." Whether he made this much-repeated remark, first reported decades after the screening, is highly doubtful, but the president certainly seemed to share much of the Dixon-Griffith view of the old South after the war. A professional historian, Woodrow Wilson, in the final volume of his five-volume *History of the American People*, gives pretty much the same account of the Reconstruction period (1865-1877) as the movie does. He describes the vigilante white-supremacist group initially at least as brave saviors of a post-war South shattered by freed blacks and Northern carpetbaggers.

A title card in the movie adapted from Wilson's book reads: "The white men were roused by a mere instinct of self-preservation.... until at last there had sprung into existence a great Ku Klux Klan, a veritable empire of the South, to protect the southern country." (Ellipsis in the original.) The elided quote, it should be noted, is misleading since Wilson does note in this volume the disparity between the KKK's initial goals and what the vigilante group became.[250]

By the same token, after assuming the presidency, the Virginia-born Wilson re-segregated much of the White House workforce. In a process begun under his administration in 1917, the government eventually named ten Southern military installations for Confederate officers. The proliferation of statues, street signs, school names, and other emblems of the Confederacy in the first few decades of the last century could lead to the conclusion that the seceding states won the Civil War.

A box office smash, this silent-screen melodrama became highly influential, among other things, contributing to the resurgence of the Ku Klux Klan only months later. By 1924, the membership of this new incarnation of the Klan had swelled to well over four million. When first organized in 1915, the group's chief goal was white supremacy, but over time, as it grew and spread from the Deep South to the Midwest and the Pacific coast, Jews, Italians, and Roman Catholics became a principal clan target in many localities. Often using *Birth of a Nation* as a recruiting tool, it drew into its white-sheeted fold mostly the poorly educated and less disciplined elements of the white Protestant community for whom membership in a group that promoted white supremacy and cast aspersions on other religions and ethnicities presumably propped up a shaky sense of self-worth.

Oscar Micheaux

By the mid-1920s, film companies run by blacks (often bankrolled by whites) had sprung up in such diverse locations as Jacksonville, St. Louis, Omaha, Philadelphia, Chicago, New York, and Los Angeles. One of the most prolific of these filmmakers was Oscar Micheaux, whose movies featured lynching, job discrimination, rape, mob violence, and economic exploitation.

The prevailing prejudice in the black community about status and shades of darkness is evident in Micheaux's movies as well. He cast light-skinned actors to play educated and professional characters, reflecting the elevated status of those of mixed-race who comprised the majority of free blacks before the Civil War. His depictions of poor blacks are invariably dark-skinned with hardly any dilution of their African ancestry.

Like other black filmmakers of the day, the multitalented Micheaux toiled on the tightest of budgets. In many of his surviving movies, the acting is amateurish, the lighting and editing crude, and the dramatic structure disjointed. Nonetheless, he was sometimes able to present racial issues and social conflicts in powerfully realistic ways that aroused anger and anxiety among both blacks and whites. As a study notes, many of the silent movies he made regularly ran into censorship difficulties.[251]

One of Micheaux's most controversial films was *Within Our Gates* (1920). The principal focus is on a mixed-race young schoolteacher with a scarred past striving to bring education to disadvantaged children and find romantic fulfillment. (No copies of this movie were believed to survive until a print was discovered in 1988 at the National

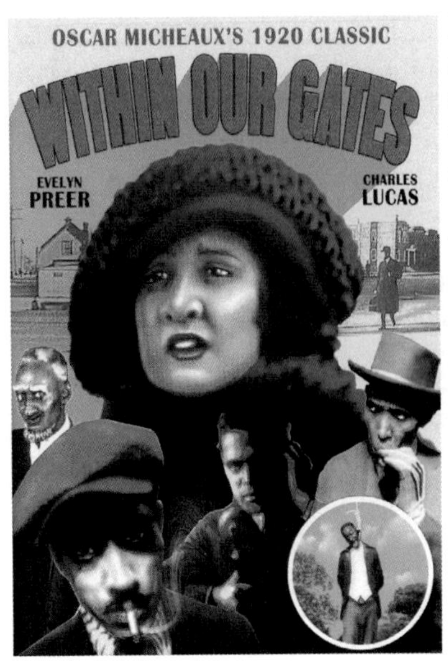

Rim Archive in Madrid, Spain.) The events depicted in the first two-thirds of the story are overshadowed by a lengthy flashback revealing the shocking details of what happened to her and her family as a result of virulent racism. In a flashback, she is shown growing up as the adopted daughter of a sharecropper. Her adoptive father, struggling to free himself from economic bondage, is falsely accused of killing a white plantation owner (Ralph Johnson). A lynch mob of ordinary townspeople, comprised of men, women and even children, organizes to exact vigilante justice on him and his family. The young woman's little brother manages to escape on horseback, but her adoptive parents are brutally beaten and then hanged for a crime they didn't commit.

In the intervening time, the plantation owner's brother comes upon her in a nearby cabin. He tries to rape her only to recoil in shock when a mark on her chest reveals that she is his own offspring. The use of parallel editing effectively links the lynching and the sexual attack, suggesting that both are employed as instruments of terror against the black community.

Black and white church and community leaders alike tried to prevent showings of *Within Our Gates*, fearing that its graphic scenes of lynching and attempted rape would rekindle the racial violence that had erupted in dozens of American cities in the summer of 1919. (In Chicago, where some of the worst rioting occurred, some 6,000 federal troops were called in to stop the bloodshed.) In the heated racial climate of the post-World War I period, fueled by fierce rivalry among whites and blacks for jobs, the movie was subject to severe censorship and even banned outright in some cities.[252]

Micheaux's movies did little to counter negative black stereotypes on the silent screen. Among other causes, such stereotypical depictions reflected longstanding fears in American society of "miscegenation." This term refers to the sexual mixing of people in different racial classifications, primarily through marriage or cohabitation between a white person and a member of another racial category.

In many states, whom one could marry was a matter of law. Anti-miscegenation laws banned the marriage of whites and non-white groups, primarily blacks, but often also Asians and Native Americans. Although routinely regarded as a Southern phenomenon, laws against interracial marriage or cohabitation were enacted in most western and plains states as well. By the 1920s, some thirty-eight of the then forty-eight states prohibited whites from marrying blacks along with other racial categories depending on the region of the country.

Virginia titled its law the Racial Integrity Act of 1924. Designed to reinforce racial hierarchies and prevent the mixing of races, it forbade interracial marriage classifying as "white" anyone without a trace of any blood other than Caucasian. During the 1950s, except in the South, laws of this type were repealed or overturned in many states. Decisively, in *Loving v. Virginia* (1967), the U.S. Supreme Court declared anti-miscegenation laws unconstitutional.[253] Of course, no ruling by the high court can erase deeply-held, often unconscious, biases and prejudices. (In 1989, the citizens of Virginia elected the first black governor in the nation, Douglas Wilder, a grandson of slaves.)

Donning Blackface

Implicit displays of white supremacy manifested themselves in many entertainment venues. White performers donning blackface theatrical makeup enjoyed enormous popularity during the nineteenth century and contributed to the spread of negative racial stereotypes that prevail to the present day. The stage adaptations of Harriet Beecher Stowe's 1852 novel, *Uncle Tom's Cabin*, about horrors of slavery, provided a layer of irony to blackface. The story centers on Uncle Tom, who, despite unspeakably cruel treatment, never wavers in his devotion to the young daughter of his white master. When the first stage production premiered in New York City in 1853, it featured an all-white cast.

The decades that followed saw hundreds of troupes crisscrossing the country, staging blackface dramatizations of the long-suffering black slave of the title and the other characters who revolve around him. By all accounts, these "Tom shows," as the traveling productions were called, generated a great deal of excitement. Spectators of all ages, sexes, races, and classes crowded the main street on the expected day of an acting company's arrival in town. In the often-makeshift kerosene-lit theatrical venues of the productions, few were likely to notice or perhaps even care if white skin of the actor playing Uncle Tom showed through his blackface makeup.[254]

White performers in a minstrel show not only blackened their skin but also exaggerated their lips, wore woolly wigs, and mangled the English language speaking in ersatz black dialects. The stereotypical traits embodied in the comic characters of blackface minstrels included the buffoonish, lazy, superstitious, cowardly, and lascivious, as well as dishonest and double-dealing. The minstrel show format, tilled in the rough-and-tumble "five points" Irish section of New York City, dominated show business into the 1890s.[255] As minstrelsy went into decline, blackface returned to its novelty act roots and became part of vaudeville and then movies.

A movie released in the fall of 1927, *The Jazz Singer*, ushered in the sound era and blackface theatrical makeup to the big screen. Based on a successful Broadway play about a cantor's son who enters show business, it's mostly a silent movie with poorly synchronized musical numbers and a few sentences of spoken words. The famed songster Al Jolson starred in the title role. In the final scene, donning blackface, on one knee, hand on his heart, he swoons his clipped-and-choppy rendition of the sentimental "My Mammy." The ring of box-office registers sounded the death knell for speechless cinema but not for the tradition of blackface theatrical makeup.

In *Check and Double Check* (1930), white radio stars Freeman Gosden and Charles Correll, who learned their trade in minstrelsy, brought their popular black characters Amos and Andy to the silver screen. The storyline has the two trying to make a go of their "open-air" taxi business, so named because the single vehicle was sans roof. They get caught up in a society hassle involving driving musicians to a fancy party. To flesh out the story the writers added a love triangle involving white characters, basically reducing Amos and Andy to minor players in what was marketed as a movie about them.

The movie featured musical numbers by Duke Ellington and his Cotton Club band, some of whose members weren't black. To avoid the impression of an integrated band, the movie's makers required the Puerto Rican trombonist and the Creole clarinetist to darken their faces and bodies. The black bandleader and composer called the movie a "crowning point" in his career. Although this was hardly the case, the association with the radio stars did greatly expand the audience for his music.

The heavily promoted movie did okay business at the box office, but it was the characters only screen appearance. Even contemporary reviewers found the blackface unsettling, although the use of such makeup was not uncommon in movies at the time. The screen stars who "blacked up" during the 1930s and early 1940s include Shirley Temple, Fred Astaire, Judy Garland, Bing Crosby, and a litany of others.

In *The Littlest Rebel* (1935), Shirley Temple appeared on screen with her hair wrapped up tight in a scarf with her skin painted pitch black. A year later, in *Dimples* (1936), she danced with two men in blackface, while other actors also in blackface watched. Fred Astaire did a tap solo in blackface for the dance number "Bojangles of Harlem" in *Swing Time* (1936) as a tribute to fellow hoofer Bill Robinson. In 1938's *Babes in Arms*, Judy Garland played an aspiring performer whose love for jazz leads to attending auditions as a blackface singer.

In *Holiday Inn* (1942), black-faced Bing Crosby and costar Marjorie Reynolds sing "Abraham," a song honoring Abraham Lincoln's birthday, backed up by "chorus girls" in lighter-toned blackface makeup. Testimony to the tenor of the times, one of composer Irving Berlin's lyrics declares that Lincoln "set the darkie free." In the 1944 romantic comedy *Here Come the Waves*, Bing and Sonny Tufts in blackface sing one of the most upbeat and popular songs of the war years, "Ac-Cent-Tchu-Ate the Positive." A chorus of women dressed as WAVES (Women Accepted for Voluntary Emergency Service) accompanies them. (This voluntary unit would refuse to admit women of color until nearly the end of 1944.) Sung in the style of a sermon, it explains that accentuating the positive is the key to happiness. In the postwar years, the movie blackface soon went the way of vaudeville. But like a monster that grows a new head each time the old is decapitated, photos of prominent political figures donning blackface keep materializing.

Docile Domestics

When black actors sought work in the movie industry, they were commonly cast in such roles as maid, mammy, manservant, and comic sidekick. They typically played kindly souls, slow moving (except when they danced), adept at only menial tasks, rarely showed any signs of sexual desire, and happy to let the white folks manage the world.

Lincoln Perry, who adopted the professional name Stepin Fetchit, lent life to stylized characters who were invariably dimwitted, tongue-tied, slow gait, and lazy. From 1929 to 1935, his career peak, he appeared in some twenty-six movies, often working on as many as three or four at a time. His caricatured slow-wittedness in such pictures as *The Ghost Talks* (1929), *David Haram* (1934), *Stand Up and Cheer* (1934), and *Charlie Chan in Egypt* (1935) spawned a bevy of black imitators, most notably Willie Best who found steady screen work at a time when his career was on the wane.

A headliner in Broadway shows, Bill "Bojangles" Robinson was the highest-paid black performer of the time. His fans included the president of the United States Franklin D. Roosevelt. Such recognition notwithstanding, the virtuoso tap dancer was relegated to the servant quarters in most movies. For example, in *The Littlest Colonel* (1935), he played a postbellum butler opposite child star sensation Shirley Temple.

In a scene the contemporary viewer is likely to find cloying and offensive, Temple's character directs the household servant to dance for the party guests celebrating her sixth birthday in the ballroom of the family plantation. In preparation for a now-iconic up-the-staircase dance number, Robinson taught the talented seven-year-old one of his exuberant, elegant tap-dancing routines entailing a rhythmically complex sequence of steps. They became the first interracial dance partners on the silver screen.

Well into middle age, Robinson appeared with prepubescent Temple in three more movies, with her characters the child of slave-owners, but rarely did the parts he played depart from the stereotype imposed by the screenwriters. While displaying his talents as an actor and tap dancer, the movies perpetuate the myth that black people are happiest when serving and entertaining whites, and have no feelings, thoughts or desires beyond those purposes. In *The Littlest Rebel*, the household slave Robinson plays even asserts that he neither wants, nor understands why others might want, to be emancipated.

Gone with the Wind

The antebellum south once again moved to the center of the cultural stage with the Civil War epic *Gone with the Wind* (1939). The striking albeit artificial-looking Technicolor images give this talkie equivalent of *The Birth of a Nation* the sheen of an alternate reality. Overseeing this make-believe historical saga, producer David O. Selznick strove for visual and aural splendor.

The costumier designed over 5,500 individual pieces of clothing for the 2000 outfits worn by the actors. He used costly Val lace for the petticoats of the southern belles. The makeup artist managed to keep the female lead's naturally blue eyes looking emerald green throughout the shooting. The actors who play the field slaves work the

plantation to a majestic offscreen musical score. An eloquent crane shot enlarges the view of the open-air, makeshift military hospital at Atlanta's railroad depot. As the camera slowly pulls up and back, it reveals countless rows of wounded and dying Confederate soldiers. It finally comes to a stop with a close-up of a torn and tattered Confederate flag waving over the human carnage. A feast to the eyes and ear, this movie perpetuates some of the worst Civil War myths and black stereotypes.

Based on the 1936 book by Margaret Mitchell of the same name, in this alternate reality of life on the plantation all is idyllic. The young white belles are elegant, the menfolk noble or at least dashing. The contented slaves seem childlike and simple-minded, incapable of independent existence. Enslaved women cool the gentilic southern ladies with peacock feather fans as they take naps in preparation for the evening's festivities. A sassy mammy (Hattie McDaniel) fusses and frets over them with loving admonitions.

Diverting attention away from the cruelty of plantation enslavement, at the movie's center is a compelling journey through Scarlett O'Hara's (Vivian Leigh) tragic life. From southern belle to refugee, to confident woman, to desperate lover, we see her fall in and out of despair, using everything she possibly can and then some to come out on top only to fail. One of the few hints of actual servitude's harshness occurs when this flawed heroine slaps her high-pitched squeaky-voice maid (Butterfly McQueen) after her admission about lying. The white characters in the movie aren't necessarily good people, but their negative qualities have nothing to do with the lives of the black slaves whose only function is to serve.

Even after the war is lost, the house servants remain devoted to their former masters. But the brave and noble southern gentlemen (KKK members in the book) must use vigilante violence to deal with rebellious ex-slaves and corrupt southern whites and unscrupulous carpetbaggers. The shortcomings of this beautifully staged and shot cinematic spectacle aside, it became the most significant box-office success in history, selling more tickets than any other movie ever made.

Dismaying Disney Characters

Negative black stereotypes turn up in all kinds of cinematic fare. The Disney studio's *Fantasia* (1940), a stunning blend of animated imagery with classical music, is comprised of eight animated segments. The Pastoral Symphony segment, featuring Beethoven's composition, contains the cringe-worthy stereotype of an odd-looking black centaur girl with braided "pickaninny" hair and over-sized lips acting as a servant to the thin, beautiful and white female centaur—a scene excised in subsequent rerelease.

The Disney studio's *Song of the South* (1946), a mostly live-action movie with animated segments interspersed, depicts happy former slaves living on a plantation in post-Civil War Atlanta. It's based on the collection of Uncle Remus stories and features black actor James Baskett as the kindly former slave. At the center of the movie, Remus touchingly teaches a little white boy a positive way to deal with his life telling him tales "in his old-timey way" of a character named Br'er Rabbit.

His kindness and gentle nature aside, the Remus character mirrors the *Uncle Tom's Cabin* stereotype, perpetuating the image of the happy, subservient black man content with his inferior lot in life. This vestige of Old South nostalgia earned an Oscar for the catchy original song "Zip-a-Dee-Doo-Dah," sung by Baskett, even though it recycles the old canard about how slaves can't have been so miserable, listen to them sing in that cottonfield. The actor got a taste of those "Zip-a-Dee-Doo-Dah" wonderful days when he was not allowed to attend the movie's premiere in racially-segregated Atlanta, Georgia.[256] (The cinema-focused podcast "You Must Remember This" did a six-episode examination of this movie.)

Some black performers were able to bring quiet strength and sensitivity to even stereotypical roles. Actor, drummer, bandleader, and Broadway star Dooley Wilson, for example, managed to invest Rick Blaine's piano-playing sidekick Sam in *Casablanca* (1943) with a high degree of dignity. But this character is only a slightly enhanced version of the asexual black servant so prevalent in this era. Wilson had tried to resist stereotyping, but there's more than a touch of Uncle Tom in his self-effacing deference to "Mister Richard" and his humble demeanor around "Miss Ilsa." Remarks like her slighting reference to the "boy at the piano," reinforce his subservience. As he sings "As Time Goes By," a sentimental love song, as a musical backdrop for Rick and Ilsa's romance, nothing suggests he might have sexual desires as well. His moods and concerns are of those of Rick's. The script doesn't give him any of his own. (In a bit of irony, Arthur "Dooley" Wilson's nickname came from singing Irish songs in "whiteface" early in his career)

Amos and Andy

One of the most popular radio programs of the 1930s and 1940s *was Amos 'n' Andy*, minstrelsy for the ear featuring two white ex-vaudevillians, Freeman Gosden and Charles Correll in blackface.[257] Sandwiched between commercials for Pepsodent toothpaste, the shows lasted about ten minutes and required from 1500 to 2000 words. Gosden and Correll initially wrote all the scripts, supplied sound effects, and timed the broadcasts. The motif composed for Lillian Gish's character in the inflammatory *Birth of a Nation* became the radio program's theme music.

All of the characters were direct descendants of the burnt-cork comics of the minstrel shows. Amos was trusting, simple, and unsophisticated, while Andy was slow and shiftless. The two owned and operated the Fresh-Air Taxi-Cab Company, whose assets included one broken-down topless automobile, one desk, and one swivel chair for the president to "rest his brains." The action often took place at the Mystic Knights of the Sea lodge presided over by a scheming fellow called "the Kingfish," a vivid character disposed to bilking Andy and fracturing the English language. He would become more central when the show switched to a half-hour weekly format in 1943.

With suspense and dramatic tension across multiple well-structured plotlines, *Amos 'n' Andy* set the standard for a new radio form: the serialized situation comedy. For a show aimed at evoking laughter, some of the early plotlines touched on the harsh realities of black life, among them Amos's brutal police interrogation about the murder of a low-level hoodlum. Following official protests by the national association of police chiefs, Correll and Gosden abandoned that plotline, improbably turning the grilling into a bad dream from which Amos gratefully awoke on Christmas Eve.

During the depths of the Depression, the show enjoyed unparalleled popularity. While assessing audience size was crude in those days, several estimates put its number of regular listeners by the early 1930s at forty million, with some episodes reaching fifty million, out of a population that was then some 120 million. A breach-of-promise suit brought against Andy by a character called Madam Queen so enmeshed audience interest that his fate became the topic of talk at dinner tables and on commuter trains across the nation. Many movie theatres would stop the projector in mid-reel at seven p.m. each weekday evening to pipe in the program to patrons who would otherwise have stayed home.

Such oft-repeated catchphrases as "I'se restin' my brain," "Holy mackerel," and "Check and double check," spoken in a bogus black dialect, became embedded in the everyday lexicon of ordinary people across the country. In addition to the movie featuring the radio stars, the *Chicago Daily News* syndicated a daily *Amos 'n' Andy* comic strip, and Victor promoted phonograph records featuring the popular pair. The recordings tend to focus on the schemes of Kingfish and his fellow fraudsters to exploit the gullibility of their black victims.

The very success of nationwide program fare lies in the manner in which it reflects and reinforces the dominant stereotypes of the majority of the population. The imaginary world of Amos, Andy, Kingfish, and the other characters was a far cry from the everyday indignities of ghetto life hinted at in the early days of the series. In the segregated society of the period, however, many people were doubtlessly unaware of the disparity.

From a present-day perspective, it is not hard to see how these black stereotypes served to legitimate segregation and discrimination by fostering the idea that blacks and whites are so different culturally that integration is undesirable and unworkable. As broadcast historian Eric Barnouw put it, the characters were "ignorant and somewhat shiftless and lazy in a lovable, quaint way, not fitting in with the higher levels of enterprise, better off where they were... essentially happy, happy."[258] Despite periodic protests, the show remained a massive hit on radio and incarnated as an early 1950s television series, where it attracted a sizable audience and even won an Emmy nomination in 1952.

Small Screen Controversy

By the time the *Amos 'n' Andy Show* aired on the CBS television network in 1951, the era in which whites played blacks on the screen had ended. After a protracted talent search, New York stage actor Alvin Childress was hired to play Amos, Spencer

Williams, a prolific director of all-black movies, was cast as Andy. The crucial role of Kingfish went to Tim Moore, a former jockey, medicine show star, and vaudevillian. Then in his early sixties, he brought the conniving Kingfish, prone to malapropisms and syntactical mishaps, to the small screen with striking vividness. With his rubbery face and a toothy but hollow smile, he could express an affecting range of moods and emotions.

As Andy, Williams excelled at playing the friendly dunce easily ensnared by even the Kingfish's most preposterous schemes. The amiable Amos personified honesty, loyalty, and good intentions. His dialect was identifiably black but not caricatured. As played by Ernestine Wade, Kingfish's wife Sapphire, who often spoke cultivated English, was strong-willed and decisive, her shrill scolding of her husband expected in view of his laziness and dishonesty. These principals along with the rest of the talented cast made this show must viewing for black and white audiences alike.

Although the show had a huge following, its racial depictions triggered a sharp debate among civil rights advocates.[259] A staunch critic of the radio show, the black-run Pittsburgh *Courier* lavishly praised the television version on its entertainment pages. But a loud chorus decrying the demeaning stereotypes soon muted such praise.

No less a figure than future Supreme Court Justice, Thurgood Marshall, the NAACP's special counsel at the time, stated that short of a complete change, *Amos 'n' Andy* and everything like it should be scrapped. After running the show biweekly in its second season, which likely contributed its downturn in ratings, CBS pulled the plug, in part because of NAACP pressure on the sponsor, the Blatz Brewing Company. In some quarters, it has become a critical truism seemingly chiseled in stone that the show's denigrating array of connivers, dimwits, quacks, slippery shysters, and bossy shrews renders it irredeemable.

Taking exception to this verdict, literary scholar Henry Louis Gates Jr. in a 1989 *New York Times* essay, said one of his favorite pastimes is screening episodes of the show for black friends who think that it was both socially offensive and politically detrimental.[260] After a few minutes, he notes, even hardliners have difficulty restraining their laughter because the highly talented black actors in the series transformed racial stereotypes into authentic black humor. The dilemma this show posed, he lamented, was that these were among the very few images of blacks that Americans could see on television at that time.

Even after the civil rights movement gained momentum, and a new era in racial relations emerged, *Amos 'n' Andy* continued to play on scores of local stations around the United States and in several foreign countries as well. The first situation comedy to be filmed with a multi-camera setup, some four months before the makers of *I Love Lucy* used the technique, some sixty-five episodes were in the can when the show was cancelled.

CBS commissioned the last thirteen of these episodes for 1953-54 network showings, but instead released them in syndication (sold on a station-by-station basis) along with reruns. Another additional thirteen episodes were produced for 1954-55 and added to the syndicated rerun package. Shooting on film insured that the show's engaging but often negative stereotypes would circulate indefinitely.

Despite the less-than-stellar quality of the shooting and editing, the show thrived in syndication until 1965, when pressure from civil rights groups forced CBS to withdraw it from distribution. In fall 1983, after a seventeen-year hiatus, reruns began to pop up on independent stations in the South. Recordings and videotapes of the show also found a brisk market. These days many of the episodes are readily available on YouTube.

After CBS canceled *Amos 'n' Andy*, a black actor would not have a leading role on a network television show again until Bill Cosby co-starred with Robert Culp in the 1965 television series *I Spy* as a team of US intelligence agents traveling undercover as international "tennis bums." A stand-up comic turned television thespian, Cosby's race was never an issue in any of the stories. He won three consecutive Emmy Awards for Outstanding Lead Actor in a Drama Series (becoming the first black actor to do so).

Shattering Negative Stereotypes

The Second World War's emotional intensity seemed to exacerbate long-existing prejudices and racial tensions. The summer of 1943 saw the eruption of violent race riots in Detroit and other cities, which not only hindered war production but also provided fodder for Nazi propaganda mills. Such racial confrontations put a national spotlight on the bigotry still plaguing the land. Not only were blacks denied decent housing and high-paying wartime civilian jobs, they were discriminated against in the armed forces as well. Although the United States was purportedly fighting against the racist doctrines of the Nazis, the American military itself was racially segregated.

Despite this harsh reality, the wartime screen image of racial relations was mostly of an America whose citizens respected one another's differences and worked together to defeat a common enemy. In the ethnically diverse military units depicted in such pictures as *Bataan* (1943), bigotry, racism, and discrimination were—if not totally absent—at least easily negotiable. This movie's rag-tag fighting team consists of a black, a Latino, and two Filipinos, as well as a West Pointer, an air force officer, a working-class sergeant, and a young sailor—all four of whom are white.

The black demolitions expert (Kenneth Spencer) is shown as an especially committed fighter who willingly sacrifices his life for God and country. He not only leads the group in a prayer service for their fallen captain but also later saves one of his white comrades from walking into enemy fire. All die valiantly in their attempt to delay faceless hordes of cruel Japanese from crossing a key bridge.

Super Sidney

Disruptions in society can bring about major shifts in stereotypes. In the post-World War II period, blacks were beginning to mobilize against oppressive conditions, initially in the South and then in the North, taking to the streets to protest, organizing sit-ins and boycotts, and bringing their grievances to the courts. Early in this changing cultural climate, the characters played set the new screen stereotype of the clean-cut, saintly-like, middle-class black who never angered and showed only patience and goodwill even toward outright racists.

In the latter half of the 1960s, when rioting erupted in the nation's inner-city ghettos, slain leader Malcolm X assumed almost mythic status, and a black power movement gained great momentum. In this context, the kind of brotherly-love pictures Poitier specialized in came under increasing attack for being out of tune with the racial tenor of times. Black and white critics alike took the actor to task for his role in *Guess Who's Coming to Dinner*, which practically parodies his saintly screen persona.

Released in 1967, the same year the U.S. Supreme Court struck down anti-miscegenation laws, this saccharine saga gingerly tackled the still touchy topic of interracial romance.[261] An idealistic young white woman (Katharine Houghton) shocks her affluent suburban parents (Spencer Tracy and Katharine Hepburn) by bringing home the black man (Poitier) she wants to marry. Although everything is thrown into turmoil, the cards are clearly stacked in favor of easy resolution. As if good looks, courtly charm, and impeccable manners were not enough, Poitier's prospective son-in-law character is also a brilliant doctor in line for a Nobel Prize. All is worked out after a meeting of the interracial couple's perplexed parents. (The peculiarly passionless couple's single kiss is shown reflected in a taxicab's rearview mirror.) By 1968, the talented actor had become the number-one box office star in the country.

East Asians

Who gets stereotyped, and how they get stereotyped, tends to reflect tensions, anxieties, or conflicts in society at large. The way East Asians were typically represented on the screen, for example, may have helped to alleviate the fears of miscegenation. Such concerns reside in legislation like the Immigration Act of 1924 (Johnson-Reed Act), which barred Japanese and Chinese from immigrating and becoming naturalized citizens. In addition to curtailing Asian immigration, this nativist-inspired legislation set ethnic quotas on the number of immigrants from the Eastern Hemisphere, ranging from 51,000 for Germany to 4,000 for Italy to 1,100 for the entire African continent.

Affable Charlie Chan

Particularly popular during the 1930s were sexually passive, unthreatening Asian sleuths, especially Charlie Chan. A total of six novels and over forty-five movies, in addition to radio programs and newspaper comics, would make this fictional character one of the most enduring icons of the twentieth century. In his first few screen appearances, the affable Chinese-American detective was mainly peripheral (two Japanese actors initially portrayed him). The Fox Film studio soon put him front and center with *Charlie Chan Carries On* (1931), and the series took off. Swedish-born actor Warner Oland played the role seventeen times before his death in 1938. Sidney Toler, a Missourian of Scottish descent, succeeded Oland and made eleven more films in the Fox series. In the basic formula, followed fairly strictly, Charlie Chan of the Honolulu Police Force, master detective and worldwide celebrity, happened upon a puzzling murder in an interesting or exotic locale, usually not Hawaii. Relying on brains rather than brawn, he gradually turned up incriminating clues, although his phlegmatic meanderings sometimes allowed for another murder or two to occur. At the climax, he would either set a trap using himself as the bait or, more commonly, gather the suspects together and reenact the crime in the invariably correct expectation that the culprit would be revealed through a rash act or slip of the tongue.

The redoubtable sleuth spoke stilted English with a singsong cadence ("May I extend courteous greeting?") and frequently rattled off faux Confucian aphorisms ("Bad alibi like dead fish can't stand the test of time."). One of his bumbling sons, who usually prefaced sentences with a "Gee, Pop," often accompanied him as he traveled the globe—from London, Egypt, Paris, Shanghai, and Monte Carlo to Reno, Panama, and Rio. Keye Luke appeared as Charlie's "number-one son" Lee eleven times.

When the Scottish-descended Toler assumed the Chan mantle, "number-two son" Jimmy, played by Victor Sen Yung, usually joined him on murder investigations. Desiring to be detectives themselves, his sons generally got in the way and provided comic relief until their father solved the case in spite of them. Lest there be any hint of miscegenation, the libidos of these otherwise Americanized youths seemed to shut down in the presence of white women.

In 1937, while the Charlie Chan series was still going strong, a diminutive Japanese detective named Mr. Moto, played by Hungarian-born Peter Lorre in eight films through 1939, made his screen debut. First penned by Pulitzer Prize-winning novelist J.P. Marquand in 1935, this seemingly timid but cunning character apparently sublimated his energies into crime fighting as well, because he, too, was essentially asexual.

Nefarious Fu Manchu

When represented on the screen at all, Asian male sexuality was generally associated with the villainy of such fictional characters as Dr. Fu Manchu. Created by journalist Sax Rohmer in 1911, he headed the "Yellow Movement," a ragtag of murderess thugs that included Asians, Arabs, and Africans.

In all his various incarnations, the wily and nefarious Fu Manchu's singular obsession was to wipe out the "whole accursed white race" with his countless Asian hordes and win world domination. In M-G-M 's *The Mask of Fu Manchu* (1932), with gaunt British-born character actor Boris Karloff (who had lately played Dr. Frankenstein's monster) as Fu Manchu, an English expedition rushes to the edge of the Gobi Desert to get the legendary golden mask and scimitar of the thirteenth-century conqueror Genghis Khan before Fu Manchu can use these relics to proclaim himself the new Khan and lead his Pan-Asian allies on a massive war westward.

Fu Manchu plans to baptize the scimitar in the blood of an English maiden (Karen Morley), who has been dressed in a slinky white nightgown and placed supine on a stone slab in preparation for the sacrifice. "Would you like to have maidens like this for your wives?" he asks his frenzied followers. "Then conquer and breed! Kill the white man and take his women."

His equally perverse daughter, Fah Lo See (Myrna Loy), has sexual designs on a captive young Englishman (Charles Starrett). She seems especially aroused watching him, stripped to the waist, getting repeatedly whipped by her Nubian slaves. Apparently relishing every lash, she exhorts excitedly, "Faster! Faster!" Little wonder the stalwart Sir Nayland Smith (Lewis Stone), Fu Manchu 's Anglo-Saxon adversary from the British Secret Service, asks "Will we ever understand these Eastern races?"

Cultural Disruption

In 1965, Congress passed the Immigration and Nationality Act. Signed into law by President Lyndon Johnson at the foot of the Statue of Liberty, this legislation, abolishing the 1924 quotas, dramatically changed the whole ethnic composition of the United States. In Queens, New York, for example, the elevated #7 train rumbles above highly diverse ethnic and immigrant neighborhoods populated by people from China, India, Korea, Mexico, Pakistan, Poland, Romania, Vietnam, Central America, and Andean South America, among other places. After a massive wave of immigration in the 1970s, the once-white working-class town of Flushing is bustling with Chinese residents. These days, note the authors of *International Express*, this town's main street, "looks a great deal like a congested section of Hong Kong."[262]

When cast in a contemporary movie or television show, East Asian male actors typically play an array of stereotypical characters such as evil geniuses, tech nerds, illegal immigrants, gangsters, and martial arts experts. In contrast, females of Asian descent usually get cast as sex workers, masseuses, or fragile, quiet, docile creatures. The practice of casting non-Chinese actors continues as well, especially in romantic roles. For example, the hugely successful satirical romantic comedy *Crazy Rich Asians* (2018) featured an English-Malaysian actor (Henry Golding) in the lead male part of the scion of a mega-rich Chinese Singaporean family. Swedish-born Warner Oland playing Charlie Chan bears more resemblance to the Han ethnic group comprising over ninety percent of China's population than does the male lead of this movie.

Enduring Categories

Such expressive forms as music, news, entertainment, advertising, and public relations affect our feelings, enhancing and amplifying aspects of our underlying beliefs and behavior. If certain things are alien to our neural connections, we may not even notice them, or they may be puzzling, or ignored, or rejected outright. This situation is so regardless of whether the believers are educated or uneducated, liberal or conservative, or something else entirely.

We are only able to understand what our brains let us comprehend, and large parts of our neural circuitry, perhaps as much as ninety-eight percent are inaccessible. One of the fundamental findings of cognitive science is that we think in terms of conceptual frames or structures. Embedded in the synapses of our brains, they're physically present in the form of neural circuitry.

When the facts don't fit the framework, we tend to keep the frame intact and ignore the facts. The deepest of our neural structures are relatively fixed. "They don't change readily or easily," cognitive scientist George Lakoff confirms. "And we are mostly unconscious of their activity and impact."[263] These findings have significant implications for assessing the way entertainment fare supplies not only the stuff of thought but also functions to reinforce and strengthen the stereotypical categories residing in the synapses shaping understanding.

Chapter 9

Gender

"All the world's a stage," wrote William Shakespeare in *As You Like It*, "and all the men and women merely players." With these insightful lines, he captured the essence of societal roles. As in the theatre, we are all actors in a drama. Our behavior stems in no small measure from the kaleidoscope of parts we play in life, and those we observe in the media shaping our identity, our thoughts, our emotions, and our ambitions.

We typically play multiple roles over a lifetime; in different contexts or with different people, a particular person might be a student, friend, lover, spouse, teacher, employee, or supervisor. Each of these roles carries its expectations about appropriate behavior, speech, attire, and so on. Beyond visible actions and accouterments, positions carry with them certain emotions and attitudes bolstered by playing the part. One feels more ardent by kissing, more pious by praying, more learned by lecturing, more studious by studying.

Most of our everyday activity involves the acting out of socially defined categories. The roles we play range from specific, applying only to a particular setting, to diffuse, applicable across a variety of situations in the grand drama of society. For instance, gender roles influence behavior in many different contexts. A woman may be a corporate attorney when she is at work. But she is a female across all settings affecting a wide array of psychological outcomes, among them behavior, attitudes, cognitions, and social interactions.

Each of our various roles has a different script for social conduct. Though we are born with certain traits that are carried by our genetic blueprint, the space for social formation within these inherited limits would appear to be quite substantial. Even what we may consider to be our essential selves is largely socially assigned within a specific cultural context. Who we are would seem to depend in large measure on the parts we're permitted to play.

Feminine/Masculine Dichotomy

The way men and women have been polarized on the silver screen has long been a sore point for many. The common gender stereotypes of the Hollywood film become more apparent when characters, situations, and actions are removed from the narrative flow and their relations of similarity and difference are analyzed. Within the typical movie, such analysis suggests, men and women are generally represented as extreme opposites. Female characters tend to be defined in terms what male characters are not; if the male is strong, then the female must be weak; if the male is rational, the female must be emotional, and so on. These divisions are transformed into a number of oppositions, such masculinity vs. femininity, public vs. private, active vs. passive, and production vs. consumption.

A masculine man is likely to be depicted as active in the public sphere, socially and sexually assertive, and a prime producer of the essential goods and services. A feminine woman, on the other hand, is more likely to be portrayed as involved primarily in the private domain, passive in societal and sexual matters, and a consumer rather than a producer. Female characters deviating from these established categories, especially with regard to sexual assertiveness, serve as sources of anxiety as well as intense erotic excitement, and are generally shown to be unstable, dangerous, and even deadly.

Although notable exceptions exist, through much of the last century, these gender divisions were mostly consistent. The plot dynamics of most movies revolve around male heroes who are the active agents. Unless they are temptresses or are at the center of such domestic melodramas as *Mildred Pierce* (1945), in which their successes are invariably compromised, female characters tend to be secondary to the male protagonist's objectives in the public sphere of work, war, missions, or expeditions.

In the romantic wartime set melodrama *Casablanca* (1942), in many ways a template for American cinema, the subordinate status of the principal female character, Ilsa Lund (Ingrid Bergmann), is firmly fixed in the finale after her erstwhile lover Rick Blaine (Humphrey Bogart) has decided to take up the Allied cause. On a fog-filled airport tarmac, he explains to her that he has a job to do, can't follow where he is going, and can't be any part of it. "I'm no good at being noble," he patronizingly explains to her, "but it doesn't take much to see that the problems of three little people don't amount to a hill of beans in this crazy world. Someday you'll understand that. Not now." He then sends her off with her remarkably patient and tolerant spouse (Paul Henreid).

After the plane carrying Ilsa and her husband is airborne, Rick and his prefect-of-police pal, the charmingly corrupt Captain Louis Renault (Claude Rains), walk off together into the Moroccan mist, and Rick remarks that this is the beginning of "a beautiful friendship." Earlier Renault had said of his companion, "He's the kind of man that, well, if I were a woman and weren't around, I should be in love with Rick." As yet another example of how cultural perch affects meaning, some critics cite Rick's decision to turn his back on heterosexual love in favor of male comradeship as evidence of the repressed homosexuality that underlies most American adventure stories.[264] We tend to see what we seek out.

Tempting Taboos

Defining male and female attributes as opposites invariably suppresses overlaps and ambiguities. The ambiguous boundary between such stark divisions is where taboos can be expected. A prevalent stereotype on the big screen has been the femme fatale, a selfish, seductive woman who uses her wiles to entrap and exploit unwitting men with the promise of unbridled passion. Appearing in many guises, she carries echoes of the mythical sirens who lured ancient mariners to their deaths.

Highly desirable but dangerous female predators leading unsuspecting males into trouble have been a screen staple since soon after the dawn of the last century. In 1915, Theda Bara making her debut in Fox Film's *A Fool There Was*, played an alluring unscrupulous character designated only as "the Vampire," taken from the name of a Rudyard Kipling poem. Before achieving stardom, she was Theodosia Goodman, the daughter of a Cincinnati tailor. The Fox publicity machine promoted her as the possessor of profoundly occult powers, conceived on the desert sands in the shadow of the Sphinx, the child of a French artist and his Arabian mistress. To enhance her exotic allure, she wore indigo facial makeup and received the press while stroking a serpent. Over four years, in some forty films, she lent her baleful eroticism to such notorious destroyers of men as Carman, Madame Du Barry, Salome, and Cleopatra.[265]

The femme fatale was central to many crime thrillers of the 1940s, with plots commonly revolving around her challenge to the values of the male-dominated society and the authority of male characters. During the Cold War, female sexual predators on the big screen frequently took on a distinct reddish hue. They could often be found using sexual wiles to dupe some politically naive male into toeing the party line. The slip straps showing beneath the transparent blouse of this scarlet temptress typically signaled her communist affinity.[266]

A standard contrast in movies is between the femme fatale and a woman who is domestic, devoted, and decidedly dull, with the two acting as magnetic poles pulling the male protagonist. In the darkly intriguing crime thriller *Out of the Past* (1947), a former Manhattan private investigator (Robert Mitchum) sought the serenity of small-town life with his steadfast but sexually unexciting fiancé (Virginia Huston). Driving to see a one-time client (Kirk Douglas), he tells her about tracking down the shady gambler's mistress (Jane Greer), who vanished with $40,000 of his money to a tawdry cantina in Acapulco. Strolling into the

bar from the sun-drenched plaza, wearing a white dress and matching hat, she seems to have materialized out of the brightness. The world-weary detective's voice-over comment on her arrival reinforces this impression. "And then I saw her coming out of the sun." He invests her with an almost ethereal essence, similarly sentimentalizing her second entrance as well: "And then she walked in out of the moonlight—smiling."

Although her otherworldly quality will turn out to be more demonic than divine, their ensuing romance is rhapsodic, enhanced by a lyrical and sensual play of light and shadow.[267] At her cozy beach bungalow, phonograph music mixes with the sound of rain hammering on the window. Kissing her on the neck, he tosses the towel, knocking the lamp to the floor. When the light goes out, there is a swirl of music, and the camera drifts toward the front door, which is blown open by a gust of wind. (Sex in mainstream movies of this era was metaphorical—rain hammering, a table lamp crushing, a clap of thunder, a door flung open by the wind.)

But far from being redeemed by love, as the plot unfolds, she turns out to be deceptive, duplicitous, and without any morals or scruples. This revelation of her deadly disposition wouldn't be as disappointing if the illusion of her during their romantic interlude weren't so captivating. After being dropped off at the gambler's estate, he sees her back living with him once again. Disappointed and disillusioned, he likens her to "a leaf that blows from one gutter to another." Once again seduced, without any of her girl-next-door pretenses, he closes the door to a passionless, uncomplicated love in a rural small town. In the climactic scene, she shoots him in the groin just before a hail of police bullets cut them both down.

Fashionable Accessory

During the twentieth century, the cigarette, a mostly useless product that stains teeth, fouls breath, shortens life spans, and lowers libidos came to play a dominant role in so many aspects of people's lives—and deaths. No other product on the market has ever been so heavily promoted or become so deeply entrenched in American culture and consciousness.[268] Early in the century, smoking cigarettes was not something women did in public or even at home. Many men viewed females lighting up a sign of lax moral standards. To expand the number of women smokers, George Washington Hill of the American Tobacco Company, makers of Lucky Strikes, decided to hire self-anointed "public relations counsel" Edward Bernays, to help him recruit female smokers.

Born in Austria in 1891, he was psychoanalysis founder Sigmund Freud's nephew twice over. His mother was Freud's sister, and his father was the brother of Freud's wife· Drawing on back-of the-envelope insights from his uncle's work, a familial link Bernays frequently exploited, he developed an approach he dubbed "the engineering of consent"—controlling and regimenting behavior by appealing not to the rational part of the mind, but the "unconscious," conceived at the time to be seething with "lust and anger, hallucinatory, primitive, and irrational," a conception roundly rejected by neuroscientists.

By emphasizing the unconscious, Freud was on the right track. But the view among neurological researchers these days is that portions of mind are inaccessible to consciousness because of the architecture of the brain rather than being subject to motivational forces such as penis envy, castration fears, repression, and the like, notes a theoretical physicist summing up the research. The inaccessibility of the "unconscious is not considered to be a defense mechanism, or unhealthy. It is considered normal."[269]

Aided by a small army of assistants, hardly requiring any of his uncle's theories of the unconscious mind, Bernays promoted the cigarette brand in inventive ways. Augmenting the company's advertising slogan, "Reach for a Lucky instead of a sweet," he enlisted photographers, artists, newspapers, and magazines to promote the slim female as the ideal of femininity, no doubt to the chagrin of confectioners.

When surveys showed that women objected to Lucky Strikes because the green package with its red bull's-eye clashed with the colors of their clothes, he swung into action to make green fashionable. There followed a green fashion luncheon, a green-themed charity ball attended by upper-crust women donning green gowns, and innumerable window displays of green suits and dresses.

To thwart traditional taboos against women smoking on the street, Bernays consulted a prominent Manhattan psychoanalyst. An avid disciple of his uncle, he explained that as a sublimation of oral eroticism, holding a cigarette in the mouth titillates the erogenous zone of the lips. And that some women regarded the cigarette as a symbol of freedom. The insights struck a chord with Bernays, notes his biographer.[270]

If not the sublimation, the symbolism of the cigarette severing the restraints of gender-specific taboos and social customs seemed on the mark. The spinmeister decided not only to promote puffing on a slender stick of rolled tobacco as fashionable but also as liberating, a feminist statement. To this end, in 1929, alerting the press in advance, he placed stylish-looking women in the annual Easter parade, a casual stroll between 34th and 57th streets along Fifth Avenue in Manhattan, instructing them to light up and flaunt their cigarettes as "torches of freedom" in a defiant show of emancipation from conventional constraints. A believer in the efficacy of testimonials, to swell the ranks of Easter torch lighters, he had paid a prominent feminist to sign a letter urging women to join the cortège.

Front page dispatches ran the next day in papers from Fremont, Nebraska, to Portland, Oregon, to Albuquerque, New Mexico. A New York Times subhead proclaimed: "Group of Girls Puff at Cigarettes as a Gesture of 'Freedom.'" The extensive coverage burnished the self-promoting PR practitioner's reputation as a media manipulator par excellence. And he helped persuade women to puff in public without anyone knowing his client picked up the tab for the pseudo-event.

Bernays pulled the same sleight of hand for more political purposes, such as putting a spin on CIA-backed coup in 1954 to topple Guatemala's president, Jacobo Árbenz

Guzman. The elected leader had confiscated more than 387,000 acres of the politically well-connected banana grower United Fruit's unplanted reserve property as part of a compulsory land purchase and redistribution plan. While on the giant fruit company's payroll, Bernays persuaded significant newspapers to carry stories cloaked in the "free world" rhetoric about the growing threat and influence of Guatemala's communists.

Smoking Signifiers

Bernays's Uncle Sigmund, seemingly seeing phallic symbols in every elongated object, is reputed to have once remarked that sometimes a cigar is merely a cigar. In the movies, a cigarette has never been solely a cigarette, but a way to visually express a range of meanings as well as give awkward actors something to do with their hands. In the tearjerker *Now, Voyager* (1942), a cigarette provides the perfect metaphor for the sexual intimacy denied to the star-crossed lovers: "Shall we just have a cigarette on it?" Jerry (Paul Henreid) asks Charlotte (Bette Davis) before he lights two cigarettes in his mouth and then passes her one, still moist and warm from his breath. When he asks her if she is happy, even if she does not have everything she wants, Charlotte responds: "Oh, Jerry, don't let's ask for the moon. We have the stars" as the camera moves through the open terrace doors and tilts upward towards the star-lite canopy of the night sky.

The wartime melodrama *Casablanca* provides another of the countless examples. Before protagonist Rick Blaine appears on screen for the first time, we see a smoldering cigarette, a champagne glass, and a chessboard. As a hand lifts the smoking thin white cylinder from the ashtray, the camera follows the movement to reveal his face as he takes a deep drag. In the context of the movie, the champagne glass, solo chess game, and cigarette suggest a world-weary sophistication.

Depending on the cultural-historical perch, very different meanings come to mind from observing Rick always with a cigarette in his hand. Imagine, for instance, how his clothes and breath must smell as a result of all that smoking. What about the carcinogenic effects of all the smoke he inhales? However, such health concerns probably never entered the minds of most moviegoers in the 1940s. Because of Big Tobacco's Machiavellian strategies to subvert the science of lung cancer and other cigarette-related diseases, the dangers of smoking wouldn't get any significant mainstream media attention until decades later.

The cinematic trope of post-coital puffing is on subtle display in a climactic scene in *Casablanca* when Ilsa (Ingrid Bergmann), desperate to secure an exit visa for her husband, threatens her former lover Rick (Humphrey Bogart) at gunpoint. Unable to pull the trigger, she drops the gun and comes into his arms, sobbing as they embrace. In the original scenario, as they kissed, a fade out and then a fade back into the interior of the apartment followed.

The industry censor thought that the time interval suggested by fading the image out and implied that their physical contact had gone far beyond mere kissing. He insisted on replacing this effect with the blurring of one vision into another. And shooting the return to the interior without any evidence of a bed in sight would remedy this impression. Whether time passed during the dissolve to a view of the circular airport tower, is left to the imagination. Rick's smoking while standing on the terrace as the blurred image fades back into sharp relief signals, at least to the initiated, that sexual activity had occurred.

In a cinematic celebration of cigarettes, the makers of the crime thriller *Out of the Past* spotlighted the spaces where characters are going to exhale, producing white plumes of smoke adding to the film-noir atmosphere. The cigarette smoking signals a range of potential meanings, among them power and dominance. Clearly in command, after Robert Mitchum's character knocks out a crooked nightclub manager and steals a briefcase from his desk, he casually pauses, taking a cigarette from the case on the desktop and lighting it. When Jane Greer's "wholesomely-seductive" character walks in out of the Acapulco sun, her first gesture is light a cigarette, suggesting she's in control of the situation. Only when no longer under her thrall does he smoke in her presence. If sought out, such symbolism seems evident across a range of fictional fare.

The notion of capping off a sexual experience with a cigarette was especially prevalent in the late 1960s early 1970s. In the groundbreaking movie *The Graduate* (1967), after a sexual encounter with the bumbling young Ben Braddock (Dustin Hoffman), the lustful, seductive and older Mrs. Robinson (Anne Bancroft), her bare tan upper body peeking out from under the white sheets, savors a long drag on a cigarette, the haze of smoke heightening her glamor and allure. The modern twist, the post-coital vape, packing a similar nicotine punch, turns out to have potentially deadly consequences.

Conflicting Images

True Women

Advertising and television following the Second World War promoted what various scholars of the era labeled the "culture of domesticity," a nineteenth century conception that "true women" possessed four cardinal virtues: piety, purity, domesticity, and submissiveness.[271] In the 1950s, many ad-makers pushed products for women as homemakers. An advertisement for a vacuum, showing a neatly attired woman on the floor touching the cleaner, proclaims, "Christmas morning, she'll be happier with a Hoover."

Another, for Chase & Sanborn coffee, depicts a woman stretched across the lap of a seated male getting a spanking. The copy warns: "If your husband ever finds out you're not 'store-testing' for coffee." These were fairly typical ads from a period when women were the primary consumers, the ones who made decisions on what was needed to run a household while being submissive to the breadwinner's needs and desires.

Advertisers tapped into a female fear in the last century of failing to find romance and marriage. Invented as a surgical antiseptic, and later sold as both a floor cleaner and a cure for gonorrhea, Listerine hit the mark with ads of instant drama, posing peril, and panacea. In the

1920s, its makers massively pitched it as a mouthwash remedy for the "heartbreak of halitosis," the ad campaign's obscure medical term for bad breath. Whether in print or onscreen, the fear-failure formula focused on forlorn young women eager for marriage but repelling potential mates with foul-smelling exhalations.

A typical Listerine advertisement from the 1920s, the theme carried over to television, tells us about someone like pathetic Edna, often a bridesmaid but never a bride. The copy reads: "Like every woman, her primary ambition was to marry. ... As her birthdays crept gradually toward that tragic thirty-mark, marriage seemed farther from her life than ever." Amplifying her agony, Edna is in tears. Why, Edna, why? Halitosis, of course. And "even your closest friends won't tell you." Bad breath soon became big business. Targeting the romance-deprived Ednas of the world propelled Listerine, now a Johnson & Johnson product, to the top of the $6-billion "oral hygiene" industry even though dental floss would be far more effective than a swish of mouthwash. But selling string doesn't generate those kinds of big bucks.

And what if a favored female "ties the knot," a revealing old metaphor for marrying? Who's binding whom? Many family sitcoms of the early television era perpetuated an "Adam's rib" marital helpmate role for women, including *Father Knows Best*, Leave it to Beaver, *The Adventures of Ozzie and Harriet*, and *The Donna Reed Show*. The mothers in these make-believe depictions of middle-class domestic life were career homemakers. Although the epitome of femininity—always neatly coiffed, wearing stylish dresses and frilly aprons, they showed no signs whatsoever of sexual desire.

The popular series *Father Knows Best* ran on network television from 1954 to 1960 and is a classic example of traditional family relationships. It features family man Jim Anderson (Robert Young), his common-sense wife Margaret (Jane Wyatt) and their children Betty (Elinor Donahue), Bud (Billy Gray), and Kathy (Lauren Chapin). Like most 1950s sitcoms, it reflects the norms and values that were deemed socially acceptable at the time.

Avoiding controversial topics, the series focuses on lighthearted and mostly positive stories about growing up and traditional rites of passage. Margaret is as level-headed and discerning as her husband but knows her place in the family hierarchy—cooking, baking, cleaning, and gardening in her full-time role as mother and wife. He, in contrast, has a good but rather vague job that earns enough money to support the family but is always on hand to offer sage advice whenever his spouse or any of their children have a problem.

What comes through in a sampling of the weekly episodes is unwavering family loyalty and mutual nurturing love and support. Wanting the "best" for their offspring, Jim and Margaret teach the girls life lessons about being ladies, including preparing for marriage, and accepting the unsuitability of pursuing careers outside of teaching, nursing, or secretarial jobs. Moralistic and sentimental, every episode tugged at least a tad at the heartstrings. This nearly all-white make-believe world contained no civil rights issues, no murders, and no molestations.

Purity Pedestal

Psychoanalytic casework suggests that many men suffer from a virgin–whore syndrome. It is inconceivable to them that a "good" woman can have "bad" sexual desires, so they split the feminine image into opposites. Traditional Freudian psychoanalysts attribute the basis for this sharp division to the unconscious need to negate childhood incestuous desire for the mother, but contemporary professionals in the field widely contest such claims. And advances in neuroscience have cast severe doubt on the existence of such specific unconscious emotional and motivational factors.

Such categorical opposites as the virgin-whore split are likely a feature of culture, not unresolved childhood conflict. When viewed through a cultural-historical lens, this cleavage more probably stems from the depictions of women as either "virgins" or "whores" in mythology and Judeo-Christian theology rather than from personal developmental disabilities. The religious doctrine of Christianity, for example, portrayed the Virgin Mary as the antithesis to Eve, that wayward temptress of man created from Adam's rib to serve as his helpmate.

Males have been trying to control and channel female hormonal urges through threat, ridicule and approbation since biblical times. Images of the Virgin Mary and child appear in paintings, murals, and sculpture reminding straying females that sexual desire is evil and virginity is the highest ideal. The sanctity of virginity is amplified in New Testament interpretations through the story of the virgin birth even though it is only recorded in two of the four gospels and is not mentioned anyplace else in this sacred text. In *Alone of All Her Sex*, Marina Warner makes a compelling case that such expressive forms as poetry, liturgy, songs, paintings, and mosaics celebrating the legends of the virgin birth have condemned actual women to perpetual inferiority.[272]

Putting purity on a pedestal is not unique to Christianity. Female virginity is prized in most other major religions as well. Although Islamic cultures widely differ in language, geography and ethnicity, they all lay supreme importance on virginity of girls, reflecting social and moral laws based on the holy book of Koran. In many Islamic societies, if a girl loses her virginity before marriage, her family is allowed by the law of the land to punish her physically and even kill her.

The surgical removal of a girl's clitoris before puberty is common in several African countries with large Muslim populations, although the practice predates both Islam and Christianity. Traditionally, part or all of the clitoris or the clitoral hood is surgically removed, resulting in reduced or no sexual feeling. In most circumstances, this ritual aims to make girls less likely to become sexually active before marriage or seek extra-marital affairs after wed. Typically performed without anesthesia under unhygienic conditions, the procedure can be excruciatingly painful.

Deeply embedded in North and West African cultures, especially prevalent in Egypt, this ancient excision practice affects the very definition of what it is to be female. In rural areas, the function of freezing female sexual urges falls to the "village cutter." As they grow up, girls suffer sweeping social constraints. A traditional Muslim nation, Egypt's guardians of morality, armed with vague laws, have recently targeted young women who appear on social media sites like the wildly popular TikTok, owned by the Beijing-based internet company ByteDance.

In mid-summer 2020, a Cairo court convicted two young women on charges of violating family values and inciting debauchery sentencing each to two years imprisonment. They had gained millions of followers for dancing alluringly in cleverly done video snippets set to catchy Egyptian club-pop tracks, tame by social media stan-

dards, and nothing that would raise the eyebrow on American over-the-air television. As Cyndi Lauper declared, "girls just want to have fun."

In the internet age, females around the globe are uniting to stop sexual subjugation, verbal and physical. A viral protest movement began in spring 2011 after a Toronto police officer told a group of college women that if they hoped to escape the sexual assault, they should avoid dressing like "sluts." The transnational participants, wanting to drain the s-word of its misogynistic venom, have marched in more than seventy cities around the world, often dressed in bras, halter tops, and garter belts. Many female marchers dressed as "sluts" in revealing, sexy attire such as short skirts, stockings, and scanty tops. Some displayed "proud slut" scrawled on their cheeks, and others donned slut-embossed facemasks.

By many accounts, albeit from anecdotal evidence, a good number of men regardless of religious upbringing remain reluctant to commit to women with considerable previous sexual experience, perhaps because of fear of cuckoldry or of the increased risk of raising someone else's child or of being denied a form of genetic immortality of sorts. Whatever the origins and reasons beyond divine dictate, such reluctance has served to perpetuate a sexual double standard by venerating female virginity.

Even in cosmopolitan cities like New York, gynecologists still perform so-called "virginity tests" to ensure that a hymen remains intact. The rapper, record producer, actor, and businessman T.I.'s disclosure that he has his eighteen-year-old daughter take such a test annually under his supervision sparked a national conversation around a painful procedure with no scientific basis. And, of course, testing for virginity is a blatant female rights violation. The legislation is in the pipeline that would prohibit medical practitioners from performing virginity examinations, subjecting them to penalties for professional misconduct as well as possible criminal charges if they breach the ban.[273]

TEENAGE TORMENT

Survey research suggests that by the early 1960s, many teenagers across social classes were sexually active even though the choices open to a pregnant high-school girl or college co-ed were illegal abortion, social disgrace, or reluctant and often disastrous marriage. Birth control devices and methods were in short supply and generally stigmatized. Taking pre-sex precautions or pushing condom use garnered girls such labels "fast" or "loose" often under the prevailing "double standard" that urged boys to sow their "wild oats." It was in this context that movies centering on teenage premarital sex and pregnancy became common.

In the overwrought "pregnancy melodrama" *A Summer Place* (1959), sixteen-year-old Molly (Sandra Dee) succumbs to her sexual impulses and goes "all the way" with Johnny (Troy Donahue). Soon after, she discovers she is pregnant, and the smitten pair run away together, planning to get married. Despite being underage, they eventually wed and presumably live happily ever after despite their parents' miserable marriages.

In *Susan Slade* (1961), the focus is again on unplanned pregnancy. A naive seventeen-year-old, Susan (Connie Stevens) has a shipboard romance with Conn White (Grant Williams), a wealthy young mountain climber. They make love in secret and plan to marry, but he wants to hold off making any announcement to their families until after he returns from his scheduled trip to Alaska to climb Mount McKinley. She waits eagerly for letters from him, but he does not write and the one time he tries to contact her, she is out and misses the call. She soon discovers that she is pregnant with his child, but keeps this a secret while urgently trying to contact him.

Susan has a breakdown after learning of his death while mountain climbing and tries to drown herself, but the stable owner and aspiring writer Hoyt Brecker (Troy Donahue), rescues her. In her delirium, she reveals to her mother that she is pregnant. Her parents decide the only way to avoid disgrace and protect her is for the family to move to remote Guatemala, where her father just got a two-year job running a mine. This way, Susan can then finish her pregnancy and have her baby in secret, and they will pass it off as their own. With the revelation of the baby's parentage, Hoyt's loving feelings for Susan have not changed. She professes her love for him, and they embrace as this plodding and predictable melodrama ends.

The focus *In Love with the Proper Stranger* (1963) is on a department store salesgirl Angie Rossini (Natalie Wood) who becomes pregnant after a one-night stand with womanizing jazz trumpeter Rocky Papasano (Steve McQueen), a man she doesn't even know. Her first and only sexual encounter, she becomes pregnant but has no expectation of marriage; she needs his help to raise the money for an illegal abortion. Although barely remembering her, by the close of the movie, he's become smitten and proposes.

The female characters in pregnancy melodramas, notes Susan Douglas, provided points on a continuum of female sexuality, from the prim to the promiscuous. "The big-breasted, out-of-control sluts on one end of the continuum and the tight-lipped ice maidens on the other served as monoliths to be rejected, while the ones in the middle, caught in the crosscurrents of discourses about 'good' and 'bad' girls, were the ones recognized as authentic teenage girls."[274]

Male/Female Figures

Breasts/Décolletage

Contradictory media depictions of women are evident in attitudes toward anatomy. A female's breasts have many non-erotic motherly functions but the hollow between them when exposed by a low-cut garment, has long had an enticingly erotic seductiveness. The postwar period witnessed a particular cultural preoccupation with cleavage, mainly on movie screens across the country. Industrialist and moviemaker Howard Hughes triggered a societal concentration on big breasts when he took over the directorial reins of *The Outlaw* (1943). In this fictional account of the exploits of Billy the Kid, he frequently focused the camera on the big bosom of his female lead, Jane Russell, a full-figured former dental office receptionist, and part-time model.

In one scene, Russell's character is tied between two trees with leather thongs. Using his engineering expertise, Hughes designed a unique brassiere for the screen

novice to accentuate her cleavage as she writhes in feigned agony. In several other scenes, the camera lingers on her loosely fitting blouse as she leans over, bends, stoops, or kneels for one contrived reason or another. A Baltimore judge upheld a ban on the movie, claiming that Russell's breasts "hung over the picture like a thunderstorm spread out over a summer landscape."[275]

Hughes orchestrated a cleavage-centered advertising campaign with the nationwide release of *The Outlaw* in 1946. Newspapers, magazines, billboards, and even skywriting proclaimed the robust proportions of the movie's female lead. An airplane wrote the words "The Outlaw" in the sky over Pasadena and then made two large circles with a dot in the middle of each. Newspaper ads for the movie asked such questions as "How would you like to tussle with Russell?" and "What are the two main reasons for Jane Russell's rise to stardom?"

In the postwar period, with metal freed for domestic use, underwire often padded bras replaced the conical designs and lower necklines became le dernier cri. Accordingly, designers produced a line of costume jewelry specifically to enhance the display of décolletage. By the 1950s, along with Marylin Monroe and her caricatured avatar Jayne Mansfield, the full-figured Russell became one of Hollywood's leading sex symbols.

Russell's décolletage is on display throughout the three-dimensional *The French Line* (1953). The movie opens with a tame striptease in which her character sidles behind furniture as she disrobes and progresses to the provocative finale number. Wearing a one-piece, black-satin tights outfit with three large leaf-shaped pieces cut from the midriff area, she does a seductive bump-and-grind dance while singing "Looking for Trouble" in which the camera and her cleavage seem to move in tandem. Advertisements for the movie proclaimed "Jane Russell in 3-D . . . it'll knock both your eyes out."

The mania over partially exposed mammary glands receded in the 1960s when flatter-chested fashion icons like former First Lady Jackie Kennedy, movie star Audrey Hepburn and emaciated-looking model Twiggy set a standard for slim silhouettes. The cultural trend of small-breasted females continued into the 1970s and eighties with stars like Diane Keaton and Jane Fonda (later to have her hope chest expanded into "plastic playthings" when she married media mogul Ted Turner).

Perhaps confirming that "beauty" as a cultural standard is entirely socially constructed, at the turn of the last century, substantial stage star Lillian Russel, weighing in at over 200 pounds, was a potent sex symbol. By the dawn of the twenty-first century, skinny, flat-chested former Spice Girl Victoria Beckham represented the ideal female body type.

Incompatible values and desires are reinforced in countless movies and other popular cultural forms. Most female characters are little more than male fantasies, asserts cultural critic Molly Haskell in *From Reverence to Rape*, stereotypes of what men want to believe about women. She charted screen depictions of women from the trembling virgins and footloose flappers of the 1920s to the demeaned and dehumanized "chicks, kooks, groupies, and cartoon pinup girls" of the 1960s and 1970s.

"Audiences, for the most part, were not interested in seeing, and Hollywood was not interested in sponsoring, a smart, ambitious woman as a popular heroine," she witheringly concludes. "A woman who could compete and conceivably win in a man's world would defy emotional gravity, would go against the grain of prevailing notions about the female sex. A woman's intelligence was the equivalent of a man's penis: something to be kept out of sight."[276] (Both have received cinematic exposure in recent years.) While the *virgin* and *whore* are the two primary leading parts Hollywood allowed women to play, Haskell elucidates the subtle and nuanced ways that female stars were able to go beyond those restrictive roles

MUSCULARITY

As the ideal female form became slender and delicate, rippling muscles emerged as the standard for male bodies. Toned and honed topless young men with ripped abs became the norm in ads and commercials. The well-built nearly naked models in Abercrombie & Fitch advertisements, for instance, rivaled the statue of Biblical hero David, Michelangelo's marble masterpiece of the masculine Platonic ideal. Targeting white, privileged, oversexed preppy kids with ads featuring muscular self-satisfied good-looking lads in low-slung boxer shorts transformed the once-staid outdoor clothier to a multibillion-dollar powerhouse.

Founded in 1973, during the height of the feminist movement, *Playgirl* provided an outlet for women to explore their sexuality. Its centerfold, a gender-reversal of *Playboy*, featured semi-nude and eventually full-frontal nude Adonis-like men. In addition to professional models, the magazine's editors use amateurs in a section called *Real Men* (formerly *Snapshots*). In June of every year, it has its "Man of the Year" issue, and in the November edition, "Campus Hunks" are the focus of attention. Most of the covers tend to be sexually charged.

The cover of the August 1990 issue, as a typical example, along with a shot of a buff lad, promises such sex tips as "69 Things to Do with Your Tongue." Another enticement on this cover is "Sleep with Donald Trump," which turns out to be a contest, albeit a deceptive one. A blurb in the table of contents proclaims: "He's rich, almost single and yours for the asking. Here's how you can get the Donald out of your dreams and into your bed!" The randomly selected twenty-five winners each receive a pillowcase--"with the Donald's face, so you can lie there whispering sweet nothings in his ear all night." Alas, no naked shots of the current Oval Office occupant appear in this issue. Only those with rock-hard muscular male bodies make the pages of this racy publication.

Much the same emphasis on heavily muscled male physiques happened in movies as well. In 1934 when Clark Gable, later proclaimed the King of Hollywood, removed his shirt in *It Happened One Night*, his bare chest and arms appeared slightly sagged, not rippled (although striking in a tailored suit). With such notable exceptions as slender Paul Newman's washboard midriff, few movies highlighted extreme male muscularity, even though entire genres, such as biblical epics, jungle adventures, and boxing films, were practically devoted to the display of the male body.

In holding sway over the African jungle, Tarzan, whose first screen appearance dates back to 1918, rarely wore more than a loincloth. Winner of multiple Olympic Gold Medals, the swimming champion Johnny Weissmuller portrayed the legendary ape-man in the movies more often than anyone else. Although the jungle adventures highlight the athlete's firm physique, he hardly bulged with sinuous muscle tissue.

Muscle Bound

The classically handsome and symmetrically muscled Steve Reeves provided little more than the pectoral background in movies like *Athena* (1954)—although he did have a big fan base among teenage readers of muscle magazines. His cinematic fortunes changed when an Italian film director cast him in *Hercules* (1958), his non-distinctive voice dubbed in postproduction. This sword-and-sandal epic showcasing his muscular physique enjoyed massive success in Europe and the United States. But his movie career never moved much beyond playing biblical and mythological figures. In a business suit, the former Mr. Universe could pass for a refrigerator.

Opportunities for heavily muscled men in the American movie industry remained meager for decades. But by the 1980s, a pumped-up Sylvester Stallone and award-winning bodybuilder Arnold Schwarzenegger gained international fame as action movie stars. Directors routinely broke down, blocked, staged, and photographed the grunt-and-groan musclemen in ways designed to put their bodies on erotic display, turning them into objects for pleasure and gratification. Since Schwarzenegger made the leap from steroid-infused bodybuilding to big-screen beefcake heroics, hugely muscled men have become de rigueur in cartoon-like action movies. But even such accomplished actors as Brad Pitt, Ryan Gosling, Hugh Jackman, and Daniel Craig are rippling with big biceps, rock-hard abdomens, and muscular chests.

Camera's Gaze

Beginning in 1975, with the publication of Laura Mulvey's highly influential essay "Visual Pleasure and the Narrative Cinema," the notion that the "look" or "gaze" of the camera in the filming situation is masculine has been central to a great deal of film theory.[277] She uses "camera" as a synecdoche, a figure of speech in which a part stands for the whole, in this instance, the entire moviemaking process. In the typical Hollywood film, according to Mulvey and the many writers who followed in her wake, moviemakers put female figures on erotic display, turning them into passive objects for the pleasure and gratification of men.

In her analysis, Mulvey draws upon the complicated, controversial postulations of the dissident French psychoanalyst Jacques Lacan, like his shifting positions on the interactions of the "gaze," "narcissism," "castration anxiety," and the "meaning structures of the symbolic order" in early childhood development—much more influential with a group of feminist film theorists than on practicing mental care professionals.

Within this exceedingly shaky theoretical framework, Mulvey hypothesizes that, although most males find such erotic displays highly pleasurable, viewing the female anatomy threatens to reawaken unconscious castration anxieties formed when perceiving sexual differences during childhood. The mainstream cinema, she claims, provides two underlying psychic mechanisms to assuage this threat: Women are either "fetishized" or "investigated."

The process of fetishization involves substituting another part of the anatomy (breasts, hair, face, legs, shoulders, backside) and making it important enough to compensate for the arousal of castration fears. Investing such body parts with power and significance supposedly exorcises the threat posed by the female anatomy, allowing heterosexual male viewers to derive pleasure from lingering close-ups, glamorous costumes, and other techniques employed in the erotic display of women.

The reduction of anxiety depends on ascertaining the guilt of a female character (invariably associated with castration) and asserting control over her through devaluation, punishment, or forgiveness. The femme fatale character seemingly intent on symbolically castrating or otherwise destroying the male protagonist is either killed, imprisoned, or saved if found to have redeeming qualities typifies this strategy. Through some unconscious process, this "demystifying" of her mystery serves to contain castration anxiety by reenacting the original traumatic discovery of presumed female castration. Why such a psychic reenactment should alleviate rather than exacerbate emasculation fears is left unexplained.

Over the past fifteen years or so, the severe limitations and shortcomings of such misleading and misdirected psychoanalytic probing into the cinematic experience have come under increasing criticism. Among other things, critics have noted that analytical frameworks stressing the male gaze tend to neglect such critical factors as class status, age, race, ethnicity, and sexual preference—all of which doubtless exert a strong influence on the meanings a movie generates.

The issue of heterosexual female pleasure at the cinema also gets short shrift. After all, women not only go to the movies often but also seem to enjoy the experience. Although the cinema indisputably provides plenty of opportunities for the erotic contemplation of the female face and form, even a cursory consideration of the camera's gaze confirms that it is decidedly bisexual. The Hollywood film has a long history of intimate close-ups of male facial and bodily parts—from silent-screen star Rudolph Valentino's smoldering stare, and Hugh Jackman's hairy muscular mutant, to Ryan Gosling's bulked-up body in *Crazy, Stupid, Love* (2011).

Male as well as female anatomy is often the focus of the sexual display. A lingering close-up of Brad Pitt's "ripped abs" in *Thelma and Louise* (1991) skyrocketed his career into the stratosphere of stardom. The

camera slowly tilts up from his tightly-muscled bare chest to his sculptured facial features like a loving caress—an ode to eroticized masculine perfection. His naked body glistens while pleasuring the unhappily-married Thelma (Gina Davis). The next morning, still disheveled, she tells her pal Louise (Susan Sarandon) about her sexual experience. "I finally understand what all the fuss is about," gleaming with a satisfied smile, "it's just like a whole 'nother ballgame!" Nearly thirty years later, *Once Upon a Time... In Hollywood* (2019) offers a rapturous paean to Pitt's mature masculine perfection. While on a roof to repair an antenna, his character strips off his shirt and cotton undergarment to become yet again the stuff of female sexual fantasy. His fortuitous arrangement of facial and physical components, a burden, as well as a benediction, the talented actor's often subtle, nuanced, and understated performances can become obscured by his striking appearance and palpable physical ease.

When grim-visage English actor Daniel Craig as James Bond in the 2006 movie *Casino Royale*, emerged from the ocean in tiny blue swim trunks, the camera embraced his muscular, highly toned body. A then thirty-seven-year-old rough-hewn actor, Craig had been a controversial choice to play the suave martini-swilling, womanizing British foreign intelligence agent. Many fans of the franchise doubted he was up to the task, so the dripping-wet-body scene proved a useful public relations tool for establishing his leading-man credentials.

The heavily promoted scene not only affected swimwear trends but also set a new standard for cinematic masculinity. The idealized depictions of human bodies in ads, movies, and television commercials have put males under more pressure than ever to attain pumped-up and rippling physiques. They are also emulating the in-vogue rugged look of many models and movie and television leading men who grow a few-days stubble.

Expanding Female Roles

In 1962, Helen Gurley Brown's nonfiction *Sex and the Single Girl* became an instant bestseller. Written as an advice book, the author encouraged women to become financially independent and experience sexual relationships before or without marriage. In chapter twelve, for instance, she provides a step-by-step guide to prepare a single girl for what will occur or should occur during the beginning, middle, and end stages of an affair.

Perhaps Brown's most shocking revelation was that unmarried women not only had sex but thoroughly enjoyed it. Quite a brazen assertion considering that on television, even married couples had to have twin beds, lest there be any hint of bodily contact, let alone sensual pleasure. And when widely-read publications like *Reader's*

Digest and *The Ladies Home Journal* insisted that a "nice" girl had only two choices: "she can marry him, or she can say no."

In 1965, Brown became editor-in-chief of the venerable but foundering *Cosmopolitan* magazine, first published in 1886 as a family magazine. She changed the emphasis on sex, work, and fashion, instructing unmarried women how to look their best, have affairs, and ultimately snag a man for keeps by being sexually pleasing. The magazine also ran cover stories on acupuncture, the birth control pill, and tips for keeping a marriage passionate. At the same time, in often breathless, aphoristic prose, Brown encouraged unmarried females to have and enjoy sex without shame in all circumstances.

The sexual liberation movement that began in earnest during the latter half of the 1960s was propelled in part by ready access to birth control pills on college campuses. This pivotal milestone, developed by Big Pharma at the dawn of the decade, unlocked a new gateway to sexual freedom and significantly changed traditional male-female roles and relationships. After centuries of captivity, a woman could now separate sex from conception and behave like a man if she so desired not only in the bedroom but also the boardroom. The ability to control reproduction has facilitated professional achievement for countless women.

Even timid over-the-air network television reflected and reinforced this change in gender relations. By the dawn of the 1970s, the role of women in sitcoms started to shift away from household chores to career concerns. In *The Mary Tyler Moore Show*, airing from 1970-1977, the setting changed from the family space, the home, to the workplace, the fictional WJM news program in Minneapolis. The show centered around the work and love life of a single woman of thirty or so, a premise that broke new ground for broadcasting.

After breaking up with a beau, unlike women of an earlier era, she has a range of options, like getting a job and staying single, forming familial bonds with friends and co-workers who become like a surrogate family. An associate news producer, she had a sex life that was not a result of marriage or even engagement, subtly revealing in one episode she took birth-control pills, a plotline that moved way beyond the typically conservative television fare of the time. And she was not determined to find a husband and take on the role of dutiful wife and mother.

An indicator of changing job opportunities, the series served as a significant salvo against the restrictive roles played by women on primetime series. Four years later, CBS introduced *Rhoda* (1974–78), a spinoff of *The Mary Tyler Moore Show* that featured Valerie Harper as a Jewish New Yorker who divorces her husband during the series. Then, in 1975, *One Day at a Time* (1975–84), the first successful series about a divorced woman, became a network hit.

By the late 1980s, network television began to showcase such offerings as *Murphy Brown*. Created by Diane English, the sitcom features Candice Bergen as the title character, a recovering alcoholic working as an investigative journalist and news anchor for a fictional CBS television newsmagazine. Over forty and divorced, she is acid-tongued, aggressive, and hard as nails having shattered many glass ceilings encountered during her career.

Propelled by excellent scripts, in many of 247 episodes over ten seasons on the air, the humor largely stems from how Murphy defies every female norm. In the show's controversial 1991–92 season, she becomes pregnant after a fling with her ex-husband. When he is unwilling to give up his lifestyle to be a parent, she decides to have the child and raise it alone. This decision made front-page news when, during the 1992 presidential campaign, Vice President Dan Quayle criticized her character for "glamorizing illegitimacy" and "mocking the importance of fathers." News media outlets were quick to ridicule him for attacking a fictional female's actions.

Feeling Grey

Several female-centered shows appeared on over-the-air network television, such as *Grey's Anatomy*, a medical drama television series that premiered in March 2005 on ABC as a mid-season replacement. A blend of workplace stresses, female accomplishment, and sexual escapades, it revolves around the title character, Dr. Meredith Grey (Ellen Pompeo), who eventually rises from intern to resident to the chief of general surgery. Each installment typically begins with her voice-over narration, which often has a philosophical bent and foreshadows the theme of the episode, usually involving the high-stress competitive lives of the racially diverse surgical interns.

A complex character, Grey is the daughter of a profoundly flawed world-renowned surgeon, neglectful and verbally abusive. Despite having a distant, indifferent mother, and a long-absent father, she maintains a steadfast, calm demeanor during medical procedures and emergencies, and her even-tempered, non-judgmental manner often prompts people to open up and confide in her. As the series progresses, sexual relationships develop among the doctors that produce conflicts between their personal and professional lives.

From the outset, who is doing it with whom, including the superiors assigning cases, gets a great deal of attention. The night before Grey's internship begins, she has a one-night stand with Derek Shepherd (Patrick Dempsey), a stranger she meets at a local watering hole only to discover the next day that he is a recently hired attending physician.

Initially resisting the married Shepard's advances, she's eventually charmed into starting an illicit relationship, whose eventual breakup leaves her devastated, falling back on old habits of consoling herself with tequila and indiscriminate sex. When she and Dereck in due course reconcile and marry, the plotline shifts to her struggles with the conflicting roles of spouse, surgeon, and mother. Well into its sixteenth season, and slated for at least one more, it remains one of the highest-rated shows among eighteen-to-forty-nine-year-olds, with a disproportionally large percentage of women viewers in that advertiser-desired demographic.

For all its sophistication, complex characters, and sexual openness, *Grey's Anatomy* has many of the old daytime serial elements, albeit expanded to a weekly format. Humorous *New Yorker* cartoonist James Thurber described the basic soap opera formula in gastronomical terms as a kind of sandwich. "Between slices of advertising, spread twelve minutes of dialogue, add predicament, villainy, and female suffering in equal measure, throw in a dash of nobility, sprinkle with tears, season with organ music, cover with a rich announcer sauce, and serve five times a week."[278] Instead of the sounds of a pipe organ, an alternative rock song often punctuates emotional scenes in *Grey's Anatomy*.

Female Fantasy

Women with multiple partners still suffer opprobrium, often denigrated with such misogynistic epithets as "sluts" or "tramps" or "whores"—the lexicon of male domination. In recent years, on premium cable channels, such female sexual behavior is not only condoned but also celebrated. The HBO series *Sex and the City* (1998–2004), based on Candace Bushnell's 1997 book of the same name, centers on the lives of a group of four single women, three in their mid-thirties and one in her forties—Carrie Bradshaw (Sarah Jessica Parker), Samantha Jones (Kim Cattrall), Charlotte York (Kristin Davis), and Miranda Hobbes (Cynthia Nixon). Carrie does the voice-over narration captioned by the typing on her laptop as she works on her weekly newspaper column. She and her friends are sexually-liberated and successful career women who hardly suffer for either shoe purchases or promiscuity.

Sex and shopping seem to be the foursome's only preoccupations. They exhibit little interest in talking about books, plays, movies, work, family matters, current affairs, or national politics. Although the conversations revolve around men's motivations as well as shortcomings (genital size matters to these gals), they stress the primacy of female bonding, which seems to surpass even fulfilling romantic relationships. The four women reside in a fantasy Manhattan that lacks crime, poverty, and sexually transmitted diseases but has an abundance of available attractive, heterosexual single men eager to satisfy every female lust and sexual appetite.

A tough career-minded lawyer, Miranda masks her vulnerability with cynicism and self-deprecating humor. Prone to promiscuity, at one point she admits to having already slept with forty-two different men. Her image softens over the years, particularly after becoming pregnant by one of her on-again, off-again boyfriends (David Eigenberg), a bartender she initially saw as just another of many one-night stands. Despite the tension caused by the disparity in social and economic status, and her spirited fling with a black sports medicine doctor (Blair Underwood), they eventually get married remaining together for the rest of the series.

At one of their regular Saturday breakfasts, the prim albeit sexually active Charlotte is shocked, shocked to learn all three of her pals have fellows they can call solely for sex with no other attachments or commitments. One of the multiple continuing storylines involves hopelessly romantic Charlotte's sex life. Her first husband, Trey MacDougal (Kyle MacLachlan), suffers from the virgin-whore complex and is unable to get sexually aroused during their intimate moments.

The resourceful Charlotte rises to the occasion and resolves the problem by touching herself in front of him. All the same, the two terminate the marriage after he ultimately decides that he's not ready for children. She then takes up with her divorce lawyer Harry Goldenblatt (Evan Handler), although initially put off by constant sweating, messy eating, shortness, baldness, and hairy body. But despite such misgivings, she ends up sleeping with him and experiencing "the best sex ever." Although she tries to keep it strictly sexual, they eventually marry and adopt a child.

The oldest and most sexually promiscuous of the foursome, Samantha, is a successful public relations practitioner. Strong, confident, and extremely outspoken, she identifies herself as a "try-sexual," meaning she'll try anything once, including sex with a lesbian artist and even a romp with Charlotte's brother. The ordinarily sweet-natured Charlotte harshly quips: "Is your vagina in the New York City guide books? Because it should be; it's the hottest spot in town, it's always open!" Yet, she soon apologizes, baking Samantha a basket of muffins to make amends.

Early on in the series, the adventurous Samantha declares she's given up on relationships. She has decided to have sex "like a man," that is, without emotions or feelings, and purely for physical gratification. Adding many notches to her bedpost, she rarely has sex with the same man more than once or twice, and especially enjoys fellatio, finding having men by the testicles empowering. In one episode, she's shown on her knees behind a man's desk, presumably feeling empowered.

A young waiter and aspiring actor many years her junior (Jason Lewis) is among her numerous conquests. A recovering alcoholic, he manages to win her heart owing to their mutually satisfying sex and patience with her commitment issues. She finds their "out-of-the-box" sex exciting and refreshing. In the final season, she is diagnosed with breast cancer and undergoes chemotherapy treatments. When the chemo sessions cause hair loss, he shaves his head to give her moral support.

Sex and Self-Loathing

Female protagonists prone to promiscuity appear across platforms. Created and written by Phoebe Waller-Bridge, who also stars in the title role, the Amazon Prime English comedy-drama series *Fleabag* (two seasons, 2016-2019) focuses on a frenzied, sexually voracious thirtyish woman residing in a fantasy London. Ideal for a feline in heat and on the prowl, this sprawling city likewise seems free of crime, privation, and fear of STDs that can put the libido in low gear.

The quirky and whimsical free spirit, albeit angry and grief-riddled, runs a small café with a guinea-pig theme—hence her sobriquet. A sign of her emotional detachment, she nicknames her hookups. In the first few minutes of the opening sequence, while being sodomized by *Arsehole Guy* (Ben Aldridge), she gleefully tells the camera—her confidant, that "after some pretty standard bouncing, you realize he's heading toward your...." One of her recurring casual sexual encounters during the season, he's named for his delight in anal sex and presumably for his preening arrogance. Combining comic artifice and unfiltered confession, the dry-witted Fleabag breaks the theatrical "fourth wall" with mischievous, and at times, sad commentary often while self-medicating with sex. In her own words, "a greedy, perverted, selfish, apathetic, cynical, depraved, morally bankrupt woman," she's also oddly endearing and enchanting.

Her "uptight and beautiful and probably anorexic" sister Claire (Sian Clifford) lives with her obnoxious alcoholic American husband, Martin (Brett Gelman), and his fifteen-year-old son (who has a habit of trying to get into the bathtub with his stepmother). For Claire's birthday, she gives her a "burrower" vibrator. Although embarrassed, her emotionally stilted and sexually frustrated sister concedes it is a very thoughtful present. During the unhappy Claire's birthday party, her insensitive husband, prone to making inappropriate remarks, tries to hit on Fleabag. He then lies to Claire about who made the first move.

Charm and eagerness for sex attract enough men to help her get through the day. But with the absence of her best and only friend, whose sudden death haunts her deeply, she is mostly alone and left to her own devices. The café is failing, the lease renewal is coming up, her efforts to secure a loan fail, and her love-life consists mainly of meaningless sex. She often picks up strangers—and then turning to the camera, comments on her sexual experiences. At one point, sitting on the toilet, she muses, "I'm not obsessed with sex. I just can't stop thinking about it. The performance of it. The awkwardness... The drama... The moment you realize someone wants your body. Not so much the feeling of it."

Like the insatiable Samantha of *Sex and the City*, Fleabag is decidedly try-sexual, open to trying anything, often multiple times with many men and occasionally women. With asides to the camera and flashbacks, she recounts the latest break-up with an on-off buffoonish live-in boyfriend Harry (Hugh Skinner). When having sex with him, she thinks about a grizzled old tattoo-covered fling (Kevin McNally) "who'd breath on every thrust." She's also inclined to pleasure herself afterward. Catching her doing so while watching a televised speech of Barack Obama, the hurt and angry Harry once again moved out of their flat.

Her clumsy attempts to repair broken relationships with her emotionally distant dad (Bill Paterson) and uptight sister only made matters worse. In an astutely shot and edited scene on the underground, reflective of her inner turmoil, she imagines the commuters rhythmically crying out in contortions of agony under the facades of their public personae. Still, the first season ends on a hopeful note. Wrestling with his demons, the bank manager (Hugh Dennis), who initially rejected her loan request, decides to give her a second chance. "Everyone makes mistakes," he sympathetically tells her.

In the opening moments of the second season, Fleabag tells the camera, "This is a love story," and it is a touching one—just not ending entirely in the way she might have expected. Over a year has passed, her once failing café is now thriving, and she's no longer using sex to, as she puts it in a therapy session, "deflect from the screaming void inside my empty heart." But she hasn't spoken to her family in ages and doesn't appear to have any friends. With the wedding of her spacey dad and obnoxious godmother (Olivia Colman) on the horizon, her dysfunctional family invites her to a celebratory dinner. She seems to be the only one at the table whose life is not in turmoil.

Angelic choruses dominate the soundtrack as she wrestles lustful impulses and attempts to save Claire from a lousy marriage. As she and her estranged sister reconnect, Fleabag finds herself falling for *Hot Priest*, the charming albeit quirky Catholic clergyman officiating the marriage ceremony. Her kind of man of the cloth, he smokes, drinks, swears, and shares many of her existential doubts. The unconventional priest seems to understand her on a level no one else ever has. Eventually, she leans into the liberating openness of connecting with someone who knows and accepts her many deviations from cultural norms.

Fortified by alcohol, while sitting in a confession booth no less, she tells him through a latticed panel about "having lots of sex outside marriage and once or twice inside someone else's." She continues, "there's been a spot of sodomy, and there's been much masturbation." Her palpable desperation, along with such spicy sexual revelations, fully awakens his barely dormant libido. They start kissing and embracing until a crash breaks the erotic spell, at least for the moment.

For some sexual distraction, reverting to her old ways, Fleabag invites a boorish black lawyer (Ray Fearon) she and her sister had earlier consulted for a little libation and licentiousness. Tagging him *Hot Misogynist*, she has low expectations after he boasts about his sexual prowess. While he's moving atop her, she turns to the camera confirming "he's really good at it." Although it's "the best sex" ever, she's still smitten with the priest. Improbable kindred spirits, with off-the-charts chemistry, after much agonizing and hesitation, they spend a sexually intimate night together, with her touching the back of his neck affectionately the next morning, without an aside to the camera.

At the bittersweet end of the final episode, the conflicted clergyman tells her he can't continue the romantic relationship. Watching him walk off, she gets up from the bus-stop bench where they were sitting and heads in the opposite direction. As the camera follows, breaking the fourth wall for the final time, rather than cracking a joke about her devastation, she holds her hands up as if to say she can handle the heartbreak on her own without confiding to the camera—in effect breaking off our relationship.

Salacious, scathingly funny, and achingly heartfelt, the hugely popular series distills the rawest human emotions into exacting dialogue, cutting directly to the quick, and wrapping it all up in glibly-delivered truths. In the process, the episodes provide a poignant window into the mind of a defective, albeit delightful work in progress, shining a sympathetic light on female sexual appetites. The palliative for self-loathing, along with the path to self-preservation, the series would seem to suggest, can only come from reckoning with our frailties and fallibilities in the inseparable agony and ecstasy of the human experience.

By many accounts, young women especially embrace the indelibly charismatic character at the center of this riveting series. The focus on her many uninhibited transient sexual relationships tends to obscure that they are mostly with equally unbridled promiscuous men eager for one-night stands. In an implicit double standard, having indiscriminate sex seems innate to the male characters, but she does so to deflect from the "screaming void" inside her empty heart.

Passion & the Postmenopausal

While the young and middle-age bounce from bed to bed, sex-prone older women who seek romance or just a pleasurable romp appear foolish or are nonexistent on most channels. A notable exception, on Netflix, with the luxury of carving out niches, the *Grace and Frankie* series features two unlikely friends brought together after their divorce-lawyer husbands announce that they are in love with each other and plan to get married. The left alone wives, everything around collapsed, Grace (Jane Fonda), a retired cosmetics executive, and Frankie (Lily Tomlin), a hippie art teacher, are forced to live together. Over time, they learn to unite and cope with difficulties; many relate to aging and attitudes toward the elderly.

Over several seasons, the show has dealt with real-life problems rarely treated on television, ranging from invisibility when seeking service and painful sexual intercourse friction from vaginal dryness to debilitating rheumatoid arthritis. One early in the series thread line concerns Frankie's homemade organic yam vaginal lube and her nibbling around the edges of a romance with the farmer growing the critical ingredient—Fleabag would tag him, Yam Man. Brainstorming yam lube names, Grace and Frankie even consider, "Yam Bam Thank You Ma'am." Having an artistic flair, Frankie paints her vagina for the box. More ethically minded than entrepreneurial, Frankie ultimately backs away from a lucrative deal after learning the maker plans to add unsavory chemicals to her formula.

When the titular characters talk about sexual matters, such as a vaginal lubricant they both admit using, they put off many around them. This ageist stigma is especially so with family members, capturing the shared cultural discomfort of confronting older women as sexually active as age and opportunity allow. Unrealistic at any age, when octogenarian Grace has cravings, chance tends to flow in her favor.

Grace decides to shed all traces of artifice when she has sex with thrice-married beau Nick (Peter Gallagher), many years her junior, telling him he'll run for cover when she strips off her youthful masquerade. Of course, he is not all disappointed by her unadorned self. Why would he be since she has a wrinkled-free face and flawless body that gives little hint of the ravages of age? After all, it's the face and body of Jane Fonda. If we believe all the reports, she's boosted her exercise regimen results with many visits over the decades to cosmetic surgeons.

Social psychology studies suggest that the sexual appeal of older women (or men) doesn't come down to youthful appearance, as the *Grace and Frankie* writers imply. All sexual attraction is more about attitude and illusion than flawless facial features and body contours. A robust sexual appetite and skin with a biography, as it were, can be highly erotic, especially to someone in a similar state. At any age, candles or soft lighting adds an all-important illusory effect, concealing non-erotic elements by misguiding the senses in pleasing ways.

Of course, even an octogenarian with the looks and stamina of Jane Fonda cannot regularly wreck the sheets. In one storyline, Grace uses a vibrator that requires a great deal of effort, and she develops a case of carpal tunnel syndrome. Inspired, she collaborates with Frankie to design a "Ménage à Moi" vibrator with bells and whistles that meets the needs of older women with shaky mobility, chronic pain, and rheumatoid arthritis. Amusingly highlighted are the obstacles they face when trying to get this new business off the ground, including difficulty getting a loan because of their advanced age.

While sex toys make fleeting appearances in other popular TV series and vague but suggestive ads push vibrators, they rarely involve older women talking openly about their experiences. An avid viewer of make-believe media might well believe that older women have lost interest in sexual pleasure, something belied by the many postings on the *Grace and Frankie* Facebook page.

Since the series debut in spring 2015, notes witty academic Susan Douglas, it's repeatedly shined a spotlight on the indignities and dismissals older women suffer without lapsing into ageist humor and insults. While refreshing to see stereotypes of other older women punctured, she cautions, the flip side is how being sexually active "might be coming to be a key indicator—almost a compulsory one—of successful aging."[279] In other words, older women are increasingly being told, in television shows, and cosmetic ads, that the conventional appearance markers of sexuality are the way to avoid being labeled old.

Cosmo Concerns

The increasing sexualizing of American culture is apparent in the way *Cosmopolitan* changed over the years with the shift in the late 1990s from the "Cosmo Girl" to the "Fun, Fearless Female" label. Under different editors, the occasional articles about pets, food, travel, and such receded before burgeoning coverage of beauty, fashion, celebrity news, and especially sexual content, practically turned the magazine into a Kama Sutra manual.

Although still highlighting busty-but-thin models and shapely stars in skimpy outfits, the cover stories have become much more erotically explicit in tone. A googled tour of recent covers turned up such fearless fun features as "Total Body Sex," "Deeper Sex," and "Kinky Sex Moves." The largest-selling young women's magazine in the world, it expanded its reach into social media with the "discover" section on Snapchat—reported to attract some three million readers daily.

The editors at *Cosmopolitan* have models photographed in three-quarter shots that call attention to their bodies. While the women displaying their bodies are typically thin, occasionally the magazine features a full-figured female on the cover. The English singer-songwriter Adele Laurie Blue Adkins appeared on the December 2011 cover, which promoted a story revealing the 100 best sex tips of the year.

Although considerably more substantial than most of the ad and cover models Adele, one of those rarified performers identified by a prename, still seems to have a reasonably flat stomach, and her cheekbones and jawbone appear firm and tight—likely accomplished through lighting, makeup and airbrushing. Inviting invidious comparisons that implicitly promote the advertised products, most of the cover models exhibit what the art critic John Berger once called skin without a biography. Conforming more to the current media-made body norm, at a Spice Girls concert in June 2019, big-breasted Adele wowed fans with her dramatic weight loss.

By the 2010s, mammary mania had once again taken hold. The new feminine ideal became Victoria Beckham's boyish-like body with a porn star's huge breasts attached. Media outlets abound these days with shapes nature never designed as well as the cosmetic products and procedures to achieve such irregular configurations.

Susan J. Douglas notes that it hasn't just been magazines like *Cosmopolitan*, filled with ads for augmenting breast size, that have stressed cleavage as essential to a woman's self-worth, and desirability. So have Wonderbras, Victoria's Secret, the covers of *Maxim*, and the "swimsuit issue" of *Sports Illustrated*. Females are busting out of their bikini tops as well on television shows like *Laguna Beach* and *Girls Gone Wild*. And "even the boss on *House*, Dr. Cuddy, and the female forensic researchers on *CSI* flash cleavage typically reserved for 'Gentlemen's clubs.'"[280]

On social media sites like Instagram, posts suggest the ongoing obsession with "perfect" contours, only achievable through cosmetic surgery. Notable exemplars of this unnatural body type include Kylie Jenner, Kim Kardashian, Cardi B, and Nikki Minaj. All well-known for being well known, the latter two are currently at the center of the highly influential hip-hop scene.

Taboo Protection

In this changing cultural climate, print ads and television commercials promoting condom use were barely evident until the 1980s, even with the sharp rise in the contraction of chlamydia, gonorrhea, human papilloma virus, genital herpes, and various other sexually transmitted diseases (STDs). The tipping point proved to be outbreak of the acquired immunodeficiency syndrome (AIDS) epidemic.

The media-shunned condom was finally allowed to wade in the mainstream. From the late 1980s on, advertising appeals for condom use have ranged from the sedate to the sexually alluring, although over-the-air television tested the waters cautiously. In 2007, for instance, FOX and CBS rejected a Trojan condom ad with a safe-sex message that featured anthropomorphized pigs because it was not about disease prevention.

A print ad for Today's condom features a wholesome-looking thirtyish or so fellow in khakis and argyle socks sitting shoeless at the edge of a bed. He is bathed in warm yellow light, enhancing to his unthreatening demeanor, while the product encased in an antiseptic blue wrapper suggests medical sterility. The copy headline blares: WOULD YOU BUY A CONDOM FOR THIS MAN. The response: More and more women would. The implicit message the model conveys is that the carriers of AIDS and other sexually transmitted diseases have no distinct look. They are neither seemly nor sinful in appearance. Anyone can have a deadly or debilitating sexually transmitted disease. Love may not last forever, but genital herpes surely does.

Although not likely intentional, reinforcing the caution against stereotyping, categorizing based on superficial traits, the model in the Today condom ad bears a striking resemblance to a young Ted Bundy (as does the young George Bush). The infamous serial killer confessed to murdering thirty women before being executed in Florida in 1989 but hinted that the true body count was far higher.

Wholesomely handsome, the one-time law student lured females to their deaths because he didn't look or sound deviant or depraved.

Sexually suggestive condom ads abound as well. An ad for Hansaplast's Long Pleasure Condoms line features a young woman in scanty bikini exhibiting rather telling tan lines, with the implication she just had protracted sex on the beach. Another less than subtle ad for the same brand depicts a firecracker with an incredibly long fuse. An ad for SKYN condoms displaying a tight shot of a prone female model with a seductive look donning black-lace panties and silk top is superimposed with the statement: "I always notice what a man is wearing." With the prophylactic no longer hidden in the shadows, consumers can now buy condoms in all sorts of fun colors, flavors, textures and materials.

Legal Status

Despite long having a lowly status, while not full-prove, the condom is an effective means of birth control and a protective measure against infections spread by sexual

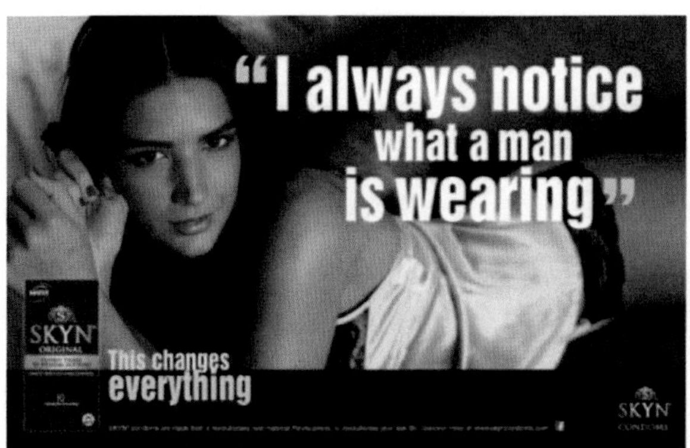

activity. Yet newspapers and networks alike refused to carry condom ads of any kind. And several states banned the use of contraceptives even by married couples.

Defying an 1879 Connecticut statute, rarely enforced, prohibiting the use of "any drug, medicinal article or instrument for the purpose of preventing conception," a gynecologist at the Yale School of Medicine, opened a birth control clinic in New Haven in conjunction with the head of Planned Parenthood in the nutmeg state. As they expected, wanting to legally challenge the antiquated legislation, the pair were arrested indicted, tried, and convicted of violating the law, and their convictions were affirmed by higher state courts.

In *Griswold v. Connecticut* (1965), the U.S. Supreme Court held that, even though not explicitly in the Constitution, a right to privacy can be inferred from several amendments in the Bill of Rights, and this right prevents states from making the use of contraception illegal.[281] Writing for the 7-2 majority, Justice William Douglas ruled that the law violated the "right to marital privacy," establishing the basis for privacy rights with respect to intimate practices.

Douglas explained that the various guarantees within the Bill of Rights create "penumbras," or partially shaded outer regions, that establish a right to privacy. "Would we allow the police," he asked rhetorically, "to search the sacred precincts of marital bedrooms for telltale signs of the use of contraceptives? The very idea is repulsive to the notions of privacy surrounding the marriage relationship." This ruling conjured up out of the "shadows" strays so far from an originalist reading that the text itself becomes irrelevant. Nonetheless, it provided the precedent for striking down anti-abortion laws and sodomy statutes.

Promoting Insecurity

Sexually active and assertive women put pressures on men of all ages. In an effort to give Viagra, its "erectile disfunction" drug, greater exposure, the pharmaceutical giant Pfizer hired war hero, former senator, and failed presidential contender Bob Dole for a television advertising campaign. Without directly promoting the little blue pill, the seventy-four-year-old spoke earnestly to the camera about sexual impotency, a stigmatized medical condition likely to be suffered in silence.

Since a somber Bob Dole explained the medical condition in 1999, ads for erectile dysfunction products have gotten increasingly racier and more youth-oriented in the battle for dominance in the $2 billion-plus market. Initially these ads were aimed at the elderly, showing a white-haired couple on a path with the caption "Walking too much?" or looking at chandeliers asking: "Antiquing too much?" In each, the now iconic blue diamond-shaped pill stamped with "Viagra" is superimposed on the couples.

A blunter 2014 Viagra ad opens with a closeup shot of a sexy blond woman in her forties lying on her stomach, with the thin strap of her dress showing on her right shoulder. "So, guys, it's just you and your honey," she whispers with a come-hither look, her sultry voice British-accented. A wide shot reveals that she's lying in an open-air cabana in a tropical location. "The setting is perfect. But, then, erectile dysfunction happens again," she goes on, purring and pouting. "You know what, plenty of guys have this issue, not just getting an erection"—raising an eyebrow—"but keeping it."

What is advertised has few limitations or boundaries these days. A billboard for a law firm showcases a woman with deep cleavage and a man with bulging muscles with the exhortation: "Life's short. Get a divorce." In a similar vein, Ashley Madison, an online dating service that marketed primarily to married people, until a 2015 hacking exposing thirty-four million accounts put it out of business, used the slogan "Life is short, have an affair" on billboards and television commercials.

Once reputed to result in hellfire and eternal damnation, the safest kind of sex also got a big media boost. Such cable TV networks as Spike, VH1, MTV, and Comedy Central carried a commercial for Trojan's Tri-Phoria, but it did not use the word "vibrator" or show the product. "Has life got you stressed out?" begins a voiceover as a woman sits stuck in traffic. "Want to have some fun? New from Trojan, a brand you trust. Introducing vibrating Tri-Phoria it's like three massagers in one."

Playing on the closing cautionary from pharmaceutical commercials, the commercial continues, "Side effects of Tri-Phoria may include screams of ecstasy, curled toes, a sudden glow and intense waves of pleasure." In the immortal words of Woody Allen in the highly acclaimed romantic comedy *Annie Hall* (1977), "Don't knock masturbation. It's sex with someone you love." In the COVID-19 era of confinement and social distancing, the whole notion of safe sex has an altogether new meaning.

Show-Biz Toxicity

In our erotically charged media environment, sexual abuse is not uncommon in workplaces of all kinds, especially in the entertainment industry. Behind the scenes, the whole system of making movies and television programs remains rife with sexual exploitation. Unlike other lines of work, the way entertainers make a living is on full public display. Wasn't succeeding all about appearances? With the right coaching and cosmetics, surely even the humblest could hope to achieve stardom.

All aspects of show business have long exerted a strong magnetic pull. Countless thousands have chased the limelight, hoping to become a famous singer, dancer, stage, movie, or television star. But for girls and women, in particular, the path to bright lights has often involved dangerous detours into the darkness of predatory sexual behavior. The pernicious practice of having to trade sexual favors to win roles in theatrical productions existed on the Great White Way from the outset. Lee Shubert, the eldest of three brothers who helped establish Broadway's theater district, demanded sex from leading ladies, promising ingenues, and chorus girls alike.[282]

Stories of the pitfalls of pursuing an acting career had circulated in the popular press early on in the movie business. Movie magazines regularly ran features describing the hard work and years of sacrifice required to succeed. Melodramas such as *A Girl's Folly* (1917), *Mary of the Movies* (1923), *Broken Hearts of Hollywood* (1926), and *Stranded* (1927) served as cautionary tales about the unscrupulous men who preyed on the star-struck girls. And yet legions of young people continued to migrate westward each year in search of stardom. Every once in a while, through some combination of charisma, chance, and calculation, an aspiring performer would attain stardom. But most ended up sorely disappointed. Unable to find work, encountering repeated rejection or exploitation, many eventually gave up in despair.

Even prepubescence did not impede mistreatment. The makers of *Baby Burlesks* cast preschoolers dressed as adults wearing diapers with oversize safety pins below the waist. When any of the pint-sized performers misbehaved, they were locked in a windowless sound box with only a block of ice on which to sit. All eight of the parodies in the series abound with sexually suggestive innuendos and unsettling slapstick such as a little girl sucking on the finger of a rubber glove. In these cynical exploitations of childish innocence, leading player four-year-old Shirley Temple appeared in such roles as a hard-boiled French bar girl clad in an off-the-shoulder blouse and satin garter. In *Kid in Hollywood*, a 1933 Fox Film release, the dimpled, precocious Shirley plays a former beauty queen reduced to scrubbing soundstage floors. After a director discovers her, she achieves stardom as under the screen name Morelegs Sweetrick.

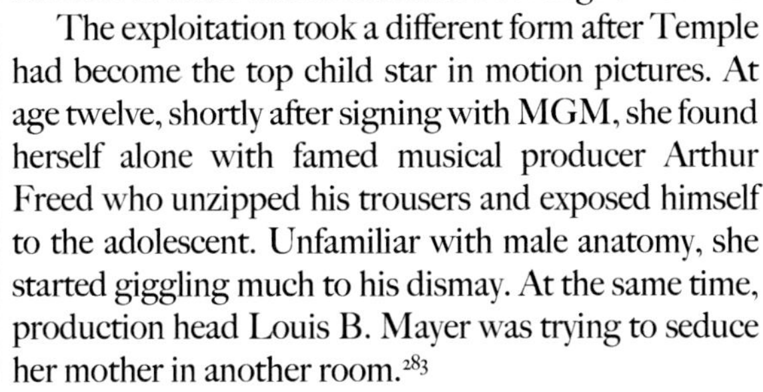

The exploitation took a different form after Temple had become the top child star in motion pictures. At age twelve, shortly after signing with MGM, she found herself alone with famed musical producer Arthur Freed who unzipped his trousers and exposed himself to the adolescent. Unfamiliar with male anatomy, she started giggling much to his dismay. At the same time, production head Louis B. Mayer was trying to seduce her mother in another room.[283]

The "casting couch" audition became emblematic of the skewed sexual politics of show business. An irresistible urge to succeed on one end, and a surplus of power on the other, make young hopefuls very vulnerable to casting-couch experiences. They go along to get along, at least while its expedient to do so. This exploitative environment, which gives a whole new meaning to the catchy lyrics "*there's no business like show business*," remained more-or-less under the radar for decades. Many groped, humiliated or even sexually assaulted women, no doubt, remained silent out of shame or fear of personal or professional backlash or retaliation. Even marquee names would be engaging in self-sabotage to reveal a predator.

Such workplace toxicity started to change with the publication of investigative reports by the *New Yorker* and the *New York Times* of Harvey Weinstein's predatory sexual behavior, backed up by meticulous research and careful editorial review. Allegations against the longtime movie mogul, producer of such cinematic touchstones as *Sex, Lies, and Videotape* (1989), *Pulp Fiction* (1994) and *Good Will Hunting* (1997), stretched back over three decades.

As the *Times* reporters, Jodi Kantor and Megan Twohey later brought to light, Weinstein hid his predation and continued to thrive through a labyrinth of secret settlements and restrictive nondisclosure agreements.[284] Scaling new heights of hypocrisy, a lawyer crusading against male predatory practices was among those whose firm profitably brokered at least one of these deals taking forty-percent off the top for its legal services.

For hefty hourly fees, another shameless spotlight-seeking female attorney even tried to intimidate his accusers or paint them as deceitful and dishonest. A nondisclosure agreement forces the victim into silence while protecting predatory behavior. Although these agreements usually prohibit employers from disparaging victims, by many accounts, whisper campaigns often follow women for years, making them unemployable in their chosen profession.

A polished high-priced male lawyer of national acclaim retained by the predatory producer for some sixteen years worked to conceal, spin and silence the mounting allegations of sexual misconduct. Among other measures, the lawyer's firm executed a contract between Weinstein and a private intelligence agency based in London, Tel Aviv, and Madrid. Bearing the evocative name Black Cube, the company, founded in 2010 by two former Israeli intelligence officers, does far more than background checks and tracing corporate assets. Its undercover agents, drawn from the ranks of Aman, Mossad and Shin Bet, engage in all sorts of deceptive and disreputable tactics against journalists and sexual-abuse accusers.

Investigative journalist Ronan Farrow reported in the *New Yorker* that the movie producer directed the Israeli intelligence firm to gather data on dozens of individuals.[285] Its agents also compiled potentially damaging psychological profiles focusing on personal or sexual histories. In an attempt to kill anything harmful to its client, the firm targeted the two *Times* reporters who eventually turned the producer into the poster boy for abusive and exploitative behavior in the movie business.

#MeToo Reckoning

Soon after the Weinstein revelations, the nascent #MeToo movement erupted with full force with women all over the world sharing their stories of sexual assault and harassment. As numerous women came forward, including several movie stars, greater public awareness of sexual abuse and exploitation prompted renewed media attention to things said and done even decades ago.

With more and more women coming out of the shadows to share personal tales of denigrating and deprecating encounters, the movement gained mind-boggling momentum. Since April 2017, several hundred powerful people, celebrities, politicians, CEOs, and others, have been credibly accused of sexual harassment, assault, or other misconduct, and the list keeps growing.

Among the high-profile media personalities taken down by charges of such behavior are TV host Tavis Smiley, *Today Show* co-anchor Matt Lauer, television interviewer Charlie Rose, political journalist Mark Halpern, and Fox News host Bill O'Reilly. Forced to resign in April 2017, O'Reilly was widely reported as having paid one of his accusers $30 million in hush money.

CBS's executive cadre made news in fall 2018 when the network announced that Jeff Fager, longtime executive producer of 60 Minutes, would be leaving the company amid allegations he touched female employees improperly and condoned a toxic culture of sexual harassment inside the storied newsmagazine's business offices. His departure came just two days after CBS corporate chief Les Moonves was ousted following two *New Yorker* exposés of sexual abuse accusations from a dozen women.

The seismic shifts set in motion by the #MeToo reckoning seemingly leave little space for fine distinctions even though transgressions run the gamut from multiple rape allegations to claims of unwanted kissing or touching.

Consider the case of former-comedian Al Franken, who was forced to resign his position as U.S. senator from Minnesota. His undoing began when a conservative talk show host released a photo of him leering at the lens of a camera with his arms outstretched toward the breasts of his sleeping U.S.O. costar, garbed in military helmet, fatigues, and a bulletproof vest.

The female in this photo, herself a host of a conservative talk show, claimed Franken had forced an unwanted kiss on her during a 2006 U.S.O. tour entertaining American troops. Several other women came forward accusing him of unwanted attempted kissing or of touching them on the buttocks or breast while having photographs taken with them.

The besieged Franken's tortured apologies only exacerbated his situation since he neither admitted guilt nor denied the claims of his accusers. This initial equivocation along with the photograph of his mischievously sophomoric behavior left him vulnerable to calls for his resignation.

The most vocal critic of his alleged offenses, Senator Kirsten Gillibrand, opposed making any distinctions between the loutish and the criminal. Adding to his woes was the no doubt well-intended but misguided #MeToo credo of "believe women." The junior senator from New York, along with others who lump all sexual impropriety together in a single category, and assume all charges of sexual misconduct are true, run the risk of creating new injustices in the service of correcting old ones.

Gray Areas

The long-overdue #MeToo comeuppances fueled already existing anxieties about accusations of assault or intimidation after any sexual act thought initially to be consensual or perhaps just a bumbling attempt at courtship. Mere mortals and celebrities have expressed a mea culpa for misreading sexual situations.

In an online piece, an angry woman using a pseudonym claimed that on a date, actor and comedian Aziz Ansari repeatedly "pressured" her to perform oral sex, missing or ignoring verbal and non-verbal cues. Her allegation sparked fierce debate across social media about gender dynamics, what constitutes consent, and appropriate sexual behavior getting into gray areas crying out for clarification. After a year and a half out of the spotlight, in his July 2019 Netflix's comedy special, the multi-talented Ansari addressed a not very funny sexual misconduct allegation that led him to recede from the public eye.

Before getting to the jokes, while not apologizing, Ansari explained to the audience, "I just felt terrible that this person felt this way." He discussed the impact the story had on his friends, saying, "If this made not just me but other people be more thoughtful, then that's a good thing, and that's how I feel about it." At the end of the special, he again addressed the sexual misconduct scandal, albeit less directly, telling the large crowd of adoring fans how grateful he is for the show of support.

Alternate Agendas

Left and right-leaning advocates too often give the criterion of verifying factual statements with several sources lip service when disruption of the status quo is at stake. The extended televised Senate Judiciary Committee Hearings in September

2018 on the nomination of Brett Kavanaugh, a likely vote to overturn *Roe v. Wade*, to the U.S. Supreme Court provide a high-profile case in point.

When Kavanaugh's appointment seemed all but certain, pro-abortion politicians demanded additional sessions to interrogate him about psychology professor Christine Blasey Ford's claims he assaulted her in the 1980s. This time around, instead of questions about judicial philosophy and past decisions, Democrats on the committee like Kamala Harris, showing off prosecutorial skills zeroed in on allegations of the attempted rape that supposedly occurred about thirty-five-years ago when he was in high school. Aside from his accuser, who made a very compelling witness, nobody could recall details of the actual incident. With the cameras rolling and millions watching, some committee members asserted Kavanaugh had committed other egregious acts (like drinking beer and misbehaving at parties). Still, they put forward no additional information about the alleged long-ago attack. Political grandstanding, less-than-subtle innuendo and outright character assassination eclipsed the respect Kavanaugh commands among many but, as might be expected, not all scholars, lawyers, and jurists. Ever since the televised hearings, whenever he tries to speak in public, his opponents stand with placards proclaiming he is a rapist lumping him together with sexual predators like the late Jeffrey Epstein.

Absence of Tributes

In this unusual historical moment, sports teams ditched derogatory Native American branding, cities dismantled Confederate statues, and makers of rice and pancake mix retired antebellum archetypes of devoted and submissive servants. Culturally significant women long denied recognition in public spaces are also getting considerable news media attention.

The magnificent 843-acre park in the middle of Manhattan, as a case in point, contains twenty-two historical figures—all are of men. The only females are fictional figures, such as Mother Goose and Alice in Wonderland. In the face of mounting pressure, the New York City parks and recreation department commissioner overturned a sixty-year-old moratorium on permanent installations.

In May of 2015, the department approved the installation of a statue of suffragists Elizabeth Cady Stanton and Susan B. Anthony, at the West 77th Street entrance of Central Park, long ago labeled "women's gate." The aim was to commemorate the women's suffrage movement in time for the Nineteenth Amendment's 100th anniversary, ensuring women's right to vote in the United States.

At the 1848 Women's Rights Convention in Seneca Falls, New York, Stanton's speech sparked the first organized woman's rights and woman's suffrage movements in the United States. Despite intimidating extralegal pressure, Stanton and Anthony, along with other bold and dedicated women, persisted in their efforts to speak in the public forum about suffrage. They often did so at great sacrifice. Though she and Stanton were prime movers in the passage of the amendment giving women the right to vote, neither would live long enough to see it implemented.

Stanton and Anthony's selection as symbols of this movement worthy of statuary celebration generated growing controversy. The tensions among black and white suffragettes escalated in the run-up to the 15th amendment, which barred the states from denying black men the right to vote. In this debate, New York Times op-ed columnist Brent Staples, a leading Stanton critic, claims that in arguing against black men preceding white women into the franchise, she invoked "white supremacist" slanders.

Drawing upon recent revisionist research, Staples asserts that racism and elitism were enduring features of the great suffragist's makeup and philosophy.[286] Among other transgressions, he contends, the Stanton-Anthony cohort rendered black suffragists nearly invisible in their six-volume *History of Woman Suffrage*, still dominate in popular thinking about the early women's rights struggle. To his chagrin, in compiling this influential work, they ignored the black activist Frances Ellen Watkins Harper's speech at the May 1866 women's rights convention in New York City, now considered visionary. A polished, self-assured writer, speaker, and teacher, Harper did not hesitate to challenge racism within the suffrage movement.

In late October 2019, New York City's Public Design Commission voted to revise the suffragist monument, adding the self-named Sojourner Truth. Born enslaved in Ulster County, New York, she became a leader in the suffrage movement and a celebrated orator. She spoke out about abolition, women's rights, prison reform, and the evils of capital punishment. The design panel city narrowly approved the monument dedicated to women—despite growing criticism that the statue wrongly links three suffragettes at opposite ends of the movement. The fourteen-foot high monument, which shows the three women seated around a table speaking and writing, appears along the Mall, a pedestrian esplanade running from 66th to 72nd street. It features statues of literary figures such as Fitz-Greene Halleck and William Shakespeare, among others. After displaying a clay model, park officials unveiled the bronze statue in late August 2020, commemorating the 100th anniversary of the ratification of the nineteenth amendment.

As with the statues in Central Park, women, actual or otherwise, are missing from paper currency as well. In the pursuit of monetary equality of sorts, the Obama administration treasury secretary initially decided to replace Alexander Hamilton on the $10 bill with Harriet Tubman, a revered antislavery and women's suffrage activist. An escaped slave, she became part of the Underground Railroad, a network of antislavery activists and safe houses. She did so while carrying a bounty for her capture and suffering lifelong dizziness, pain, and spells of hypersomnia from a head blow that suffered at age thirteen when a slave master threw a metal weight at someone else and fractured her skull instead.

The treasury department scrapped replacing Hamilton following the immense success of Lin-Manuel Miranda's rap Broadway musical featuring this founding father, one of the few who was not a slave owner. Attention then turned to Andrew Jackson; the controversial seventh president featured on the $20 bill had a pervasive influence on American politics before and after his office (1829 to 1837). An admired Army general in some circles, Jackson sought to advance the rights of everyday citizens as president. Of course, American men of European descent were the primary beneficiaries of the democratic reforms instituted during his presidency.

The connection between whiteness, freedom, and autonomy would grow stronger during Jackson's presidency. To be white in the Jacksonian era was to have the "liberty" not only to enslave West Africans but also to confiscate native land. After the discovery of gold in northern Georgia on Cherokee territory, the slave-owning Jackson signed the 1830 Indian Removal Act leading to the tribe's forced relocation (along with their African slaves) to what became in 1907 the state of Oklahoma.[287] In what came to be called the "trail of tears," some 4,000 died from hunger, exposure, and disease.

A preliminary design with Harriet Tubman's image on the $20 bill was completed in late 2016 to be unveiled in 2020 to celebrate the 100th anniversary of women's right to vote. This planned currency change was not without opposition, either. A portrait of the seventh president hangs in the Oval Office. In May 2019, President Trump's treasury secretary decided to delay plans to reproduce and circulate the $20 bill bearing Tubman's face for six years.

Fighting Words

In many venues, male-female interactions remain fraught. Sexist taunts and personal insults are still blood sport in the nation's political arena. Mired in misogyny, the vitriol toward Hillary Clinton has been relentless from her stints as First Lady, U.S. Senator, and Secretary of State to her 2016 presidential run. During the campaign for the nation's highest office, she took a lot of flak for referring to half of her opponents' supporters as a "basket of deplorables." Elaborating, she said, "They're racist, sexist, homophobic, xenophobic—Islamophobic—you name it." Within a day, she expressed regret for "saying half," while insisting that Trump had deplorably amplified "hateful views and voices." Her politically inept, inelegant metaphor notwithstanding, she was hardly off the mark about expanding hateful expression. As recently as late May 2020, the president re-tweeted a congressman calling her "a skank."

The beloved-by-many former First Lady Michelle Obama famously once remarked, "When they go lower, we go higher." Some younger female politicians have taken that to mean, "go for the jugular, not the groin," in a dignified way. In 2018, a one-time bartender, Alexandria Ocasio-Cortez, defeated a ten-term incumbent to become among the first female members of the Democratic Socialists of America elected to serve in Congress. Although skillful fundraisers, getting lots of small donations, they have a rough cultural terrain ahead in their grassroots campaign. The term "socialism" carries heavy political baggage, as Michael Harrington documented decades ago, associated with the odious regimes of Adolph Hitler and Josef Stalin, to mention the more extreme examples.[288]

Like the left-leaning Harrington, Ocasio-Cortez and her congressional cohorts have in mind a benevolent movement. They seek to make capitalism less authoritarian and more humane through the electoral process—pushing a progressive platform that includes issues concerning climate change, healthcare, housing, care of children, immigration, campaign-finance reform, taxation, and income inequality. Harnessing social media's power, they have moved the Democratic Party decidedly leftward, even though its standard-bearer is an old white guy with a track record that's anything but progressive.

Right-wingers have labored hard to cast the congresswoman as an avatar of leftist evils. The Bronx-born Ocasio-Cortez, no shrinking violet, is exceptionally skilled at capitalizing from her many detractors, some quite vicious, to enhance her political strength and resilience. In late July 2020, Ted Yoho, a veteran Republican from Florida, approached Ocasio-Cortez on the Capitol steps to inform her that she was, among other things, "disgusting" and "out of your freaking mind," his wrath ignited by her public statements that poverty and unemployment are root causes of the recent spike in crime rates in New York. Yoho did not cease to express his disdain for her even as she walked away. Believing her out of earshot, he reportedly described his congressional colleague as a "fucking bitch."

The Florida Republican will think twice before again denigrating a congressional colleague, especially one smart and media-savvy with a practiced actor's command of political platforms. Summoning her considerable thespian skills, the congresswoman sprang into performance mode, turning his vulgar, sexist slur into a group theatre event by inviting her fellow lawmakers to express solidarity. Thirteen women and three men, including the Democratic majority leader, appeared on the House floor to speak on her behalf. For over an hour, in a mesmerizing moment of televised drama, the women shared stories of condescension, harassment, and mistreatment.

Speaking first, most spellbinding was Ocasio-Cortez herself. The former waitress and bartender, offspring of a poor Puerto Rican family, stepped to the microphone in the House chamber and shredded Yoho, who had hidden behind the cloak of family and given an implausible denial and defense. With measured cadence, artful construction, and acidic flourishes, she stated: "This issue is not about one incident. It is cultural. It is a culture of lack of impunity, accepting violence and violent language against women and an entire structure of power that supports that." She had heard all the racist and sexual slurs before, on the subway, working as waitress, and bartending to a rough-and-tough cliental. But she wasn't going to let this pass, not from a fellow-member of Congress: "I could not allow my nieces, I could not allow the little girls that I go home to, I could not allow victims of verbal abuse, and worse, to see that. See that excuse, and see our Congress accept it as legitimate and accept it as an apology and accept silence as a form of acceptance. I could not allow that to stand."

The first-termer was incensed that Yoho used his family as a "shield" for his barrage. "Having a daughter does not make a man decent. Having a wife does not make a decent man. Treating people with dignity and respect makes a decent man. And when a decent man messes up, as we all are bound to do, he tries his best and apologizes," she said forcefully. "I am someone's daughter, too."[289]

Firmly Fixed

Such rhetorical dynamism denouncing sexism, bigotry, and the deliberate septicity of division is likely to have a powerful cultural and political impact. But a century of depicting females as idealized, subordinate, deceptive, dangerous, or as innately less capable, competent, or rational as men, undoubtedly has taken a hard toll. The very familiarity of such female stereotypes circulating in media outlets over generations operates to make these depictions unseen as an influencing agent.

Given the heavy emotional freight traditional gender roles often carry, they may be highly resistant to contradictory evidence or logical argument. Three women are now serving on the nation's highest tribunal; innumerable others hold prominent positions; female moviemakers have made significant strides, over a quarter of Congress is female, and the #MeToo reckoning is still gaining momentum. Nonetheless, women are still vulnerable to exploitation and workplace sexual harassment—the weaponizing of hurtful slurs to diminish female achievement or sexual desires persists. For a woman to have the word *ambitious* attached to her is still stigmatizing in some circles. And the nation always seems eons away from a future little girl innocently asking her mother whether men can be president.

Chapter 10

Web Culture

Most people in the United States—child or adult, male or female—like a modern-day Aladdin, click on the large screen at home or a smaller one while in transit and command, "Inform, entertain, titillate me!" The past several decades witnessed the spread of an intricate global web of internet connections and the sophisticated software to negotiate this nexus and sparking new laptop and smartphone devices.

As stationary commuters mentally move across the digitally borderless brave new world—typing, reading, looking, listening, and watching, they've shattered the cultural confines of corporate-controlled theatrical movies, radio broadcasting, and over-the-air television. In an amazingly short amount of time, cyberspace, a regrettably out of fashion term for the internet, has become the domain of global digital interaction, offering an unparalleled array of cultural spaces.

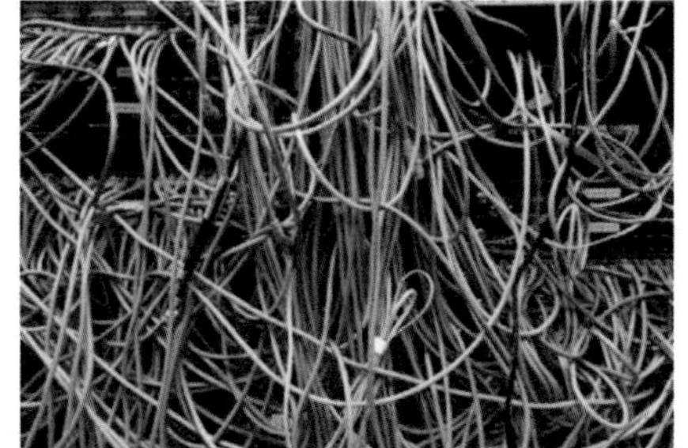

The compelling notion of cyberspace, lifted from science fiction, conjures up some exotic and alluring alternate universe. A place to share stories, provide social support, conduct business, play games, create art works, have political debates, and even engage in virtual lovemaking. Of course, the internet is not a place. It is an unglamorous collection of interwoven wires and routers and computer servers. They transmit billions of bits of data back and forth, fostering disembodied communities and social separation and fragmentation.

Origins of the Internet

The origins of the internet trace back to a Department of Defense division called the Advanced Research Project Agency (ARPA). In the fall of 1969, this agency linked four universities to coordinate military-related research projects. This modest network employed "packet switching," cutting messages into little pieces and sending them on along the easiest route to their final destination.

The receiving computers reassembled these messages, which could originate from any point. The network expanded and eventually joined in the 1980s with one designed and operated by the National Science Foundation. As private parties gained access via browsers like Mosaic or Netscape and, later, Chrome or Firefox, the internet grew from a specialized scientific network to a significant engine of commerce and communication with little deliberate government oversight.

Early in January 1983, engineers launched the basic protocol for sharing bits between computers and, a decade or so later, Tim Berners-Lee created software that organizes and standardizes the data flowing through the internet's electronic pathways letting individual computers tap into one another—now the core of the online experience. This software, called the World Wide Web, can present data as text, graphics, audio, and video. An array of dedicated software along with the ever-increasing processing power of modern personal computers allows for the connection of billions of people around the globe.

Most private individuals connect through Internet Service Providers, or "ISPs." Along with connection, in return for a fee, they provide e-mail and other basic technology. Information travels to and from the individual's computer through the ISP's computer, which in turn forwards that information up the hierarchy and on to the internet. In short, the ISP acts as the individual's gateway into cyberspace—chats, games, and custom-built forums being among the original aims and destinations. Just as a book permits reaching back across the decades, centuries, and millennia, the internet provides paths transcending physical boundaries into an abstract realm communicating with unknown others in far-off places across endless time and space.

Early Era

The internet offers a global megaphone for voices that might otherwise be heard only feebly, if at all. It invites and facilitates multiple points of view and dialogue in ways the traditional, one-way, mass media cannot. Like early point-to-point radio communication, many found the internet's initial openness, its room for a diversity of voices and its earnest amateurism exhilarating. A blind faith seemed to prevail that "netizens" were somehow different, transformed as it were, and that the culture of the web was intrinsically better. Unfortunately, that excessive faith in "web culture" left a void, one that became filled by the lowest forms of human conduct—trolling, clickbait, security breaches, and excessive and intrusive advertising demands, adopting a standard of corporate attention—a business model with unrelenting demands for constant expansion of the bottom line.

Like the printing press for its time, the internet had a protracted adolescence ranging from the first bulletin boards, to the early days of blogging, to the emergence of social platforms like Friendster, and eventually to the online world dominated by tech giants like Google, Facebook, Amazon, and Apple that touch every corner of our digital lives. In the looser, chaotic, and creative period of the internet starting in the late 1970s, bulletin board systems (BBS), partitioned and mostly regional, functioned like a corkboard of sorts, containing local notices, stuff for sale, forums, and the like. The forums were similar to current ones but an emphasis on location shaped the inter-

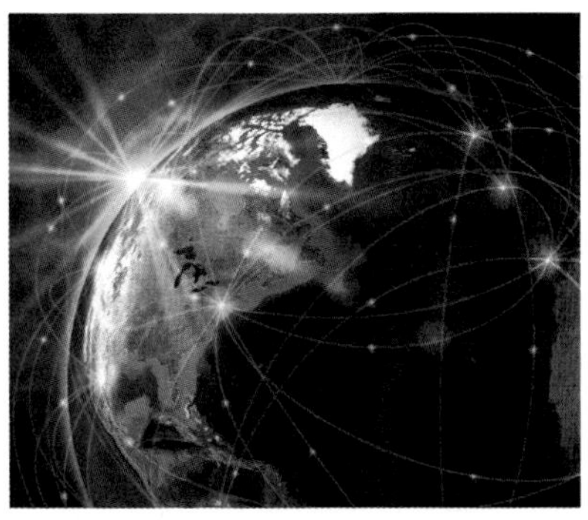

actions. Unlike a BBS or web forum, Usenet (user network), established in 1980, has a central server and dedicated administrator that distribute to one or more categories, known as newsgroups. Moderated from the top, the distribution network lets individual users read messages from and post messages to a local server, which may be operated by anyone. In the 1990s, before access to the internet became commonly affordable, its connections made long-distance or worldwide discussions and other communication widespread, not requiring a server, just (local) telephone service. This vast network consists of tens of thousands of interconnected sub-networks with no single owner or controlling authority that links together millions of computers around the world. Copper wires, switches, routers, wireless connections link its infrastructure, and increasingly fiber optics—thin glass strands designed for light transmission. A single hair-thin fiber is capable of transmitting trillions of bits per second.

Wiki World

Virtually anything in cyberspace can be updated, changed, or erased at any moment. The mutable quality of internet-based information has permitted the rise of vast user-maintained databases such as Wikipedia, the brainchild of Jimmy Wales, and his first hire Larry Sanger, a Ph.D. candidate in philosophy. They launched the user-editable encyclopedia website in 2001, but by the end of the year, self-styled "chief organizer" Sanger was laid-off. His imperial manner reportedly offended many participants. To keep the nonprofit afloat, Wales sought donations, not advertiser support.

Coined from the Hawaiian word for "quick," wikis are enabled by software that allows the creation of content without any defined owner or leader. Wikipedia is not a single wiki but rather a collection of hundreds of wikis, each with a specific language. The English Wikipedia has the most extensive user base among wikis, making it among the world's most visited websites. The open philosophy of Wikipedia, allowing anyone to edit content, does not ensure that every participant's intentions are benevolent. The website established strict standards and protocols to safeguard against changing content to something offensive, adding nonsense, or incorrect information, or hyperlinks to sites hosting malicious code. New knowledge adds new insights, and the information this site contains is forever evolving.

Disembodied Intimacy

The possibilities now available to typical cyberspace travelers seem boundless. The multi-media capabilities of browsers allow for viewing a virtually unlimited number of files that display text, images and sound. Hyperlinking means that a simple click of a button takes them from files stored in one computer to those stored on another. Through texting and e-mailing, users are able to "chat" or otherwise communicate with each other interactively. They can make virtual friends, fall in love, and even adopt a new identity as well as buy goods and services for their "real-space" environment.

Advances in media technology have made it possible to tell more engaging stories, and to more directly connect with communities and audiences through platforms such as Facebook and Instagram. Digital media enables of all kinds of activities to be endlessly and cheaply reproduced without loss of quality. Such sites as YouTube allow people to make and distribute videos on the internet creating transnational communities.

Hugely popular around the globe, with young and not-so-young, the TikTok video-sharing social networking service owned by Beijing-based ByteDance, allows

users to create short dance, lip-sync, comedy and talent videos. Sports fanatics, pet enthusiasts or those just looking for a laugh are likely to find something worth watching. With its number of active users rising toward a billion, the app has spawned numerous viral trends, cyberspace celebrities, and musical crazes worldwide. Such bands as Fitz and the Tantrums built fanbases as far off as South Korea, despite never having toured in that region. The app's virtual videos draw millions of preteens and teenagers. A feature permitting a video's addition to an existing one with the original content's audio sparked many innovative combinations. The youthful exuberance on display causes crackdowns in conservative countries, in extreme cases leading to prosecution and imprisonment. And the platform provides a sturdy launching pad for lies, deceptions, and farfetched conspiracy claims.

Shifting News Landscape

Once upon a time, and seemingly long ago, in a strange land whose residents didn't don facemasks, trained reporters using various types of recorders, cameras, and notebooks gathered and wrote about what they deemed newsworthy. Such reports were, in turn, edited, published, and distributed through basically three types of mass media, namely, print, radio, and television. For the most part, profit-driven corporations oversaw these traditional or "legacy" media outlets with an eye toward the bottom line. With high entry fees and a handful of firms competing with one another, the rest of the population listened, watched, or read passively, unable to participate.

These once estimable news outlets no longer have a tight hold on publishing power. The advent and widespread use of the internet turned this news world upside down, making it more participatory, social, diverse, and often highly partisan. Armed with easy-to-use online publishing tools, always-on connections, and ever-more powerful mobile devices, once passive participants now have the means to create and disseminate news, information, and viewpoints of all kinds. The affordability of digital media, along with ease of use, has democratized news production and dissemination.

Whether benign or benighted, many of those assuming the essential reporter role lack professional training, and what they publicize hasn't gone through the standard process of oversight, editing, and fact-checking. As a result, at a time of pandemic when expertise is most needed, baseless often-farfetched conspiracy theories echo across the outer reaches of cyberspace. These include a variety of false claims that governments are faking the public health crisis to distract the public and push through dangerous new technologies.

Fanning the flames of doubt and distrust, imagined machinations migrated from fringe internet communities into more mainline news and opinion venues. As the coronavirus, and the deadly Covid-19 disease it causes, arrived and spread across the United States and around the globe, reactionary talk show hosts like Medal—of-Freedom recipient Rush Limbaugh, consistently misinformed listeners about the dangers of the outbreak. At the Fox News Channel, morning "friends" and evening pundits like Sean Hannity along with Jeanine Pirro and Laura Ingraham, neither likely to test positive for empathy, joined the discordant rightwing ensemble discharging highly toxic distortions and disinformation.

Even among the many deniers and distorters of scientific evidence, the smooth-talking primetime television star and radio talk show host Sean Hannity stands out. This highly paid presidential cheerleader, not at all averse to amplifying White House talking points, frequently misled his audiences early on downplaying the coronavirus. He's also engaged in flawed and faulty amateur analysis and armchair epidemiology promoting unproven treatments like the anti-malarial drug hydroxychloroquine whose side effects include potentially fatal consequences, especially for those with cardiovascular disease.

Not only at high-rated cable channels like Fox News, but also at the highest levels of government, credentials and credibility no longer seem to matter. So much of what the commander-in-chief says that gets broadly reported in this war against an insidious, invisible enemy is overly simplistic, misleading, or just flat-out wrong. Staring down not only a pandemic and possible economic collapse but also a political crisis of his own, he too has touted the anti-malarial drug as a silver-bullet cure while infectious-disease experts were urging caution. Yet again, prioritizing gut feelings over scientific research and factual evidence, he even suggested that injecting disinfectants could treat Covid-19.

Amid deepening levels of administration dysfunction, the Oval Office occupant's impulses are guiding what he tells a distraught, increasingly shelter-in-place nation yearning for the return of some semblance of normalcy. According to insider accounts, his clashes with or undercutting of scientists leading the effort against the virus provoked a contentious divide within a White House already besieged as it struggles to make up for wasted time in dealing with the crisis.

The uncertainty, even in the scientific community about the pandemic's causes and the most beneficial courses of action to thwart its spread, leaves us all susceptible to entanglement in an intricate web of distortions and deceptions. The nightmare of this topsy-turvy surreal world heightens the need for professionally trained analytical, albeit nonpartisan, reporters and editors, cautiously vetting and verifying confusing and contradictory statements about such matters as the efficacy of wearing facemasks or the risks of taking ibuprofen.

The advent of the internet offered young and old alike a broad new panoply of choices, altering the whole character of news, information and entertainment as audiences become ever more fragmented. The plethora of portable laptops, smartphones, tablets, and the like has significantly increased the use of social media. The open and unfettered flow of information is an essential component of a fully functioning democratic society. As repressive measures multiply around the globe, the news media in the United States are under threat from many quarters—not only in the alternate online reality information free-for-all, but from the White House as well. President Donald Trump routinely degrades journalists, declaring the press the "enemy of the people."

Institution or Copying Machine

As if the journalist didn't have enough challenges, the assumed special constitutional protection of the profession is at issue. The stark differences between journalism today and what it was like when the Congress ratified the First Amendment in 1789 raises questions about the meaning of the word "press" in the mandate that "Congress shall make no law... abridging the freedom of speech or of the press...." The answers have wide-ranging implications in such areas as election-related expression, libel law, reporter's privilege, shield laws, and access to government property.

Judges, justices, and legal scholars have long debated whether the founders singled out the press as an *institution* to play an essential role in the discussion of public affairs, a "fourth estate" outside the government as an additional check on the three official branches; or if this provision protects everyone's use of the printing press (or its modern equivalents) as a *technology* with the institutional news media enjoying no special privileges to take part in public discourse.

In an essay on the press clause's original meaning, a UCLA law professor provides strong evidence that the founders were referring to the printing press and by implication, any future communications technology.[290] He draws on the prominent writers these framers of constitutional mandates often cited to make his argument that history and case law refute the idea that freedom of the press refers only to the institutional news media. The essay covers what the phrase likely meant during the time of the First Amendment's ratification, at the adoption of the Fourteenth Amendment in 1868, and what it has come to mean in the modern era.

Citing an extensive number of court cases, the author demonstrates that courts have consistently interpreted the press clause as protecting any individuals who use the printing press, including newspaper advertisers and authors of letters to the editor, pamphlets, magazines, and books. In other words, this clause protects an activity, not a particular set of actors like bona-fide journalists. The latter meaning has received some legal support since the 1970s, he notes, but this interpretation conflicts with the preponderance of precedent.

Facebook Forums

With the attention of a quarter of the world's population to sell to advertisers, Facebook has hugely expanded the penny-press model for making money. But its various forums, a source of significant revenue, have been plagued with a range of problems in recent years. In an attempt to sway elections, foreign agents from countries like Russia have used them to publish disinformation. Along with many other cyberspace polluters, the anti-vaccination advocates have similarly spread misleading and inaccurate information. While it employs a large team to review content whose veracity is challenged, it makes an exception for posts by political candidates.

As a consequence, during the 2016 presidential election, its platform was overrun with partisan lies and distortions, some of it Russian, that was amplified by its own algorithms. After months of indecisiveness, the social platform's executive cadre announced that unlike Google, which restricted the targeting of political ads in 2019, or Twitter, which barred political ads entirely, it would not change its basic rules for political advertising ahead of the 2020 election. Politicians will continue to be exempt from Facebook's fact-checking program. And their campaign staff and backers will still be allowed to spend millions of dollars on ads targeted to narrow slices of the electorate. They may also upload voter files to build custom audiences, and use all the other such crucial tools available through the site.

Facebook has been criticized in many circles for maintaining its policy of not fact-checking or censoring advertising and other content that political candidates post on its platforms. Mark Zuckerberg, its chief executive since the company was founded in 2004, asserted on a number of occasions that Facebook should take a hands-off approach to what people post, including lies from elected officials and others in power. In the name of free speech, the social network would not police what politicians said in political ads — even if they lied. It is not the business of being an "arbiter of truth," nor does it want to be, repeatedly saying the public should be allowed to decide what to believe.

The social platform's stance has parallels in over-the-air broadcasting. Congress long ago imposed a "no censorship" requirement on broadcasters for ads by federal, state, and local candidates. Once a candidate is legally qualified, and a station decides to accept advertising for a political race, it cannot reject candidate ads based on their content or modify them in any way. And for federal candidates, broadcasters must accept those ads once a political campaign has started. As with social media sites like Facebook, broadcasters are immune from any legal claims that may arise from the content of over-the-air candidate ads. If a candidate's ad is defamatory, or if it infringes on someone's copyright, the aggrieved party has a remedy against the candidate who sponsored the ad. Still, that party has no legal recourse against the broadcaster.

Although Facebook gives wide latitude to politicians and campaigns, the platform does occasionally act on hateful expression. The Trump campaign had been running ads blaming, without any evidence, the far-left network known as Antifa (pronounced "an-TEE-fuh") for the looting and rioting that rose during anti-police-brutality protests in cities across the nation. In June 2020, after public backlash, Facebook, which had approved the ads, deactivated dozens of them featuring an inverted red triangle. The Nazis used the symbol to mark political prisoners and people who rescued Jews. Contrary to Trump administration claims of its extensive use by Antifa, supporters of the loose-knit anti-fascist network tend to use a different symbol—two flags surrounded by a circle—that dates back to opponents of the Nazis in 1930s Germany.

Businesses ranging from social networking services to little-known data brokers collect all kinds of information about consumers, often without their knowledge or consent. In 2014, the upstart Cambridge Analytica, backed Robert Mercer, a wealthy Republican donor, harvested private information from Facebook's profiles of more than fifty million users without their permission to create voter profiles of a huge swath of the American electorate, developing techniques that underpinned its work on Donald Trump's presidential campaign in 2016.

Among many downsides in Facebook's digital environment is the proliferation of scams. The social network's fastest growing demographic in the United States is people over fifty-five, a group especially vulnerable to "love scams." As two *Times* reporters explain, users of the popular site—often young men in Nigeria—steal the digital photos and identities of American military personnel.[291] Posing as the service members, the scammers make a "friend request" to seek out vulnerable and lonely older women, forming an emotional connection with the aim of tricking them out of money. The emotional toll these scams take on the victims, who often send the scammer much of their life savings, is depicted in a recent episode of the paper's *Weekly* television series.

Anyone with a hidden agenda can potentially don the cloak of anonymity to set up a site and spew false or misleading stories. As one example among many, the surreptitiously Kremlin-backed serious-sounding Internet Research Agency interfered in the 2016 election, stealing the identities of American citizens and spreading incendiary messages on Facebook and other social media platforms to stoke discord on race, religion and other issues aimed at influencing voters, with misspellings, and grammatical and syntactical mishaps exposing the nefarious machinations.

Computer programs have gotten much better at processing vast amounts of text, making them more effective at ferreting telltale social media manipulation signals such as semantic errors and common hashtags. Undeterred, the Russian operatives at the agency are using different tactics to cancel itself more effectively. Among these tactics are publishing "fake news" stories, then using legions of fake social media accounts to amplify those and other messages. They boost their ranking in search results — and to spread them across social media platforms and in groups on private messaging apps. The fake accounts also make comments designed to give false weight to specific sentiments, both positive and negative, in line with their clients' interests. (This form of artificial grassroots expression is known as "astroturfing.")

While Facebook has struggled with issues such as election interference and privacy concerns in recent years, its juggernaut digital ads business continued to power the company's social media platforms. But facing pressure from the Anti-Defamation League, the NAAP, and other civil rights groups, the issues of hate speech and disinformation have catapulted to ad agency agendas. The big-name advertisers object to the world's largest social media company's handling of these hot-button matters. With an eye toward the bottom line, Mark Zuckerberg is striking a more conciliatory approach. Among other measures, he banned 250 white supremacist organizations from its core Facebook site and its photo-sharing site, Instagram.

The birthers are back centering on a candidate of color soon after Joe Biden selected Kamala Harris as his vice-presidential running mate. Social networking sites, including Facebook, were buzzing with memes and conspiracy postings, claiming she is ineligible to serve. The paper-thin argument about her status has no constitutional basis. That neither of her parents was a legal resident for five years before her birth, and they didn't raise her in the United States during childhood are irrelevant. The land's highest elected office requirements are straightforward and have nothing to do with one's parents' naturalization status. One must be born in the United States or to a parent who is a citizen of this country, be thirty-five years of age or older, and have been a resident in the United States for at least fourteen years. Harris meets all of these requirements.

Legislation enacted when the Facebook founder was a lad of eleven prevents the government from removing sites that harbor hate. A provision in Title V of the Telecommunications Act of 1996, Section 230 of the mostly defunct Communications Decency Act, provides immunity from liability for interactive computer services that publish information provided by others. In *Zeran v. America Online*, a defamation case involving the 1995 Oklahoma City bombing, the fourth circuit court of appeals held that Congress considered the weight of the speech interests implicated and chose to immunize service providers to avoid any such restrictive effect.[292] The courts have repeatedly sided with internet firms, invoking a broad interpretation of immunity.

Tweeting Time

One of the most recognizable and influential social media platforms on the planet, Twitter, emerging in 2006 from the ashes of a failed podcast startup, incorporates instant messaging technologies to create networks of users who can communicate throughout the day with brief messages, or "tweets." To turn a profit, Twitter, four years later, inaugurated "promoted tweets." A company pays so that a tweet, account, or trend (such as a particular hashtag) will show up on users' feeds, with money paid out on a per-click and per-retweet basis. According to several reports, within five years, this attention-selling model generated around $400 million in revenue. Creating a dialogue of sorts in cyberspace, this self-proclaimed offspring of co-founder Jack Dorsey, savvy at selling himself, attracts over three million monthly active users. They post a staggering 500 million tweets a day. The bluebird logoed Twitter, as a matter of first necessity and then branding, initially limited its users to 140-word count, doubled to 280 in November 2018. The tweets range from jokes to news to nastiness.

The platform's reach and influence can be enormous, not just for pundits and politicians but for anyone, even an avian enthusiast subject to racial prejudice. In late May 2020, a fifty-seven-year-old black birdwatcher searched for sparrows, scarlet tanagers, swallows, and other songbirds that wing their way into Central Park's Ramble. This lush woodland comprising thirty-eight acres is an unusually rich habitat for birds. Its meandering pathways are also popular with dog walkers, including a fortyish white woman with a blond cocker spaniel.

Startled from his quiet birding by this woman loudly calling after her dog, he asked her to leash the clamorous canine, as the park rules required. When she refused the request, they exchanged words. As he recorded on his smartphone, she threatened to report: "An African-American man is threatening my life," a blatantly false accusation. Before and during her 911 "emergency" call, as his video clip shows, she referred to him as "African-American" three times, seemingly using the term as a weapon. His sister later posted the clip to Twitter, where it went viral getting more than forty million hits.

The posted encounter touched a nerve, evoking for many a long history of white women making false charges against black men, sometimes with deadly consequences. A few hours after this incident, George Floyd would be killed in Minneapolis when a white police officer pressed his knee on the black man's neck. The two events captured on video represent two facets of what too often black people experience; one police brutality, the other routine bigotry.

For years the San Francisco-based company took a hands-off approach to moderating the posts on its platform. That brought it acclaim when it enabled dissidents to tweet about political protests, like the Egyptian revolution in 2011. But it also allowed trolls, bots and malicious operatives onto the site. Serving as the epicenter for harassment, misinformation and abuse has put it at the forefront of controversy. Hardly a day goes by where it doesn't find itself in the headlines, usually resulting from President Donald Trump's extensive use of the social media platform. Having some 80 million followers, his tweets—bullying, cajoling and spreading falsehoods—have sparked commentary on all sides of the political spectrum.

For its part, the company repeatedly responded that the president's messages did not violate its terms of service and that while he may have skirted the line of what was accepted under its rules, he never crossed it. That changed in May 2020 after the president repeatedly implicated former Republican congressman and MSNBC commentator Joe Scarborough in the death of an intern, Lori Klausutis. The young woman died in 2001 from complications of an undiagnosed heart condition while in his employ. He was over 800 miles away at the time.

In mid-August 2020, Twitter temporarily blocked the Trump election campaign account from tweeting until it removed a post with a video clip from a Fox News interview in which the president urged schools to reopen, falsely claiming that children are "almost immune from this disease." Facebook also removed a post containing the same video from Trump's personal page. Both Facebook and Twitter said the post violated their rules on Covid-19 misinformation.

Later in the month, after years of pressure over its inaction on the president's false and threatening posts, Twitter added links to two of his tweets in which he had posted about mail-in ballots. He falsely claimed that they would cause the November presidential election to be "rigged." In blue lettering at the bottom of the posts and punctuated by an exclamation mark, they urged its users to "get the facts" about voting by mail. Clicking on the links led to a CNN story that said the president's claims were unsubstantiated and to a list of bullet points that Twitter had compiled rebutting the inaccuracies.

In a tweet, the president, advocating violence, murder and imminent threat against looters said the company was "interfering in the 2020 Presidential Election." He added, in another post, that it was "completely stifling FREE SPEECH." A few days later, he signed an executive order directing federal regulators to crack down on companies like

Twitter and to consider taking away the legal protections under Section 230 shielding them from liability for what gets posted on their platforms.

The company has also cracked down on QAnon, shutting down some 7,000 of its Twitter accounts. The loose-knit rightwing group, whose adherents are starting to win elective office, promotes a baseless conspiracy theory alleging a "deep state" apparatus run by pedophile political elites, business leaders, and Hollywood celebrities. Extreme even by social media standards, many of its followers believe that this "worldwide cabal of satanic pedophiles" runs "all the major levers of power," including government, news media, big business, and the movie industry. Despite the Tweeter shutdowns, the boogaloo movement is gaining momentum.

The role of Twitter in social discourse has come under increasing scrutiny across the globe. In Europe, where some of the strictest laws against the sharing of hate speech, violent content, and misinformation exist, Twitter has found itself struggling to balance its company's policies with the laws of the countries it operates in. In 2018, Twitter received over 500,000 complaints about posts that violated German hate speech laws. After years of shrugging off concerns about the negative effects of hateful and inflammatory content on its platform, it took down ten percent of the flagged posts. Like other social media sites, Twitter is grappling with how to moderate content and take responsibility without losing legal protections.

The immensely popular platform is also struggling with security breaches. In mid-July 2020, someone hacked into the accounts of the social media network's most vibrant and most famous tweeters, including former President Barack Obama, presumptive Democratic presidential nominee Joe Biden, Amazon CEO Jeff Bezos, and rapper Kanye West. The celebrity accounts posted the same strange message: Send Bitcoin and double your money. The hacker managed to scam more than $100,000 in Bitcoin from duped users. The principal suspects include a teenager who recently graduated high school. Many kids these days are skilled computer users. But this was a highly sophisticated hack on a magnitude not seen before showing even the mighty are vulnerable in cyberspace.

Weaving Pleasing Masks

Communications philosopher Marshall McLuhan's maxim that the printing press helped release the ego by extending the dimensions of space and time is a million times truer for the internet. A plethora of photo-posting sites tap into narcissistic tendencies, an all-consuming, all but erotic self-absorption—practical in a pandemic. The term traces its origin in Greek mythology. Narcissus was a beautiful lad who harshly rejected the love of a nymph. As vengeance, the gods made him fall hopelessly in love with himself. He couldn't take his eyes from his reflection on the water's glassy surface as he bent to slake his thirst at a spring and pined away until he turned into the narcissus flower.

The range of global platforms in cyberspace, and the prospect of many "like" clicks, has let loose a "narcissism epidemic," as millions create a photo persona that inflates the sense of self-worth and youthfulness, including sexually discarded victims of ageism. Many women of a certain age, perhaps taking a cue from septuagenarian superstar rocker Cher, with nips and tucks, fat sucked from the hips, thighs, and abdomen, Botox injections, and an abundance of makeup masquerade as thirty-somethings. The

careful selection of online images and thoughtful comments and reactions for profile enhancement bears on the insights of Erving Goffman decades ago. The still widely-read sociologist used the metaphor of theatrical performance as a framework for analyzing social actions and interaction.[293] His basic premise is that in ordinary social discourse, we present ourselves to others in attempts to guide and control the impressions. We form and employ specific techniques to sustain performances, just as a professional actor inhabits a character aided by makeup, lighting, costumes, and set designs.

Goffman conceives social life in theatrical terms as a "performance" carried out by groups or troupes of participants in three places: "front stage," "backstage," and "off stage." We play different roles during our daily lives and display various kinds of behavior depending on where we are, and the time of day. All of us fellow actors, as it were, whether consciously or otherwise, behave somewhat differently as our stage selves than we do off stage. The front stage behavior of exhibitionists, and more reserved types as well, generally follows an imitated or internalized social script.

Waiting in line for something, boarding a bus and flashing a transit pass, and exchanging pleasantries about the weekend with fellow students or colleagues are examples of highly routinized and scripted front-stage performances. The routines of our daily lives—traveling to and from work, shopping, dining out, or going to a museum or gallery—all fall into the category of front stage behavior. The "performances" we put on with those around us follow established rules and expectations for what we should do and discuss in each setting. We also engage in front stage behavior in less public places such as among colleagues at work and as students in classrooms.

Whatever the setting of front stage behavior, we tend to be aware of how others perceive us and what they expect, and this knowledge guides our practice, hoping for perpetual "like" clicks. Such expectations shape not just what's said and done in social settings but how we dress and style ourselves, the consumer items we carry around, and our behavior (assertive, demure, pleasant, hostile, etc.). When we engage in backstage performances, we feel freer from the norms and expectations dictating our onstage act. We are often more relaxed and comfortable when backstage; we let our guard down and behave in ways that reflect our uninhibited or "true" selves. Casting off elements of onstage appearance, we may even change how we speak and comport our bodies or carry ourselves.

Even when backstage, our lives involve others, such as partners, family members, and comfortable colleagues. We may not behave formally as standard frontstage behavior dictates, but don't entirely let down our guards. Our backstage actions mirror the way professional actors behave in the wings of a theater, waiters in the kitchen of a restaurant, or those admitted to "employee only" areas of retail shops. We are still conscious of norms and expectations, although they likely vary depending on the circumstance. In private, offstage moments, we sometimes behave in ways that we never would in public or even backstage.

This theatrical framework is all the more applicable to the digital age. Wayfarers traversing cyberspace offer a particular self on one platform. Other aspects of personality are full-throttle on another platform—although, as in real life, the different people may bleed into one another across platforms and friendships. In a process coined "context collapse," a social media user with a particular public mask may share an incongruent feeling or make crude remarks but expects that the intended group's special social norms and practices are at play. Then another social media user, not part of the peer group, might encounter it using a different set of standards, values, and practices.

This phenomenon can often occur among political leaders when private remarks contradict a carefully crafted persona. During a 2020 "Pod Save America" interview, recently revealed, former UN ambassador Susan Rice, President Obama's point person on Benghazi, made remarks she thought would stay in her circle. When co-host and former deputy national security adviser Ben Rhodes commented, "You have to understand Benghazi to understand [President] Trump." Another advisor chimed in, "Right, because Lindsey Graham isn't just a piece of shit now," before Rice interrupted. "He's been a piece of shit," she agreed. "He's a piece of shit." The salty language offers a contrasting peek behind the theatrical mask she dons on interview shows like NPR's Morning Edition during which her performances are forceful but dignified.

Curiously, for many, part of the president's appeal seems to be his authenticity. When his offstage bragging, say about crotch-grabbing, moves onstage, owing to a copying machine, his fans both male and female might see such remarks as in character, merely the boasting they typically hear at a neighborhood tavern. After the revelation, several tavern news interviews seemed to confirm this interpretation, although such anecdotes hardly comprise a systematic survey.

All the same, they point to a pattern. To prop up a shaky real estate enterprise, as an example in point, Trump made some money on the side as a promoter of professional wrestling, a close cousin to the old circus "freak shows," shamelessly exploiting abnormalities. Even his most sycophant enthusiasts might gasp at his backstage behavior revealed in books like *Fire and Fury*.[294] Having ready access to the White House inner sanctums, the author shows a level of cattiness, cynicism, and cruelty that rarely moves to the center stage.

Profit-Producing Personae

The theatrical masks public figures don can have considerable monetary value. A fairly recent tort called the "right of publicity" can make their image, name, likeness, or other defining aspects very marketable. Tracing its roots to a 1950s court ruling about baseball cards, this "property right" has become a lot more complicated and difficult to control in the internet age. Virtually anyone can combine pages of text, photos, audio, and video for almost no cost. And they can share them with the entire world, all at once. This ease of creating, copying, and circulating occurred as the property value of specific public figures, alive or dead, skyrocketed.

The right of publicity is a creature of state law, either arising under statute or at common law. Some thirty-five states protect the economic value of the name or likeness of well-known persons. A photo or drawing of the celebrity or even something more ephemeral like an idiosyncratic gesture or the distinctive sound and style of a singer may qualify for protection.

To put it in legal sounding language, a cause of action seeking redress for violation of the right of publicity is not the exclusive purview of the famous. Indeed, fame per se is not an element that needs to be proven. But the courts do focus on the value of the property in question and tend not to find in favor of those without public figure status, often, it seems because there is no perceived value in the persona of the average person. A plaintiff must show the recognizable aspects of his or her identity—visage, voice, general appearance—has economic value.

Some eighteen states recognize a right of publicity that continues after death. This posthumous commercial value can be assigned or licensed or bequeathed by will. The after-death right's duration varies from ten years from the date of the demise to 100 years in states like Indiana and Oklahoma. California provides for the right to survive seventy years after the end of a celebrity's life. Some have statutes that cover both the living and the dead, and others, like New Jersey, recognize a common law right of publicity. The estate of rocker and movie star Elvis Presley has driven much of Tennessee's law on the right of publicity. Since 1984 a statutory right has been in place that protects both the living and, unsurprisingly, the dead indefinitely.

For public figures and celebrities of all kinds, visits from the Grim Reaper can prove to be very profitable. Of course, the expired, departed, gone, lost, lamented, perished, fallen, slain, slaughtered, killed, or murdered won't see a penny after the expiration of corporal existence. The heirs reap the rewards from such "passing away," a euphemism many find oddly comforting. This form of postmortem immortality has created a whole new industry built on acquiring and marketing dead people. The images, old movie clips, and voices of long-deceased social figures or celebrities have become ubiquitous, enjoying an immortality of sorts. The 1950s Civil Rights pioneer Rosa Parks sells Chevy trucks, and renowned physicist Albert Einstein peddles everything from baby products to Apple computers.

The marketing, licensing, and commercial use of dead celebrities has become a multi-billion business. Based in Los Angeles and serving clients in more than fifty countries, GreenLight is the duly appointed exclusive licensing agent for the Hebrew University of Jerusalem. It is authorized to secure new business ventures related to all utilizations of the Albert Einstein persona, including name, voice, signature, photographs, likeness, and image of Albert Einstein. It also is charged with vigorously pursuing all unauthorized uses of Albert Einstein's creations, appellations, copyrights, right of publicity, photographs, trademarks and characterizations, and to prosecute and maintain trademark and copyright registrations on behalf of The Hebrew University of Jerusalem.

Einstein made the university the beneficiary of all of his intellectual property rights, including his publicity rights. The November 2009 "Sexiest Man Alive" issue of *People* magazine carried an ad to promote the GMC Terrain SUV, explaining, "THAT'S WHY WE GAVE IT MORE IDEAS PER SQUARE INCH." The Hebrew Uni-

versity of Jerusalem sued for misappropriation of Einstein's rights of publicity. In Los Angeles, a federal judge ruled that an automobile manufacturer's unauthorized use of an altered image of Nobel laureate Albert Einstein in an advertisement, though "tasteless," was not unlawful. The court determined that New Jersey courts would limit that state's postmortem right of publicity to a maximum period of fifty years. Because the famed physicist died in 1955, the claimant could no longer enforce his persona's publicity rights.

Had the great physicist last resided in New York, he would have had no descendible right of publicity, as this state doesn't recognize postmortem publicity rights. The fading star Marilyn Monroe had residences in both New York City and Brentwood, California. When she expired at age thirty-six from an overdose of barbiturates, to avoid substantial California estate, inheritance, and income taxes, her lawyer and executor declared she died a New York citizen. At Monroe's death, neither New York nor California recognized a descendant, posthumous right of publicity. As the District Court explained, the California legislature didn't make publicity rights inheritable until 1984, decades after Monroe's 1962 death. The Ninth Circuit Court of Appeals confirmed that the late movie star's heirs had no right of publicity over her image.[295]

A New York federal district court came to the same conclusion. After the death of the photographer who took some of the famous star's images, including the iconic image of her standing above a subway grate with her white skirt billowing in the wind, family members asserted that they could sell the photos for commercial use without paying a license fee. The U.S. District Court for the Southern District of New York agreed. It held that because Monroe died before the passage of California's Celebrity Rights Act in 1985 and because New York does not recognize a postmortem right of publicity, her name, image and voice were in the public domain in New York and California. As she or a ghostwriter once prophetically proclaimed: "I knew I belonged to the public and the world, not because I was talented or even beautiful but because I had never belonged to anyone else." Her sexy persona sells hundreds of different products worldwide.

Because the states primarily govern the right of publicity, the degree of recognition of the publicity rights can vary. Corporate owners

of these rights tend to settle in states with extensive property rights protection like Indiana. The Hoosier state provides recognition for 100 years after the death and protecting not only the usual "name, image and likeness," but also signature, photographs, gestures, distinctive appearances, and mannerisms. Headquartered in Indiana, CMC Worldwide's dead-people client roster includes everyone from Billie Holiday, Malcolm X, and Amelia Earhart to Mark Twain, Chuck Berry, Ingrid Bergmann, and Frank Lloyd Wright.

One of the global company's most valuable properties is James Dean, who died at the age of twenty-four when he crashed his Porsche Spyder convertible. When authorities brought his mangled body to the morgue, he had appeared in only three major movies, *East of Eden* (1955), *Rebel Without a Cause* (1955), and *Giant* (1955), the latter two released posthumously. Dean's amorphous, seemingly real-life, rhythms struck an unusually strong emotional chord with teenagers of the 1950s. He seemed to become the embodiment of restless American youths, an expression of all their anguish and alienation. The admiration of his fans grew posthumously to legendary proportions. His father, and ultimately his father's relatives, reap millions of dollars each year from his name, likeness, and image on everything from posters and apparel to fridge magnets. Dean's enduring appeal to advertisers pursuing the youth market lies in the fact that he never grew old.

After the right of publicity cases baffled lower courts for decades, the United States Supreme Court in 1977 took up the matter. The plaintiff, Hugo Zacchini, renowned for his fifteen-second "human cannonball" act, brought a claim against the defendant, an Ohio broadcasting company, for wrongfully appropriating his "professional property" by taping and broadcasting his death-defying feat without his consent. The Ohio trial court granted the defendant's motion for summary judgment. The state court of appeal unanimously reversed, holding that no First Amendment privilege guarded the defendant against the plaintiff's copyright infringement claims. The Ohio Supreme Court recognized the state common law "right to the publicity" value of his performance, but found that the defendant had a privilege to report "matters of legitimate public interest."

Justice Byron White, writing for the 5-4 majority, reversed the Ohio Supreme Court.[296] He explained that a state law right of publicity functions to compensate entertainers for the time and effort dedicated to performing and provides an economic incentive to create future creative acts. He emphasized the importance of the defendant's broadcasting the full human cannonball performance, finding that this wholesale appropriation went to the heart of his ability to earn a living as an entertainer. It's the only high court ruling on rights of publicity, and it served to confirm the overall validity of the doctrine and the interests it protects. Whether implicated by video games, nationwide advertising campaigns, or platinum-selling records, a wide swath of expression across a broad range of media platforms is potentially subject to "right of publicity" protections.

Before cyberspace's population explosion, celebrity rights were mostly about distributing print, tangible items, audiovisual materials, and broadcasts. The economics of these significant media meant that legal disputes mostly involved celebrities against businesses. Only businesses, not consumers, had the equipment and resources to create an infringing work worth pursuing in court. The costs of distribution meant that most infringing works were small-scale and contained in a particular region. The parties, jurisdiction, and scope of legal disputes were all easily defined.

In the digital age, with even society's youngest members connected by smartphones and social media services, fewer barriers to celebrities exist than ever before. Holograms, avatars, and CGI of alive and deceased celebrities circulate across cyberspace. Celebrities in one country are often pursuing claims against defendants in another, forcing courts to determine if they even have jurisdiction over the subject-matter and also personal jurisdiction over the parties.

While advances in technology make fame easier to attain, at the same time, they make it more challenging to maintain it for moneymaking purposes. As fame becomes more fluid, celebrities, those well-known for being well-known, now aggressively guard images and identities to protect their publicity rights against encroachment. Protecting against this form of identity thief implicates another kind of expression: freedom of expression under the First Amendment. The tension between these rights is not new. Still, the digital age makes interactions far more complicated for celebrities seeking to preserve property rights over images, likenesses, and personae.

An attempt at resolving the global issues concerning disputes over the right to publicity on the internet is the Uniform Domain-Name Dispute-Resolution Policy, a process established by the Internet Corporation for Assigned Names and Numbers to resolve disputes regarding the registration of internet domain names. When internet domain names are registered, registrants effectively agree by contract to resolve disputes as to the "rightful ownership" by arbitration. The UDRP eliminates much of the preliminary matters of determining a proper jurisdiction or venue because it contracts with the domain name registrant. It mandates that a single referee handle the dispute.

Cyberspace Distortions

Cyberspace is awash in rumors, innuendos, outright falsehoods, and crazy conspiracy theories. Internet surfers may seek out the consensus and deviance that reinforces their worldviews residing, as it were, in information bubbles or cultural echo chambers. Activists and aspiring entertainers as well as hate mongers of any political bent find each other and link up on a global scale. All too often, fringe group attacks and risky maneuvers impede psychic exploration of cybervillage waystations. A looming threat is the confluence of social media, algorithmic news selection, bots, artificial intelligence, and big data analysis. A computer program or "bot" that performs an automatic repetitive task intended for malicious purposes can quickly infest news outlets and major platforms like Twitter, Facebook, and Instagram. Innovations in machine learning and artificial intelligence allow for ever-more realistic bots targeting people precisely with the kind of propaganda they'll believe.

The advent of digital photography offers a whole new realm of opportunity for the manipulation, reproduction, and transmission of images. As one example out of many, in the aftermath of the shooting at Marjory Stoneman Douglas High School in Parkland, Florida on February 2018, a number of the students emerged as potent voices in the national debate over gun control. Emma Gonzalez, a student who survived the attack, in particular, gained prominence thanks to the closing speech she delivered during the "March for Our Lives" protest in Washington, D.C. She also wrote a contemporaneous article for *Teen Vogue.* The magazine piece incorporated a video entitled "This Is Why We March," including a visually arresting sequence in which Gonzalez rips up a large sheet displaying a bullseye target. Soon someone generated a fake version in which the torn sheet is not a bullseye, but rather a copy of the Constitution of the United States. The doctored video went viral, triggering many threats to the young woman's life.

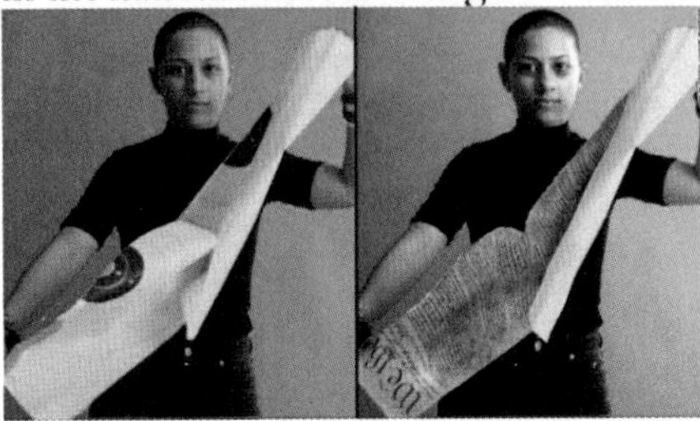

The cover of the *New York Daily News* featured a photo of an almost-two-year-old Honduran girl crying as her mother is questioned near the U.S.-Mexico border on June 12, 2018, in McAllen, Texas. Superimposed over the image are the words: Callous, Soulless, Craven, Trump. At the bottom of the pages is the sentence: "Prez's edict led to 2,000 children ripped from parents at the border in the past six weeks." This image of a crying toddler was widely used by online outlets to illustrate stories about children taken from their parents after attempting to cross the border.

A bright red cover of *Time* featured the toddler isolated from her original surroundings with president Donald Trump towering over her with the caption "Welcome to America." As was later revealed, the toddler and her mother were not separated. Agents patted down the mother for less than two minutes, and she immediately picked up her daughter, who then stopped crying. As might be expected, the misleading image prompted a round of media criticism from the White House and other supportive outlets.

Doctored images of teenage climate-change activist Greta Thunberg circulate about cyberspace. One bogus meme has her posing for a photograph with a member of ISIS. In the manipulated image of her with Al Gore at a United Nations climate conference in Poland in December 2018, multi-billionaire George Soros, a bugaboo for many right-wingers, replaces the vice-president. She also appears on the cover of a non-existent magazine, "People with Money" with the false claim she is the highest-paid activist. A satirical news website included this fake magazine cover in a phony article making this fabricated claim with few disclaimers.

Computer-generated bogus videos made with cutting-edge artificial intelligence software, dubbed "deepfakes," challenge assumptions about what is real and what is not. With the potential to set the world afire with falsehood, this software could do irreparable damage, smearing politicians, fabricating revenge porn, perverting celebrities, and deceitfully incriminating someone. The potential for misbehavior is boundless. Teams of researchers at internet firms like Google and Facebook are creating tools to detect digital skullduggery. But development in artificial intelligence technologies is streamlining the process, reducing the cost, time, and skill needed to doctor digital images. Morphing one person's facial features and expressions on another's body, leaving very few traces of manipulation, is becoming commonplace.

A deepfake porn video circulating in cyberspace features former first-lady Michelle Obama's digital doppelgänger. She is wearing a low-cut top with a black bra visible underneath, lustily writhing while accentuating her deep cleavage in front of the camera before matters become more hardcore.

With the technology so rapidly advancing, the fight against deepfakes and other forms of online trickery will require nearly constant vigilance along with reinvention. Along with other sites, Facebook has worked at deleting deepfakes and limiting the reach of hoax-purveying sites in users' news feeds, inhibiting but not by any means eradicating the spread of fake news stories as well as distorting and damaging digital doppelgängers. The problem seems intractable. Many more bogus sites pop up by the time one is taken down.

Virtual Vigilantes

The ubiquity of the internet, making it possible to gather, publish, and distribute news with breakneck speed at little or next to no cost, also fosters inaccuracies, distortions, conspiracy claims, and even outright attacks and threats. The venom and vitriol that virtual vigilantes are inflicting upon Dr. Anthony S. Fauci, the director of the National Institute of Allergy and Infectious Diseases and a thirty-year veteran of dealing with global epidemics have been relentless.

As a member of the Trump administration's coronavirus task force, Fauci is one of two doctors, along with Dr. Deborah Birx, assigned by the White House to explain this emergency to the public through daily briefings and interviews. In the face of hospitals exceeding capacity, nurses and doctors overstretched, insufficient medical supplies and equipment, mounting deaths, and loss of livelihoods, accurate information from creditable scientists has never been more essential.

The federal government's top infectious-disease expert since 1984, Fauci's willingness to correct or qualify the president's misinformation, flights of fancy, and perhaps well-intended palliative but specious assertions about containing the virus unleashed a barrage of vitriol and vilification on Facebook, Twitter, and YouTube. The doctor's detractors not only discredited him but also dismissed scientific expertise in general as unreliable and dishonest. An analysis by the *New York Times* found over seventy accounts on Twitter that have promoted the hashtag #FauciFraud, with some tweeting as frequently as 795 times a day.[297] The severity of the threats prompted the government to enhance his security. On a brighter note, Dr. Fauci has inspired some clever videos (click box).

The campaign against one of the world's leading infectious disease experts as states and agencies of the federal government battle a deadly pathogen spreading with unnerving speed is not only deluded and self-destructive but also downright dangerous. Such fanatical support for a leader—especially one so seemingly over his head, ego absorbed, and promoting his prospects for reelection to a second term with unabashed bluster and boastful bravado—turning a blind eye to the pandemic and denigrating those battling it for telling the truth defies all logic and even the survival instinct itself.

To less fiercely partisan, more analytical observers, albeit highly critical and at times acerbic, the "foot-spur-deferred" commander-in-chief, once again seemed fearful of entering the fray even though he likely knew of the deadly disease's dire threat in January 2020. As *New York Times* reporter Maggie Haberman points out in a well-documented article, a White House trade adviser warned in a detailed memo that the coronavirus crisis could cost the United States trillions of dollars and put millions of Americans at risk of illness or death.[298] It circulated inside the West Wing during a period when the president was playing down the risks to the United States, and he would later go on to say that no one could have predicted such a devastating outcome.

The self-proclaimed "wartime president" was still downplaying the danger at the time of a widely circulated second trade advisor memo almost a month later predicting a full-blown Covid-19 pandemic. A *Washington Post* reporting team noted that his denials, delays, and dysfunction sowed significant public confusion and contradicted the urgent messages of public health experts. By leaving the spread of the virus unchecked, he likely contributed to thousands of deaths, tens of thousands of infections, and perhaps paralyzing many aspects of American life for the foreseeable future.[299]

Spurred on by inflammatory presidential tweets, some linking jobs and gun rights, the self-identified "back-to-work" protesters in several states have demanded that restrictions on businesses and public gatherings be lifted, insulting not only state and municipal political leaders seeking to protect the public health but also the army of health professionals putting life on the line to keep a cap on the pandemic's spread. The dilemma is that long overdue widespread testing may implode the economy and shatter already frayed nerves. Putting individual rights over community responsibility undercuts public health practices that only work in a pandemic if broadly followed. One person's "liberty" may translate into ventilators for many others.

Lincoln Project

Derisive remarks about the president's many faults may seem partisan, but they are about the man himself, not any particular party or social cause. Democrats and Republicans have been highly critical of him. The Lincoln Project, for example, is an American political action committee formed in late 2019 by disenchanted Republicans. Its advisory board includes pollical operative Steve Schmidt, who worked on a slew of major Republican political campaigns, including those of President George W. Bush and Arizona Senator John McCain. As might be expected, hardly everyone in the grand old party is marching in lockstep behind the "renegade" Republicans.

THE LINCOLN PROJECT

In a *New York Times* op-ed piece, three of the founders explained the rationale for the project: "Patriotism and the survival of our nation in the face of the crimes, corruption and corrosive nature of Donald Trump are a higher calling than mere politics. As Americans, we must stem the damage he and his followers are doing to the rule of law, the Constitution and the American character."[300]

The project produced several anti-Trump advertisements that attracted attention across the political spectrum. The *Washington Post*'s conservative political columnist, Jennifer Rubin, a harsh critic of Trump, called the project's ads "devastating for several reasons: They are produced with lightning speed, and thereby catch the public debate at just the right moment. They hammer Trump where he is personally most vulnerable... and they rely to a large extent on Trump himself—his words and actions."[301]

Its release entitled "Chyna" attacks Trump on his China policy, with narration saying, "They know who Donald Trump is: weak, corrupt, ridiculed, China beats him every time. No matter what he says, China's got his number." The ad attacks Trump for his handling of the trade war with China and refers to his daughter Ivanka Trump's business dealings in China, including the Chinese government's grant of trademarks. The release drew upon Trump's former National Security Adviser, archconservative John Bolton's excerpt from his memoir, *The Room Where It Happened,* a scathing critique of Trump's arrogance, narcissism, and sheer incompetence.[302]

Among many damning revelations, Bolton states that Trump asked Chinese president Xi Jinping to assist him in getting elected and had told the Communist leader that he should continue building internment camps detaining Uyghurs. Native to northwest China, the Turkic-speaking Muslims have long-experienced persecution, with over a million of them confined in re-education camps to ensure adherence to national ideology.

Harboring Hate

Such metaphors as hives, bubbles, cocoons, and echo chambers capture quite well the way websites serve to isolate people from contradictory facts and points of views, and endlessly reinforce existing beliefs, attitudes, and opinions, along with percolating morbid thoughts and toxic fantasies. Within the confines of such sites, fanatics, malcontents, and conspirators of all kinds are weaponizing social media, connecting with, among others, marginalized white supremacists and alienated Muslim youths worldwide.

For several decades, Dallas-born extremist radio host Alex Jones has been spreading dark and bizarre theories through airwaves and across cyberspace. These include that the federal government caused the 1995 Oklahoma City bombing, the 2012 Sandy Hook Elementary School, and the 2018 Stoneman Douglas High School shootings were hoaxes, and Democrats run a worldwide child-sex ring. Among many other incredible claims, he asserted global warming is part of a plot by the World Bank to control the world economy through a carbon tax.

By the time Apple, Google, Facebook, and Spotify severely restricted his Infowars website's reach in August 2018, Jones drew some ten million monthly visits, making his range more extensive than many of the bona fide media news websites. These days he's peddling overpriced vitamin products claiming they cure the coronavirus, attributing its source to American-made biological weapons.

The anonymous message board of the forum website 8chan provides a place for airing and spreading violent and often racist messages. The deadly attacks on the shopping mall in El Paso, Texas, the mosques in Christchurch, New Zealand, and the synagogue in Poway, California, were all announced on 8chan's message board before they began. Like other websites, 8chan relies on a complex network of internet infrastructure businesses crucial to keeping sites up and running. Dozens of these companies provide web addresses, cloud computing power, and other underlying mechanisms that websites need to be quickly and easily accessible at a low cost.

A San Francisco-based security firm called Cloudflare provides the tools that protect websites from cyber-attacks and allows them to load content more quickly. The more than nineteen million internet properties that use its service have ranged from 8chan and the neo-Nazi-run *Daily Stormer* to Twitter and Facebook, where extremists also gather. Without this kind of protection, sites can be barraged by automated, hard-to-prevent attacks from its critics, making it nearly impossible to stay online.

Although it has no legal requirement to do so, Cloudflare succumbed to enormous social pressure to remove cyberattack protection first from *Daily Stormer* and then from 8chan essentially rendering them inoperable. Such internet infrastructure companies fill the ever-growing need for services. The termination of accounts because of social or political pressure rarely proves useful. After being denied protection in 2017, following the violent rally in Charlottesville, Virginia, the *Daily Stormer* quickly came back online using a competitor. These private infrastructure companies or platforms like Facebook playing the role of content arbiter puts us on a slippery slope toward censorship without any constitutional safeguards.

True Threats

The proliferation of private, encrypted messaging makes legal surveillance based on reliable information all the more necessary, as hateful rhetoric and threatening remarks of all kinds circulate throughout cyberspace. The difficulty of discerning what legally constitutes genuine threat from exaggerated rhetoric or hyperbole exacerbates the problem of monitoring potentially dangerous behavior and acting to prevent it from actualizing. In 1939, Congress enacted a law, now 18 U.S.C. § 875(c), that prohibits interstate communications that contain a threat to kidnap or injure another person. The statute has raised fundamental free speech concerns over what constitutes a "true threat," especially over the internet.

Significant in the history of the true threat First Amendment exemption is the case involving the University of Michigan student Jake Baker (given name Abraham Jacob Alkhabaz). In 1995, he posted on the electronic bulletin board of the "alt.sex.stories" newsgroup, publicly available via the internet, graphic details of the imagined rape, torture, and murder of one of his female classmates living in the same dorm. Baker also exchanged violent sexual fantasies with a Canadian correspondent. The two men planned to meet in Ann Arbor to fulfill their fantasy of sexually attacking girls and women. Both agreed, for starters, hurting the body and defiling the innocence of a thirteen or fourteen-year-old girl would be especially fun.

A grand jury indicted Baker under the 1939 federal statute. Still, a federal district court quashed this indictment stating "only unequivocal, unconditional and specific expressions of intention immediately to inflict injury may be punished."[303] The government appealed this decision. The Sixth U.S. Court of Appeals upheld lower court dismissal of charges against Baker ruling no reasonable person would see his sexual musings, no matter how unsavory, as constituting a true threat.

Over the years, federal courts in various jurisdictions have dealt with threatening speech cases with contradictory outcomes. A central question dividing the courts concerning true threats has been whose point of view matters, the maker or the target of the threatening speech. The issue finally came before the U.S. Supreme Court stemming from a case involving the Facebook posts of Anthony Douglas Elonis. A former amusement park employee, Elonis had been arrested in December 2010 and charged with violating the federal anti-threat statute by menacing his estranged wife, among others, on his Facebook page, posting crude, degrading, and violent material. In one post he states, "If I only knew then what I know now, I would have smothered your ass with a pillow, dumped your body in the back seat.... and made it look like a rape and murder." In another post, some five months after his wife left him, he writes: "There's one way to love ya but a thousand ways to kill ya. I'm not gonna rest until your body is a mess, soaked in blood and dying from all the little cuts." He also threatened children.

At his trial, his soon-to-be ex-wife testified that his posts made her fearful for her life. He testified in his defense, asking the court to dismiss the charges because the Facebook comments were not true threats. Among other things, he argued that he was an aspiring rap artist and that his remarks were merely a form of artistic expression. Elonis's attorney asked the trial judge to instruct the jury that the government is required to prove his client intended to communicate a true threat. The Judge disagreed, telling jurors that the proper legal test for determining whether someone made a threat is whether reasonable people hearing the comment would perceive it to be a threat.

Elonis was convicted and sentenced to imprisonment for forty-four months, and three years of supervised release. On appeal, the U.S. Court of Appeals for the Third Circuit affirmed his conviction. The U.S. Supreme Court granted certiorari (agreed to hear the case). The question before the justices was whether a conviction for threatening another person under the federal anti-threat statute required proof of the defendant's subjective intent to threaten.

In a stunning eight-to-one decision, the high court reversed the conviction.[304] It did not address the First Amendment issues presented by the case. Instead, it based the ruling on its interpretation of the statute. Writing for the majority, Chief Justice Roberts held that the law requires proof of the defendant's intent to threaten, not how a reasonable person would understand his posts. "Federal criminal liability," he stated, "does not turn solely on the results of an act without considering the defendant's mental state." To warrant a conviction, "wrongdoing must be conscious to the criminal." This interpretation, which sets no standard for assessing mental health, makes online terror threats and fear mongering extremely difficult to prosecute under the true-threats doctrine.

Surveillance

Cyberspace behemoths like Facebook are not in the business of selling merchandise. Like the old *New York Sun*, they sell attention—yours and mine—to advertisers. Its business model and other such social networking sites depend on personal data users provide, whether knowingly or not. The more time we spend on their websites, the more advertising revenue they generate, so they benefit from serving up content that will keep us sticking around. They capture as much of our attention as possible to encourage us to create and share more information about who we are and who we want to be. This policy results in immense amounts of data, not just likes and dislikes, but how many seconds we watch a particular video — that firms like Facebook use to refine its targeted advertising. Facebook's unprecedented cache of data allows marketers—both commercial and political—to test various approaches and identify users who are most susceptible to their message. When political ads with false claims circulate only among the people who will be most receptive to them, there is little chance of assessing such advertisements' integrity. Such data includes essential details like what websites they visit, what they purchase online and in retail stores and with whom they interact. The information is most commonly used to help companies deliver targeted ads, but it can also be amassed into detailed profiles for purchase by anybody, including for political purposes.

On its YouTube channel, the "recommendation" algorithm is a common denominator in many cyberspace chambers. The software determines videos appearing on users' home pages, and inside the "Up Next" sidebar next to a video that is playing.

It is a business model that rewards provocative videos with exposure and advertising dollars. The algorithms guide users down personalized paths as people become ever more enveloped in comforting cocoons of the likeminded. Once the bane of high-school algebra classes, algorithmic calculations direct more than seventy percent of all time spent on sites, meant to keep space travelers glued to their screens.

Through social media sites and smartphones, we provide a great deal of data voluntarily, even though we don't know who's getting it or for what purposes. The prying algorithms at Amazon, the world's biggest merchandiser, look over our shoulders, as it were, and are quick to exploit our tastes: If you enjoyed *Cult of the Spankers*, you'll positively delight in reading *Mistress of Leather*, *Screaming Flesh*, and *Dance of the Dominant Whip*.

FISA STATUTE

The federal government likewise has a long history of collecting personal information of all kinds, although without permission. In 1978, after revelations of illegal spying on dissidents by the Nixon Administration, Congress approved, and President Jimmy Carter signed into law the Foreign Intelligence Surveillance Act (FISA) to provide oversight of the government's covert domestic surveillance activities.

Under this statute, the Chief Justice of the United States, without congressional confirmation appoints, eleven federal district court judges to the FISA court, which sits in a secure federal courtroom in the in Washington D.C. Each judge serves for a maximum of seven years, and terms are staggered to ensure continuity. The chief justice must draw the judges from at least seven of the judicial circuits, and three of them must reside within twenty miles of the capital.

Judges typically sit for one week at a time, on a rotating basis. They consider requests for surveillance warrants by federal law enforcement and intelligence agencies, usually the National Security Agency (NSA) and the Federal Bureau of Investigation (FBI), against suspected foreign spies and terrorists inside the United States. The FISA court typically scrutinizes warrant requests through informal telephone calls and meetings with the government rather than through formal hearings.

Civil libertarians have frequently criticized the court's structure and secrecy as ripe for abuse by government officials. A FISA review panel and the high court itself can assess its decisions, but such oversight is rare. Also rare are FISA rejections of surveillance requests. How often it insists on modifications before approval is uncertain. The record of proceedings is maintained under security measures established by the chief justice in consultation with the attorney general and the director of national intelligence.

Criticism of the FISA court swelled in 2013 when whistleblower Edward Snowden leaked highly classified information from the NSA when he was an agency subcontractor. The computer whiz's disclosures revealed numerous FISA-approved global and domestic surveillance programs in violation of personal freedoms. As first reported in the British *Guardian*, and picked up and expanded upon by news media nationwide, virtually every telephone company in the United States had been providing the NSA with phone metadata for millions of business customers.

Other revelations included a program called PRISM that involved the NSA accessing the emails, documents, photographs, and other sensitive data of users from Facebook, Google, Microsoft, Yahoo, YouTube, and Apple, among other major internet companies. The program had become the NSA's top source of raw intelligence. The nearly ubiquitous smartphone records an enormous amount of data, including personal matters preferably kept private such as visiting casinos, abortion centers, drug treatment facilities, dens of iniquity, or other places that may carry a social stigma.

A hero in some circles and vilified in others, Snowden had worked on network security for the CIA before becoming a systems administrator for Booz Allen Hamilton on contract to the National Security Agency. In both capacities, he had pledged not to divulge state secrets. He had also taken an oath to "defend the Constitution against all enemies, foreign and domestic." The Chinese government's decision to let him pause in Hong Kong while fleeing arrest, and the Kremlin's grant of asylum, guarantee that he would be charged under the 1917 Espionage Act as a traitor if he returned to the United States. Acting in the public interest is not a permissible defense under this legislation.

Across the political spectrum, the Snowden revelations heightened wariness of unwarranted government intrusion into citizens' private lives, especially since the secrecy shrouding the FISA approval process continues to breed abuse. Justice Department Inspector General Michael Horowitz's high-profile report released in late 2019 about the F.B.I.'s investigation into Russia meddling to the 2016 presidential election unearthed problems that point to deeper issues with the cloaked-in-secrecy security apparatus.

The report found the investigation lawful and legitimate, and no improper "spying" on the Trump campaign. It did reveal the error-ridden and dysfunctional way the F.B.I., an improbable darling these days of some left-leaning media outlets, went about obtaining and renewing FISA court permission to wiretap a former Trump campaign adviser. To get the special intelligence court's benediction, the federal agency made serious and repeated errors and omissions, selectively-picking the evidence, providing information that made the advisor look suspicious, and leaving out material that cut the other way.

When seeking renewal of its surveillance warrant, the F.B.I had already uncovered information that cast doubt on some of its original assertions but neglected to tell the FISA court. In exact terms, the application included sloppy, deceitful cherry picking from the already discredited dossier prepared by Christopher Steele, a former British intelligence agent whose "research" was funded by Democrats. The inspector general's report contains many more examples of errors, omissions, and misstatements.

The irregularities discovered in the F.B.I.'s FISA application process may well prompt a needed overhaul of the standards for intrusive surveillance of American citizens lest the systemic failures fester at the expense of national security matters involving terrorism or espionage. The tension between the government's constitutional commitment to the privacy of individuals and its responsibility for the safety of the nation remains an acute problem.

Media Upheaval

In recent decades, concentration over the contents and news and entertainment contours has reached unprecedented levels. Most of the parent companies of the major news and entertainment outlets became or were absorbed by corporate configurations, conglomerate in orientation and transnational in size and scope. The same firms that turn out newspapers now also operate publishing houses, television stations and networks, cable TV systems, movie studios, and other media-related enterprises. The directors of most media organizations also serve on the boards of big banks, insurance companies, investment firms, and major industries that organize and manage much of the world's resources.

The development of radio, movies, and television in all its forms followed what antitrust law professor Tim Wu in *The Master Switch* calls "the cycle." Invention begets industry, corporate battles give rise to empire. In time, government or technology or societal shifts disrupt a closed domain, and the process begins anew. Each of the modern communications media—from movies to radio to television to cable—started as open, chaotic, diverse, and intensely creative; each stimulated utopian visions of the future. In the end, they all wound up being controlled by profit-oriented corporations. "Without exception," notes Wu, "the brave new technologies of the twentieth century... eventually evolved into privately controlled industrial behemoths.... through which the flow and nature of the content would be strictly controlled for reasons of commerce."[305]

Cycle Is Unbroken

The one significant exception to the hegemony of big business over the communications media had been the internet. Would this network of networks usher in a reign of industrial openness, Tim Wu asked rhetorically? Or would it become "the object of the most consequential centralization yet?"[306] The answer is no longer a matter of conjecture. In its infancy, the internet was chaotic and volatile. Search engines and social media sites rose and fell like satellites that failed to achieve orbit. Such online operations as Bigfoot and MySpace were household names one moment and gone the next.

During the 2010s, government oversight agencies and departments allowed more than 500 start-up acquisitions to go unchallenged. This loose merger policy resulted in a roll-up of internet space. From 2004 to 2014, Google spent at least $23 billion buying 145 companies, including the marketing giant DoubleClick, which uses cookies to gather data from computers that visit any of the thousands of websites affiliated with the network. These cookies include a unique identifier for each computer that visits a site. This data gives DoubleClick the power to track users across websites to build well-rounded profiles it then uses to target them with ads for its clients.

Around the same time frame, Facebook spent a similar amount buying sixty-six companies, including critical acquisitions allowing it to attain dominance in mobile social networking. None of these acquisitions got blocked as anti-competitive.

The massive telecom Verizon has been buying fading web presences like AOL and HuffPost on the cheap. But so far, this strategy has yet to pay dividends. In January 2019, it announced the layoff of some 800 personnel at theses once-thriving online operations.

"Suddenly," notes Wu writing in 2018 in *The Curse of Bigness*, "there weren't a dozen search engines, each with a different idea, but one search engine.... And to avoid Facebook was to make yourself a digital hermit. There stopped being a next new thing, or at least, a new thing that was a serious challenge to the old thing."[307] Amazon, Apple, Facebook, Google, and Microsoft, all hitting a trillion-dollar milestone market value in recent years, command everything from app stores to operating systems to cloud storage to an already large and growing share of the online ad business. And behemoths AT&T/Warner Media, Spectrum/Charter, Comcast/NBC Universal, and Verizon now provide virtually all the internet connections to American homes and smartphones.

Such concentration and consolidation of control arises as we enter a period in which all communications media may well become part of the vast and connected world of cyberspace. Hardly boding well for creating an alert, critical, and informed citizenry, such crucial matters as the privileges of power, immense corporate corruption, unjust wars, or the inequities of the justice system are likely to get short shrift. This dissection from logic and reason is accelerating as more and people turn to social media for comfort and consolation.

In the face of traditional media's decline in popularity—when the nation no longer consists of a dominant culture and related subcultures—no unifying center or mainstream exists, just an expansion of tribal formations worldwide with increasingly stronger allegiances. They are nurtured and sustained by transnational conglomerates with bottom lines that depend on cultural division. The chaotic sphere of cyberspace leaves us all susceptible to entanglement in an intricate web of distortions and deceptions. This uncertainty about what lies ahead heightens the necessity for sharpening rhetorical skills and acquiring a more refined sense of how the interactions among media, meaning, culture, and history affect our environment and ourselves.

Endnotes

1. Barbara W. Tuchman, *A Distant Mirror: The Calamitous 14th Century* (New York: Alfred A. Knph, 1978) p. xviii.
2. Lucien Febvre and Henri-Jean Martin, *The Coming of the Book: The Impact of Printing 1450–1800*, trans. David Gerard (London, New Left Books, 1976). p. 17.
3. Harold Innis, *Empire and Communications* (Toronto, University of Toronto Press, 1972) p. 138.
4. Fernand Braudel, *The Structures of Everyday Life*, trans. Sian Reynolds, vol. 1 (New York: Harper and Row, 1981) p. 401.
5. Marshall McLuhan, *The Gutenberg Galaxy: The Making of Typographic Man* (Toronto: University of Toronto Press, 1962) p. 161.
6. Elizabeth L. Eisenstein, "Some Conjectures about the Impact of Printing on Western Society and Thought: A Preliminary Report," *Journal of Modern History* 40 (1968), p. 8
7. See Elizabeth L. Eisenstein, *The Printing Press as an Agent of Change: Communications and Cultural Transformations in Early-Modern Europe*, vol. 1 (Cambridge, Eng.: Cambridge University Press, 1979)
8. Aristotle, *Rhetoric* (Overland Park, KS: Digireads.com, 2020) W. Rhys Roberts translator.
9. See Agnes Callard' "Should We Cancel Aristotle?" *New York Times*, July 21, 2020 and Iain Murrray, "Why Are We Even thinking of Canceling Aristotle? *National Review* July 22, 2020.
10. See *Looking for Richard:* https://www.youtube.com/watch?v=nVgdtcNwIGQ
11. Barbara Leaming, *Orson Welles: A Biography* (New York: Viking Penguin, 1983) pp. 43-44.
12. In film theory and practice, pure cinema refers to creating a more emotionally intense experience using autonomous film techniques instead of stories, characters, or actors.
13. S.H. Steinberg, *Five Hundred Years of Printing* (Harmonsworth, Eng. Penguin Books, 1961), p. 27.
14. Lawrence Stone, "Literacy and Education in England, 1640-1900," *Past and Present* 42 (February 1969), p. 86.
15. Quoted in Frank Luther Mott, *American Journalism: A History*, 3rd ed. (New York: Macmillan, 1962), p. 6.
16. See Vincent Buranelli, ed., *The Trial of Peter Zenger* (New York : New York University Press, 1957). See also Leonard W. Levy, ed., *Freedom of the Press from Zenger to Jefferson* (Indianapolis: Bobbs-Merrill, 1966).
17. Actor James Earle Jones's video reading of the speech that raises matters still applicable today is available at https://www.youtube.com/watch?v=E2YYEce01HI
18. Eric Burns, *Infamous Scribblers: The Founding Father and the Rowdy Beginnings of American Journalism* (New York: PublicAffairs, 2006) p.3
19. See Ron Chernow, *Alexander Hamilton* (New York: Penguin Books, 2005). This comprehensive biography was the principal source for Lin-Manuel Miranda's hugely successful rap Broadway musical featuring this founding father.
20. Richard Rosenfeld and Edmund S. Morgan, *American Aurora: A Democratic-Republican Returns: The Suppressed History of Our Nation's Beginnings and the Heroic Newspaper That Tried to Report It* (New York: St. Martin's Press, 1997) p. 33.

21. Quoted in Geoffrey R. Stone, *Perilous Times: Free Speech in Wartime, From the Sedition Act of 1798 to the War on Terrorism* (New York: W.W. Norton & Co., 2004), p. 62.
22. *Community for Creative Non-Violence v. Reid,* 490 U.S. 730 (1989).
23. *Bright Tunes Music Corp. v. Harrisongs Music, Ltd.* 420 F. Supp. 177 (S.D.N.Y. 1976).
24. *Harper & Row v. Nation Enterprises,* 471 U.S. 539 (1985)
25. *Sony Corp. of America v. Universal City Studios, Inc.* (1984).
26. *Campbell v. Acuff-Rose Music, Inc.,* 510 U.S. 569 (1994)
27. *Leibovitz v. Paramount Pictures Corp.*, 137 F.3d 109 (2d Cir. 1998)
28. *Cariou v. Prince,* 714 F.3d 694 (2d Cir. 2013)
29. *Suntrust Bank v. Houghton Mifflin Co.,*US District Court for the Northern District of Georgia, 136 F. Supp. 2d 1357 (N.D. Ga. 2001)
30. *Suntrust Bank v. Houghton Mifflin Co.*, 268 F.3d 1257 (11th Cir. 2001)
31. *Lenz v. Universal Music Corp.* 801 F.3d 1126 (9th Cir. 2015)
32. *Viacom International, Inc. v. YouTube, Inc.* 676 F.3d 19 (2nd Cir.2012)
33. *Solid Oak Sketches, LLC v. 2K Games, Inc. and Take-Two Interactive Software, Inc,* 1-30 (S.D.N.Y. 2020)
34. *MGM Studios, Inc. v. Grokster,* Ltd., 545 U.S. 913 (2005)
35. *Authors Guild v. Google, Inc.*, 804 F.3d 202 (2d Cir. 2015)
36. Tim Wu, *The Attention Merchants: The Epic Scramble to Get Inside Our Heads* (New York: vintage Books, 2017) p. 6.
37. See Gerald J. Baldasty, *The Commercialization of News in the Nineteenth Century* (Madison, Wis.: University of Wisconsin Press, 1992)
38. Quoted in Matthew Goodman, *The Sun and the Moon: The Remarkable True Account of Hoaxers, Showmen, Dueling Journalists, and Lunar Man-Bats in Nineteenth Century New York (New York, Basic Books,* 2008), p. 276.
39. Tali Sharot, *The Influential Mind: What the Brain Reveals About Our Power to Change Others* (New York: Henry Holt and Co. 2017), p. 17.
40. Harold L. Nelson, ed., *Freedom of the Press from Hamilton to the Warren Court* (Indianapolis: Bobbs-Merrill, 1967) p. 175
41. Russel B. Nye, *Fettered Freedom: Civil Liberties and the Slavery Controversy, 1830-1860* (East Lansing: Michigan State College Press, 1949) p. 119.
42. See James L. Crouthamel, *Bennett's New York Herald and the Rise of the Popular Press* (New York: Syracuse University Press, 1989).
43. The explosion of digital news sources in the internet age obliterated the daylong "news exclusive" prized by the print press.
44. "Awful Calamity. Wild Animals Broken Loose from Central Park," *New York Herald* (Nov 9, 1874).
45. T.B. Connery, "A Famous Newspaper Hoax," *Harper's Weekly* (June 3, 1893), pp. 534-535.
46. "Wild Beasts," *New York Herald* (November 10, 1874).
47. "The Heartless Newspaper Hoax," *New York Times* (November 11, 1874).
48. Anthony Smith, *The Geopolitics of Information: How Western Culture Dominates the World* (New York: Oxford University Press, 1980) p. 25.
49.Matthew Josephson, *The Robber Barons* (New York: Harcourt, Brace, and World, 1962), p. 208.
50. The legislation's roots are in an obscure passage in the U.S. Constitution, Article I, Section 9, which stipulates that importing slaves could be prohibited twenty-five years after this law of the land's ratification.
51. See James McGrath Morris, *Pulitzer: A Life in Politics, Print, and Power* (New York: Harper, 2010).
52. See Anna-Lisa Cox *The Bone and Sinew of the Land: America's Forgotten Black Pioneers and the Struggle for Equality* (New York: PublicAffairs, 2018).
53. Renamed Welfare Island in 1921; in 1972, it got the name it still has today, Roosevelt Island.
54. Quoted in Matthew Goodman, *Eighty Days: Nellie Bly and Elizabeth Bisland's History-Making Race Around the World* (New York: Ballantine Books, 2013) p. 33.
55. Daniel Boorstin, *The Image* (New York: Harper and Row, 1961), p. 12.
56. See David Nasaw, *The Chief: The Life of William Randolph Hearst* (Boston, MA: Mariner Books 2001).
57. This racial epithet reflects white supremacist fears that barbarian hordes of Asians, in particular the Chinese, would invade Europe and America and disrupt Western values, such as democracy, Christianity, and technological innovation.
58. See Jay Risen, *The Crowded Hour: Theodore Roosevelt, the Rough Riders, and the Dawn of the American*

Century, (New York, Scribner, 2019).
59. See Brent Staples, "When Newspapers Justified Lynching," *New York Times*, May 6, 2018.
60. David Zucchino, *Wilmington's Lie: The Murderous Coup of 1898 and the Rise of White Supremacy* (New York: Atlantic Monthly Press, 2020).
61. See Randy Krehbiel, *Tulsa, 1921: Reporting a Massacre* (Norman, Okla: University of Oklahoma Press, 2019), and Russell Cobb, *The Great Oklahoma Swindle: Race, Religion, and Lies in America's Weirdest State* (Lincoln, NE: Bison Press, 2020)
62. For an in-depth look at the crusading newspaper publisher in the context of the cultural and intellectual currents of mid-nineteenth-century America see Adam Tuchinsky, *Horace Greeley's New-York Tribune: Civil War-Era Socialism and the Crisis of Free Labor* (Ithaca, N.Y., 2009).
63. His journalistic endeavors remain pertinent to present-day political and cultural concerns. See James Ledbetter, ed., *Dispatches for the New York Tribune: Selected Journalism of Karl Marx* (New York: Penguin Classics, 2008).
64. Gay Talese, *The Kingdom and the Power: The Story of the Men Who Influence the Institution That Influences the World—The New York Times* (New York: World Publishing Company, 1969) p. 168.
65. See John M. Barry, *The Great Influenza: The Story of the Deadliest Pandemic in History* (New York: Penguin Books, 2005).
66. James W. Loewen, *Lies My Teacher Told Me: Everything Your American History Textbook Got Wrong* (New York: The New Press; reprint edition 2018) p. 354.
67. Karl E. Meyer, "The Editorial Notebook; Trenchcoats, Then and Now," *New York Times* (June 24, 1990).
68. See Amisha Padnani and Jessica Bennett, *New York Times*, Times Insider, March 8, 2018, p.2
69. Jennifer Harlan, "Overlooked No More: Emma Stebbins, Who Sculpted an Angel of New York," New York Times, May 29, 2019.
70. "Charlotte Cushman," *New York Times*, February 19, 1876
71. Excerpts from Michael Goodwin's lecture at Hillsdale College, a private conservative college in Hillsdale, Michigan appears in the *New York Post* on November 30, 2019.
72. Jim Rutenberg, "Trump Is Testing the Norms of Objectivity in Journalism," *New York Times,* August 7, 2016
73. See William Cullen Bryant II, *Power for Sanity: Selected Editorials of William Cullen Bryant, 1829-61* (New York: Fordham University Press, 1994).
74. Michael Schudson, *Discovering the News: A Social History of American Newspapers* (New York: Basic Books, 1978 p. 7
75. See Dan Schiller, *Objectivity and the News: The Public and the Rise of Commercial Journalism* (Philadelphia: University of Pennsylvania Press, 1981)
76. Jan Ransom, "Case Against Amy Cooper Lacks Key Element: Victim's Cooperation," *New York Times* July 8, 2020.
77. Tali Sharot, *The Influential Mind: What the Brain Reveals About Our Power to Change Others* (New York: Henry Holt and Co. 2017) pp. 3-5.
78. Neil Postman, *Amusing Ourselves to Death: Public Discourse in the Age of Show Business* (New York: Viking Penguin, 1985) p. 72
79. His irreverent account is detailed in Tom Wolfe, *Radical Chic & Mau-Mauing the Flak Catchers* (New York: Picador 2009).
80. See Daniel C. Hallin, *The Uncensored War: The Media and Vietnam* (Oakland, CA: University of California Press, 1989)
81. Michael J. Arlen, *Living Room War* (New York: Viking, 1969) p. 45.
82. Fred W. Friendly, *Due to Circumstances Beyond Our Control…* New York: Random House, 1967) p. 215.
83. David Halberstam, *The Best and the Brightest* (New York: Random House, 1972).
84. Marvin Barrett, ed., *Survey of Broadcast Journalism* 1969-1970 (New York: Grosset & Dunlap, 1970), pp. 31-32.
85. David Paul Kuhn, *The Hardhat Riot: Nixon, New York City, and the Dawn of the White Working-Class Revolution* (New York: Oxford University Press, 2020).
86. See Richard Zoglin, *Hope: Entertainer of the Century* (New York: Simon & Schuster, 2014)
87. See Joe McGinniss, *The Selling of the President 1968* (New York: Trident, 1969). See as well the "Living Room Candidate" website (http://www.livingroomcandidate.org/), which includes all of the TV and web ads American presidential campaigns deployed since 1952.

88. See Roberta Smith, "The Case for Keeping San Francisco's Disputed George Washington Murals," *New York Times*, January 29, 2019, Arts, pp. 1-2.
89. See Richard Gambino, *Vendetta: The True Story of the Largest Lynching in U.S. History* (Montreal, Quebec: Guernica Editions, 1998).
90. Kirkpatrick Sale, *The Conquest of Paradise: Christopher Columbus and the Columbian Legacy* (New York: Knopf 1990) pp. 153-154.
91. For a riveting firsthand account of their reporting read Bob Woodward and Carl Bernstein *All the President's Men*, reissue edition (New York: Simon & Schuster, 2014). Applications to journalism schools rose significantly when the movie version of the book achieved notable success.
92. *United States v. Johnson*, 221 U.S. 488 (1911)
93. Eric Barnouw, *The Sponsor: Notes on a Modern Potentate* (New York: Oxford University Press, 1978) p. 90.
94. John Heilemann and Mark Halperin, *Game Change: Obama and the Clintons, McCain and Palin, and the Race of a Lifetime* (New York: Harper, 2010) p. 142.
95. Margaret Sullivan, "Is this strip-mining or journalism? 'Sobs, gasps, expletives' over latest Denver Post layoffs" *Washington Post* March 15, 2018.
96. Richard W. Stevenson, *New York Times*, "How We Fact-Check Politicians," July 31, 2019, p.2.
97. Ben Smith, *New York Times*, "Why the Success of The Times May Be Bad News for Journalism," March 2, 2020, p.B1.
98. Craig Whitlock, "The Afghanistan Papers: A Secret History of the War," *Washington Post*, December 9, 2019.
99. Ben Smith, *New York Times*, "Bail Out Journalists. Let Newspaper Chains Die," March 29, 2020, p. B1.
100. See Leonard W. Levy, *Legacy of Suppression* (Cambridge, Mass: Harvard University Press, 1960). For a more recent version of Levy's views, see his *Emergence of a Free Press* (New York: Oxford University Press, 1985).
101. *Schenck v. United States*, 249 U.S. 47 (1919).
102. *Debs v. United States*, 249 U.S. 211 (1919)
103. Zechariah Chafee, Jr. *Free Speech in the United States* (Cambridge Mass.: Harvard University Press, 1941) p. 52.
104. *Gitlow v. New York*, 268 U.S. 652 (1925).
105. Santa Clara County v. Southern Pacific R. Co., 118 U.S. 394 (1886)
106. West Coast Hotel Co. v. Parrish, 300 U.S. 379 (1937)
107. *Citizens United v. Federal Election Commission*, 558 U.S. 310 (2010)
108. Jane Mayer, *Dark Money: The Hidden History of the Billionaires Behind the Rise of the Radical Right* (New York: Anchor/paperback, 2016) p. 281.
109. *Lemon v. Kurtzman*, 403 U.S. 602 (1971)
110. *American Legion v. American Humanist Association*, 588 U.S. ___ (2019)
111. See Irin Carmon and Shana Knizhnik, *Notorious RBG: The Life and Times of Ruth Bader Ginsburg* (New York: HarperCollins, 2015).
112. Fred Friendly, *Minnesota Rag The Dramatic Story of the Landmark Supreme Court Case That Gave New Meaning to Freedom of the Press* (New York: Random House, 1981) p.
113. *Near v. Minnesota*, 283 U.S. 697 (1931)
114. *Mutual Film Corp. v. Ohio Industrial Commission*, 236 U.S. 230 (1915); *Mutual Film Corp. v. Ohio Industrial Commission*, 236 U.S. 236 (1915); *Mutual Film Corp. v. Kansas*, 236 U.S. 248 (1915).
115. Burstyn v. Wilson, 343 U.S. 495 (1952).
116. *Kingsley International Pictures v. Regents*, 360 U.S, 684 (1959).
117. *Times Film Corporation v. Chicago*, 365 U.S. 43 (1961).
118. *Freedman v. Maryland*, 380 U.S. 51 (1965).
119. *Star v. Preller*, 419 U.S. 955 (1974) sustained the federal courts below, which had declared the revised statute constitutional.
120. *New York Times Co. v. United States*, 403 U.S. 713 (1971)
121. *New York Times Co. v. Sullivan*, 376 U.S. 254 (1964)
122. Anthony Lewis, *Make No Law: The Sullivan Case and the First Amendment* (New York: Random House, 1991)
123. *Gertz v. Robert Welch, Inc.*, 418 U.S. 323 (1974)

124. Samuel Warren and Louis Brandeis, "The Right to Privacy," 4 *Harvard Law Review* 193 (1890).
125. *Sipple v. Chronicle Publishing Company*, 201 Cal. Rptr. 665 (Ct. App. 1984).
126. See Ryan Holiday, *Conspiracy: Peter Thiel, Hulk Hogan, Gawker, and the Anatomy of Intrigue* (New York: Portfolio, 2018)
127. Catherine Allgor, *A Perfect Union: Dolley Madison and the Creation of the American Nation.* (New York: Macmillan, 2006), p. 34. The author notes that the actual accusations from the newspapers are not preserved although several references to them exist.
128. See *Rosen v. United States*, 161 U.S. 29 (1896).
129. See *Butler v. Michigan*, 352 U.S. 380 (1957)
130. *Roth v. United States* and *Alberts v. California*, 354 U.S. 476 (1957). The high court heard the appeals in these cases involving violations of federal and state obscenity statutes together.
131. Bob Woodward and Scott Armstrong describe "movie day" at the high court in *The Brethren: Inside the Supreme Court* (New York: Simon & Schuster, 1979), p. 198.
132. *Jacobellis v. Ohio*, 378 U.S. 184 (1964).
133. Memoirs v. Massachusetts, 383 U.S. 413
134. *Mishkin v. New York*, 383 U.S. 502 (1966)
135. *Ginzburg v. United States*, 383 U.S. 463 (1966)
136. Redrup v. New York, 386 U.S. 767 (1967)
137. *Stanley v. Georgia*, 394 U.S. 557 (1969)
138. *Cohen v. California*, 403 U.S. 15 (1971)
139. See Richard Smith, *Getting into Deep Throat* (Chicago: Playboy Press, 1973) for a detailed discussion of this decision.
140. *Miller v. California*, 413 U.S. 15 (1973).
141. *Pope v. Illinois*, 481 U.S. 497 (1987).
142. *Jenkins v. Georgia*, 418 U.S. 153 (1974).
143. *Cruz v. Ferre*, 755 F.2d 1415 (11th Cir. 1985)
144. See Marvin R. Bensman , "The Zenith Case and the Chaos of 1926-27," *Journal of Broadcasting* 14 (Fall 1970), pp. 423-40.
145. Federal Radio Commission, "In the Matter of the Application of Great Lakes Broadcasting Co.," in the Third Annual Report (Washington, D.C.: Government Printing Office, 1929).
146. See Pope Brock, *Charlatan: America's Most Dangerous Huckster, the Man Who Pursued Him, and the Age of Flimflam* (New York: Crown Publishing, 2008).
147. Gerald Carson, *The Roguish World of Doctor Brinkley* (New York: Rinehart, 1960), pp. 101-102.
148. *KFKB Broadcasting Association, Inc. v. Federal Radio Commission*, 47 F. (2d) 670 (1931).
149. Ibid., p. 672. See also Andrew G. Haley, "The Law on Radio Programs," *George Washington Law Review* 5 (January 1937), pp. 1-46.
150. *Chevron U.S.A., Inc. v. Natural Resources Defense Council, Inc.*, 467 U.S. 837 (1984).
151. 8 F.C.C. 333 (1940).
152. Editorializing by Broadcast Licensees, 13 F.C.C. 1246 (1949).
153. Quoted in *Illinois Citizens Committee for Broadcasting v. Federal Communications* Commission 515 F. (2d) 397 (1975).
154. *Federal Communications Commission v. Pacifica Foundation* 438 U.S. 726 (1978).
155. *Federal Communications Commission v. Fox Television Stations, Inc.*, 556 U.S. 502 (2009)
156. *Federal Communications Commission v. Fox Television Stations, Inc.*, 567 U.S. 239 (2012)
157. *Reno v. American Civil Liberties Union*, 521 U.S. 844 (1997)
158. 18 U.S.C. Sections 1461, 1462, 1465 (2019).
159. See Michael Freedland, *Men Who Made Hollywood: The Lives of the Great Movie Moguls* (London, UK: Aurum Press 2009).
160. Karl Marx and Friedrich Engels, *The German Ideology*, trans. R. Pascal (New York: International Publishers, 1947), p.39.
161. F.D. Klingender and Stuart Legg, *Money Behind the Screen* (London: Lawrence & Wishart, 1937), p.79.
162. See Cari Beauchamp, "Wall Street Awaits Kennedy's Findings," *Joseph P. Kennedy Presents: His Hollywood Years* (New York: Vintage Books, 2010) pp. 334-349.
163. See Lea Jacobs, *The Wages of Sin: Censorship and the Fallen Woman Film*, 1928-1942 (Berkeley: University of California Press, 1997), pp. 69-81.

164. See Neal Gabler, *An Empire of Their Own: How the Jews Invented Hollywood* (New York: Crown, 1988).
165. Quoted in Gregory Black, *Hollywood Censored: Morality Codes, Catholics, and the Movies* (New York: Cambridge University Press, 1994), p. 170.
166. See Raymond Fielding, *The American Newsreel: A Complete History, 1911-1967* 2nd ed. (New York: McFarland, 2006)
167. See Raymond Fielding, *The March of Time: 1935-1951* (New York: Oxford University Press, 1978).
168. Quoted in Otto Friedrich, *City of Nets: A Portrait of Hollywood in the 1940s* (New York: Harper & Row, 1986) p.47.
169. See Thomas Doherty, *Hollywood and Hitler, 1933-1939* (New York: Columbia University Press, 2013).
170. David Nasaw, *The Patriarch: The Remarkable Life and Turbulent Times of Joseph P. Kennedy* (New York: Penguin Books, 2013) p. 502.
171. Gerald P. Nye, "War Propaganda: Our Madness Increases As Our Emergency Shrinks," *Vital Speeches*, 7 (September 1941), pp. 720-723.
172. U.S. Congress, Senate Subcommittee of the Committee on Interstate Commerce, Propaganda in Motion Pictures, 77th Congress, 1st Session, September 9-26, 1941 (Washington, DC: Government Printing Office, 1942).
173. Erik Barnouw, *Documentary: A History of the Non-Fiction Film* (New York: Oxford University Press, 1974), p. 160.
174. C. J. Hovland, A. A. Lumsdaine, and F. D. Sheffield, *Experiments on Mass Communication, Vol. III of Studies of Social Psychology in World War II* (New York: John Wiley & Sons, 1965).
175. See Shearon Lowery and Melvin L. De Fleur, *Milestones in Mass Communication Research* (New York: Longman, 1983), chapter five, for a summary and analysis of these studies.
176. See Iris Chang, *The Rape of Nanking: The Forgotten Holocaust of World War II* (New York: Basic Books, 1997)
177. "How to Tell the Japs from the Chinese," *Life*, December 22, 1941, p. 81.
178. Geoffrey R. Stone, *Perilous Times: Free Speech in Wartime From the Sedition Act of 1798 to the War on Terrorism.* (New York: W.W. Norton & Co., 2004) p. 287.
179. *Korematsu v. United States*, 323 U.S. 214 (1944).
180. Cited in "Walt Disney: Great Teacher," *Fortune*, August 1942, p.94.
181. Richard R. Lingeman, *Don't You Know There's a War On? The American Homefront 1941-1945* (New York: Capricorn Books, 1976), pp. 333-334.
182. Clayton R. Koppes and Gregory D. Black, "What to Show the World: The Office of War Information and Hollywood 1942-1945," *The Journal of American History*, 64 (1977), p.l03.
183. Leonard J. Leff and Jerold L. Simmons, *The Dame in the Kimono: Hollywood, Censorship, and the Production Code from the 1920s to the 1960s* (New York: Anchor Books, 1990), p. 151.
184. Quoted in Anthony Holden, *Behind the Oscar: The Secret History of the Academy Awards* (New York: Simon & Schuster, 1993), p. 408.
185. *Ginsberg v. New York*, 390 U.S. 629 (1968).
186. *Interstate Circuit v. Dallas*, 390 U.S. 676 (1968).
187. See *United States v. Paramount Pictures, Inc. et al.*, 344 U.S. 131 (1948).
188. See Steven Bach, *Final Cut: Dreams and Disaster in the Making of Heaven' s Gate* (New York: William Morrow, 1985).
189. For a scathing ultimately uplifting account of the ageism women face at work and across media outlets, see Susan J. Douglas, *In Our Prime: How Older Are Reinventing the Road Ahead* (New York: W.W. Norton, 2020).
190. See David Bordwell, "The Classical Hollywood Style 1917-60," in David Bordwell, Janet Staiger, and Kristin Thompson, eds. *The Classical Hollywood Cinema: Film Style & Mode of Production to 1960* (New York: Columbia University Press, 1985), p. 3.
191. David Bordwell, *The Way Hollywood Tells It: Story and Style in Modern Movies* (Berkeley, CA: University of California Press, 2006) p. 28.
192. See Syd Field, *Screenplay: The Foundations of Screenwriting* (New York: Delta rev. ed., 2005)
193. See Robert B. Ray, *A Certain Tendency of the Hollywood Cinema, 1930-198*0 (Princeton, NJ: Princeton University Press, 1985)
194. See Jim Kitses, *Horizons West: Anthony Mann, Budd Boetticher, Sam Peckinpah: Studies of Authorship Within the Western* (Bloomington: Indiana University Press,1970), p. 11.

195. See Gary Wills, *John Wayne's America: The Politics of Celebrity* (New York: Simon & Shuster, 1997).
196. Richard Slotkin, *Gunfighter Nation: The Myth of the Frontier in Twentieth-Century America* (New York: Atheneum, 1992).
197. Tim Wu, *The Master Switch: The Rise and Fall of Information Empires* (New York: Alfred A. Knoph, 2010) p. 12.
198. James Rorty, *Our Master's Voice: Advertising* (New York: John Day, 1934), pp. 73- 74.
199. See Gleason Archer, *History of Radio to 1926* (New York: American Historical Society, 1938), pp. 397- 98, for the full text of the first sponsored message.
200. See William Peck Banning, *Commercial Broadcasting Pioneer: The WEAF Experiment 1922-1926* (Cambridge , Mass.: Harvard University Press, 1946), pp. 149-50.
201. Hans V. Kaltenborn, "Radio: Dollars and Nonsense," in *Problems and Controversies in Television and Radio*, eds. Harry J. Skornia and Jack William Kitson (Palo Alto, Calif: Pacific Books, 1968), p. 303.
202. See Robert Metz, *CBS: Reflections in a Bloodshot Eye* (Chicago: Playboy Press, 1975) for a detailed history of this organization under Paley's stewardship.
203. Susan J. Douglas, Listening In: Radio and the American Imagination (New York: Times Books, 1999), p. 28.
204. Bruce Barton, *The Man Nobody Knows* (Indianapolis: Bobbs-Merrill, 1924), pp. i-v.
205. Charles F. McGovern, *Sold American: Consumption and Citizenship, 1890-1945* (Chapel Hill, N.C. University of North Carolina Press, 2006) p. 25.
206. Hubbell Robinson and Ted Patrick, "Jack Benny," in *American Broadcasting: A Source Book on the History of Radio and Television*, eds. Lawrence W. Lichty and MalachiC.Topping (New York:Hastings-House,1975), p.334.
207. See Joseph Boskin, *Sambo: The Rise and Demise of an American Jester* (New York: Oxford University Press, (1988) pp. 175-187.
208. J . Fred MacDonald, *Don't Touch That Dial: Radio Programming in American Life from 1920 to 1960* (Chicago: Nelson-Hall, 1979), p. 158.
209. Herta Herzog, "On Borrowed Experience: An Analysis of Listening to Daytime Sketches," *Studies in Philosophy and Social Science* 9 (1941), pp. 65-95
210. See A. Brad Schwartz, *Broadcast Hysteria: Orson Welles's War of the Worlds and the Art of Fake News* (New York: Hill and Yang, 2016).
211. Hadley Cantril, *The Invasion from Mars: A Study in the Psychology of Panic* (New York: Harper & Row, 1940)
212. See Sheldon Marcus, *Father Coughlin: The Tumultuous Life of the Priest of the Little Flower* (Boston: Little, Brown, 1973).
213. Richard M. Ketchum, *The Borrowed Years: 1938-1941 America on the Way to War* (New York: Random House, 1989), p. 124.
214. Alan Brinkley, *Voices of Protest: Huey Long, Father Coughlin, and the Great Depression* (New York: Alfred A. Knopf, 1982) p. 261.
215. See Stanley Cloud and Lynne Olson, *The Murrow Boys: Pioneers on the Front Lines of Broadcast Journalism* (Boston: Houghton Mifflin Harcourt, 1996).
216. See Philip Seib. *Broadcasts from the Blitz: How Edward R. Murrow Helped Lead America into War.* (New York: Potomac Books, 2006).
217. See Allan M. Winkler, *The Politics of Propaganda: The Office of War Information* 1942-1945 (New Haven, Ct.: Yale University Press, 1978)
218. See George A. Willey, "The Soap Operas and the War," *Journal of Broadcasting* 7 (Fall 1963), pp. 339-52
219. Charles A. Siepmann, *Radio's Second Chance* (Boston: Little, Brown, 1946), pp. 186-87.
220. *National Broadcasting Co. v. United States*, 319 U.S. 190 (1943).
221. Gary, Giddens, Bing Crosby: A Pocketful of Dreams—The Early Years, 1903-1940 (New York: Little, Brown and Company, 2001). p. 228.
222. The movie's producer, Hal B. Wallis, once said that its director Michael Curtiz's camera setups were unmistakable, that they "had a stamp as clearly marked as a Matisse." Aljean Harmetz, *Round Up the Usual Suspects: The Making of Casablanca-Bogart, Bergman, and World War II* (New York: Hyperion, 1992), p.64.
223. Eric Barnouw, *The Image Empire: A History of Broadcasting in the United States*, Volume III: From 1953 (New York: Oxford University Press, 1970), p. 33.
224. See Robert Metz, *CBS: Reflections in a Bloodshot Eye* (New York: Playboy Press, 1975) p.202.
225. See Naomi Oreskes and Erik H. Conway, *Merchants of Doubt: How a Handful of Scientists Obscured the*

Truth on Issues from Tobacco Smoke to Global Warming (New York: Bloomsbury Press, 2010).
226. See John Cogley, *Report on Blacklisting II: Radio-Television* (New York: Fund for the Republic, 1956). See also J . Fred MacDonald, *Television and the Red Menace: The Video Road to Vietnam* (New York: Praeger Publishers, 1985).
227. Quoted in ibid., pp. 89-91.
228. Les Brown, *Television: The Business behind the Box* (New York: Harcourt Brace Jovanovich, 1971), p. 58.
229. Michael Parenti, *Make-Believe Media: The Politic of Entertainment* (New York: St. Martin's Press, 1992) pp. 72-73.
230. See Donald T. Critchlow, *Phyllis Schlafly and Grassroots Conservatism: A Woman's Crusade* (Princeton, NJ: 2008) for a sympatric portrait of the most consequential woman in American politics since Susan B. Anthony.
231. James Aronson, *The Press and the Cold War* (Boston: Beacon Press, 1973) p. 71.
232. Fred W. Friendly, *Due to Circumstances Beyond Our Control* (New York: Random House, 1967), p. 48.
233. Cited in Alexander Kendrick, *Prime Time: The Life of Edward R . Murrow* (Boston: Little, Brown , 1969), p. 60.
234. See A. M. Sperber, *Murrow: His Life and Times* (New York: Freundlich Books, 1986).
235. Incident related in Kendrick, *Prime Time*, p. 378.
236. The struggling Dumont network also had too few affiliates for nationwide coverage. It offered a daily newscast only sporadically before expiring in 1956.
237. Perhaps undercutting his credibility, Daly continued moderating the popular CBS television game show *What's My Line*? after he became an ABC news anchor.
238. Quoted in "Longer News: A Bitter Pill Stations Brace to Swallow," *Broadcasting*, June 28, 1976, p. 19.
239. John R. MacArthur, *Second Front: Censorship and Propaganda in the 1991 Gulf War* (New York: Hill and Wang, 1992) p. 58.
240. See George Lakoff and Mark Johnson, *Metaphors We Live By* (Chicago, Il., University of Chicago Press, 2003).
241. For a description of the seven techniques of propaganda developed by the Institute for Propaganda Analysis in the late 1930s see J. Michael Sproule, *Propaganda and Democracy: The American Experience of Media and Mass Persuasion* (New York: Cambridge University Press, 1996) pp. 129-177.
242. Frank Rich, *The Greatest Story Ever Sold: The Decline and Fall of Truth from 9/11 to Katrina* (New York: Penguin Press, 2006).
243. *United States v. Southwestern Cable Company* 392 U.S. 157 (1968).
244. For the full Wallace interview click: https://www.youtube.com/watch?v=aXqEcUoW5JI
245. Tammy Duckworth, "Tucker Carlson Doesn't Know What Patriotism Is," *New York Times*, July 9, 2020
246. Go to this link for the Swan/Trump interview: https://www.youtube.com/watch?v=zaaTZkqsaxY
247. Susan Crawford, *Captive Audience: The Telecom Industry and Monopoly Power in the New Gilded Age* (New Haven, CT: Yale University Press, 2013).
248. For *Dark Waters* trailer link go to: https://www.youtube.com/watch?v=RvAOuhyunhY
249. The father-daughter duo, known as "the Dancing Cansinos," posed as husband and wife, art imitating sordid life, since he sexually abused her for several years. See Barbara Leaming, *If This Was Happiness: A Biography of Rita Hayworth* (New York: Viking, 1989)
250. Wilson, Woodrow, *A History of the American People*. vol. 5 (New York: Harper & Brothers, 1916) p. 64.
251. See Charlene Regester, "Black Films, White Censors: Oscar Micheaux Confronts Censorship in New York, Virginia and Chicago;" in Francis G. Couvares, ed., *Movie Censorship and American Culture* (Washington, DC: Smithsonian Institution Press, 1996), pp. 170-171.
252. See Pearl Bowser and Louise Spence, *Writing Himself into History: Oscar Micheaux, His Silent Films, and His Audiences* (New Brunswick, NJ: Rutgers University Press, 2000).
253. *Loving v. Virginia*, 388 U.S. 1 (1967).
254. See John W. Frick, *Uncle Tom's Cabin on the American Stage and Screen* (New York: Palgrave Macmillan, 2012) chapter one.
255. John Strausbaugh, *Black Like You: Blackface, Whiteface, Insult & Imitation in American Popular Culture* (New York: TarcherPerigee 2007), Chapter Three.
256. Ronald H. Bayor, "Roads to Racial Segregation: Atlanta in the Twentieth Century," *Journal of Urban*

History, Vol. 15, No. 1, 3–21 (1988).
257. For a detailed study of this show on both radio and television, see Melvin Patrick Ely, *The Adventures of Amos 'n' Andy: A Social History of an American Phenomenon* (New York: Free Press, 1991).
258. Erik Barnouw, *A Tower in Babel: A History of Broadcasting in the United States, Volume I: To 1933* (New York: Oxford University Press, 1966), p. 230.
259. See Melvin Patrick Ely, *The Adventures of Amos 'n' Andy: A Social History of an American Phenomenon* (New York: Free Press, 1991), chapter ten.
260. Henry Louis Gates Jr., *New York Times*, November 12, 1989.
261. *Loving v. Virginia*, 388 U.S. 1 (1967)
262. Stéphane Tonnelat and William Kornblum, *International Express: New Yorkers on the 7 Train* (New York: Columbia University Press, 2017) p. 5
263. George Lakoff, *The All New Don't Think of an Elephant! Know Your Values and Frame the Debate* (White River Junction, VT: Chelsea Green Publishing, 2014) p. xi.
264. See William Donelley, "Love and Death in *Casablanca*" in Joseph McBride, ed. *Persistence of Vision: A Collection of Criticism* (Madison: Wisconsin Film Society Press, 1968),p. 103.
265. See Eve Golden, *Vamp: The Rise and Fall of Theda Bara* (New York: Vestal Press, 1998).
266. See Nora Sayer, *Running Time: Films of the Cold War* (New York: Doubleday, 1982).
267. Director Jacques Tourneur and director of photography of Nicholas Musuraca created this movie's compellingly romantic and baleful ambiance.
268. See Allan Brandt, *The Cigarette Century: The Rise, Fall, and Deadly Persistence of the Product That Defined America* (New York: Basic Books, 2007).
269. Leonard Mlodinow, *Subliminal: How Your Unconscious Mind Rules Your Behavior* (New York, Patheon Books 2012) p. 17.
270. Larry Tye, *The Father of Spin: Edward L. Bernays and the Birth of Public Relations* (New York: Crown, 1999) p. 27–28
271. See Lisa A. Keister, Darby E. Southgate, *Inequality: A Contemporary Approach to Race, Class, and Gender. Cambridge*: (New York Cambridge University Press, 2011) p. 228
272. Marina Warner, *Alone of All Her Sex: The Myth and the Cult of the Virgin Mary* (New York: Vintage, 1983).
273. "New York State May Ban 'Virginity tests'," *New York Times*, December 4, 2019, p. A23.
274. Susan Douglas, *Where the Girls Are: Growing Up Female with the Mass Media* (New York: Three Rivers Press, 1995) p. 74.
275. Quoted in Murray Schumach, *The Face on the Cutting Room Floor: The Story of Movie and Television Censorship* (New York: William Morrow, 1964), p. 59.
276. Molly Haskell, *From Reverence to Rape: The Treatment of Women in the Movies*, 2nd ed. (Chicago: University of Chicago Press, 1987), p. 4.
277. Laura Mulvey "Visual Pleasure and the Narrative Cinema," *Screen* 16, 3, Autumn 1975, pp. 6-18; reprinted in Mulvey, *Visual and Other Pleasures* (Bloomington: Indiana University Press, 1989). This volume also contains two reconsiderations of her original essay.
278. James Thurber, "Onward and Upward with the Arts," *New Yorker*, May 15, 1948, p. 34.
279. Susan J. Douglas, *In Our Prime: How Older Women Are Reinventing the Road Ahead* (New York: W.W. Norton & Company, 2020) p. 138.
280. Susan J. Douglas, *The Rise of Enlighten Sexism: How Pop Culture Took Us from Girl Power to Girls Gone Wild* (New York: Times Books, 2010), p. 217
281. *Griswold v. Connecticut*, 381 U.S. 479 (1965)
282. See Foster Hirsch, *The Boys from Syracuse: The Shuberts' Theatrical Empire* (New York, Cooper Square Press, 2000).
283. For the former child star's oddly upbeat take on everything from *Baby Burlesks* to genital exposure and middle-aged male costars see, Shirley Temple Black, *Child Star: An Autobiography*, (New York: Warner Books, 1988).
284. See Jodi Kantor and Megan Twohey, *She Said: Breaking the Sexual Harassment Story That Helped Ignite a Movement* (New York: Penguin Press, 2019)
285. Ronan Farrow, "Harvey Weinstein's Army of Spies," *New Yorker* (November 6, 2017).
286. Brent Staples, "How the Suffrage Movement Betrayed Black Women," *New York Times*, July 28, 2018.
287. Steve Inskeep, *Jacksonland: President Jackson, Cherokee Chief John Ross, and a Great American Land Grab.* (New York: Penguin Press, 2015) pp. 332–333

288. Michael Harrington, *Socialism: Past and Future* (New York: Signet, 1992), first published two years earlier.
289. Her floor speech is available at: https://www.youtube.com/watch?v=hgAXM7TqZU8
290. Eugene Volokh, "The Freedom...of the Press, From 1791 to 1869 to Now - Freedom for the Press as an Industry, or the Press as a Technology?" *University of Pennsylvania Law Review*, Vol. 160 (2011).
291. Pui-Wing Tam and Jim Kerstetter, "Romance Rip-Offs and Accountability," *New York Times*, August 5, 2019, p. B2.
292. *Zeran v. America Online, Inc.*, 129 F.3d 327 (4th Circuit. 1997)
293. Erving Goffman, *Presentation of Self in Everyday Life* (New York: Anchor, 1959).
294. Michael Wolff, *Fire and Fury: Inside the Trump White House* (New York: Henry Holt and Co. 2018).
295. *Milton H. Greene Archives v. Marilyn Monroe* LLC 692 F.3d 983 (2012)
296. Zacchini v. Scripps-Howard Broadcasting Co., 433 U.S. 562 (1977).
297. Davey Abla and Sheera Frenkel, "Chief Scientist Draws Venom from the Right," *New York Times*, March 29, 2020, p.11.
298. Maggie Haberman, "Trade Adviser Warned White House in January of Risks of a Pandemic," *New York Times*, April 6, 2020.
299. See Yasmeen Abutaleb, Josh Dawsey, Ellen Nakashima and Greg Miller, "'What do you have to lose?': Inside Trump's Embrace of a Risky Drug Against Coronavirus," *Washington Post*, April 4, 2020.
300. George T. Conway III, Steve Schmidt, John Weaver and Rick Wilson, "We Are Republicans, and We Want Trump Defeated," New York Times, December 17, 2019.
301. Jennifer Rubin, "'Distinguished pols of the week: They may beat Trump all by themselves," *The Washington Post*, June 21, 2020.
302. John Bolton, *The Room Where It Happened: A White House Memoir* (New York: Simon & Schuster, 2020).
303. *United States v. Baker*, 890 F. Supp, 1375 (E.D. Michigan, 1995), affirmed by *United States v. Alkhabaz*, 104 F.3d 1492 (6th Circuit. 1997).
304. *Elonis v. United States*, 575 U.S. ___ (2015)
305. Tim Wu, *The Master Switch: The Rise and Fall of Information Empires* (New York: Alfred A. Knoph, 2010) p. 6.
306. Ibid. Wu, p. 12.
307. Tim Wu, *The Curse of Bigness: Antitrust in the New Gilded Age* (New York: Columbia Global Reports, 2018) p. 121.

Made in the USA
Middletown, DE
30 August 2020

16910403R00203